Building
Structures:

Elementary analysis and design

Prose requires the use of grammar;
POETRY requires an understanding of grammar.

Building requires the use of structure;
ARCHITECTURE requires an understanding of structure.

Prentice-Hall, Inc. *Englewood Cliffs, New Jersey   07632*

R. E. SHAEFFER

School of Architecture
Florida A & M University

Consulting Engineer
Tallahassee, Florida

With full-page illustrations by Pat Pinnell

Building Structures:
Elementary analysis and design

Library of Congress Cataloging in Publication Data

Shaeffer, R. E
    Building structures.

    Bibliography: p.
    Includes index.
    1. Structures, Theory of.   2. Structural design.
I. Title.
TA645.S479   1980   624'.17   79-21912
ISBN 0-13-086561-3

Editorial/production supervision and interior design
   by Barbara A. Cassel
Cover design by Pat Pinnell
Manufacturing buyer: Gordon Osbourne

Printed in the United States of America

10 9 8 7 6 5 4 3 2

PRENTICE-HALL INTERNATIONAL, INC., *London*
PRENTICE-HALL OF AUSTRALIA PTY. LIMITED, *Sydney*
PRENTICE-HALL OF CANADA, LTD., *Toronto*
PRENTICE-HALL OF INDIA PRIVATE LIMITED, *New Delhi*
PRENTICE-HALL OF JAPAN, INC., *Tokyo*
PRENTICE-HALL OF SOUTHEAST ASIA PTE. LTD., *Singapore*
WHITEHALL BOOKS LIMITED, *Wellington, New Zealand*

A.B.
Amy
Connie
Eleanor
Howard
Jane
Joan
Joe
John
Joseph
Kathy
Kristin
Mary
Poppy
Tim

You know what you have given.

FOREWORD   *xi*

PREFACE   *xiii*

1   OVERVIEW   *1*

1-1   Definition of Structure, *1*   1-6   Structural Forms in Nature, *5*
1-2   Structure of Buildings, *1*   1-7   Structural Forms in Buildings, *6*
1-3   Structural Planning and Design, *3*   1-8   Cost, *10*
1-4   Types of Loads, *4*   1-9   Building Codes, *10*
1-5   Types of Stress, *4*   1-10   Accuracy of Computations, *11*

2   STATICS   *12*

2-1   Introduction, *12*   2-9   Equilibrium of Single Members, *24*
2-2   Forces, *12*   2-10   Two-Force Members, *27*
2-3   Components and Resultants, *12*   2-11   Graphical Techniques, *30*
2-4   Force Polygons, *14*   2-12   Stability and Determinacy, *31*
2-5   Equilibrium of Concurrent Forces, *16* 2-13   Three-Hinged Arches, *33*
2-6   Moments and Couples, *19*   2-14   Pinned Frames, *35*
2-7   Replacement of a Force by a Force   2-15   Simple Cable Statics, *37*
       and a Couple, *22*   2-16   Conclusion and Procedure, *41*
2-8   Ideal Support Conditions, *22*

3   STRUCTURAL PROPERTIES OF AREAS   *42*

3-1   Introduction, *42*   3-4   Parallel Axis Theorem, *49*
3-2   Centroids, *42*   3-5   Radius of Gyration, *52*
3-3   Moment of Inertia, *45*

Contents

4   STRESS AND STRAIN   53

4-1   Types of Stress, *53*
4-2   Basic Connection Stresses, *54*
4-3   Strain, *54*
4-4   Lateral Strain, *55*
4-5   Stress versus Strain, *55*

4-6   Stiffness, *56*
4-7   Total Axial Deformation, *57*
4-8   Indeterminate Axially Loaded Elements, *57*
4-9   Thermal Stresses and Strains, *60*
4-10   Allowable Stress Design and Strength Design, *62*

5   PROPERTIES OF STRUCTURAL MATERIALS   65

5-1   Introduction, *65*
5-2   Nature of Wood, *65*
5-3   Concrete and Reinforced Concrete, *65*
5-4   Structural Steel, *66*

5-5   Masonry and Reinforced Masonry, *67*
5-6   Structural Plastics, *67*
5-7   Stress Concentration, *68*
5-8   Creep, *68*

6   TORSION   72

6-1   Torsion in Building Structures, *72*
6-2   Basic Torsional Stress, *73*
6-3   Magnitude of the Torque Force, *74*
6-4   Angle of Twist, *74*
6-5   Cross-Shears, *75*

6-6   Diagonal Tension and Compression, *76*
6-7   Torsional Stresses in Rectangular Sections, *77*
6-8   Torsional Stresses in Closed Sections, *77*
6-9   Torsional Stresses in Open Sections, *79*
6-10   Shapes That Are Effective in Torsion, *81*

7   SHEAR AND MOMENT   82

7-1   Definitions and Sign Conventions, *82*
7-2   Shear and Moment Equations, *83*
7-3   Significance of Zero Shear, *87*
7-4   Load, Shear, and Moment Relationships, *88*

7-5   Unusual Loads, *91*
7-6   Determinate Frames, *93*
7-7   Tension Side Moment Diagrams, *96*
7-8   Cable Analogy, *97*

8   BENDING   99

8-1   Introduction to Bending, *99*
8-2   Flexural Strain, *99*
8-3   Flexural Stress, *100*

8-4   Section Modulus, *104*
8-5   Shearing Stresses Due to Bending, *106*

9   SPECIAL CONSIDERATIONS IN BEAM ANALYSIS   110

9-1   Introduction, *110*
9-2   Lateral Buckling and Stability, *110*
9-3   Lateral Stability in Timber Beams, *111*
9-4   Size Effect in Timber Beams, *113*
9-5   Compactness in Steel Beams, *113*
9-6   Lateral Stability in Steel Beams, *114*
9-7   Allowable Bending Stresses above $\frac{2}{3}F_y$, *117*

9-8   Horizontal Shearing Stresses in Timber Beams, *117*
9-9   Horizontal Shearing Stresses in Steel Beams, *119*
9-10   Forces in Beams on a Pitch, *120*
9-11   Beams of Variable Moment of Inertia, *123*
9-12   Shear Center, *124*
9-13   Loads Acting at Angles to the Principal Axes, *127*
9-14   Beams of Two Materials, *129*

10   DEFLECTION   133

10-1   Introduction, *133*
10-2   Organization, *134*
10-3   Radius of Curvature, *134*
10-4   Curvature and Bending Moment, *135*
10-5   Double-Integration Method, *135*
10-6   Moment-Area Method, *137*

10-7   Principle of Superposition, *140*
10-8   Conjugate Beam Method, *141*
10-9   Point of Maximum Deflection, *144*
10-10 Deflection Formulas, *145*
10-11 Superposition and Indeterminate Structures, *146*

11   BEAM DESIGN AND FRAMING   149

11-1   Introduction, *149*
11-2   Shape of Beam Cross Sections, *149*
11-3   "Ideal" Beams, *150*
11-4   Properties of Materials, *150*

11-5   Tributary Area, *151*
11-6   Framing Direction, *152*
11-7   Selecting Wood and Steel Beams, *155*
11-8   Design Aids for Wood and Steel, *163*

12   COMBINED STRESSES   164

12-1   Axial Stresses in Bending Members, *164*
12-2   Eccentric Loading, *166*
12-3   Torsion and Horizontal Shear, *168*
12-4   Principal Stresses, *170*

12-5   The Mohr Circle, *174*
12-6   Torsion and Flexure, *175*
12-7   Flexure and Horizontal Shear, *176*

13   COLUMN ANALYSIS AND DESIGN   178

13-1   Columns as Building Structural Elements, *178*
13-2   Column Failure Modes, *179*
13-3   The Euler Theory, *179*
13-4   Influence of Different End Conditions, *181*
13-5   Intermediate Lateral Bracing, *184*
13-6   Limits to the Applicability of the Euler Equation, *187*

13-7   Axial Loads on Timber Columns, *187*
13-8   Axial Loads on Steel Columns, *191*
13-9   Intermediate Axial Loads, *195*
13-10 Beam-Columns, *197*
13-11 Combined Loading on Timber Columns, *197*
13-12 Combined Loading on Steel Columns, *201*

14   TRUSSES   207

14-1   Introduction, *207*
14-2   Analysis by Joint Equilibrium, *210*
14-3   Graphical Techniques, *213*

14-4   Method of Sections, *216*
14-5   Preliminary Determination of Depth, *219*
14-6   Special Types of Trusses, *220*

15   INDETERMINATE BEAMS AND FRAMES   222

15-1   Introduction, *222*
15-2   Theorem of Three Moments, *223*
15-3   Loading Patterns, *228*
15-4   Moment Distribution Concepts and Development, *228*
15-5   Pinned-End Stiffness Reduction, *236*

15-6   Moment Distribution in Frames, *238*
15-7   Deflection, *242*
15-8   Support Settlement, *243*
15-9   Estimating Frame Moments, *246*
15-10 Introduction to Sidesway, *250*

16 CONSIDERATION OF LATERAL LOADS   252

16-1 Introduction, *252*
16-2 Wind Loads and Distribution, *252*
16-3 Earthquakes, *254*
16-4 Earthquake Loads and Distribution, *255*

16-5 Earthquake Design Principles, *259*
16-6 Lateral Load Bracing Systems, *260*
16-7 Portal Method for Approximate Analysis, *262*

17 REINFORCED CONCRETE AND PRESTRESSED CONCRETE CONCEPTS   267

17-1 Introduction to Reinforced Concrete, *267*
17-2 Load Factors, *268*
17-3 Ultimate Moment Capacity, *268*
17-4 Amount of Reinforcement, *272*
17-5 Design for Flexure, *272*
17-6 Introduction to Beam Shear, *276*

17-7 Introduction to Beam Deflection, *276*
17-8 Considerations in Column Design, *277*
17-9 Introduction to Prestressing, *279*
17-10 Basic Analysis of Prestressed Beams, *282*
17-11 Initial and Final Stresses, *283*

APPENDICES   286

A. Introduction to the SI Metric System, *286*
B. Selected Bibliography, *289*
C. Derivation of Basic Torsional Stress Expressions, *290*
D. Derivation of Basic Flexural Stress Equation, *291*
E. Derivation of Basic Horizontal Shearing Stress Equation, *293*
F. Proof of Moment-Area Theorems, *294*
G. Derivation of Principal Stress Equations, *295*
H. Derivation of Euler Column Buckling Equation, *297*
I. Derivation of Theorem of Three Moments, *298*
J. Derivation of Ultimate Moment Capacity Terms, *299*

K. Mass Densities of Selected Building Materials, *300*
L. Properties of Materials, *300*
M. Properties of Areas, *301*
N. Load Intensity, *303*
O. Minimum Live Load Values, *306*
P. Allowable Stress Values for Selected Woods, *307*
Q. Wood Section Properties, *307*
R. Values for Steel Column Analysis, *308*
S. Steel Section Properties, *310*
T. Reinforcing Bar Sizes, *316*
U. Values for Strength Design of Reinforced Concrete Beams, *316*
V. Shear, Moment, and Deflection Equations, *317*
W. Answers to Problems, *319*

INDEX   331

Building Structures comes at a time when a clear, concise textbook on structural design and analysis is needed. In the world of structural engineering, we are experiencing rapid and profound changes in design methods. To have published, at this time, a structural book such as this is most fortunate.

However, even though the author deals with the changes taking place in structural design methods, one of the strong points in this book is that he does not neglect the old basics—those old tenets that all great engineers "teethed on" and "live by." For example: the simple, but very beautiful, concept of replacing a "force" with a "force and a couple," and Varignon's theorem; the author also points out that carrying loads via bending is the least efficient method of support and therefore the most costly. These, and others, are important lessons, indeed, for the serious student of architecture.

The importance of theory is stressed and many examples of well-thought-out problems and solutions are offered. Only the metric system is used throughout. We seem inexorably headed toward joining the rest of the world in its use. This is an issue that many of us have been ducking for years. However, new students of architecture and engineering will be the transition group, and the author's complete reliance on the metric system without conversions seems appropriate.

The basic problems involved in building are presented in such a way as to sustain the interest of the student. Even though the subject is complicated and many-faceted, it is presented in a straightforward manner.

The author has prepared a vast amount of well-organized material. I have never used a textbook that I felt contained all the material needed for a course. However, here in *Building Structures* the author has assembled virtually all the data necessary for the selection of course material. This allows teachers to use their own creativity and assemble courses to meet the specific needs and backgrounds of their particular students.

The chapters progress in an organized way, and the appropriate subjects flow logically, in smooth sequence. The related charts, tables, and derivations included in the appendix I found most useful, as will the student. Rarely have I seen so many appropriate references assembled in a single volume.

This is a well-documented book that reflects the author's great knowledge and skill in his field. The text is new in format and concept, and will be an invaluable textbook for the student of architecture and a good reference for the engineering student interested in a consulting career.

Herman D. J. Spiegel

Professor of Architectural Engineering
School of Architecture
Yale University

Principal, Spiegel and Zamecnik, Inc.
Structural Engineers
New Haven, Connecticut

Foreword

This beginning text has been written primarily for students of architecture and building construction. It should also be appropriate for some engineering courses and could provide the text material needed for several courses in certain technology programs. It is hoped that the major subject areas will maintain their continuity even when selected articles are deleted and that this will permit the book to be used for several different levels of required depth. The presentation is basically quantitative but attempts to go beyond the traditional and sometimes narrow approach taken by most texts in structural analysis. It will be most effective when used in conjunction with a book emphasizing a qualitative approach to structural behavior.

The text is written completely in the SI metric system of units and the author regrets that much of the required reference data has had to be converted from the customary values. It is certain that these values will change in the near future as more metric standards become available.

A brief introduction to the SI system is given in Appendix A, and those not familiar with it will find it surprisingly simple. In the interest of trying to achieve a conceptual conversion to SI as well as a numerical one, no customary units accompany the metric values in this book. It is felt that "thinking in metric" will come about more rapidly if the student is unhindered by the "old" units.

Many illustrative examples are included, which have been fully worked out. It is most definitely an example-oriented book, as this is the teaching methodology preferred by the author. Real comprehension in any learning experience is best accomplished by following the advice given in an old Chinese proverb:

I hear, I forget;
I see, I remember;
I do, I understand.

There are numerous sections in which the author has deliberately included material of considerable depth and engineering rigor, either by personal preference or as it is needed for reference by other sections. In many instances, these can and should be deleted from study, depending upon the goals of the particular course, teacher, or degree program. As an organizing example, a beginning year of structures in a professional architecture program might typically include the following, with reference to the table of contents:

All of Chapter 1
All of Chapter 2
   with Sections 14 and 15 optional
All of Chapter 3
All of Chapter 4
All of Chapter 5
Sections 1 through 6 of Chapter 6
Sections 1 through 4 of Chapter 7
All of Chapter 8
Sections 1, 8, 9, and 10 of Chapter 9
Sections 1 through 11 of Chapter 10
All of Chapter 11
Sections 1 and 2 of Chapter 12
Sections 1 through 8 of Chapter 13
All of Chapter 14

A minimal background in calculus and physics has been assumed in writing this material, and one- or two-semester courses in both areas will suffice. Most of the mathematical derivations of the equations have been placed in the appendices, as they are usually not absolutely essential to the proper use of the equations, themselves. Better students will find these derivations essential, by individual preference, and will study the appropriate appendix as it is referenced.

It is assumed that the student has a background in

Preface

methods and materials of construction from prior coursework or individual experience. Chapter 5 provides a brief review of the essential characteristics of the more common structural materials but is not sufficient in depth or diversity of coverage.

Most of the examples and problems in this text utilize elastic theory with wood or steel as the primary structural material. Some treatment of reinforced concrete elements and strength design techniques is provided in Chapter 17, but most programs of study will require a more comprehensive approach to these subjects.

Portions of the material included herein have been adapted from classroom materials previously developed by the author. Specifically, Chapter 2 is partially based on a study guide written in 1964; Chapter 7 was adapted from a similar study guide produced in 1967; and Chapter 13 is based on the manual, *Column Behavior and Analysis*, copyrighted in 1976.

I wish to express my gratitude to several offices and individuals within the University of Maryland at College Park. The offices of the Provost of the Division of Arts and Humanities and of the Dean for Undergraduate Studies provided assistance in the form of an Improvement of Instruction grant, which provided funds for part of the initial production costs. I am most grateful to the Dean of the School of Architecture and the Vice Chancellor for Academic Affairs for granting me sabbatical leave for a semester, which enabled this project to be realized.

R. E. SHAEFFER

Building
Structures:

Elementary analysis and design

1-1 DEFINITION OF STRUCTURE

The word "structure" has many meanings. Dictionaries usually define it in very general terms such as the following: "the organization or interrelation of all the parts of a whole; manner of construction." Structures or structured things exist almost everywhere and any definition will apply more aptly to some than others. Without confining our use of the word to buildings or other engineered objects, we find that almost everything has structure. It is very difficult to think of anything that is totally without structure. Certainly, every material object has a basic molecular structure, if nothing else. Even outer space, closer to a true vacuum than anything we know, is somewhat defined by the relatively few objects in it. It has been suggested that electrical discharge in the form of lightning has no structure. If we narrow our general terms slightly, we say that lightning seems to behave as if it has no structure. However, it has direction, and this in itself indicates the presence of some structure.

Even intangible things such as thoughts, emotions, and social relationships frequently have definite patterns. Almost everything we do or think has a structure. It is important for us to realize that in this text and our related studies, we are dealing with a very specific and narrow use of the term.

1-2 STRUCTURE OF BUILDINGS

Considering only the engineering essentials, the structure of a building can be defined as the assemblage of those parts which exist for the purpose of maintaining shape and stability. Its primary purpose is to resist any loads applied to the building and to transmit those to the ground.

In terms of architecture, the structure of a building is and does much more than that. It is an inseparable part of the building form and to varying degrees is a generator of that form. Used skillfully, the building structure can establish or reinforce orders and rhythms among the architectural volumes and planes. It can be visually dominant or recessive. It can develop harmonies or conflicts. It can be both confining and emancipating. And, unfortunately in some cases, it cannot be ignored. It is physical.

From a philosophical standpoint, the design of structure can be defined as the *art* of making *w(holes)* or the *science* of making *form*. We shall see that building structures, whether they be free-form shells or right-angled skeletal frames, serve as the surrounding elements for holes (spaces). Some structures are themselves a collection of holes (e.g., a truss or cable network or a bone). At the same time, the structure must possess its own integrity. It must be complete or whole. It must be an entity, independent of anything except for its connection to the earth. Deciding where and how to make holes and/ or wholes can be a complex task involving both skill and judgment.

The structure must also be engineered to maintain the architectural form. The principles and tools of physics and mathematics provide the basis for differentiating between rational and irrational forms in terms of construction. Artists can sometimes generate shapes that obviate any consideration of science, but architects cannot.

There are at least three items that must be present in the structure of a building:

> stability
> strength and stiffness
> economy

Taking the first of the three requirements, it is obvious that *stability* is needed to maintain shape. An unstable building structure implies unbalanced forces or

Overview

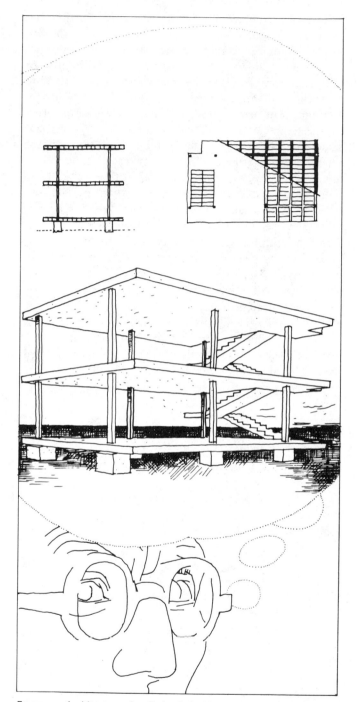

"Structure" is the assembly of parts which maintain the stability of a building. The desire to make the distinction between "working" and secondary elements, and the increasing ability to make it correctly, underlay the origins and growth of modern architecture. The primitive hut's essential structural naturalness was held up as a model of ideal clarity for architecture by the Abbe Laugier in his 1753

Essay on Architecture; Le Corbusier's Maisons Dom-ino of 1914, conceived as basic housing, followed Laugier's thinking by identifying slab, column, and footing as the minimum essential structure. Note that the actual structure, revealed in plan and sections, is disguised in the desire for a forceful diagram; the "slab" is a system of beams and joists.

a lack of equilibrium and a consequent acceleration of the structure or its pieces. (The nature of structural stability is covered in more detail in Section 2-12.)

The requirement of *strength* means that the materials selected to resist the stresses generated by the loads and shapes of the structure(s) must be adequate. Indeed, a "factor of safety" is usually provided so that under the anticipated loads, a given material is not stressed to a level even close to its rupture point. The material property called *stiffness* is considered with the requirement of strength (i.e., the structure designed must be of sufficient strength *and* stiffness). Stiffness is different from strength in that it directly involves how much a structure strains or deflects under load. A material that is very strong but lacking in stiffness will deform too much to be of value in resisting the forces applied.

Economy of a building structure refers to more than just the cost of the materials used. Construction economy is a complicated subject involving raw materials, fabrication, erection, and maintenance. Design and construction labor costs and the costs of energy consumption must be considered. Speed of construction and the cost of money (interest) are also factors. In most design situations, more than one structural material requires consideration. Competitive alternatives almost always exist, and the choice is seldom obvious.

Apart from these three primary requirements, several other factors are worthy of emphasis. First, the structure or structural system must *relate* to the building's function. It should not be in conflict in terms of form. For example, a linear function demands a linear structure, and therefore it would be improper to roof a bowling alley with a dome. Similarly, a theater must have large, unobstructed spans but a fine restaurant probably should not. Stated simply, the *structure* must be *appropriate* to the *function* it is to *shelter*.

Second, the structure must be *fire-resistant*. It is obvious that the structural system must be able to maintain its integrity at least until the occupants are safely out. Building codes specify the number of hours for which certain parts of a building must resist the heat without collapse. The structural materials used for those elements must be inherently fire-resistant or be adequately protected by fireproofing materials. The degree of fire resistance to be provided will depend upon a number of items, including the use and occupancy load of the space, its dimensions, and the location of the building.

Third, the structure should *integrate* well with the building's circulation systems. It should not be in conflict with the piping systems for water and waste, the ducting systems for air, or (most important) the movement of people. It is obvious that the various building systems must be coordinated as the design progresses. One can design in a sequential step-by-step manner within any one system, but the design of all of them should move in a parallel manner toward completion. Spatially, all the various parts of a building are interdependent.

Fourth, the structure must be *psychologically safe* as well as physically safe. A high-rise frame that sways considerably in the wind might not actually be dangerous but may make the building uninhabitable just the same. Lightweight floor systems that are too "bouncy" can make the users very uncomfortable. Large glass windows, uninterrupted by dividing mullions, can be quite safe but will appear very insecure to the occupant standing next to one 40 floors above the street.

Sometimes the architect must make deliberate attempts to increase the apparent strength or solidness of the structure. This apparent safety may be more important than honestly expressing the building's structure, because the untrained viewer cannot distinguish between real and perceived safety.

1-3 STRUCTURAL PLANNING AND DESIGN

The building designer needs to understand the behavior of physical structures under load. An ability to intuit or "feel" structural behavior is possessed by those having much experience involving structural analysis, both qualitative and quantitative. The consequent knowledge of how forces, stresses, and deformations build up in different materials and shapes is vital to the development of this "sense."

Beginning this study of forces (statics) and stresses and deformations (mechanics of materials) is most easily done through quantitative methods. These two subjects form the basis for all structural planning and design and are very difficult to learn in the abstract.

In most building design efforts, the initial structural planning is done by the architect. Ideally, the structural and mechanical consultants should work side by side with the architect from the conception of a project to the final days of construction. In most cases, however, the architect must make some initial assumptions about the relationships to be developed between the building form and the structural system. A solid background in structural principles and behavior is needed to make these assumptions with any reasonable degree of confidence. The shape of the structural envelope, the location of all major supporting elements, the directionality (if any) of the system, the selection of the major structural materials, and the preliminary determination of span lengths are all part of the structural planning process.

Structural design, on the other hand, is done by both the architect and the engineer. The preliminary determination of the size of major structural elements, providing a check on the rationality of previous assumptions, is done by the architect and/or the engineer. Final structural design, involving a complete analysis of all the parts and components, the working out of structural details, and the specifying of structural materials and methods of construction is almost always done by the structural engineer.

Of the two areas, structural planning is far more complex than structural design. It involves the previously mentioned "feeling for structure" or intuition that comes through experience. Structural design can be learned from lectures and books, but it is likely that structural planning cannot. Nevertheless, some insight and judgment can be developed from a minimal background in structural analysis and design. If possible, this should be gained from an architectural standpoint, emphasizing the relationship between the quantities and the resulting qualities wherever possible, rather than from an engineering approach.

This study of quantitative structures can be thorough enough to permit the architect to do completely the analysis for smaller projects, although such depth is not absolutely necessary. At the very least it should provide the knowledge and vocabulary necessary to work with the consulting engineer. It must be remembered that the architect receives much more education that is oriented toward creativity than does the engineer, and therefore needs to maintain control over the design. It is up to the architect to ask intelligent questions and suggest viable alternatives. If handicapped by structural ignorance, some of the design decisions will, in effect, be made by others.

1-4 TYPES OF LOADS

In general, loads that act on building structures can be divided into two groups: those due to gravitational attraction and those resulting from other natural causes and elements. Gravity loads can be further classified into two groups: live load and dead load. Building *live loads* include people and most movable objects within the structure or on top of it. Snow is a live load. So is a grand piano, a safe, or a water bed. Appendix O provides some typically recommended live loads for various types of occupancy within building structures. Research bears out that these figures represent probable maximum values for live loads during the lifetime of a structure. Such loads are seldom realized. What is more likely is an unexpected change in the use of the space. One can sense the problems that might result if an abandoned school is purchased for use as a warehouse (to store bowling balls). *Dead loads*, on the other hand, generally include the immovable objects in a building. The walls (both interior and exterior), floors, mechanical and electrical

equipment, and the structural elements themselves are examples of dead loads.

The snow map of Appendix N gives the maximum *snow load* that can reasonably be expected in various parts of the United States. Like the live-load values, such large snowfalls seldom occur. Nevertheless, we must design for some level of probability and should not forget such occurrences as the more-than-500-millimeter snowfall that hit the southeastern United States in 1974, resulting in many small building failures.

Natural forces not due to gravity that act on buildings are provided by wind and earthquakes. *Wind load* is a lateral load that varies in intensity with height as discussed in Section 16-2. (Hurricanes and tornadoes present special design problems, and local building codes often require certain types of resistive construction.) A probable wind pressure map is given in Appendix N.

Earthquakes are also treated as lateral loads (at least for preliminary design purposes), but it is well known that buildings in earthquakes are subjected to vertical forces as well. Design methods are not fully developed for *disaster loadings* such as tornadoes and earthquakes, and research continues in these areas. Design guidelines for building in earthquake-prone localities are given in Section 16-5, and an earthquake zone map for the United States appears in Appendix N.

One final type of load is an *impact load*, usually due to moving equipment, which occurs within or on the structure. Most structural materials can withstand a sudden and temporary load of higher magnitude than a load that is applied slowly. For this reason, the specified permissible stress magnitudes are substantially increased when such loads govern the design. No permanent damage is done by a moderate impact load provided that it does not occur repeatedly. (An earthquake is a good example of a severe and repeating impact load.)

All the tables and maps referred to in this text, as part of the appendices, provide rough data only. The designer should consult local building codes, which always take precedence. The designer also bears the professional responsibility for increasing any recommended design loads when the situation warrants it.

1-5 TYPES OF STRESS

A fundamental concept in the structural analysis of buildings is that objects are in a state of *equilibrium*. This means there are no unbalanced forces acting on the structure or its parts at any point. All forces counteract one another, and this results in equilibrium. The structural element or object does not accelerate because the net force acting on it is zero, but it does respond to these forces internally. It is pushed or pulled and otherwise deformed, giving off energy as heat as it resists the forces. Internal stresses of varying types and magnitudes accompany the deformations to provide this resistance.

These stresses are named by their action or behavior (i.e., tension, compression, shear, and bending). *Tensile* and *compressive* stresses which act through the axis or center of mass of an object are evenly distributed over the resisting area and result in all the material fibers being stressed to like amounts. *Shearing* stresses and, more important, *bending* stresses are not uniform and usually result in a few fibers of material being deformed to their limit while others remain unstressed or nearly so. Bending is, by far, the structurally least efficient way to carry loads.

Assuming for the moment that we have a material equally strong in tension, compression, shear, and bending, it would be best to load it in tension to achieve its maximum structural capacity. Compressive forces, if applied to a long slender structure, can cause buckling as illustrated in Figure 13-2(b). Buckling always occurs under less load than would be required to fail the materials in true compression (i.e., crushing). Of course, materials are not equal in strength when loaded in different ways. Some materials have almost no tensile strength, and generalizations are very difficult to make. As explained in succeeding chapters, shearing stresses will cause tension and compression; and bending is actually a combination of shear, tension, and compression. Because of the previously mentioned uneven distribution of stress intensity, however, bending is always the most damaging load that can be applied to any resisting structural material.

1-6 STRUCTURAL FORMS IN NATURE

Some of the most sophisticated and efficient structures are found in plants, animals, and animal houses. Through adaptation to specific environments over time, natural forms may be refined until they are nearly perfect responses to a given set of forces. Countless examples of this type of form response or form resistance, some less successful than others, may be found all around us. Only a few are cited here, to provide a representative sample. Natural forms can be very complicated in terms of structural analysis, and the reader should not be discouraged at being unable to understand them right away.

As an educational exercise, one may wish to select two or three plant or animal structures and record some preliminary thoughts or ideas about them. What forces act on them? What types of stresses are developed? What parts are strong, weak, stiff, or flexible; and why? The same forms could then be analyzed several months

or a year later after completing some formal education in structures. In some cases an object that appears simple and straightforward at first glance becomes quite complex as we learn more about structural behavior.

The egg is one of the classic examples of good structure both in terms of form and material. It is a thin shell which is very strong in compression when loaded uniformly. It is doubly curved, which provides some resistance to compression buckling, a problem with all thin shells. In contrast to its strength under uniform loads, the egg is virtually defenseless against point loads. In this case, of course, the development of resistance to point loads would be totally self-defeating.

The scallop shell sketched in Figure 1-1 is considerably stronger than the egg shell. It is much more of a permanent structure and is subject to much greater loads. It is also doubly curved but is much thicker, to provide some resistance to impact loads from predators. Of

Figure 1-1. Scallop shell.

greater significance, however, is the fluting or small undulations in the surface of the shell. This greatly stiffens the shell and enables it to withstand large loads without buckling. Any type of folding or ribbing of a surface (convolution) adds stiffness, and this principle is used frequently in man-made structures—from building roofs to guard rails.

The ordinary blade of grass provides an interesting example of a form that changes shape constantly over its length. Its cross section goes from a very strong and stiff tube at the bottom through a V or arc shape at midheight and finally to a very flexible flat shape at the tip. As illustrated in Figure 1-2(b), the V shape is sometimes further refined by a stiffening rib.

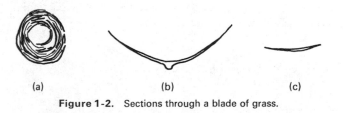

(a)   (b)   (c)

Figure 1-2. Sections through a blade of grass.

A blade of grass acts much like a cantilever beam sticking vertically out of the ground. It deflects when subjected to lateral loads (such as the wind) but resists failure by having its greatest strength located at the bottom, where it is needed to resist the bending.

The common spider web is an ingenious tensile structure, light yet very strong and easily maintained. It is very redundant, possessing many extra members, and parts of it can be completely torn away and the rest will not collapse. Because every member is tensile, the structure is extremely efficient in terms of its self-weight. It is quite flexible and its highly elastic nature is well suited to the impact loads it must sustain.

One of the most sophisticated natural structures is the walnut shell. It has a double curvature and its surface has many convolutions. Figure 1-3 compares half of the shell to a dome. In general, a dome tends to thrust outward at the bottom edge as the load tries to flatten it. This circular bottom edge must be prevented from moving outward or it will develop numerous vertical cracks.

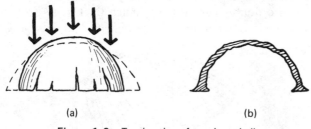

(a)   (b)

Figure 1-3. Tension ring of a walnut shell.

One way to contain this edge is with a tension ring around the bottom. The walnut shell provides this in the form of a thickened tapered edge. This thick edge ring also helps to maintain the boundary shape against loads applied in that plane.

As if this were not enough protection for the meat inside, the interior is crossed by several paperlike tensile diaphragms which help to maintain the overall spherical shape of the shell. It is not surprising that great force must be applied to fail such a structure.

Because of the success of many natural forms, they are often copied in the design of buildings and artifacts. Sometimes this is done without much thought and even less skill and the resulting design is most unfortunate. Success is more likely when we borrow the *principles* of "resistance to loads through form" from nature and apply those principles to suit the needs of a particular design problem.

1-7 STRUCTURAL FORMS IN BUILDINGS

There are several basic structural elements found in buildings, each of which embodies a different type of structural behavior. The more complicated forms are made up of combinations of the basic ones or are exten-

sions of the same concepts. The basic elements and the stresses they develop under load are as follows:

cable—pure tension

post —compression (and bending under certain loads)

beam—bending and shear[1]

truss —tension and compression

arch —compression (and bending under certain loads)

shell —membrane (tension and/or compression evenly distributed through the shell thickness)

A considerable portion of this text is devoted to the analysis of each of these structures, except the last two. A proper discussion of arches and shells rightly belongs in a more advanced treatment of the subject, after the basic concepts are understood and some background has been established. Even so, the beginning student can develop some insight into the behavior of these and the more complicated systems from the chapters that follow.

Table 1-1 attempts to provide some data on different types of building structures. Some of these are quite conventional, while others are used only under very special circumstances. The table has been restricted to systems or parts of systems that form spans, as opposed to supporting elements, such as columns, bearing walls, or vertical cables. This has been done only because of the frequent commonality of pertinent data within the two categories of spanning and supporting. (This separation is somewhat arbitrary and, as seen in the table, many spanning systems act integrally with their supports.)

The tabulation is not to be considered an exhaustive classification of structural systems, and the sketches, especially, are merely representative of the class of structure listed. The figures for span range and span ratios vary widely in many cases and the values given can only be considered as guidelines. No unusual loads or support conditions have been considered in this table.

The floor systems in the flat-deck category of Table 1-1 occur more frequently than the structures of other groups by virtue of required spans and ease of construction. Each one is compatible with one or more support systems, and these relationships are shown in Figure 1-4.

---

[1]*Beam* is a generic term. The name applies to (in order of decreasing size and load capacity): girder, beam, joist, and purlin.

Success in the application of natural forms to architecture is more likely when the forms are regarded not as models for copying but as types of solution, demonstrations of principle, or suggestive metaphors. We are now quite accustomed to calling the structural frame a "skeleton," and to seeing the various other systems in buildings as also having purposes rather like those in animal anatomy. It was the principles on display in such places as Georges Cuvier's early 19th century museum, not the literal shapes and assemblies of bones, which inspired the analogy. The increased clarity of thinking which resulted contributed to the development of true, skeleton-frame, skyscraper construction.

TABLE 1-1 Characteristics of Selected Spanning Systems

Primary means of resisting loads	Spanning system		Usual materials and types	Usual span range (m)	Typical span/depth ratio	Typical span/thickness ratio	Advantages	Disadvantages	Comments
Tension	Cable		Steel with joist or concrete panel deck	30–150	DNA	300+	Long span	High technology; must provide for wind stability	Roof construction only
Compression	Arch		Timber, glued-laminated	20–40	DNA	35	Appearance (wood finish)	Large pieces to transport	Roof construction only; usually circular or parabolic in shape
			Timber truss	30–70	DNA	40	Low technology	Not good for concentrated loads	
			Steel truss	40–100	DNA	40		Not good for concentrated loads	
			Reinforced concrete, convoluted or ribbed	20–70	DNA	30	Low maintenance	Slow construction	
Bending and shear	Flat deck, floor		Wood — Joist with plywood subfloor	2–6	20	DNA	Versatile plan and section shapes; low technology	High noise transmission	Popular for residential construction
			Wood — Beam with planks	4–9	18	DNA	Open walls; simple foundations; low technology	High noise transmission	Popular for residential construction
			Steel — Beam w/steel subfloor or concrete slab	5–15	22	DNA	Can have composite action	Limited availability in some areas	
			Steel — Bar joist with steel subfloor	4–20	22	DNA	Wide range of available spans	No heavy loads	Deep long-span joists span much farther
			Reinf. concrete — Flat plate w/ or w/o drop panels	3–6	30	DNA	Low airborne noise transmission	Short spans; openings limited	Popular for high-rise construction
			Reinf. concrete — Beam with flat slab	5–10	15	DNA	Low airborne noise transmission; ease of construction	Openings limited	
			Reinf. concrete — Pan joist	5–10	20	DNA	Low airborne noise transmission	Openings limited	Strong directionality
			Reinf. concrete — Waffle pan	7–14	22	DNA	Low airborne noise transmission; appearance (concrete finish)	Poor integration w/mechanical system	Can cantilever both directions at a corner
			Reinf. concrete — Precast plank	6–12	38	DNA	Low airborne noise transmission; rapid construction high span/depth ratio	Requires repetitive bay sizes	Usually prestressed
Tension and compression	Truss		Timber members	7–30	5–12	DNA	Long span	Low span/depth ratio	Popular for residential roof construction
			Steel members	20–60	5–15	DNA	Long span	Low span/depth ratio	Popular for industrial roof construction

TABLE 1-1 (continued)

Primary means of resisting loads	Spanning system	Usual materials and types	Usual span range (m)	Typical span/depth ratio	Typical span/thickness ratio	Advantages	Disadvantages	Comments
Membrane action (tension and compression)	Dome	Reinforced concrete thin shell	15–50	DNA	200	Low stresses	Slow construction; poor acoustics; no point loads	Strong directionality
		Reinforced concrete (convoluted or ribbed)	30–100	DNA	40	Can accept moderate point loads	Slow construction	Popular form for sports stadia
		Steel truss	40–150	DNA	60	Long span	Requires skin for stability	Popular form for sports stadia
Membrane action (tension and compression)	Vault	Reinforced concrete thin shell	20–60	DNA	175	Many shapes possible	Slow construction; openings limited; poor acoustics; no point loads	Dominant forms; usually circular or parabolic in shape; roof construction only
Bending and shear	Barrel vault and folded plate	Reinforced concrete thin shell	20–40	12	200	Many shapes possible	Slow construction; openings limited	Dominant forms; roof construction only; strong directionality
Tension and compression	Space frame	Steel members	20–80	30	DNA	High span/depth ratio; long span	High technology	Roof construction only
Membrane action (tension and compression)	Warped surface	Reinforced concrete thin shell	20–60	DNA	200	Many shapes possible; low stresses	Slow construction; openings limited	Dominant forms; roof construction only
Tension	Cable net	Steel	30–100	DNA	600+	Long span; rapid consturction; many shapes possible	High technology; needs flexible skin system	Dominant forms; roof construction only
Membrane action (tension)	Air	Fabric-supported	40–200	DNA	1000+	Long span; rapid construction; low air pressure	High noise transmission; needs air locks; fabric deterioration	Roof construction only
		Fabric-inflated	20–60	DNA	30	No air locks needed; rapid construction	High noise transmission; needs air locks; fabric deterioration	Roof construction only

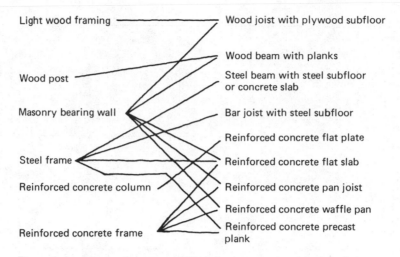

Figure 1-4. Construction compatibility between support and deck systems.

1-8 COST

Probably the question that is asked most frequently of structural consultants is one involving the relative cost of alternative structural systems. As might be suspected, it is also one of the most difficult to answer.

First, the costs of materials, fabrication, and erection are constantly changing and vary considerably with geographic location. The availability of materials and needed construction trades varies widely and transportation costs can be very high. As mentioned previously, compatibility with other building systems must also be considered (e.g., it might be costly to select a structural system that causes difficulty in the installation of mechanical ducts).

Second, and much harder to assess, is the ultimate or life-cycle cost of one system compared to another when one considers the effects that each has upon the other building systems. For example, the lowest-cost structural system might result in the greatest amount of unused building volume, which would have to be heated and cooled needlessly. The same choice could result in the highest insurance premiums. On the other hand, a low first cost might be better because the cost of money (interest) to construct the building would be less. The general subject of engineering economy treats these issues, and they will not be examined here. For the time being, it will have to be sufficient to realize that a proper determination of true cost is not simple.

On the other hand, what is not often understood by beginning designers is how low the cost of a typical building structural system, per se, really is. If we consider superstructure alone (because the cost of a foundation depends so much upon the individual site conditions), we find that it constitutes about 15 to 20% of the total construction cost. This percentage becomes even less

if we consider all the costs of a project, including land, interest, fees, and overhead. The 15 to 20% range must be compared to about 35% for the mechanical and electrical systems and about 20% for the nonbearing partitions and interior finishes. These figures all vary greatly with the building type. For example, a hospital would have a high mechanical cost, driving the structural percentage down. On the other hand, a sports stadium with little interior finish costs and very long spans would have a large portion of its cost in the structure. In any event, the cost of the structural system for the great majority of buildings should probably not be a major design determinant. The beginning designer, at least, can derive greater benefits by concentrating less on structural costs and more on the relationships among structure, form, function, and space. Cost may have to compromise these relationships but should not establish them.

1-9 BUILDING CODES

Throughout this text reference is made to various codes and specifications, which provide data on design loads, allowable stresses in materials, properties and dimensions of standard cross sections, and so on. These documents also frequently spell out standard design procedures, construction tolerances, factors of safety, and in some cases even provide the appropriate design equations. Most of these are developed for the use of design professionals by the materials industry associations, which have as one of their purposes the promotion of the proper and safe use of their material.

In the United States, the large general building codes, such as that provided by the Building Officials and Code Administrators International, Inc., and the International Conference of Building Officials, and the many municipal codes often include and/or make reference to the specifications of the materials industries. In such cases these specifications, like the rest of the code, must be followed or the design professional has the responsibility of proving the equality or superiority of a different or new procedure. The intent of all building codes is the protection of the health, safety, and welfare of the public; and while some provisions may seem arbitrary or overly restrictive, they cannot be taken lightly. Indeed, the provisions of a code will generally represent minimum acceptable standards and not design ideals. As mentioned previously there are cases where the design professional has the cause and responsibility to be more stringent than the code.

A clearly written and rational building code can be of real assistance to the designer, and it is well to remember that far fewer failures occur in jurisdictions where good codes are present and enforced.

1-10 ACCURACY OF COMPUTATIONS

One of the largest inconsistencies of structural analysis and design procedures is in the determination of a proper accuracy level for computations. The author believes that sometimes it is unfortunate that we possess the machine capability to rapidly produce answers to many decimal places. In structural engineering such precision is seldom, if ever, necessary. In most cases, any values written with more than three significant digits are misleading as to the actual accuracy level and can generate an undeserved sense of confidence.

To put the matter of required precision in prospec-

tive, one has only to look at the often-used live-load values in Appendix O. Many structural calculations start with these suggested values as estimates of the expected maximum loading. It is completely false to assume that 5 kN/m² means 5.00 kN/m², yet that is what the analyst does when the answer derived from that loading is given to three significant places. This is not to suggest that calculations must be done in an approximate way and, above all, analytical procedures should never be handled in a careless or sloppy manner. Quite the contrary, good procedures and precise work will always prevent errors, never promote them. It is merely that we should be aware of the true accuracy level in our work, taking into account the various idealistic assumptions made as to load, dimensions, and physical conditions.

For most purposes the levels of precision given in Table 1-2 will probably suffice and may become "too accurate" if not cut off at three significant digits.

TABLE 1-2 *Accuracy Levels*

Quantity	Sufficient precision
Member lengths	Nearest tenth of a meter
Cross-sectional dimensions	Nearest millimeter
Force	Nearest tenth of a kilonewton
Moment	Nearest kilonewton-meter
Stress	Nearest kilopascal
Angles	Nearest degree
Deflections	Nearest millimeter
Temperature	Nearest degree Celsius

In this book the writer has attempted to round off quantities to the appropriate level except where clarity would be reduced by so doing.

2-1 INTRODUCTION

Statics is one part of a more general subject called mechanics. *Mechanics* involves the study of forces and the effects of those forces upon the bodies on which they act. When the forces acting on a body are balanced such that no acceleration is taking place, a state of equilibrium exists. The subject of *statics* is limited to forces acting on bodies in equilibrium.

The branch of mechanics that treats unbalanced systems of forces involving acceleration is called *dynamics*. A third area, which deals with the physical deformations and internal effects in bodies caused by forces, is called *mechanics of materials* or, somewhat incorrectly, strength of materials. Mechanics of materials provides the theory behind most of the procedures used in structural analysis and design and, as such, is extensively covered in succeeding chapters of this book.

The subject matter treated in statics rarely poses any difficulty for the majority of students. Much of it is repetitious, merely repeating what has already been covered in a physics course. In some topical sequences, little emphasis is placed on statics and a thorough understanding of loads and their reactive forces is never really achieved. The reader is cautioned that statics forms the basis for all structural analysis, and all professionals in the field consider it the most important part of any study of quantitative structures.

2-2 FORCES

For our purposes, a *force* is a push or pull provided by one object upon another. It can act at a point, such as a concentrated column load upon a spread footing, or be distributed, such as the uniform dead load of a slab carried by a beam.

Force is a *vector* quantity, meaning that it has both magnitude and direction. If we let the magnitude of a force be represented graphically by the length of an arrow, the *direction* can be established from its line of action, as seen in Figure 2-1. The line of action extends infinitely in front of and behind the force. Each force also has a *sense*, which becomes the sign (+ or −) in

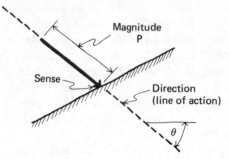

Figure 2-1. Description of a force.

algebraic computations. Sense is represented by the arrowhead in Figure 2-1. It is important not to confuse sense and direction, and it may be helpful to remember that for each direction there are two possible senses. For example, if a certain gravity load acts vertically downward, its direction is vertical and its sense is down.

In statics, we consider only external forces exerted by one body upon another. Internal forces, more properly called *stresses*, are those exerted by one part of a body upon another part of the same body. The body must be "cut open," in a figurative manner, before such forces can be examined or quantified.

2-3 COMPONENTS AND RESULTANTS

When two or more forces act at one point on a body (concurrent forces), it may be convenient to replace such forces by a single force which will have the same external effect on the body. This replacement force is called a

2

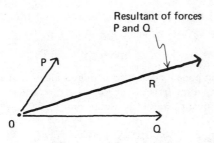

Figure 2-2. Resultant of two forces.

resultant. Figure 2-2 shows a system of two forces being replaced by a resultant. Graphically, it is represented as the diagonal of a parallelogram, which includes the two given forces as adjacent sides. More than two concurrent forces could be treated by successive parallelograms.

It should be apparent that, by following the reverse procedure, one could resolve a given force *R* into two components along any two lines of action. Figure 2-3 illustrates three such sets of components. The force *R* could be replaced by any one of these pairs without any change in the action of the particle at *O*. The most useful pair is that shown in Figure 2-3(b), which are called the *rectangular components*.

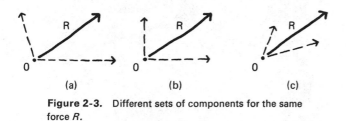

(a)   (b)   (c)

Figure 2-3. Different sets of components for the same force *R*.

The force *F* in Figure 2-4 may be replaced by two forces, which act in the horizontal (*x*) and vertical (*y*) directions, by noting that

$$F_x = F \cos \theta \qquad (2\text{-}1)$$

and

$$F_y = F \sin \theta \qquad (2\text{-}2)$$

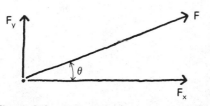

Figure 2-4. Rectangular force components.

where θ is the angle made by the parent force with the *x* axis. Conversely, if given the two forces F_x and F_y, one could find the magnitude of their resultant by using the *Pythagorean theorem*:

$$F = \sqrt{(F_x)^2 + (F_y)^2} \qquad (2\text{-}3)$$

The direction of this resultant could be found from the fact that

$$\tan \theta = \frac{F_y}{F_x} \qquad (2\text{-}4)$$

The resultant of a system of several concurrent forces can be determined by first resolving each force into its rectangular components as shown in Figure 2-5.

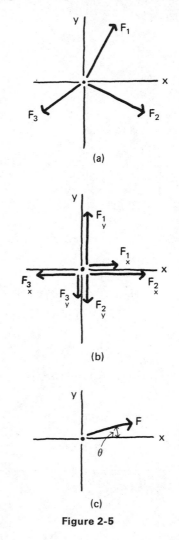

Figure 2-5

These components can then be treated algebraically as indicated by Equations (2-3a) and (2-4a).

$$F = \sqrt{(\textstyle\sum F_x)^2 + (\textstyle\sum F_y)^2} \qquad (2\text{-}3a)$$

$$\tan \theta = \frac{\sum F_y}{\sum F_x} \qquad (2\text{-}4a)$$

EXAMPLE 2-1

Determine the resultant of the three forces shown in Figure 2-6(a).

Solution: Resolve each force into its rectangular components by using Equations (2-1) and (2-2). For the 50-kN force,

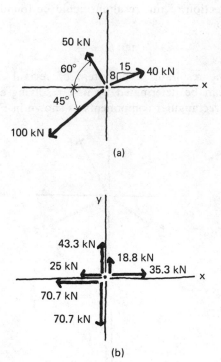

(a)

(b)

Figure 2-6

$$F_x = 50(0.500) = 25.0 \text{ kN}$$
$$F_y = 50(0.866) = 43.3 \text{ kN}$$

For the 40-kN force,

$$F_x = 40(\tfrac{15}{17}) = 35.3 \text{ kN}$$
$$F_y = 40(\tfrac{8}{17}) = 18.8 \text{ kN}$$

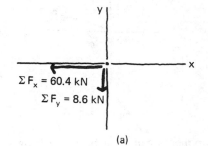

(a)

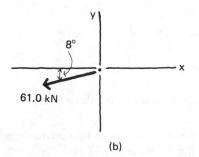

(b)

Figure 2-7

For the 100-kN force,

$$F_x = 100(0.707) = 70.7 \text{ kN}$$
$$F_y = 100(0.707) = 70.7 \text{ kN}$$

These components can then be algebraically summed in their respective directions to get the net components in Figure 2-7(a). Substituting into Equations (2-3a) and (2-4a), we obtain

$$F = \sqrt{(\textstyle\sum F_x)^2 + (\textstyle\sum F_y)^2}$$
$$= \sqrt{(60.4)^2 + (8.6)^2}$$
$$= 61.0 \text{ kN}$$

$$\tan \theta = \frac{\sum F_y}{\sum F_x}$$
$$= \frac{8.6}{60.4}$$
$$\theta = 8°$$

Problems

2-1. Determine the magnitude, sense, and direction of the resultant of the concurrent system in Figure 2-8.

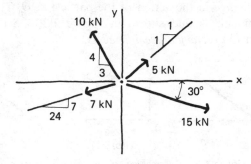

Figure 2-8

2-2. Determine the magnitude, sense, and direction of the resultant of the three forces acting at the top of the pole in Figure 2-9.

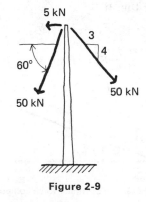

Figure 2-9

2-4 FORCE POLYGONS

By using the fact that the opposite sides of a parallelogram are equal, we see that a force triangle (Figure 2-10) may be formed instead of the parallelogram of Figure

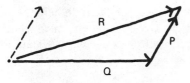

Figure 2-10. Force triangle.

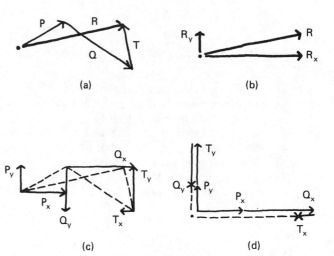

(a)

(b)

2-2. The components *P* and *Q* form a head-to-tail arrangement by transposing the force *P*. The resultant *R* which closes the triangle does not follow this head-to-tail order. This same procedure may be used to determine graphically the resultant of more than two concurrent forces. The forces shown in Figure 2-11(a) may be taken

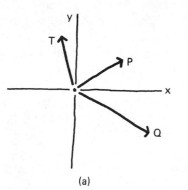

(a)

(c)

(d)

Figure 2-12

a given system in equilibrium. It negates or balances the effects of the other forces. Figure 2-13(b) shows the equilibrant *E* of the previous three-force system. Graphically, the equilibrant will close a polygon of forces by continuing the head-to-tail relationship. In fact, each of the forces shown in Figure 2-14 is the equilibrant of the other three.

(b)

Figure 2-11. Forces with rectangular components.

in any order to form a head-to-tail pattern. The force needed to close the polygon is the resultant of the system. Reversing the head-to-tail sequence will give the resultant the proper sense. Figure 2-12 shows how the rectangular components of the forces *P*, *Q*, and *T* will add to have the same net effect as the components of the resultant force *R*. Figure 2-12(d) shows two polygons (with coincident or overlapping lines), which could be formed by the rectangular components of the forces. The dashed resultants are, of course, the same as the components R_x and R_y shown in Figure 2-12(b).

The force that is equal in magnitude, but opposite in sense, to the resultant is called the *equilibrant*. It is, as its name suggests, the one force that is needed to put

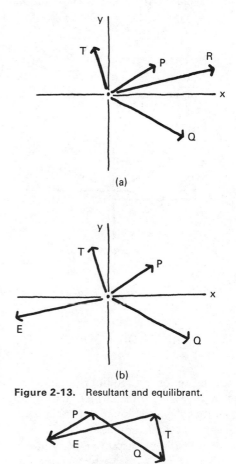

(a)

(b)

Figure 2-13. Resultant and equilibrant.

Figure 2-14

EXAMPLE 2-2

Graphically determine the resultant of the force system in Example 2-1.

Solution: The accuracy of any graphical solution depends upon the care and skill provided by the analyst and the scale of the drawings. Large figures will always yield a smaller percentage of error. Even so, one can seldom achieve the accuracy inherent in an algebraic solution (if such precision is necessary). In this case, the force scale is given in Figure 2-15. The answers shown in Figure 2-15 were obtained by measuring directly from the drawing with a scale and a protractor.

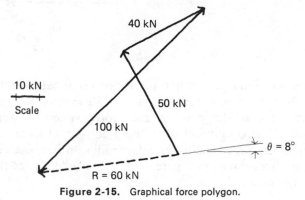

Figure 2-15. Graphical force polygon.

Problems

2-3. Work Problem 2-1 graphically.

2-4. Work Problem 2-2 graphically.

2-5. Graphically determine the equilibrant of the force system in Figure 2-16.

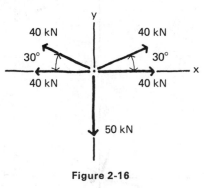

Figure 2-16

2-5 EQUILIBRIUM OF CONCURRENT FORCES

As stated in Section 2-1, equilibrium is a state of balance created by opposing forces which act on a body in such a manner that their combined net effect is zero. *Newton's first law* states, in effect, that when a body is at rest (or is moving with a constant velocity in a straight line), the resultant of the force system acting on the body is equal to zero.

If we consider, for the time being, only those force systems which are concurrent, such that there is no tendency for rotation to occur, then equilibrium can be established by setting

$$\sum F = 0 \qquad (2\text{-}5)$$

To ensure force equilibrium in all directions, it is usually easier to work with the two rectangular component equations:

$$\sum F_x = 0 \qquad (2\text{-}5a)$$
$$\sum F_y = 0 \qquad (2\text{-}5b)$$

(These two equations will suffice for coplanar systems; however, a third one in the z direction would be necessary for three-dimensional situations.)

The simplest structural systems are those which are concurrent and coplanar, and the two equations above will enable us to analyze such systems for two unknowns. Consider the load W suspended by the two ropes in Figure 2-17. The system is a concurrent one of only three forces, A and B and the load W, as shown in Figure 2-17(b).

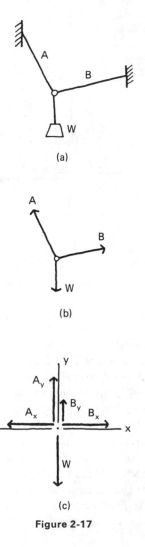

Figure 2-17

Assuming that the load W is known and the angles of the cables A and B are known, the forces A and B can be readily determined by using the x and y components. With reference to Figure 2-17(c) and using the standard convention that forces upward and to the right are positive in sense, we get

$$\Sigma F_x = 0 \qquad \Sigma F_y = 0$$
$$B_x - A_x = 0 \qquad B_y + A_y - W = 0$$

If the components are then expressed in terms of their parent forces A and B, the two equations can be solved simultaneously.

Problems of this type are not limited to tensile members, and the cables at A and B could just as well have been rigid bars capable of taking tension or compression. Where the sense of the force carried by such a member is uncertain, it must be assumed and then verified as the answer is obtained. A negative sign accompanying the answer will mean an incorrect sense assumption.

EXAMPLE 2-3

Determine the magnitude and sense of the forces in the members A and B in Figure 2-18.

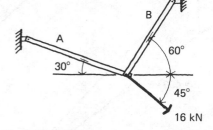

Figure 2-18. Two bars supporting a 16-kN load.

Solution: If we assume that both bars are in tension, we get the concurrent forces shown in Figure 2-19(a). Their components appear as in Figure 2-19(b). Writing the two x and y equations from the components, we get

$$\Sigma F_x = 0 \qquad \qquad \Sigma F_y = 0$$
$$B_x + 0.707(16) - A_x = 0 \qquad B_y + A_y - 0.707(16) = 0$$

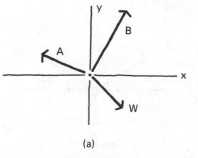

(a)

Figure 2-19

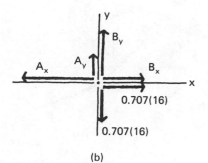

(b)

Figure 2-19 (continued)

In terms of forces A and B,

$$0.500B - 0.866A + 11.3 = 0$$
$$0.866B + 0.500A - 11.3 = 0$$

Solving simultaneously will yield $A = +15.5$ and $B = +4.2$. The plus signs indicate that our sense assumptions were correct.

$$A = 15.5 \text{ kN tension}$$
$$B = 4.2 \text{ kN tension}$$

EXAMPLE 2-4

Determine the magnitude and sense of the forces in bars A and B in Figure 2-20.

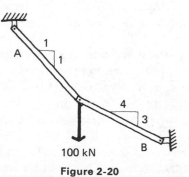

Figure 2-20

Solution: For purposes of illustration, we shall assume that bar A is in tension and bar B is in compression. Tension force arrows will act away from the point of concurrency and compression arrows will act in toward it (Figure 2-21). (After an inspection of the horizontal force components, the reader should be able to ascertain that these sense assumptions cannot both be correct.)

$$\Sigma F_x = 0 \qquad \qquad \Sigma F_y = 0$$
$$-B_x - A_x = 0 \qquad B_y + A_y - 100 = 0$$
$$-0.800B - 0.707A = 0 \qquad 0.600B + 0.707A - 100 = 0$$

Solving for A and B, we get $A = +566$ kN and $B = -500$ kN. The minus sign indicates that bar B is actually in tension, not compression as we had assumed.

$$A = 566 \text{ kN tension}$$
$$B = 500 \text{ kN tension}$$

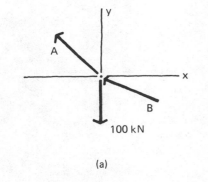

(a)

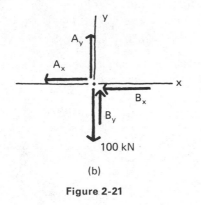

(b)

Figure 2-21

These types of problems can also be solved graphically. In each case, the three forces, load plus two unknowns, are in equilibrium. This means that each one is the equilibrant of the other two, and we must be able to form a head-to-tail triangle. The only magnitude given is that of the applied load, but the directions of all three lines of action are known. Given the three forces, for example, of Figure 2-17(b) and drawing the load vector to scale, only two possible triangles can be formed. These are shown in Figure 2-22. If we place the sense arrows on the triangles in head-to-tail fashion as in Figure 2-23, we see that either triangle will give us the correct results. In each case, the sense arrows point away from the original point of concurrency, indicating tensile forces in

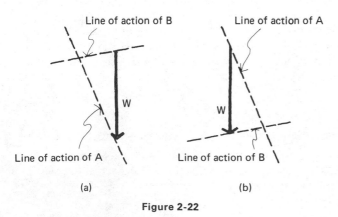

(a)   (b)

Figure 2-22

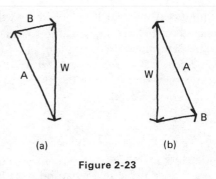

(a)   (b)

Figure 2-23

both members. The magnitudes are simply measured with the force scale used to draw *W*.

EXAMPLE 2-5

Use graphical techniques to check the results of Example 2-4.

Solution: The answers in Figure 2-24(a) were obtained by measuring the polygon and are less than 5% off the values obtained in the algebraic solution. Placing the arrows so they act on the original joint, as in Figure 2-24(b), we see that both arrows represent tension.

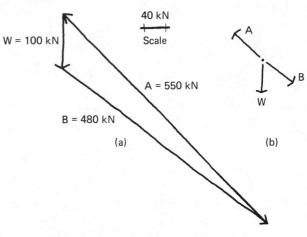

(a)   (b)

Figure 2-24. Force polygon for Example 2-5.

Problems

2-6. Determine the magnitude and sense of the forces in cables *A* and *B* of Figure 2-25.

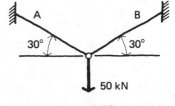

Figure 2-25

2-7. Determine the magnitude and sense of the forces in bars *A* and *B* of Figure 2-26. Use the algebraic method and then check your results graphically.

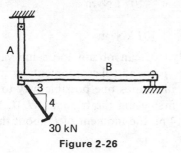

Figure 2-26

2-8. Determine the magnitude and sense of the forces in bars *A* and *B* in Figure 2-27.

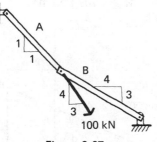

Figure 2-27

2-9. With reference to Figure 2-25, what will be the limiting value of the forces in bars *A* and *B* as the two angles labeled 30° approach zero?

2-6 MOMENTS AND COUPLES

A *moment* is a tendency to rotate or twist. When a force acts on a certain object, that object has a tendency to move in the direction of the force. This is called *translation*. Figure 2-28 shows the force *P* having a line of action that passes through the particle at *C*. Under the action of the force, the particle will tend to move along that line of action. However, the particles at *A* and *B* do not lie along the line of action. Under the influence of the force, they will not only tend to translate, but will also tend

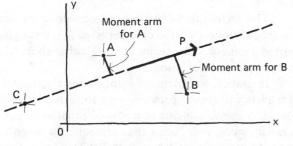

Figure 2-28. Moment of a force.

to rotate (i.e., the force *P* has moment with respect to those two points).[1] Indeed, a force tends to cause rotation or has moment about every point which does not lie along its line of action.

The *magnitude* of the moment of a force acting about some point is defined as the product of the force and the perpendicular distance from its line of action to the point. Such a perpendicular distance is often called a *moment arm* and is, in effect, a lever arm. The units of moment are force times distance and in structural analysis this is usually expressed in kilonewton-meters (kN·m). Moment also has sense; it either acts clockwise or counterclockwise.

Most moments from forces tend to bend structural objects; for example, when two children sit on a seesaw, they bend the board, and how much it is bent depends upon the location (distance) and the weight (force) of a child. Some moments, however, act to twist an object about its long axis, and these forces are generally called *torques* or *torsional moments*. The effects of bending moments and their importance are covered in Chapters 8 and 9, and torsion is treated in Chapter 6.

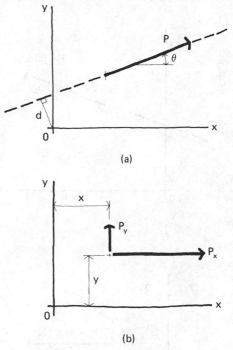

Figure 2-29. Varignon's theorem.

In order to obtain the magnitude of the moment of a force, with respect to a certain point, it is sometimes easier to work with the components of the force rather than with the force itself. Figure 2-29(a) shows a force *P*

---

[1]The phrases "tend to move" or "tend to rotate" are used because in statics there are generally other forces present which act to balance out or prevent the actual motion.

which has a moment arm of distance d with respect to the origin O. The magnitude of this moment is P times d, and it is clockwise in sense. This value may also be found by using the components shown in Figure 2-29(b). The moment of a force with respect to a point is equal to the algebraic sum of the moments of the components of the force taken with respect to that same point. This means that the moment of P with respect to the point O can also be found as the net effect of $P_y(x)$ counterclockwise and $P_x(y)$ clockwise. [Credit for this observation is given to Pierre Varignon (1654–1722), a French mathematician.]

For algebraic purposes, we shall let counterclockwise moments be positive and clockwise moments be negative. (There is no consistency among writers in the mechanics field for this sign convention, and this selection is quite arbitrary. It is only important that one be consistent throughout a given analysis.)

To illustrate *Varignon's theorem*, let us assign values to the quantities as shown in Figure 2-30. The components in Figure 2-30(b) are found as functions of the 20° angle, and the net moment about the origin O of those components is

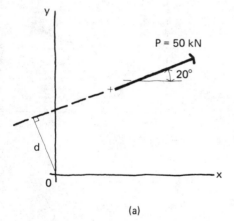

(a)

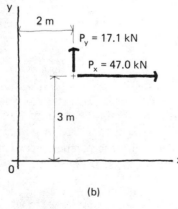

(b)

Figure 2-30

$$M_0 = +P_y(2\text{ m}) - P_x(3\text{ m})$$
$$= +17.1\text{ kN}(2\text{ m}) - 47.0\text{ kN}(3\text{ m})$$
$$= -107\text{ kN·m}$$

or

$$M_0 = 107\text{ kN·m } \circlearrowright$$

Alternatively, we can obtain the same value by determining the perpendicular moment arm distance d. Figure 2-31 illustrates one possible way to quantify this distance by first using the triangle KLM. With d established as 2.14 m, the moment of P about the origin is

$$M_0 = -P(d)$$
$$= -50\text{ kN}(2.14\text{ m})$$
$$= -107\text{ kN·m}$$

or

$$M_0 = 107\text{ kN·m } \circlearrowright$$

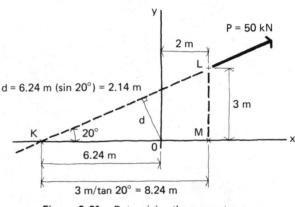

Figure 2-31. Determining the moment arm.

The reader should notice that the moment of the force P, being a function of the perpendicular distance to the line of action, is independent of the location of the force along its line of action. For example, if we relocate P so that it acts at the point K in Figure 2-31, then using Varignon's theorem, we get

$$M_0 = P_x(0\text{ m}) - P_y(6.24\text{ m})$$
$$= -17.1\text{ kN}(6.24\text{ m})$$
$$= -107\text{ kN·m}$$

or

$$M_0 = 107\text{ kN·m } \circlearrowright$$

This technique of moving a force along its line of action until one of its components passes through the desired moment center can be a valuable shortcut for many moment calculations.

In statics, we frequently encounter a special kind of tendency to rotate, provided by a force system called a couple. A *couple* consists of a pair of equal and opposite parallel forces, two forces that are equal in magnitude, opposite in sense, and have parallel lines of action. It produces only rotation, no translation. It is pure moment. Its magnitude is given by the product of one of the forces, and the perpendicular distance between the forces and its sense is clockwise or counterclockwise. The most important characteristic of a couple is that its effect (magnitude and sense of the moment) is the same with respect to every point in its plane. Its tendency to cause rotation of a point is a constant and is *independent* of the distance between the couple and the point. The student should verify arithmetically that each couple in Figure 2-32 has the same 20-kN·m clockwise effect upon the point O. Given the dimensions to any other point in the plane of Figure 2-32, we could show that the same 20-kN·m rotation acts there also.

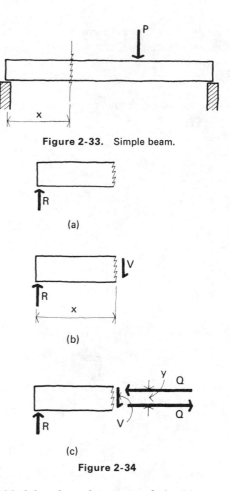

Figure 2-33. Simple beam.

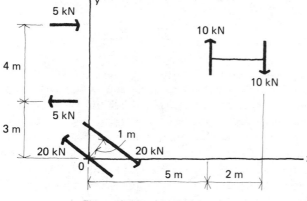

Figure 2-32. Identical couples.

Figure 2-34

From the standpoint of static equilibrium, the effect of a couple can only be negated or balanced by a second couple of identical magnitude but opposite sense. The equilibrant couple must lie in the same (or parallel) plane. The moment of a couple cannot be balanced by a single force because the value of moment for a force is dependent upon the location of the moment center. Similarly, the action of a single force cannot be negated by a couple, for a couple provides no translation.

An understanding of what a couple is enables us to look more closely at what happens inside a bending member (beam). In Chapter 1, mention was made of the inefficiency of bending as a means to carry load. Not only are the stresses distributed very unevenly within a beam, but the small structural depth of most beams necessitates large couple forces to maintain equilibrium. Figure 2-33 shows a beam with a single concentrated load carried between two bearing walls. The beam itself is assumed to be weightless. Let us cut through the beam near the load to examine the internal forces. Isolating the left-hand portion of the beam from the rest of the system, we will see the upward reaction R provided by the wall as in Figure 2-34(a). An internal downward force called V in Figure 2-34(b) develops as a response to R. This force

V is provided by the other part of the beam and, for vertical equilibrium, would have to be exactly equal to R.

These two forces constitute a couple of magnitude V times x (or R times x), which can only be balanced by an opposing couple. In other words, the beam portion might be in force (translational) equilibrium ($\sum F = 0$), but it is not in moment (rotational) equilibrium. The second or opposing couple can only be provided by the other beam part upon the cut face as shown in Figure 2-34(c). Because the moment arm of this opposing couple is limited by the beam depth, the forces Q will be quite large. For moment equilibrium ($\sum M = 0$), Q times y must equal V times x. The two forces Q, of course, are equal according to the definition of a couple. This also assures force equilibrium in the horizontal direction.

The preceding explanation introduced the third equation of static equilibrium, which joins the previous two discussed in Section 2-5 dealing with concurrent forces. Since a beam involves forces that are not concurrent, all three equations were involved.

$$\sum F_x = 0 \qquad (2\text{-}5a)$$
$$\sum F_y = 0 \qquad (2\text{-}5b)$$
$$\sum M = 0 \qquad (2\text{-}6)$$

These are the only three equations of statics that are applicable to coplanar structures.

Problems

2-10. Determine the magnitude and sense of the moment of the force in Figure 2-35 with respect to points O, A, and B.

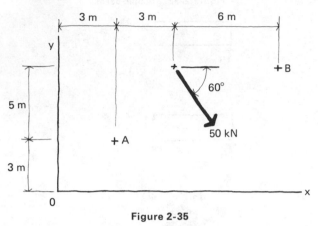

Figure 2-35

2-11. Show that the four forces in Figure 2-36 have a net moment of zero with respect to points O and A and a third point of your choice.

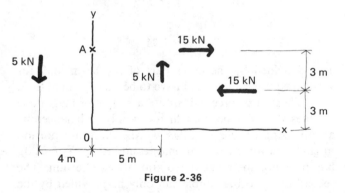

Figure 2-36

2-7 REPLACEMENT OF A FORCE BY A FORCE AND A COUPLE

Sometimes it is computationally convenient to replace a force with a force and a couple, which have the same effect upon the member. Equilibrium is maintained if we proportion the new force and couple correctly. For example, Figure 2-37(a) shows an eccentric load acting on the top of a pier. The effect on the pier consists of a downward force (P) and a clockwise moment (P times e). In Figure 2-37(b), two collinear forces P (shown dashed) have been added to the pier. These forces cancel each other and we have, in effect, added zero to the system. However, the two forces P which are circled constitute a clockwise couple of magnitude P times e. The replacement system is shown in Figure 2-37(c) with the couple

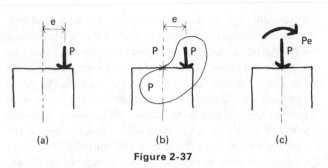

Figure 2-37

represented as a moment arc of value $P(e)$. This new concentric force and couple have the same action upon the pier as did the original eccentric load. Almost all problems involving eccentric loads can be conceptually simplified using such equivalent systems.

2-8 IDEAL SUPPORT CONDITIONS

The actual support conditions and member connections in real building structures are quite complicated. The proper design of connections, if all the various forces were considered, would be a lengthy and exacting process. An accurate determination of the amount of friction and slip, for example, which occurs under load at a given beam to column joint would be almost impossible. Nevertheless, the behavior of the supports can have a critical effect upon the structure proper, and the designer cannot ignore the end conditions of any member.

In actual practice, it is necessary to make certain idealized simplifications regarding the nature of connections and supports. The designer must be aware of the fact that these simplifications are false and may or may not approximate the actual construction conditions. Judgment must be used to increase the factors of safety involved in the design whenever it is suspected that an assumed condition departs markedly from the actual one. It is too easy to forget that, while it is simple to draw frictionless rollers or fully rigid, inflexible connections, they are literally impossible to fabricate.

The symbols presented in Figures 2-38 through 2-41 for various ideal support conditions are standard and universally accepted. What is not universally accepted is the determination of characteristics needed, by actual field connections and conditions, for the symbols to be valid representations. In spite of this, some attempt has been made in the following discussion to indicate a few types of real connections which would correspond to the various symbols.

The *hanger* can take no compression and is assumed to provide a single force of known sense and direction. The *rod* or *angles* are assumed to be long and slender, having no resistance to compression buckling and negligible bending resistance. If the tension member is placed

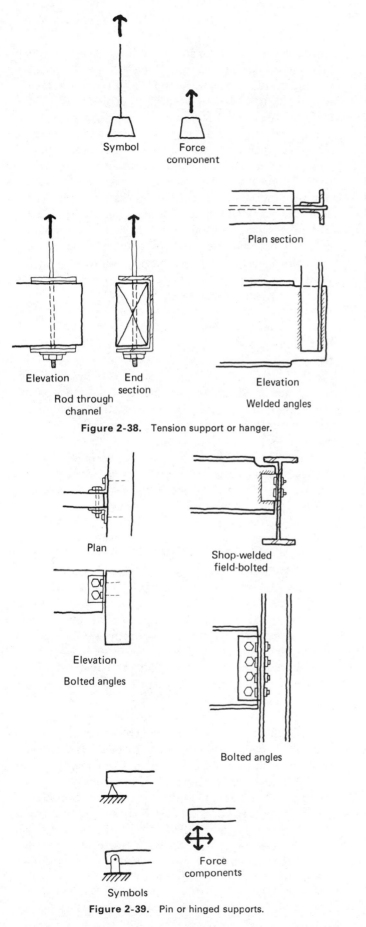

Figure 2-38. Tension support or hanger.

at an angle, its force can be represented as two rectangular components, but these components are not independent. They are related to each other by the direction of their resultant, which acts along the member.

The *pin* can take one force of unknown sense and direction (Figure 2-39). In theory, it offers no resistance to rotation (moment). The single force is usually represented by two rectangular components, since this will cover any possible line of action. The two components are independent as to both magnitude and sense and will constitute two unknowns.

The *roller* provides a single force of known direction (Figure 2-40). Its sense is unknown (i.e., it is assumed that the member cannot "lift off" a roller). Like the tension hanger, if the roller or link is on an angle, its force

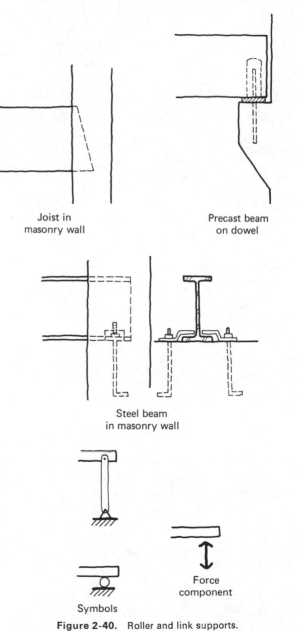

Figure 2-39. Pin or hinged supports.

Figure 2-40. Roller and link supports.

is usually represented as two rectangular components. These two components are dependent both as to magnitude and sense and constitute but one unknown. Once either component is determined, the other is known by trigonometry. The pin and roller are called *simple supports*.

The *link support* is really more of a separate structural member than a support, but it acts very much like a roller. To provide a force of known direction, the link must have a pin (or hinge) at both ends and carry no load in between. Sometimes called a *strut*, it is a special case of a larger group of structural elements, described later (Section 2-10) as two-force members.

The *fixed* or *rigid* or *built-in support* can take one force of unknown sense and direction (Figure 2-41). In theory, it also has full moment resistance (of either sense) and will not change its angle of attachment. Like the pin, the single force is usually represented as two com-

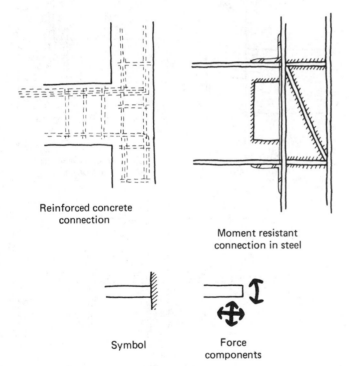

Reinforced concrete connection

Moment resistant connection in steel

Symbol   Force components

Figure 2-41. Fixed or moment-resistant support.

pletely independent components. A fixed connection has the potential of three unknowns (i.e., two independent components and a couple). This couple is sometimes called a *moment reaction* or *fixed-end moment*.

2-9 EQUILIBRIUM OF SINGLE MEMBERS

Before looking further into the subject of static equilibrium, the concept of the *rigid body* should be introduced. In statics, it becomes convenient, if not necessary, to

ignore the small deformations and displacements which take place when a member is loaded. To do this, we pretend that the materials used for all structural elements and supports are rigid, having the property of infinite stiffness. We assume that members do not stretch, compress, or bend in any way and that their geometry, therefore, remains constant. This is, of course, never true. Even though structural materials are very stiff, they all deform slightly even under small loads. However, the assumption that structural bodies are rigid greatly simplifies many situations in terms of static equilibrium and, in most cases, introduces an insignificant amount of error. An example of the type of minute change, which is generally ignored, is the shortening of span that takes place when a beam deflects into an arc. Depending upon the type of loading, minor changes in the upward reactions at the supports would also occur. Not only would such changes be insignificant if expressed in percentage terms, but would also be difficult to consider quantitatively because, like other deformations, they vary with the load.

Once all of the external forces have been resolved in terms of statics, the stresses and strains within the various elements of the structure are examined. At this point, it is critical that material deformations are not ignored. The rigid-body concept is useful only for the determination of external forces. (It is generally valid but can require modification when applied to the statics of more complicated structural problems.)

While the idea of a structure that is rigid for some analytical operations but not for others may seem incongruous to the novice, a little experience will quickly provide the rationale and judgment behind this concept.

In structural analysis, the principles of statics are used to determine reactive forces, which are responses to the applied loads. These reactions always develop the appropriate magnitudes and directions, such that the end result is one of equilibrium. In other words, under the combined action of the loads and reactions, each element of the structure has zero tendency to translate and zero tendency to rotate.

Determining the needed reactive forces is made easier if the analyst makes a sketch of the structure or element, showing all the forces involved (known and unknown). Such a sketch is called a *free-body diagram* (FBD), and most structural designers consider making such a diagram the first step in any statics problem. A free-body diagram shows the body in isolation or cut "free" from everything adjacent to it. The effects of all such removed objects are shown as forces acting at the appropriate locations. We have already used these diagrams in this chapter without calling them by name. Figure 2-17(b) is, in effect, a free-body diagram of the central joint. The portion of beam shown in Figure

2-34(c) is another free-body diagram. The examples that follow will all utilize an FBD.

EXAMPLE 2-6

Determine the reaction components for the simply supported beam in Figure 2-42.

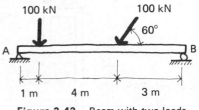

Figure 2-42. Beam with two loads.

Solution: The free-body diagram is shown in Figure 2-43. The senses of the unknown reactions must be assumed. A negative sign on the answer will mean an incorrect sense assumption. The load that acts at an angle has been resolved into its rectangular components. The three equations of equilibrium are then used to find the unknown force components.

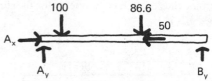

Figure 2-43. Free-body diagram for Example 2-6.

(Whenever practicable, moment equations are written for more than one point, and one of the two force equations is left for use as an independent check on the answers. It should be noted that regardless of the number of moment centers selected, however, there remain only three independent equations in planar statics, and thus a maximum of three independent unknowns can be determined. Other techniques must be used to supplement these three equations whenever the number of independent reaction components exceeds three.)

$$\Sigma F_x = 0$$
$$A_x - 50 = 0 \qquad\qquad A_x = 50 \text{ kN} \atop \rightarrow$$
$$\Sigma M_A = 0$$
$$B_y(8) - 86.6(5) - 100(1) = 0 \qquad B_y = 66.6 \text{ kN}\uparrow$$
$$\Sigma M_B = 0$$
$$-A_y(8) + 100(7) + 86.6(3) = 0 \qquad A_y = 120 \text{ kN}\uparrow$$
$$\Sigma F_y = 0 \quad \text{check}$$
$$-100 - 86.6 + 120 + 66.6 = 0 \quad \checkmark$$

Notice that each answer specifies magnitude, direction, and sense of the force.

EXAMPLE 2-7

Determine the reaction components for the structure in Figure 2-44(a).

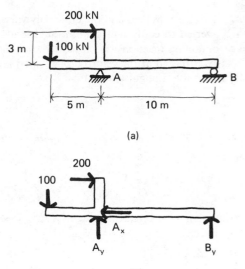

(a)

(b)

Figure 2-44. T-frame and free-body diagram.

Solution:

$$\Sigma F_x = 0$$
$$200 - A_x = 0 \qquad\qquad A_x = 200 \text{ kN} \atop \leftarrow$$
$$\Sigma M_A = 0$$
$$100(5) - 200(3) + B_y(10) = 0 \qquad B_y = 10 \text{ kN}\uparrow$$
$$\Sigma M_B = 0$$
$$100(15) - 200(3) - A_y(10) = 0 \qquad A_y = 90 \text{ kN}\uparrow$$
$$\Sigma F_y = 0 \quad \text{check}$$
$$-100 + 90 + 10 = 0 \quad \checkmark$$

EXAMPLE 2-8

Determine the reaction components for the beam in Figure 2-45(a).

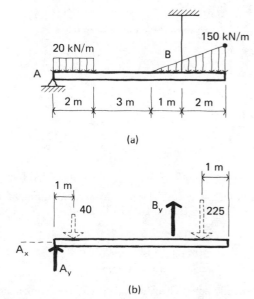

(a)

(b)

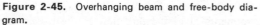

Figure 2-45. Overhanging beam and free-body diagram.

Solution: The uniform load and the uniformly varying load are both converted to equivalent concentrated loads for the purpose of obtaining reactions. Each load shown dashed in Figure 2-45(b) is placed at the centroid of its load area. (See Appendix M for the triangular load.)

$\Sigma F_x = 0$ \qquad\qquad\qquad\qquad $A_x = 0$

$\Sigma M_A = 0$

$B_y(6) - 40(1) - 225(7) = 0$ \qquad\qquad $B_y = 269.2$ kN↑

$\Sigma M_B = 0$

$-A_y(6) + 40(5) - 225(1) = 0$

$A_y = -4.2$ \qquad\qquad\qquad\qquad $A_y = 4.2$ kN↓

(The negative sign means that the sense of A_y as shown on the FBD is incorrect.)

$\Sigma F_y = 0$ \qquad check

$-40 - 225 + 269.2 - 4.2 = 0$ ✓

EXAMPLE 2-9

Determine the reaction components for the frame in Figure 2-46(a).

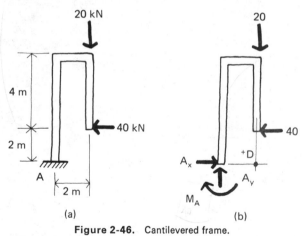

(a) \qquad\qquad\qquad\qquad\qquad\qquad (b)

Figure 2-46. Cantilevered frame.

Solution:

$\Sigma F_x = 0$

$A_x - 40 = 0$ \qquad\qquad\qquad\qquad $A_x = 40$ kN →

$\Sigma F_y = 0$

$A_y - 20 = 0$ \qquad\qquad\qquad\qquad $A_y = 20$ kN↑

$\Sigma M_A = 0$

$-M_A - 20(2) + 40(2) = 0$ \qquad\qquad $M_A = 40$ kN·m ↺

To accomplish a check, select a convenient moment center such as point *D* in Figure 2-46(b).

$\Sigma M_D = 0$ \qquad check

$-M_A - A_y(2) + 40(2) = 0$

$-40 - 20(2) + 40(2) = 0$ ✓

A theoretically better check would be made by using a moment center that eliminates A_x and A_y. The magnitudes of those two components gives the direction of the parent force *A*

shown in Figure 2-47. Thus, the moment center *E* will eliminate everything except the 40-kN load and the moment reaction.

$\Sigma M_E = 0$ \qquad check

$-40 + 40(1) = 0$ ✓

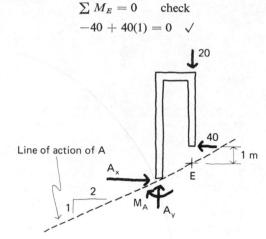

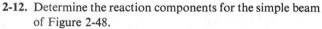

Figure 2-47

Problems

2-12. Determine the reaction components for the simple beam of Figure 2-48.

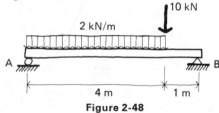

Figure 2-48

2-13. Determine the reaction components for the U-shaped frame of Figure 2-49.

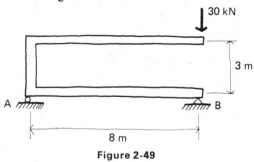

Figure 2-49

2-14. Determine the reaction components for the frame loaded by wind in Figure 2-50.

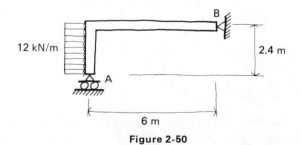

Figure 2-50

2-15. Determine the reaction components for the beam in Figure 2-51. (*Hint:* Separate the load into two parts.)

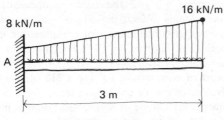

Figure 2-51. Cantilever beam.

2-16. Determine the reaction components for the beams of Figure 2-52. The connection at *B* may be assumed to act like a pin in both beams. (*Hint:* The components of the sloped cable force are related to each other by the angle of the cable.)

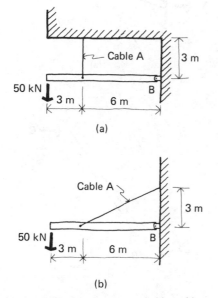

(a)

(b)

Figure 2-52. Beams suspended by cables.

2-10 TWO-FORCE MEMBERS

When a structural element is hinged or pinned at each end and carries no load in between, it is called a *two-force member*. Such elements have only two forces acting on them, one applied at each of the two pins. To maintain equilibrium, these forces must be equal, opposite, and collinear. If forces are resolved into components, the components are dependent upon the line of action of the parent force. In this case, the line of action must connect the two pins. In other words, the direction of the two forces is known by inspection.

Member *DB* in Figure 2-53 is a two-force member. Provided that no intermediate load is placed on it, any force acting at *D* or *B* must have the line of action shown. The magnitude and sense of such forces will be a function of the loading on member *AC*. There are only two pos-

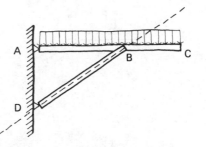

Figure 2-53. Two-force member.

sibilities for equilibrium, as shown in Figure 2-54(a) and (b). Any components drawn must be consistent as to sense, as in Figure 2-54(c) or (d). This means that if one of the four components is determined, the others are known automatically. Likewise, if one of the four components is assumed as to sense, the other three sense assumptions are made without choice.

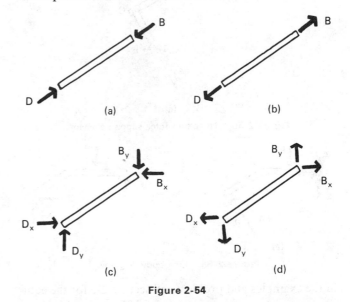

Figure 2-54

A *cable* is a two-force member of limited sense (i.e., only tension). A roller is the simplest of all two-force members and the link support is by definition a two-force member. The determination of force direction by two-force members is a very useful tool in statics. It means, for example, that the reactions of the three structures of Figure 2-55 will be identical. In each case, the reaction at *B* (which passes through *C*) will be as shown in Figure 2-56(a). For algebraic determination, it is probably easiest to deal with the dependent components shown in Figure 2-56(b). The components in this case will have the relationship

$$\frac{B_x}{B_y} = \frac{3}{4}$$

Because the equilibrium determination of a two-force member is trivial, it is best to remove it from free-body diagrams just as if it were a support. This was done

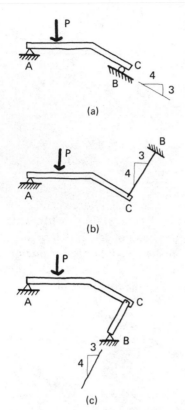

(a)

(b)

(c)

Figure 2-55. Three two-force support elements.

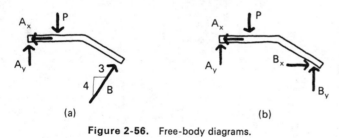

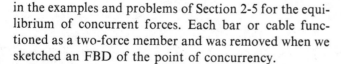

(a)   (b)

Figure 2-56. Free-body diagrams.

in the examples and problems of Section 2-5 for the equilibrium of concurrent forces. Each bar or cable functioned as a two-force member and was removed when we sketched an FBD of the point of concurrency.

EXAMPLE 2-10

Determine the reaction components at A and B for the structure in Figure 2-57.

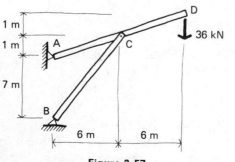

Figure 2-57

Solution: The member BC is a two-force member which holds up the bar AD. (In this case, it is fairly obvious that BC acts in compression, and the force components will be assumed accordingly. When the sense is not so obvious, it may be guessed as either tension or compression, consistent with the options of Figure 2-54.) The reader should recognize from Figure 2-58(b) that $B_x = C_x$ and $B_y = C_y$. When writing the equations of equilibrium for the FBD of member AD, these equivalencies will be used. Also recognize that the two-force member is on a slope of 8 m vertical on 6 m horizontal, and therefore $B_x = \frac{3}{4}B_y$ or $B_y = \frac{4}{3}B_x$.

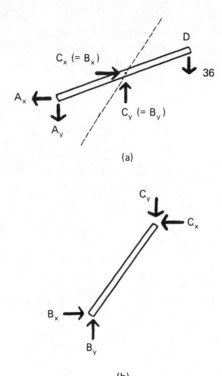

(a)

(b)

Figure 2-58. Free-body diagrams for Example 2-10.

$$\sum M_A = 0$$
$$-B_x(1) + B_y(6) - 36(12) = 0$$

But

$$B_x = \frac{3}{4}B_y$$
$$-\frac{3}{4}B_y(1) + 6B_y - 432 = 0 \qquad\qquad B_y = 82.3 \text{ kN}\uparrow$$

If B_y is 82.3, then

$$B_x = \frac{3}{4}(82.3) \qquad\qquad\qquad B_x = 61.7 \text{ kN} \atop \rightarrow$$

The two force equations can be used to get A_x and A_y from an FBD of member AD or an FBD of the whole structure as in Figure 2-59.

$$\sum F_x = 0$$
$$-A_x + 61.7 = 0 \qquad\qquad A_x = 61.7 \text{ kN} \atop \leftarrow$$
$$\sum F_y = 0$$
$$-A_y + 82.3 - 36 = 0 \qquad\qquad A_y = 46.3 \text{ kN}\downarrow$$

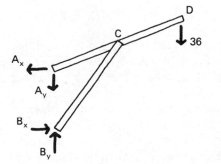

Figure 2-59. FBD of whole structure.

A check on our work is essential because, in this case, all the answers were made dependent upon the first answer for B_y. Using Figure 2-59 and taking moments about B, we get

$$\sum M_B = 0 \qquad \text{check}$$
$$61.7(7) - 36(12) = 0$$
$$431.9 - 432 \approx 0 \quad \checkmark$$

EXAMPLE 2-11

Determine the reaction components at A and B for the structure in Figure 2-60(a).

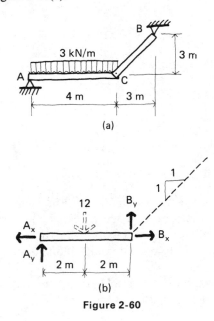

(a)

(b)

Figure 2-60

Solution: The two-force member BC acts on a 45° slope, which means that $B_x = B_y$. Using the free-body diagram in Figure 2-60(b),

$$\sum M_A = 0$$
$$-12(2) + B_y(4) = 0 \qquad\qquad B_y = 6 \text{ kN}\uparrow$$
$$\text{From the slope of } BC,\ B_x = 6 \text{ kN}$$
$$\rightarrow$$

$$\sum M_B = 0$$
$$-A_y(4) + 12(2) = 0 \qquad\qquad A_y = 6 \text{ kN}\uparrow$$

$$\sum F_x = 0$$
$$-A_x + 6 = 0 \qquad\qquad A_x = 6 \text{ kN}$$
$$\leftarrow$$

$$\sum F_y = 0 \qquad \text{check}$$
$$+6 - 12 + 6 = 0 \quad \checkmark$$

From the previous example, one can see that the length of the two-force member does not affect the external forces involved; only the slope (or geometry) is important. The line of action of the forces acting on a two-force member always connects the two pins present at each end of the member. It then becomes apparent that the shape of the two-force member between the pins is arbitrary. The shape of the two-force member will *not* affect the statics of the structure. This means that the three structures shown in Figure 2-61 would have the same external reactions as we found in Example 2-11.

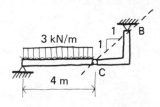

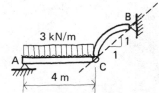

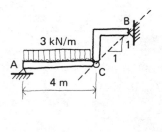

Figure 2-61. Three structures that have the same reactions as the structure in Figure 2-60(a).

Problems

2-17. Determine the reaction components for the structure in Figure 2-62.

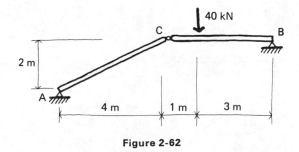

Figure 2-62

2-18. Determine the reaction components for the structure in Figure 2-63. (*Hint:* Make an FBD of member *BC* to prove that B_y and C_y are both zero.)

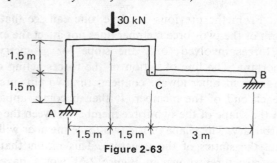

Figure 2-63

2-19. With reference to the structure in Figure 2-63, move the load so that it acts in the middle of member *BC*, and then determine the reaction components.

2-20. Determine the reactions for the structure in Figure 2-64.

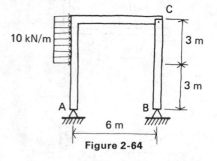

Figure 2-64

2-21. Determine the reaction components for the frame in Figure 2-65.

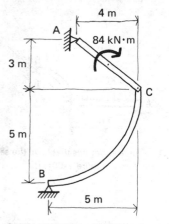

Figure 2-65. Structure acted upon by a couple.

2-22. Determine the reaction components for the structure in Figure 2-66.

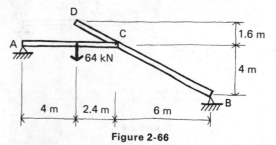

Figure 2-66

2-11 GRAPHICAL TECHNIQUES

If a member acted upon by only two forces is to be in equilibrium, it is necessary for those two forces to be collinear. It is similarly true that if a member or structure is acted upon by only three forces, equilibrium requires that those forces be concurrent. If this is the case, the three forces will make a *force polygon* that will have head-to-tail vectors like those of the simple structure in Section 2-5. For example, the structure in Figure 2-57 was proven to be in equilibrium under the action of three forces: the load, the reaction at *A*, and the reaction at *B*. An accurately drawn scale figure will show the point of concurrency. Since the line of action of the reaction at *B* is known, this point is easy to find. It is labeled p.o.c. in Figure 2-67. The line of action of the reactive force at *A* must pass through the p.o.c. to ensure equilibrium. With all lines of action known, the magnitude and sense of each reaction can be found by a force polygon.

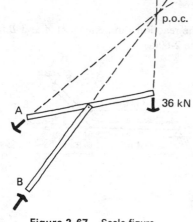

Figure 2-67. Scale figure.

The answers given in Figure 2-68 were measured directly from the drawing. The reader should verify that, within reasonable limits of accuracy, these values are the resultants of the *x* and *y* components found in Example 2-10.

The graphical force polygon is a powerful tool in statics which can be used to find reactions directly or as

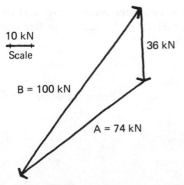

Figure 2-68. Force polygon.

a check on algebraic solutions. The writer frequently uses this technique to provide a quick and approximate visual determination of the sense and direction of reactions. With a little practice, the analyst can even get rough magnitudes by visualizing the appropriate force polygon and mentally scaling off distances on that image.

Force polygons are never as accurate as algebraic solutions, but they almost invariably provide a better conceptual grasp of the forces involved. In the problems that follow, the student should try to guess at the answers by making mental (or, better yet, actual freehand) sketches before drafting the solution.

(There are graphical methods for solving almost every type of problem in statics and only an introduction is attempted here. Applied couple loads, such as in Figure 2-65, have not been discussed nor has any method been provided to deal with parallel forces (point of concurrency at infinity). These and other problems can be solved graphically, but the techniques are sometimes not as fundamental to the understanding of equilibrium as is the basic force polygon.)

Problems

2-23. Graphically verify the results obtained in Example 2-11.

2-24. Graphically determine the reactions for the structure in Figure 2-66.

2-25. Graphically determine the reactions at *A* and *B* for the arch in Figure 2-69. (*Hint:* First resolve the two loads into one.)

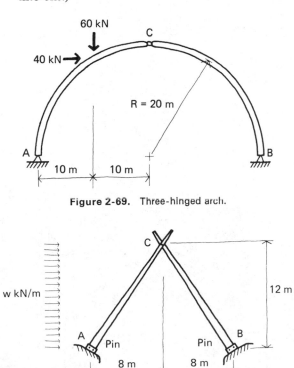

Figure 2-69. Three-hinged arch.

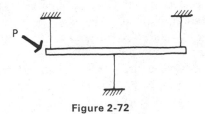

Figure 2-70. Timber frame.

2-26. The bolted connection at *A* in Figure 2-70 can withstand a tensile force of 40 kN. Determine the safe maximum wind load (*w* kN/m) which can be applied to the frame as shown. (*Hint:* Assume that the uniform wind load can be resolved into one horizontal force that acts halfway up the member *AC*.)

2-12 STABILITY AND DETERMINACY

In order to be in a state of static equilibrium, a structure must meet the requirements of stability. Loads and reactions bear no meaningful relationship to one another in an unstable structure. Structural stability is accomplished through the geometry of the members and the support (or boundary) conditions present. First, a stable structure is one that will remain at rest under any realistic loading pattern. For example, the simple beam in Figure 2-71(a) is generally unstable. Even though it might remain at rest under a specific load, such as in Figure 2-71(b), it is still

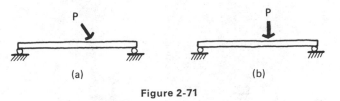

Figure 2-71

judged unstable. Second, the structure must be capable of carrying load without requiring an angular change in its geometry. The structure held in place by cables in Figure 2-72 is unstable because its load-carrying ability depends upon a change in geometry—in this case, a small motion to the right. The amount of motion is not important. The fact that such motion must take place before the structure can accept load is important.

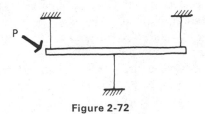

Figure 2-72

It may be helpful to consider the three concurrent force structures in Figure 2-73. The horizontal bars of Figure 2-73(b) are unstable because, as two-force members, they cannot develop the vertical components needed to equilibrate the load *P*. In other words, an angle change is necessary. But, if we accept the concept of rigid bodies, such an angle change is impossible because the "rigid" bars cannot elongate to accommodate this change.

Structural stability, for the purposes of equilibrium, is a theoretical concept, and it should be remembered that bodies are considered weightless as well as rigid and that rollers and pins are assumed to be frictionless.

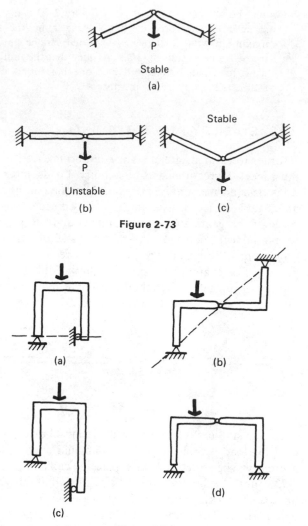

Figure 2-73

Figure 2-74

Examine each of the structures in Figure 2-74 with respect to the previous discussion. By our rules, the two shown in Figure 2-74(a) and (b) are unstable, while those of Figure 2-74(c) and (d) are stable.

Once a structure has satisfied the conditions of stability, it can then be classified as determinate or indeterminate with respect to its reactions. A member or structure is statically *determinate* if the number of independent reaction components does not exceed the number of applicable independent equations of equilibrium. (This is really just a precise way of stating the familiar axiom, "the number of unknowns cannot exceed the number of equations.") If this is true, then those reaction components can be determined using the techniques of statics alone. If, on the other hand, there exist extra or redundant reaction components, then the structure is said to be statically *indeterminate*. This means that, in order to determine the reactions, the analyst will have to consider more than the basic equilibrium of forces. In general, this means that the deformation or deflection of a structure or member must be examined.

One procedure for analyzing such structures is briefly introduced in Chapter 10 (dealing with deflection), and others are examined in Chapter 15.

If an indeterminate structure has only one redundant force component, it is described as being indeterminate to the first degree; with two redundant components, to the second degree; and so on. Some structures, such as a light timber frame of stud and joist construction, have mostly determinate members. Others, such as the typical cast-in-place reinforced concrete frame, are highly indeterminate. There are advantages and disadvantages inherent in both classes of structure, and these are discussed in Chapter 15. All the examples and problems presented for quantitative solution in this chapter are statically determinate.

Problems

2-27. Determine whether or not each of the structures in Figure 2-75 is stable. If stable, then ascertain if it is determinate or indeterminate. If indeterminate, to what degree?

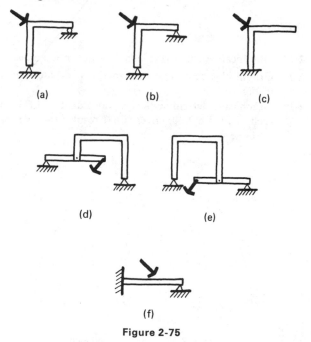

Figure 2-75

2-28. Each of the structures in Figure 2-76 is either unstable or indeterminate. Change or remove one of the support conditions in each case so that the resulting structure will be stable and determinate.

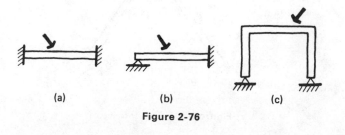

Figure 2-76

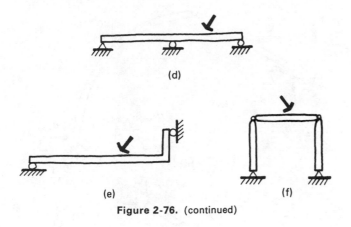

(d)

(e)   (f)

Figure 2-76. (continued)

2-13 THREE-HINGED ARCHES

The frame shown in Figure 2-77 appears to be indeterminate by virtue of its four independent reaction components, two at each pin. The fact that both members are loaded means that there are no two-force members involved. With four independent unknowns present, four independent equations are needed for static determinacy.

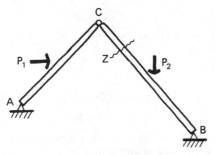

Figure 2-77. Three-hinged arch, loaded both sides.

A fourth equation can be found, in this case, because of the hinge at joint C. If the two members were continuous or rigidly joined at this point, the frame would be truly indeterminate. However, the hinge or pinned connection will transmit no moment from one member to the other (i.e., regardless of the amount of internal moment in the members at other points, such moments must go to zero at joint C). From the standpoint of statics, this means that a free-body diagram of either member will show no moment acting at C. Figure 2-78 shows the difference between cutting the frame at C and cutting it at some arbitrary point Z. A moment equation written for member CB with C as the moment center will have two unknowns, B_x and B_y. On the other hand, a moment equation for the point Z on the free body in Figure 2-78(b) will have three unknowns, B_x, B_y, and M_z.

The pin at C makes it possible to remove one of the members from the structure (much as we remove two-force members) and treat the remaining member as a second free body. Figure 2-79 shows two free-body

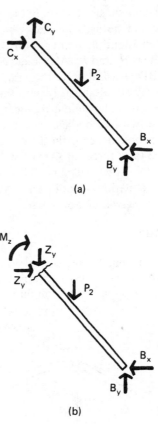

(a)

(b)

Figure 2-78

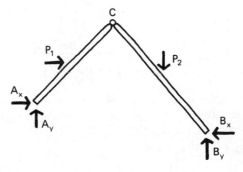

FBD I

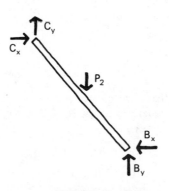

FBD II

Figure 2-79. Free-body diagrams.

diagrams that can be used to find the reactions. (The member CA could be used instead of CB.) A moment equation written about the point A on FBD I will involve the two unknowns B_x and B_y. A moment equation written about C on FBD II will involve the same two unknowns and can be solved simultaneously with the first equation. Thus, we have two independent moment equations, one for each of the two free bodies. It is a simple matter to complete the problem using the force equations to get A_x and A_y. The joint forces at C may be found if desired from an FBD of either member. This method of generating another equation of equilibrium has been referred to as the *three-hinged-arch* approach.

EXAMPLE 2-12

Determine the reactions for the structure in Figure 2-80. It is acted upon by a snow load (uniform on the horizontal projection) and a wind load (uniform on the vertical projection).

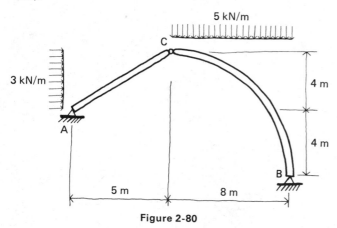

Figure 2-80

Solution: Member AC is arbitrarily selected to get the second moment equation. Writing moment equations using Figure 2-81 to obtain A_x and A_y, we get

FBD I: $\sum M_B = 0$

$$-A_y(13) + A_x(4) - 12(6) + 40(4) = 0$$

FBD II: $\sum M_C = 0$

$$-A_y(5) - A_x(4) + 12(2) = 0$$

Solving simultaneously yields

$A_x = -1.78$ $A_x = 1.78$ kN
                                    $\rightarrow$

and

$A_y = 6.22$ $A_y = 6.22$ kN$\uparrow$

This means that the sense of A_x was assumed incorrectly. Writing the force equations to get B_x and B_y, we have

FBD I: $\sum F_x = 0$

$$-A_x + 12 - B_x = 0$$

$$-(-1.78) + 12 - B_x = 0$$

$$B_x = 13.78 \text{ kN}$$

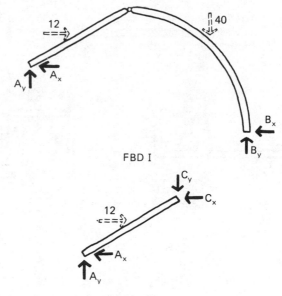

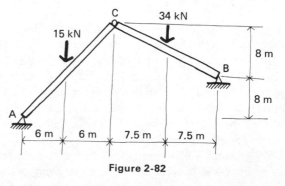

Figure 2-81. Free-body diagrams for Example 2-12.

FBD I: $\sum F_y = 0$

$$A_y - 40 + B_y = 0$$

$$6.22 - 40 + B_y = 0$$

$$B_y = 33.78 \text{ kN}$$

The final answers will be

$$A_x = 1.78 \text{ kN}$$
$$A_y = 6.22 \overset{\rightarrow}{\text{ kN}}\uparrow$$
$$B_x = 13.78 \text{ kN}$$
$$B_y = 33.78 \overset{\leftarrow}{\text{ kN}}\uparrow$$

A valid check can be made by taking moments about some point on FBD I other than support B.

FBD I: $\sum M_A = 0$ check

$$-12(2) - 40(9) + B_y(13) - B_x(4) = 0$$

$$-24 - 360 + 33.78(13) - 13.78(4) = 0$$

$$-439.1 + 439.1 = 0 \quad \checkmark$$

Problems

2-29. Determine the reaction components for the frame in Figure 2-82.

Figure 2-82

2-30. Determine the reaction components at *A* and *B* for the structure in Figure 2-83. Also find the force components at joint *C* as they act on member *DA*.

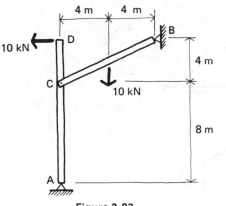

Figure 2-83

2-31. Determine the reactions for the beam in Figure 2-84. Support *A* is a pin, while walls *B* and *D* function as rollers.

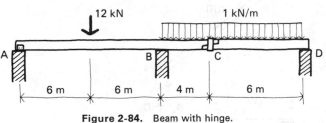

Figure 2-84. Beam with hinge.

2-14 PINNED FRAMES

In this chapter, we have considered many structures that utilize pinned joints to transmit forces from one member to another. In reality, such joints are seldom really pinned but do have enough flexibility such that they can be considered moment-free for the purposes of statics. Even when such joints are continuous and moment-resistant (and the structure is therefore usually indeterminate), it sometimes helps to make the temporary and fictitious assumption of pinned connections. This can aid the designer in doing a preliminary visual analysis of the basic manner in which a completed structure might carry its loads. The effects of continuity can then be imposed on this qualitative analysis to achieve a higher degree of accuracy and understanding. An initial pin-joint assumption can serve as a starting point in the study of many structures.

The statics of any structure is made simpler if there is no moment at the joints. For example, at a joint involving only two members, it is logical to conclude that the force exerted by the first member upon the second is equal and opposite to and collinear with the force exerted by the second member upon the first. This is essential for equilibrium of the pin itself.

Before any member can be designed, it is necessary to determine all the forces acting upon it. A structural analysis of the A-frame in Figure 2-85 would start with a complete determination of all the force components acting on each member. In this case, the external reactions at *A* and *B* could be easily obtained using a free

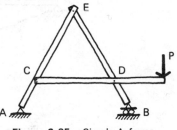

Figure 2-85. Simple A-frame.

body of the whole structure. Note that there would be no A_x component. The joint forces at *C*, *D*, and *E* can be found by using an FBD for each member as in Figure 2-86. The forces are assumed to act with arbitrary sense except that, of course, they must act in an opposite manner on the two members meeting at a given joint.

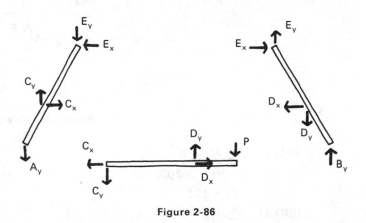

Figure 2-86

The equations of equilibrium can be applied to each member in turn, moving from one free body to another as the various forces become known. An incorrect sense assumption will provide a negative answer as usual, but it must be remembered that any sense change will affect *two* free bodies.

EXAMPLE 2-13

Determine all the force components acting on each member of the pin-jointed frame in Figure 2-87.

Solution: The four external reactions components cannot be simply obtained from an FBD of the whole, so the structure will be taken apart as in Figure 2-88. Sense assumptions are made by attempting to trace the pattern each load might take to the supports. Recognition of the two-force member *CD* is essential to the solution.

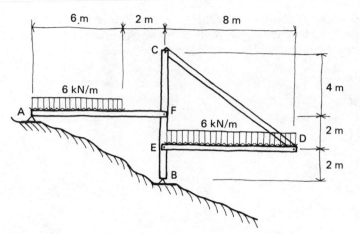

Figure 2-87. Schematic section of a hillside dwelling.

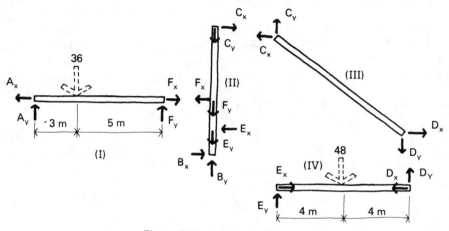

Figure 2-88. Free-body diagrams.

FBD I: $\quad \sum M_A = 0$

$\quad -36(3) + F_y(8) = 0$

$\quad F_y = 13.5$

FBD I: $\quad \sum M_F = 0$

$\quad 36(5) - A_y(8) = 0$

$\quad A_y = 22.5$

FBD IV: $\quad \sum M_E = 0$

$\quad -48(4) + D_y(8) = 0$

$\quad D_y = 24$

FBD IV: $\quad \sum M_D = 0$

$\quad 48(4) - E_y(8) = 0$

$\quad E_y = 24$

FBD III: $\quad D_x = \frac{4}{3}D_y$

$\quad = \frac{4}{3}(24)$

$\quad D_x = 32$

FBD III: $\quad \sum F_x = 0$

$\quad -C_x + D_x = 0$

$\quad C_x = 32$

FBD III: $\quad \sum F_y = 0$

$\quad C_y - D_y = 0$

$\quad C_y = 24$

FBD IV: $\quad \sum F_x = 0$

$\quad -E_x + D_x = 0$

$\quad E_x = 32$

FBD II: $\quad \sum M_B = 0$

$\quad -C_x(8) + F_x(4) + E_x(2) = 0$

$\quad -32(8) + 4F_x + 32(2) = 0$

$\quad F_x = 48$

FBD II: $\quad \sum M_F = 0$

$\quad -C_x(4) - E_x(2) + B_x(4) = 0$

$\quad -32(4) - 32(2) + 4B_x = 0$

$\quad B_x = 48$

FBD II: $\quad \sum F_y = 0$

$\quad -C_y - F_y - E_y + B_y = 0$

$\quad -24 - 13.5 - 24 + B_y = 0$

$\quad B_y = 61.5$

FBD I: $\quad \sum F_x = 0$

$\quad\quad\quad -A_x + F_x = 0$

$\quad\quad\quad A_x = 48$

Using the entire structure for a check, we obtain

$\sum F_x = 0 \quad$ check

$48 - 48 = 0 \quad \checkmark$

$\sum F_y = 0 \quad$ check

$22.5 - 36 - 48 + 61.5 = 0 \quad \checkmark$

The correct answers are provided in Figure 2-89.

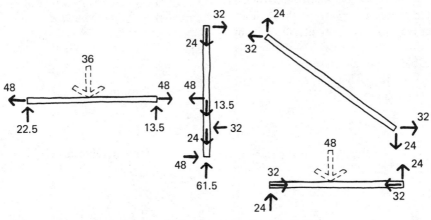

Figure 2-89. Answers to Example 2-13.

Problems

2-32. Determine all the force components acting on each member of the frame in Figure 2-90.

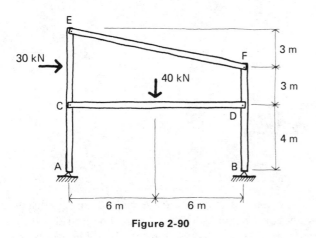

Figure 2-90

2-33. Determine all the force components acting on each member of the frame in Figure 2-91.

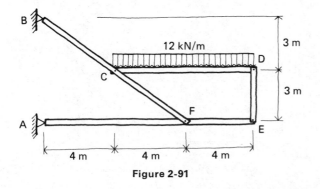

Figure 2-91

2-34. Determine all the force components acting on the main carriage member, *AD*, in Figure 2-92.

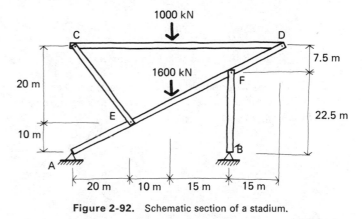

Figure 2-92. Schematic section of a stadium.

2-15 SIMPLE CABLE STATICS

A flexible cable will assume a specific geometry when acted upon by one or more point loads. This geometry is dependent upon the relative magnitude and location of each load, the length of the cable, and the height of the supports. The designer usually has little control over the loads but can select the length of the cable, thereby controlling the sag, and the support locations. In general, the greater the sag, the less will be the force in the cable. For reasons of equilibrium discussed previously, a taut cable of very slight sag will have to withstand tremendous internal forces.

Analysis of one-way cable systems is made simple by the fact that a cable has effectively zero moment resistance. It acts like a link chain and, if assumed weightless, will take a straight-line geometry between the loads. Each cable segment then acts like a two-force tension member. Each load point is held in concurrent equilibrium by the load and two internal cable forces, one on each side of the load.

If the loads are applied vertically, the horizontal component of the cable force is a *constant* throughout the cable, and only the vertical component varies from segment to segment. Since the vertical component is dependent upon the cable slope, the largest tension in the cable will occur where the cable slope is greatest, usually at the highest cable support.

EXAMPLE 2-14

Determine the distance y and the magnitude of the force in each segment of the cable in Figure 2-93.

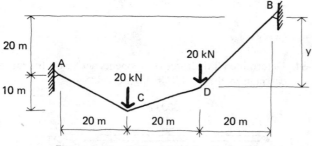

Figure 2-93. Cable with third-point loading.

Solution: First determine the external reactions. The ratio of the components A_x and A_y will be 2:1, following the slope of the cable segment AC.

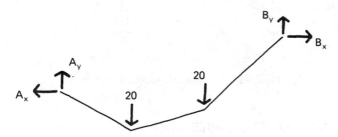

Figure 2-94. Free-body diagram.

Using the FBD in Figure 2-94, we obtain

$$\sum M_B = 0$$
$$-A_x(20) - A_y(60) + 20(40) + 20(20) = 0$$
$$-2A_y(20) - 60A_y + 800 + 400 = 0$$
$$A_y = 12 \qquad\qquad A_y = 12 \text{ kN}\uparrow$$
$$A_x = 24 \qquad\qquad A_x = 24 \text{ kN} \atop \leftarrow$$
$$\sum F_x = 0$$
$$-A_x + B_x = 0$$
$$B_x = 24 \qquad\qquad B_x = 24 \text{ kN} \atop \rightarrow$$

$$\sum M_A = 0$$
$$-20(20) - 20(40) + B_y(60) - 24(20) = 0$$
$$B_y = 28 \qquad\qquad B_y = 28 \text{ kN}\uparrow$$
$$\sum F_y = 0 \qquad \text{check}$$
$$12 - 20 - 20 + 28 = 0 \quad \checkmark$$

The distance y must be such that the cable segment BD has a slope that fits the component ratio of B_y to B_x. Therefore,

$$\frac{28}{24} = \frac{y}{20}$$
$$y = 23.3 \qquad\qquad y = 23.3 \text{ m}$$

The cable force in segment AC is

$$T_{AC} = \sqrt{(12)^2 + (24)^2}$$
$$= 26.8 \qquad\qquad T_{AC} = 26.8 \text{ kN}$$

The cable force in segment BD is

$$T_{BD} = \sqrt{(24)^2 + (28)^2}$$
$$= 36.9 \qquad\qquad T_{BD} = 36.9 \text{ kN}$$

The vertical component of the force in CD can be determined by considering its slope or from the vertical equilibrium of either point C or D, as shown in Figure 2-95. The force in segment CD will then be

$$T_{CD} = \sqrt{(24)^2 + (8)^2}$$
$$= 25.3 \qquad\qquad T_{CD} = 25.3 \text{ kN}$$

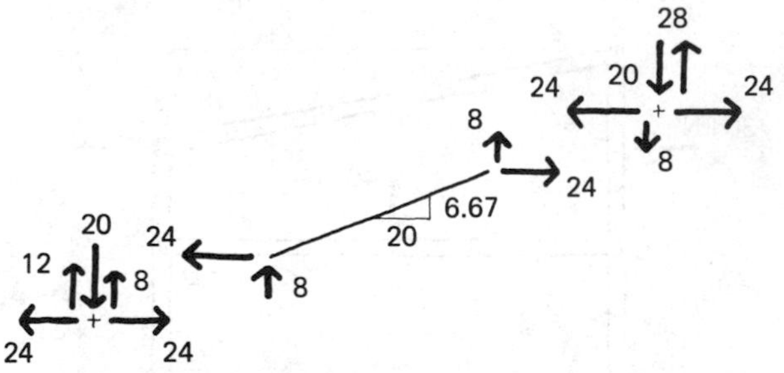

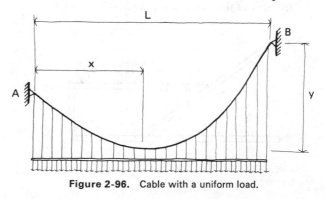

Figure 2-95. Statics of the central portion of the cable in Example 2-14.

When the load points get very close together and are of equal magnitude, the load may be considered to be uniform. If it is uniform along the horizontal projection as in Figure 2-96, the cable will assume a parabolic

Figure 2-96. Cable with a uniform load.

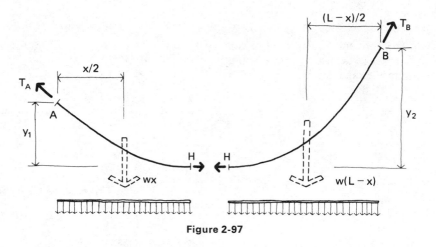

Figure 2-97

shape. The maximum sag and its location, labeled y and x, respectively, will depend upon the cable length and the relative support heights as before. Given the value of the uniform load, the designer can vary the span and sag and easily check the influence of such changes on the cable force. With a uniformly loaded cable, the lowest point will usually have a slope of zero, and thus the force in the cable at that point will have no vertical component. This means that, referring to Figure 2-97 and assuming known loads and support locations, we can write two independent moment equations, one about A and the other about B. The equations will have the same two unknowns, H and x, and can be solved simultaneously. Once x is known, the vertical components of each reaction can be obtained from equilibrium in the vertical direction. Since H is constant throughout the cable, the largest cable force will again be at the uppermost support.

EXAMPLE 2-15

Determine the highest tension in the uniformly loaded cable of Figure 2-98.

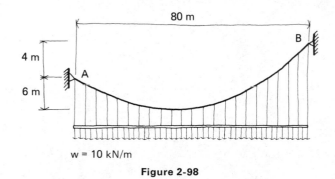

Figure 2-98

Solution:

FBD I: $\sum M_A = 0$

$$-10x\left(\frac{x}{2}\right) + H(6) = 0$$

$$6H - 5x^2 = 0$$

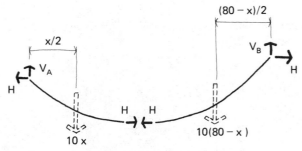

Figure 2-99. Free-body diagrams for Example 2-15.

FBD II: $\sum M_B = 0$

$$-H(10) + 10(80 - x)\left(\frac{80 - x}{2}\right) = 0$$

$$-H + 3200 - 80x + \frac{x^2}{2} = 0$$

Solving the two equations will yield the quadratic

$$\frac{x^2}{3} + 80x - 3200 = 0$$

$$x = \frac{-b \pm \sqrt{b^2 - 4ac}}{2a}$$

$$= \frac{-80 \pm \sqrt{(80)^2 - 4(\frac{1}{3})(-3200)}}{2(\frac{1}{3})}$$

$$= -275 \text{ and } 34.9$$

The maximum tension will occur at point B. From previous work,

$$H = \tfrac{5}{6}x^2$$

$$= \tfrac{5}{6}(34.9)^2$$

$$= 1015$$

FBD II: $\sum F_y = 0$

$$V_B - 10(80 - x) = 0$$

$$V_B - 10(80 - 34.9) = 0$$

$$V_B = 451$$

$$T_B = \sqrt{(451)^2 + (1015)^2}$$

$$= 1110 \qquad\qquad T_B = 1110 \text{ kN}$$

EXAMPLE 2-16

Determine the value of H, the horizontal component of the cable force, in terms of w, L, and y as defined in Figure 2-100. The two cable supports are on the same level.

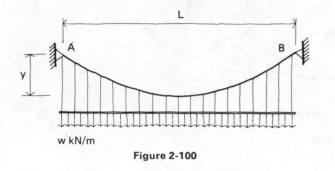

Figure 2-100

Solution: The slope is zero at midspan. Using the free body in Figure 2-101, we get

$$\sum M_B = 0$$

$$\frac{wL}{2}\left(\frac{L}{4}\right) - H(y) = 0$$

$$H = \frac{wL^2}{8y} \qquad (2-7)$$

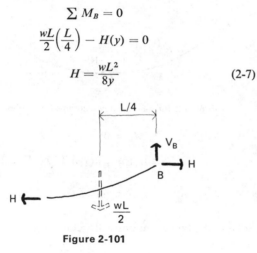

Figure 2-101

Problems

2-35. Determine the maximum sag and the largest tension in the symmetrically loaded cable of Figure 2-102.

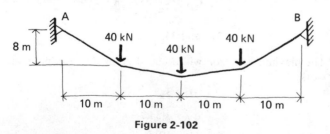

Figure 2-102

2-36. One-half of a suspension structure is shown in Figure 2-103. How much tension will be in the tie-back cable *AB* and how much compression in the mast *BC*?

2-37. A total of 60 kN must be supported by the cable in Figure 2-104. How much should be placed at each of the two load points to achieve the geometry shown?

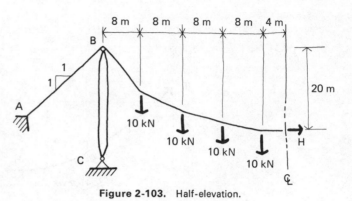

Figure 2-103. Half-elevation.

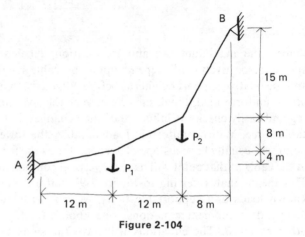

Figure 2-104

2-38. With reference to Figure 2-100, if $L = 100$ m and $w = 10$ kN/m, determine the maximum tension in the cable when
(a) $y = 100$ m
(b) $y = 50$ m
(c) $y = 25$ m
(d) $y = 10$ m
(e) $y = 5$ m

2-39. Determine the maximum tension in the cable of Figure 2-105.

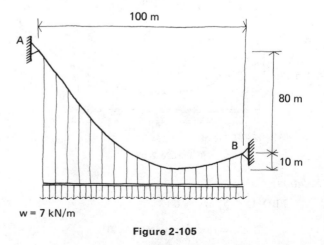

Figure 2-105

2-40. The cables shown in Figure 2-106 carry a uniform load (on the horizontal projection) of 40 kN/m over the entire 80 m. Determine the required values of H_L and x in order to maintain equilibrium.

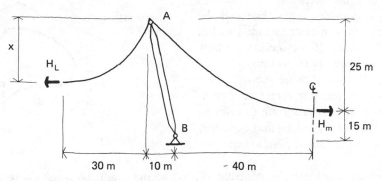

Figure 2-106. Half-elevation of a uniformly loaded cable.

2-16 CONCLUSION AND PROCEDURE

The preceding sections have provided an introduction to concepts of static equilibrium in planar force systems. The principles can easily be extended to three-dimensional systems by increasing the number of equilibrium equations to six, one force equation and one moment equation for each of the three coordinate axes. Problem examples have not been included for three-dimensional systems because no new and fundamental concepts would be involved.

Statics is a subject, like most areas of structural analysis, that cannot be learned by reading about it. The few concepts involved are deceptively simple, but any real understanding comes only through practice. The forces of statics have very real effects on all structures, and the designer must become familiar with the action of such forces and the responses (reactions) made by the structures. While the directions and relative magnitudes of reactive forces are far more important to the architect than their actual quantitative values, no purely qualitative approach to the study of physical forces has proven to be sufficient. It is also important not to confine one's study of the subject to text or classroom examples. The beginning student is urged to attempt to conceptualize or sense the forces that provide equilibrium to the objects in his or her immediate environment. Because of the presence of gravity, such forces can be found everywhere. Begin to examine the statics of ordinary objects such as chairs, doors, signposts, bridges, trees, spider webs, playground equipment, and buildings.

Success in quantitative problem analysis comes only through experience, but that experience should be directed so there is a minimum of wasted effort. The writer's own mistakes and those of his students have resulted in the recommendations that follow.

1. Always take time to thoroughly review the given situation. Read the problem carefully, noting what it is that you are to find. What is it that the client is asking you to do?

2. To study forces, always sketch free-body diagrams. Do not attempt to work without them. The mere process of sketching can help you to "see" the forces. If you are a visually minded person, you need a picture.

3. Check your assumptions and your answers as you proceed. Make qualitative estimates. Make graphical polygon checks. Are the results rational? Arithmetic may be neat and precise, but common sense is more valuable.

4. Attempt to work slowly and carefully at the beginning of any analysis. Charging into a problem seems to generate more errors than does racing to finish it.

5. Record your work in neat and orderly fashion. Always include units and senses with numerical answers. State assumptions clearly and make notes explaining your procedure as you work. Always work as though someone were going to review your records and follow your steps at a later date. Most often, that someone will be you.

3-1 INTRODUCTION

This chapter is devoted to two concepts that have to do with certain properties of cross sections. In structural analysis, it is necessary to consider more than just the number of square millimeters or meters included within a cross-sectional area. The shape of the section (or how the material is distributed) is equally important.

In this discussion, the term "cross section" is a general one applying to any element or even to a section through an entire structure. It is appropriate to refer to the cross-sectional areas of not only beams and columns, but also trusses, footings, walls, folded plates, segments of shells, and so on.

Two very important concepts are the centroid of an area, which is analogous to the center of mass of a volume; and the moment of inertia of an area, which is most simply described as a measure of resistance to bending and buckling.

3-2 CENTROIDS

The center of mass or center of gravity may be visualized as the location of the resultant of a set of parallel forces. Figure 3-1 illustrates a thin, flat plate of homogeneous material, lying in a horizontal plane. Each element dA, located by coordinates x and y, will be acted upon by a vertical force due to gravity. The resultant of all these parallel forces will be located at the center of gravity of the plate. Conceptually, this point would be the place where we could attach a vertical string to hang the plate and have the plate remain horizontal. It is dimensioned by $\bar{x}$ and $\bar{y}$ in Figure 3-1.

If we let the thickness approach zero, the plate becomes an area and the center of gravity is then called a *centroid*. The centroid is sort of an average location of

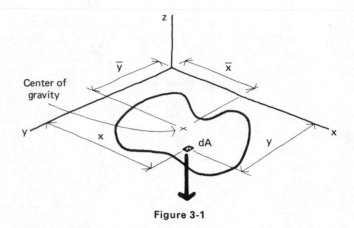

Figure 3-1

all the small elemental areas, dA. Mathematically, it can be located with respect to any reference axes by two equations.

$$\bar{x} = \frac{\int_0^A x \, dA}{\int_0^A dA} \tag{3-1}$$

$$\bar{y} = \frac{\int_0^A y \, dA}{\int_0^A dA} \tag{3-2}$$

The denominator in each of these expressions is, of course, the total area and the numerator is called the *first moment* of the area, being a summation of areas times distances. The numerator is also sometimes called the *statical moment* of the area.

The concept of the centroid is used in most of the principles found in the study of mechanics of materials and is, therefore, critical to the understanding of structures. As indicated, the center of gravity is an easier concept to grasp, as it can be experimentally determined. For example, if we cut a shape out of cardboard, the shape will balance on the end of a pencil placed under its

3 Structural Properties of Areas

center of gravity. If the cardboard is uniform in thickness, the center of gravity will be at the centroid of the area. (This experiment will not always be practical because the centroid, and center of gravity for that matter, do not have to be located physically within the area or on the object. For example, the centroid of a doughnut shape would be at the center of the hole.)

For most structural applications, the areas involved are regular geometric shapes, portions of such shapes, or combinations of them. This means that it is seldom necessary to use the calculus to determine a centroid location. Since the centroid of a regular shape is usually known by inspection, the integrals become algebraic sums of the statical moments and areas involved.

$$\bar{x} = \frac{\sum (x_i A_i)}{\sum A_i} \qquad (3\text{-}1a)$$

$$\bar{y} = \frac{\sum y_i A_i}{\sum A_i} \qquad (3\text{-}2a)$$

These versions of the basic equations will be used in the examples that follow. Appendix M will be useful in obtaining the centroids of often used shapes.

After the centroid of an area has been determined, it is good practice to sketch a rough scale figure of the area, showing the location of the centroid. Gross errors will appear readily in such a sketch.

EXAMPLE 3-1

Determine the centroid location of the T shape in Figure 3-2. (*Note:* Unless otherwise indicated, dimensions on cross sections have units of millimeters throughout this book.)

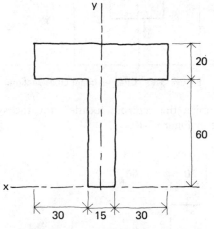

Figure 3-2. T-shaped cross section.

Solution: The shape is comprised of two rectangles with their centroids as shown in Figure 3-3. By symmetry, the centroid of the T will lie along the y axis, and $\bar{x}$ must be zero (Figure 3-4). Note that the statical moment of an area will be zero whenever the reference axis passes through the centroid. The distance, $\bar{y}$, however, has a value between 30 and 70 mm and can be found by Equation (3-2a).

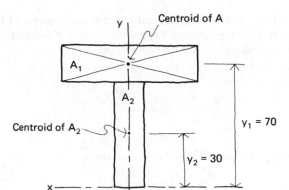

Figure 3-3. Two rectangles in the T shape.

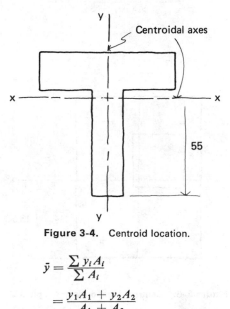

Figure 3-4. Centroid location.

$$\bar{y} = \frac{\sum y_i A_i}{\sum A_i}$$

$$= \frac{y_1 A_1 + y_2 A_2}{A_1 + A_2}$$

$$= \frac{70(20)(75) + 30(15)(60)}{20(75) + 15(60)}$$

$$= 55 \text{ mm}$$

EXAMPLE 3-2

Find $\bar{x}$ and $\bar{y}$ for the shape in Figure 3-5.

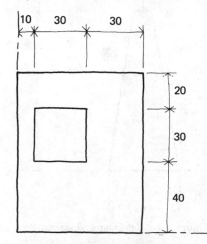

Figure 3-5. Rectangular shape with a square hole.

Solution: Subtract the statical moment and the area of the hole. If we let the subscript 1 represent the area of the rectangle and 2 represent the square hole, we get

$$\bar{x} = \frac{x_1 A_1 - x_2 A_2}{A_1 - A_2}$$

$$= \frac{35(70)(90) - 25(30)(30)}{70(90) - 30(30)}$$

$$= 37 \text{ mm}$$

(Figure 3-6). Similarly, for the y direction,

$$\bar{y} = \frac{y_1 A_1 - y_2 A_2}{A_1 - A_2}$$

$$= \frac{45(90)(70) - 55(30)(30)}{90(70) - 30(30)}$$

$$= 43 \text{ mm}$$

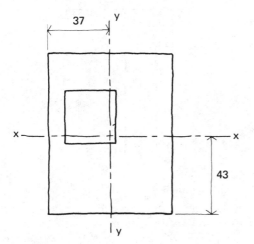

Figure 3-6. Centroid location for Example 3-2.

EXAMPLE 3-3

Determine the $\bar{y}$ for the section shown in Figure 3-7.

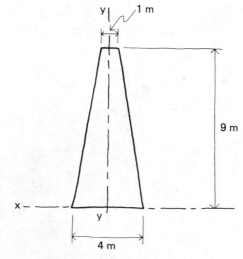

Figure 3-7. Retaining-wall section.

Solution: Assume the area to be made up of two triangles (subscript 2) and one rectangle (subscript 1).

$$\bar{y} = \frac{y_1 A_1 + 2 y_2 A_2}{A_1 + 2 A_2}$$

$$= \frac{4.5(1)(9) + 2(3)(\frac{1}{2})(1.5)(9)}{(1)(9) + 2(\frac{1}{2})(1.5)(9)}$$

$$= 3.6 \text{ m}$$

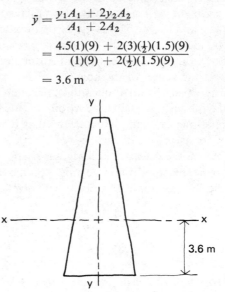

Figure 3-8. Centroid location for Example 3-3.

Problems

3-1. Determine $\bar{y}$ for the cross section in Figure 3-9.

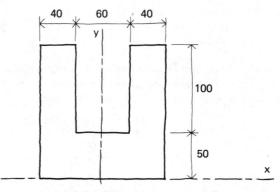

Figure 3-9. Channel beam cross section.

3-2. Determine the centroid location for the symmetrical angle in Figure 3-10.

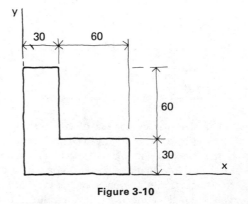

Figure 3-10

3-3. Determine $\bar{y}$ for the shape in Figure 3-11.

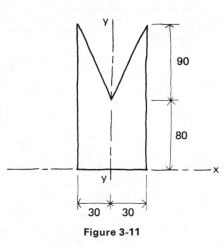

Figure 3-11

3-4. Determine the centroid location for the group of footing pads shown in Figure 3-12. Each square is 3 m on a side and each circle is 3 m in diameter.

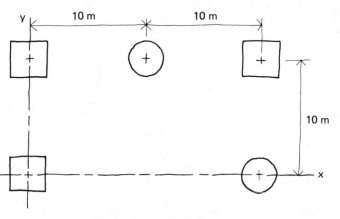

Figure 3-12. Footing plan.

3-5. Locate the centroid of the prestressed single-T in Figure 3-13.

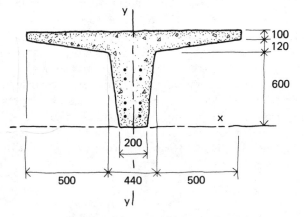

Figure 3-13. Prestressed beam cross section.

3-6. Figure 3-14 shows a cross section through a timber beam taken where a hole 50 mm in diameter was drilled to permit the passage of a pipe. Determine $\bar{y}$ with respect to the *x* axis, which was a centroidal axis before the hole was drilled. (*Hint:* First determine $\bar{y}$ with respect to the base of the section.)

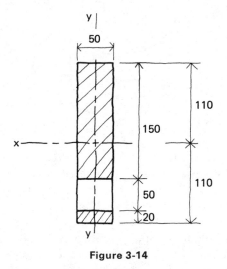

Figure 3-14

3-3 MOMENT OF INERTIA

The *moment of inertia* of an area is a mathematical concept that is used to quantify the resistance of various sections to bending or buckling. It is a shape factor that measures the relative location of material in a cross section in terms of effectiveness. A beam section with a large moment of inertia, or *I* value, will have smaller stresses and deflections under a given load than one with a lesser *I* value. A thin shell will have less tendency to buckle if its surface is shaped so that a large moment of inertia is present. A long, slender column will not buckle laterally if the moment of inertia of its cross section is sufficient.

The concept of moment of inertia is vital to understanding the behavior of most structures, and it is unfortunate that it has no accurate physical analogy or description. Mathematically it is easy to compute, and in structural analysis it is easy to use, but beginning students often have difficulty with its abstract nature.

A moment-of-inertia value can be computed for any shape with respect to any reference axis. Figure 3-15 shows this general situation. The moment of inertia of an area about a given axis is defined as the sum of the products of all the elemental areas and the square of their respective distances to that axis. Thus, we get the following two equations from Figure 3-15.

$$I_x = \int_0^A y^2 \, dA \qquad (3\text{-}3)$$

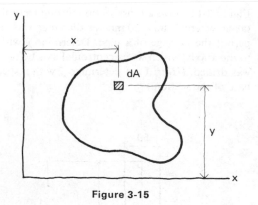

Figure 3-15

$$I_y = \int_0^A x^2 \, dA \qquad (3\text{-}4)$$

An I value has units of length to the fourth power, because the distance from the reference axis is squared. For this reason, the moment of inertia is sometimes called the *second moment* of an area. More important, it means that elements that are relatively far away from the axis will contribute substantially more to an I value than those which are close by. Assuming that each element has the same area dA, then one located at twice the distance of another will have four times the moment of inertia.

For structural analysis purposes, usually only two I values are important, the ones that can be computed with respect to the centroidal x and y axes. These are called the *principal axes*. Figure 3-16 shows a simple wood

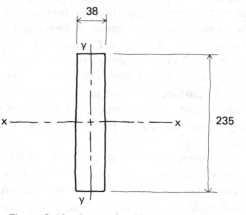

Figure 3-16. Rectangle with centroidal axes.

joist of rectangular cross section. Following the previous discussion, this shape has a much larger moment of inertia about the x axis than it does about the y axis. This confirms what we already know from experience, that a rectangular shape has more resistance to bending if used as a joist than if used as a plank. Laid on its side, as in Figure 3-17(b), so that the load would be parallel to the x axis, the rectangle would deflect and break under relatively low load. Like many structural elements, the rectangle has a strong axis and a weak axis. It is far more efficient to load the cross section so that bending occurs about the strong axis.

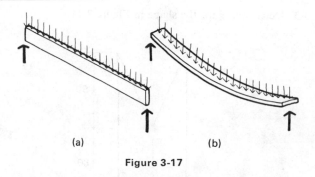

Figure 3-17

It may help to understand the concept of moment of inertia if we draw an analogy based upon real inertia due to motion and mass. Imagine the two shapes in Figure 3-18 to be cut out of heavy sheet material and placed on an axle (xx) so they could spin about it. The two shapes have equal areas, but the one in Figure 3-18(a) has a much higher moment of inertia (I_{xx}) with

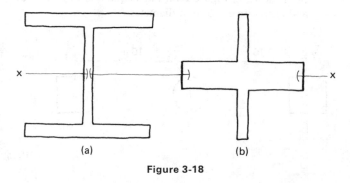

Figure 3-18

respect to the axis of spin. It would be much harder to start it spinning, and once moving, much harder to stop. The same principle is involved when a figure skater spins on the ice. With arms held close in, the skater will rotate rapidly, and with arms outstretched (creating increased resistance to spin and/or more inertia), the skater slows down.

Similarly, a beam section shaped as in Figure 3-18(a), with flanges located far from the centroidal axis, will have far more resistance to bending than the cruciform shape in Figure 3-18(b).

As with centroidal determinations, it is seldom necessary to use the calculus to find moments of inertia for the shapes commonly used in building structures. Most often, I values for regular shapes can be expressed in terms of the section dimensions. For example, the centroidal moment of inertia (I_{xx}) of a simple rectangle of dimensions b and h is found from Figure 3-19.

$$I_{xx} = \int_0^A y^2 \, dA$$

$$= \int_{-h/2}^{h/2} y^2 b \, dy$$

$$= b\left[\frac{y^3}{3}\right]_{-h/2}^{h/2}$$

$$= \frac{b}{3}\left[\frac{h^3}{8} + \frac{h^3}{8}\right]$$

$$I_{xx} = \frac{bh^3}{12}$$

centroid
rectangle

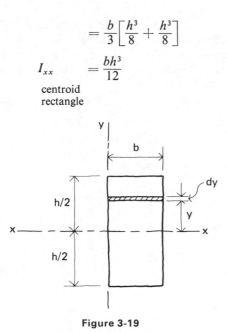

Figure 3-19

The moment of inertia expressions for several geometric shapes appear in Appendix M and will be used in the example problems. The values with respect to an axis located along an edge or base are also given, as these are sometimes useful.

We can now quantify the previous illustration of how a rectangular joist has greater resistance to bending if used upright as opposed to flat. For the joist in question and referring to Figure 3-20, the centroidal moments of inertia are

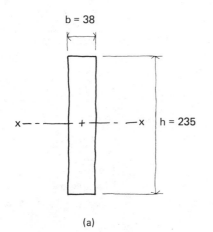

(a)

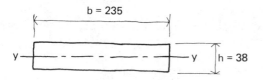

(b)

Figure 3-20

$$I_{xx} = \frac{bh^3}{12} \qquad\qquad I_{yy} = \frac{bh^3}{12}$$

$$= \frac{38(235)^3}{12} \qquad\qquad = \frac{235(38)^3}{12}$$

$$= 41.1(10)^6 \ mm^4 \qquad = 1.07(10)^6 \ mm^4$$

The figures indicate that the same 38×235 mm section has a strong-axis moment of inertia that is almost 40 times larger than its weak-axis moment of inertia. The strong- and weak-axis moments of inertia for this and other timber rectangular sections may be found in Appendix Q. The same values for steel beam shapes appear in Appendix S.

EXAMPLE 3-4

Determine the centroidal moments of inertia for the wide-flange shape in Figure 3-21.

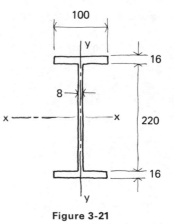

Figure 3-21

Solution: The I_{yy} computation is merely the summation of the I values of three rectangles. To compute I_{xx}, it will be necessary to subtract the I values of two rectangles of "space," located on either side of the web, from the I value of the enclosing rectangle.

$$I_{yy} = [I_{yy}]_{web} + 2[I_{yy}]_{flange}$$

$$= \left[\frac{bh^3}{12}\right]_{web} + 2\left[\frac{bh^3}{12}\right]_{flange}$$

$$= \frac{220(8)^3}{12} + 2\left[\frac{16(100)^3}{12}\right]$$

$$= 2.68(10)^6 \ mm^4$$

$$I_{xx} = [I_{xx}]_{gross} - 2[I_{xx}]_{space}$$

$$= \left[\frac{bh^3}{12}\right]_{gross} - 2\left[\frac{bh^3}{12}\right]_{space}$$

$$= \frac{100(252)^3}{12} - 2\left[\frac{46(220)^3}{12}\right]$$

$$= 51.7(10)^6 \ mm^4$$

EXAMPLE 3-5

Determine the moment of inertia with respect to the xx axis of the 89-mm square, which has been rotated 45° as in Figure 3-22.

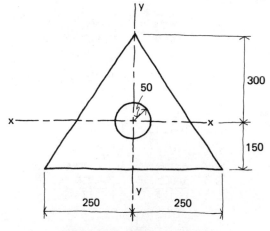

Figure 3-22. Rotated square section.

Solution: The section is comprised of two triangles attached at their bases. From Appendix M, for each triangle,

$$I_x = \frac{bh^3}{12}$$
base
triangle

The dimensions b and h can be computed because of the 45° relationship.

$$h = 89(\sin 45°)$$
$$= 63 \text{ mm}$$
$$b = \frac{89}{\sin 45°}$$
$$= 126 \text{ mm}$$
$$I_x = 2\left[\frac{bh^3}{12}\right]$$
$$= 2\left[\frac{126(63)^3}{12}\right]$$
$$= 5.25(10)^6 \text{ mm}^4$$

EXAMPLE 3-6

Compute the centroidal moments of inertia of the shape in Figure 3-23.

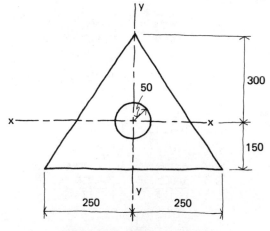

Figure 3-23. Triangle with hole.

Solution: I_{xx} can be obtained by subtracting the I of the circular hole from the I of the gross triangle. (Note that this

direct subtraction is only possible because the triangle and the circle share the same xx centroidal axis.) I_{yy} can be computed by subtracting the I of the hole from a larger I computed by adding two values for triangles about a common base. The common base in this case is the vertical yy axis.

$$I_{xx} = [I_{xx}]_{\text{gross}} - [I_{xx}]_{\text{hole}}$$
$$= \left[\frac{bh^3}{36}\right]_{\text{gross}} - \left[\frac{\pi R^4}{4}\right]_{\text{hole}}$$
$$= \frac{500(450)^3}{36} - \frac{\pi(50)^4}{4}$$
$$= 1260(10)^6 \text{ mm}^4$$
$$I_{yy} = 2[I_y]_{\text{base}} - [I_{yy}]_{\text{hole}}$$
$$= 2\left[\frac{bh^3}{12}\right]_{\text{base}} - \left[\frac{\pi R^4}{4}\right]_{\text{hole}}$$
$$= 2\left[\frac{450(250)^3}{12}\right] - \frac{\pi(50)^4}{4}$$
$$= 1170(10)^6 \text{ mm}^4$$

Problems

3-7. Determine the centroidal moments of inertia for the beam cross section of Figure 3-24.

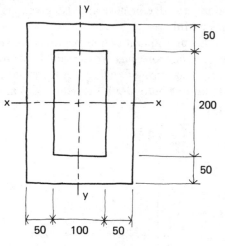

Figure 3-24. Hollow rectangle.

3-8. Determine the centroidal moments of inertia for the T-beam cross section of Example 3-1.

3-9. Determine the I_{xx} value for the tapered section in Figure 3-25.

3-10. Determine the I_{xx} value for the precast plank cross section of Figure 3-26. Each hole is 150 mm in diameter.

3-11. Determine the moment of inertia, with respect to the centroidal xx axis, of the section in Figure 3-27. It is built up from two skins, each 12 mm thick, and six 38×139 mm flange pieces.

3-12. With reference to the T shape of Figure 3-28, first locate the xx centroidal axis by finding $\bar{y}$, and then compute the value of I_{xx}.

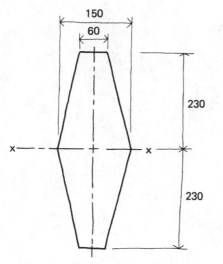

Figure 3-25

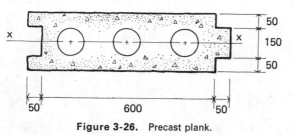

Figure 3-26. Precast plank.

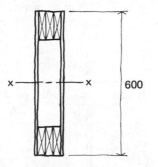

Figure 3-27. Plywood box beam.

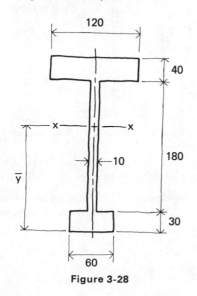

Figure 3-28

3-4 PARALLEL AXIS THEOREM

The addition and subtraction of moment of inertia values for parts of complex shapes can become confusing and lead to errors. The parallel axis theorem provides a simple way to compute the moment of inertia of a shape about any axis parallel to a centroidal one. Its use not only saves time but eliminates most of the confusion. It is easily derived. Assume that we wish to find the moment of inertia of the general shape in Figure 3-29 with respect

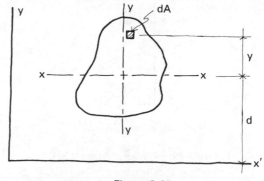

Figure 3-29

to an x' axis which is parallel to the centroidal xx one and located d distance away. The general expression will give us

$$I_{x'} = \int_0^A (y + d)^2 \, dA$$

$$= \int_0^A (y^2 + 2yd + d^2) \, dA$$

$$I_{x'} = \int_0^A y^2 \, dA + 2d \int_0^A y \, dA + d^2 \int_0^A dA$$

The integral in the second term of this expression is the statical moment of the shape with respect to one of its own centroidal axes and, as such, must be zero-valued. Since the first term is a centroidal moment of inertia for the shape, the parallel axis theorem is reduced to

$$I_{x'} = I_{xx} + Ad^2 \qquad (3\text{-}5)$$

where $I_{x'}$ = moment of inertia of the shape about a remote x' axis

I_{xx} = moment of inertia of the shape about the centroidal xx axis

A = area of the shape

d = perpendicular distance between the xx and x' axes

In almost all applications of this theorem, the x' or remote axis is actually the centroidal axis of a composite section made up of several geometric shapes. The parallel axis theorem is applied to each of the shapes in turn to find the total or composite moment of inertia. In every case, the axes of the individual shapes must be centroidal ones. The following examples will illustrate the theorem's use.

EXAMPLE 3-7

Determine the moment of inertia about the xx centroidal axis for the shape shown in Figure 3-30.

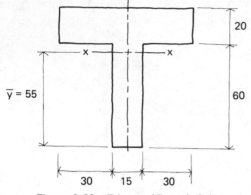

Figure 3-30. T-beam of Example 3-1.

Solution: Since neither rectangle has its centroid coincident with the centroid of the entire section, two applications of the parallel axis theorem will be used. The d distances are as given in Figure 3-31.

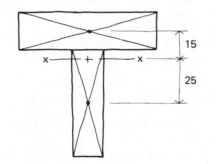

Figure 3-31. Parallel axis distances for Example 3-7.

$$I_{xx} = [I_{xx} + Ad^2]_{\text{flange}} + [I_{xx} + Ad^2]_{\text{stem}}$$

$$= \left[\frac{bh^3}{12} + Ad^2\right]_{\text{flange}} + \left[\frac{bh^3}{12} + Ad^2\right]_{\text{stem}}$$

$$= \left[\frac{75(20)^3}{12} + 75(20)(15)^2\right] + \left[\frac{15(60)^3}{12} + 15(60)(25)^2\right]$$

$$= 1.22(10)^6 \text{ mm}^4$$

EXAMPLE 3-8

Determine the I_{yy} value for the retaining-wall section of Figure 3-7.

Solution: The d distances are given in Figure 3-32. The central rectangle has its yy axis coincident with the yy axis of the entire shape, but the triangles do not.

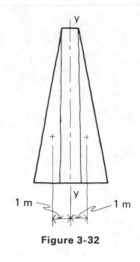

Figure 3-32

$$I_{yy} = [I_{yy}]_{\text{rectangle}} + 2[I_{yy} + Ad^2]_{\text{triangle}}$$

$$= \left[\frac{bh^3}{12}\right]_{\text{rectangle}} + 2\left[\frac{bh^3}{36} + Ad^2\right]_{\text{triangle}}$$

$$= \left[\frac{9(1)^3}{12}\right] + 2\left[\frac{9(1.5)^3}{36} + \frac{1}{2}(9)(1.5)(1)^2\right]$$

$$= 15.9 \text{ m}^4$$

EXAMPLE 3-9

To get additional bending resistance, a plate is welded to the top flange of a W360 × 32.9 as shown in Figure 3-33. The shape itself has an I_{xx} value of $82.8(10)^6$ mm^4, an area of

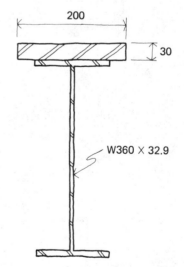

Figure 3-33. Wide-flange beam with plate.

4190 mm², and is 349 mm in actual depth. Determine the centroidal xx moment of inertia for this built-up section.

Solution: First determine the location of the centroidal xx axis by finding $\bar{y}$. Selecting a reference axis through the bottom edge of the beam, we get

$$\bar{y} = \frac{\sum y_i A_i}{\sum A_i}$$

$$= \frac{174(4190) + 363(30)(200)}{4190 + 30(200)}$$

$$= 285 \text{ mm}$$

$$I_{xx} = [I_{xx} + Ad^2]_{\text{wide flange}} + [I_{xx} + Ad^2]_{\text{plate}}$$

With reference to Figure 3-34, we get

$$I_{xx} = [82.4(10)^6 + 4190(111)^2] + \left[\frac{200(30)^3}{12} + 30(200)(78)^2\right]$$
$$= 171(10)^6 \text{ mm}^4$$

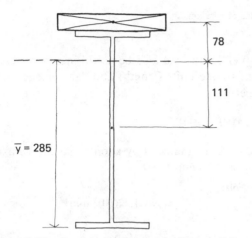

Figure 3-34. Parallel axis distances for Example 3-9.

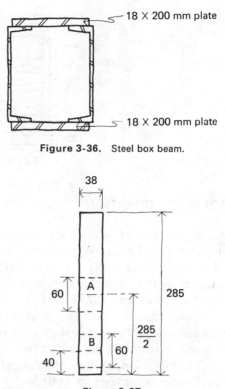

Figure 3-36. Steel box beam.

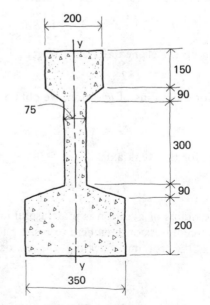

Figure 3-37

Problems

3-13. Two 38 × 235 mm joists enclose a 38 × 89 mm member to make the beam section in Figure 3-35. Determine the centroidal moment of inertia, I_{xx}.

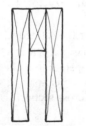

Figure 3-35. Built-up timber beam.

3-14. Knowing that $\bar{y}$ has a value of 160 mm in Figure 3-28, determine I_{xx} for the shape by using the parallel axis theorem.

3-15. Determine the I_{xx} value for the steel box beam of Figure 3-36. It is made from two C250 × 37 channels and two plates as shown. Each channel has an I_{xx} of 38.0(10)^6 mm^4, an area of 4740 mm^2, and is 254 mm in actual depth.

3-16. The 38 × 285 mm joist of Figure 3-37 has an I_{xx} value of 73.3(10)^6 mm^4, as given in Appendix Q. What will be the percentage decrease in this value if a hole 60 mm in diameter is drilled through it at
(a) location A?
(b) location B?

3-17. The wide-flange beam shape of Example 3-4 must be cut in half at the xx axis to make two structural T shapes, each 126 mm in depth. Compute the I_{xx} value for one of the T sections. What percentage does this represent of the total I_{xx} previously computed in that example?

3-18. Locate the centroidal xx axis and determine I_{xx} for the concrete shape in Figure 3-38.

Figure 3-38. Prestressed concrete section.

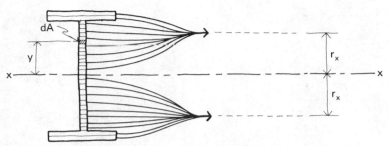

Figure 3-39. Concept of radius of gyration.

3-5 RADIUS OF GYRATION

The radius of gyration (*r*) is a concept that expresses a relationship between the area of a cross section and a centroidal moment of inertia. It is a shape factor, which measures resistance to bending (or buckling) about a certain axis, and accounts for both *I* and *A*.

Continuing the concept of rotational inertia discussed in Section 3-3, the radius of gyration represents the location of two parallel lines, one on each side of the axis of spin, at which all of the mass of an object could be concentrated with no change in inertia. For a cross section instead of a mass, we say that all the area may be placed in two lines with no change in the moment of inertia. The *r* value with respect to a centroidal axis, as indicated in Figure 3-39, is a perpendicular distance from the axis to one of the imaginary lines of concentration. For the shapes most frequently encountered in structural analysis, there are two *r* values, r_x and r_y, one each for the strong and weak axes, respectively.

If, by definition, the moment of inertia for the shape does not change, then from Figure 3-39,

$$I_{xx} = \int_0^A y^2 \, dA = r_x^2 \int_0^A dA$$

If we sum up the elemental areas, we get

$$I_{xx} = r_x^2 A$$

Solving for the radius of gyration, we obtain

$$r_x = \sqrt{\frac{I_{xx}}{A}} \qquad (3\text{-}6)$$

Similarly, for the weak axis,

$$r_y = \sqrt{\frac{I_{yy}}{A}} \qquad (3\text{-}7)$$

The radius of gyration is most useful in the design of slender compression members to resist buckling. It is central to the column buckling theory developed in

Chapter 13 but can also be useful in other ways because it has simple units (length) and can replace two section properties.

EXAMPLE 3-10

Determine the radius of gyration about the *xx* axis for the T shape of Example 3-7.

Solution:

$$I_{xx} = 1.22(10)^6 \text{ mm}^4$$

$$r_x = \sqrt{\frac{I_{xx}}{A}}$$

$$= \sqrt{\frac{1.22(10)^6 \text{ mm}^4}{2400 \text{ mm}^2}}$$

$$= 23 \text{ mm}$$

Problems

3-19. Determine r_x and r_y for the wide-flange shape of Example 3-4.

3-20. Determine r_x for the rotated square of Example 3-5.

3-21. Figure 3-40 shows two 38 × 139 mm pieces which are to be fastened together to make a column. What should be the center-to-center spacing *s* so that r_y will equal r_x for the column cross section?

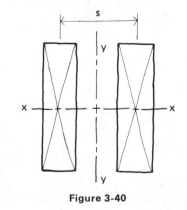

Figure 3-40

In simple terms, *stress* is merely the intensity of force. It is force per unit area. The levels and types of stress at different points throughout a building structure are of prime concern to the structural designer. Forces are generated in response to applied loads, dead and live, and those forces always result in a stressed body or an accelerating body. Since most building elements are not meant to accelerate, they develop internal stresses. These stresses, if they become too large, can cause rupture or excess deformation.

Figure 4-1(a) shows a simple bar in tension. The free-body cut in Figure 4-1(b) exposes the stress inside the bar. Even though the loads P are point loads applied

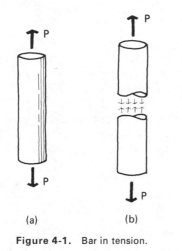

(a)   (b)

Figure 4-1. Bar in tension.

along the central axis of the bar, the stress is constant over the cross section except in a zone right next to the end of the bar. The intensity of the stress is simply

$$f_a = \frac{P}{A} \qquad (4\text{-}1)$$

where f_a = axial stress (Pa)[1]
       P = axial force (N)
       A = cross-sectional area (m²)

If the stress is too great, it can be reduced by increasing the area of the member. However, it is usually preferable to reduce the force. This can sometimes be done through a change in geometry or manner in which the loads develop the force (i.e., a change in the statics of the design).

There are really only two kinds of stress, normal and tangential. *Normal stresses* act at right angles to the surface of the stressed area, while *tangential stresses* act parallel to that surface. Shearing stresses are tangential while the axial stress shown in Figure 4-1 is normal. Reference is frequently made to torsional stress and bending stress as being separate types, but it will be

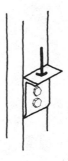

Figure 4-2

shown later that these are types of tangential and normal stress, respectively. The bolts in Figure 4-2 are being subjected to shear by the load P. The stresses will act tangentially on a transverse section through each bolt.

[1]Pa stands for pascal (a stress magnitude of one newton per square meter) after Blaise Pascal (1623–1662), a French scientist.

Stress and Strain

Problems

4-1. Determine the average axial tensile stress in the bar of Figure 4-1 if $P = 50$ kN and the cross-sectional area of the bar is 400 mm².

4-2. Determine the average shearing stress in the bolts of Figure 4-2 if $P = 75$ kN and the diameter of each bolt is 25 mm.

4-2 BASIC CONNECTION STRESSES

A simple bolted connection can serve to illustrate several different examples of normal and tangential stresses. The bolted connection of Figure 4-3 could fail in any one of four different ways if subjected to overload. Aside from the obvious bolt shear failure shown in Figure

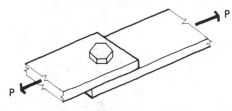

Figure 4-3. Bolted connection.

4-4(a), the hole in the plate could elongate by a compression bearing failure as in Figure 4-4(b). In this case the crushing area to be used for design purposes is the projected rectangle, dimensioned by the bolt diameter for one side and the plate thickness for the other. Bearing stress is a normal stress.

The plate might also fail by excess normal tensile stresses on the area of the plate left after the hole was drilled, as in Figure 4-4(c). This type of stress is called "tension on the net section."

Likewise, if the hole was located too close to the

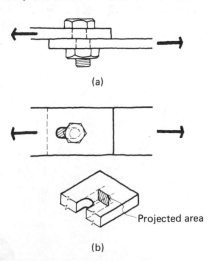

(a)

(b)

Figure 4-4. Stresses in a bolted connection: (a) shear through the bolt; (b) excess bearing (crushing) of the plate at the hole.

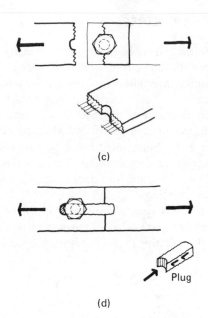

(c)

(d)

Figure 4-4. (continued) (c) tension on the net section of the plate; (d) end shear-out of the plate.

end of one of the plates, the tangential failure of Figure 4-4(d) might result. Here the stressed area is actually two parallel sides of a "plug" of material pushed out of the plate by the bolt.

4-3 STRAIN

Stresses are usually accompanied by a *strain*, which is a physical change in the size or shape of the stressed body. *Normal stresses* result in a shortening or lengthening of the fibers of that body, while *tangential* or *shearing strain* indicates an angle change. It is interesting to note that stress can never be seen, whereas strain can be seen and precisely measured.

Figure 4-5 shows two types of strain. The normal strain in Figure 4-5(a), called δ, is the *total strain*, and in this case it is elongation. This total strain is the sum of the smaller strains occurring in each individual unit length of the bar. The average unit strain is designated as ϵ.

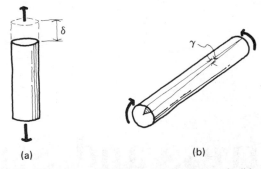

(a)   (b)

Figure 4-5. Normal strain (a) and shearing strain (b).

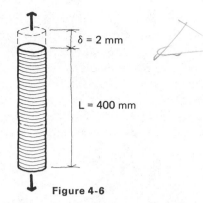

Figure 4-6

Figure 4-6 illustrates a bar with a total strain (shown greatly exaggerated) of 2 mm. Each of the 400 units of the original bar got a tiny bit longer, so that the total effect over the aggregate length summed to 2 mm. ϵ is the amount of strain experienced by each unit length. δ is the total strain and equal to ϵ times the number of units in the original length.

$$\delta = \epsilon L \qquad (4\text{-}2)$$

Solving this for the unit strain, we get

$$\epsilon = \frac{\delta}{L}$$

and for the case in question,

$$\epsilon = \frac{2 \text{ mm}}{400 \text{ mm}} = 0.005$$

Notice that the average unit strain will always be a pure number, as δ and L must have like units.

A similar relationship exists for the shearing strain of torsion in Figure 4-5(b), and this is discussed in Chapter 6.

Problems

4-3. A reinforced concrete column is 5 m long and under load it shortens 3 mm. Determine its average unit strain.

4-4. A 100-m-long steel cable is loaded in tension until the average unit strain is 0.004. Determine the total elongation under this load.

4-4   LATERAL STRAIN

As an object gets longer or shorter due to normal stresses, it also gets thinner or fatter in the transverse dimension. This is readily observable by stretching a rubber band or piece of chewing gum and noting the change in cross-sectional area. This can be explained in a simplistic way by assuming that the volume of a body must remain essentially constant, so that a change in one dimension requires a change in another.

This lateral strain is called the *Poisson effect*, after S. D. Poisson (1781–1840), the French scientist who first

quantified it. *Poisson's ratio* is defined as the average unit lateral strain divided by the average unit strain in the direction of load.

4-5   STRESS VERSUS STRAIN

In 1678, Robert Hooke, an Englishman, observed that most materials were essentially *elastic*, that is, the deformations in a stressed body would disappear upon removal of the load. Furthermore, the relationship between stress and strain (or between load and deformation) was a linear one. Many materials are "springlike," in that if we place a 10-kN load on a member, it will strain a certain amount, and if we add an additional 10-kN load, an additional strain of that same amount will take place. If we continue this loading process, of course, the material will eventually rupture or more usually *yield* (permanently deform), and proportionality between stress and strain will no longer exist. Some materials have definite yield points or stress levels beyond which additional load will cause a great increase in strain. Most steels have very definite yield points, and a graph plotting stress versus strain will show a straight line up to the yield stress and then show an abrupt departure from linearity as failure begins. Other materials, such as concrete (in compression), have no definite yield point, and stress is not proportional to strain except at low levels of stress.

Figure 4-7 illustrates the sharp yield point of mild

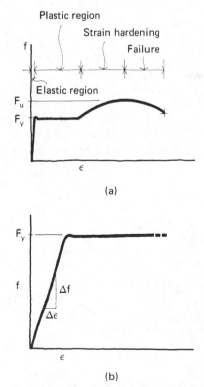

(a)

(b)

Figure 4-7. Stress–strain curve for mild steel in tension.

steel. Figure 4-7(b) is merely an enlarged picture of the elastic region in Figure 4-7(a). The ultimate strength of steel is designated as F_u and the yield strength is called F_y. This particular curve is interesting because it shows a large plastic region where strain continues with no increase in load, demonstrating the "taffylike" nature of the material. Also indicated is the "strain-hardening" property of mild steel, which causes an increase in strength just before failure.

The curve for a structural concrete in compression is shown in Figure 4-8. Notice that the curve for concrete has no real straight-line portion and that stress is only approximately linear with strain and then only for low loads. The ultimate strength of concrete in compression is designated as f'_c.

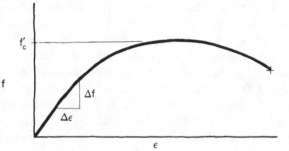

Figure 4-8. Stress–strain curve for concrete in compression.

Notice that the curves drop downward, indicating a loss of strength near the material failure point. This happens by virtue of the manner in which the materials are tested and merely illustrates the inability of a testing machine to keep load upon a rapidly disintegrating material.

By definition, once a material has experienced any appreciable yield, it will not return to its original shape when the load is removed, but will show some permanent deformation. For all practical purposes, such a material has failed. Therefore, we strive to keep stress levels well below such values when designing structural elements.

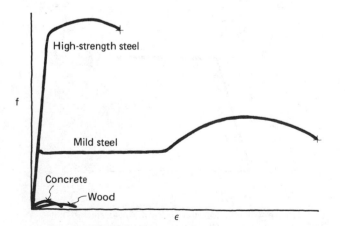

Figure 4-9. Stress–strain curves.

The curves of four different materials have been drawn at the same scale in Figure 4-9 so the reader can sense the relative strengths. The curves for concrete and wood are in compression, while those for steel were taken from tensile tests. (Steel tested in compression behaves much as it does in tension, but in practical applications, buckling failures preclude a true compressive yield. Buckling is discussed in some detail in Chapter 13.)

4-6 STIFFNESS

The stiffness of a material is a measure of how much that material strains for a given amount of stress. If we place equal loads upon like pieces of wood and steel, the wood will undergo a much larger strain than will the steel. This happens because steel is much stiffer than wood. Because stronger materials are usually stiffer, we tend to confuse stiffness with strength, when in reality the two properties are quite different. The strength of a material can be ascertained as the highest stress achieved during a test of the material (i.e., the largest ordinate at any point on the stress–strain curve). The stiffness, on the other hand, is the slope of the stress–strain curve, given as $\Delta f/\Delta\epsilon$ in Figure 4-7(b) and 4-8. The magnitude of this slope is called the *modulus of elasticity* [or *Young's modulus*, after Thomas Young (1773–1829), an English scientist[2]] and is designated by the symbol E. It has the same units as stress because it is defined as incremental stress divided by incremental strain, and, of course, strain has no units. Values of E and ν (Poisson's ratio) for several common materials are tabulated in Appendix L.

The E value or stiffness of concrete is about one-tenth that of steel, while structural wood is about one-half as stiff as concrete. This important property helps to tell us how much a given material will deform or deflect under load. How much will a certain cable stretch? How much will a steel girder deflect? How "bouncy" will a wood joist floor be? The answers to these questions are independent of the material strength but are directly related to material stiffness.

The following example illustrates how E can be quantified.

EXAMPLE 4-1

A sample of steel is being stressed in a tensile testing machine. Stress is found to be linear with strain in the elastic region and when $f = 50$ MPa, $\epsilon = 0.000\,25$. At a greater load, $f = 150$ MPa and $\epsilon = 0.000\,75$. Determine the E value for steel.

[2]Actually, it was Claude L. M. H. Navier (1785–1836) a French engineer, who first stated the relationship the way we use it today.

Solution:

$$E = \frac{\Delta f}{\Delta \epsilon}$$

$$= \frac{150 \text{ MPa} - 50 \text{ MPa}}{0.000\ 75 - 0.000\ 25}$$

$$= \frac{100 \text{ MPa}}{0.000\ 50}$$

$$= 200\ 000 \text{ MPa}$$

or

$$E = 200 \text{ GPa}$$

Problems

4-5. A concrete cylinder with a cross-sectional area of 18 200 mm² is to be tested in axial compression. Before loading, two marks are scribed on the cylinder precisely 200.0 mm apart, as in Figure 4-10. When the load is 182 kN, the marks are measured and found to be 199.9 mm apart. Determine the E value for this concrete. Assume an approximately linear relationship between stress and strain.

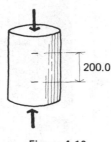

Figure 4-10

4-6. The modulus of elasticity for the steel cable of Problem 4-4 is 160 GPa. Determine the average stress in the cable under the applied load. Assume a linear stress–strain curve.

4-7 TOTAL AXIAL DEFORMATION

A unique relationship can be drawn between load and deformation by combining some of the relationships developed in previous sections. The total deformation of an axially loaded member is given by equation

$$\delta = \epsilon L \tag{4-2}$$

The average unit strain ϵ can be expressed in terms of the average unit stress and the modulus, because $E = f/\epsilon$ or $\epsilon = f/E$. Substituting, we get

$$\delta = \frac{fL}{E} \tag{4-3}$$

This equation is only valid, of course, if the relationship between stress and strain, is essentially linear. For this reason, it is more useful for materials such as steel and less useful for concrete.

EXAMPLE 4-2

The first-story column of a tall steel building is 6 m long and must carry an axial load of 22 000 kN. If $E = 200$ GPa and the cross-sectional area of the column is 140 000 mm², determine its total shortening.

Solution:

$$\delta = \frac{PL}{AE}$$

$$= \frac{22\ 000 \text{ kN}(6 \text{ m})}{(0.140 \text{ m}^2)[200(10)^6 \text{ kN/m}^2]}$$

$$= 4.71(10)^{-3} \text{ m}$$

or

$$\delta = 5 \text{ mm}$$

Problems

4-7. A 150-m-long roof cable cannot be permitted to stretch more than 800 mm or the roof geometry will change too greatly. If $E = 155$ GPa and the load is 8000 kN, determine the required cable diameter needed to avoid excessive elongation.

4-8. An 8-m-long wood column is stressed in compression to 5000 kPa. If $E = 9600$ MPa, determine the total shortening of the column.

4-8 INDETERMINATE AXIALLY LOADED ELEMENTS

Figure 4-11 shows a composite post in which both materials are stressed by the axial load P. To determine how much of the load is carried by each material, we must look beyond statics. Only one equation of equilibrium is useful here,

$$\sum F_y = 0$$

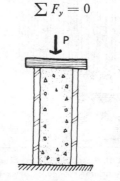

Figure 4-11. Concrete-filled steel pipe.

which gives us

$$P = P_c + P_s$$

or

$$P = f_c A_c + f_s A_s \tag{4-4}$$

where f_c = concrete stress (Pa)
  f_s = steel stress (Pa)
  A_c = concrete area (m²)
  A_s = steel area (m²)

Intuitive understanding of the development of axial stresses and the corresponding strains—and their dependencies upon cross-sectional area and material stiffness—can be used by the architect to promote the reading of a certain kind of character into a building. Such manipulations, though they make use of our visual knowledge of structural behavior, may or may not have anything to do with the actual stability of the structure. Thus the builders of Cologne Cathedral chose to make the front faces of the massive nave piers look like almost-independent columns, the only things visibly connecting the vaults above with the ground below. The "columns" are so slender as to seem incapable of taking any appreciable load from the vaults; they hint, even, at being in tension, not columns at all but cables tying down the upward-ballooning roof. At the other extreme, Frank Furness used visual expectations of normal column proportions, and of behavior under axial compression, to suggest that his façade possesses an almost intimidating weight and density.

Assuming that the total load and the areas of each material are given, Equation (4-4) has two unknowns, f_c and f_s, and cannot be solved alone. This problem is indeterminate because we must examine the deformations as well as the statics of the situation. If the plate at the top of the post is completely rigid (or effectively so), then the total shortening, δ, will be equal for the two materials.

$$\delta_s = \delta_c$$

or

$$\epsilon_s L_s = \epsilon_c L_c$$

If the original lengths of the two materials were equal, then $\epsilon_s = \epsilon_c$, or

$$\frac{f_s}{E_s} = \frac{f_c}{E_c}$$

or

$$f_s = \frac{E_s}{E_c} f_c \qquad (4-5)$$

Equation (4-5) is the second equation (independently obtained) which can be solved simultaneously with Equation (4-4) to get the stresses in the two materials. The following example should help to clarify this procedure.

EXAMPLE 4-3

With reference to Figure 4-11, the short pipe column must support an axial load of 200 kN. The cross-sectional areas of the concrete and steel are 17 000 mm and 1200 mm, respectively. If $E_c = 25$ GPa and $E_s = 200$ GPa, determine the compressive stress in each material.

Solution:

$$\sum F_y = 0$$
$$200 \text{ kN} = f_c(0.017 \text{ m}^2) + f_s(0.0012 \text{ m}^2)$$

Equation (4-5):

$$f_s = \frac{E_s}{E_c} f_c$$
$$= \frac{200 \text{ GPa}}{25 \text{ GPa}} f_c$$
$$= 8 f_c$$

Substituting into the equation of statics, we get

$$200 \text{ kN} = f_c(0.017 \text{ m}^2) + 8 f_c(0.0012 \text{ m}^2)$$

Solving for f_c, we get

$$f_c = 7520 \text{ kPa}$$

or

$$f_c = 7.52 \text{ MPa}$$

From Equation (4-5),

$$f_s = 8(7.52 \text{ MPa})$$
$$= 60.2 \text{ MPa}$$

Notice that owing to its high modulus of elasticity, the steel carries a disproportionate share of the load relative to its area.

$$P_s = f_s A_s$$
$$= 60\ 200 \text{ kPa } (0.0012 \text{ m}^2)$$
$$= 72.2 \text{ kN}$$

whereas

$$P_c = f_c A_c$$
$$= 7520 \text{ kPa } (0.017 \text{ m}^2)$$
$$= 127.8 \text{ kN}$$

The steel carries about one-third of the load but occupies only one-fifteenth of the cross-sectional area.

EXAMPLE 4-4

A precast concrete housing module is suspended from two identical cables and rests on the building core as shown in Figure 4-12. The module is rigid and has a total weight of $W = 1600$ kN. Determine the force in each cable.

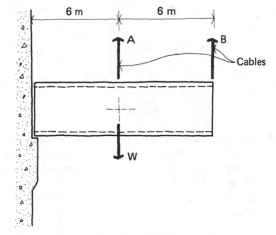

Figure 4-12. Suspended precast concrete unit.

Solution: Taking moments about point C (Figure 4-13), we get

$$\sum M_c = 0$$
$$1600 \text{ kN}(6 \text{ m}) = P_a(6 \text{ m}) + P_b(12 \text{ m})$$

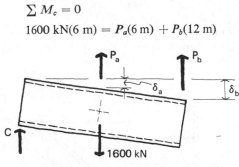

Figure 4-13. Free-body diagram.

From the geometry of the stretched cables and the fact that the concrete unit may be considered rigid, we get

$$\delta_b = 2\delta_a$$
$$\left(\frac{PL}{AE}\right)_b = 2\left(\frac{PL}{AE}\right)_a$$

Since the cables are identical, L, A, and E will drop out of each term, leaving

$$P_b = 2P_a$$

Substituting this relationship into the moment equation, we get

$$9600 \text{ kN·m} = P_a(6 \text{ m}) + 2P_a(12 \text{ m})$$

Solving for P_a gives us

$$P_a = 320 \text{ kN}$$

and therefore $P_b = 640$ kN.

Problems

4-9. A short reinforced concrete column has the cross section shown in Figure 4-14. It is reinforced by four steel bars, each of which has an area of 600 mm. It must support an axial load of 1000 kN and is loaded such that that the two materials will deform equally. Determine the stress in each material. Assume that $E_s = 200$ GPa and $E_c = 20$ GPa.

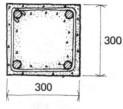

Figure 4-14

4-10. Two steel cables are loaded by an 800-kN force as in Figure 4-15. Before the load is applied, cable B is 500 mm longer than cable A. The area of each cable is 800 mm². Determine the force in each cable after the load is applied. Assume that $E = 160$ GPa for both cables.

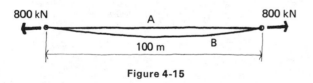

Figure 4-15

4-11. With reference to Figure 4-16, two steel cables at A and B both help to support the rigid crane beam. If they

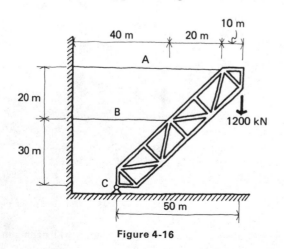

Figure 4-16

have identical E values and areas, how much force is in each cable?

4-9 THERMAL STRESSES AND STRAINS

Whenever a structure is heated or cooled, it changes shape. Most materials expand when heated and contract when cooled. Long building structures must have joints in them to allow these changes to take place. Exposed exterior structural elements often undergo great temperature variations compared to interior ones and large differential movements can result. If these movements are restrained, stresses can build up in the members themselves and connecting elements.

In many building structures, the small range of ambient temperatures and/or the absence of long uninterrupted structural elements serve to minimize thermal effects and they can be safely ignored. It is helpful to study the magnitudes of thermal movements and stresses to be able to judge when they deserve design attention.

The total change in length of a body due to a temperature change is

$$\delta = \alpha \, \Delta t(L) \qquad (4\text{-}6)$$

where δ = total change in length (m)
  α = thermal coefficient for the material (°C⁻¹)
  Δt = temperature change (°C)
  L = original length (m)

The coefficient α is usually expressed in terms of strain per degree of temperature change (e.g., m/m per degree Celsius). With Δt expressed in degrees Celsius, it then becomes convenient to think of $\alpha \, \Delta t$ as equivalent to ϵ, the unit strain.

EXAMPLE 4-5

A 40-m-long masonry wall undergoes a temperature rise from 0°C to 40°C. Determine the total change in length if α for the material is $6.1(10)^{-6}$ m/m per °C.

Solution:

$$\delta = \alpha \, \Delta t(L)$$
$$= [6.1(10)^{-6} \text{ °C}^{-1}](40\text{°C})(40 \text{ m})$$
$$= 9.76(10)^{-3} \text{ m}$$
$$= 10 \text{ mm}$$

Without intermediate joints to allow movement in the plane of the wall, this motion will accummulate, possibly causing damage to attached walls or other constructions. The real difficulties, however, will develop during the contraction or cooling cycle of the same wall. Masonry and concrete lack the requisite tensile strength needed for large thermal contractions, and vertical cracks will develop in a long unjointed wall.

EXAMPLE 4-6

A high-rise building 220 m tall has an exposed steel frame. On a given sunny day in winter, the columns on the south side reach 50°C while those on the north side remain at −10°C. Under these extreme conditions, what will be the overall difference in length of the columns? Assume that $\alpha = 11.7(10)^{-6}$ °C^{-1}.

Solution:

$$\delta = \alpha \, \Delta t(L)$$
$$= [11.7(10)^{-6} \text{ °}C^{-1}](60\text{°C})(220 \text{ m})$$
$$= 0.154 \text{ m}$$
$$= 154 \text{ mm}$$

Unlike the contraction of a material such as masonry, unrestrained thermal elongation seldom results in a structural failure of the piece itself. However, as soon as that element is attached to others or restrained in any way, stresses will develop. A fully restrained bar fixed at the ends will build up compressive stress while attempting to elongate during a temperature increase. The resulting stress will have the same magnitude as if the bar had been allowed to expand and then axially loaded until it was "squeezed" back to its initial length. In other words, the change in length under free thermal expansion would be

$$\delta_{\text{case 1}} = \alpha \, \Delta t(L)$$

The change in length due to an applied compressive load will be

$$\delta_{\text{case 2}} = \frac{PL}{AE}$$

or

$$\delta_{\text{case 2}} = \frac{fL}{E}$$

Since the actual elongation for a "fixed" end bar is zero,

$$\delta_{\text{case 1}} - \delta_{\text{case 2}} = 0$$

or

$$\delta_{\text{case 1}} = \delta_{\text{case 2}}$$

$$\alpha \, \Delta t(L) = \frac{f}{E}L$$

Solving for the axial stress, we get

$$f = E\alpha \, \Delta t \qquad (4\text{-}7)$$

This stress would, of course, be tensile if we cooled the bar instead of heating it.

Equation (4-7) is interesting in that it illustrates that axial stresses, which develop in a restrained body due to a temperature change are independent of any dimension of the body.

EXAMPLE 4-7

A straight concrete bridge is restrained by two canyon walls. If $E = 25$ GPa and $\alpha = 10(10)^{-6}$ °C^{-1}, determine the compressive stress developed during a temperature increase of 35°C.

Solution:

$$f = E\alpha \, \Delta t$$
$$= 25 \text{ GPa}[10(10)^{-6} \text{ °}C^{-1}](35\text{°C})$$
$$= 8.75(10)^{-3} \text{ GPa}$$
$$= 8750 \text{ kPa}$$

EXAMPLE 4-8

A steel cable 25 mm in diameter is stretched tightly between two massive supports. If $E = 175$ GPa and $\alpha = 11(10)^{-6}$ °C^{-1}, determine the force in the cable developed due to a temperature drop of 40°C.

Solution:

$$P = fA$$
$$= E\alpha \, \Delta t A$$
$$A = \pi r^2 = \pi(0.0125 \text{ m})^2$$
$$= 491(10)^{-6} \text{ m}^2$$
$$= 175 \text{ GPa}[11(10)^{-6} \text{ °}C^{-1}](40\text{°C})[491(10)^{-6} \text{ m}^2]$$
$$= 37.8(10)^{-6} \text{ GN}$$
$$= 37.8 \text{ kN}$$

Problems

4-12. An unloaded steel roof cable is 125.0 m long at 25°C. Determine its length at −10°C and at 70°C. Assume that $\alpha = 11(10)^{-6}$ °C^{-1}.

4-13. A long concrete bearing wall has vertical expansion joints placed every 22 m. Determine the required width of the gap in a joint if it is wide open at −5°C and just barely closed at 40°C. Assume that $\alpha = 10(10)^{-6}$ °C^{-1}.

4-14. A large steam pipe is built with no provision for thermal expansion. If the ends are fixed, what is the level of compressive stress developed as the pipe goes from 20°C to 120°C? Assume that buckling does not occur. Assume that $E = 200$ GPa and $\alpha = 11.7(10)^{-6}$ °C^{-1}.

4-15. An expansion loop is placed in the pipe of Problem 4-14 as shown in Figure 4-17. The loop is 2.0 m long at 20°C. How long is it at 120°C?

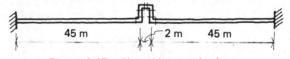

Figure 4-17. Pipe with expansion loop.

4-16. An aluminum curtain wall panel is attached to large concrete columns when the temperature is 18°C. No provision is made for differential thermal movement. Because of insulation between the two, the sun heats the wall to 55°C but the column only gets to 33°C. Determine the consequent compressive stress in the curtain wall. (Ignore the effect of small tensile stresses in the concrete columns.) Assume that E of the aluminum is 70 GPa, α for the concrete is $10(10)^{-6}$ °C^{-1}, and α for the aluminum is $22(10)^{-6}$ °C^{-1}.

4-10 ALLOWABLE STRESS DESIGN AND STRENGTH DESIGN

Structural problems are basically of two types: analysis or design. *Analysis* (sometimes called review) is the process of determining the types and magnitudes of stresses and deformations in a *given* structure when it is subjected to known or assumed loads. Most of the problems in this chapter have been of the analysis type. The process of design has quite a different goal. In a *design* situation we are trying to proportion the size and shape of a structure so that it can carry the known or assumed loads in a safe manner.

These two attitudes are not as distinct and separate as they might appear at first glance, because often the design process becomes an analytical trial-and-error procedure in order to determine the "best" size or configuration for a structure. (The phrase "trial and error," while much used and generally understood, can be misleading, as there really is no "error" involved. The writer prefers "trial-and-check" or "select-and-try" as being more descriptive terminology.)

What determines the "best" structure for a given architectural and construction endeavor is quite an impossible question to answer definitively. In pure structural design terms, the word "best" can sometimes be interpreted as "efficiency," that is, efficient use of the material(s) involved through (a) optimum manipulation of the geometry or statics present, and (b) loading the materials with types of stress which they can most easily "take" or resist. Here the word "efficiency" is used, in a narrow sense, to mean just enough material to do the job without waste. Too much material would be "over-design" and not enough for proper safety would be "underdesign."

As with any type of design, many orders and sequences of compromises are involved and it is a rare (or nonexistent) effort in which the structural, constructional, and functional considerations become coincident. The structural design process can never be accomplished in isolation and becomes a mixture of efficiency and compatibility determinations.

There are two different approaches to structural design currently in use. One is called the *allowable stress method*, in which the structure is shaped and the elements are proportioned so that certain "allowable" stresses are not exceeded. (This approach is also referred to as the *working stress method* or *service load method*.) These allowable stresses are determined as percentages of the failure strengths of materials under various kinds of stress. For example, the allowable stress in shear for a certain species and grade of wood might be 500 kPa, whereas its failure stress in shear might be 1000 kPa.

The allowable bending stress in structural steel might be determined as two-thirds of its yield value (i.e., steel that has a yield strength of 250 MPa can be safely stressed to 165 MPa). The difference between the two values in each case constitutes a "margin of safety" or factor of safety obtained by dividing the failure stress by the allowable stress. This design method is used for wood structures and for most steel structures. Elements are proportioned so that the computed stresses present under the expected loads (both dead and live) will be less than the allowable stresses. The behavior of the structure under overload or failure load is not considered. Representative allowable stresses for several types of wood are given in Appendix P. Allowable stresses for different steels are given as required in various chapters.

The other approach to design is called *strength design*, in which the factor of safety is applied in a manner quite different from the allowable stress concept. In the strength design method, various factors of safety are applied directly to the loads which are known or assumed to be acting on the structure. Thus, we conceptually increase the loads that the structure must be proportioned to take by multiplying those loads by specific factors. Such increased or factored loads are called *ultimate loads* and we then design the member or structure to *fail* under the application of these increased loads. (This approach is also called *ultimate strength design* or *ultimate load design*.)

Strength design is quite distinct from allowable stress design in that the strength approach proportions a structure to fail under a specified overload and the actual stresses present in the structure under normal loads are not computed. The margin of safety is present in the degree of overload specified. Strength design is widely used for reinforced concrete structures, and overload load factors of 1.4 for dead loads and 1.7 for live loads have been specified by the American Concrete Institute. A brief introduction to reinforced concrete and this design approach is given in Chapter 17.

(Various sections of this chapter have focused on the fact that structures might become unusable because of excess deformation or deflection as well as by actual material rupture. The two different approaches to structural design presented here concern only the stresses in a loaded structure and are not involved with "failure" by excess deformation. This is guarded against by specifying certain permissible values of deformation or deflection which may not be exceeded when the expected loads act on the structure. There is no easily quantifiable factor of safety involved.)

It is important to note that no matter which design approach is adopted, the stresses and deformations due to the actual loads will be reasonably close in magnitude.

The strength design approach can take advantage of the redundancy of indeterminate structures and is therefore preferred by many analysts in such cases.

The factors of safety in each case are not up to the designer but are usually specified by code bodies and industry associations and are based upon research and experience with the particular materials. These factors can vary in magnitude and are determined by considering the answers to such questions as:

How statistically consistent are the properties of the material?

How homogeneous is the material?

What is the statistical frequency of flaws in the material?

What level of supervision and inspection will be present?

How easy is it to make errors when fabricating the material?

How disastrous is the failure that might occur?

How important is this piece to the integrity of the whole structure?

How accurately can the probable loads be predicted?

How accurate are the assumptions that have been made in the structural design process?

How good or proven is the theory used in the structural design?

One can see from the last three questions that a factor of ignorance is needed within the factor of safety. Many structures are standing today because the effects of errors were safely negated by providing for an overload which never occurred.

EXAMPLE 4-9

A 150-m-long steel elevator cable must carry a load of 45 kN. The tensile stress must not exceed an allowable 150 MPa and the total elongation must not exceed 20 mm. Determine the required diameter of the cable. Assume that $E = 175$ GPa.

Solution: Determine separately the area needed to meet the two requirements.

(a) $A_r = \dfrac{P}{f_{\text{allow}}}$ ref. Eq. (4-1)

$= \dfrac{45 \text{ kN}}{150\ 000 \text{ kN/m}^2}$

$= 0.0003 \text{ m}^2$

(b) $A_r = \dfrac{PL}{\delta E}$ ref. Eq. (4-3)

$= \dfrac{45 \text{ kN}(150 \text{ m})}{0.020 \text{ m}[(175)(10)^6 \text{ kN/m}^2]}$

$= 0.001\ 93 \text{ m}^2$

The elongation limitation will govern.

$$A_r = 1930 \text{ mm}^2$$

$$D = \sqrt{\frac{4A}{\pi}}$$

$$= \sqrt{\frac{4(1930 \text{ mm}^2)}{\pi}}$$

$$= 50 \text{ mm}$$

EXAMPLE 4-10

The cross section of a concrete-filled short tubular steel column is shown in Figure 4-18. The area of the steel tube is 1400 mm², while the concrete core has an area of 12 000 mm². Determine the maximum safe axial load that can be applied to this column such that the following allowable stresses will not be exceeded. Allowable stress for concrete, 10 MPa; allowable stress for steel, 150 MPa. Assume that $E_c = 20$ GPa and $E_s = 200$ GPa.

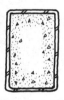

Figure 4-18

Solution:

$$\Sigma F_y = 0$$

$$P - f_c A_c + f_s A_s \qquad \text{ref. Eq. (4-4)}$$

$$= f_c(0.012 \text{ m}^2) + f_s(0.0014 \text{ m}^2)$$

$$f_s = \frac{E_s}{E_c} f_c \qquad \text{ref. Eq. (4-5)}$$

$$= \frac{200 \text{ GPa}}{20 \text{ GPa}} f_c$$

$$= 10 f_c$$

Therefore, the concrete allowable stress will control. Let f_c reach its allowable of 10 MPa; f_s will then be 100 MPa.

$$P = 10 \text{ MN/m}^2(0.012 \text{ m}^2) + 100 \text{ MN/m}^2(0.0014 \text{ m}^2)$$

$$= 0.26 \text{ MN}$$

or

$$P = 260 \text{ kN}$$

Problems

4-17. A wood post must carry an axial load of 50 kN. The failure stress due to buckling has been determined to be 2000 kPa. If a factor of safety of 2.7 is desired, determine the required cross-sectional area.

4-18. A first floor steel column in a high-rise building delivers its load of 4700 kN to the top of a concrete pier. If the permissible bearing stress of the concrete is 4000 kPa, determine the required area of the bearing plate.

4-19. Determine the required diameter of the cable in the structure of Figure 4-19 if it cannot be permitted to elongate more than 0.1% of its length. Assume that $E = 160$ GPa.

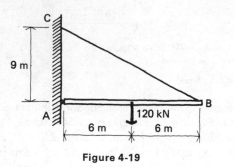

Figure 4-19

4-20. The short reinforced concrete column of Figure 4-20 must carry an axial load of 2000 kN. The steel area constitutes 3% of the gross area of the column; the concrete occupies the remaining 97%. Determine the required dimension D if the allowable stresses are 12 MPa for the concrete and 165 MPa for the steel. Assume that $E_c = 25$ GPa and $E_s = 200$ GPa.

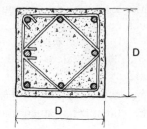

Figure 4-20. Reinforced concrete column cross section.

5-1 INTRODUCTION

It is important for the structural designer to realize that different engineering materials have different characteristics and will exhibit different behaviors under load. A knowledge of such characteristics or properties will help to ensure proper use of these materials, both architecturally and structurally.

It is assumed that the reader will have already been exposed to the study of materials through courses in building construction or materials science. This chapter will only highlight a few selected structural materials in the interest of emphasizing the range of structural characteristics and their diversity. A table of properties of structural materials is given in Appendix L.

5-2 NATURE OF WOOD

Wood is a natural material and has a broad range of physical properties because of the different characteristics of its many species. Softwoods such as fir, pine, and hemlock are most often used for structural applications because they are more plentiful (grow fast and tall) and are easier to fabricate. These woods are generally strong in tension and compression in a direction parallel to the grain and weak when stressed perpendicularly to the grain. Wood is also weak in shear because of its tendency to split along the natural grain laminations. The allowable stresses for a few selected species are given in Appendix P.

Wood is light and soft compared to most other structural materials and is easily shaped and fastened together. A minimum of materials-handling equipment is needed to erect wood structures because of their weight. It is also very versatile in terms of its adaptability to the making of geometric shapes and even nonlinear forms.

Most softwoods are fairly ductile and will not fail suddenly when overloaded. Because of their lack of homogeneity or uniformity, the allowable stresses are quite low compared to failure stresses. Consequently, when wood structures are properly engineered, a statistically high margin of safety is present. Wood is often known as the "forgiving" material because of its apparent ability to sustain loads not accounted for when the structure was designed.

Wood, on the other hand, is not very stiff. It is subject to excessive deflection and creep deformation if not designed with these characteristics in mind. It is prone to damage by fire and to deterioration by moisture and insects. It expands and contracts with variations in humidity, markedly so in the direction perpendicular to the grain. Timber structures that are to be exposed to the elements must be carefully treated or highly maintained to preserve their integrity.

The American Institute of Timber Construction publishes the *Manual of Timber Construction* and the reader is referred to it for more extensive information on the properties and use of wood. The National Forest Products Association publishes some excellent design aids and data books for use by the structural designer.

5-3 CONCRETE AND REINFORCED CONCRETE

Concrete is a man-made conglomerate stone composed of essentially four ingredients: portland cement, water, sand, and coarse aggregate. The cement and water combine to make a paste that binds the sand and stones together. Ideally, the aggregates are graded so that the volume of paste is at a minimum, merely surrounding every piece with a thin layer. Most structural concrete is stone concrete, but structural lightweight concrete (roughly two-thirds the density of stone concrete) is becoming increasingly popular.

Properties of Structural Materials

Concrete is essentially a compressive material having almost no tensile strength. As explained in Chapter 6, shearing stresses are always accompanied by tension, so concrete's weakness in tension also causes it to be weak in shear. These deficiencies are overcome by using steel bars for reinforcement at the places where tensile and shearing stresses are generated. Under load, reinforced concrete beams actually have numerous minute cracks which run at right angles to the direction of major tensile stresses. The tensile forces at such locations are being taken completely by the steel "re-bars."

The compressive strength of a given concrete is a function of the quality and proportions of its constituents and the manner in which the fresh concrete is cured. (*Curing* is the process of hardening during which time the concrete must be prevented from "drying out," as the presence of water is necessary for the chemical action to progress.) Coarse aggregate that is hard and well graded is particularly essential for quality concrete. The most important factor governing the strength, however, is the percentage of water used in the mix. A minimum amount of water is needed for proper hydration of the cement. Additional water is needed for handling and placing the concrete, but excess amounts cause the strength to drop markedly.

These and other topics are fully covered in the booklet, "Design and Control of Concrete Mixtures," published by the Portland Cement Association. This is an excellent reference, treating both concrete mix design and proper construction practices. The American Concrete Institute publishes a widely adopted code specifying the structural requirements for reinforced concrete.

Concrete is known as the "formable" or "moldable" structural material. Compared to other materials, it is easy to make curvilinear members and surfaces with concrete. It has no inherent texture but adopts the texture of the forming material, so it can range widely in surface appearance. It is relatively inexpensive to make, both in terms of raw materials and labor, and the basic ingredients of portland cement are available the world over. (It should be noted, however, that the necessary reinforcing bars for concrete may not be readily available in less-developed countries.)

The best structural use of reinforced concrete, in terms of the characteristics of the material, is in those structures requiring continuity and/or rigidity. It has a monolithic quality which automatically makes fixed or continuous connections. These moment-resistant joints are such that many low-rise concrete buildings do not require a secondary bracing system for lateral loads. In essence, a concrete beam joins a concrete column very differently from the way steel and wood pieces join, and the sensitive designer will not ignore this difference.

(These remarks do not apply to precast structural elements, which are usually not joined in a continuous manner.)

Concrete is naturally fireproof and needs no separate protection system. Because of its mass, it can also serve as an effective barrier to sound transmission.

In viewing the negative aspects, concrete is unfortunately quite heavy and it is often noted that a concrete structure expends a large portion of its capacity merely carrying itself. Attempts to make concrete less dense, while maintaining high quality levels, have generally resulted in increased costs. Nevertheless, use of lightweight concrete can sometimes result in overall economies.

Concrete requires more quality control than most other building materials. Modern transit-mixed concrete suppliers are available to all U.S. urban areas and the mix is usually of a uniformly high quality. Field- or job-mixed concrete requires knowledgeable supervision, however. In any type of concrete work, missing or mislocated reinforcing bars can result in elements with reduced load capacities. Poor handling and/or curing conditions can seriously weaken any concrete. For these and other reasons, most building codes require independent field inspections at various stages of construction.

Proper concrete placement is also somewhat dependent upon the ambient weather conditions. Extremely high temperatures and, more important, those below (or near) freezing can make concrete work very difficult.

5-4 STRUCTURAL STEEL

Steel is the strongest and stiffest building material in common use today. Relative to wood and concrete, it is a high-technology material made by highly refined and controlled processes. Structural steel has a uniformly high strength in tension and compression and is also very good in shear. It comes in a range of yield strengths made by adjusting the chemistry of the material in its molten state. It is the most consistent of all structural materials and is, for all practical purposes, homogeneous and *isotropic*, meaning it has like characteristics in all directions. (By contrast, wood is *anisotropic*.)

The greatest asset to steel is its strength and "plastic reserve," as shown in Figure 4-7. It is highly ductile and deforms greatly before failing if overloaded. Because of steel's strength, the individual members of a frame are usually small in cross section and have very little visual mass.

Steel is a linear material and can be economically made into a visual curve only by using a segmented geometry. It is most appropriately used in rectilinear structures where bolted or welded connections are easy to make. The structural shapes (i.e., pipes, tubes, channels, angles, and wide-flange sections) are manufactured to uniform dimensions having low tolerances. They are fully prepared (cut, trimmed or milled, drilled or punched, etc.) in a fabrication shop, remote from the site, and then delivered ready for erection. Such structures go up rapidly with a minimum of on-site labor. The most popular form of construction used today is referred to as shop-welded, field-bolted. In this method the various clip angles, beam seats, and so on, are welded to the members in a shop and then the members are bolted together in the field.

A major disadvantage to structural steel is its need to be fire-protected in most applications. It loses its strength at around 500°C and will then yield rapidly under low loads. A few municipalities require that all structural steel be fire-protected, and most codes will not permit any exposed elements to be within approximately 4 m of a combustible fire source.

The making of steel requires large physical plants and a high capital outlay, and therefore relatively few countries of the world have extensive mill facilities. The cost of manufacturing, coupled with the cost of transportation, can make steel a relatively expensive material. Just the same, in most urban areas, concrete and steel are quite competitive with one another in terms of in-place construction costs.

Continuity in the connections is much harder to achieve in steel than in concrete, and most buildings are constructed with simple connections or ones that are only partially moment-resistent. Some type of lateral load bracing system is almost always required in a steel-framed building and must be considered early in the design process.

Rolled steel is manufactured in a wide range of strengths. The standard low-carbon, mild steel in use today has a yield strength of 250 MPa. Steel plate can be obtained with an F_y value of almost 700 MPa, and most standard shapes can be rolled in steel as strong as 450 MPa, although this can be expensive. Examples and problems in this text are limited to shapes of $F_y = 250$ MPa and $F_y = 345$ MPa. These particular values are the most common ones, with the lower 250-MPa strength being the most frequently specified.

Information about the various kinds of steel available can be obtained directly from manufacturers and fabricators. The reader is also advised to purchase the latest edition of the *Manual of Steel Construction*, published by the American Institute of Steel Construction. It is an indispensable reference work for the design professional.

5-5 MASONRY AND REINFORCED MASONRY

Like concrete, brick and concrete masonry units are strong in compression and weak in tension. These materials have traditionally been used in walls, both bearing and nonbearing. Usually, wall thicknesses required by code specifications to prevent lateral instability are such that the actual compressive stresses are low. Crushing is seldom an important design constraint.

Masonry walls are more permanent than wood walls and provide effective barriers to both fire and noise. They are less expensive and often more attractive than formed concrete walls. Brick generally has more variation of pattern and texture than does concrete block, but is also more expensive.

It is becoming increasingly common to use reinforced concrete block for retaining walls and structural pilasters. In this construction, individual reinforcing bars are grouted in some of the vertically aligned cells of the concrete units and serve as tensile reinforcement. This greatly increases the lateral load capacity of the block. Reinforcing can also be placed in special channel-shaped blocks to serve as lintels and tie beams. Brick can be reinforced by using two wythes to create a cavity for grout and reinforcing bars. The brick not only serves as formwork but also carries compressive forces under load.

5-6 STRUCTURAL PLASTICS

Polyester resin reinforced by glass fibers can be a versatile structural material. The glass reinforcing makes this composite very strong in tension. It can be molded or sprayed into a form-resistant geometric or warped surface and can serve as the tensile skin for a sandwich panel with a paper honeycomb or foam core. Additionally, it has been quite successfully used as a forming material for both precast and cast-in-place concrete.

Like most plastics, however, reinforced polyester has a low modulus of elasticity, and any usable resistance to deflection or buckling must come from its shape and/or adjoining materials. It is also susceptible to stress concentration (see the next section) and should be designed without sharp corners or discontinuities.

Polyurethane foam is another plastic with potential use as a structural material. Innovative curvilinear shapes can be sprayed from this lightweight foam. It comes in a wide range of densities and some varieties are even "self-skinning," developing a hard surface as they cure.

In spite of the architectural advantages inherent in a lightweight formable material, it is doubtful that the immediate future will bring about a great increase in the use of plastics structurally. Those which are inexpensive enough for structural use usually have little resistance to fire, and some even give off toxic fumes. Widespread use, at least in urban areas, will not occur without further advances in the chemistry of synthetics and/or the economics of production. The widespread use of plastics in pipe, membranes, coatings, and insulation, where stability in fire conditions is not so critical, will continue to increase.

5-7 STRESS CONCENTRATION

Among experts who study structural engineering failures, a statement is used which calls attention to an obvious truism: "The member breaks where the stress is greatest." When examining a failed member, the analyst must face up to the fact that independent of theoretical niceties, the stress became very high at the point of rupture or crushing. A flaw or defect in the material is often present at the point, thus precipitating the failure there rather than somewhere else.

Stresses tend to build up or concentrate around such flaws or discontinuities, be they natural or man-made. A bolt hole or a fillet or a sharp corner can serve as a place for stresses to concentrate. This can best be understood by observing what happens to an otherwise uniform stress state when it is interrupted by a hole.

Figure 5-1 shows the stress distributions at two different points in an axially loaded bar. The concentration of stress around the sides of a hole has been quanti-

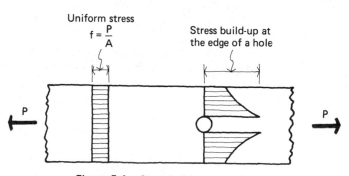

Figure 5-1. Stress build up around a hole.

fied by experimental photoelastic studies. One would expect the stress to be somewhat greater because the axial tension must be computed with the load acting on the *net* section remaining after the hole has been made. What is not expected is a sharp buildup of stress right at the face of the hole. Similar concentrations exist at all changes of cross section and at sharp corners.

It is important to note that this phenomenon is not as dangerous to building structures as one might think

at first. As previously stated, most structural materials are somewhat ductile and will yield to varying degrees when overstressed. This means that the most highly stressed fibers will yield without rupture and, rather than take more load, will continue to strain while neighboring fibers become more stressed. In mild steel the overstressed fibers continue to yield plastically, and this effect can be used to advantage in some design applications. Concrete, which is brittle under most types of loading, can overcome the dangerous effects of stress concentration through the proper placement of extra reinforcing bars. Cracks will develop at the highly stressed discontinuities, but the integrity of the member will be maintained because of the bond between the steel and the concrete.

Glass and gypsum board are examples of materials that possess little ductility and are quite prone to the effects of stress concentration. These, of course, are rarely used as primary structural materials.

There is one note of caution with respect to assuming that ductile materials or constructions have no problem with stress concentration. Under a cyclical or often repeated loading, materials will lose their ductility and become brittle. Members that are subjected to continued flexing or many cycles of loading deserve special attention.

5-8 CREEP

Sections 4-3 and 4-4 explained how structural elements change their size and shape upon application of load. This is called *elastic strain* and, provided that we do not stress the material too greatly, such deformation will disappear upon removal of the load. Most materials, if left under load for a long time, will exhibit an additional strain referred to as *creep*. In some cases these strains will remain after removal of the load.

The amount of creep, which takes place under long-term load, seems to vary directly with the stress level present and the ambient temperature and inversely with the material stiffness. Many plastics creep considerably in just a short period of time. Steel exhibits very little creep except at elevated temperatures. Concrete and wood both creep appreciably if stressed highly for long periods of time.

Members that must support constantly applied loads such as dead weight should be "overdesigned" so that the stresses will be low. For example, the increased deflection (over a couple of years) of a reinforced concrete beam carrying a heavy masonry wall can be double the initial elastic deflection. Many cantilevered portions of wood structures develop an unsightly sag with time which could have been prevented or minimized through the proper consideration of creep.

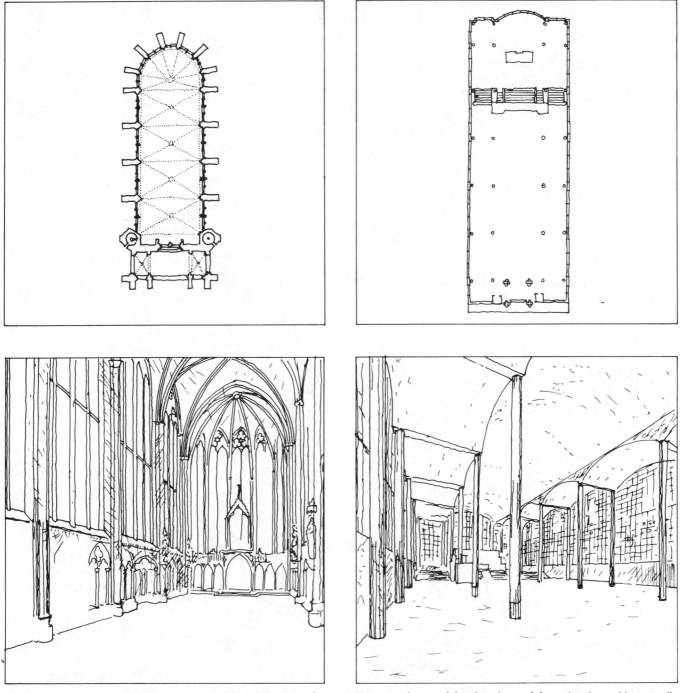

In considering the properties of structural materials, it is important for the architect to realize that although an understanding is necessary to make a successful building, the materials themselves do not usually *dictate* architectural form. This may be illustrated by two contrasting sets of comparisons.

Here are plans and interior views of four churches with generally the same architectural intent; the Ste. Chapelle in Paris, constructed in stone; Notre-Dame du Raincy, outside Paris, built in concrete by Auguste Perret; Otto Bartning's Steel Church in Germany; and Richard Munday's wooden Trinity Church in Newport, Rhode

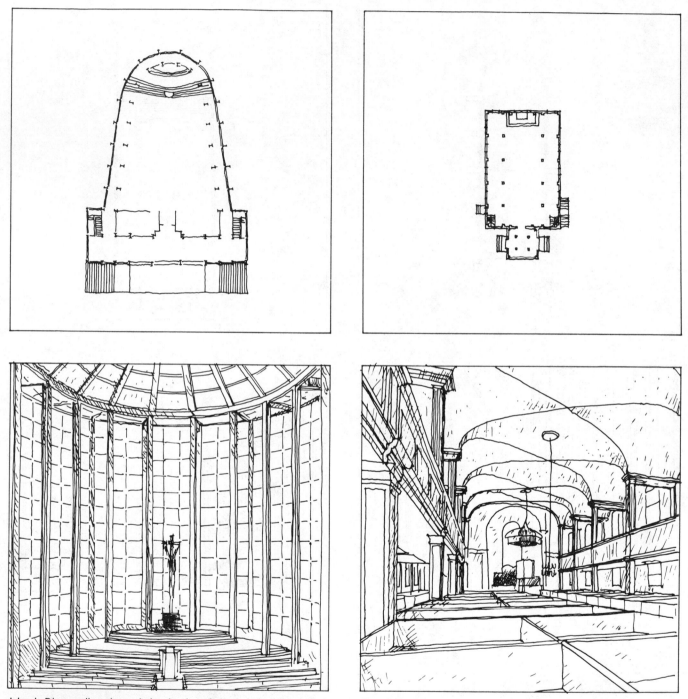

Island. Disregarding the variation in size of the four buildings, they are very similar in plan. In fact on the basis of plan alone, it would be hard to tell which church is of which material. The reason is this; despite the fact that all four seek to make the lightest possible impression on the interior, none of the designs strains the structural capacities of its material. Formal desires, rather than the structural properties of materials, by and large determine the nature of architectural mass and space relations.

In bridges, on the other hand, conditions are generally more extreme, formal preconceptions fewer, and concern for economy of materials high, and so bridge forms and the characteristics of the materials making the forms are often highly correlated. Stone works best in compression and is conveniently transported in pieces, so arched bridges of stone are a natural result. Wooden bridges take into account the facts that their material will come in sticks, of greater or lesser, but certainly of limited, size, and will take compression or tension with equal capacity. Suspension bridges are unthinkable without some homogeneous material, quite good in tension and available in extreme lengths, like steel cable or rope. Spans in reinforced concrete, at least the best of them, take advantage of its compressive strength and its ability to make large continuous elements and smooth connections.

6-1 TORSION IN BUILDING STRUCTURES

Torsional forces are those that tend to twist individual building elements or whole structures. The stress that results is a tangential shear that initiates upon a cross-sectional plane. The magnitude of this stress depends upon the torsional forces involved and the geometry of the cross section. These forces are easiest to visualize when the twisting action takes place about the longitudinal axis of a single linear element such as a beam or column.

Figure 6-1 shows examples of loads that develop torsional stresses. The angled beam shown in 6-1(b) is of particular interest because it represents schematically the situation that occurs whenever two beams frame together at right angles with a moment-resistant connection. As beam AC bends it twists beam BC, and when beam BC bends, it must twist AC. The members framing into the spandrel girders in Figure 6-1(c) and (d) cause torsional stresses in the girders as they themselves bend under load. The continuous connection of Figure 6-1(d) will cause more torsion than the clip angle connection shown in Figure 6-1(c). In both cases, the masonry curtain wall is eccentrically loading the girders, applying a torque of the opposite sense from that of the beams. In some cases these twisting forces are of small magnitude relative to other loads and can be ignored. Other structures require special analysis and design measures to provide the needed torsional resistance.

Entire building frames can twist under lateral loads as exaggerated in Figure 6-2. Many high-rise buildings are designed as vertical cantilevers that bend, shear, and twist under lateral loads from wind or earthquake.

Torsional stresses also develop at the corners of concrete floor slabs under gravity load because of continuity and bending deformations. As represented in

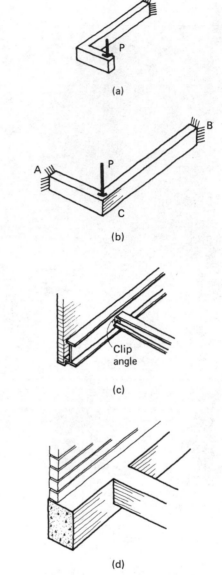

Figure 6-1. Axial torsion on building elements.

6

Torsion

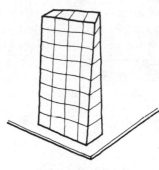

Figure 6-2

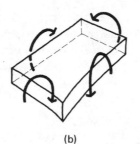

(a)

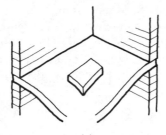

(b)

Figure 6-3. Torsional forces in a floor slab.

Figure 6-3(b), these forces act tangentially on various cross sections of a slab and can sometimes require the placement of additional reinforcing bars.

6-2 BASIC TORSIONAL STRESS

The theory behind the development of torsional stresses can best be explained by examining a simple solid circular shaft, even though such elements are rare in building structures. Basically, the shearing stresses act on a transverse plane as shown in Figure 6-4, varying linearly from zero at the central axis to a maximum at the outside face. The magnitude of this stress is given by

$$f_v = \frac{Tr}{J} \tag{6-1}$$

where f_v = torsional shearing stress (Pa)
T = applied external torque (N·m)
r = radial distance from the center of bar out to the point where the stress is desired (m)
J = polar moment of inertia (m⁴)

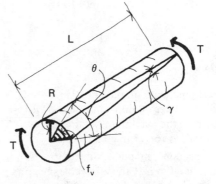

Figure 6-4. Torsion on a circular cross section.

The maximum value of f_v will occur at the outermost fiber, where r takes the value of R, the radius of the bar. The polar moment of inertia J is very similar to the rectangular moments of inertia discussed in Chapter 3, except that in this case the axis of imagined rotation is a polar one, normal to the section. The value of J is a constant for a given section and can be determined quantitatively as

$$J = \frac{\pi R^4}{2}$$

Proof of this and Equation (6-1) are offered in Appendix C. It is important to note, from Equation (6-1), that the shearing stress due to torsion is independent of the length of the member.

EXAMPLE 6-1

The timber sign post of Figure 6-5 is loaded by wind pressure, which generates a torque of 1 kN·m. If the post is a solid section of 200 mm diameter, determine the maximum shearing stress.

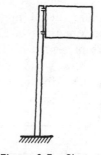

Figure 6-5. Sign post.

Solution:

$$J = \frac{\pi R^4}{2}$$

$$= \frac{\pi (0.100 \text{ m})^4}{2}$$

$$= 157(10)^{-6} \text{ m}^4$$

$$f_v = \frac{TR}{J}$$

$$= \frac{1 \text{ kN·m}(0.100 \text{ m})}{157(10)^{-6} \text{ m}^4}$$

$$= 637 \text{ kPa}$$

Problems

6-1. A steel pipe, with an outside diameter of 100 mm and an inside diameter 70 mm, is twisted by a 10-kN·m torque. Determine the maximum torsional stress. (*Hint:* Subtract two *J* values to get the effective *J*.)

6-2. A precast concrete pile is subject to a torque of 10 kN·m during handling. If the allowable shearing stress for the concrete is 2 MPa, determine the required radius *R*.

6-3. Compare the torque capacities of two circular shafts of the same material and diameter, one having a hole drilled through its center. The diameter of the hole is one-half the outside diameter of the shaft.

6-3 MAGNITUDE OF THE TORQUE FORCE

In some cases, such as the vertically cantilevered post of Example 6-1, the amount of torque applied to a building element is relatively easy to determine. In other situations [e.g., beams loaded as in Figure 6-1(c) and (d)], the determination of the torsional force becomes less clear. It is obvious that the torque force (really a moment acting about the axis of the member) will increase as the eccentricity of the load increases. What is not so obvious is how to quantify the effects of point loads versus uniform loads or the effects of member end conditions. Such determinations are complicated by the fact that most beam cross sections warp when they twist (see Section 6-9). The effects of warping vary greatly with the length of the member, properties of the material, and the shape of the cross section. To provide even the minimal accuracy needed for preliminary design purposes is a difficult task. Very rough approximations of torque loads for a few common cases are presented in Table 6-1, but the reader is cautioned that these values can be very much in error, depending upon the individual design situation.

The investigation of torsional stresses is included in this elementary text so that novice designers can become acquainted with the nature of torsional loads and their effects on building elements. This approach will help the designer to know when a torsional problem exists but cannot develop the competency needed to solve that problem.

6-4 ANGLE OF TWIST

Figure 6-6 shows the development of torsional strain between two transverse sections a short distance *dL* apart. This amount of unit strain, γ, can be expressed as ab/dL in Figure 6-6(c) or as AB/L in Figure 6-6(a), where *L* is the total length of the bar. The amount of strain is related to the stress by the modulus of elasticity in shear for the material, which is given the symbol *G*. (This property is sometimes called the *modulus of rigidity*.)

$$G = \frac{f_v}{\gamma} \tag{6-2}$$

Values of *G* for various materials are given in Appendix L.

For a given stress, the rotation developed will be inversely proportional to the *G* value for the material. The total angle of twist for the bar of length *L* is designated as θ in Figure 6-6(a). The value of this angle in radians is

$$\theta = \frac{AB}{R}$$

However, *AB* is equal to γL as previously stated, so

$$\theta = \frac{\gamma L}{R}$$

From Equation (6-2), $\gamma = f_v/G$. Therefore,

$$\theta = \frac{f_v L}{GR}$$

and from Equation (6-1), the torsional stress on the surface of the bar is

$$f_v = \frac{TR}{J}$$

TABLE 6-1 *Approximate Values of Torque Force*

Midspan concentrated load		Uniform load	
Pinned ends	*Fixed ends*	*Pinned ends*	*Fixed ends*
$T \approx \frac{3}{4} Pe$	$T \approx \frac{1}{2} Pe$	$T \approx \frac{3}{8} wLe$	$T \approx \frac{1}{4} wLe$

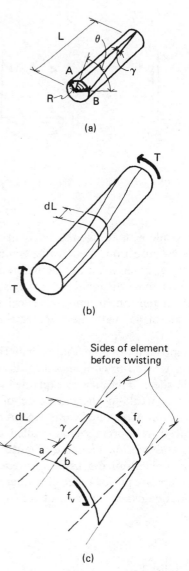

(a)

(b)

Sides of element
before twisting

(c)

Figure 6-6. Torsional strain.

Substituting for f_v, we get

$$\theta = \frac{TL}{JG} \qquad (6\text{-}3)$$

which is an expression for the amount of twist in a circular shaft. It is interesting to note the parallel between the form of this equation and the one for axial elongation developed in Chapter 4.

EXAMPLE 6-2

If the timber post in Example 6-1 is 8 m tall, determine its angle of twist in degrees. Assume that $G = 1000$ MPa.

Solution:

$$\theta = \frac{TL}{JG}$$

$$= \frac{1 \text{ kN}\cdot\text{m}(8 \text{ m})}{[157(10)^{-6} \text{ m}^4][1000(10)^3 \text{ kN/m}^2]}$$

$$= 0.051 \text{ rad}$$

$$= 0.051\left(\frac{180}{\pi}\right)$$

$$= 3°$$

Problems

6-4. An eccentrically loaded steel balcony beam in a theater is subjected to a torque of 8 kN·m. Its torsional stiffness can be approximated as being the same as that of a hollow tube 150 mm in diameter with a wall thickness of 10 mm. How much will it twist in a length of 10 m? Assume that $G = 85$ GPa.

6-5. A 2-m-long fiber glass light fixture support has a diameter of 40 mm. How much torque can be applied to it if it should not twist more than 15°? Assume that $G = 2$ GPa.

6-5   CROSS-SHEARS

The small element of Figure 6-6(c), taken from the bar in torsion, is shown in elevation in Figure 6-7. The two stresses, f_v, must be equal in magnitude and opposite in sense to ensure vertical equilibrium. However, under the action of those two stresses alone, the element would rotate in a counterclockwise manner. Clearly, this couple

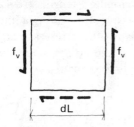

Figure 6-7.   Shearing stress.

must be negated by the action of another couple, shown as the dashed stress arrows. Assuming that the differential element is square, the value of the dashed stresses would be equal in magnitude to f_v. This principle is sometimes phrased as "cross-shears are equal." In other words, shearing stress cannot exist on an element without a like stress located 90° around the corner. Figure 6-8 illustrates this for the bar in torsion.

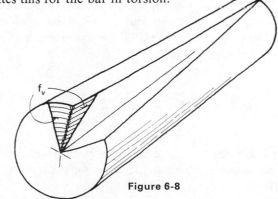

Figure 6-8

This explains why a piece of wood, if twisted to failure, will not break on the transverse plane but will split longitudinally. Wood has a grain that creates planes of weakness, and if equal shears exist on both transverse and longitudinal planes, the shear failure will take place parallel to the grain. The reader should verify this with a scrap piece of balsa or other weak wood. The cross section need not be circular.

6-6 DIAGONAL TENSION AND COMPRESSION

Shearing stresses can be developed from other types of applied load and do not require the presence of torsion. Chapter 4, for example, shows shear in basic connections. Shearing stresses due to bending forces are almost always present in beams, and these are treated in some detail in Chapter 8. In this section it will be shown that shear will always be accompanied by tension and compression. These stresses are often more important in beam design than are the direct shear stresses.

The square element in Figure 6-9(a) is being acted upon by four shearing stresses as explained in Section 6-5. The stressed element will appear as in Figure 6-9(b) as it deforms, developing a tensile stress along a line from a to b and compressive stress along a line joining c and d. In the absence of any other stresses acting on the element, the lines of tension and compression will be oriented at 45° to the original shear planes.

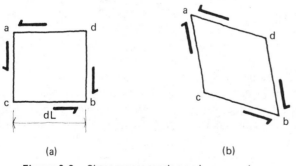

Figure 6-9. Shear causes tension and compression.

If the thickness of the element is designated as dz, then an equation of equilibrium in the ab direction can be used to solve for the magnitude of f_t, the tensile stress. Referring to Figure 6-10(b),

$$\sum F_{ab} = 0$$

$$f_t(\sqrt{2}) \, dL(dz) - 2\left[\frac{\sqrt{2}}{2}(f_v)\right] dL(dz) = 0$$

$$f_t = f_v$$

which illustrates that the diagonal tension developed by shearing stress is equal to the shearing stress itself. A

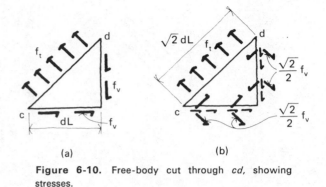

Figure 6-10. Free-body cut through *cd*, showing stresses.

similar proof could be made for the diagonal compression stress in the *cd* direction. The reader should break a piece of chalk, or other weak brittle material, in torsion to ascertain that these diagonal stresses exist. The chalk should break in tension, forming a helical surface that makes an angle of 45° with the transverse and longitudinal planes.

It is important to note that a material which is weak in either tension or compression will also be effectively weak in shear. Thus, it was explained in Chapter 5 that concrete is weak in shear because of its lack of strength in tension. Concrete beams are strengthened by specially placed reinforcing bars (called *stirrups*) to prevent diagonal tension cracking. Figure 6-11 shows potential diagonal tension cracks being crossed by several stirrups. (Stirrups are placed vertically rather than normal to the potential cracks for reasons of construction ease.)

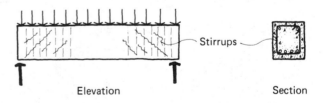

Figure 6-11. Concrete beam reinforced for shear.

Some deep steel girders have relatively thin webs, which tend to buckle in compression along 45° lines, as shown happening on the left-hand beam of Figure 6-12. Vertical plate stiffeners shown welded in place on the right-hand sketch constitute one way to prevent such failure. The reader can "see" diagonal buckling as it occurs in a thin member by applying shearing forces along the opposite edges of a piece of paper.

(The shearing forces in the beams of Figure 6-11 and 6-12 result more commonly from bending loads than from torsional loads.)

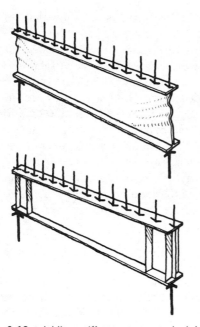

Figure 6-12. Adding stiffeners to a steel girder for shear.

6-7 TORSIONAL STRESSES IN RECTANGULAR SECTIONS

Rectangular cross sections are far more common in building construction than are circular ones. When a rectangle is twisted, the maximum stresses will develop at the centers of the longer sides. At this point the boundary edge of the section comes closest to the center of rotation. This is in direct contrast to a circular section, in which the maximum stresses occur at the most distant point from the axis.

The twisted bar of Figure 6-13 shows how torsional stresses vary from maximum at the center of a side to zero at a corner. The presence of zero shear at these corners is consistent with the equilibrium of cross-shears as explained in Section 6-5. When there is no more material or no external forces at the edge to provide for one of

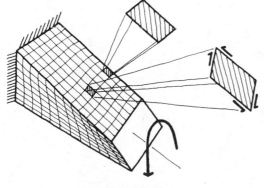

Figure 6-13

the four required shear stresses, then all four must go to zero. The maximum stress can be approximated as

$$f_v \approx \frac{4.5T}{b^2 h} \tag{6-4}$$

where b = length of shorter side (m)
h = length of longer side (m)

The exact solution for torsional stresses in such a section is more involved and this approximation, first presented in 1924 by C. Bach, a German engineer, will suffice for our purposes. Its percentage of error increases as the ratio h/b increases, but is always on the conservative side.

EXAMPLE 6-3

Determine the approximate maximum torsional stress in an 89×235 mm timber beam, which is subjected to a midspan concentrated load of 2 kN. The load is eccentric by 0.2 m. Assume pinned ends.

Solution: Table 6-1 indicates that an approximate value for T is

$$T \approx \tfrac{3}{4} Pe$$
$$\approx \tfrac{3}{4}(2 \text{ kN})(0.2 \text{ m})$$
$$\approx 0.3 \text{ kN} \cdot \text{m}$$

$$f_v \approx \frac{4.5T}{b^2 h}$$
$$\approx \frac{4.5(0.3 \text{ kN} \cdot \text{m})}{(0.089 \text{ m})^2 (0.235 \text{ m})}$$
$$\approx 725 \text{ kPa}$$

Problems

6-6. Determine the approximate maximum torsional stress in the post of Example 6-1 if the circular cross section is replaced by a 180-mm square section.

6-7. A concrete beam, 300×600 mm, is reinforced with stirrups for the shearing stresses which result from both bending and torsion. The beam has an ultimate shearing stress capacity of 4000 kPa. If half of this capacity is needed for shear due to bending, determine the ultimate value of torque that can be applied to this section.

6-8 TORSIONAL STRESSES IN CLOSED SECTIONS

Closed structural sections behave quite differently in torsion from solid sections. If the wall thickness is small relative to the overall dimensions of the section, the shearing stress developed will be essentially constant over this thickness.

In Figure 6-15, shearing stresses called f_v act on the small element which has an area of $t \, dp$, where dp is a

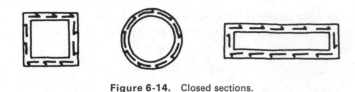

Figure 6-14. Closed sections.

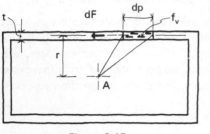

Figure 6-15

differential length of the perimeter. The small force on this element is then

$$dF = f_v t\, dp$$

and the torque of the force acting about the center of rotation is

$$dT = rf_v t\, dp$$

The moment arm r varies in magnitude depending upon the location of the element. The sum of the torques dT must be equal to the externally applied torque, T. Computing the area of the triangle in Figure 6-15, which has an altitude of r and a base of dp, we get

$$dA = \tfrac{1}{2} r\, dp$$

or

$$r\, dp = 2dA$$

Substituting this value into the expression for dT gives us

$$dT = f_v t\, 2dA$$

Integrating both sides, we get

$$T = 2f_v tA$$

or

$$f_v = \frac{T}{2tA} \qquad (6\text{-}5)$$

where A is the total area enclosed by the midline of the wall thickness (m²).

Credit for the format of this derivation is given to Glenn Murphy.[1]

(This equation was derived assuming that the shearing stress remained constant through the wall thickness. Since this is not actually the case, error will accrue if the equation is applied to other than thin-walled members. The error will *not* be in the conservative direction.)

[1]Glenn Murphy, *Advanced Mechanics of Materials* (New York: McGraw-Hill Book Company, 1946), p. 174.

Use of Equation (6-5) will show that hollow sections are quite efficient compared to solid ones, which makes sense when we consider the stress distribution of the torsional stresses in a solid circular section. The material located near the central axis has too small a moment arm to be very effective. Hollow sections are more efficient; however, as discussed in Section 6-6, normal stresses always exist on planes 45° away from the shearing stress planes and thin-walled sections can fail prematurely as a result of compression buckling. The reader should also be aware that, as discussed in Chapter 5, depending upon the nature of the loading and the material involved, the effects of stress concentration at corners may have to be considered.

EXAMPLE 6-4

A rectangular steel tube has outside dimensions of 100 mm by 200 mm. The wall thickness is 6 mm. Determine the maximum safe torque that may be applied to this section if the allowable shearing stress is 100 MPa. Ignore the possible effects of stress concentration.

Solution:

$$\begin{aligned}
A &= bh \\
&= (94\ \text{mm})(194\ \text{mm}) \\
&= (0.094\ \text{m})(0.194\ \text{m}) \\
&= 0.0182\ \text{m}^2 \\
T &= 2f_v tA \\
&= 2[100(10)^3\ \text{kN/m}^2](0.006\ \text{m})(0.0182\ \text{m}^2) \\
&= 21.8\ \text{kN} \cdot \text{m}
\end{aligned}$$

Problems

6-8. A steel pipe section having an outside diameter of 100 mm and an inside diameter of 90 mm is subjected to a torque of 7 kN·m. Determine the shearing stress.

6-9. The two shafts in Figure 6-16 have equal cross-sectional areas. Assuming that the permissible stress is the same for both shafts and that buckling will not govern, compare their safe torque capacities.

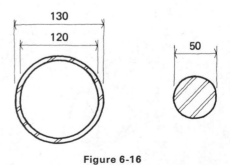

Figure 6-16

6-9 TORSIONAL STRESSES IN OPEN SECTIONS

As seen in Figure 6-17, the lack of continuity (in this case caused by a cut in the circular cross section) will change the manner in which the torsional stresses distribute themselves over the cross section. The open section cannot develop a uniformity of stress through the wall thickness and is, therefore, not very efficient. Similarly, open sections do not have the rigidity of closed sections and will twist through greater angles under the same applied loads.

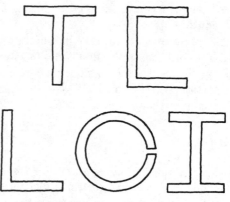

Figure 6-18. Open cross sections.

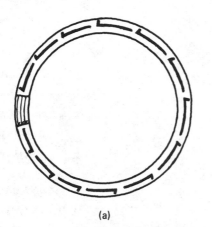

(a)

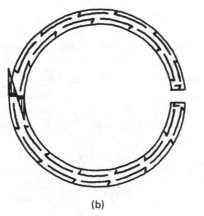

(b)

Figure 6-17. Shearing stress distributions.

In addition to developing higher shearing stresses due to a reduced stiffness or moment of inertia, open sections are also subject to increased stresses caused by warping. All sections other than continuous circular ones are subject to warping when twisted. This means essentially that transverse sections, which are plane before they are twisted, are deformed upon twisting and do not remain plane. Figure 6-13 shows the warping of a rectangular section and the accompanying longitudinal deformation. These effects are small compared to the basic nonwarping torsional stresses for sections other than

those of the type shown in Figure 6-18. In such sections, additional shearing and normal (longitudinal) stresses are caused by the warping deformations. Analytically, such problems are mathematically involved and certainly beyond the scope of this text. Several steel companies have published some useful design handbooks on the subject to aid the practicing engineer, and these publications can be consulted when rigorous engineering solutions are needed.

The complexities involved in mathematically precise solutions have led to numerous attempts to find an approximate approach to determining the torsional stresses in open sections. Most of these center around trying to find an equivalent polar moment of inertia for use in some form of Equation (6-1). A frequently suggested value for this section property is

$$J_{equiv} = \tfrac{1}{3} \sum ht^3$$

where h = width of each segment (m)

t = average thickness of each segment (m) $(t \ll h)$

This value for the polar moment of inertia can be used directly in a modified version of a formula developed by Lyse and Johnston in 1936.[2] If the effects of stress concentration can be ignored, the maximum torsional stress can be approximated as

$$f_v \approx \frac{3Tt_1}{\sum (ht^3)} \qquad (6\text{-}6)$$

where t_1 is the average thickness of the thickest segment (m). The maximum stress is usually located at a junction or corner.

If the various segments have about the same thickness, then Equation (6-6) reduces to

$$f_v \approx \frac{3T}{\sum (ht^2)} \qquad (6\text{-}6a)$$

[2]Inge Lyse and B. G. Johnson, "Structural Beams in Torsion," *Transactions of the American Society of Civil Engineers*, Vol. 62, 1936, p. 857.

A curved segment can be handled by letting h equal the curved length.

These formulas do not take into account the effects of warping and are only first-order approximations. Indeed, the writer has seen similar approximate evaluations of torsional stress which will yield values either 50% larger or smaller than Equation (6-6).

EXAMPLE 6-5

The idealized section of Figure 6-19 is used as a fixed-end beam 4 m long. It carries an eccentric load of 5 kN/m located 0.4 m off the beam center line. Determine the approximate value of the torsional shearing stress developed. Stress concentration effects are to be ignored.

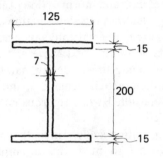

Figure 6-19. Idealized W shape.

Solution:

$$\Sigma (ht^3) = 2(ht^3)_{\text{flange}} + (ht^3)_{\text{web}}$$
$$= 2(0.125 \text{ m})(0.015 \text{ m})^3 + (0.200 \text{ m})(0.007 \text{ m})^3$$
$$= 0.91(10)^{-6} \text{ m}^4$$

$$f_v \approx \frac{3Tt_1}{\Sigma (ht^3)}$$

From Table 6-1,

$$T \approx \frac{weL}{4}$$
$$\approx \frac{5 \text{ kN/m}(0.4 \text{ m})(4 \text{ m})}{4}$$
$$\approx 2 \text{ kN} \cdot \text{m}$$
$$f_v \approx \frac{3(2 \text{ kN} \cdot \text{m})0.015 \text{ m}}{0.91(10)^{-6} \text{ m}^4}$$
$$\approx 98.9(10)^3 \text{ kPa}$$
$$\approx 98.9 \text{ MPa}$$

EXAMPLE 6-6

Compare the torque capacities of the two cross sections in Figure 6-20. They are identical except for the longitudinal slit in one of them.

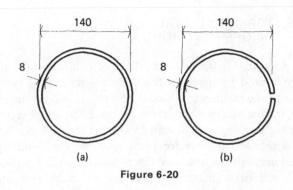

Figure 6-20

Solution:

For section (a)

$$T = 2f_v tA$$
$$A = \pi r^2$$
$$= \pi(0.066 \text{ m})^2$$
$$= 0.0137 \text{ m}^2$$
$$T = 2f_v(0.008 \text{ m})(0.0137 \text{ m}^2)$$
$$= 219(10)^{-6} \text{ m}^3(f_v)$$

For section (b)

$$T \approx \frac{f_v \Sigma (ht^2)}{3}$$

Σ is unity in this case

$$h = 2\pi r$$
$$= 2\pi(0.066 \text{ m})$$
$$= 0.415 \text{ m}$$
$$T \approx \frac{f_v(0.415 \text{ m})(0.008 \text{ m})^2}{3}$$
$$\approx 8.85(10)^{-6} \text{ m}^3(f_v)$$

The torque capacity of the closed section is roughly 25 times that of the open section.

Problems

6-10. A $100 \times 100 \times 9$ mm steel angle is tressed in torsion when used as a lintel. If the allowable shearing stress is 100 MPa, determine the approximate value of torque that can safely be applied.

6-11. The rectangular steel tube of Example 6-4 is replaced by two channel shapes as shown in Figure 6-21. By approximately what percentage is the torque capacity reduced?

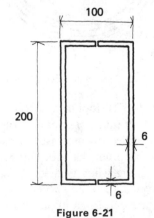

Figure 6-21

6-12. Compare the torque capacities of the three beams of approximately equal area shown in Figure 6-22.

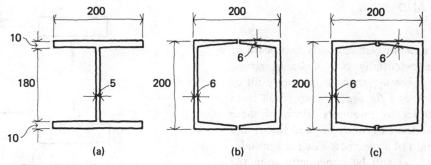

Figure 6-22. Three beam shapes: (a) wide-flange; (b) channels not welded; (c) channels welded.

6-10 SHAPES THAT ARE EFFECTIVE IN TORSION

Certain conclusions can be drawn from the examples and problems presented in previous sections. It has been shown that the strength of a member in torsion is highly related to the configuration of its cross section. Any increase in J (or the effective J) tends to decrease the shearing stress due to torsion. Although torsional deformation or angle of twist was only considered for circular sections, it is easy to extend Equation (6-3), in concept, to include other sections. This would indicate that an increase in J would reduce the angle of twist as well.

Using the principles involved in determining the shape factor, J, one can show that a circular tube section would be very good in torsion, whereas a wide thin rectangular section would be quite weak. Sections that are closed allow a continuity of shear stresses, sometimes called *shear flow*, and the uniform stresses that result indicate an efficient use of the material (see Figure 6-17). Open sections with wide thin extensions outstanding from the center tend to be poor in torsion. In general, segments of open sections should be thick and bulky and preferably turned back in on one another to approximate a tube or tubes. W shapes used as spandrel beams, as shown in Figure 6-1(c), must often carry torsional loads, and shallow sections with wide, heavy flanges are usually preferable to deep narrow sections.

Building structures in earthquake zones can be subjected to both torsional racking and lateral shear by the forces of ground motion. Earthquake design recommendations always include some sort of statement about the desirability of continuity not only in member con-

nections, but also in building plan and shape. It is also usually indicated that outstanding wings and sharp reentrant corners are to be avoided in such designs. It is clear that some of the concepts of torsional resistance can be applied directly to overall building envelopes. In some cases very tall buildings, which have lateral forces (from wind or earthquake) as primary design determinants, have been configured to act as tubes. The reader will find that the torsional stiffness of structures such as the World Trade Center in New York or the Hancock or Sears Towers in Chicago is very high. Indeed, the structural system of the Sears Tower is called a "bundled tube," being composed of nine square tubes with shared interior sides (Figure 6-23). The nine tubes, of course, provide much more torsional resistance than would a single large tube. The interior tube walls also serve to stiffen the long exterior walls against compression buckling.

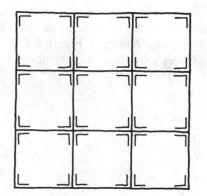

Figure 6-23. Schematic plan of bundled tube.

7-1 DEFINITIONS AND SIGN CONVENTIONS

A transverse load on a linear element such as a beam or column will generate essentially two kinds of stress, shearing and flexural. *Shearing stresses* are the result of internal shearing forces, and *flexural stresses* result from internal resisting couples or moments. Both of these effects are responses to the externally applied forces and will vary along the length of a member. Their magnitudes and senses at any section will be dependent upon the loads, span, and support conditions of the member.

Usually, the structural designer is interested in the maximum values of these shears and moments, which exist in the many elements or parts of a structure. These maximum values will help to make judgments as to the soundness of the overall scheme and in the planning of the geometry of the various structural elements. Member sizes are also determined and spans sometimes modified on the basis of maximum shear and moment values.

In order to study these forces, we use free-body diagrams and the techniques of statics. By cutting a transverse section through a beam or column, we expose the internal forces and make them external via a free-body diagram (see Figure 2-34). Statics can then be applied to solve for the magnitudes and senses of the unknown values. Graphs or plots are made to show how forces change from section to section. A plot illustrating how the internal shearing force *V* varies over the length of a member is called a *shear diagram* or *V diagram*. A *moment diagram* or *M diagram* is a similar plot showing the variation of the internal moment throughout the member. Shears and moments are plotted according to the following sign conventions.

Shearing forces that tend to cause the slippage failures shown in Figure 7-1 will be denoted by the sign accompanying them. Notice in Figure 7-2 that for positive shear, forces exist (for equilibrium) which are *up*

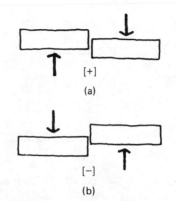

Figure 7-1. Sign convention for shearing forces.

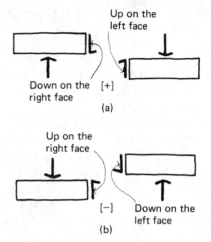

Figure 7-2. Internal shearing forces.

on the left-hand face and *down* on the right-hand face of an element. The opposite forces act on the cut faces when they are subjected to negative shear. (*Note:* The sign convention for shear is somewhat arbitrary and the opposite plus and minus associations are preferred by some writers.)

The sign convention for internal bending moment is considerably more straightforward, as Figure 7-3 shows.

7

Shear and Moment

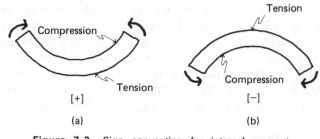

Figure 7-3. Sign convention for internal moment forces.

Positive moment generates concave upward curvature, causing compression in the top fibers and tension in the bottom fibers. Negative moment causes concave downward curvature and, of course, the opposite types of fiber strain. This convention is the standard one for curvature in mathematics and is universally accepted. Since the convention is related to strain, it is possible to look at the probable deflected shape of a beam under load, for example, and determine what portions of the span have positive or negative internal moments. The uniformly loaded beam in Figure 7-4 has an overhang, and from the deflected shape we can see that negative internal moments exist over part of the beam's length and positive internal moments are present in another portion. The implication here is that there is likely a transverse section or portion of the span where the bending moment is zero to accommodate the required sign change. Such a section, termed a *point of inflection*, is almost always present in overhanging beams.

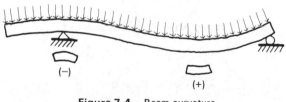

Figure 7-4. Beam curvature.

The most important feature of these sign conventions is that they are different from the conventions used in statics. When using the three equations of equilibrium, forces up and to the right are plus and counterclockwise moments are plus. The new sign conventions are used only for plotting the shear and moment diagrams. It is important that the two conventions not become confused.

7-2 SHEAR AND MOMENT EQUATIONS

The most basic way to obtain V and M diagrams is to graph specific values from statics equations which have been written so they are valid for appropriate portions of the member. (In these explanations we shall assume

that the member is a beam, acted upon by downward loads, but actually the member could be turned at any angle. In the general case, we are determining shears and moments due to transverse loads.) The following examples will illustrate how we can write and plot V and M equations. In each case, the uniform load of the beam's own weight has been neglected.

EXAMPLE 7-1

Construct the V and M diagrams for the beam in Figure 7-5.

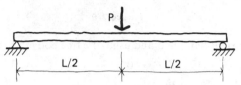

Figure 7-5. Simple beam with a concentrated load at midspan.

Solution: If we let x designate any point along the length of a beam and assume the origin to be at the left end ($x = 0$ there), we can write expressions for V and M in terms of constants (the external loads and reactions) and the distance x. To examine V_x and M_x in the left-hand half of the beam in Figure 7-6, we cut through that portion. This will make the

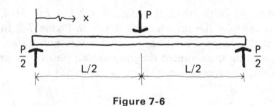

Figure 7-6

unknowns external and we can use statics on the resulting free body of Figure 7-7. Notice that the unknowns have been assumed positive by the new convention. This will mean that answers yielded by statics which come out plus (as assumed)

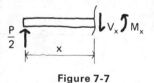

Figure 7-7

will be plotted as positive ordinates, and those that turn out with minus signs (not as assumed) must be plotted as negative values. Now, applying the equations of equilibrium to find the unknowns, we get

$$\sum F_y = 0$$

$$\frac{P}{2} - V_x = 0$$

$$\left(0 \le x \le \frac{L}{2}\right) \qquad V_x = \frac{P}{2}$$

Taking moments at the cut face (thereby eliminating V_x), we get

$$\sum M_x = 0$$

$$-\frac{P}{2}(x) + M_x = 0$$

$$\left(0 \leq x \leq \frac{L}{2}\right) \qquad M_x = \frac{P}{2}x$$

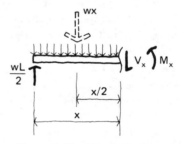

Figure 7-8

For the right-hand half and using the free body in Figure 7-8,

$$\sum F_y = 0$$

$$\frac{P}{2} - P - V_x = 0$$

$$\left(\frac{L}{2} \leq x \leq L\right) \qquad V_x = \frac{P}{2} - P$$

$$\sum M_x = 0$$

$$-\frac{P}{2}(x) + P\left(x - \frac{L}{2}\right) + M_x = 0$$

$$\left(\frac{L}{2} \leq x \leq L\right) \qquad M_x = \frac{P}{2}(x) - P\left(x - \frac{L}{2}\right)$$

Substituting finite values of x (e.g., $x = 0$, $L/4$, $L/2$, $3L/4$, and L), we can plot the equations as shown in Figure 7-9. In this case the V diagram does not vary with x except in sign. The ordinates on the moment diagram are all positive, as might be verified by the deflected shape of this beam.

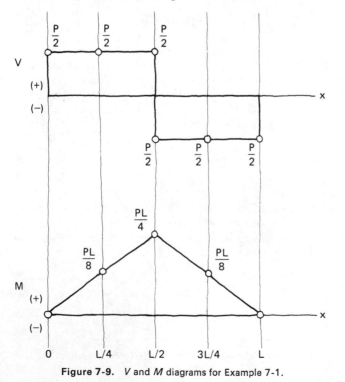

Figure 7-9. V and M diagrams for Example 7-1.

From the diagrams we can also see the necessity for writing an equation for each half of this beam. Any type of load change or application (including reactions) will cause discontinuities in the diagrams so that each set of V and M equations is only valid for a specific part of the beam length. However, equations with appropriate interval limits can always be written for each beam portion.

EXAMPLE 7-2

Construct the V and M diagrams for the beam in Figure 7-10.

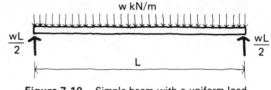

Figure 7-10. Simple beam with a uniform load.

Solution: Since the uniform load is constant over the entire span, only one set of equations will be necessary. Using Figure 7-11, we get

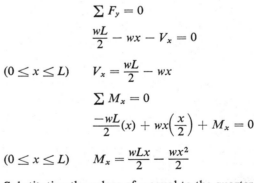

Figure 7-11. Free-body diagram.

$$\sum F_y = 0$$

$$\frac{wL}{2} - wx - V_x = 0$$

$$(0 \leq x \leq L) \qquad V_x = \frac{wL}{2} - wx$$

$$\sum M_x = 0$$

$$\frac{-wL}{2}(x) + wx\left(\frac{x}{2}\right) + M_x = 0$$

$$(0 \leq x \leq L) \qquad M_x = \frac{wLx}{2} - \frac{wx^2}{2}$$

Substituting the values of x equal to the quarter points of the span, we get the diagrams shown in Figure 7-12. Ordinates that lie above the reference line are taken as positive and those below, as negative.

The shear diagram reflects the linear variation with x as required by the shear equation. The moment diagram is a parabolic curve, which follows the second-power function of x present in the moment equation. This can be confusing, as one is led to think that bending is a

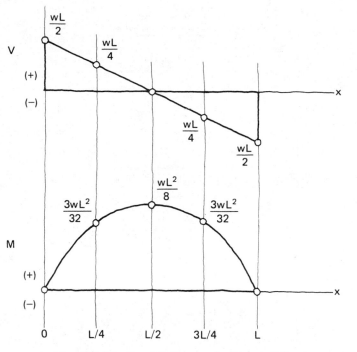

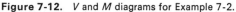

Figure 7-12. *V* and *M* diagrams for Example 7-2.

second-power function of the span alone. Moment is always linear with span; it is just that with a uniform load, as opposed to a concentrated one, a change in length means a change in load. For this reason the plot becomes parabolic. To understand this better, compare the maximum moment for the concentrated load of Example 7-1 (i.e., $M = PL/4$) to the maximum moment for the uniform load, which is $M = wL^2/8$. Since P is the total load in the first case, let $wL = W$ to get a comparable load for the uniform case. Then M will be $WL/8$, indicating that moment varies linearly with span and linearly with load. This also shows clearly that concentrated loads will generate double the moment caused by uniform loads.

EXAMPLE 7-3

Construct the *V* and *M* diagrams for the beam in Figure 7-13.

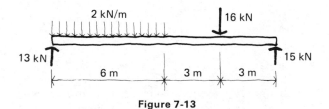

Figure 7-13

Solution: Three separate sets of *V* and *M* equations will be used.

$$\sum F_y = 0$$
$$13 - 2x - V_x = 0$$

$$(0 \leq x \leq 6) \qquad V_x = 13 - 2x$$
$$\sum M_x = 0$$
$$-13x + 2x\left(\frac{x}{2}\right) + M_x = 0$$
$$(0 \leq x \leq 6) \qquad M_x = 13x - x^2$$

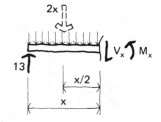

Figure 7-14. FBD for interval $(0 \leq x \leq 6)$.

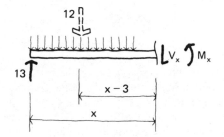

Figure 7-15. FBD for interval $(6 \leq x \leq 9)$.

$$\sum F_y = 0$$
$$13 - 12 - V_x = 0$$
$$(6 \leq x \leq 9) \qquad V_x = 1$$
$$\sum M_x = 0$$
$$-13x + 12(x - 3) + M_x = 0$$
$$(6 \leq x \leq 9) \qquad M_x = 13x - 12x + 36$$

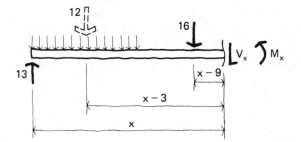

Figure 7-16. FBD for interval $(9 \leq x \leq 12)$.

$$\sum F_y = 0$$
$$13 - 12 - 16 - V_x = 0$$
$$(9 \leq x \leq 12) \qquad V_x = -15$$
$$\sum M_x = 0$$
$$-13x + 12(x - 3) + 16(x - 9) + M_x = 0$$
$$(9 \leq x \leq 12) \qquad M_x = 13x - 28x + 180$$

Using these equations and values of x as needed, the diagrams of Figure 7-17 can be drawn. Notice that equations which

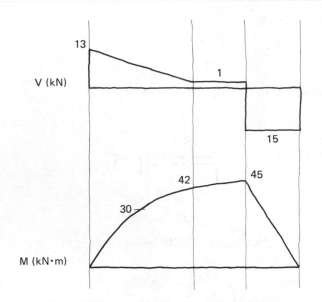

Figure 7-17. *V* and *M* diagrams for Example 7-3.

contain the variable *x*, plot as straight horizontal lines; that equations containing *x* raised only to the first power plot as straight sloping lines, and that equations involving x^2 plot as parabolic curves. Note also that the points of curve change on the diagrams are common to two equations, and either equation may be used to find the ordinate value. Downward-acting uniform loads will result in moment curves that are concave downward, as verified by the value at $x = 3$ on the *M* diagram. Concentrated loads will always cause a sudden change in ordinate on the shear diagram and require two values of *V* at that section. (Actually, these two values of *V*, differing by the magnitude of the concentrated load, are a small distance apart because the load does occupy a short length of beam. In theory, however, we assume a true point load and the distance becomes infinitesimal.

Using the guidelines given above, it is usually possible to construct shear and moment diagrams using only the values of *x* at the points of load change (i.e., the interval limits).

EXAMPLE 7-4

Construct the *V* and *M* diagrams for the beam in Figure 7-18(a).

Solution: The external reactions are found in Figure 7-18(b) and the FBD needed to write the equations appears in Figure 7-18(c).

$$\sum F_y = 0$$
$$36 - 12x - V_x = 0$$
$$(0 \leq x \leq 3) \quad V_x = 36 - 12x$$
$$\sum M_x = 0$$
$$54 - 36x + 12x\left(\frac{x}{2}\right) + M_x = 0$$
$$(0 \leq x \leq 3) \quad M_x = -54 + 36x - 6x^2$$

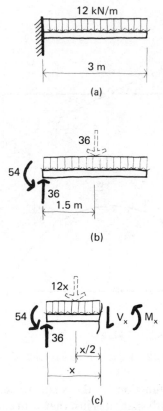

Figure 7-18. Cantilever beam with a uniform load.

This example serves well to illustrate the difference in the two sign conventions. In the FBD of Figure 7-18(c), the 54-kN·m moment reaction is counterclockwise or plus in the $\sum M_x = 0$ statics equation. It causes tension in the top fiber, however (as the deflected shape of the beam would be concave downward) and is plotted as a negative ordinate on the moment diagram (Figure 7-19). Also notice that, just as a point load

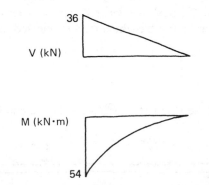

Figure 7-19. *V* and *M* diagrams for Example 7-4.

(or reaction) causes a sudden jump in the shear diagram, an externally applied moment will cause a sudden jump in the moment diagram. (Actually, this is the only way that such a change can occur in a moment diagram, which means that the moment will always be zero at the end of a beam unless there is an applied moment load or a wall reaction at that point.)

As an exercise the student should turn the cantilever beam of Example 7-4 end for end and again construct the V and M diagrams. Since the origin is always kept at the left end, x will then equal zero at the free end and the two equations will change. The moment diagram remains all negative and is merely turned right about, as would be expected, but the shear diagram changes sign illustrating that the shear sense is not related to the beam's physical behavior.

Problems

7-1. Construct the V and M diagrams for the simple beam in Figure 7-20.

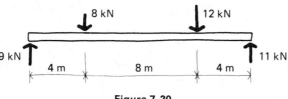

Figure 7-20

7-2. Construct the V and M diagrams for the overhanging beam in Figure 7-21.

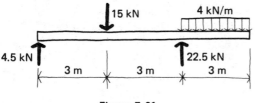

Figure 7-21

7-3. Determine the reactions and construct the V and M diagrams for the beam in Figure 7-22.

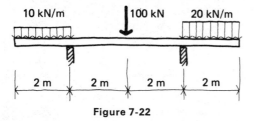

Figure 7-22

7-4. Determine the reactions and construct the V and M diagrams for the cantilever beam in Figure 7-23.

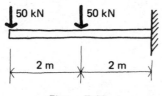

Figure 7-23

7-5. The beam in Figure 7-24 is partially restrained by its supports, resulting in applied couple loads at its ends. Determine the reactions and construct the V and M diagrams.

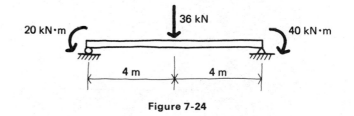

Figure 7-24

7-3 SIGNIFICANCE OF ZERO SHEAR

The examples and problems of the previous section had shear and moment diagrams that could be drawn by connecting the ordinates at the various points of curve change with either straight or curved lines. With the exception of Example 7-2, the maximum value of moment in each case occurred at one of these points. (For Example 7-2, the location of the maximum bending was obviously at midspan by symmetry.) For many loading situations, the point of maximum moment cannot be found so conveniently. However, it must be located before the magnitude of the maximum moment can be determined. Example 7-5 illustrates this situation.

EXAMPLE 7-5

Construct the V and M diagrams for the partially loaded beam of Figure 7-25.

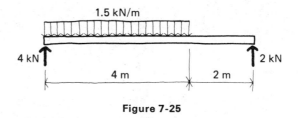

Figure 7-25

Solution: The V and M equations for the two intervals will be

$(0 \leq x \leq 4)$	$V_x = 4 - 1.5x$
$(0 \leq x \leq 4)$	$M_x = 4x - 0.75x^2$
$(4 \leq x \leq 6)$	$V_x = -2$
$(4 \leq x \leq 6)$	$M_x = 12 - 2x$

The location of the point of maximum moment is not obvious from Figure 7-26. The distance x can be found rather easily, however, by remembering that the first derivative of an equation represents the slope. Borrowing the maxima–

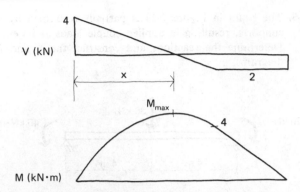

Figure 7-26.   V and M diagrams for Example 7-5.

minima concept from calculus, we can find where the slope levels off to zero by taking dM_x/dx and setting it equal to zero. For the interval $0 \leq x \leq 4$, we have

$$M_x = 4x - 0.75x^2$$

and

$$\frac{dM_x}{dx} = 4 - 1.5x$$

Setting this expression equal to zero, we get

$$4 - 1.5x = 0$$

$$x = 2.67 \text{ m}$$

By substitution, the value of the maximum moment is then

$$M_{x_{max}} = 4(2.67) - 0.75(2.67)^2$$

$$= 5.33 \text{ kN} \cdot \text{m}$$

It is most important to notice that the first derivative of the moment equation is equal to the V equation. Hence, when the moment becomes a maximum (or minimum) between points of curve change, it will do so where the shear is zero. This means that the value of x could have been determined from the V diagram using similar triangles. From Figure 7-27,

$$\frac{6}{4} = \frac{4}{x}$$

$$x = 2.67 \text{ m}$$

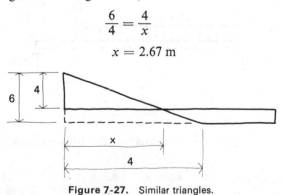

Figure 7-27.   Similar triangles.

The relationships between the two diagrams will be explored more fully in the next section.

Problems

7-6. Construct the V and M diagrams for the beam in Figure 7-28.

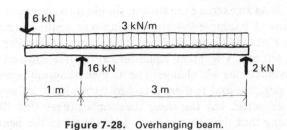

Figure 7-28.   Overhanging beam.

7-7. What is the value of maximum moment in the beam of Figure 7-29? It carries a uniform load and is subjected to an applied moment at its left end.

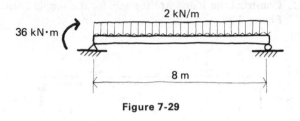

Figure 7-29

7-4   LOAD, SHEAR, AND MOMENT RELATIONSHIPS

Let us look further at what goes on inside a beam by studying the forces acting on a small length of the uniformly loaded simple span of Example 7-2. In Figure 7-30, we have added a load diagram which is nothing more than a plot of the transverse loads (including reactions) that act on the beam. Up loads are taken as positive and down loads as negative.

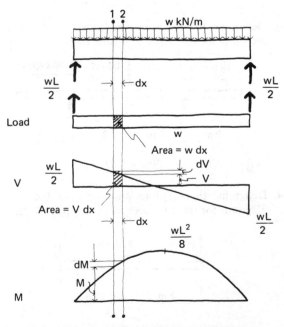

Figure 7-30.   Load, shear, and moment diagrams.

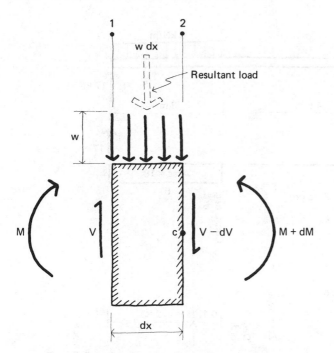

Figure 7-31. Free-body diagram.

$w = \dfrac{dV}{dx}$	At any point along the length of the beam, the *ordinate* on the load diagram is equal to the *slope* of the shear diagram.
$V = \dfrac{dM}{dx}$	At any point along the length of the beam, the *ordinate* on the shear diagram is equal to the *slope* of the moment diagram.

This slope–ordinate relationship holds for both magnitude and sign. (A positive slope is one that is up and to the right; a negative slope is down and to the right.) Looking at the diagrams, we see that, in the left half of the beam, the ordinate of the V diagram and the slope of the M diagram are both positive and decreasing as we move from left to right. At midspan, the ordinate of the V diagram and the slope of the M diagram are both zero. Moving from left to right for the right half of the beam, we find that the ordinate of the V diagram and the slope of the M diagram are both negative and increasing.

Now look at Equations (7-1) and let the distance dx in Figure 7-30 be a small but finite interval.

Figure 7-31 shows a small elemental length of beam taken from between sections 1 and 2. This element must be in equilibrium under the forces shown; therefore,

$$\sum F_y = 0$$
$$V - w\,dx - (V - dV) = 0$$
$$dV = w\,dx \tag{7-1a}$$

or

$$w = \frac{dV}{dx} \tag{7-2a}$$

Likewise, for rotational equilibrium, we can take moments about any point. Point c conveniently eliminates a force, and thus

$$\sum M_c = 0$$

$$M + dM + w\,dx\left(\frac{dx}{2}\right) - V\,dx - M = 0$$

Considering the third term to be small enough to be neglected gives us

$$dM = V\,dx \tag{7-1b}$$

or

$$V = \frac{dM}{dx} \tag{7-2b}$$

The four equations, (7-1) and (7-2), establish some very useful relationships among the load, shear, and moment diagrams. They enable us to construct the diagrams rapidly, without writing the shear and moment equations.

Look first at Equations (7-2) and let the distance dx in Figure 7-30 approach zero.

$dV = w\,dx$	Over any beam length interval, the *net area* under the load curve is equal to the *change in ordinate* on the shear diagram.
$dM = V\,dx$	Over any beam length interval, the *net area* under the shear curve is equal to the *change in ordinate* on the moment diagram.

For the left half of the beam, the area under the shear curve is

$$A = \frac{1}{2}\left(\frac{wL}{2}\right)\left(\frac{L}{2}\right) = \frac{wL^2}{8}$$

This is the change in ordinate on the M diagram from $x = 0$ to $x = L/2$, that same interval. For the entire beam length, the *net* area under the shear curve is zero because the positive area equals the negative area. The change in ordinate on the M diagram from $x = 0$ to $x = L$ is zero, both points having a value of $M = 0$.

These relationships support and verify the point made previously concerning maximum moment and zero shear. We can also now state that, for a beam portion having no load ($w\,dx = 0$), the shear must be constant ($dV = 0$). Furthermore, if the moment is constant over a beam length ($dM = 0$), then no shear can exist ($V\,dx = 0$).

The reader should study the illustrations in Figure 7-32 to become familiar with the diagram relationships. It is recommended that Problems 7-1 through 7-7 be

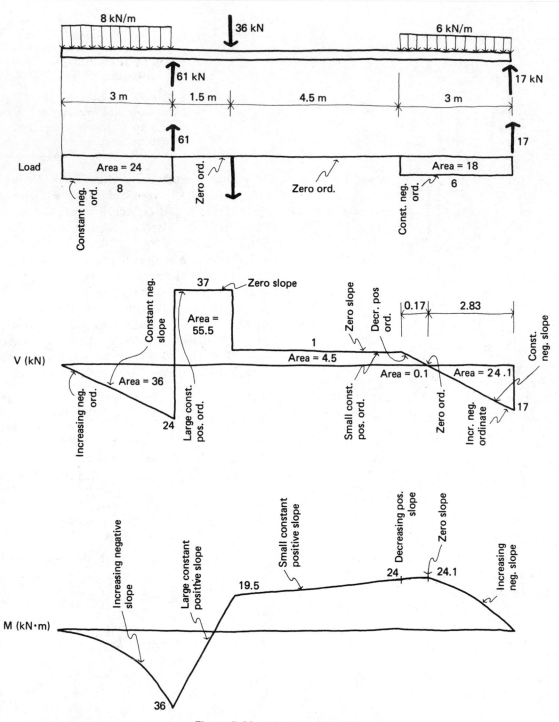

Figure 7-32. Diagram relationships.

reworked for practice using the new techniques before attempting any new problems.

Always remember to sketch the probable deflected shape and make sure it can be rationalized with the moment diagram in each case. Many careless errors can be found or prevented this way.

Problems

7-8. Construct the *V* and *M* diagrams for the long-span girder of Figure 7-33.

7-9. Construct the *V* and *M* diagrams for the beam in Figure 7-34.

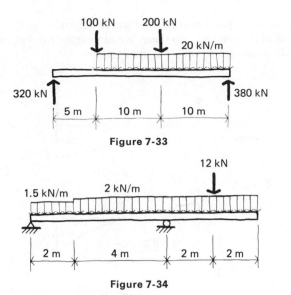

Figure 7-33

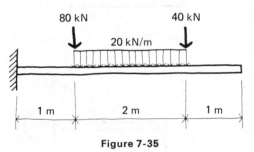

Figure 7-34

7-10. Construct the *V* and *M* diagrams for the cantilever beam in Figure 7-35.

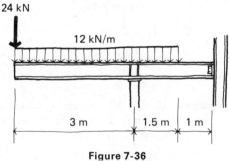

Figure 7-35

7-11. Construct the *V* and *M* diagrams for the beam in Figure 7-36. Pinned connections may be assumed.

Figure 7-36

7-12. A simple beam of length *L* (m) supporting a uniform load of *w* (kN/m) has a midspan moment of $wL^2/8$ (kN·m). How much moment, *M* (in terms of *w* and *L*), should be applied to the ends of the beam in Figure 7-37 to reduce that midspan moment by a factor of three?

7-13. Construct the *V* and *M* diagrams for the hinged beam of Figure 7-38. (*Hint:* Make sure that the moment diagram goes to zero at the hinge.)

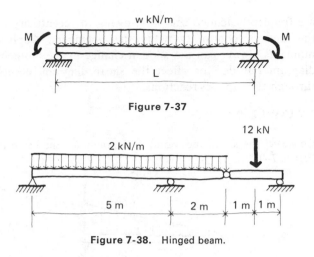

Figure 7-37

Figure 7-38. Hinged beam.

7-5 UNUSUAL LOADS

The uniformly varying load of Figure 7-40 may be thought of as the type of load provided by a pile of sand in a storage bin or the horizontal pressure of water against a dam. More frequently, however, such loads in building structures result from structural framing layouts, which employ diagonal elements or openings. Chapter 11 treats tributary areas for different framing patterns, and this will not be discussed here. At this point we are interested only in the shears and moments that result from such loads. Basically, the uniformly varying load causes each diagram to move up one order so that the *V* diagram has parabolic curves and the *M* diagram, cubic curves. This means that in some instances it is necessary to evaluate the areas under parabolic curves to utilize the area–ordinate relationship. Appendix M provides the areas for two parabolic cases with the stipulation that the curve pass through the apex of the parabola.

Another type of load is an applied moment or couple which is located at some point other than a support. Torsional loads and lateral loads on cantilevers, as seen in Figure 7-39, will cause such moments. Columns

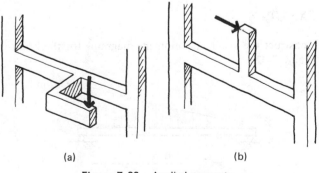

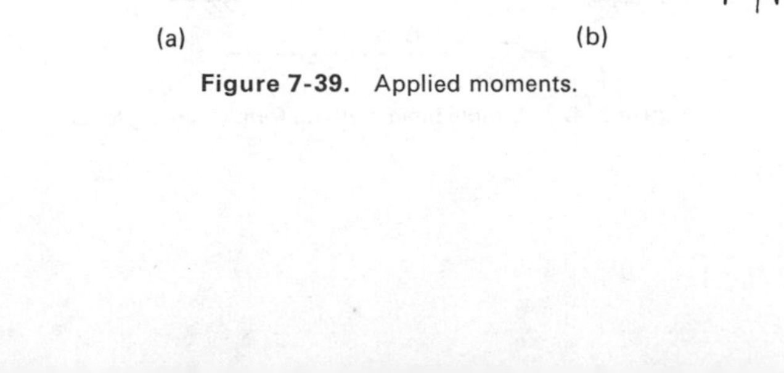

(a)   (b)

Figure 7-39. Applied moments.

are frequently loaded this way, owing to eccentricity of the load or continuity with other members. Applied moments always cause a sudden change in the moment diagram but do not affect the shear diagram, except through the support reactions.

EXAMPLE 7-6

Construct the shear and moment diagrams for the beam in Figure 7-40.

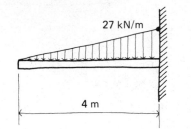

Figure 7-40.　Cantilever with uniformly varying load.

Solution (see Figure 7-41):

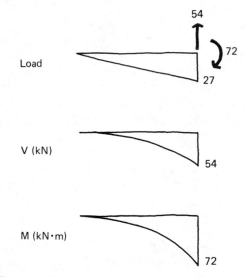

Figure 7-41.　Load, shear, and moment diagrams for Example 7-6.

EXAMPLE 7-7

Construct the shear and moment diagrams for the beam in Figure 7-42.

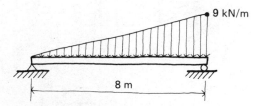

Figure 7-42.　Simple beam with uniformly varying load.

Solution: To find M_{max} we need to determine x, the location of the point of zero shear. We can use the FBD of Figure 7-43(b) and let V_x take a value of zero.

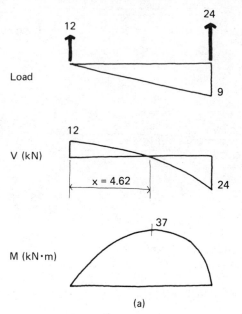

(a)

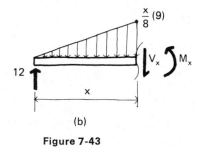

(b)

Figure 7-43

$$\Sigma F_y = 0$$

$$12 - \frac{1}{2}\left(\frac{x}{8}\right)(9)x = 0$$

$$x = 4.62 \text{ m}$$

The half-parabola in the V diagram (altitude = 12 kN, base = 4.62 m) *does* include an apex at its left end, and according to Appendix M, its area will be

$$A = \tfrac{2}{3}bh$$
$$= \tfrac{2}{3}(12)(4.62)$$
$$= 37.0 \text{ kN·m}$$

In this case, the maximum moment will have the same value. This can be verified from case 6 in Appendix V, where

$$M_{max} = \frac{wL^2}{9\sqrt{3}}$$
$$= \frac{9(8)^2}{9\sqrt{3}}$$
$$= 37.0 \text{ kN·m}$$

EXAMPLE 7-8

Construct the shear and moment diagrams for the beam in Figure 7-44.

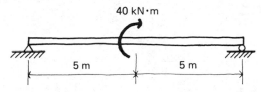

Figure 7-44. Simple beam with applied moment load.

Solution (see Figure 7-45):

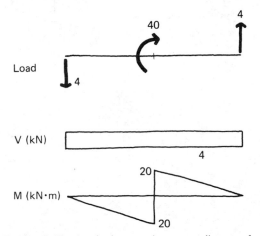

Figure 7-45. Load, shear, and moment diagrams for Example 7-8.

Problems

7-14. Construct the *V* and *M* diagrams for the beam in Figure 7-46.

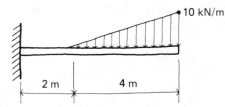

Figure 7-46. Cantilever beam with uniformly varying load.

7-15. Construct the *V* and *M* diagrams for the beam in Figure 7-47.

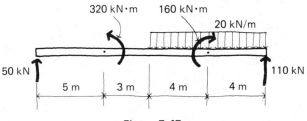

Figure 7-47

7-16. Construct the *V* and *M* diagrams for the beam in Figure 7-48.

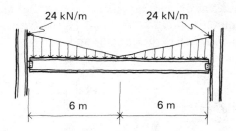

Figure 7-48. Steel beam with pin connections.

7-17. Construct the *V* and *M* diagram for the beam in Figure 7-49.

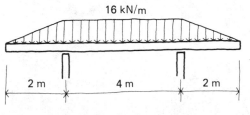

Figure 7-49. Overhanging beam.

7-18. Construct the *V* and *M* diagrams for the concrete beam in Figure 7-50. The columns may be assumed to provide fixed ends and the connections to act as hinges.

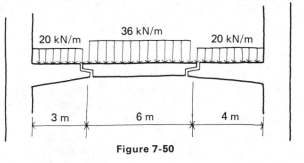

Figure 7-50

7-6 DETERMINATE FRAMES

The majority of continuous frames are indeterminate and cannot be resolved by the simple equations of statics alone. Chapter 15 is devoted to an investigation of indeterminate beams and frames, but an introduction to shear and moment in frame members will be provided in this section.

Plotting the diagrams for vertical members presents no problems if we adopt the standard drafting convention that a drawing is read from the bottom and from the right. In other words, the positive (top) side of a vertical member is the left side and the negative (bottom) side is the right side.

Pinned joints in frames act like hinges in that they can transmit shear but no moment. If a beam-to-column corner connection is pinned, the moment in both members will be zero at the joint. However, if the beam is pinned to a column that passes through the connection, the column is continuous and may have internal moment at that point. See Figure 7-51(a) and (b).

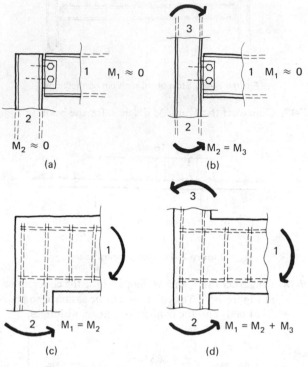

Figure 7-51. Beam-to-column connections.

Moment resistant or continuous joints such as shown in Figure 7-51(c) and (d) can transmit both moment and shear. In every case the internal moments at the intersection must have magnitudes and senses that will hold the joint in rotational equilibrium. (The moments acting on the joints in Figure 7-51 are only intended to be representative and could all be reversed, depending upon the applied loads, and provided that equilibrium was maintained.)

EXAMPLE 7-9

Construct the shear and moment diagrams for the frame in Figure 7-52.

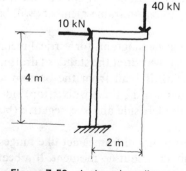

Figure 7-52. L-shaped cantilever.

Solution (see Figure 7-53):

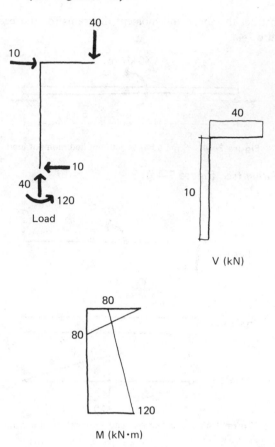

Figure 7-53. Load, shear, and moment diagrams for Example 7-9.

EXAMPLE 7-10

Construct the shear and moment diagrams for the frame in Figure 7-54.

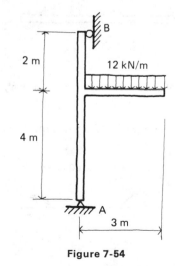

Figure 7-54

Solution: Make a free-body diagram of the continuous joint to check equilibrium [Figure 7-55(b)].

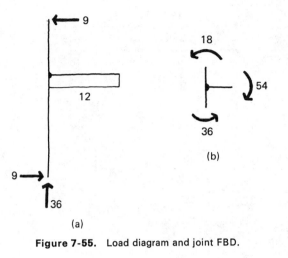

(a)

(b)

Figure 7-55. Load diagram and joint FBD.

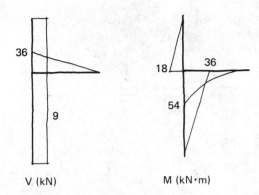

Figure 7-56. Shear and moment diagrams for the frame of Example 7-10.

EXAMPLE 7-11

Construct the V and M diagrams for the members in the structure of Figure 7-57. Assume that all connections are pins.

Solution: First determine all the forces on each member (Figure 7-58), making note of the two-force members, AC and EF. There will be neither shear nor moment in these two members (Figure 7-59).

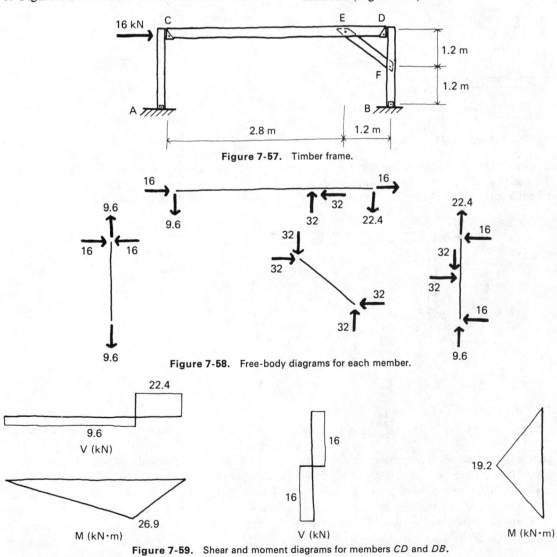

Figure 7-57. Timber frame.

Figure 7-58. Free-body diagrams for each member.

Figure 7-59. Shear and moment diagrams for members CD and DB.

Problems

7-19. Construct the *V* and *M* diagrams for the continuous frame of Figure 7-60.

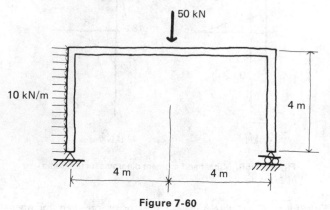

Figure 7-60

7-20. Construct the *V* and *M* diagrams for the continuous frame of Figure 7-61.

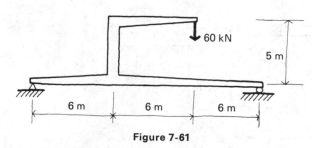

Figure 7-61

7-21. Construct the *V* and *M* diagrams for the L-shaped member in Figure 7-62. Assume that the support at *A* is a pin and that the wall at *B* acts as a roller.

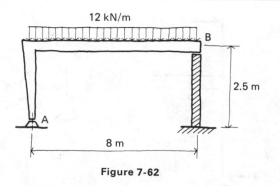

Figure 7-62

7-22. Construct the *V* and *M* diagrams for the vertical member in Figure 7-63.

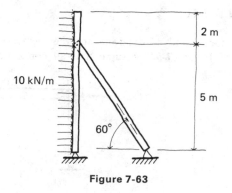

Figure 7-63

7-23. Construct the *V* and *M* diagrams for the beam in the frame of Figure 7-64. Assume that all joints are pinned. Because of symmetry, the horizontal reactions at the supports may be assumed to be equal.

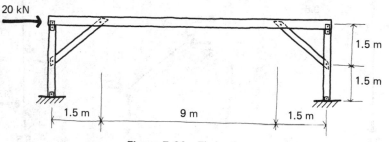

Figure 7-64. Timber frame.

7-7 TENSION SIDE MOMENT DIAGRAMS

Because the sign convention for moment is related to member curvature or deflected shape, all moment diagrams presented so far have been plotted on the compression side of each member. When the top of a beam is in compression, the moment diagram is positive and the ordinates graph upward from a line representing the *x* axis. When the bottom fibers of a beam go into compression, as in a cantilever, the moment diagram falls below the *x* axis.

It is sometimes advantageous, particularly for the moment diagrams of continuous frames, to reverse this convention and plot the bending moment on the tension side of members. Figure 7-65 shows two possible diagrams for a pinned end frame. In many cases a diagram on the tension side is easier to read because it has less

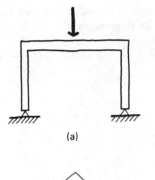

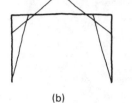

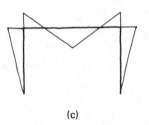

Figure 7-65. Compression and tension side moment diagrams.

overlap at the corners. It can also look more like the deflected shape of a structure, as illustrated by the frame with fixed supports shown in Figure 7-66.

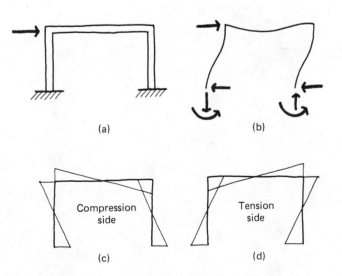

Figure 7-66. Compression and tension side moment diagrams.

7-8 CABLE ANALOGY

When the moment diagram for a simple beam carrying a uniform load is plotted on the tension side of the beam (i.e., below the x axis), it forms a concave upward, parabolic curve. This is the same shape taken by a cable when it is similarly loaded. Comparing Figure 7-67 with the results of Example 2-16, we find that the horizontal force throughout the cable is equal to the maximum moment (of an analogous beam) divided by the cable sag. This relationship holds true for concentrated loads as well.

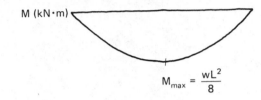

Figure 7-67. Simple beam moment diagram.

EXAMPLE 7-12

Given that the horizontal force H in the cable of Figure 7-68(b) must not exceed 16 kN, determine the minimum length of cable required.

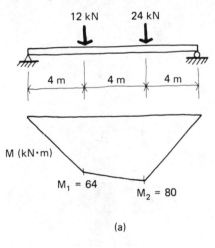

Figure 7-68. Cable and simple beam moment geometry.

Solution: Since the cable shape must be that of the analogous simple beam moment diagram, the values of y_1 and y_2 can be found using the moment ordinates at those points.

$$y_1 = \frac{M_1}{H} \qquad y_2 = \frac{M_2}{H}$$

$$= \frac{64 \text{ kN} \cdot \text{m}}{16 \text{ kN}} \qquad = \frac{80 \text{ kN} \cdot \text{m}}{16 \text{ kN}}$$

$$= 4 \text{ m} \qquad\qquad = 5 \text{ m}$$

The overall length of the cable can then be found by adding the lengths of its three segments.

$$L = \sqrt{(4)^2 + (4)^2} + \sqrt{(1)^2 + (4)^2} + \sqrt{(5)^2 + (4)^2}$$

$$= 16.2 \text{ m}$$

8-1 INTRODUCTION TO BENDING

Chapter 1 makes reference to the structural inefficiency of bending as a means to carry load. Compared to axial tension and compression, bending generates much higher stresses in members, because the fibers of material are not stressed uniformly. We know from experience that if we want to break something in half, it is much easier to break it in bending than to try to pull it apart in tension or buckle it in compression.

Although it might be nice (for the sake of structural efficiency) to eliminate bending stresses in our structures, clearly this is not possible. To attempt to carry all loads in direct tension or compression would lead to some very awkward configurations and/or very small spans. The fact is that true structural efficiency, in many cases, would result in a false economy, because of the resulting spatial or architectural inefficiencies. (It is also true that bending action takes place in most structural elements anyway, even those designed and configured to carry loads by other means. As soon as we build stiffness into a structure, by thickness or shape (I), it will have a tendency to carry load by bending.)

Many functions require clear spans in the short-to-moderate range of 5 to 20 m, and most often some form of beam construction is preferable to arches, cables, vaults, folded plates, or other "more efficient" structures. A post-and-beam system will usually provide more usable building volume than the more form-resistant structures. For anything but the longer spans, beams will give the largest span/depth ratio, enabling the designer to reduce the space between the ceiling and the finish floor above. This can be essential in high-rise buildings.

Beams are also relatively insensitive to the type and location of loads they can receive. For example, trusses will only take concentrated loads at the panel points, and vaults and domes are quite unsuitable for either concentrated or line loads. Although it is true that bending action results in high stresses and deflections, it is equally true that strong, stiff structural materials are both readily available and inexpensive, particularly when compared to some nonstructural building materials and labor.

A beam can be loosely defined as any structural element that carries transverse loads and has two of its dimensions much less than the third. Most beams are straight and of constant cross section, but some are curved or angled and some have varying cross sections. All beams develop two kinds of stress: flexural (sometimes called bending), which is a normal stress, and shearing, which is tangential. All beams also deflect under load, and these three items—flexural stress, shearing stress, and deflection—are the parameters by which we determine the required size and/or shape of the cross section. Of these, flexural stress governs most frequently. The remainder of this chapter will be devoted to analyzing and understanding beam stresses. Special aspects and applications required for beam design are considered in Chapter 9, and deflection is covered in Chapter 10. Finally, beam design and framing are treated in Chapter 11.

8-2 FLEXURAL STRAIN

Beams bend under load such that transverse sections remain plane as represented by the lines on the beam in Figure 8-1(b). There is a compression zone and a tension zone, which are separated by a horizontal neutral plane. The neutral plane (called the *neutral axis*) is located at the centroid of the cross section and the beam fibers are squeezed or stretched in direct proportion to their distance from this neutral axis. The top and bottom fibers, or extreme fibers, undergo the most strain and do the most work, while those close to the neutral axis have strain levels near zero and are least effective. A fiber

Bending

8

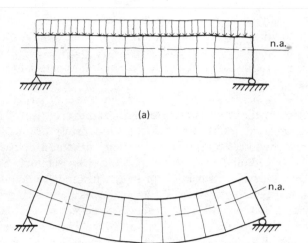

(a)

(b)

Figure 8-1. Flexural strain.

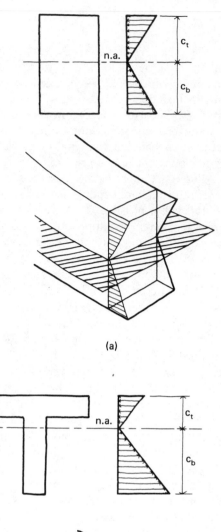

(a)

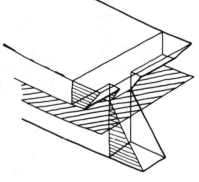

(b)

Figure 8-2. Bending stress distribution.

located halfway between the neutral axis and the top or bottom edge of a beam will have half the strain of a fiber located at that edge. (Verify this by making a small beam of an easy-to-bend material, such as polyurethane foam or balsa wood and drawing parallel lines on one of its sides.) It is important to understand the linearity of bending strain and the corresponding stresses that develop, and this subject is fully examined in Appendix D.

The correct location of the neutral axis, critical to the proper understanding of flexural stresses, was theorized in 1713 by Antoine Parent (1666–1716), a French scientist. However, it remained largely unknown until the extensive work by Claude L. M. H. Navier, also French, in 1826.

8-3 FLEXURAL STRESS

External bending loads are resisted by internal stresses that build up in the beam fibers. These stresses are directly related to flexural strain by the stiffness of the material. Their direction is always normal to the transverse section. Assuming that the beam is made of a reasonably homogeneous material, the stresses will vary as the strains do (i.e., linear with the distance from the neutral axis). Bending stress distributions for two different beam shapes are illustrated in Figure 8-2. Because of symmetry, the top and bottom fiber stresses in a rectangular section will be equal in magnitude (opposite in sense). This is not true for the T shape, where higher stresses exist at the stem edge than in the flange, because of the greater distance to the neutral axis.

Flexural stresses are a direct response to bending moments and therefore will vary over the length of a beam as well as with the distance from the neutral axis. The general flexure formula is

$$f_y = \frac{My}{I} \tag{8-1}$$

where f_y = flexural stress at fiber level, y (Pa)

M = bending moment at the transverse section being examined (N·m)

y = vertical distance from neutral axis to level y (m)

I = moment inertia of the cross section with respect to the neutral (centroidal) axis (m⁴)

When we are interested only in the maximum bending stresses at a given transverse section, we can use

$$f_b = \frac{Mc}{I} \qquad (8\text{-}1a)$$

where f_b = extreme fiber bending stress (Pa)
c = distance to extreme fiber (m)

[In Equation (8-1a), c will have the value illustrated as distance c_t or c_b in Figure 8-2, and f_b will then be a top fiber stress or a bottom fiber stress, respectively.]

The derivation of these formulas and certain restrictions concerning their use are given in Appendix D. The reader will notice that the sense of the bending stress at a given point in a beam depends upon the sense of the bending moment and whether the point is above or below the neutral axis.

(In some of the examples and problems that follow, the effects of member self-weight as part of the dead load have been ignored. Although this is not recommended as sound engineering practice, the writer's own experience indicates that this component of the load seldom controls the member size in short-span building structures of timber or steel. Larger spans in these materials and all reinforced concrete beams, however, have significant self-weights, which cannot be ignored.)

EXAMPLE 8-1

The wood joist in Figure 8-3 is 38 × 235 mm in section.
(a) Determine the maximum bending stress.
(b) Determine the stress due to bending at a point 1.5 m in from one of the ends and 100 mm below the top edge.

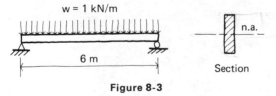

w = 1 kN/m

n.a.

6 m

Section

Figure 8-3

Solution:

(a) By symmetry the neutral axis (n.a.) is located at mid-depth. The maximum bending stress will occur where the moment is a maximum and will be compressive in the top fiber and tensile in the bottom fiber. From Appendix Q, $I = 41.1(10)^6$ mm⁴.

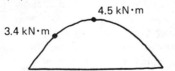

4.5 kN·m

3.4 kN·m

Figure 8-4. Moment diagram for the beam in Figure 8-3.

$$f_b = \frac{Mc}{I}$$

$$= \frac{4.5 \text{ kN·m}(0.118 \text{ m})}{41.1(10)^{-6} \text{ m}^4}$$

$$f_b_{\text{top}} = 12\ 900 \text{ kPa compression}$$

$$f_b_{\text{bottom}} = 12\ 900 \text{ kPa tension}$$

(b) The point is above the neutral axis, and in the presence of positive moment the stress will be compressive.

$$f_y = \frac{My}{I}$$

$$= \frac{3.4 \text{ kN·m}(0.018 \text{ m})}{41.1(10)^{-6} \text{ m}^4}$$

$$= 1490 \text{ kPa compression}$$

EXAMPLE 8-2

Determine the maximum bending stress in the beam of Figure 8-5.

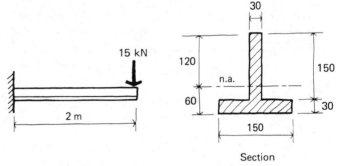

30

15 kN

120

n.a.

60

150

150

30

Section

Figure 8-5. Inverted T-beam used as a cantilever.

Solution: The maximum bending stress will be at the cross section where the moment maximizes and at the fiber level farthest from the n.a. In this case, these conditions are met at the top fiber, where the beam enters the wall. The stress will be tensile.

30 kN·m

Figure 8-6. Moment diagram for the beam in Figure 8-5.

Using the parallel axis theorem, we get

$$I = 27(10)^6 \text{ mm}^4$$

The maximum moment is 30 kN·m.

$$f_b = \frac{Mc}{I}$$

$$= \frac{30 \text{ kN·m}(0.120 \text{ m})}{27(10)^{-6} \text{ m}^4}$$

$$= 133(10)^3 \text{ kPa}$$

$$= 133 \text{ MPa}$$

EXAMPLE 8-3

A steel W310 × 21 is used for the beam in Figure 8-7. Determine the maximum tensile and compressive stresses due to bending.

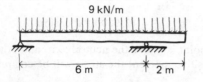

Figure 8-7. Overhanging beam with uniform load.

Solution: As with the rectangle, the symmetrical W shape has its *c* distance to the top fiber equal to the *c* distance to the bottom fiber, so that (for any given section) the top and bottom stresses are equal in magnitude. This means that the maximum tensile and compressive stresses must both occur where the moment is a maximum, in this case, 32 kN·m. From Appendix S, $I = 36.9(10)^6$ mm⁴ and $d = 303$ mm.

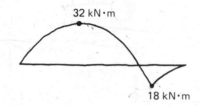

Figure 8-8. Moment diagram for the beam in Figure 8-7.

$$f_{b_{top}} = \frac{Mc}{I}$$
$$= \frac{32 \text{ kN·m}(0.152 \text{ m})}{36.9(10)^{-6} \text{ m}^4}$$
$$= 132 \text{ MPa compression}$$

and

$$f_{b_{bottom}} = \frac{Mc}{I}$$
$$= \frac{32 \text{ kN·m}(0.152 \text{ m})}{36.9(10)^{-6} \text{ m}^4}$$
$$= 132 \text{ MPa tension}$$

EXAMPLE 8-4

To save construction depth with a precast plank system, a structural T is used in lieu of the W shape in Example 8-3. Its properties are given in Figure 8-9. Determine the maximum tensile and compressive stresses due to bending.

Solution: The structural T is not symmetrical with respect to its extreme fiber distances, and the possibility exists that one of the maximum stresses (tensile or compressive) may occur where the moment is not at its maximum absolute value. The compression stress will maximize at fibers 1 and 2 in Figure 8-10, and the tension stress will maximize at fibers 3 and 4. For illustrative purposes we shall examine all four points in this example. (The moment diagram from Example 8-3 is, of course, still valid.)

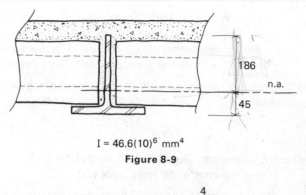

$I = 46.6(10)^6$ mm⁴

Figure 8-9

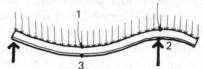

Figure 8-10. Deflected shape of structural T beam.

For the maximum positive moment section,

$$f_{b_1} = \frac{Mc}{I}$$
$$= \frac{32 \text{ kN·m}(0.186 \text{ m})}{46.6(10)^{-6} \text{ m}^4}$$
$$= 128 \text{ MPa compression}$$

and

$$f_{b_3} = \frac{Mc}{I}$$
$$= \frac{32 \text{ kN·m}(0.045 \text{ m})}{46.6(10)^{-6} \text{ m}^4}$$
$$= 30.9 \text{ MPa tension}$$

For the maximum negative moment section,

$$f_{b_4} = \frac{Mc}{I}$$
$$= \frac{18 \text{ kN·m}(0.186 \text{ m})}{46.6(10)^{-6} \text{ m}^4}$$
$$= 71.8 \text{ MPa tension}$$

and

$$f_{b_2} = \frac{Mc}{I}$$
$$= \frac{18 \text{ kN·m}(0.045 \text{ m})}{46.6(10)^{-6} \text{ m}^4}$$
$$= 17.4 \text{ MPa compression}$$

A comparison of the four values just determined shows that the maximum compression occurs where the moment is maximum (i.e., at point 1). The tensile stress, however, maximizes at point 4, where the moment is only 18 kN·m. This happens, of course, because of the different *c* distances involved in the asymmetrical T shape. Accordingly, when sections having dissimilar *c* distances are used for beams that have both positive and negative curvature, the largest bending stress of a specified sense will not necessarily occur where the moment is maximum. In order to determine the maximum bending stresses in such cases, one either has to check the stress levels at four points (as we did) or compare the ratio of *M* values to the ratio of *c* distances to ascertain where the equation *Mc/I* will maximize. What remains true, however, is that the *absolute* maximum value of bending stress (128 MPa in our example) will always occur at the section having the *absolute* maximum moment.

Problems

8-1. Assume that the joist of Example 8-1 has a hole bored through it at midspan. If the hole is located as in Figure 8-11, determine the extreme fiber bending stresses.

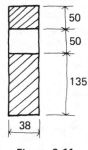

Figure 8-11

8-2. A W610 × 101 is used as a simple beam spanning 9 m. It must carry a uniform load of 12 kN/m and two concentrated loads at the third points of 40 kN each. Determine the maximum bending stress.

8-3. Douglas fir joists, 38 × 285 mm, span 5.5 m between two bearing walls. Determine the permissible total uniform load in kN/m. Use the repetitive member bending stress in Appendix P as the allowable stress.

8-4. Determine the maximum permissible simple span for the joists of Problem 8-3 if the total uniform load is 1 kN/m. Assume that bending stress controls.

8-5. The built-up timber beam of Figure 8-12 is made of two 38 × 285 mm members enclosing a 38 × 185 mm member. The beams are spaced 2.4 m in a direction normal to the page and must carry a floor load of 1.5 kN/m². Determine the maximum tensile and compressive stresses due to bending. (*Hint:* Each meter of beam length must support 2.4 m² of floor area.)

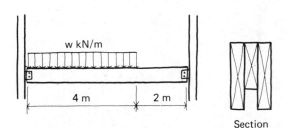

Figure 8-12. Balcony beam simply supported by two columns.

8-6. A W530 × 74 is used for the overhanging beam of Figure 8-13. Assuming pinned connections, determine the magnitude and sense of the extreme fiber stresses

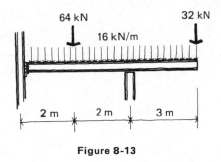

Figure 8-13

(a) at the section where the moment is a maximum.
(b) under the left-hand concentrated load.

8-7. The 8-m-long timber 89 × 285 beams of Figure 8-14 are spaced 1.2 m on center. They must carry a total floor load of 2 kN/m² and a wall load (from the roof) of 5 kN per running meter of wall. Determine the maximum bending stress.

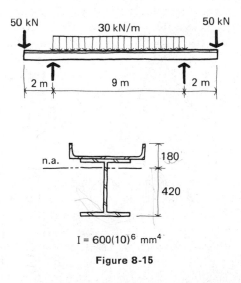

Figure 8-14. Section through a residential floor.

8-8. The steel beam of Figure 8-15 is composed of a W section and a channel welded together and has the *I* value given. Determine the maximum compressive and tensile stresses due to bending.

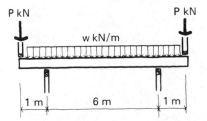

$$I = 600(10)^6 \text{ mm}^4$$

Figure 8-15

8-9. The beam in Figure 8-16 is fabricated from two 38 × 185 mm members and one 38 × 139 mm member. The three pieces have coincident centroidal axes.
(a) Determine the maximum bending stress.
(b) At that same section, determine the bending stress at the extreme edge of the 38 × 139 mm member.

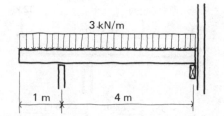

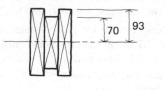

Section

Figure 8-16. Overhanging wood beam.

8-4 SECTION MODULUS

The general formula for flexural stress, $f_b = Mc/I$, can be simplified slightly if we restrict our analyses to problems involving only extreme fiber stresses. (Since these are the stresses that usually control, this restriction is of little consequence.) Notice that the maximum flexural stress is really a function of only two items, the bending moment and the dimensions of the cross section. If we can combine the two cross-sectional factors c and I into one term, the general equation will be easier to use, particularly when applied in a design situation. The quantity I/c has been given the special name of section modulus and the symbol S. It is a measure of bending resistance which includes both the moment of inertia and the depth. Its units are length cubed. The formula for maximum flexural stress will then be

$$f_b = \frac{M}{S} \qquad (8-2)$$

In a section that is symmetrical about the neutral axis, the c distances to the tensile and compressive fibers will be equal and the section modulus will have only one value. For a T shape or other unsymmetrical section, where the neutral axis is not at middepth, the larger c dimension should be used in S so that formula (8-2) will compute the larger of the two extreme fiber stresses. (It is probably just as easy to use the straight Mc/I formula for unsymmetrical shapes.)

For a rectangular section, S can be stated in terms of the width and depth, bypassing the I computation.

$$S = \frac{I}{c}$$

$$= \frac{bd^3/12}{d/2}$$

$$= \frac{bd^2}{6} \qquad (8-3)$$

The section modulus values for both strong and weak axes of some common timber rectangles are given in Appendix Q. For steel wide-flange shapes and channels, the S values have been computed and are listed in Table 1 of Appendix S.

EXAMPLE 8-5

Determine the maximum bending stress in an 89 × 235 mm timber, which is used as a uniformly loaded cantilever 2 m long. The total load is 4 kN/m.

Solution:　From Appendix Q, $S = 819(10)^3$ mm³.

$$f_b = \frac{M}{S}$$

$$= \frac{8\ \text{kN·m}}{819(10)^{-6}\ \text{m}^3}$$

$$= 9770\ \text{kPa}$$

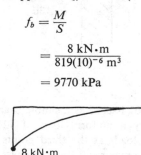

8 kN·m

Figure 8-17. Moment diagram for the beam of Example 8-5.

EXAMPLE 8-6

The W920 × 365 beam in Figure 8-18 must carry three column loads of 300 kN each. Determine the maximum bending stress.

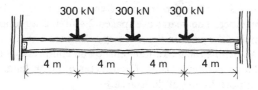

Figure 8-18. Simply supported steel beam.

Solution:　From Appendix S, $S = 14\ 700(10)^3$ mm³.

$$f_b = \frac{M}{S}$$

$$= \frac{2400\ \text{kN·m}}{14\ 700(10)^{-6}\ \text{m}^3}$$

$$= 163(10)^3\ \text{kPa}$$

$$= 163\ \text{MPa}$$

This is very close to the allowable bending stress of 165 MPa for mild steel, and the size of the span indicates that the bending stress due to the dead weight of the beam itself should not be ignored. The self-weight is a uniform load that (in this case) causes a maximum moment at midspan which should be

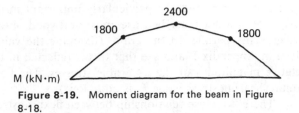

Figure 8-19. Moment diagram for the beam in Figure 8-18.

added to the applied load moment at that point. The self-weight moment is

$$M_{s.w.} = \frac{wL^2}{8}$$

where w is the self-weight of the beam (kN/m). To obtain this weight, we must convert from the mass value given by the shape designation. Because of the earth's gravity, a mass of 1 kg will exert a force of about 9.8 N. Therefore, the weight of the steel beam can be obtained as

$$w = (365 \text{ kg/m})(9.8 \text{ N/kg})$$

$$= 3580 \text{ N/m}$$

$$= 3.58 \text{ kN/m}$$

$$M_{s.w.} = \frac{3.58 \text{ kN/m}(16 \text{ m})^2}{8}$$

$$= 115 \text{ kN·m}$$

The actual bending stress after inclusion of the self-weight moment will be, by ratio,

$$f_{b_{new}} = \frac{M + M_{s.w.}}{M}(f_b)$$

$$= \frac{2400 + 115}{2400}(163 \text{ MPa})$$

$$= 171 \text{ MPa}$$

This is an overstress of about 4% and a larger beam should be used.

EXAMPLE 8-7

A hem-fir joist must span 4.8 m and carry a total uniform load of 1 kN/m. Assuming that flexure controls the design, select the smallest adequate 38 × ? mm section. Use the allowable stress for repetitive members. (Note that this is a design problem as opposed to analysis or review.)

Solution:

$$M = \frac{wL^2}{8}$$

$$= \frac{1 \text{ kN/m}(4.8 \text{ m})^2}{8}$$

$$= 2.88 \text{ kN·m}$$

$$S_{required} = S_r = \frac{M}{F_b}$$

The value of allowable stress F_b from Appendix P is 9600 kPa.

$$S_r = \frac{2.88 \text{ kN·m}}{9600 \text{ kN/m}^2}$$

$$= 0.0003 \text{ m}^3$$

or

$$S_r = 300(10)^3 \text{ mm}^3$$

From Appendix Q, a 38 × 235 mm joist with an S value of $350(10)^3$ mm³ is the smallest adequate size.

Problems

8-10. Determine the maximum bending stress in a W460 × 60 steel beam that carries a midspan concentrated load of 85 kN on a simple span of 8 m.

8-11. A large steel beam simply spans 24 m and carries an applied load of 20 kN/m. Assuming that an allowable bending stress of $F_b = 165$ MPa will control the beam size, select the lightest adequate W shape. Include the effect of member self-weight.

8-12. A triangular opening in a building floor causes the total load on a W460 × 52 to be as illustrated in Figure 8-20. Determine the maximum bending stress.

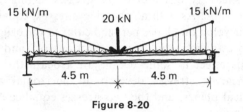

Figure 8-20

8-13. Select Douglas fir 38 × ? mm floor joists for each of the following conditions. Assume that bending will control and that repetitive member stresses apply.
(a) $w = 1$ kN/m, $L = 6$ m
(b) $w = 1$ kN/m, $L = 4$ m
(c) $w = 0.8$ kN/m, $L = 6$ m
(d) $w = 0.8$ kN/m, $L = 3$ m

8-14. Ignoring any deflection limitation and other controlling factors, how far can a W920 × 446 span before the flexural stresses from its own weight will reach an allowable value of 165 MPa?

8-15. The beam in Figure 8-21 is a hemlock 100 × 250 mm. Determine the flexural stress
(a) at the right-hand support.
(b) under the point load.
(*Hint:* Use $S = bd^2/6$.)

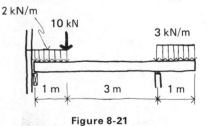

Figure 8-21

8-16. The beam in Figure 8-22 is built up of three 38 × 285 mm pieces as shown.
(a) Determine the maximum flexural stress in the upright stems.

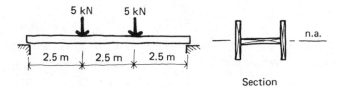

Figure 8-22. Timber beam with two point loads.

(b) Determine the maximum flexural stress in the crossweb.

(*Hint:* Use $f = My/I$ because the individual S values are not additive.)

8-5 SHEARING STRESSES DUE TO BENDING

The vertical shear force varies along the length of a beam as indicated by a V diagram. At each section the appropriate shear is distributed as stresses acting on the vertical plane. As with all shearing stresses, equal cross-shears develop on planes perpendicular to the originating ones to establish equilibrium. (Sections 6-5 and 6-6 go into this effect in some detail.) In a beam this means that shearing stresses develop on horizontal as well as vertical planes, and the two stresses equal each other at any point.

In some ways it is easier to visualize these stresses acting on horizontal planes than upon vertical ones. For example, if you make a beam by laying several planks flatwise on top of one another, there would exist horizontal slippage planes as shown in Figure 8-23. As the top fibers of each plank get shorter in compression, they have to "slip past" the bottom fibers of the plank above. The bottom fibers, in each case, are themselves getting longer because of the bending tensile strain. Now if we glued all the planks together, so as to simulate a solid one-piece cross section, there would be less deflection, and horizontal shearing stresses would develop in the glue planes. These same stresses occur in solid

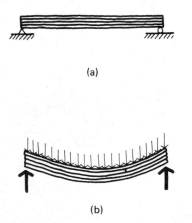

(a)

(b)

Figure 8-23. Beam made of planks.

pieces, of course, and are particularly important in the design of wood beams because most softwood shears rather easily parallel to the grain. (Examine the values given in Appendix P and see that this is reflected in the relative magnitudes of the allowable stresses. The horizontal shearing stress value F_v is quite low.)

There is a close relationship between flexural stress and shearing stress. Clearly, the slippage deformations of Figure 8-23(b) would not take place in the absence of bending. Indeed, the derivation of the general shearing stress formula in Appendix E proves that such stresses are caused by the *change* in moment from one beam section to the next. This is also implied in Chapter 7, where it is stated that the magnitude of the ordinate on the V diagram (the shear force) is equal to the slope of the moment diagram. Zero shear can only exist when the slope of the moment diagram is zero.

As explained in Chapter 6, shearing stresses cannot develop on planes parallel and close to a surface because of the absence of one of the four cross-shears needed for equilibrium. Unlike flexural stresses, shearing stresses tend to maximize near the center of a beam cross section and go to zero at the top and bottom edges. The general formula for horizontal (or vertical) shearing stress in beams is

$$f_v = \frac{VQ}{Ib} \qquad (8\text{-}4)$$

where f_v = shearing stress (Pa)

V = vertical shear force at the transverse section being examined (N)

Q = statical moment of that area of cross section between the horizontal plane under investigation and the near edge of the beam, taken with respect to the neutral axis (m³)

I = moment of inertia of the cross section with respect to the neutral axis (m⁴)

b = width of cross section at the horizontal plane under investigation (m)

The term represented by Q in the formula is not nearly so complicated as its written definition implies. Q is really nothing more than a shape factor that represents how bending forces (which cause the shear) are distributed with respect to the neutral axis. Bending stress is linear, but bending force is a function of the stressed area as well and is not linear. As illustrated in Appendix E, this will cause the shear stress in beams to vary as a square function, or parabolically, over the depth of the cross section. A few examples will illustrate this more clearly.

EXAMPLE 8-8

The 38 × 235 mm wood joist of Example 8-1 has the shear diagram shown in Figure 8-24. Determine the distribution of

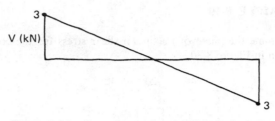

Figure 8-24. Shear diagram for wood joist in Example 8-1.

horizontal shearing stresses on a transverse section just inside either support.

Solution: The shearing force V has its maximum value of 3 kN at these two locations. For a given transverse section, V and I are constants and the shearing stress varies with the value of the ratio Q/b. For this cross section b is a constant also, so f_v will vary over the depth directly with the value of Q.

At the neutral axis, using Figure 8-25(a),

$$Q = 38(118)(59)$$
$$= 265\ 000\ \text{mm}^3$$

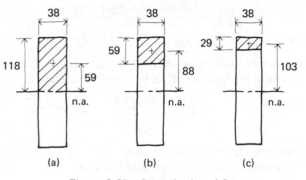

Figure 8-25. Determination of Q.

and the shearing stress will be

$$f_{v_{\text{n.a.}}} = \frac{VQ}{Ib}$$
$$= \frac{3\ \text{kN}[265(10)^{-6}\ \text{m}^3]}{[41.1(10)^{-6}\ \text{m}^4](0.038\ \text{m})}$$
$$= 509\ \text{kPa}$$

Halfway to the edge of the section, at the $d/4$ level, Q is obtained using Figure 8-25(b).

$$Q = 38(59)(88)$$
$$= 197\ 000\ \text{mm}^3$$

The shearing stress is

$$f_{v_{d/4}} = \frac{VQ}{Ib}$$
$$= \frac{3\ \text{kN}[197(10)^{-6}\ \text{m}^3]}{[41.1(10)^{-6}\ \text{m}^4](0.038\ \text{m})}$$
$$= 378\ \text{kPa}$$

At the $d/8$ level, where Q is obtained using Figure 8-25(c),

$$Q = 38(29)(103)$$
$$= 114\ 000\ \text{mm}^3$$

$$f_{v_{d/8}} = \frac{VQ}{Ib}$$
$$= \frac{3\ \text{kN}[114(10)^{-6}\ \text{m}^3]}{[41.1(10)^{-6}\ \text{m}^4](0.038\ \text{m})}$$
$$= 219\ \text{kPa}$$

The values will be identical at symmetrical levels below the neutral axis, and a plot of the shearing stress is given in Figure 8-26. The distribution would look the same at the other transverse sections of the beam, but the values would be less because of the decrease in V. Note that no sign distinction is made for shearing stress.

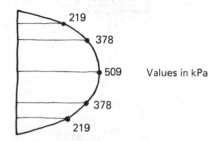

Values in kPa

Figure 8-26. Shearing stress distribution for the rectangle of Example 8-8.

EXAMPLE 8-9

Determine the shearing stress distribution for the beam in Figure 8-27.

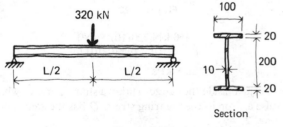

Figure 8-27

Solution: V is constant for this beam at 160 kN. I can be determined as $1320(10)^6$ mm⁴. Using Figure 8-28, Q at level 1 (the neutral axis) is found to be

$$Q = 100(10)(50) + 20(100)(110)$$
$$= 270\ 000\ \text{mm}^3$$

and

$$f_{v_1} = \frac{VQ}{Ib}$$
$$= \frac{160\ \text{kN}[270(10)^{-6}\ \text{m}^3]}{[1320(10)^{-6}\ \text{m}^4](0.010\ \text{m})}$$
$$= 3270\ \text{kPa}$$

At level 2, b remains the same but

$$Q = 20(100)(110)$$
$$= 220\ 000\ \text{mm}^3$$

and

$$f_{v_2} = \frac{VQ}{Ib}$$

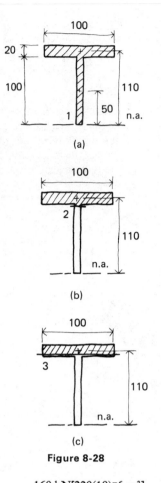

(a)

(b)

(c)

Figure 8-28

$$= \frac{160 \text{ kN}[220(10)^{-6} \text{ m}^3]}{[1320(10)^{-6} \text{ m}^4](0.010 \text{ m})}$$

$$= 2670 \text{ kPa}$$

At level 3, just inside the flange, b takes a sharp increase, which will cause a drop in the shearing stress. Q has the same value as at level 2.

$$f_{v_3} = \frac{VQ}{Ib}$$

$$= \frac{160 \text{ kN}[220(10)^{-6} \text{ m}^3]}{[1320(10)^{-6} \text{ m}^4](0.100 \text{ m})}$$

$$= 267 \text{ kPa}$$

The final distribution is shown in Figure 8-29. It varies according to the ratio Q/b.

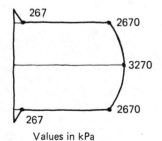

Values in kPa

Figure 8-29. Shearing stress distribution for the wide-flange shape of Example 8-9.

EXAMPLE 8-10

Determine the plane of maximum shear stress for the cross section in Figure 8-30.

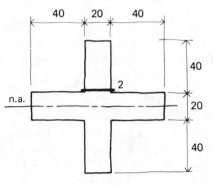

Figure 8-30. Cruciform beam cross section.

Solution: The stress will maximize at the plane where the ratio Q/b maximizes. Q will always be a maximum at the neutral axis; therefore,

$$\left(\frac{Q}{b}\right)_1 = \frac{10(100)(5) + 20(40)(30)}{100}$$

$$= 290$$

The other possible place for Q/b to reach its largest value would be at the junction of the two rectangles, plane 2.

$$\left(\frac{Q}{b}\right)_2 = \frac{20(40)(30)}{20}$$

$$= 1200$$

Clearly, the shearing stess will maximize at this junction. A distribution plot would appear as in Figure 8-31.

Figure 8-31. Qualitative shearing stress distribution for the cruciform shape of Example 8-10.

EXAMPLE 8-11

Assume that the 38×235 mm joist of Example 8-8 was fabricated from two pieces of wood as shown in Figure 8-32. If the nails are spaced every 100 mm apart, determine the shearing force on each nail. Use $V = 3$ kN as in Example 8-8.

Solution: From the work of that example, Q for that "nailed-together" plane is 114 000 mm³, and the shearing stress (that would exist in a solid piece) is 219 kPa. Each nail must take the shearing force that would be present at that

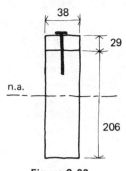

Figure 8-32

level in a 100-mm length of solid joist, as shown in Figure 8-33.

$$F = f_v A$$
$$= 219 \text{ kPa } (0.038 \text{ m})(0.100 \text{ m})$$
$$= 832 \text{ N}$$

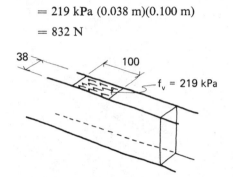

Figure 8-33. Cutaway showing the stressed area for one nail.

With reference to Figure 8-24, notice that the spacing of the nails can be farther apart as we come in from the ends of the joist. Where V is zero, no nails would be needed.

Problems

8-17. Determine the shearing stress distribution for the beam in Figure 8-5. Give values in 30-mm increments of depth.

8-18. Show by taking successive trial planes (or by the calculus) that the shearing stress of a triangular cross section, such as that of Figure 8-34, maximizes at $h/2$.

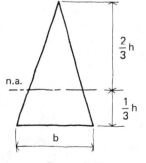

Figure 8-34

8-19. Using the beam in Figure 8-16, determine the maximum value of V and then find the corresponding value of
  (a) f_v at the n.a.
  (b) f_v on a horizontal plane taken just above or below the enclosed 38×139 mm member.

8-20. If $V = 10$ kN, plot the shearing stress distribution for the rotated square section of Figure 8-35. Give values in 30-mm increments of depth.

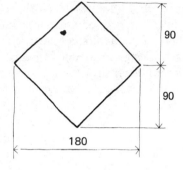

Figure 8-35

8-21. Locate the plane of maximum shearing stress for the cross section of Figure 8-36.

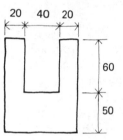

Figure 8-36. Channel shape.

8-22. If each nail in the section shown in Figure 8-37 can take 500 N of force, determine the required spacing of each set of four nails in
  (a) the left portion of the beam.
  (b) the right portion of the beam.

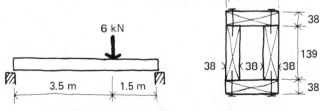

Figure 8-37. Wood box-type beam.

8-23. A Douglas fir rectangular timber 285 mm deep is used as a simple beam spanning 6 m. If the total load is a uniform 4.8 kN/m, determine the required safe minimum width.

9-1 INTRODUCTION

Certain properties of materials and unusual loading conditions can have considerable influence on beam design. In some cases these secondary or specialized considerations can outweigh the determinations of the more general aspects presented in Chapter 8. Many are of lesser consequence. This chapter is devoted to examining a few of these considerations, selected for their frequency of occurrence and/or importance. Nothing more than an overview is intended and the student should realize that further study of these factors is needed before any development of a working knowledge in beam design can be assumed. Nevertheless, such an overview in a beginning text can serve to broaden the background of information needed to make basic structural choices. Certain issues discussed will serve to answer some of the more frequently asked "what if" questions, while others will increase the general awareness of how structures behave under load.

9-2 LATERAL BUCKLING AND STABILITY

Whenever a long, slender column is loaded in compression along its axis, it tends to deflect sideways, or *buckle*. This buckling phenomenon occurs even though the stresses remain well within the elastic range of the material. It occurs rapidly once a certain critical load is reached and is a function of the modulus of elasticity and cross-sectional shape rather than of material strength. (Elastic column buckling is discussed in considerable detail in Chapter 13.) This same behavior occurs in the compression zones of long slender beams.

Whenever compressive stresses exist over a length of beam, such as in the top of a simple beam or along the bottom of a cantilever, there exists a tendency for the compressive fibers to buckle laterally or "get out of

the way of the compressive forces" (Figure 9-1). It makes no difference whether the loads are applied from above or below. The buckling is caused by the horizontal force resultant of the internal moment couple, not by the fact that loads push downward from above. Even though the tension fibers tend to remain straight, the section still undergoes a rotation or twisting action, which reduces both the effective depth and the moment of inertia.

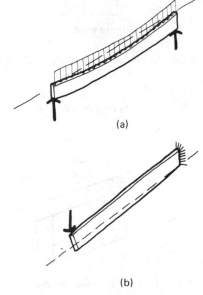

(a)

(b)

Figure 9-1. Lateral buckling.

The examples and problems presented in Chapter 8 all assumed that lateral buckling was not a factor or was prevented from happening in some manner. Certain beams are inherently stable against any lateral buckling tendency by virtue of cross-sectional shape. For example, a rectangle with a width greater than its depth and loaded vertically in a plane of symmetry will have no lateral stability problem. A wide-flange beam having a compression flange that is both wide and thick, so as

9 Special Considerations in Beam Analysis

to provide a resistance to bending in a horizontal plane, will have considerable resistance to buckling.

A beam that is not laterally stiff in cross section must be braced every so often along its compressive side in order to develop its full moment capacity. Sections not so braced or laterally supported by secondary members will fail prematurely (or at best be unsafe in terms of maintaining a proper factor of safety). Sometimes such lateral bracing occurs naturally because of other design considerations. The plywood subfloor nailed (and frequently glued) to the tops of wood joists of simple residential spans provides excellent lateral support. Open web bar joists, with their ends welded to the top flanges of the beams that carry them, provide lateral bracing for those flanges. Other situations, such as the overhanging beams of Figure 9-2, require specific bracing elements. In this case, the four beams are tied together by the spandrel channels at their ends and one bay has X-bracing (of rods or angles) connecting the critical compression flanges.

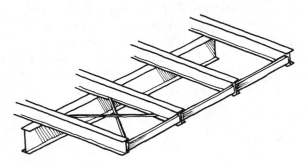

Figure 9-2. Lateral stability for overhanging steel beams.

In a few design situations it may become desirable not to use full moment capacity of a section but rather to use reduced allowable stresses (calling for lower loads or larger members) in order to maintain the same margin of safety. An excellent illustration of this approach is found in Crown Hall (on the Illinois Institute of Technology campus) by Mies van der Rohe (see Figure 9-3). Here the large clear-span steel plate girders that frame

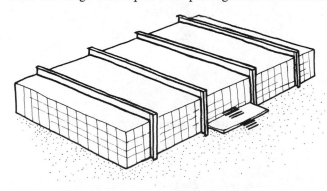

Figure 9-3. Concept sketch of Crown Hall.

the roof are exposed, with the roof deck attached to the bottom or tension flange.

Clearly, the architect desired a strong statement of the horizontal structure, achieved by exposing these girders, and was similarly not concerned by the increase in their size required by the absence of lateral support elements.

9-3 LATERAL STABILITY IN TIMBER BEAMS

Because of the infrequency of long unbraced simple spans, timber joists and small beams seldom have lateral buckling problems. They are also usually wide enough to possess sufficient stability against the buckling of the bottom edge on short cantilevers. In large deep beams, however, as might be found in glued-laminated lumber, sufficient lateral support may not be present, and the allowable bending stress must be reduced in such cases. The percent reduction depends upon the relative lack of lateral support and the dimensions of the cross section. The American Institute of Timber Construction (AITC) recommends that this reduction be a function of a *slenderness factor*, C_s.

$$C_s = \sqrt{\frac{L_e d}{b^2}} \qquad (9\text{-}1)$$

where $b =$ width of the section (m)
   $d =$ depth of the section (m)
   $L_e =$ effective unbraced length (m)

The term L_e has to do with the effectiveness of lateral bracing members and their locations, the loading pattern, and the overall buckling mode of a beam. It is usually between 1.5 and 2.0 times the actual distance between points of lateral support for the compression side of a beam. It is conservative to take L_e as being twice the distance between such points (or twice the length of a cantilever, if that be the case).

The AITC divides beams into three categories on the basis of lateral support: short, intermediate, and long. Short beams are those where $C_s < 10$ and no reduction in allowable bending stress is required. Intermediate beams are those in which C_s exceeds 10 but is less than C_k, a constant depending upon the type of wood used.

$$C_k = \sqrt{\frac{3E}{5F_b}} \qquad (9\text{-}2)$$

where $E =$ modulus of elasticity (Pa)
   $F_b =$ allowable bending stress (Pa)

If $10 < C_s < C_k$, the allowable bending stress shall be reduced to a new allowable stress, F_b', as follows:

$$F_b' = F_b\left[1 - \frac{1}{3}\left(\frac{C_s}{C_k}\right)^4\right] \qquad (9\text{-}3)$$

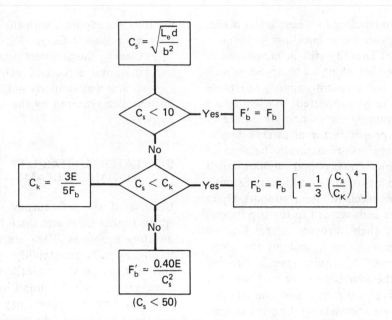

Figure 9-4. Flowchart for allowable bending stress as a function of lateral stability.

Long beams are those where the value for C_s exceeds C_k and the lateral stability problem becomes severe. In such cases, the reduced allowable stress is

$$F_b' = \frac{0.40E}{C_s^2} \qquad (9\text{-}4)$$

(C_s values above 50 are not permitted by the AITC.) Note that the allowable stress, as given by Equation (9-4), is no longer a function of material strength.

The lack of proper lateral support can have a significant effect on beam size. Equation (9-3) results in reductions in allowable stress of up to about 25%, and Equation (9-4) can result in much larger reductions. The flowchart of Figure 9-4 can help establish which equation to use, and a plot of the relative stress values is given in Figure 9-5.

The reader is referred to the *Manual of Timber Construction*, published by the AITC, for further infor-

mation on slenderness effects, particularly concerning the effective length parameter. The allowable stresses resulting from the consideration of lateral stability are subject to the usual modifications for duration of load and moisture content as outlined in Appendix P, but are not cumulative with the size-effect reductions outlined in the next section.

EXAMPLE 9-1

A glu-lam beam 130 × 457 mm is used to simply span 9 m and is laterally supported at the third points. If $F_b = 16\ 500$ kPa and $E = 12\ 400$ MPa, determine the allowable bending stress F_b' after lateral stability has been considered.

Solution: Take L_e, conservatively, as twice the distance between points of lateral support.

$$C_s = \sqrt{\frac{L_e d}{b}}$$

$$= \sqrt{\frac{(6\ \text{m})(0.457\ \text{m})}{(0.130)^2}}$$

$$= 12.7$$

$$C_k = \sqrt{\frac{3E}{5F_b}}$$

$$= \sqrt{\frac{3(12\ 400)(10)^3\ \text{kPa}}{5(16\ 500\ \text{kPa})}}$$

$$= 21.2$$

$10 < C_s < C_k$, so use Equation (9-3).

$$F_b' = F_b\left[1 - \frac{1}{3}\left(\frac{C_s}{C_k}\right)^4\right]$$

$$= 16\ 500\ \text{kPa}\left[1 - \frac{1}{3}\left(\frac{12.7}{21.2}\right)^4\right]$$

$$= 15\ 800\ \text{kPa}$$

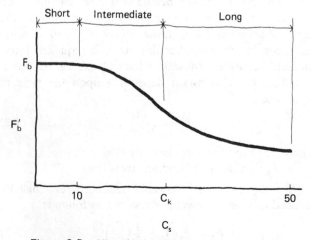

Figure 9-5. Allowable bending stress versus slenderness factor.

Problems

9-1. Determine the value of F'_b for the beam of Example 9-1 if it has lateral support only at the ends and at midspan.

9-2. A glu-lam 79 × 457 section is used as an unbraced cantilever beam 4 m long. Determine the appropriate value of F'_b. Assume that $E = 12\ 400$ MPa and $F_b = 15\ 100$ kPa.

9-4 SIZE EFFECT IN TIMBER BEAMS

Empirical studies have shown that large deep sections are subject to failure at loads slightly less than those predicted by theory. Such deep sections do not follow precisely the assumptions made regarding bending strain, on which the general flexure equation is based. Depth is not the only parameter, as this effect is also seen to increase with the span/depth ratio.

The American Institute of Timber Construction recommends a reduction in the allowable flexural stress for members deeper than 305 mm and provides a factor to accomplish this, C_f.

$$C_f = \left(\frac{305}{d}\right)^{1/9} \tag{9-5}$$

where d is the member depth (mm). When d is less than 305 mm, the value of C_f should be taken as unity.

Values of C_f, as computed by Equation (9-5) for a few depths, are presented in Table 9-1. The equation is based on test results achieved using beams having span/depth ratios of 21. When that ratio is much smaller, say 10, the values in Table 9-1 may be increased by about 3%. If the span/depth ratio is much larger, say 40, the values should be reduced by that same percentage. Straight-line interpolation may be used in the table and for the span/depth changes.

The tabulated values are also based on the assumption of uniform loading and when other loading patterns are used, the reduction factors given will be slightly in error. The reader should consult the previously cited *Manual of Timber Construction* for further information.

TABLE 9-1 *Size Factors for Deep Timber Beams*

Depth (mm)	C_f
305	1.00
381	0.98
457	0.96
533	0.94
610	0.93
686	0.91
762	0.90
838	0.89
914	0.88
1219	0.86
1524	0.84
1829	0.82

The size-factor reduction should not be applied cumulatively with the slenderness factor of the preceding article. Final allowable stresses are, of course, still subject to duration of load and moisture modifications.

Problem

9-3. For the beam in Example 9-1, show that the reduction in allowable stress due to insufficient lateral support is about the same as that for size.

9-5 COMPACTNESS IN STEEL BEAMS

As mentioned in Chapters 4 and 5, mild structural steel has a large plastic reserve capacity. The fibers do not rupture or crush after reaching the yield stress and will continue to strain, meaning that considerable deformation is observable in most steel structures before actual collapse. It has been proven by tests that the entire cross section of a steel beam will actually go into the plastic strain region without failure. A so-called "plastic hinge" develops, before failure, which has a certain "plastic moment" capacity.

Figure 9-6 shows the various stress distributions that exist in a steel beam as it is overloaded. For clarity, compressive stresses are shown to the right and tensile

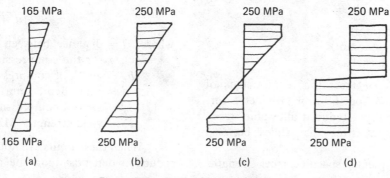

165 MPa · 250 MPa · 250 MPa · 250 MPa

165 MPa · 250 MPa · 250 MPa · 250 MPa

(a)　　　(b)　　　(c)　　　(d)

Figure 9-6. Overload in a steel beam.

stresses are plotted to the left. Figure 9-5(a) shows a distribution indicating extreme fiber stress values of 165 MPa, the highest allowable value ($\frac{2}{3}F_y$) for a steel that yields at 250 MPa. As the load increases, the extreme fibers will reach yield and then continue to strain without further increase in stress. Additional capacity, however, is developed as fibers closer to the neutral axis enter the plastic region, until finally a full plastic hinge is developed, as shown in Figure 9-6(d).

Part of the margin of safety in steel beams is contingent upon a given cross section being able to develop its full plastic moment capacity without any premature local failures. If a beam shape has long, thin projections or other elements as part of the cross section, these might be subject to elastic compression buckling, which will take place before the fibers reach yield. Such an effect is called *local buckling* and can happen to either the flanges or webs of W sections. If the dimensions of a section and the yield level of the steel are such that local buckling will not occur before the full plastic capacity can be developed, the section is said to be *compact*. If, on the other hand, local buckling failure precludes such development, the shape is said to be *noncompact*. Logically, certain beam shapes will be compact in lower strengths of steel, but noncompact when made from high-strength steel because of the potentially larger moment capacity of the stronger material. If a section is noncompact, the allowable bending stress must be reduced by up to 10% from the maximum value of $\frac{2}{3}F_y$.

The American Institute of Steel Construction (AISC) has specified how to determine compactness for a W shape. Only the more commonly applicable parameters will be given here and the reader is referred to the *Manual of Steel Construction*, published by the AISC, for a more complete treatment of this subject. In essence, a W section loaded only by transverse loads will be compact if its flanges are not too slender. (With the levels of steel strengths and shapes used currently, all sections are compact with respect to web buckling provided that there are no axial forces on the member.)

With respect to the slenderness of the compression flange, compactness requires that

$$\frac{b_f}{2t_f} \leq \frac{170}{\sqrt{F_y}} \tag{9-6}$$

where b_f = flange width (mm)
         t_f = flange thickness (mm)
         F_y = yield strength (MPa)

If a section does not meet the requirements of Equation (9-6), the AISC Specification provides a formula to determine the proper reduced allowable stress. The formula computes a stress that slides between $0.60F_y$ and $\frac{2}{3}F_y$.

The two most frequently specified steel strengths

are F_y = 250 MPa (the most common by far) and F_y = 345 MPa. Because of its low yield strength, all but one of the W shapes are compact in 250-MPa steel, and most sections remain compact even in F_y = 345-MPa steel. For this reason, it is probably easier to set F_b = $0.60F_y$ for the few shapes that do not meet the compactness criteria rather than be concerned with the above-mentioned "sliding" formula.

9-6 LATERAL STABILITY IN STEEL BEAMS

As discussed in Section 9-2, the compression side of a beam tends to buckle laterally like a slender column. Because of the greater material strength and consequently smaller cross-sectional requirements, steel beams have much greater lateral stability problems than do timber sections. Actual design situations encountered by the author have seldom called for any substantial reduction in the allowable stresses for wood beams. This is not the case with steel W shapes, however, and significant stress reductions can occur whenever the compression side lacks lateral support even for only a few meters of the span.

From the standpoint of structural efficiency and construction economy, the deeper and more narrow sections are the best selections for beam use. They have the highest section modulus and moment of inertia values per unit mass (or per unit cost since steel is sold by the kilogram). Unfortunately, these efficient shapes are the ones that behave poorly in terms of lateral stability because they have little resistance to torsion or lateral deformation. The flanges are narrow and highly stressed, and the overall section is quite deep. These factors can be seen in the AISC formulas that follow.

To ensure against the reduction of a proper factor of safety, the AISC Specification requires that the allowable bending stress be reduced below $\frac{2}{3}F_y$ for all beams in which the frequency of lateral support does not meet the following restrictions.

$$l \leq \frac{200b_f}{\sqrt{F_y}} \tag{9-7}$$

and

$$l \leq \frac{138(10)^3}{(d/A_f)F_y} \tag{9-8}$$

where l = distance between points of lateral support for the compression flange (mm)
         b_f = width of compression flange (mm)
         d = beam depth (mm)
         A_f = area of compression flange (mm²)
         F_y = yield strength (MPa)

When these limits are not met, the amount of stress reduction depends upon the properties of the section, the strength of the steel, the degree of lateral support that is present, and the variation in moment over the span. As with timber beams, it is possible to classify such beams as short, intermediate, or long, depending upon their relative slenderness and lack of lateral support. The determination of reduced allowable bending stresses as presented here is simplified somewhat and the reader should consult the AISC Specification directly for more complete information.[1]

If a beam is not braced sufficiently as indicated by Equation (9-7) or (9-8), the allowable stress drops to a maximum value of $0.60F_y$, whether the section is compact or not. This very small reduction (about 10%) is permissible only if the compression zone of the cross section has a specified resistance to lateral deformation as measured by

$$\frac{l}{r_T} \le \sqrt{\frac{703(10)^3}{F_y}} \qquad (9\text{-}9)$$

where l = distance between points of lateral support for the compression flange (mm)

r_T = radius of gyration of the compression flange plus one-third of the compression area of the web, taken about the weak axis (mm)

F_y = yield strength (MPa)

For W shapes, if the slenderness ratio l/r_T exceeds this limit, F_b will be reduced further and the situation can be classified as intermediate rather than short. *Intermediate beams* are defined as those in which the parameter l/r_T exceeds the value given by Equation (9-9) but is still less than a similar quantity which forms the boundary between intermediate and long beams. That is, for the intermediate degree of lateral support, l/r_T is bounded as follows:

$$\sqrt{\frac{703(10)^3}{F_y}} \le \frac{l}{r_T} \le \sqrt{\frac{3510(10)^3}{F_y}} \qquad (9\text{-}10)$$

If this is the case, the allowable bending stress is the larger of the two values computed by Equations (9-11) and (9-12).

$$F_b = \left[\frac{2}{3} - \frac{F_y(l/r_T)^2}{10\ 500(10)^3}\right]F_y \qquad (9\text{-}11)$$

$$F_b = \frac{82.7(10)^3}{ld/A_f} \qquad (9\text{-}12)$$

Long beams are those where l/r_T exceeds the previously given $\sqrt{3510(10)^3/F_y}$, and in such cases the allowable stresses are greatly reduced and can be taken as the larger value computed by Equations (9-12) and (9-13).

$$F_b = \frac{1170(10)^3}{(l/r_T)^2} \qquad (9\text{-}13)$$

---

[1]For example, the variation in moment term C_b has been deleted from this presentation.

Notice that the allowable stress as determined by the equations for long beams is no longer a function of the material strength.

Equations (9-11) and (9-13), for intermediate and long beams, respectively, give the permissible bending stress to avoid failure by lateral deformation of the compression flange. (This is why they contain the term r_T.) Equation (9-12), on the other hand, is an expression dealing more with the torsional stiffness of the cross section and its contribution to lateral stability. For both the intermediate and long categories of lateral support, the Specification indicates taking the larger of two values as the allowable bending stress. Since it is normal to think of the smaller of two allowable values as controlling or being more restrictive, a note of explanation is in order. These equations are gross simplifications of much more complicated theoretical and empirical expressions which predict different types of failure due to lateral instability. Because each equation applies to a large range of support and rigidity conditions, it becomes more accurate in some cases than in others. In general, the formulas have been developed so that as any one equation becomes less accurate, the error occurs in the conservative direction. This means, in effect, that the larger of the two values computed will be more correct. In each case the constant in the equation is such that length quantities can be used in units of mm and the stress values will be in MPa.

The reader should notice the similarities between the treatment of laterally unsupported timber and steel beams. The wood parameter C_s (defined as $\sqrt{L_e d/b^2}$) serves the same function as that of l/r_T for steel. The boundary between the intermediate and long ranges is $\sqrt{3E/5F_b}$ for wood and $\sqrt{3510(10)^3/F_y}$ for steel. Quite logically, that important measure of buckling resistance, E, appears in the wood equations because it varies by species, and is numerically hidden in the steel equations because it has the same value for all rolled steels.

The flowchart of Figure 9-7 and the graph of Figure 9-8 should help to reduce some of the confusion produced by the many different equations. In actual engineering design work such equations are seldom used directly because of the many design aids available. For example, the *Manual of Steel Construction* contains quantitative curves similar to Figure 9-8 for each beam shape and two different steel strengths.

EXAMPLE 9-2

A 12-m-long steel girder must carry concentrated loads at the third points. If lateral bracing can only be supplied at the load points, determine the proper allowable bending stress for the cross section in Figure 9-9. Assume that $F_y = 250$ MPa.

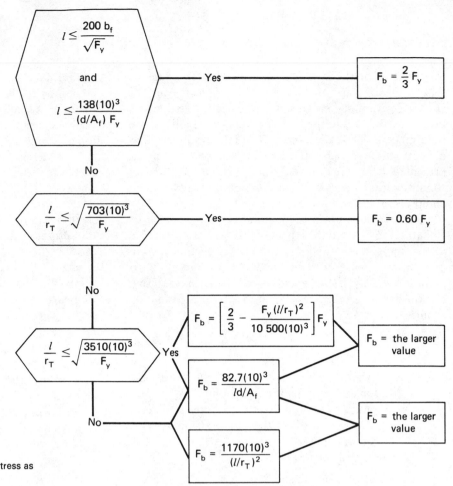

$$l \le \frac{200\,b_f}{\sqrt{F_y}}$$

and

$$l \le \frac{138(10)^3}{(d/A_f)\,F_y}$$

Yes → $F_b = \frac{2}{3}\,F_y$

No

$$\frac{l}{r_T} \le \sqrt{\frac{703(10)^3}{F_y}}$$

Yes → $F_b = 0.60\,F_y$

No

$$\frac{l}{r_T} \le \sqrt{\frac{3510(10)^3}{F_y}}$$

Yes → $F_b = \left[\frac{2}{3} - \frac{F_y\,(l/r_T)^2}{10\,500(10)^3} \right] F_y$ → F_b = the larger value

$$F_b = \frac{82.7(10)^3}{l d/A_f}$$

No → $F_b = \frac{1170(10)^3}{(l/r_T)^2}$ → F_b = the larger value

Figure 9-7. Flow chart for allowable bending stress as a function of lateral stability.

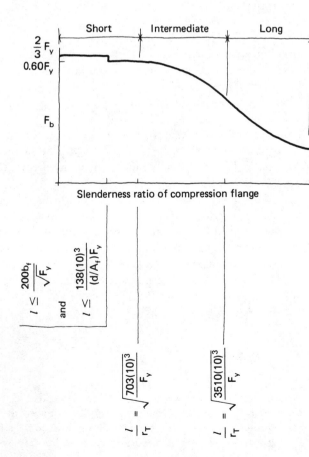

Figure 9-8. Allowable bending stress versus slenderness ratio.

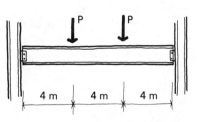

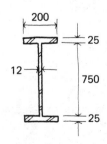

Figure 9-9

116

Solution: Following the flowchart of Figure 9-7,

$$\frac{200 b_f}{\sqrt{F_y}} = \frac{200(200)}{\sqrt{250}} = 2530$$

$$\frac{138(10)^3}{(d/A_f)F_y} = \frac{138(10)^3}{(800/5000)(250)} = 3450$$

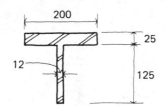

Figure 9-10. Area needed for determining r_T.

For our case $l = 4000$ mm, so neither criterion is met when both must be to avoid bending stress reduction.

$$r_T = \sqrt{\left(\frac{I}{A_T}\right)}$$

$$I_T = \left(\frac{bh^3}{12}\right)_{\text{flange}} + \left(\frac{bh^3}{12}\right)_{\text{web}}$$

$$= \frac{25(200)^3}{12} + \frac{125(12)^3}{12}$$

$$= 16.7(10)^6 \text{ mm}^4$$

$$A_T = (bh)_{\text{flange}} + (bh)_{\text{web}}$$

$$= 25(200) + 12(125)$$

$$= 6500 \text{ mm}^2$$

$$r_T = \sqrt{\frac{16.7(10)^6 \text{ mm}^4}{6500 \text{ mm}^2}}$$

$$= 50.7 \text{ mm}$$

$$\frac{l}{r_T} = \frac{4000 \text{ mm}}{50.7 \text{ mm}}$$

$$= 78.9$$

Comparing this ratio to the specified limit of

$$\sqrt{\frac{703(10)^3}{F_y}} = \sqrt{\frac{703(10)^3}{250}} = 53.0$$

We find that $l/r_T = 78.9$, which is larger than 53.0, and therefore our situation falls outside the short region. The upper limit for l/r_T in the intermediate region is

$$\sqrt{\frac{3510(10)^3}{F_y}} = \sqrt{\frac{3510(10)^3}{250}} = 118$$

and since this is larger than our l/r_T of 78.9, our case is intermediate, not long. Checking the two applicable equations for this region,

$$F_b = \left[\frac{2}{3} - \frac{F_y(l/r_T)^2}{10\,500(10)^3}\right]F_y \quad \text{and} \quad F_b = \frac{82.7(10)^3}{ld/A_f}$$

$$= \left[\frac{2}{3} - \frac{250(78.9)^2}{10\,500(10)^3}\right]250 \qquad = \frac{82.7(10)^3}{(4000)(800)/5000}$$

$$= 130 \text{ MPa} \qquad = 129 \text{ MPa}$$

Since the specification permits us to use the larger of the two values, $F_b = 130$ MPa.

Problems

9-4. Using the beam of Example 9-2, determine the allowable bending stress if the concentrated loads come from columns that provide no lateral support (i.e., $l = 12\,000$ mm).

9-5. Determine the maximum permissible magnitude of the loads P in
(a) Example 9-2.
(b) Problem 9-4.

9-6. A wide-flange beam frames across an open well in a building and is loaded as shown in Figure 9-11. Determine if a W410 × 67 of $F_y = 250$-MPa steel is sufficient under these conditions. Use $d = 410$ mm, $b_f = 179$ mm, $r_T = 47.0$ mm, and $A_f = 2555$ mm².

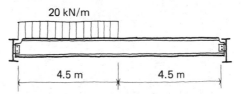

20 kN/m

4.5 m   4.5 m

Figure 9-11. Partially loaded steel beam.

9-7 ALLOWABLE BENDING STRESSES ABOVE $\frac{2}{3}F_y$

The AISC Specification permits an allowable bending stress of $0.75F_y$ on solid, square, and circular sections and on solid rectangles bent about a minor axis. Compact W shapes can also be stressed to $0.75F_y$ if they are loaded in bending about a minor axis. This increase is permitted because such shapes have considerably more plastic reserve strength when turned on their sides. In this position they also have little tendency to twist or buckle laterally.

9-8 HORIZONTAL SHEARING STRESSES IN TIMBER BEAMS

The general expression for stress due to bending is $f_v = VQ/Ib$, as presented in Section 8-5. For a rectangular section, as most timber beams are, the maximum value of shearing stress occurs at the neutral axis. Since Q and I can both be expressed in terms of b and d for a rectangular section, a simpler expression for this maximum f_v can be developed.

$$f_{v_{\text{max}}} = \frac{VQ_{\text{max}}}{Ib}$$

$$Q_{\text{max}} = b\left(\frac{d}{2}\right)\left(\frac{d}{4}\right)$$

$$= \frac{bd^2}{8}$$

$$I = \frac{bd^3}{12}$$

$$= \frac{Vbd^2(12)}{bd^3(8)b}$$

$$bd = A$$

$$= \frac{3V}{2A} \qquad (9\text{-}14)$$

From Equation (9-14), the maximum shearing stress is 50% larger than the average value, which can be represented by a rectangular block. The total shearing force resistance or shear capacity is stress times area, and this is represented as a volume in Figure 9-12. The area under a parabola is $\frac{2}{3}$ the base times the height, so its altitude must be 50% greater to achieve a "stress volume" equal to a rectangular volume.

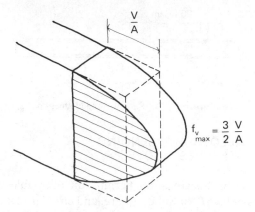

Figure 9-12. Shearing stress distribution.

From previous work it is known that the maximum value of shearing force will usually occur at a reaction. Local compressive forces due to the transfer of the load to the support are also very high at this point and test results have shown that shear failures will almost never occur at or adjacent to a support. Accordingly, the American Institute of Timber Construction permits us to ignore all stationary loads within a distance from the support equal to the depth of the beam, when calculating the reactive force V (Figure 9-13). The design value of V, then, for a uniform load will not be $V = wL/2$ but can be expressed as

$$V = \frac{wL}{2}\left(1 - \frac{2d}{L}\right) \qquad (9\text{-}15)$$

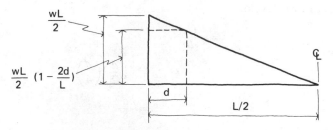

Figure 9-13. Permissible reduction in V.

This provision is of more importance whenever a large concentrated load falls close to a support. In the absence of this reduction, such loads, which generate little moment or deflection, would almost certainly cause the beam size to be controlled by shear. Likewise, it can be helpful to apply this reduction to the interior supports of continuous beams, where the shear forces tend to build up because of the negative moments. (This is discussed in Chapter 15.)

(Loads on reinforced concrete beams within d distance of a support can also be neglected in shear because the buildup of local compressive stresses helps to resist the opening of diagonal tension cracks. The provision does not apply to steel sections, however, where overload in shear can result in diagonal buckling of the web, a compression failure.)

EXAMPLE 9-3

A hem-fir 89×185 mm beam spans 3.5 m and supports a uniform load of 3 kN/m. Is it adequate in shear?

$$V = \frac{wL}{2}\left(1 - \frac{2d}{L}\right)$$

$$= \frac{(3 \text{ kN/m})(3.5 \text{ m})}{2}\left[1 - \frac{2(0.185 \text{ m})}{3.5 \text{ m}}\right]$$

$$= 4.70 \text{ kN}$$

$$f_v = \frac{3V}{2A}$$

$$A = 16\ 500 \text{ mm}^2$$

$$= \frac{3(4.70 \text{ kN})}{2(0.0165 \text{ m}^2)}$$

$$= 427 \text{ kPa}$$

From Appendix P the allowable shear stress for hem-fir is 500 kPa, so the section is adequate in shear.

Problems

9-7. The beam in Figure 9-14 is a doubled 38×185 mm section of Douglas fir. Is it adequate in shear?

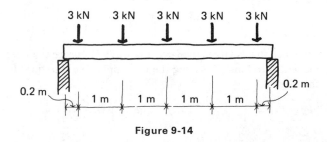

Figure 9-14

9-8. A uniformly loaded southern pine joist must span 5 m and carry a total load of 0.8 kN/m. Will a 38×235 mm section be OK in shear?

9-9. (a) Determine the design value of the vertical shear force V, if the depth of the joist in Figure 9-15 is estimated at 285 mm.

(b) Compute the corresponding shear stress if a 38 × 285 is used.

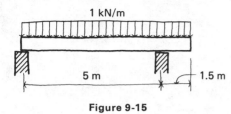

Figure 9-15

9-9 HORIZONTAL SHEARING STRESSES IN STEEL BEAMS

As developed in Chapter 8, the distribution of shearing stresses in a W shape is as shown in Figure 9-16. Almost all of the shearing force is resisted by stresses in the web, and very little work is done by the flanges—the opposite, of course, being the case for flexural stresses. The calculation of the exact maximum stress magnitude using

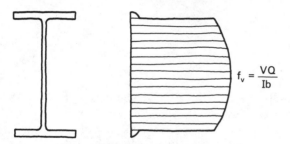

Figure 9-16. Shearing stress distribution in a wide-flange beam.

VQ/Ib can become difficult because of the presence of fillets where the flanges join the web. A high level of accuracy is even harder to achieve in channels or I shapes which have sloping flange surfaces. Accordingly, the American Institute of Steel Construction recommends the use of a much simpler approximate formula for the common steel shapes.

$$f_v = \frac{V}{th} \qquad (9\text{-}16)$$

where t = web thickness (m)

h = total beam depth (m)

This formula gives the average unit shearing stress for the web over the full beam depth, ignoring any contribution of the flange projections (Figure 9-17). Depending upon the particular steel shape, this formula can be as much as 20% in error in the nonconservative direction. This means that when a shearing stress computed by

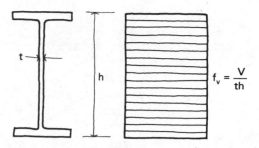

Figure 9-17. Simplified shearing stress distribution.

Equation (9-16) gets to within 20% of the maximum allowable stress, the actual maximum stress (computable by VQ/Ib) might be exceeding the allowable by a small amount.

Fortunately, this low level of accuracy is seldom a problem for two reasons:

1. Structural steel is very strong in shear.
2. Most beams and girders in buildings, unlike those in some machines, have very low shearing stresses.

A rolled steel beam has to be very short and very heavily loaded, or have a large concentrated load adjacent to a support, in order for shear to control. In determining the size of a steel beam, flexural stresses will usually govern. Excessive deflection will occasionally dictate the use of a larger section, but shear will almost never govern the design.

When shearing stresses do become excessive, steel beams do not fail by ripping along the neutral axis as might happen in wood. Rather, it is the compression buckling of the relatively thin web which constitutes a shear failure. This can be diagonal buckling, as discussed in Chapter 6, or a type of vertical buckling, illustrated in Figure 9-18. The AISC has provided several design formulas for determining when extra bearing area must be provided at concentrated loads or when web stiffeners are needed to prevent such failures (Figure 9-19).

Most beams of normal depth seldom present any major problems, and detailed design considerations will not be given here. A word of caution is given with respect to large built-up plate girders, however. Such sections usually have deep thin webs and are particularly susceptible to buckling action. For these beams, shear can be

Figure 9-18. Web buckling in steel beams.

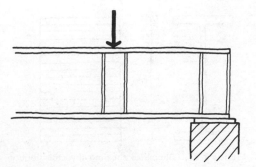

Figure 9-19. Bearing plate and web stiffeners.

a determining factor in the overall structural design. The reader may wish to consult the *Manual of Steel Construction* for further material on web buckling.

EXAMPLE 9-4

Determine the average shearing stress for the W460 × 89 beam in Figure 9-20 if $V = 100$ kN.

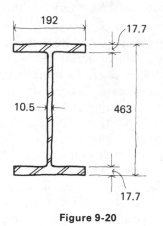

Figure 9-20

Solution:

$$f_v = \frac{V}{th}$$

$$= \frac{100 \text{ kN}}{(0.0105 \text{ m})(0.463 \text{ m})}$$

$$= 20\ 600 \text{ kPa}$$

or

$$f_v = 20.6 \text{ MPa}$$

Problems

9-10. Ignoring the fillets, determine the percentage error that accrues by using the average shearing stress formula instead of the exact one for the beam in Example 9-4.

9-11. A W760 × 257 of $F_y = 250$-MPa steel has been selected for the beam in Figure 9-21. The actual bending stress is very close to the maximum allowable bending stress. The allowable in shear is 100 MPa. If $h = 773$ mm and $t = 16.6$ mm, determine the average shearing stress.

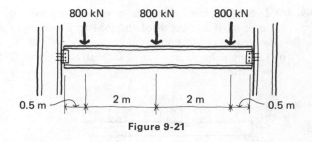

Figure 9-21

9-10 FORCES IN BEAMS ON A PITCH

Beams such as those illustrated in Figure 9-22 occur commonly in roof construction and are usually subject to uniform loads from snow and wind. (Design considerations of wind loads are discussed in Chapter 16.) Loads from snow are uniform along the horizontal projection of the span and are different from dead loads, such as the roof deck, which are uniform along the sloped length. A very steep roof has little projected plan area but may have a high dead load per unit run of horizontal span.

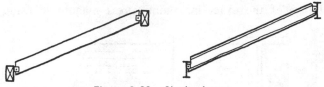

Figure 9-22. Sloping beams.

In Figure 9-23, a convenient angle of slope has been chosen to show the difference between load on a slope and load on the projection. Assume that the spacing of the roof beams is such that the snow load is 2 kN per meter of horizontal projection, for a total load of 8 kN. Likewise, take the structural dead load of the roof, including an allowance for beam self-weight, as 2 kN per meter of sloped length, for a total of 10 kN. Both loads are gravity loads and act vertically downward, so each reaction will be 9 kN upward. If the beams are supported equally by girders at each end as in Figure 9-22, there

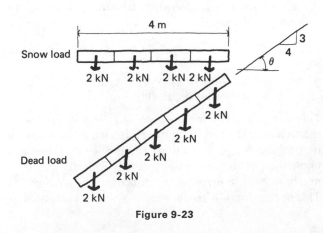

Figure 9-23

will be no horizontal thrust, only down load. To illustrate that this is the case, we will break the load into components that act perpendicularly and tangentially to the beam. The snow load, if spread over the sloped length, will be 8 kN/5 m or 1.6 kN/m. Adding this to the dead load, the total load per meter of slope will then be 3.6 kN, as in Figure 9-24(a). If this value is broken into com-

ponents as in Figure 9-24(b), these components will sum to perpendicular and tangential reactions at each end of the span as shown in Figure 9-24(c). The resultant of these two reactions is, of course, vertical as in Figure 9-24(d) and equal to the originally computed 9 kN.

The transverse forces will cause the usual shears and moments, and the axial forces, in this case, will cause tension in the top half of the beam and compression in the lower half. These axial forces maximize at the ends for the uniform load of our example. (Generally, the axial stresses from such forces are negligible compared to the bending stresses and may be ignored. However, this would not be the case with heavy dead loads on steep angles. In such cases, the axial stresses should be accounted for and added to the bending stresses as explained in Section 12-1.)

The maximum bending moment will occur at midspan and be figured from the uniform load of 2.88 kN/m on a 5-m span.

$$M = \frac{wL^2}{8}$$

$$= \frac{[2.88 \text{ kN/m}](5 \text{ m})^2}{8}$$

$$= 9 \text{ kN} \cdot \text{m}$$

Alternatively, this value could have been achieved more simply by figuring all the loads to act on a horizontal projection with a span of 4 m. The dead load will be 10 kN/4 m or 2.5 kN/m. The total load per meter of horizontal projection will then be 4.5 kN/m. The value of M in Figure 9-25 can be computed by taking moments about the cut section,

$$M = 9(2) - 4.5(2)(1)$$
$$= 9 \text{ kN} \cdot \text{m}$$

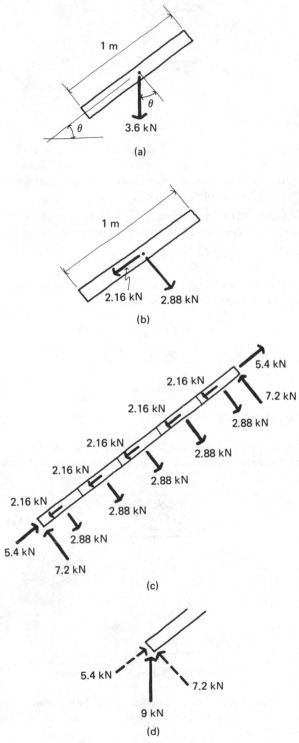

(a)

(b)

(c)

(d)

Figure 9-24. Sloped beam components.

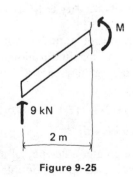

Figure 9-25

or from the formula

$$M = \frac{wL^2}{8}$$

$$= \frac{[4.5 \text{ kN/m}](4 \text{ m})^2}{8}$$

$$= 9 \text{ kN} \cdot \text{m}$$

The resolution of forces is not so straightforward if the sloping surfaces are configured to carry load by the development of a horizontal thrust. If there is no beam at the top end to provide the vertical reactive force, horizontal forces must be present. This situation might be typified by a residential attic space as illustrated in Figure 9-26, where the ridge member has a negligible capacity. In such cases, the attic floor serves as a tensile

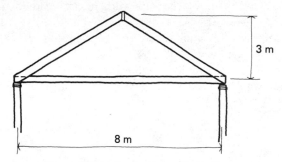

Figure 9-26. Roof rafters and attic tie.

tie to resist the outward thrust of the rafters and the structure acts like a simple truss. Using the numbers from our previous shed roof beam and the free-body diagram of Figure 9-27, we can solve for the V and H

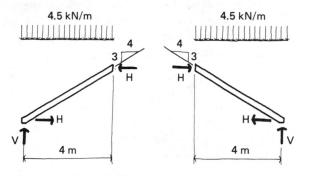

Figure 9-27. Free-body diagrams.

forces by the equations of statics. V will be 18 kN and H will equal 12 kN. The maximum moment will again be at midspan and taking moments at the cut section of Figure 9-28, we get

$$M = 18(2) - 12(1.5) - 4.5(2)(1)$$

$$= 9 \text{ kN} \cdot \text{m}$$

This illustrates the greater efficiency of a gable roof with a tie over a shed roof; the span is double yet the moment is no greater. Of course, the effective structural depth is much greater because the clear ceiling volume is interrupted by the tie beams.

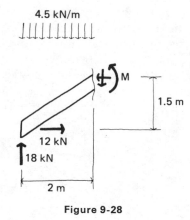

Figure 9-28

EXAMPLE 9-5

A shed roof has a 4-on-10 slope over a horizontal span of 6 m. Determine the maximum moment in a roof beam if the snow load is 4 kN/m of horizontal projection and the dead load is 2.5 kN/m of roof slope.

Solution: The hypotenuse of a 4-on-10 triangle is 10.77, so the unit dead load on the horizontal projection will be

$$\frac{10.77}{10}(2.5) = 2.69 \text{ kN/m}$$

Adding the snow load, we get a total uniform load on the horizontal projection of 6.69 kN/m.

$$M = \frac{wL^2}{8}$$

$$= \frac{[6.7 \text{ kN/m}](6 \text{ m})^2}{8}$$

$$= 30 \text{ kN} \cdot \text{m}$$

EXAMPLE 9-6

The roof rafters of Figure 9-29 carry a total load 1 kN/m on the horizontal projection. Determine the thrust in the collar beam.

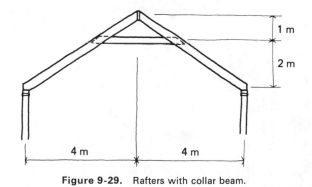

Figure 9-29. Rafters with collar beam.

Solution: Each vertical reaction is one-half the total load, or 4 kN. Taking moments about the ridge line in Figure 9-30, we get

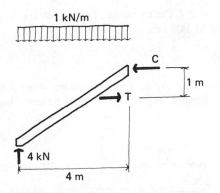

Figure 9-30. Free-body diagram.

$$\Sigma M_{r.l.} = 0$$

$$T(1) + 4(1)(2) - 4(4) = 0$$

$$T = 8 \text{ kN}$$

Problems

9-12. For the shed roof of Example 9-5, if the unit loads and span remain the same, determine the maximum moment if the slope is
(a) 8 on 10.
(b) 2 on 10.

9-13. The roof rafters in Figure 9-31 are supported by a wall that runs down the center of the building. The snow load is 1.5 kN/m² of horizontal plan and the dead load is 1.0 kN/m² of sloped roof. Determine the horizontal thrust that each rafter will exert at the top of an outer wall if the central partition is accidentally removed.

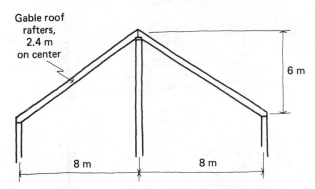

Figure 9-31. Gable with central support.

9-14. Determine the maximum bending moment in the rafters of Example 9-6 if
(a) the collar beam is located as it is in Figure 9-29.
(b) the collar beam is moved to the eave height.
(c) the collar beam is moved to the ridge height, in effect "fixing" the ridge joint.

9-11 BEAMS OF VARIABLE MOMENT OF INERTIA

In some instances, it is desirable to change the cross section of a beam within a given span length. This can be done for many reasons, such as efficiency, aesthetics, and construction ease. In most cases, the problem is easily handled if we remember that stresses vary with changes in section modulus (or moment of inertia) just as they vary with moment. This means that bending stress will not necessarily maximize where the moment maximizes. Some combination of lesser moment at a smaller cross section may provide the critical combination.

(It is worth noting that, while the moment diagram for determinate structures is independent of the beam rigidity (*EI*), this is not the case with indeterminate structures. Chapter 15 shows how heavier cross sections will take more moment, relieving the stresses in sections of less capacity. It is in such structures that variable cross sections may be used to advantage by distributing the stresses more evenly throughout the members.)

A simple way to guard against possible overstress is to check the stresses at various intervals. Whenever a beam undergoes an abrupt change of cross section, the designer can suspect that stresses might maximize there. If appropriate, the effects of stress concentration discussed in Section 5-7, may also need to be considered at that point.

Beam cross sections that undergo gradual changes by tapering or gentle curvature can usually be treated with standard formulas (i.e., ignoring the possible effects of having a sloping edge at a given section). Use of the regular formulas on beams that taper or change rapidly can result in considerable error, however, and some form of curved beam theory should be used to investigate the stresses. (Curved-beam theory involves transverse sections that do not remain plane, and will not be considered in this text. The reader may wish to consult an engineering text on strength of materials for a proper approach to such problems.)

Beams that have variable cross sections develop stresses in one significant way that straight beams do not—the shear stress will usually not go to zero at the sloping edge. The derivation of the general shearing stress formula as given in Appendix E makes use of an element placed in an unbalanced state of forces by changing moment. The horizontal shearing force that restores the element to equilibrium cannot be provided at an edge because of a lack of material at that point. However, there is material at the "edge" in the case of a tapered beam and the shearing stresses need not go to zero (Figure 9-32).

This can be a particular problem with rectangular

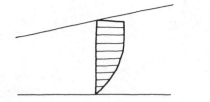

Figure 9-32. Shearing stress distribution in a tapered beam.

or other nonflanged sections, where the stresses might be highest at an edge. (Sections such as W shapes usually have thin webs, which ensure that the shearing stresses will maximize in the web rather than at a top or bottom edge.) When the shearing and bending stresses maximize at the same fiber in a cross section, they can combine to produce tensile and compressive stresses which are higher than those due to bending alone. Such combinations are called *principal stresses* and are treated briefly in Chapter 12, but it is sufficient here to be aware of the problem (i.e., to recognize that stresses found by Mc/I may not be the maximum normal stresses).

EXAMPLE 9-7

Determine the maximum bending stress in the beam of Figure 9-33. The section is cut from a 139×285 mm member and tapers to a depth of 160 mm at the small end.

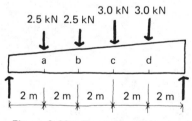

Figure 9-33. Tapered wood beam.

Solution: Check the bending stress by the select-and-try process at the load points. Establish the beam depth at those points by proportion and compute the various section modulus values by $S = bd^2/6$.

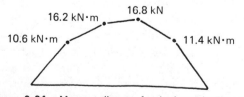

Figure 9-34. Moment diagram for the beam in Figure 9-33.

TABLE 9-2 *Data for Example 9-7*

Section	Depth (mm)	S (10^3 mm^3)	M (kN·m)	f_b (kPa)
(a)	185	793	10.6	13 400
(b)	210	1020	16.2	15 900
(c)	235	1280	16.8	13 100
(d)	260	1570	11.4	7 260

From Table 9-2, the maximum bending stress occurs at point (b) and is 15 900 kPa.

Problems

9-15. Determine the maximum bending stress for the W460 $\times$ 68 beam with the rectangular hole in Figure 9-35.

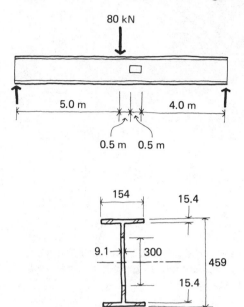

Figure 9-35. Steel beam with a hole cut for a mechanical duct.

9-16. The steel beam of Figure 9-36 was made by cutting a W shape longitudinally and then welding it end for end. Determine the maximum bending stresses at 1-m intervals of span. The web is 10 mm thick and each flange is 16 mm by 100 mm.

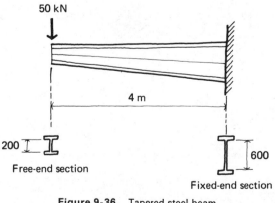

Figure 9-36. Tapered steel beam.

9-12 SHEAR CENTER

One of the assumptions made in deriving the general flexural stress equation in Appendix D is that the loading of the beam was such that no twisting occurs. This implies a plane of loading that passes through an axis

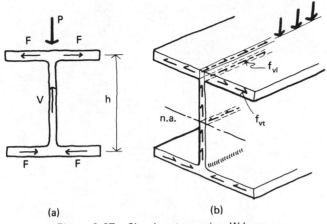

(a)   (b)

Figure 9-37. Shearing stresses in a W beam.

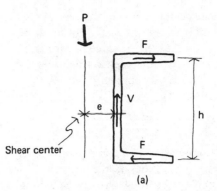

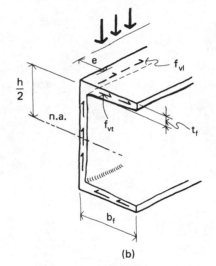

Figure 9-38. Shearing stresses in a channel.

of symmetry. A look at the shearing stresses in Figure 9-37(b) will prove why there is no tendency to twist with this kind of loading. The stresses labeled f_{vl} occur on vertical planes in the flanges as required for equilibrium due to varying bending stresses along the beam length (see Appendix E). As usual, there is the equal accompanying shear, f_{vt}, on the orthogonal, transverse planes. These f_{vt} stresses act over an area of the flange creating a force, called F in Figure 9-37(a). These forces, in turn, act as opposing couples that equate each other so that no twisting occurs. In a channel shape, on the other hand, only one of the couples is present and the load P should be placed out of the plane of the web, as in Figure 9-38(a), in order to keep the section from twisting. For equilibrium

$$Pe = Ve = Fh \qquad (9-17)$$

The point located by the distance e, which represents the intersection of the loading plane and the neutral plane, is called the *shear center*.

Making a few approximations, it is easy to determine the magnitude of the distance e needed to avoid twist in a given channel. First, solve for the longitudinal shearing stress, f_{vl}, by using VQ/Ib. To make the determination of Q easier, we shall assume that the distance between the center lines of the two flanges, h, is the same as the overall depth.

$$f_{vl} = \frac{VQ}{Ib}$$

where Q = statical moment of the flange taken about the n.a., $Q = b_f t_f (h/2)$

b = width or thickness of the stressed element (t_f in this case)

$$f_{vl} = \frac{V b_f t_f}{I t_f} \frac{h}{2}$$

$$f_{vl} = \frac{V b_f h}{2I} \qquad (9-18)$$

This is equal to the transverse stress, 90° away, which causes the twisting force F.

$$f_{vt} = \frac{V b_f h}{2I}$$

The magnitude of F can be obtained by noting that f_{vl} (also f_{vt}) varies linearly from zero at the outstanding edge of the flange to a maximum at the root or junction with the web. This variation must be linear because the only item that can change in Equation (9-18) is the amount of flange width b_f accumulated as we move toward the web.

$$F = \tfrac{1}{2} f_{vt} b_f t_f$$

(This assumes with slight error, that f_{vt} is constant over the flange thickness.) Substituting for f_{vt}, we get

$$F = \frac{V b_f^2 t_f h}{4I}$$

Using this evaluation of F in Equation (9-17), where we will let V be the entire shearing force, gives us

$$Ve = \frac{V b_f^2 h^2 t_f}{4I}$$

Solving for e, we obtain

$$e = \frac{b_f^2 h^2 t_f}{4I}$$

The shear center for other shapes having no vertical plane of symmetry may be located by similar techniques. It may be proven that the shear center for the H shape of Figure 9-39(a) is located closer to the larger flange by the ratio of the moments of inertia of the flanges,

$$\frac{x_1}{x_2} = \frac{I_2}{I_1}$$

Similarly, with the shapes of Figure 9-39(b) and (c), the plane of loading should lie within the vertical element, as the moment of inertia of the horizontal leg can be considered negligible. It is theoretically interesting to note that the shear center for any cross section composed of linear elements that intersect at a common point (such

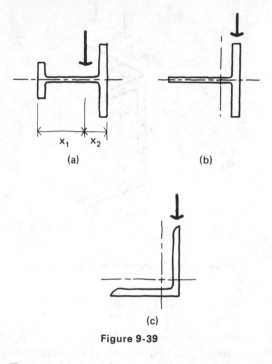

(a)   (b)

(c)

Figure 9-39

as the T or angle) must be located at the point of intersection. This remains true even if the section is rotated and can be illustrated by making the appropriate shear force sketches such as that of Figure 9-38(a). It will be clear that, if no twist is desired, the plane of loading cannot be eccentric with respect to the point of force concurrency.

While the shear center for an angle is located at its corner, this does not mean that the ideal loading position is one with the legs horizontal and vertical. In fact, the major and minor bending axes (called *principal axes*) for a single L shape will be at some angle with the legs. Since it is seldom practical to tilt such angles, they are quite difficult to load so that they comply with bending theory. Loaded by P_1 the angle in Figure 9-40 will twist; loaded by P_2 it will deflect laterally along a $y'y'$ axis.

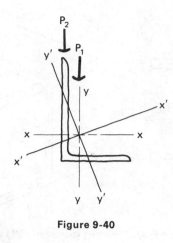

Figure 9-40

The equal leg angle of Figure 9-41 is shown loaded along its principal axes, which are at 45° to the legs. The loading in (a) will tend to twist the angle, whereas that of (b) will not.

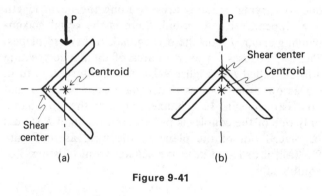

(a)   (b)

Figure 9-41

Problems

9-17. Locate the shear center, by determining e, for each of the channels in Figure 9-42.

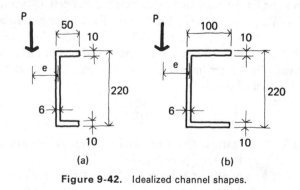

(a)   (b)

Figure 9-42. Idealized channel shapes.

9-18. A lintel beam section built up from two channels has been idealized in Figure 9-43(b). Locate the shear center by using the approximate methods of the preceding section.

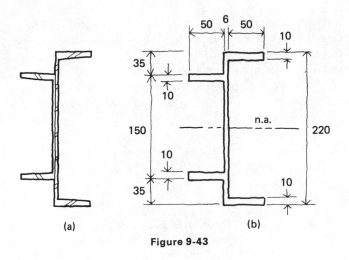

Figure 9-43

9-13 LOADS ACTING AT ANGLES TO THE PRINCIPAL AXES

A rectangular section, loaded through its centroid but at an angle to the principal axes, is shown in Figure 9-44. The bending stress distribution may be readily determined by using the x and y components of the moment provided by the vertical loading such that

$$f_b = \left(\frac{Mc}{I}\right)_x \pm \left(\frac{Mc}{I}\right)_y \qquad (9\text{-}19)$$

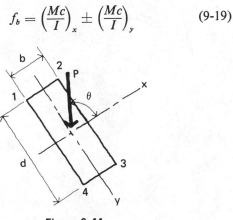

Figure 9-44

The maximum compression will be at point 2 and the maximum tension will occur at point 4.

EXAMPLE 9-8

Let the member of Figure 9-44 be an 89×185 mm section subjected to a moment of 4 kN·m acting at an angle of $\theta = 70°$. Determine the extreme fiber stresses and the location of the neutral plane.

Solution:

$$M_x = M \sin\theta \qquad M_y = M \cos\theta$$
$$= 4(0.940) \qquad\quad = 4(0.342)$$
$$= 3.76 \text{ kN·m} \qquad = 1.37 \text{ kN·m}$$

From Appendix Q,

$$I_x = 47.0(10)^6 \text{ mm}^4 \qquad I_y = 10.9(10)^6 \text{ mm}^4$$

$$f_b = \pm\left(\frac{Mc}{I}\right)_x \pm \left(\frac{Mc}{I}\right)_y$$

At a given point the sign will be plus or minus, depending upon whether the moment causes tension or compression, respectively.

At point 1,

$$f_b = -\frac{3.76 \text{ kN·m}(0.093 \text{ m})}{47.0(10)^{-6} \text{ m}^4} + \frac{1.37 \text{ kN·m}(0.045 \text{ m})}{10.9(10)^{-6} \text{ m}^4}$$

$$= -7440 \text{ kPa} + 5660 \text{ kPa}$$

$$= 1780 \text{ kPa compression}$$

At the other points the same two numerical values are combined. At point 2,

$$f_b = -7440 \text{ kPa} - 5660 \text{ kPa}$$

$$= 13\ 100 \text{ kPa compression}$$

At point 3,

$$f_b = +7440 \text{ kPa} - 5660 \text{ kPa}$$

$$= 1780 \text{ kPa tension}$$

At point 4,

$$f_b = +7440 \text{ kPa} + 5660 \text{ kPa}$$

$$= 13\ 000 \text{ kPa tension}$$

Since all of the bending stresses vary linearly, the points of intersection of the neutral plane with the sides of the beam may be determined by ratio. With respect to Figure 9-45,

$$\frac{p}{q} = \frac{p}{185 - p} = \frac{13\ 100}{1780}$$

$$p = 163 \text{ mm}$$

and

$$q = 185 - 163 = 22 \text{ mm}$$

Also from Figure 9-45,

$$\tan\phi = \frac{(163 - 185/2)}{89/2}$$

$$= 1.58$$

$$\phi \approx 58°$$

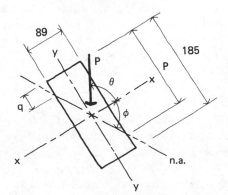

Figure 9-45. Neutral plane for the angled load of Figure 9-44.

Note that the angle ϕ, in general, is not the complement of the angle θ. The beam is bending about an axis that makes an angle of 58° with the horizontal and will deflect downward and to the left as it bends. This behavior is called *biaxial bending*.

The situation as presented in Example 9-8, while theoretically neat and readily analyzed, seldom occurs in actual structures. In practically all cases, the beam is loaded from the top and not through its centroid. This loading, usually from a roof deck, is illustrated in Figure 9-46(a) and can be separated into three component

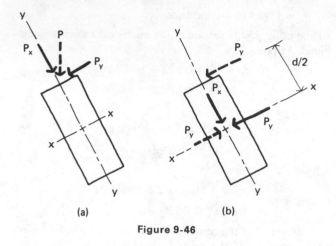

(a)   (b)

Figure 9-46

effects. Figure 9-46(b) shows that the force P_y has been relocated, so that it acts through the centroid, requiring the addition of a couple, represented by the dashed vectors. The three load components are P_x and P_y, which act centroidally, and the torsional moment, $P_y(d/2)$. Fortunately, the shearing stress from the torque usually does not maximize at a location near the maximum bending stress and the two effects can be handled separately. (If the torsion and bending stresses do become critical near one another, it may be necessary to consider using principal stress techniques, introduced briefly in Chapter 12.) For the section shown, the torsional stress will be greatest at the middle of the long side of the cross section, as explained in Section 6-7. As a shearing stress, it must be added to the horizontal shear stress, also a maximum at that point, generated by bending component P_x.

The net effect of permitting a member to be eccentrically loaded about its weak axis is a great reduction in capacity, and all such sections will be much larger than would otherwise be required. It is far superior to orient members on a roof slope so that they run *with* the slope rather than across it. With steel sections the problem becomes even more severe because of the very low bending resistance such shapes have with respect to their weak axes. The twisting of open sections, such as a wide-flange and channel shapes, is a complicated phe-

nomena and results in considerable warping, which causes longitudinal normal stresses in addition to those from biaxial bending. In lieu of a proper torsional analysis, a simpler approximate approach is to consider the entire weak-axis bending resistance as having to be provided by the loaded flange. This seems rational for steel sections, in that the twisting effect probably prevents the lower flange from being effectively utilized. Credit for this approach, which is illustrated by the following example, is given to Crawley and Dillon.[2]

EXAMPLE 9-9

The W150 × 18 roof purlin of Figure 9-47(a) spans 3 m. Determine the approximate maximum bending stress.

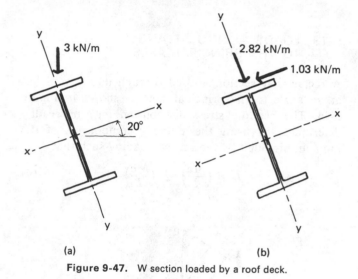

(a)   (b)

Figure 9-47. W section loaded by a roof deck.

Solution:

$$w_x = (3 \text{ kN/m}) \cos 20° \qquad w_y = (3 \text{ kN/m}) \sin 20°$$
$$= (3 \text{ kN/m})0.940 \qquad = (3 \text{ kN/m})0.342$$
$$= 2.82 \text{ kN/m} \qquad = 1.03 \text{ kN/m}$$
$$= \frac{w_x L^2}{8} \qquad M_y = \frac{w_y L^2}{8}$$
$$M_x = \frac{(2.82 \text{ kN/m})(3 \text{ m})^2}{8} \qquad = \frac{(1.03 \text{ kN/m})(3 \text{ m})^2}{8}$$
$$= 3.2 \text{ kN·m} \qquad = 1.2 \text{ kN·m}$$

Since there is virtually no contribution to the weak-axis section modulus from the web, the S_y for the loaded upper flange may be taken as one-half of the section modulus for the entire shape.

$$f_b = \pm \frac{M_x}{S_x} \pm \frac{M_y}{S_y/2} \qquad (9\text{-}20)$$

Obtaining the section modulus values from Appendix S, we get

[2]S. W. Crawley and R. M. Dillon, *Steel Buildings: Analysis and Design* (New York: John Wiley & Sons, Inc., 1970), p. 93.

$$f_b = \pm \frac{3.2 \text{ kN·m}}{120(10)^{-6} \text{ m}^3} \pm \frac{1.2 \text{ kN·m}}{[24.6(10)^{-6} \text{ m}^3]/2}$$

For maximum compression in the top corner and tension at the bottom corner,

$$f_b = 26\ 700 \text{ kPa} + 97\ 600 \text{ kPa}$$
$$= 124 \text{ MPa}$$

Problems

9-19. How much uniform load could the W150 × 18 of Example 9-9 accept if it is turned upright on the same span and stressed to the same 124-MPa level?

9-20. The eastern hemlock 38 × 285 mm roof joists of Figure 9-48 span 4 m and must support a *total* (snow plus dead weight) roof load of 2 kN/m² on the horizontal projection.
  (a) Determine if the section is adequate in extreme fiber bending. (*Hint:* Assume that the load acts at the centroid.)
  (b) Determine if the section is adequate in shear, including that due to torsion. (*Hint:* Refer to section 6-7 and Table 6-1.)

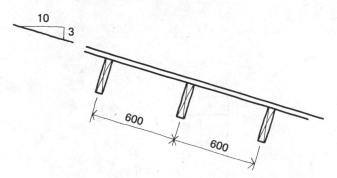

Figure 9-48. Wood joists at right angles to roof slope.

9-21. W360 × 91 beams of $F_y = 250$-MPa steel span 7 m between triangular roof trusses. The top chord of each truss has a pitch of 6 on 10 and the beams are turned so that their flanges have this same slope. If the *total* loading, including all dead weight, is 2.2 kN/m² of sloped area, determine the required center-to-center spacing of the beams. Use the approximate method of Example 9-9.

9-14 BEAMS OF TWO MATERIALS

In some design situations it is desirable to fabricate beams from more than one material. (Reinforced concrete is the obvious combination of two materials, and this will be discussed in Chapter 17.) Occasionally, the design requirements in a wood structure will stipulate that one of the beams be much more heavily loaded than the others. Increasing the capacity of a wood beam by attaching steel plates, commonly called *flitch plates*, is a viable alternative to reducing the span or using one steel beam in an otherwise wood structure. The plates can be attached to the top and bottom edges or to the sides. More bending efficiency will result from top and bottom plates, but attachment is easier with side plates, which can be through-bolted.

The determination of stresses in a member of two materials requires some adjustment in method because the general flexural stress equation assumes a homogeneous material in its derivation. The most common approach is to temporarily imagine the beam as being composed all of one material; compute the stresses using the regular formulas, and then adjust the stresses to account for the difference between the real and imagined materials. This temporary and fictitious, homogeneous cross section is called the *transformed section*.

The key to generating the proper transformed section is to remember that it must have the same stiffness or bending resistance as the real beam. This means that if we transform a combination wood and steel beam into one of all wood, the fictitious section will have to be larger because a unit of wood is less stiff than a unit of steel. Likewise, it is important that the bond between the two materials be good (i.e., that no slippage takes place). This is essential to the transformed section concept, which requires that the two materials in the real beam undergo the same strain while bending. For example, at any level y in Figure 9-49(b), we assume that

$$\epsilon_s = \epsilon_w$$

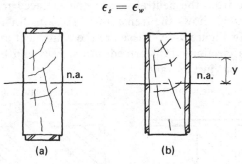

Figure 9-49. Beam sections of combined wood and steel.

Since strain may be expressed in terms of stress and the modulus of elasticity,

$$\left(\frac{f}{E}\right)_s = \left(\frac{f}{E}\right)_w$$

This relationship enables us to express the stress in one material in terms of the other.

$$f_s = \frac{E_s}{E_w} f_w$$

(The ratio of E values has been given a special name, the *modular ratio*, and is often designated as n.

In general, n is equal to the stiffer modulus divided by the less stiff modulus.)

In our case, then,

$$f_s = nf_w \qquad (9\text{-}21)$$

which simply states that if two materials strain like amounts, they will pick up stress in proportion to their respective E values. (The student should notice that exactly the same relationship was developed in Section 4-8 treating elements of two materials subject to axial loads.)

If the transformed section must have the same bending resistance as the real beam, it will have to deflect (and strain) the same amount and carry the same bending forces. Since stress equals force divided by area, Equation (9-21) may be written in terms of the bending force, F, at a given point in the beam.

$$\left(\frac{F}{A}\right)_s = n\left(\frac{F}{A}\right)_w$$

If the bending forces must be equal, they can be canceled and we get

$$\frac{1}{A_s} = \frac{n}{A_w}$$

or

$$A_w = nA_s \qquad (9\text{-}22)$$

In other words, to replace an area of steel by its equivalent in wood we must use an area of wood equal to n times the area of steel. For the bending strain to be equal at all levels, the new material must be placed at the same distance from the neutral axis as the replaced material. Figure 9-50 shows the transformed sections for the real beams in Figure 9-49. These are the equivalent all-wood sections; sections transformed into steel would be quite narrow but just as valid.

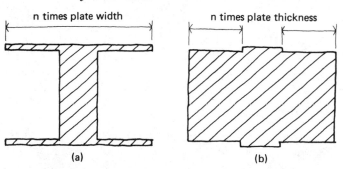

Figure 9-50. Transformed sections.

Once the section is transformed, bending stresses at any level can be computed using My/I. Whenever steel exists in the real beam, the transformed section stresses must be multiplied by n to obtain the real stresses. The deflection of the real beam will, by definition, be the same as that of the transformed section.

(The concepts developed here form the basis for elastic design of reinforced concrete elements. This method, called working stress design, is no longer the preferred procedure in reinforced concrete but is still in use. Reinforced masonry design is exclusively done by these techniques but will not be treated in this text.)

EXAMPLE 9-10

A sandwich beam is made from three 38×235 mm pieces. The two side members are southern pine and the inner one is eastern hemlock. If the beam is subjected to a moment of 10 kN·m, determine the bending stress in each material.

Solution:

To get the width of the equivalent all-hemlock beam,

$$n = \frac{E_{s.p.}}{E_h.}$$

$$= \frac{12\ 400\ \text{MPa}}{8900\ \text{MPa}}$$

$$= 1.39$$

The transformed width b of each outer joist will be 1.39 times 38 mm. The new section modulus is

$$S = \frac{bd^2}{6}$$

$$= \frac{(53 + 38 + 53)(235)^2}{6}$$

$$= 1330(10)^3\ \text{mm}^3$$

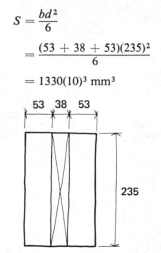

Figure 9-51. Transformed section for the beam of Example 9-10.

The extreme fiber bending stress in the all-hemlock section will be

$$f_b = \frac{M}{S}$$

$$= \frac{10\ \text{kN·m}}{1330(10)^{-6}\ \text{m}^3}$$

$$= 7520\ \text{kPa}$$

This will also be the actual stress in the eastern hemlock in the real beam.

$$f_{b_{e.h.}} = 7520\ \text{kPa}$$

To get the actual southern pine stresses, multiply by n.

$$f_{b_{s.p.}} = nf_b$$

$$= 1.39(7520\ \text{kPa})$$

$$= 10\ 500\ \text{kPa}$$

EXAMPLE 9-11

Determine the increase in bending capacity achieved by the addition of two $F_y = 250$-MPa steel plates, each 12×80 mm, as shown in Figure 9-52.

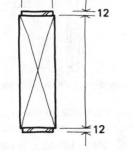

Figure 9-52. Douglas fir 89 × 285 mm reinforced by two steel plates.

Solution: The bending capacity for the timber beam alone is

$$M = f_b S$$
$$= 10\ 300\ \text{kPa}[1200(10)^{-6}\ \text{m}^3]$$
$$= 12.4\ \text{kN·m}$$

To get the transformed section (Figure 9-53),

$$n = \frac{E_s}{E_w}$$
$$= \frac{200\ 000\ \text{MPa}}{12\ 400\ \text{MPa}}$$
$$= 16.1$$

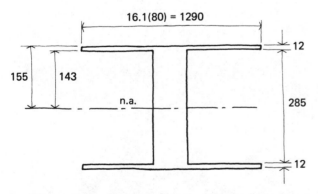

Figure 9-53. Transformed section for the beam in Example 9-11.

The moment of inertia is obtained by adding the I value of the two new flanges to that of the original wood beam.

$$I = (I)_{89 \times 285} + 2\left[\frac{bh^3}{12} + Ad^2\right]$$
$$= 172(10)^6\ \text{mm}^4 + 2[\text{negligible} + 12(1290)(149)^2]$$
$$= 859(10)^6\ \text{mm}^4$$

The bending stresses are, for the extreme fibers,

$$f_b = \frac{Mc}{I}$$
$$= \frac{M(0.155\ \text{m})}{859(10)^{-6}\ \text{m}^4}$$
$$= 180M$$

and for the junction of flange and web (extreme fibers of real wood),

$$f_y = \frac{0.143}{0.155}(180M)$$
$$= 166M$$

To obtain the stresses in the steel plates of the real beam, we use the modular ratio. The maximum stress in the steel will be

$$f_b = n(180M)$$
$$= 16.1(180M)$$
$$= 2900M$$

Beam capacity will be determined as the smaller of two values of M based upon the allowable bending stress for each material.

$$M = \frac{F_{b\ \text{steel}}}{2900} \qquad M = \frac{F_{b\ \text{wood}}}{166}$$
$$= \frac{165\ 000\ \text{kPa}}{2900} \qquad = \frac{10\ 300\ \text{kPa}}{166}$$
$$= 56.9\ \text{kN·m} \qquad = 62.0\ \text{kN·m}$$

So the capacity is limited by the steel stress and the final stress distribution at full load would be as shown in Figure 9-54. Adding the plates increased the bending capacity 360%, from 12.4 kN·m to 56.9 kN·m.

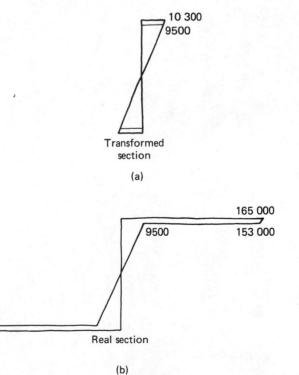

Figure 9-54

Problems

9-22. The box beam of Figure 9-55 is used as a simple beam spanning 5 m and supporting a uniform load of 2.0 kN/m. It is fabricated from two 38×89 mm studs of eastern spruce sandwiched between two southern pine shelving boards. Assume that $E_{e.s.} = 8300$ MPa and $E_{s.p.} = 12\ 800$ MPa Determine the bending stress in each material.

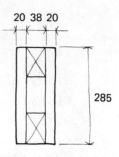

20 38 20

285

Figure 9-55.   Box beam.

9-23. The flitch-plate beam of Figure 9-56 spans 6 m and carries a concentrated load of 90 kN at each third point. It is fabricated from two Douglas fir 38×285 mm

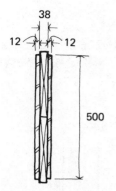

38

12   12

500

Figure 9-56.   Flitch-plate beam.

joists and two steel side plates. Determine the maximum bending stress in each material.

9-24. A Douglas fir 89×185 mm beam must span 5 m, carrying a uniform load. To increase its bending capacity, an 8×80 mm plate of $F_y = 248$ steel is firmly attached to its bottom edge by lag screws. Assume that the member is nonrepetitive.

(a) Determine the permissible load w in kN/m as controlled by the given materials.

(b) Determine the same permissible w without the plate.

10-1 INTRODUCTION

The *deflection* of beams is an important topic in structural design. As noted previously, the design of a beam for a particular load generally involves the investigation of bending stresses, shearing stresses, and deflection. Building codes limit the permissible deflection of a beam just as stresses or loads are limited. Some typical values are given in Table 10-1.

TABLE 10-1 *Typical Deflection Limitations Expressed as a Fraction of the Span*

	Total load	Live load only
*Roof beams	$\dfrac{L}{180}$	$\dfrac{L}{240}$
Floor beams	$\dfrac{L}{240}$	$\dfrac{L}{360}$

*Floor-beam values should be used in place of these if a plaster ceiling is attached directly to the structural members.

Excessive deflection can cause cracking of nonstructural materials that are attached to beams. Many cracks in nonbearing partition walls are due to such deflection. Doors and windows can bind up or become inoperable due to distortion of their openings by structural deflection. More important, flat or nearly flat roof surfaces are subject to "ponding," a continued buildup of water that can result eventually in a dishlike collapse.

Deflection is particularly critical in situations where a large portion of the total load is dead as opposed to live. Timber or concrete beams will both creep if subjected to permanent loading and will eventually sag enough to become unsightly and possibly unsafe. Therefore, when a beam supports a heavy wall or roof, for example, special design consideration needs to be given to deflection control.

Floor beams that are closely designed for bending stresses but not adequately limited in deflection can often be too "springy" or "bouncy" when loaded by impact or vibrated by a machine or vehicle to a natural frequency. This "springiness," although seldom a real structural safety problem, can be most annoying and in some cases make a space unfit for occupancy.

In the last 50 years we have been able to produce steels that are very strong in tension and compression; however, the stiffness (E) of these steels remains at about 200 GPa, the stiffness of mild steel, and is independent of strength. This means that as the strength increases, a large percentage of steel beams will be designed with deflection controlling (or governing) as opposed to flexure or shear.

Beam deflections may be calculated easily by using deflection formulas available in a number of structural handbooks and design aids. A few simple cases are given in Appendix V. These formulas can also be used to approximate deflection magnitudes, for more complicated loading patterns and conditions, by "modifying" the actual conditions in the conservative direction so as to "fit" one of the tabled situations. The results so obtained will be overestimates of actual deflections and will enable the designer to ascertain if further and more accurate computations are necessary. To do this with any accuracy, it helps to understand deflection theory, and for this reason further discussion of this technique will be deferred to a later section.

The most important reason for studying beam deflection theory, however, does not concern the rather narrow and specific task of finding the amount of sag in a loaded beam or girder. Rather, it is that deflection theory is vital to the understanding of indeterminate structures! It is deformation that must be considered, over and above the forces of static equilibrium, in order to solve indeterminate or "redundant" structures.

A knowledge of deflection theory will also help the designer to visualize more easily the deflected shapes of beams, frames, and other structures, determinate or indeterminate. Often a reasonably accurate image (or

Deflection

sketch) of how a structure deforms under load will help immeasurably in understanding how the loads are being resisted. Points of high and low stress can be ascertained, and this in turn can help decide whether a given structural choice is rational or irrational for those loads.

10-2 ORGANIZATION

In this chapter basic deflection theory is covered in the beginning sections, and more-applied material is treated after some background has been established. Three general methods of obtaining beam deflections are discussed and of these, the writer feels that the moment-area approach is the most useful for future studies. In Chapter 15, two approaches to the solution of indeterminate structures are presented and both are developed with the aid of moment-area concepts. Consequently, in this chapter more examples are presented to explain this method than the other two.

The examples and problems illustrate the accurate determination of beam deflections, but this is really only a convenient tool used to help approach the goal of understanding how these deformations take place. In actual beam design situations, the approximate techniques introduced in Section 10-10 are more than sufficient in almost every case. Although the theoretical techniques are quite capable of producing answers to many decimal places, the uncertainties of design and construction obviate the need for such accuracy.

10-3 RADIUS OF CURVATURE

It is assumed from beam theory that planes a and b in Figure 10-1, which were parallel before loading, will remain plane after bending so as to include a small angle $d\theta$. If the curvature is small (which is always true considering the stiff materials from which beams are made), we may assume that $R_a = R_b$, the radius of curvature of the neutral axis. The shape of the deflected neutral axis is called the *elastic curve*.

The length of line ab is designated as L_{ab}, and if

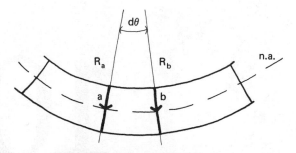

Figure 10-1. Beam bending under load.

$d\theta$ is very small and R is very large, then $L_{ab} = R\,d\theta$, since for small angles $\sin\theta = \tan\theta = \theta$. From Figure 10-2, then, $L_{a''b''} = (R + c)\,d\theta$ by the same reasoning. The total elongation that the bottom fiber undergoes is

$$\delta_c = L_{a''b''} - L_{ab}$$

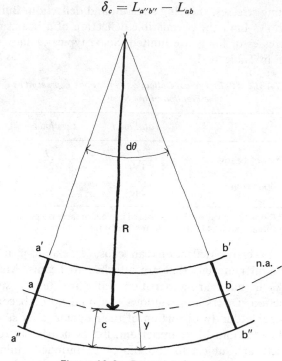

Figure 10-2. Exaggerated curvature.

Substituting the values given above, we get

$$\delta_c = (R + c)\,d\theta - R\,d\theta = R\,d\theta + c\,d\theta - R\,d\theta$$
$$= c\,d\theta$$

From $\epsilon = \delta/L$, we get

$$\epsilon_c = \frac{L_{a''b''} - L_{ab}}{L_{ab}} = \frac{c\,d\theta}{R\,d\theta}$$
$$= \frac{c}{R}$$

Similarly, it can be shown that the unit strain at any distance y from the neutral axis can be written as

$$\epsilon_y = \frac{y}{R}$$

We know that $\epsilon_y = f_y/E$ and $f_y = My/I$, so

$$\epsilon_y = \frac{My}{EI}$$

Equating the two expressions for ϵ_y, we get

$$\frac{My}{EI} = \frac{y}{R}$$

or

$$R = \frac{EI}{M} \qquad (10\text{-}1)$$

Since the flexure formula was used to obtain this relationship, it will be valid only for those members that meet the assumptions made in the derivation of the flexure formula (see Appendix D). E and I will usually be constants for a given beam.

EXAMPLE 10-1

Determine the radius of curvature of the cantilever steel beam in Figure 10-3 at the point where it enters the wall.

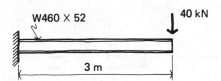

Figure 10-3. Cantilever beam with a point load.

Solution:

$$E = 200 \text{ GPa}$$

$$I = 212(10)^6 \text{ mm}^4$$

$$M_a = 40(3) = 120 \text{ kN·m}$$

$$R = \frac{EI}{M} = \frac{[200(10)^6 \text{ kN/m}^2][212(10)^{-6} \text{ m}^4]}{120 \text{ kN·m}}$$

$$= 357 \text{ m}$$

Problems

10-1. A simply supported W610 × 82 steel beam 12 m long carries two equal concentrated loads symmetrically placed at the third points. Each load is 60 kN. Determine the radius of curvature at midspan for this beam.

10-2. A 25 mm × 25 mm strip of southern pine is to be bent into an arc as a trim piece. Determine the minimum radius of curvature permitted if the bending stress developed must not exceed 20 000 kPa.

10-4 CURVATURE AND BENDING MOMENT

The radius of curvature at any point along a curve whose equation is $y = f(x)$ (Figure 10-4) can be expressed as

$$R = \frac{[1 + (dy/dx)^2]^{3/2}}{d^2y/dx^2}$$

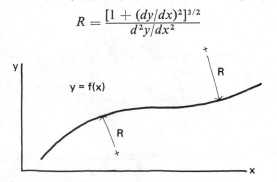

Figure 10-4. General curve.

In beams, the slopes of elastic curves are always very small, and for this reason the term $(dy/dx)^2$ is insignificant and may be taken as zero. Therefore,

$$R = \frac{1}{d^2y/dx^2}$$

where d^2y/dx^2 is merely the rate of change of the slope. It is a measure of the change in slope between two points on the elastic curve as we shall use it. If the points a and b in Figure 10-5 are allowed to approach each other, then θ_{ab} can be represented by d^2y/dx^2.

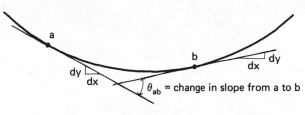

θ_{ab} = change in slope from a to b

Figure 10-5

If we equate the two values obtained for R,

$$R = \frac{EI}{M} = \frac{1}{d^2y/dx^2}$$

we get

$$EI\frac{d^2y}{dx^2} = M \qquad (10\text{-}2)$$

Credit for the development of this equation is given to Leonhard Euler (1707–1783), a Swiss mathematician.

10-5 DOUBLE-INTEGRATION METHOD

From Figure 10-6 we see that by integrating an equation representing one curve, we can obtain the curve immediately below it. The M/EI curve is merely the usual

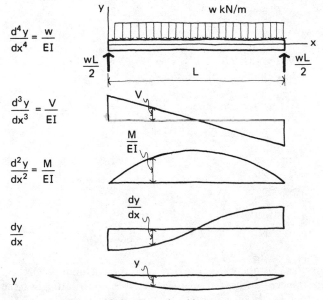

Figure 10-6. Five related beam curves.

moment diagram with each ordinate having been divided by the stiffness constant *EI*. If we integrate the *M/EI* equation once, we get an equation that will plot the slope of the elastic curve. If we integrate a second time, we get an equation that represents the deflected shape.

EXAMPLE 10-2

Determine the maximum values of slope and deflection for the beam in Figure 10-7.

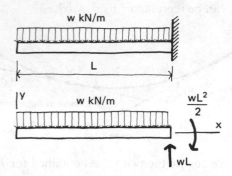

Figure 10-7. Cantilever beam with uniform load.

Solution: With the origin at the left end, the moment at any point *x* along the length of the beam is given by

$$(0 \leq x \leq L) \qquad M_x = -\frac{wx^2}{2}$$

Substituting into Equation (10-2), we get

$$EI\frac{d^2y}{dx^2} = -\frac{wx^2}{2}$$

Integrating once,

$$EI\frac{dy}{dx} = -\frac{wx^3}{6} + C_1$$

Evaluating the constant by the support conditions (where $x = L$, $dy/dx = 0$), we get

$$C_1 = \frac{wL^3}{6}$$

Therefore,

$$EI\frac{dy}{dx} = -\frac{wx^3}{6} + \frac{wL^3}{6}$$

Integrating a second time yields

$$EIy = -\frac{wx^4}{24} + \frac{wL^3x}{6} + C_2$$

C_2 can also be evaluated at the fixed end (where $x = L$, $y = 0$); therefore,

$$C_2 = -\frac{wL^4}{8}$$

and

$$EIy = -\frac{wx^4}{24} + \frac{wL^3x}{6} - \frac{wL^4}{8}$$

In this case the maximum slope and the maximum deflection both occur at the free end, where $x = 0$. Substituting into the

two expressions above and solving for the slope and deflection, we get

$$\theta_{max} = \frac{wL^3}{6EI}$$

and

$$\Delta_{max} = -\frac{wL^4}{8EI}$$

EXAMPLE 10-3

Determine the maximum values of slope and deflection for the beam in Figure 10-8.

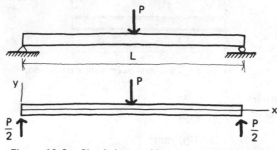

Figure 10-8. Simple beam with a concentrated load at midspan.

Solution: Because of symmetry only one-half of the beam will be examined. Selecting the origin at the left end, the moment at any point *x* in the left half of the beam is given by

$$\left(0 \leq x \leq \frac{L}{2}\right) \qquad M_x = \frac{Px}{2}$$

Substituting into Equation (10-2), we get

$$EI\frac{d^2y}{dx^2} = \frac{Px}{2}$$

Integrating once yields

$$EI\frac{dy}{dx} = \frac{Px^2}{4} + C_1$$

Evaluating the constant by noting that the slope is zero at midspan (where $x = L/2$, $dy/dx = 0$), we get

$$C_1 = -\frac{PL^2}{16}$$

Therefore,

$$EI\frac{dy}{dx} = \frac{Px^2}{4} - \frac{PL^2}{16}$$

Integrating again gives us

$$EIy = \frac{Px^3}{12} - \frac{PL^2x}{16} + C_2$$

This second constant can be evaluated at the support (where $x = 0$, $y = 0$); therefore,

$$C_2 = 0$$

and

$$EIy = \frac{Px^3}{12} - \frac{PL^2x}{16}$$

For this case, the maximum slope occurs at the left end, and it is

$$\theta_{max} = -\frac{PL^2}{16}$$

The identical value (with a sign change) will exist at the right end of the beam. The maximum deflection is at midspan, and using $x = L/2$, we get

$$\Delta_{max} = -\frac{PL^3}{48EI}$$

The double-integration method, while simple in concept, becomes impractical in use for any but the simplest of loading situations. For example, whenever the loading or end conditions are such that a point of zero slope is not known, constant evaluation becomes cumbersome. Furthermore, separate moment equations must be written for each change of condition, such as the starting or stopping of a uniform load or an intermediate hinge or support. Fortunately, simpler methods are available.

Problems

10-3. Determine expressions for the maximum slope and deflection of a uniformly loaded cantilever beam whose left end is fixed and whose right end is free.

10-4. Determine expressions for the maximum slope and deflection of a uniformly loaded simple beam.

10-5. Sketch the five related beam curves for the beams of Examples 10-2 and 10-3.

10-6 MOMENT-AREA METHOD

The moment-area method of determining beam slopes and deflection is both the simplest and the most useful. This semigraphical method was first developed in 1864 by Barré de Saint-Venant, a French scientist. The entire method can be stated in two theorems with reference to Figure 10-9. In general, the method finds slopes and

deflection only *indirectly*, and careful attention should be paid to the equivalencies presented in the theorems.

> *First moment-area theorem:* The change in slope between any two points, *A* and *B*, on the elastic curve is equal to the net area under the *M/EI* curve between those two points.

(Note that this theorem finds only a *change* in slope and does not directly find a slope.)

> *Second moment-area theorem:* The vertical distance from point *B* on the elastic curve to a tangent line from point *A* is equal to the statical moment of the net area under the *M/EI* curve between points *A* and *B* taken about the vertical line through *B*.

(Note that this theorem finds only a vertical distance, often called a *tangential deviation*, and does not directly find a deflection.)

The theorems and the notes will both become clear after a couple of example problems. There is one pertinent restriction placed upon the application of moment-area theory: it cannot be applied across an interior hinge. Such a beam must be broken into segments for deflection analysis. This is true because in the development of the principles, we assumed a continuous curve with no discontinuities or sudden change in slope. Proof of the moment-area theorems are offered in Appendix F.

(The symbol ∇, normally a differential operator, is here used to mean "triangle side.")

EXAMPLE 10-4

Determine the slope at the left end and the deflection at midspan for the beam in Figure 10-10.

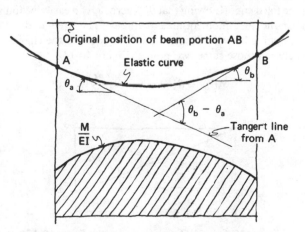

Figure 10-9. Portion of elastic curve and *M/EI* diagram.

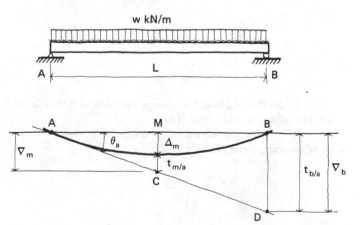

Figure 10-10. Simple beam with a uniform load.

Solution: To find θ_a, note that $\tan \theta_a = \theta_a$, as assumed previously, and that

$$\tan \theta_a = \frac{\nabla_b}{L}$$

in Figure 10-10, where ∇_b, the triangle side BD of triangle ABD, is geometrically equal to $t_{b/a}$, a tangential deviation. $t_{b/a}$ is a "vertical distance from point B on the elastic curve to a tangent line from point A," and we can use the second moment-area theorem to find it.

The M/EI curve for the beam is shown in Figure 10-11, and it is easy to compute its statical moment about a vertical line through B. See Appendix M for areas and centroidal distances of parabolic curves.

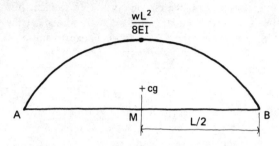

Figure 10-11. M/EI curve for the beam in Figure 10-10.

$$t_{b/a} = \frac{2}{3}\left(\frac{wL^2}{8EI}\right)(L)\frac{L}{2} = \frac{wL^4}{24EI} = \nabla_b$$

$$\tan \theta_a = \theta_a = \frac{\nabla_b}{L} = \frac{wL^4/24EI}{L}$$

$$\theta_a = \frac{wL^3}{24EI}$$

(The sign of θ_a is not evident from the computations but is negative by inspection.)

To find the midspan deflection, Δ_m (also negative by inspection), we will find the values of ∇_m and $t_{m/a}$ as shown in Figure 10-10. A subtraction will then give us Δ_m. First find ∇_m, the triangle side MC, by using θ_a.

$$\theta_a = \tan \theta_a = \frac{\nabla_m}{L/2}$$

or

$$\nabla_m = \theta_a\left(\frac{L}{2}\right) = \frac{wL^3}{24EI}\left(\frac{L}{2}\right)$$

$$= \frac{wL^4}{48EI}$$

(Note that ∇_m could also have been found by using the similar triangles AMC and ABD.)

The value $t_{m/a}$ can be found using the second moment-area theorem. From Figure 10-12,

$$t_{m/a} = \frac{2}{3}\left(\frac{wL^2}{8EI}\right)\frac{L}{2}\left(\frac{3}{8}\right)\frac{L}{2}$$

$$= \frac{wL^4}{128EI}$$

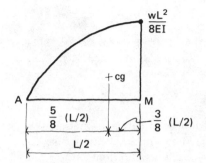

Figure 10-12. M/EI curve between A and M.

Then

$$\Delta_m = \nabla_m - t_{m/a}$$

$$= \frac{wL^4}{48EI} - \frac{wL^4}{128EI}$$

$$= \frac{5wL^4}{384EI}$$

EXAMPLE 10-5

Determine the slope and deflection at the free end of the cantilever beam in Figure 10-13.

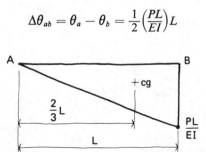

Figure 10-13.   Cantilever beam with a point load.

Solution: Notice that the slope of the elastic curve is zero at the fixed end. Knowing that θ_b is zero, θ_a can easily be found using the first moment-area theorem. The area under the M/EI curve between points A and B is equal to the change in θ between those same two points (Figure 10-14).

$$\Delta\theta_{ab} = \theta_a - \theta_b = \frac{1}{2}\left(\frac{PL}{EI}\right)L$$

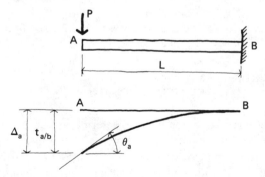

Figure 10-14. M/EI curve for the beam in Figure 10-13.

Since $\theta_b = 0$,

$$\theta_a = \frac{PL^2}{2EI}$$

The sign is plus by inspection.

To find Δ_a, notice that a tangent line drawn from B will be coincident with the initial position of the beam before loading. This means that deflections can be found directly because they are geometrically equal to tangential deviations.

$$\Delta_a = t_{a/b} = \frac{1}{2}\left(\frac{PL}{EI}\right)L\left(\frac{2}{3}L\right)$$

$$= \frac{PL^3}{3EI}$$

The selection of the tangent line location in Example 10-5 gives us a hint as to how we could have set up the simple beam of Example 10-4 so as to reduce the numerical work involved.

In Figure 10-15, we see that the slope of the beam is zero at midspan due to symmetry. With θ_m equal to zero, θ_a can be found directly as the difference between θ_m and θ_a. The midspan deflection Δ_m can also be found

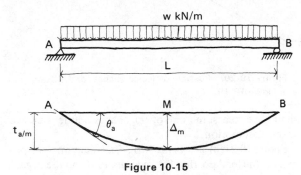

Figure 10-15

directly by noting that it is geometrically equal to $t_{a\,m}$, which can be found by one application of the second moment-area theorem. Referring to Figure 10-12 and taking the statical moment about a vertical line through A, we get

$$\Delta_m = t_{a/m} = \frac{2}{3}\left(\frac{wL^2}{8EI}\right)\frac{L}{2}\left(\frac{5}{8}\right)\frac{L}{2}$$

$$= \frac{5wL^4}{384EI}$$

Moment-area computations can often be simplified through judicious selection of tangent-line locations.

EXAMPLE 10-6

Determine θ_b and Δ_m for the beam in Figure 10-16.

Solution: (It is easier to work with the symbols E and I in the computations and replace them with numerical values as a final step.)

The slope at midspan is zero; therefore,

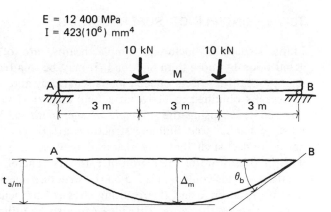

Figure 10-16. Simple beam with two concentrated loads.

$$\theta_b = \theta_b - \theta_m = \frac{30\ \text{kN}\cdot\text{m}}{EI}(1.5\ \text{m}) + \frac{1}{2}\left(\frac{30\ \text{kN}\cdot\text{m}}{EI}\right)3\ \text{m}$$

$$= \frac{90\ \text{kN}\cdot\text{m}^2}{EI}$$

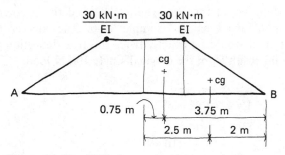

Figure 10-17. M/EI diagram for the beam in Figure 10-16.

The deflection at midspan is equal to $t_{a\,m}$.

$$t_{a/m} = \frac{30\ \text{kN}\cdot\text{m}}{EI}(1.5\ \text{m})(3.75\ \text{m}) + \frac{1}{2}\left(\frac{30\ \text{kN}\cdot\text{m}}{EI}\right)(3\ \text{m})2\ \text{m}$$

$$\Delta_m = \frac{259\ \text{kN}\cdot\text{m}^3}{EI}$$

Substituting the actual values for E and I, we get

$$\theta_b = \frac{90\ \text{kN}\cdot\text{m}^2}{[12\ 400(10)^3\ \text{kN/m}^2][423(10)^{-6}\ \text{m}^4]}$$

$$= 1.72(10)^{-2}$$

This is the slope of the beam at B in radians. If degrees are desired, it can be multiplied by $180/\pi$ to get

$$\theta_b = 1°$$

To find the deflection,

$$\Delta_m = \frac{259\ \text{kN}\cdot\text{m}^3}{[12\ 400(10)^3\ \text{kN/m}^2][423(10)^{-6}\ \text{m}^4]}$$

$$= 0.049\ \text{m}$$

or

$$\Delta_m = 49\ \text{mm}$$

10-7 PRINCIPLE OF SUPERPOSITION

Many structures, including simple beams, are often acted upon by more than one load. It may be to advantage to treat the effects of such loads separately and add the results obtained to arrive at a final answer. This is referred to as using the *principle of superposition*. We must remember that building structures are (hopefully) never loaded such that any material reaches its yield limit or passes out of the region of elasticity. Therefore, the design loads could be placed on the structure one at a time or all at once and the resulting stresses and deflections would be the same. This idea can also be utilized from the opposite standpoint.

Suppose, for example, that we were asked to obtain the midspan deflection of the beam in Figure 10-18. Since there is no known point of zero slope, we could not obtain the answer with a single application of the second moment-area theorem. However, if we added a fictitious load of 10 kN at a point 3 m from the right end, the loading would then be symmetrical and the problem is simply solved as in Example 10-6. The answer thus obtained would be exactly twice the true deflection that would result from the original single 10-kN load.

$E = 12\ 400$ MPa
$I = 423(10)^6$ mm⁴

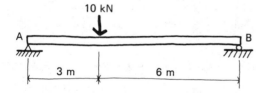

Figure 10-18. Simple beam with one concentrated load.

The principle of superposition cannot be applied to every structure, however. Structures whose behavior is significantly affected by changes in geometry, such as most cable systems, do not respond linearly to load application and superposition becomes invalid.

Superposition is used to simplify the computations in Example 10-7. Here a single uniform load is treated as two separate loads, so the M/EI diagram will not involve cumbersome centroid locations. The separate diagrams are sometimes called *component diagrams*.

EXAMPLE 10-7

Determine the deflection at the overhanging end C of the beam in Figure 10-19.

Solution: In this case we do not know by inspection whether the deflection at C is up or down; that is, we do not know which of the deflected shapes shown in Figure 10-20 is correct.

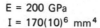

$E = 200$ GPa
$I = 170(10)^6$ mm⁴

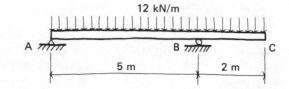

Figure 10-19. Overhanging beam with a uniform load.

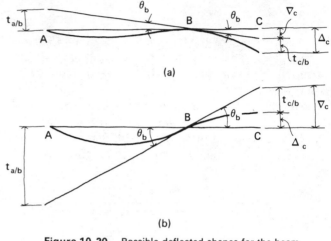

Figure 10-20. Possible deflected shapes for the beam in Figure 10-19.

We shall have to assume one of the shapes and let our work check our assumption.

Figure 10-21(b) shows the two M/EI diagrams (the positive one for the load portion between A and B and the negative one for the load between B and C), which can be used in place of the diagram in Figure 10-21(a).

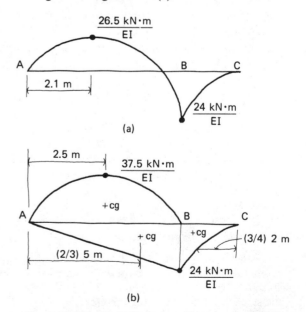

Figure 10-21. (a) M/EI diagram; (b) component M/EI diagrams.

First, we will obtain a value for θ_b. This, in turn, will enable us to get ∇_c, which can be used to obain Δ_c. To begin, we shall assume that the elastic curve of Figure 10-20(a) is correct (i.e., that θ_b is negative).

$$\theta_b = \tan \theta_b = \frac{t_{a/b}}{5 \text{ m}}$$

Using Figure 10-21(b),

$$t_{a/b} = \frac{2}{3}\left(\frac{37.5 \text{ kN·m}}{EI}\right)(5 \text{ m})(2.5 \text{ m})$$
$$- \frac{1}{2}\left(\frac{24 \text{ kN·m}}{EI}\right)(5 \text{ m})\left(\frac{2}{3}\right)5 \text{ m}$$
$$= \frac{312 \text{ kN·m}^3}{EI} - \frac{200 \text{ kN·m}^3}{EI}$$

Here it must be noticed that the left-hand term represents action of the load between A and B (which causes a positive slope at B) and the right-hand term represents the overhanging load between B and C (which causes a negative slope at B).

The *net* statical moment is

$$t_{a/b} = \frac{112 \text{ kN·m}^3}{EI}$$

and indicates that our assumption as to the deflected shape was not correct. The angle at B is *positive*, as shown in Figure 10-20(b).

$$\theta_b = \frac{t_{a/b}}{5 \text{ m}}$$
$$= \frac{112 \text{ kN·m}^3}{EI(5 \text{ m})}$$
$$= \frac{22.4 \text{ kN·m}^2}{EI}$$

Now we can get ∇_c by using

$$\nabla_c = \theta_b(2 \text{ m})$$
$$= \frac{22.4 \text{ kN·m}^2}{EI}(2 \text{ m})$$
$$= \frac{44.8 \text{ kN·m}^3}{EI}$$

Then $t_{c/b}$ comes from the second moment-area theorem and Figure 10-21(b),

$$t_{c/b} = \frac{1}{3}\left(\frac{24 \text{ kN·m}}{EI}\right)(2 \text{ m})\left(\frac{3}{4}\right)2 \text{ m}$$
$$= \frac{24 \text{ kN·m}^3}{EI}$$

The fact that ∇_c is larger than $t_{c/b}$ confirms that the deflection at C is up, not down. A subtraction will give us its value.

$$\Delta_c = \nabla_c - t_{c/b}$$
$$= \frac{44.8 \text{ kN·m}^3}{EI} - \frac{24 \text{ kN·m}^3}{EI}$$
$$= \frac{20.8 \text{ kN·m}^3}{EI}$$

Substituting for EI gives us

$$\Delta_c = \frac{20.8 \text{ kN·m}^3}{[200(10)^6 \text{ kN/m}^2][170(10)^{-6} \text{ m}^4]}$$
$$= 0.6(10)^{-3} \text{ m}$$

or

$$\Delta_c = 0.6 \text{ mm}$$

Problems

10-6. Determine the free-end slope and deflection values in terms of $w, L, E,$ and I for a cantilever beam with a uniform load.

10-7. The beam in Figure 10-22 is an 89×285 mm section of Douglas fir. Will the deflection due to the concentrated loads be within a code limitation of $L/240$?

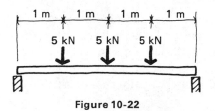

Figure 10-22

10-8. Determine the free-end deflection of the beam in Figure 10-23.

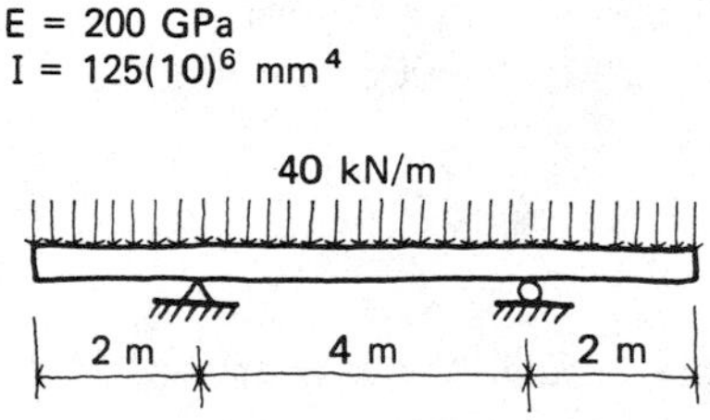

E = 200 GPa
I = 125(10)^6 mm^4

40 kN/m

2 m   4 m   2 m

Figure 10-23

10-9. A simply supported W610 × 113 is 16 m long and carries a uniform load of 30 kN/m over the left half of its span. Determine the midspan deflection.

10-8 CONJUGATE BEAM METHOD

The conjugate beam method utilizes the relationships of the five related beam curves presented in Section 10-5. From previous work the student should be quite familiar with the relationships among the load, shear, and moment diagrams. These same relationships involving the slope and ordinates of the diagrams continue to apply to the M/EI diagram and the slope and deflection diagrams. This implies that if one had an imaginary beam with the proper support conditions and loaded it with an imaginary load whose shape and intensity was that of the real M/EI curve, this imaginary beam would develop shears and moments that would equal the slopes and deflections of the real beam. In other words, we are merely moving two notches on the five related beam curves such that an imaginary beam, called a *conjugate beam*, is loaded by the M/EI diagram and the appropriate shear and moment curves drawn for that loading. The shear and moment diagrams of the conjugate beam will be, respectively, the slope and deflection diagrams of the real beam. The steps involved in this procedure are as follows:

1. Set up the conjugate beam with the appropriate boundary conditions (see explanation below).
2. Load the beam with the M/EI diagram of the real beam. Positive ordinates will constitute upward-acting loads and negative ordinates will mean down loads.
3. Compute shears and moments at specific points in the beam, and these will equal the slopes and deflections at those points in the real beam. Use free-body sections of the conjugate beam, and the equilibrium equations to do this.

To set up the appropriate support conditions on the conjugate beam (sometimes called "designing the conjugate beam"), we make use of the following relationships. The subscript r indicates real beam and the subscript c stands for conjugate beam.

$$\theta_r = V_c$$
$$\Delta_r = M_c$$

As an example, assume that a beam has a fixed-end condition. What kind of end condition on a corresponding conjugate beam will meet the equalities above? A fixed end is a support that has zero slope and zero deflection. Therefore, that end of the conjugate beam must have zero shear and zero moment. Only a free end will satisfy those requirements.

Table 10-2 will assist you in designing the conjugate beams in the examples and problems that follow. In working through the examples, notice that it is rarely, if ever, necessary to draw the complete shear and moment diagrams for the conjugate beam; rather, it is necessary only to compute specific values at sections where the slope or deflection is desired in the real beam. Notice also that some real beams will have conjugate beams that appear to be unstable. Such beams will be placed in equilibrium by the M/EI diagram loads acting upon them.

It is interesting to note that while the entire approach or concept for this method is very different from moment-area theory, the numerical computations are essentially the same.

TABLE 10-2 *Support Conditions for Conjugate Beams*

Real beam		Conjugate beam	
Fixed end	$\theta = 0$ $\Delta = 0$	$V = 0$ $M = 0$	Free end
Free end	$\theta \neq 0$ $\Delta \neq 0$	$V \neq 0$ $M \neq 0$	Fixed end
Pin or roller end	$\theta \neq 0$ $\Delta = 0$	$V \neq 0$ $M = 0$	Pin or roller end
Interior pin or roller	$\theta \neq 0$ $\Delta = 0$	$V \neq 0$ $M = 0$	Hinge
Hinge	$\theta \neq 0$ $\Delta \neq 0$	$V \neq 0$ $M \neq 0$	Interior pin or roller

EXAMPLE 10-8

Determine the slope and deflection at the free end of the beam in Figure 10-24.

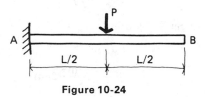

Figure 10-24

Solution: Referring to Figure 10-25 and using the equations of equilibrium, we can establish that

$$V_b = \frac{PL^2}{8EI}$$

and

$$M_b = \frac{PL^2}{8EI}\left(\frac{5}{6}\right)L$$
$$= \frac{5PL^3}{48EI}$$

For the real beam, then,

$$\theta_b = \frac{PL^2}{8EI}$$

and

$$\Delta_b = \frac{5PL^3}{48EI}$$

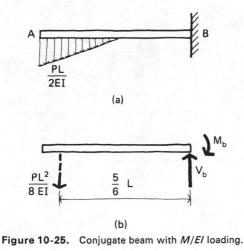

(a)

(b)

Figure 10-25. Conjugate beam with *M/EI* loading.

EXAMPLE 10-9

Determine the deflection at point *A* of the beam in Figure 10-26.

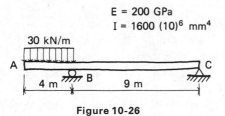

E = 200 GPa
I = 1600 (10)^6 mm^4

Figure 10-26

Solution: In order to find the moment at *A*, it will be necessary first to determine the shearing force across the hinge at *B*. Taking moments about *C* in Figure 10-28(b),

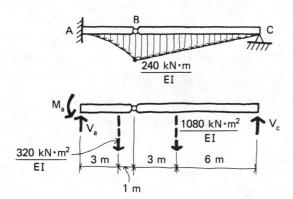

Figure 10-27. Conjugate beam with *M/EI* loading.

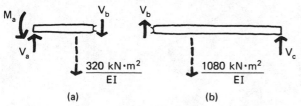

(a)   (b)

Figure 10-28. Free-body diagram to determine hinge shear.

$$\Sigma M_c = 0$$

$$-V_b(9) + \frac{1080}{EI}(6) = 0$$

$$V_b = \frac{720 \text{ kN} \cdot \text{m}^2}{EI}$$

Referring to Figure 10-28(a), we can then take moments to get

$$M_a = \frac{320 \text{ kN} \cdot \text{m}^2}{EI}(3 \text{ m}) + \frac{720 \text{ kN} \cdot \text{m}^2}{EI}(4 \text{ m})$$

$$= \frac{3840 \text{ kN} \cdot \text{m}^3}{EI}$$

or for the real beam,

$$\Delta_a = \frac{3840 \text{ kN} \cdot \text{m}^3}{EI}$$

Substituting for *E* and *I* yields

$$\Delta_a = \frac{3840 \text{ kN} \cdot \text{m}^3}{[200(10)^6 \text{ kN/m}^2][1600(10)^{-6} \text{ m}^4]}$$

$$= 1.2(10)^{-2} \text{ m}$$

or

$$\Delta_a = 12 \text{ mm}$$

EXAMPLE 10-10

Determine the midspan deflection for the beam in Figure 10-29.

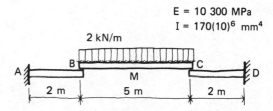

E = 10 300 MPa
I = 170(10)^6 mm^4

Figure 10-29. Simple beam supported by two cantilevers.

Solution: The connections at *B* and *C* act like internal hinges in terms of shear and moment, so the conjugate beam will have interior supports at those points (Figure 10-30). The total load will be

$$\frac{2}{3}\left(\frac{6.25 \text{ kN} \cdot \text{m}}{EI}\right)5 \text{ m} - \frac{20.8 \text{ kN} \cdot \text{m}^2}{EI}$$

and each reaction will be 10.4 kN·m^2/*EI*.

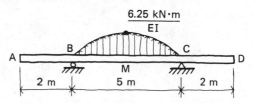

Figure 10-30. Conjugate beam with *M/EI* loading.

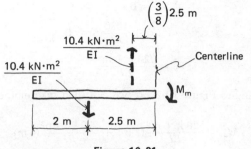

Figure 10-31

Referring to Figure 10-31 and solving for M_m, we get

$$M_m = \frac{10.4 \text{ kN·m}^2}{EI}(2.5 \text{ m}) - \frac{10.4 \text{ kN·m}^2}{EI}\left(\frac{3}{8}\right)2.5 \text{ m}$$

$$= \frac{16.3 \text{ kN·m}^3}{EI}$$

or for the real beam,

$$\Delta_m = \frac{16.3 \text{ kN·m}^3}{EI}$$

Substituting for E and I yields

$$\Delta_m = \frac{16.3 \text{ kN·m}^3}{[10\ 300(10)^3 \text{ kN/m}^2][170(10)^{-6} \text{ m}^4]}$$

$$= 9.31(10)^{-3} \text{ m}$$

or

$$\Delta_m = 9 \text{ mm}$$

Problems

10-10. A W310 × 60 is used as a 6-m-long cantilever beam. It carries a uniform load of 15 kN/m for the first 3 m of its length, starting at the fixed end. Determine the free-end deflection.

10-11. Determine the midspan deflection for the beam in Figure 10-32.

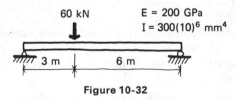

Figure 10-32

10-12. Determine the maximum deflection of the beam in Figure 10-32. (*Hint:* Make use of the conjugate beam shear diagram to locate the point of zero slope in the real beam.)

10-9 POINT OF MAXIMUM DEFLECTION

Maximum deflection for a simply supported beam will occur where the slope is zero. Referring to Figure 10-33 and using the double-integration techniques of Section

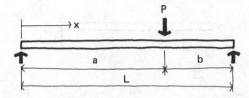

Figure 10-33. Simple beam with a concentrated load.

10-5, the expression for the slope of the beam in the interval $0 \leq x \leq a$ is given by

$$EI\frac{dy}{dx} = \frac{Pb}{6L}[3x^2 - (L^2 - b^2)]$$

Setting this expression equal to zero will locate the point of zero slope or maximum deflection at

$$x = \sqrt{\frac{L^2 - b^2}{3}} \qquad (10\text{-}3)$$

This expression tells us how the point of maximum deflection moves when the position of the load changes. Taking $b = L/2$ as an example, x will equal $L/2$, verifying that the maximum deflection occurs under the load for a midspan load location. It can be shown that the greatest deflection of a simple beam will always occur between the load and midspan. The greatest deviation away from midspan will occur as the load approaches a support (i.e., b approaches zero). When $b = 0$ in Equation (10-3), $x = L/\sqrt{3}$ or $0.57L$. This tells us that, regardless of loading pattern, maximum deflection will occur within 7% of the beam length from midspan.

Similarly, it can be shown that, owing to the very slight curvature in beams, the central deflection will be only slightly smaller than the maximum deflection. In fact, as the load approaches one of the supports, the midspan deflection approaches 97.4% of the maximum deflection. This is shown in greatly exaggerated fashion in Figure 10-34.

The implication of the foregoing is that, for any pattern of vertical loading on a simple beam, it is suffi-

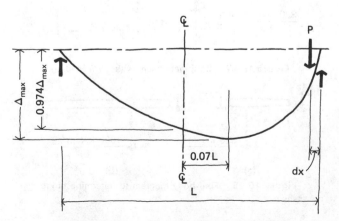

Figure 10-34. Location of maximum deflection.

ciently accurate to compute the midspan deflection as an approximation of the maximum deflection. Credit for this concept is given to Roland Trathen.[1]

10-10 DEFLECTION FORMULAS

Many loading patterns and support conditions occur so frequently in construction that reference manuals and engineering handbooks tabulate the appropriate formulas for their deflections. A few such cases are given in Appendix V. More often than not, the required deflection values in a beam design situation can be obtained via these formulas, and one does not have to resort to deflection theory. Even when the actual loading situation does not match one of the tabulated cases, it is sufficiently accurate for most design situations to approximate the maximum deflection by using one or more of the formulas.

EXAMPLE 10-11

Determine the approximate maximum deflection for the beam in Figure 10-35.

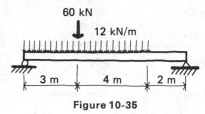

Figure 10-35

Solution: The real maximum value could be obtained by any of the three theoretical methods presented previously. However, from Section 10-9 we know that the central deflection will be very close to the maximum. Furthermore, it would be conservative in this case to treat this beam as though it had a uniform load over the full span *and* had the concentrated load located at midspan. The midspan deflection for this fictitious situation can be computed by using cases 3 and 4 in Appendix V.

$$\Delta_{max} = \frac{PL^3}{48EI} + \frac{5wL^4}{384EI}$$

or

$$\Delta_{max} = \frac{60 \text{ kN}(9 \text{ m})^3}{48EI} + \frac{5(12 \text{ kN/m})(9 \text{ m})^4}{384EI}$$

$$= \frac{911 \text{ kN} \cdot \text{m}^3}{EI} + \frac{1025 \text{ kN} \cdot \text{m}^3}{EI}$$

$$= \frac{1936 \text{ kN} \cdot \text{m}^3}{EI}$$

The value thus obtained will be very close to and slightly larger than the actual deflection.

[1]Roland Trathen, *Statics and Strength of Materials* (New York: John Wiley & Sons, Inc., 1954), p. 150.

EXAMPLE 10-12

Determine the approximate maximum deflection for the 10-m portion of the beam in Figure 10-36.

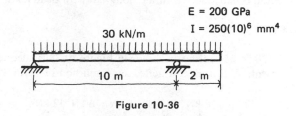

Figure 10-36

Solution: In this case, it would be "safe" to ignore the overhang and assume a 10-m uniformly loaded simple span.

$$\Delta_{max} = \frac{5wL^4}{384EI}$$

$$= \frac{5(30 \text{ kN/m})(10 \text{ m})^4}{[384(200)(10)^6 \text{ kN/m}^2][250(10)^{-6} \text{ m}^4]}$$

$$= 7.81(10)^{-2} \text{ m}$$

$$= 78 \text{ mm}$$

EXAMPLE 10-13

The Douglas fir joist in Figure 10-37 has been designed for moment and shear as a doubled 38×285 mm. If the deflection is limited to $L/240$, is this section adequate?

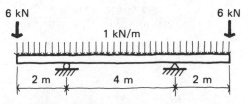

Figure 10-37. Overhanging joist with loads from floor and walls.

Solution: One conservative approach is to treat the joist as a true cantilever, ignoring the tempering effect of the central span. Using cases 1 and 2 of Appendix V, we get

$$\Delta_{max} = \frac{PL^3}{3EI} + \frac{wL^4}{8EI}$$

$$= \frac{6 \text{ kN}(2 \text{ m})^3}{3EI} + \frac{(1 \text{ kN/m})(2 \text{ m})^4}{8EI}$$

$$= \frac{18 \text{ kN} \cdot \text{m}^3}{EI}$$

$$= \frac{18 \text{ kN} \cdot \text{m}^3}{[12 \ 400(10)^3 \text{ kN/m}^2][2(73.3)(10)^{-6} \text{ m}^4]}$$

$$= 9.90(10)^{-3} \text{ m}$$

$$= 10 \text{ mm}$$

$$\Delta_{code} = \frac{L}{240} = \frac{2000 \text{ mm}}{240} = 8 \text{ mm}$$

The code would limit the deflection to about 8 mm, while our solution gave a deflection of 10 mm. In view of the conservative assumptions made, this 25% excess deflection would probably not occur, and the actual deflection might be very close to the allowable. However, in view of the problems associated with creep in timber structures, the writer would suggest further checking if a significant portion of the applied load could be classified as either "long-term" or dead load.

EXAMPLE 10-14

The W530 × 65 roof beam shown in Figure 10-38 is adequate in moment. Will it meet a deflection limitation of $L/180$?

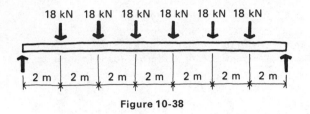

Figure 10-38

Solution: The total load on the beam is 6 times 18, or 108 kN. If this load were uniformly spread out, the unit load would be $w = 7.71$ kN/m. The deflection due to this fictitious load will be less than the actual deflection. If the loads were all gathered into one load of 108 kN and applied at midspan, the deflection thus generated would be considerably greater than the actual.

$$\Delta_{\min} = \frac{5wL^4}{384EI}$$

$$= \frac{5(7.71 \text{ kN/m})(14 \text{ m})^4}{384[200(10)^6 \text{ kN/m}^2][351(10)^{-6} \text{ m}^4]}$$

$$= 5.49(10)^{-2} \text{ m}$$

$$= 55 \text{ mm}$$

$$\Delta_{\max} = \frac{PL^3}{48EI}$$

$$= \frac{108 \text{ kN}(14 \text{ m})^3}{48[200(10)^6 \text{ kN/m}^2][351(10)^{-6} \text{ m}^4]}$$

$$= 8.79(10)^{-2} \text{ m}$$

$$= 88 \text{ mm}$$

We now know that the actual beam deflection is between 55 and 88 mm and, in view of the loading pattern, is probably closer to the lesser value. The code limit is

$$\Delta_{\text{code}} = \frac{L}{180} = \frac{14\ 000 \text{ mm}}{180} = 78 \text{ mm}$$

Examining the upper and lower limits of the actual deflection versus the code allowable, this beam is probably OK in deflection.

Problems

10-13. A W410 × 46.1 serves as a simple beam 9 m long. It supports a uniformly varying load that varies linearly from zero at one end to 25 kN/m at the other. Determine the approximate maximum deflection.

10-14. A Douglas fir 89 × 285 mm beam spans 7 m and is loaded only over its central 3 m by a 4-kN/m uniform load. Determine the approximate maximum deflection.

10-11 SUPERPOSITION AND INDETERMINATE STRUCTURES

In Section 10-1 it was mentioned that one of the prime reasons for studying beam deflection was that it could be used in the analysis of indeterminate structures. Moment-area concepts, in particular, are used in Chapter 15 to develop methods for solving continuous beams and frames. Certain indeterminate structures, however, can be approached directly without further theory and solved through use of the deflection equations in combination with statics. For example, beams that are indeterminate to the first degree (those having only one redundant support component) are easily analyzed through the concepts of superposition.

EXAMPLE 10-15

Determine the vertical reactions for the indeterminate beam in Figure 10-39.

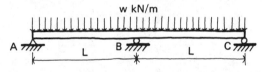

Figure 10-39.   Two-span continuous beam.

Solution: From statics we know that $A_y + B_y + C_y = 2wL$. Moment equations, however, cannot be used directly because any selected moment center will only eliminate one of the three forces and still leave two independent unknowns in each equation (Figure 10-40). It is noted that if any one of the three forces could be obtained by some other means, the remaining two can be easily evaluated. For example, if we denote reaction B_y as the redundant force and remove it, the beam will deflect as shown in Figure 10-41.

If we now apply a force P vertically upward at B, the beam will be pushed back toward its original position. Indeed, if we apply just the right amount of P, say equal in magnitude

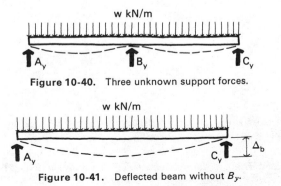

Figure 10-40.   Three unknown support forces.

Figure 10-41.   Deflected beam without B_y.

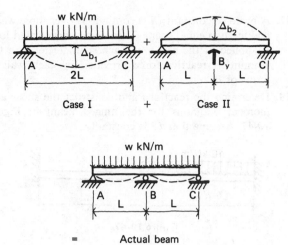

Figure 10-42. Loading cases for Example 10-15.

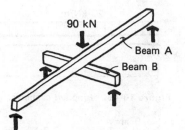

Figure 10-43. Crossed simple beams.

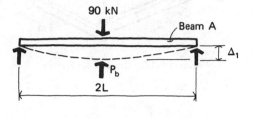

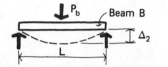

Figure 10-44. Free-body diagrams.

to B_y, we will then have the deflected shape as shown in Figure 10-40, having reduced Δ_b to zero. In other words, the amount of P necessary to remove the deflection Δ_b is called B_y.

The procedure is to first remove the redundant force and calculate the deflection at that point, Δ_{b_1}. The deflection must be equal to Δ_{b_2}, the upward deflection due to B_y acting alone, if we are to get back to the real beam situation of zero deflection at B.

$$\Delta_{b_1} = \Delta_{b_2}$$

Using the appropriate deflection equations from Appendix V, we get

$$\frac{5w(2L)^4}{384EI} = \frac{B_y(2L)^3}{48EI}$$

E, I, and L^3 will drop out, leaving us with

$$B_y = 1.25wL$$

Through symmetry and statics we can then find that

$$A_y = C_y = 0.375wL$$

It should be noted any one of the three vertical support forces could have been declared as the redundant in this example. Owing to a lack of symmetry, the arithmetic would be a bit more involved if we had chosen A_y or C_y.

The concept of equating deflections (really superposition of loads) is a very useful tool in structural analysis. The following example will illustrate its application to a very different kind of indeterminate structure.

EXAMPLE 10-16

Figure 10-43 shows two beams crossed at midspan and having the same EI value. Beam A, however, is twice as long as beam B. How much of the 90 kN is carried by each beam?

Solution: The key to the solution is to recognize that the midspan deflection of the two beams will be equal. From statics the amount of load carried by the two beams must sum to 90 kN. If the load carried by beam B is called P_b, the *net* load carried by beam A is $90 - P_b$, as shown in Figure 10-44. Beam A is simultaneously acted upon by 90 kN down and the

contact force P_b up, whereas beam B is loaded only by P_b downward.

$$\Delta_1 = \Delta_2$$
$$\frac{(90 - P_b)(2L)^3}{48EI} = \frac{P_b(L)^3}{48EI}$$

Solving for P_b yields

$$P_b = 80 \text{ kN}$$

This indicates that the long beam is very lightly loaded, carrying only 10 kN. This is not surprising once we realize that the short beam is much stiffer; consequently it takes considerably more load to deflect than does the long beam. The support reactions will be 40 kN and 5 kN for the short and long beams, respectively.

Example 10-16 is often used to explain the behavior of a rectangular monolithic concrete slab supported on all four edges. The more rectangular or less square is the slab, the greater is the fraction of the load taken by the long edge supports that make the short span. While the bending and torsional forces in a monolithic slab are more involved than this, the idea is essentially correct.

Problems

10-15. Determine the reactions and the shear and moment diagrams for the beam in Figure 10-45. (*Hint: EI* need not be known.)

10-16. In Figure 10-46, beams A and B are crossed at 90° in plan. The two beams are made of the same wood, but beam A has twice the I value of beam B. Determine how much of the load is taken by each beam.

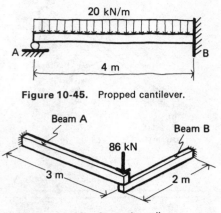

Figure 10-45. Propped cantilever.

Figure 10-46. Crossed cantilevers.

10-17. A beam of constant *EI* is continuous over three walls, making two equal spans. There is a concentrated load *P* applied at the center of each span. Determine the amount of reactive force provided by each wall in terms of *P*.

10-18. Determine the reactions and construct the shear and moment diagrams for the hinged beam in Figure 10-47. Assume that *EI* is constant.

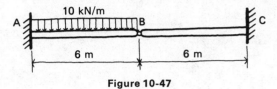

Figure 10-47

11-1 INTRODUCTION

Most conventional building structures involve a vertical support system and a horizontal spanning system. The configuration of such systems and the determination of the required sizes for elements in these systems is an integral part of building design. The horizontal framing or deck system is of particular importance because it almost always involves bending as the primary structural behavior. Its members can become quite large relative to those of the support system, which carries loads in an axial manner. Proper attention to the framing directions of joists, beams, and girders can save both depth and weight in a structural deck. Any excessive structural depth is to be avoided, particularly in multistoried structures where the overall building height and square area of exterior wall can be significantly increased by repetition of the floors. The location and shape of openings in a floor system can present unusual loading patterns and may require special attention structurally. The planning of such openings with the framing system in mind will usually avoid unnecessary conflicts. Similarly, the selection of structural materials is best made with due consideration for the proper span range for such materials and their relative capabilities to resist different kinds of stresses.

Novice designers all too frequently move too far along in the architectural planning process without attention to the structural planning process. Most attempts to "structure" building designs after the major spatial relationships and configurations have been determined result in contorted constructions and/or unsatisfactory compromises. The situation becomes even more disastrous when the preliminary design work was done by manipulating plans and elevations without sufficient attention to what was happening in building section. It has been the author's experience that many framing problems can be easily detected at an early stage by frequent sketches of building sections showing major structural elements.

11-2 SHAPE OF BEAM CROSS SECTIONS

Beams are designed for moment and shearing forces and deflections, all of which are brought about by the loads and spans of a given building structure. In designing bending members, it is helpful to remember that stresses and deflections are developed as functions of cross-sectional shape as well as being responses to externally applied loads. The equations developed in Chapters 8, 9, and 10 illustrate the relationships between beam shape and the magnitude of stresses and deflections.

The general flexure formula, $f_b = Mc/I$, indicates that bending stress is directly proportional to the extreme fiber distance and inversely proportional to the moment of inertia. Since I may be considered a product of cross-sectional area and distance to the neutral axis squared, the approximate net effect is that bending stress decreases linearly as either area or depth is increased. Bending stress in not an inverse function of depth squared, as it is often misrepresented. It *is* true, of course, that bending resistance is increased more by adding material that is remote to the neutral axis rather than near it.

The general shear formula, $f_v = VQ/Ib$, involves Q (a function of area and depth) and I (area and depth squared), which partially offset one another, and b, the section width. These factors tell us that shearing stress is inversely proportional to the area, as measured by b and d. As either b or d gets smaller, the shearing stresses increase. An adequate depth is usually maintained to control flexural stresses, so with shear it becomes critical that an adequate width is maintained.

Deflection is inversely proportional to both E and I. E is independent of cross-sectional shape, but I

Beam Design and Framing

is, once again, a product of area and its location squared. Deflection will be greatly decreased by adding material to the section at points far from the neutral axis but will be decreased to an even greater degree by increasing the section depth.

In conclusion, it is important to notice that the moment of inertia occurs in the denominator of all three cases. It can be concluded that maintaining a large I value per unit of cross-sectional area will almost always result in a structurally efficient beam design.

11-3 "IDEAL" BEAMS

Over the years, various structural analysts have attempted to determine the theoretically most efficient or "ideal" beam shapes to meet certain loading conditions. Although such exercises have little practical value, they are useful in understanding how forces in beams vary and how materials could be shaped to respond in purely structural terms.

The two beams in Figure 11-1(a) and (b) have been shaped so that the depth responds to moment diagrams for uniform and concentrated loads, respectively. As the depth reduces, the width must increase at the ends in order to maintain enough shear capacity. Actually, the uniformly loaded beam should increase its area in a linear manner from midspan to support in an ideal response to shear alone. A variation on this same theme would have a wide-flange section using flanges that increase in thickness slightly as the overall beam depth

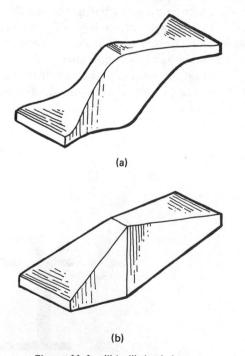

(a)

(b)

Figure 11-1. "Ideal" simple beams.

decreases. In each case, deflection could be controlled by maintaining a high moment of inertia in regions of high bending moment.

The cantilever beams of Figure 11-2 are shaped so they have constant bending stress under concentrated free end loads. The beam of constant depth in Figure 11-2(a) must taper so the section modulus, $S = bd^2/6$, will change in direct proportion to the linear change in moment. To have the same uniform bending stress, the

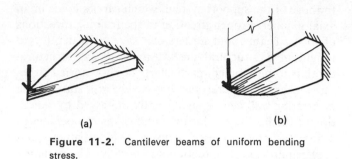

(a)   (b)

Figure 11-2. Cantilever beams of uniform bending stress.

beam of constant width must also have a section modulus that varies with the moment diagram. Since the moment varies with the distance x, as in Figure 11-2(b), the depth of the cross section must vary with the square root of x. In other words, if d is some constant times the square root of x, the section modulus will vary directly with x.

Any number of similar examples can be devised and manipulated to suit particular loading situations and shape constraints. As an exercise, the reader may wish to determine the proper shapes dictated by uniform rather than point loads acting on the cantilevers.

11-4 PROPERTIES OF MATERIALS

In designing framing systems or the individual elements of such systems, it is well to keep in mind the particular characteristics of the material being used. Such knowledge can help prevent irrational schemes and enable the designer to predict areas of probable high stress before any computations are done.

A brief review of the structural nature of each of the three major materials follows. There are always exceptions, of course, to these very general comments.

Wood is quite light and soft. It is generally weak perpendicular to the grain and strong parallel to it. It is very weak in shear, and this stress should always be checked. It is also subject to creep deformations.

Bending stress usually controls member size except for short, heavily loaded spans and overhangs, where shear can govern. The span range is normally up to about 6 m, and deflection will often control the design when the span is this great. Glued laminated sections, plywood box beams, and large timbers can span much farther, of course. Wood is a versatile framing material and minor changes on the job are relatively easy to accomplish. Structure self-weight is seldom a design factor except for large members.

Steel is the strongest of all building materials and is both homogeneous and isotropic. Bending stress will usually control member size, but deflection should be checked. On longer simple spans and cantilevers, deflection limitations can readily govern. The increasing use of high-strength steels, requiring smaller I values for flexure, also increases the proportion of beams designed for deflection. Shear almost never controls member size, but excess shear at selected points can require web stiffeners.

The normal span range for rolled steel sections is about 5 to 15 m. Longer spans frequently employ trusses or plate girders. Steel building frames erect rapidly because of prior shop fabrication, but field modifications are not easily accommodated. Structure self-weight can be a significant part of the design load on longer spans.

Concrete, being an artificial stone, is quite heavy. Although not as dense as steel, much larger cross sections are required in reinforced concrete, and the self-weight of slabs and beams is always significant. Bending stress almost always controls member size. (Bending theory is treated in Chapter 17.) Excess shear is generally resisted by stirrups rather than increased member size. Concrete is subject to creep deformations, and members that are highly stressed on a constant basis may be governed by deflection limitations. The same is true of cantilevers, where deflection is naturally large.

Connections are inherently moment resistant, and advantage should be taken of the consequent indeterminacy of concrete structures. Continuous members require smaller sections than simple ones. The usual span range for reinforced concrete beams is about 5 to 10 m. Longer spans become less efficient but can be accomplished using large member depths. Prestressing is a viable alternative for longer spans.

Reinforced concrete is formable and cross-sectional shape is less restricted than in wood or steel. It is also naturally fire-resistant.

11-5 TRIBUTARY AREA

Every structural element in a framing system has a tributary area, sometimes called a *contributing area*. In conventional structures, it is an area in horizontal plan from which a given member receives all its load. In previous examples and problems, this concept has been introduced by reference to parallel beams or joists spaced a certain distance apart.

Figure 11-3 illustrates how one beam in a parallel

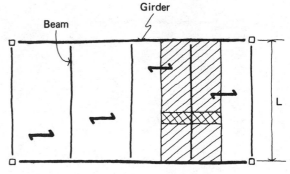

Figure 11-3. Tributary area.

system must accept the loads on that portion of floor or roof deck which extends halfway to the neighboring beams. (The assumption is made here that the deck is constructed such that it acts structurally as shown by the arrows. For our purposes, these arrows may be assumed to represent plank or bar joists or the primary reinforcing of a one-way slab.) The larger, lightly shaded area constitutes the total load on the beam, W. The smaller and more heavily shaded area, called a *tributary strip*, would generate w, the load per running meter of beam. W, of course, equals wL.

In such a framing system, the girders are essentially point-loaded by the beam reactions. The only uniform load acting on the girder would be the girder self-weight. The small strip of dead and live load directly above the space occupied by the girder is usually included in the tributary areas of the beams. Exterior beams have half the deck loading of interior beams but often end up being just as large, for reasons of repetition, economy, or exterior wall loads and torsional effects.

As shown in Figure 11-4, angled beams in plan will generate triangular loading patterns. In this case, both AB and AC have angled tributary areas.

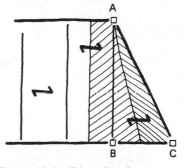

Figure 11-4. Triangular tributary areas.

The open well is framed in Figure 11-5(a) so that the girder AB will have the loading pattern shown in Figure 11-5(b). The concentrated load at midspan is the sum of two equal beam reactions from CM and DM. The student should investigate what happens to this

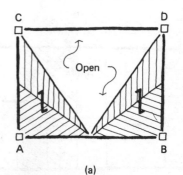

(a)

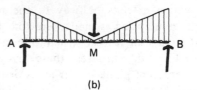

(b)

Figure 11-5. Tributary areas caused by a triangular opening.

loading pattern if the deck structure acts in the other direction (i.e., parallel to *AB*).

Any sort of opening in the horizontal system can usually be framed in more than one manner. The tributary areas and loading patterns on the framing elements will change, depending upon the alternative selected. Figure 11-6 demonstrates two ways to frame a rectangular opening in a structural bay. The loading patterns that result are also shown. Such framing decisions should be made considering all of the influencing factors. If the structure is exposed, the beam directions can have a strong effect upon the character of the space. Mechanical duct runs may require beams to be shallow in one direction but not in the other. Structural efficiency, however, might best be served by a uniformity of depth.

Smaller beam sizes are usually possible if large concentrated loads can be avoided. When this is not practical, it is best to keep loads away from midspan regions, if possible.

The proper location of any type of opening can depend on the framing material. For example, with reinforced concrete, it is very important not to interrupt the structure where continuity is required. In steel, it is important to avoid laterally unsupported spans which can require heavier sections.

Deck construction can also help to determine opening placement. In concrete slabs with beams framing between columns, an opening can be placed in the slab right next to a column. If there are no beams, as in a flat plate deck, all the material around a column is needed for shear and should not be interrupted.

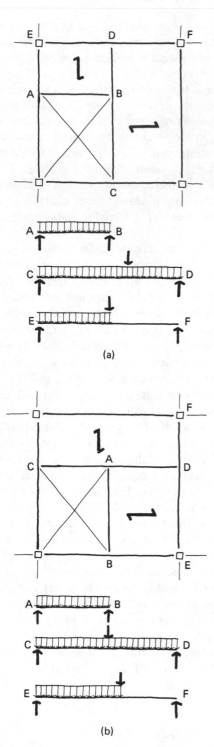

(a)

(b)

Figure 11-6. Opening framing and loading patterns.

11-6 FRAMING DIRECTION

One of the most frequently asked questions concerning framing refers to the optimum way to structure a rectangular bay. Figure 11-7 shows four possibilities without considering any dimensions. In some cases, one or more

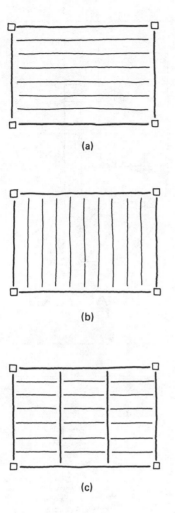

(a)

(b)

(c)

(d)

Figure 11-7. Spanning the long or short distance.

possibilities may be ruled out by calling for unreasonably long or short spans for the material. For example, running the joists in the long direction as in Figure 11-7(a) would not be feasible in wood for spans more than about 6 m. Common joist sizes are unavailable or expensive in longer lengths. Likewise, the long heavily loaded beams of Figure 11-7(b) may not be feasible in reinforced concrete at distances greater than about 15 m. Without prestressing, such long members can become very large and inefficient.

As mentioned in the previous section, one of the foremost determinants of framing direction should be the mechanical system. With a little advance planning, beam directions and large duct runs can be compatibly placed, reducing the overall finish ceiling to finish floor dimension. Smaller ducts and pipes can sometimes pass through holes in beams or girders at acceptable locations. Figure 11-8 shows the better locations for removal of material in a uniformly loaded simple beam, for example.

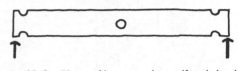

Figure 11-8. Places of low stress in a uniformly loaded simple beam.

The writer's experience has been that many architects make the mechanical system "fit around" the structure by considering it too late in the design process. This is probably a mistake, as the structure should be made to compromise in the interest of total building design and economy. It should be recognized that there are alternative methods to structure a space just as there are alternative ways to heat and cool it.

There is no universally correct way, from a structural standpoint, to frame such rectangular bays. It is easy to observe, however, that long, lightly loaded joists delivering their loads to shorter beams will lead to a uniformity of structural depth. Conversely, short joists creating heavy loads on the longer members will mean shallow joists and deep beams. It can also be noted that some of the load on certain beams can be reduced by one of the techniques of Figure 11-7(c) or (d), should this be beneficial. Such intermediate beams must be used, of course, whenever the deck or slab span becomes too great.

Diagonal framing is possible with reinforced concrete because of the natural continuity between intersecting elements, and this is shown in Figure 11-9. The author considers this to be more novel than practical, owing to the difficult intersections that can occur if bay sizes are not held constant or manipulated to fit the pattern. However, powerful axes can be developed (or obscured) for the space below when such a system is left exposed, and this may be desirable. Diagonal framing

Figure 11-9. Diagonal framing.

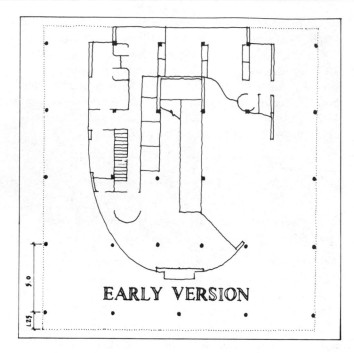

EARLY VERSION

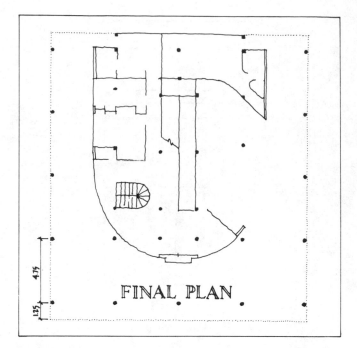

FINAL PLAN

no transverse beams
no cantilever beams
no beams on outside column lines

Adaptability and cleverness in framing a design, whether in order to integrate structure properly with other building systems or to acknowledge, as a matter of principle, that a single perfect geometric system can seldom accommodate all the empirical demands of a given program, have been hallmarks of many good architects. It is instructive, for example, to look at the early and the as-built versions of Le Corbusier's Villa Savoye. Externally, the building presents a very simple structural system, a 4 × 4 m grid of equally-spaced round columns, with cantilevers whose proportion to bay span is such that minimum moment is imparted to the end columns. In both the early and as-built versions, matters on the interior become less diagrammatic and more responsive. The early plan shows the central column line split to make room for a central ramp, and a column in the garage is simply dropped, but the house as a whole still presents an almost regular pattern. The Villa as built is more complicated, but the complexity is *systematic*. To cite a few items: a whole extra row of columns has been added inside, cantilever beams along the main axis of the house have been eliminated (presumably for the sake of a clearer volume above the piloti), and the external bay size lessened without a corresponding reduction of the cantilever. The final plan suggests that what appears to be a platonically-ideal, two-way grid of columns and beams is actually a quite pragmatic one-way system, whose columns can be shifted and whose beams can be expressed or suppressed as circumstances, including esthetic circumstances, demand.

154

can also be helpful in resisting lateral loads on simply connected structures, since a stiff diaphragm plane results from the triangulation.

In "framing out" a building plan, it is helpful to remember the effects of span lengths and load types on the parameters that govern member size. Any increase in span almost always increases load by gathering more tributary area for the member, so the effects of load and span are difficult to differentiate. Assuming for purposes of this discussion, however, that change in span does not necessarily mean change in load, we can state the following with respect to simple beams.

1. Increasing the span alone will cause a proportional change in moment, no change in shear, and will increase deflection as the cube of the relative span change.
2. Increasing a load while making no other changes will cause a proportional increase in moment, shear, and deflection.
3. Changing a uniform load to a concentrated one of the same magnitude will cause the moment to double, no change in shear, and a deflection increase of about 50%.

11-7 SELECTING WOOD AND STEEL BEAMS

Selecting member sizes of rectangular wood sections is a simple matter of:

1. Providing enough section modulus so that the allowable bending stress is not exceeded.
2. Providing enough cross-sectional area so that the allowable shearing stress is not exceeded.
3. Providing enough moment of inertia so that the deflection limitation is not exceeded.

The writer prefers to size the member to meet the bending and shear requirements in a single step and then check the deflection once I is known for the trial section. Alternatively, one could also solve for the I required as part of the initial determination.

With wood, it is important to remember that the allowable stress values (but not the modulus of elasticity) should be modified for duration of loading and the presence of moisture if warranted by the situation (see Appendix P).

The first procedure in selecting steel beams usually involves finding the lightest member having an adequate section modulus. For a given section modulus, the lightest beam is usually the deepest and, in the absence of other factors, this would be the one selected. Frequently,

there are other considerations, which make a shallower and less efficient section more suitable. The optimum choice can only be made by including the various nonstructural factors as well.

After a trial section has been selected, deflection is checked (except in such cases where it is obvious that deflection will not be excessive). As previously indicated, shear is seldom very great and need not be checked under normal loading circumstances. In any event, it will seldom control member size.

With steel, in particular, the designer must be alert for any unbraced lengths of compression flange that can necessitate large reductions in allowable bending stress and a corresponding increase in member size.

EXAMPLE 11-1

Design the residential floor system of Figure 11-10. The live load is 2 kN/m² and the total dead load, including an allowance for the members, is 0.5 kN/m². Use hem-fir. Assume that the deflection due to live load is limited to $L/360$.
(a) Select a typical joist.
(b) Design a header beam for the 3-m span. Use side-by-side $38 \times ?$ mm pieces.

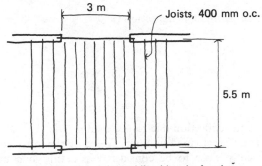

Figure 11-10. Joist and lintel header framing.

Solution:

(a) T.L. $= 2 + 0.5 = 2.5$ kN/m². In terms of tributary area,

$$w = \frac{400}{1000}(2.5) = 1 \text{ kN/m}$$

$$M = \frac{wL^2}{8} \qquad\qquad V = \frac{wL}{2}$$

$$= \frac{(1 \text{ kN/m})(5.5 \text{ m})^2}{8} \qquad = \frac{(1 \text{ kN/m})5.5 \text{ m}}{2}$$

$$= 3.78 \text{ kN·m} \qquad\qquad = 2.75 \text{ kN}$$

$$S_r = \frac{M}{F_b} \qquad\qquad A_r = \frac{3V}{2F_v}$$

$$= \frac{3.78 \text{ kN·m}}{9600 \text{ kPa}} \qquad = \frac{3(2.75 \text{ kN})}{2(500 \text{ kPa})}$$

$$= 0.000\ 394 \text{ m}^3 \qquad = 0.008\ 25 \text{ m}^2$$

or

$$S_r = 394(10)^3 \text{ mm}^3 \qquad A_r = 8250 \text{ mm}^2$$

To meet these requirements, try a 38×285 mm joist from Appendix Q. A 38×235 mm section would be OK in shear but inadequate in moment. If shear had been controlling, the value of V could be reduced after the approximate joist depth become known. Since loads within d distance of a support can be ignored (see Section 9-8), the actual V for design could be taken as

$$V = \frac{wL}{2}\left(1 - \frac{2d}{L}\right)$$

To check deflection, first find the live load. We can ratio the total load downward,

$$w = \frac{2.0}{2.5}(1 \text{ kN/m})$$
$$= 0.8 \text{ kN/m}$$

For a uniformly loaded simple beam,

$$\Delta_{max} = \frac{5wL^4}{384EI}$$

For a 38×285 mm joist, $I = 73.3(10)^6$ mm^4, so

$$\Delta_{max} = \frac{5(0.8 \text{ kN/m})(5.5 \text{ m})^4}{384[10\ 300(10)^3 \text{ kN/m}^2][73.3(10)^{-6} \text{ m}^4]}$$
$$= 0.0126 \text{ m}$$
$$= 13 \text{ mm}$$

The permissible deflection is

$$\Delta_{code} = \frac{L}{360}$$
$$= \frac{5500 \text{ mm}}{360}$$
$$= 15 \text{ mm}$$

So the deflection due to live load is OK.

(b) The discrete load points provided by the joists are sufficiently close to be considered as acting in a uniform manner. The tributary strip for one header is one-half of the joist span, or 2.75 m.

$$w = 2.75 \text{ m}(2.5 \text{ kN/m}^2)$$
$$= 6.88 \text{ kN/m}$$

$$M = \frac{wL^2}{8} \qquad\qquad V = \frac{wL}{2}$$
$$= \frac{(6.88 \text{ kN/m})(3 \text{ m})^2}{8} \qquad = \frac{(6.88 \text{ kN/m})3 \text{ m}}{2}$$
$$= 7.74 \text{ kN·m} \qquad\qquad = 10.3 \text{ kN}$$

$$S_r = \frac{M}{F_b} \qquad\qquad A_r = \frac{3V}{2F_v}$$
$$= \frac{7.74 \text{ kN·m}}{8300 \text{ kPa}} \qquad = \frac{3(10.3 \text{ kN})}{2(500 \text{ kPa})}$$
$$= 0.000\ 932 \text{ m}^3 \qquad = 0.0309 \text{ m}^2$$

or

$$S_r = 932(10)^3 \text{ mm}^3 \qquad A_r = 30\ 900 \text{ mm}^2$$

From Appendix Q, the required area for shear

will control, so V should be reduced as previously discussed.

$$V = \frac{wL}{2}\left(1 - \frac{2d}{L}\right)$$

Assuming that d will be 285 mm, we get

$$V = 10.3 \text{ kN}\left[1 - \frac{2(0.285 \text{ m})}{3.0 \text{ m}}\right]$$
$$= 8.34 \text{ kN}$$

Reducing the previously determined value of A_r by ratio,

$$A_r = \frac{8.34}{10.3}(30\ 900 \text{ mm}^2)$$
$$= 25\ 000 \text{ mm}^2$$

A doubled 38×285 mm member will provide only 21 600 mm^2. To try three 38×235 mm pieces, the shear reduction will have to be modified.

(*Note:* For ease of construction and in spite of the overdesign, it might be more practical to use three 38×285 mm, since the joists being supported have that depth. However, we will continue to check out the shallower beam for this example.)

$$V = \frac{wL}{2}\left(1 - \frac{2d}{L}\right)$$
$$= 10.3 \text{ kN}\left[1 - \frac{2(0.235 \text{ m})}{3.0 \text{ m}}\right]$$
$$= 8.69 \text{ kN}$$
$$A_r = \frac{8.69}{10.3}(30\ 900 \text{ mm}^2)$$
$$= 26\ 100 \text{ mm}^2$$

Three 38×235 mm will give us $A = 26\ 800$ mm^2 and $S = 1050(10)^3$ mm^3. Both are sufficient.

Check live-load deflection even though it is doubtful that deflection would control on such a short span.

$$w = \frac{2.0}{2.5}(6.88 \text{ kN/m})$$
$$= 5.5 \text{ kN/m}$$
$$I = 123(10)^6 \text{ mm}^4$$
$$\Delta_{max} = \frac{5wL^4}{384EI}$$
$$= \frac{5(5.5 \text{ kN/m})(3.0 \text{ m})^4}{384[10\ 300(10)^3 \text{ kN/m}^2][123(10)^{-6} \text{ m}^4]}$$
$$= 0.0046 \text{ m}$$
$$= 5 \text{ mm}$$

The permissible deflection is

$$\Delta_{code} = \frac{L}{360}$$
$$= \frac{3000 \text{ mm}}{360}$$
$$= 8 \text{ mm}$$

The actual deflection is less than that permitted.

EXAMPLE 11-2

Design the roof members of Figure 11-11 using Douglas fir. The snow load is 1.2 kN/m² and the allowance for total dead load is 0.7 kN per square meter of slope.

(a) Select a beam 89 mm thick and assume that Δ may be ignored.

(b) Select a 139-mm-thick member for the girder AB. Assume that the total deflection must not exceed $L/180$.

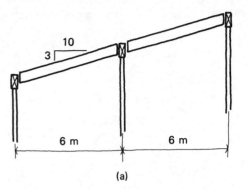

(a)

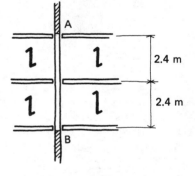

(b)

Figure 11-11. Roof framing: (a) section; (b) partial plan.

Solution: First, convert the dead load to get its equivalent on the horizontal projection. The hypotenuse of the slope is 10.44; therefore, $(0.7 \text{ kN/m}^2)/(10.0/10.44) = 0.73$ kN/m². The total design load is 1.2 plus 0.73, or 1.93 kN/m².

(a) The tributary strip for a beam is 2.4 m. Thus,

$$w = 1.93 \text{ kN/m}^2 (2.4 \text{ m})$$
$$= 4.63 \text{ kN/m}$$

$$M = \frac{wL^2}{8} \qquad\qquad V = \frac{wL}{2}$$

$$= \frac{(4.63 \text{ kN/m})(6 \text{ m})^2}{8} \qquad = \frac{(4.63 \text{ kN/m})(6 \text{ m})}{2}$$

$$= 20.8 \text{ kN·m} \qquad\qquad = 13.9 \text{ kN}$$

$$S_r = \frac{M}{F_b} \qquad\qquad A_r = \frac{3V}{2F_v}$$

The allowable stresses may be increased by 15% for the temporary snow load, following Appendix P.

$$S_r = \frac{20.8 \text{ kN·m}}{1.15(10\ 300 \text{ kPa})} \qquad A_r = \frac{3(13.9 \text{ kN})}{2(1.15)(650 \text{ kPa})}$$

$$= 0.001\ 76 \text{ m}^3 \qquad\qquad = 0.0279 \text{ m}^2$$

or

$$S_r = 1760(10)^3 \text{ mm}^3 \qquad A_r = 27\ 900 \text{ mm}^2$$

An 89×385 mm beam is required by moment. Shear is no problem. As specified, deflection may be ignored. (This is often done on roof slopes, where "ponding" would not be a problem.)

(b) The girder AB is loaded by a single concentrated load at midspan, which is equal in magnitude to two beam reactions.

$$P = 2R$$
$$= 2\left(\frac{wL}{2}\right)$$
$$= 2(13.9 \text{ kN})$$
$$= 27.8 \text{ kN}$$

$$M = \frac{PL}{4} \qquad\qquad V = \frac{P}{2}$$

$$= \frac{(27.8 \text{ kN})4.8 \text{ m}}{4} \qquad = \frac{27.8 \text{ kN}}{2}$$

$$= 33.4 \text{ kN·m} \qquad\qquad = 13.9 \text{ kN}$$

$$S_r = \frac{M}{F_b} \qquad\qquad A_r = \frac{3V}{2F_v}$$

$$= \frac{33.4 \text{ kN·m}}{1.15(8900 \text{ kPa})} \qquad = \frac{3(13.9 \text{ kN})}{2600 \text{ kPa}}$$

$$= 0.003\ 26 \text{ m}^3 \qquad\qquad = 0.0302 \text{ m}^2$$

or

$$S_r = 3260(10)^3 \text{ mm}^3 \qquad A_r = 30\ 200 \text{ mm}^2$$

A 139×385 mm girder is needed with moment controlling. Since such a large section is being used and the required section modulus is quite close to that provided, the self-weight of the girder should be included. The approximate density of wood is 550 kg per cubic meter and 1 kg exerts a force of 9.8 N. The weight of wood is then about 5.4 kN/m³. The self-weight per running meter for the girder cross section is

$$(0.139)(0.385)(5.4 \text{ kN/m}^3) = 0.289 \text{ kN/m}$$

The moment from this uniform load maximizes at midspan, where that of the concentrated load does, and is given by

$$M_{\text{s.w.}} = \frac{wL^2}{8}$$
$$= \frac{(0.289 \text{ kN/m})(4.8 \text{ m})^2}{8}$$
$$= 0.83 \text{ kN·m}$$

The total moment is then 33.4 plus 0.8, or 34.2 kN·m. The new S_r is by ratio,

$$S_{r_{\text{new}}} = \frac{34.2}{33.4}(3260)(10)^3 \text{ mm}^3 = 3340(10)^3 \text{ mm}^3$$

This is still less than the S provided of $3430(10)^3$ mm³.

The deflection can be computed using case 3 from Appendix V.

$$\Delta_{\text{max}} = \frac{PL^3}{48EI}$$

$$= \frac{(27.8 \text{ kN})(4.8 \text{ m})^3}{48[(11\ 000)(10)^3 \text{ kN/m}^2][661(10)^{-6} \text{ m}^4]}$$

$$= 0.0088 \text{ m}$$

$$= 9 \text{ mm}$$

The permissible deflection is

$$\Delta_{\text{code}} = \frac{L}{180}$$

$$= \frac{4800 \text{ mm}}{180}$$

$$= 27 \text{ mm}$$

which is well beyond the actual. The additional deflection due to member self-weight would, of course, be negligible.

EXAMPLE 11-3

Select the steel W shapes designated as *AB*, *CD*, and *EF* in Figure 11-12. The plan shows two adjacent open wells on either side of *EF*. The live load is 4 kN/m² and the dead load is 1 kN/m², which is sufficient to include the beams themselves. Use $F_y = 250$ MPa steel and a deflection limitation due to live load of $L/360$. The maximum depth permitted is a nominal 530 mm, owing to the mechanical system requirements.

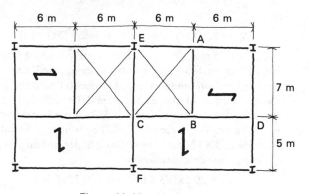

Figure 11-12. Framing plan.

Solution: The total load is 5 kN/m². The allowable stress for beams *AB* and *CD* is 165 MPa, assuming full lateral support from the floor deck. Girder *EF* is unbraced for 7 m. For beam *AB*,

$$w = (3 \text{ m})(5 \text{ kN/m}^2)$$

$$= 15 \text{ kN/m}$$

$$M = \frac{wL^2}{8}$$

$$= \frac{(15 \text{ kN/m})(7 \text{ m})^2}{8}$$

$$= 91.9 \text{ kN} \cdot \text{m}$$

$$S_r = \frac{M}{F_b}$$

$$= \frac{91.9 \text{ kN} \cdot \text{m}}{165\ 000 \text{ kPa}}$$

$$= 0.000\ 557 \text{ m}^3$$

or

$$S_r = 557(10)^3 \text{ mm}^3$$

From Appendix S, the lightest adequate section is a W360 × 39 with an *S* value of 578(10)³ mm³. The deflection can be checked by

$$\Delta_{\text{max}} = \frac{5wL^4}{384EI}$$

Using a live load of

$$\tfrac{4}{5}(15 \text{ kN/m}) = 12 \text{ kN/m}$$

$$\Delta_{\text{max}} = \frac{5(12 \text{ kN/m})(7 \text{ m})^4}{384[200(10)^6 \text{ kN/m}^2][102(10)^{-6} \text{ mm}^4]}$$

$$= 0.0184 \text{ m}$$

$$= 18 \text{ mm}$$

The code permits a live-load deflection of

$$\Delta_{\text{code}} = \frac{L}{360}$$

$$= \frac{7000 \text{ mm}}{360}$$

$$= 19 \text{ mm}$$

Beam *CD* receives a concentrated load from *AB* at *B* and also carries a uniform load from a strip of floor deck. The concentrated load is one-half the total load on *AB* [i.e., (3.5 m)(15 kN/m) equals 52.5 kN]. The tributary strip for the uniform load is 2.5 m wide and

$$w = (2.5 \text{ m})(5 \text{ kN/m}^2)$$

$$= 12.5 \text{ kN/m}$$

The loading pattern is given in Figure 11-13. The maximum moment from the combined loading is

$$M = \frac{PL}{4} + \frac{wL^2}{8}$$

$$= \frac{(52.5 \text{ kN})(12 \text{ m})}{4} + \frac{(12.5 \text{ kN/m})(12 \text{ m})^2}{8}$$

$$= 158 \text{ kN} \cdot \text{m} + 225 \text{ kN} \cdot \text{m}$$

$$= 383 \text{ kN} \cdot \text{m}$$

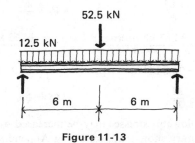

Figure 11-13

$$S_r = \frac{M}{F_b}$$

$$= \frac{383 \text{ kN} \cdot \text{m}}{165\ 000 \text{ kPa}}$$

$$= 0.002\ 32 \text{ m}^3$$

or

$$S_r = 2320(10)^3 \text{ mm}^3$$

The lightest fully adequate section is a W610 × 101. However, this exceeds the stated depth restriction, so a W530 should be selected. A W530 × 101 has an S value of $2290(10)^3$ mm³, almost enough and is just as light as the deeper W610. The percentage overstress can be computed by the ratio

$$\frac{S_{\text{required}} - S_{\text{provided}}}{S_{\text{provided}}} = \frac{2320(10)^3 \text{ mm}^3 - 2290(10)^3 \text{ mm}^3}{2290(10)^3 \text{ mm}^3}$$

$$= 0.013 \quad \text{or} \quad 1.3\%$$

This is within the accuracy of our assumptions, especially the live-load value. The W530 × 101 will be checked for deflection.

$$\Delta_{\max} = \frac{PL^3}{48EI} + \frac{5wL^4}{384EI}$$

The portion of the total load that is live can be obtained by ratio.

$$\tfrac{4}{5}(52.5 \text{ kN}) = 42 \text{ kN}$$

$$\tfrac{4}{5}(12.5 \text{ kN/m}) = 10 \text{ kN/m}$$

$$\Delta_{\max} = \frac{(42 \text{ kN})(12 \text{ m})^3}{48[200(10)^6 \text{ kN/m}^2][616(10)^{-6} \text{ m}^4]}$$

$$+ \frac{5(10 \text{ kN/m})(12 \text{ m})^4}{384[200(10)^6 \text{ kN/m}^2][616(10)^{-6} \text{ m}^4]}$$

$$= 0.0123 \text{ m} + 0.0219$$

$$= 34 \text{ mm}$$

The permitted live-load deflection is

$$\Delta_{\text{code}} = \frac{L}{360}$$

$$= \frac{12\ 000 \text{ mm}}{360}$$

$$= 33 \text{ mm}$$

The deflection is slightly excessive but not enough to justify selecting a heavier section. The W530 × 101 will be used.

Girder *EF* is loaded only by a concentrated load at *C*, equal to the sum of two reactions, one each from *CD* and its counterpart in the opposite bay.

$$P = 2R$$

$$= 2\left[\tfrac{1}{2}P_B + \frac{wL}{2}\right]$$

$$= 2\left[\tfrac{1}{2}(52.5 \text{ kN}) + \frac{(12.5 \text{ kN/m})(12 \text{ m})}{2}\right]$$

$$= 203 \text{ kN}$$

The loading pattern and the shear and moment diagrams for *EF* are given in Figure 11-14. Since the girder is

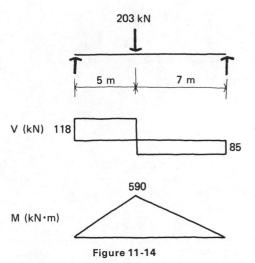

Figure 11-14

unbraced for a significant portion of its span, the allowable stress must be reduced. The final allowable stress is based upon the unbraced length (7 m in this case) and the lateral stability of the trial cross section. The AISC *Manual of Steel Construction* provides graphs for the direct solution of this type of problem and also tabulates the values of r_T and A_f, used in the formulas of Section 9-6. Without such design aids, the problem becomes a lengthy one involving select-and-try procedures. Even then, a table of dimensions for all the steel sections would be required. In the absence of such information, we will assume a conservative value for F_b and proceed to find at least an approximate beam size.

Since the girder is unbraced for more than half its length, the allowable stress will probably be quite low. For this example, we shall take it as one-half the fully braced allowable stress of 165 MPa.

$$S_r = \frac{M}{\tfrac{1}{2}F_b}$$

$$= \frac{590 \text{ kN} \cdot \text{m}}{82\ 500 \text{ kPa}}$$

$$= 0.007\ 15 \text{ m}^3$$

$$= 7150(10)^3 \text{ mm}^3$$

This will require a W360 × 421, which has a section modulus of $7520(10)^3$ mm. (It is probable that more exacting procedures would yield a lighter shape.)

Although it is unlikely that deflection will be a problem because of the low value of F_b used, we will check it anyway in the interest of completeness. Rather than compute an exact value, we shall approximate the maximum deflection by pretending the load is at midspan (see Section 10-10).

$$\Delta_{\max} = \frac{PL^3}{48EI}$$

The live load is

$$\tfrac{4}{5}(203 \text{ kN}) = 162 \text{ kN}$$

$$\Delta_{\substack{\max \\ \text{approx}}} = \frac{(162 \text{ kN})(12 \text{ m})^3}{48[200(10)^6 \text{ kN/m}^2][1600(10)^{-6} \text{ m}^4]}$$

$$= 0.0182 \text{ m}$$

or

$$\Delta_{\substack{max \\ approx}} = 18 \text{ mm}$$

The permitted live-load deflection by code is

$$\Delta_{code} = \frac{L}{360}$$

$$= \frac{12\ 000 \text{ mm}}{360}$$

$$= 33 \text{ mm}$$

The W360 × 421 will suffice.

EXAMPLE 11-4

Select a W shape for the beam *AB* (Figure 11-15). The live load on the floor is 5 kN/m² and the dead load, including all structural elements, is 1 kN/m². There is also a 3-m-high masonry wall which bounds the opening from *A* to *C* to *D*. The wall has a mass of 400 kg per square meter of elevation. The deflection due to live load is limited to *L*/360 and that due to total load is limited to *L*/240. Use high-strength $F_y =$ 345-MPa steel.

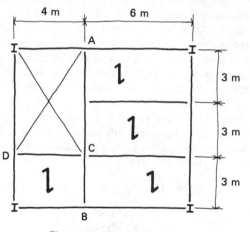

Figure 11-15. Framing plan.

Solution: The beam *AB* is loaded by two unequal concentrated loads at the third points plus a uniform load from that portion of the wall from *A* to *C*. The total floor load is 6 kN/m². The wall load per square meter is 9.8 N/kg times 400 kg or 3.92 kN. The wall is 3 m tall, so the wall load is

$$w = (3 \text{ m})(3.92 \text{ kN/m}^2)$$

$$= 11.8 \text{ kN/m}$$

The beam *DC* carries the wall directly above it plus a 1.5-m tributary strip of floor. Its uniform load is 11.8 kN/m plus 1.5 m (6 kN/m²), for a total of 20.8 kN/m. The reaction at *C* is (20.8 kN/m)(2 m), or 41.6 kN.

The two beams coming into *AB* from the right each have a tributary area of 18 m², and half of this gets to beam *AB*. The magnitude of each reaction upon *AB* is, therefore, ½(18 m²)(6 kN/m²), or 54 kN, so the loads end up as shown in Figure 11-16(b). Figure 11-17 provides the *V* and *M* diagrams.

With full lateral support, the allowable bending stress for $F_y =$ 345-MPa steel is 230 MPa.

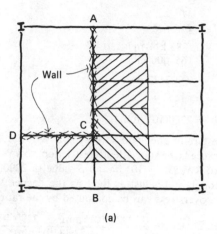

(a)

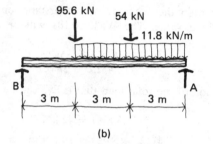

(b)

Figure 11-16. Tributary areas and final loading pattern.

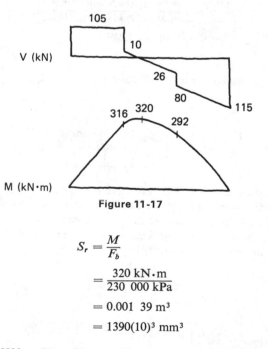

Figure 11-17

$$S_r = \frac{M}{F_b}$$

$$= \frac{320 \text{ kN} \cdot \text{m}}{230\ 000 \text{ kPa}}$$

$$= 0.001\ 39 \text{ m}^3$$

$$= 1390(10)^3 \text{ mm}^3$$

A W530 × 74 will provide a section modulus of 1550(10)³ mm³.

To make an approximate check on the total deflection, we shall simplify the loading pattern in the conservative direction as shown in Figure 11-18.

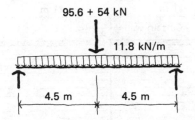

Figure 11-18. Loading pattern for approximate deflection computation.

$$\Delta_{\substack{max \\ approx}} = \frac{5wL^4}{384EI} + \frac{PL^3}{48EI}$$

$$= \frac{5(11.8 \text{ kN/m})(9 \text{ m})^4}{384[200(10)^6 \text{ kN/m}^2][410(10)^{-6} \text{ m}^4]}$$

$$+ \frac{149.6 \text{ kN}(9 \text{ m})^3}{48[200(10)^6 \text{ kN/m}^2][410(10)^{-6} \text{ m}^4]}$$

$$= 0.0123 \text{ m} + 0.0277 \text{ m}$$

or

$$\Delta_{\substack{max \\ approx}} = 40 \text{ mm}$$

The permitted total deflection is

$$\Delta_{code} = \frac{L}{240}$$

$$= \frac{9000 \text{ mm}}{240}$$

$$= 38 \text{ mm}$$

Our approximate deflection exceeds the allowable value by 3 mm, but since the computation was in the conservative direction, the actual deflection will almost surely be OK.

We still need to check the deflection due to live load alone against $L/360$. The live loads are shown in Figure 11-19(a) and can be combined into one load to overestimate their effect, as we have done previously. Referring to Figure 11-19(b), we get

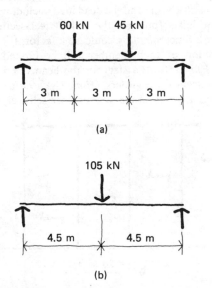

(a)

(b)

Figure 11-19. Simplification of live load for approximate deflection computation.

$$\Delta_{\substack{max \\ approx}} = \frac{PL^3}{48EI}$$

$$= \frac{105 \text{ kN}(9 \text{ m})^3}{48[200(10)^6 \text{ kN/m}^2][410(10)^{-6} \text{ m}^4]}$$

$$= 0.0194 \text{ m}$$

or

$$\Delta_{\substack{max \\ approx}} = 19 \text{ mm}$$

This compares to a live-load limitation of

$$\Delta_{code} = \frac{L}{360}$$

$$= \frac{9000 \text{ mm}}{360}$$

$$= 25 \text{ mm}$$

The W530 × 74 will be OK.

Problems

11-1. Design the members for the balcony floor in Figure 11-20. The live load is 0.5 kN/m² and the dead load is 0.5 kN/m². Use hem-fir members of 38-mm stock. Two or more may be used to make beams as needed. The maximum depth allowed is 235 mm and the live-load deflection is limited to $L/300$ by local code. Assume full lateral support for all members.

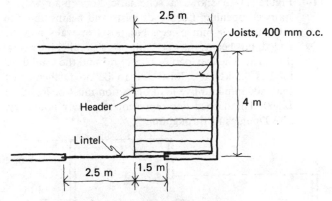

Figure 11-20. Balcony framing.

11-2. With reference to Figure 11-21, size the joists (for the 4.5-m span) and determine how many 38 × 285

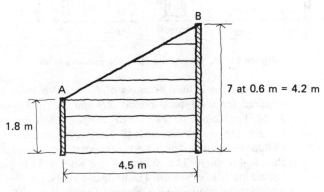

Figure 11-21. Roof framing plan.

members are required for the beam *AB*. The snow load is 1.5 kN/m² and the dead load is 0.65 kN/m². Use eastern spruce and assume a total deflection limit of *L*/180.

11-3. Beams *AB* shown in Figure 11-22 are spaced 1 m apart. The girder at *C* is 3 m long and supports two of the beams at its third points. Select an 89-mm member for the beams and a 139-mm member for the girder. The snow load is 1.2 kN/m² and the dead load is 0.8 kN/m², both taken on the horizontal projection. Assume that deflection is not a concern for the beam but that the girder deflection should be limited to *L*/180. Use Douglas fir.

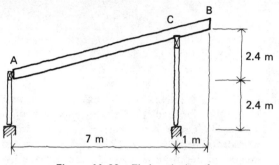

Figure 11-22.   Timber shed roof.

11-4. Figure 11-23 shows a schematic floor plan with a stairwell opening. Locate all joists and beams and size them using 38-mm pieces. No posts or walls may be added, but beams may be built up of parallel members, if needed. The live load is 2.0 kN/m² and the total dead load is 0.5 kN/m². Joists are to be no farther apart than 400 mm and live-load deflection must be less than *L*/360. The dashed line represents the floor boundary. Use Douglas fir throughout.

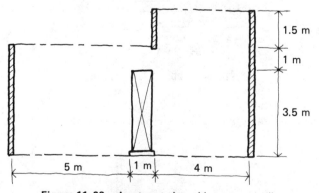

Figure 11-23.   Apartment plan with masonry walls.

11-5. Determine the lightest sections of $F_y = 250$-MPa steel required for the typical beams *AB* and *AC* in Figure 11-24. The dashed lines represent bar joists 800 mm on centers. The spandrel beams *AC* carry only a small strip of floor but must support a precast concrete curtain wall that is 4 m high. The weight of the wall is 2 kN per square meter of elevation. The floor live load is 4 kN/m², and the total dead load is 1 kN/m². The live-load deflec-

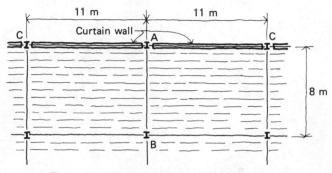

Figure 11-24.   Portion of a steel framing plan.

tion of beam *AB* must be less than *L*/360 and the total load deflection of *AC* must be less than *L*/270.

11-6. Beam *AB* in Figure 11-25 is limited in depth to a nominal 530 mm. The live load is 3 kN/m² and the total dead load is 1.5 kN/m². The code limit on total deflection is *L*/240. Select a section for beam *AB* using $F_y = 250$-MPa steel.

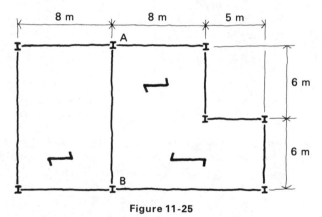

Figure 11-25

11-7. Figure 11-26 shows a long-span, flat roof structure designed using bar joists, beams, and girders. The snow load is 1.5 kN/m² and the dead load, including the weight of the joists (but not the rolled steel section), is 1.3 kN/m². Since ponding could be a factor, the dead-load deflection of each member will be limited to *L*/360. Use $F_y = 250$-MPa steel for the beams and $F_y = 345$-MPa steel for the girders. (*Hint:* Use accurate deflection computations and include member self-weight.)

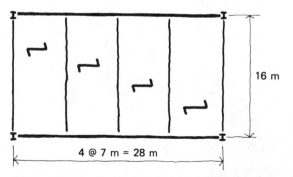

Figure 11-26.   Framing plan for a long-span steel frame.

11-8. Locate and size all the beams and girders for the office building floor plan in Figure 11-27. Note the absence of a column at the center of the east side. Closely spaced joists, which deliver uniform loads to beams, may be used for the floor deck, but these must span neither less than 4 m nor more than 10 m. The live load is 4 kN/m² and the dead load is 1 kN/m², which includes an allowance for the self-weight of all structural elements. There is a masonry wall around each stairwell and along the periphery as shown. Its mass is 306 kg/m² of elevation and it is 4 m high. The live-load deflection of the interior beams is limited to $L/360$ and the total load deflection of all spandrel beams must not exceed $L/270$. The dashed line represents the exterior face of the building. Assume that the floor deck provides full lateral support for all members and use $F_y = 250$ MPa throughout.

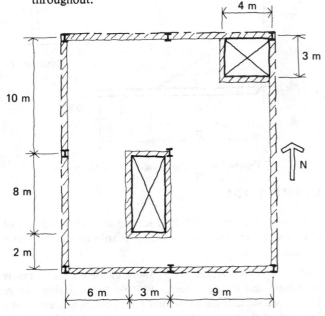

Figure 11-27. Office building schematic plan.

11-8 DESIGN AIDS FOR WOOD AND STEEL

The process of beam sizing can be accelerated considerably by the proper use of design aids published by manu-facturers' associations. Much of the data needed concerning member selection have been printed in the form of convenient graphs, charts, and tables. In many cases, beams can be selected with almost no computational work.

The often-mentioned AISC *Manual of Steel Construction* is an absolute necessity for any steel design work. Beam selection involves only a determination of the loads or the maximum moment. Even deflection magnitudes are tabulated for common load situations.

For timber design, the National Forest Products Association publishes an inexpensive, bound volume of tables called *Wood Structural Design Data*. For each nominal beam size and many different values of F_b, the permissible uniform loads are tabulated for a range of spans. The resulting maximum shear stress is given for each load and the required E value for an $L/360$ deflection limit has been computed. Common uniformly loaded joists and header beams can often be sized without making a single written computation.

Open-web steel joists are so standardized that their design is almost always done by selection from allowable load tables. These tables are prepared by the Steel Joist Institute and include values of permissible uniform loads by section and span as limited by bending, end reaction, and deflection.

As with any design aid or shortcut, the designer must be aware of how the data were generated and when the actual situation departs from the one used to get the data. Many unfortunate errors have occurred through a misunderstanding or misapplication of tabled values. Similarly, the designer should always be wary of making decisions and leaving no record of how the choice was made or the options that were available. Good design is an iterative process, often accomplished over a substantial period of time, and unless good records are kept, much of the work ends up being done over and over again.

At this writing, most of these publications are available only in the customary system of units, but it is only a matter of time before all industries will have similar items available in SI units.

12-1 AXIAL STRESSES
IN BENDING MEMBERS

Building structures are subjected to a great variety of loading patterns, and frequently a number of different types of stress will act upon the same member or cross section at the same time. Probably the most frequent combination is that of two types of normal stress, axial and flexural. Axial stresses, except when they are present in long, slender compression members or concentrated at connections, are usually of small consequence. An axial load is distributed evenly over the entire cross section and the resulting stresses can be quite low. However, these stresses must be added algebraically to any other normal stresses acting on a given section, such as flexural stresses. Since bending results in both tensile and compressive stress, any additional stress that is uniform over the cross section will be additive to one sense of bending stress and subtractive from the other. This is illustrated in Figure 12-1, which shows what

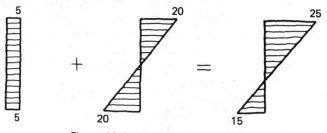

Figure 12-1. Axial plus flexural stress.

happens to the extreme fiber stresses when two normal stresses combine at the same cross section. Notice from Figure 12-1(c) that the effective neutral axis has moved from its centroidal position. Its location will depend largely on the relative magnitude and sense of the applied loads and will vary over the member length.

When flexure occurs about one of the principal axes and combines with the axial load (applied through the centroid of the cross section), the general equation for extreme fiber stresses is

$$f = \pm \frac{P}{A} \pm \frac{Mc}{I} \qquad (12\text{-}1)$$

In using Equation (12-1) we shall take the positive sign to represent tension and the negative sign to mean compression. Where applicable, the section modulus may be used instead of c and I.

When the axial load is applied to only part of a member, as in Figure 12-2, the maximum tensile and compressive stresses will usually occur at two different transverse sections.

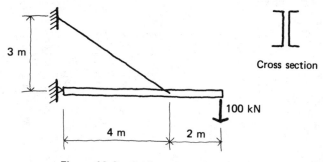

Figure 12-2. Cable-supported cantilever.

EXAMPLE 12-1

The beam in Figure 12-2 is made up of two C380 × 50.4 channels. Determine the maximum tensile and compressive stresses.

Solution: From Appendix S, the area of each channel is 6430 mm² and its S_x value is $688(10)^3$ mm³. Using Figure 12-3(a), we see that the axial load P acts compressively on the first 4 m of the beam. The maximum moment is 200 kN·m. Just to the left of the point where the cable attaches to the

12

Combined Stresses

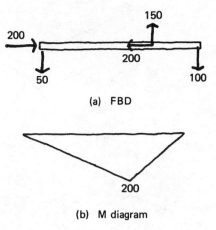

(a) FBD

(b) M diagram

Figure 12-3. (a) FBD ; (b) *M* diagram.

beam, we get the stress distribution shown in Figure 12-4. Compressive stresses are plotted to the right of the reference line and tensile stresses to the left. The magnitudes are computed using Equation (12-1).

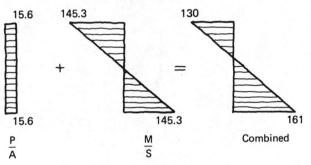

Figure 12-4. Stress distributions (MPa).

$$f_{top} = -\frac{P}{A} + \frac{M}{S}$$

$$= -\frac{200 \text{ kN}}{2(0.006\ 43) \text{ m}^2} + \frac{200 \text{ kN·m}}{2(0.000\ 688) \text{ m}^3}$$

$$= -15\ 600 \text{ kPa} + 145\ 300 \text{ kPa}$$

$$= 130 \text{ MPa}$$

$$f_{bottom} = -15.6 \text{ MPa} - 145.3 \text{ MPa}$$

$$= -161 \text{ MPa}$$

The maximum compressive stress is 161 MPa, at the bottom edge of the beam just to the left of the cable connection. The maximum tensile stress, however, occurs just to the right of that connection, where bending alone exists. It is 145 MPa and is, of course, at the top edge of the beam.

Problems

12-1. With reference to the structure in Figure 12-5, determine the top and bottom fiber stresses at the section where the 40-kN load is applied.

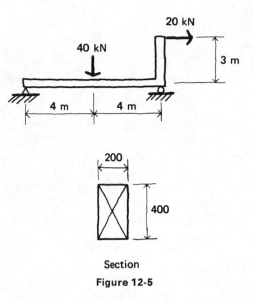

Section

Figure 12-5

12-2. With reference to Figure 12-2, rework Example 12-1 but change the slope of the cable by moving its top end downward 2 m. The cable will now have a slope of one on four.

12-3. Determine the maximum tensile and compressive stresses in the member *AB* of the structure in Figure 12-6. Ignore the material removed in order to make the connections.

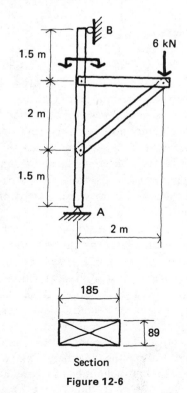

Section

Figure 12-6

12-4. The glu-lam beam in Figure 12-7 is supported by a cable that passes through it to attach at a bottom corner edge. Determine the maximum tensile and compressive stresses.

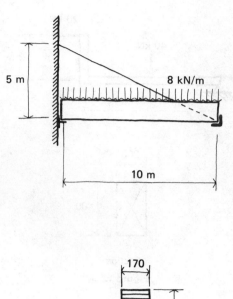

Section

Figure 12-7. Cable-supported cantilever.

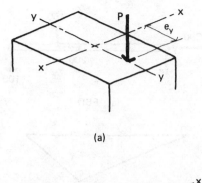

(a)

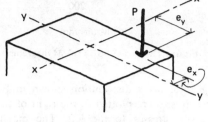

(b)

Figure 12-8. Eccentric loads.

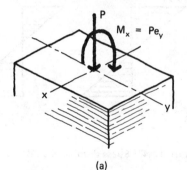

(a)

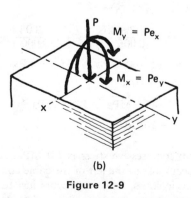

(b)

Figure 12-9

12-2 ECCENTRIC LOADING

It is almost always desirable to load compression elements in an axial manner so that the stresses assume an even P/A value over the entire cross section. Whenever a pier or column is loaded eccentrically, bending results, and even a small amount of bending can cause relatively high stress values. The effect of the eccentricity becomes much worse if the member is long and slender, because then the applied moment greatly increases the lateral buckling tendencies. Eccentrically loaded long columns are treated in Chapter 13.

Eccentric loads can be off-center with respect to one or both centroidal axes, as illustrated in Figure 12-8. The load in Figure 12-8(b) will cause bending about both x and y axes, whereas that of 12-8(a) will cause bending only about the x axis. In addition, there will always be an axial stress from the load. Using the technique explained in Section 2-7, we can convert an eccentric load to an axial load and one or two couples without changing its effect on the member. This will make it easier to isolate the component bending and axial stresses that result. Figure 12-9(a) shows only an M_x couple, because the original load in Figure 12-8 was not eccentric with respect to the y axis. In Figure 12-9(b), two couples are shown (at right angles to one another in plan) because, in that case, the load did not lie along either principal

axis. Considering a parallel cross-sectional plane located somewhat below the level where the load is applied, we can expect the corner nearest the load to have the highest compression and the diagonally opposite corner to have very low compression or even go into tension. Notice that as such loads become more eccentric, the bending effects increase and, in relative terms, the axial effect decreases. The member is then acting more like a beam and less like a column, and a considerable part of the section may have tensile stresses.

Assuming that the extreme fiber stresses are of primary concern, the following equation uses section modulus rather than moment of inertia for bending resistance. The stresses at the four corners can be obtained by using the appropriate terms from

$$f = \pm \frac{P}{A} \pm \frac{M_x}{S_x} \pm \frac{M_y}{S_y} \qquad (12\text{-}2)$$

The moments can be expressed in terms of the load and its eccentricities.

$$f = \pm \frac{P}{A} \pm \frac{Pe_y}{S_x} \pm \frac{Pe_x}{S_y} \qquad (12\text{-}2a)$$

The double sign on the axial term indicates that the original load might act up or down (i.e., creating axial tension or compression).

In some situations involving loads which are essentially compressive, it is desirable to limit the eccentricity in any direction so that no tension will result for any point in the entire cross section. If we let the rectangle have the dimensions b and d as shown in Figure 12-10, we can obtain the S_x and S_y values in terms of those dimensions.

$$S_x = \frac{bd^2}{6}$$

$$S_y = \frac{db^2}{6}$$

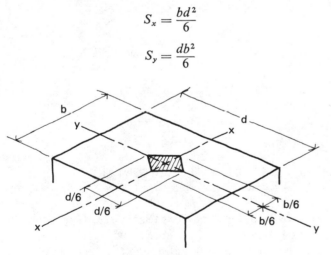

Figure 12-10. Location of the kern for a rectangle.

Equation (12-2a) will then become

$$f = -\frac{P}{bd} \pm \frac{6Pe_y}{bd^2} \pm \frac{6Pe_x}{db^2}$$

Setting the value of f at zero for one corner (no tension permitted) and letting the load be applied in the diagonally opposite quadrant, we get

$$\frac{P}{bd} = \frac{6Pe_y}{bd^2} + \frac{6Pe_x}{db^2}$$

which can be reduced to

$$\frac{1}{6} = \frac{e_y}{d} + \frac{e_x}{b} \qquad (12\text{-}3)$$

If Equation (12-3) is written for each of the four quadrants, it will bound the shaded area of Figure 12-10, called the *kern*. The two eccentricities, expressed as fractions of the section dimensions, cannot sum to more than one-sixth if no tensile stresses are permitted. This concept is sometimes referred to as the *middle-third rule*.

EXAMPLE 12-2

Determine the stress distribution for the plane *abcd* in Figure 12-11.

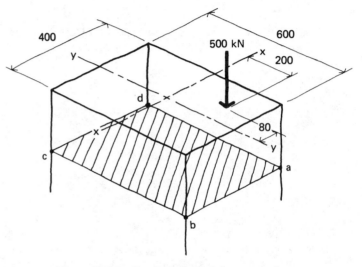

Figure 12-11. Eccentrically loaded concrete pier.

Solution:

$$A = 0.400(0.600)$$
$$= 0.24 \text{ m}^2$$

$$S_x = \frac{0.400(0.600)^2}{6} \qquad S_y = \frac{0.600(0.400)^2}{6}$$
$$= 0.024 \text{ m}^3 \qquad = 0.016 \text{ m}^3$$

$$f = \pm \frac{P}{A} \pm \frac{Pe_y}{S_x} \pm \frac{Pe_x}{S_y}$$

$$= -\frac{500 \text{ kN}}{0.24 \text{ m}^2} \pm \frac{500 \text{ kN}(0.200 \text{ m})}{0.024 \text{ m}^3} \pm \frac{500 \text{ kN}(0.080 \text{ m})}{0.016 \text{ m}^3}$$

$$= -2080 \text{ kPa} \pm 4170 \text{ kPa} \pm 2500 \text{ kPa}$$

$$f_a = -2080 - 4170 - 2500 = -8750 \text{ kPa}$$
$$f_b = -2080 - 4170 + 2500 = -3750 \text{ kPa}$$
$$f_c = -2080 + 4170 + 2500 = 4590 \text{ kPa}$$
$$f_d = -2080 + 4170 - 2500 = -410 \text{ kPa}$$

These stresses are plotted in Figure 12-12. The neutral (or zero stress) line is labeled *fg*. (It should be noted that the tensile stress level of 4590 kPa in this pier is somewhat unrealistic. The cracking strength of normal structural concrete in bending is on the order of 1500 to 3000 kPa, and reinforcing bars would always be used to carry most of the tensile forces.)

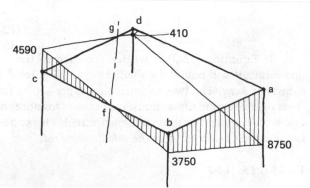

Figure 12-12. Stress distribution for Example 12-2.

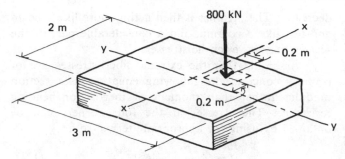

Figure 12-15. Footing pad.

Problems

12-5. Determine the stresses in the pier of Figure 12-13 at the four edges below the corners *a*, *b*, *c*, and *d*.

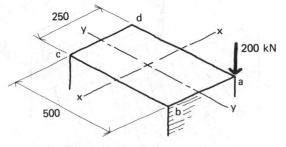

Figure 12-13. Rectangular pier.

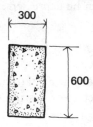

Section

12-6. Determine the maximum allowable eccentricity, e_y, for the T-shaped pier of Figure 12-14 if no tensile stresses are permitted.

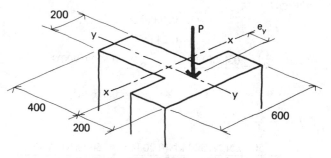

Figure 12-14. T-shaped pier.

12-7. The allowable safe bearing pressure for the soil under the footing in Figure 12-15 is 200 kN/m². Will this limit be exceeded if the 800-kN column load is brought in with a 0.2-m eccentricity in each direction?

12-8. Determine the size of the kern for a circular cross section of radius *R*. Express the answer as a fraction of *R*.

12-9. The three-hinged arch of Figure 12-16 carries only the 60-kN load. Ignoring self-weight, determine the maximum compressive stress in the arch.

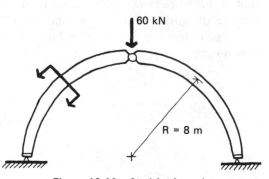

Figure 12-16. Semicircular arch.

12-3 TORSION AND HORIZONTAL SHEAR

Eccentricity of bending loads usually results in torsional shearing stresses as the member is twisted about its own axis. Any load not passing through the shear center of a cross section is considered eccentric (see Section 9-12). Unfortunately, such loads also cause horizontal shearing stresses due to bending. The two kinds of shear can be directly additive, depending upon the loading and support conditions. This can be of prime concern if the structural material is weak in shear. (In the example that follows, it has been assumed that the two kinds of shear will maximize at the same beam cross section. The validity of this approach may be questionable, but a conservative approach is consistent with the approximate nature of the torsional formulas used. As stated in

Chapter 6, a thorough treatment of torsional behavior is beyond the scope of this elementary text.)

EXAMPLE 12-3

The 89 × 285 mm Douglas fir beam in Figure 12-17 is simply supported and has lateral support at its two ends. The wall load of 3 kN/m is eccentric by 75 mm for the beam's full span of 5 m. Determine the approximate maximum shear stress due to combined torsion and bending.

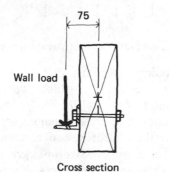

Figure 12-17. Timber beam with eccentric wall load.

Solution: From Section 9-8, the maximum horizontal shearing stress due to bending is

$$f_v = \frac{3V}{2A}$$

$$A = 25\ 400\ \text{mm}^2$$

Let V take its maximum value at one end of the beam.

$$V = \frac{wL}{2}$$

$$= \frac{(3\ \text{kN/m})(5\ \text{m})}{2}$$

$$= 7.5\ \text{kN}$$

$$f_v = \frac{3(7.5\ \text{kN})}{2(0.0254\ \text{m}^2)}$$

$$= 443\ \text{kPa}$$

From Table 6-1,

$$T \approx \tfrac{3}{8}wLe$$

$$\approx \tfrac{3}{8}(3\ \text{kN/m})(5\ \text{m})(0.075\ \text{m})$$

$$\approx 0.422\ \text{kN} \cdot \text{m}$$

and from Section 6-7, the torsional stress at the neutral axis is

$$f_v \approx \frac{4.5T}{b^2h}$$

$$\approx \frac{4.5(0.422\ \text{kN} \cdot \text{m})}{(0.089\ \text{m})^2(0.285\ \text{m})}$$

$$\approx 841\ \text{kPa}$$

Therefore, the combined shearing stress will be

$$f_{v_{\text{total}}} \approx 443 + 841$$

$$\approx 1320\ \text{kPa}$$

(Notice that this design is unacceptable, as the total stress is about double the allowable shearing stress for Douglas fir of 650 kPa.)

Problems

12-10. Determine the approximate maximum permissible load P that can be placed as shown on the square cantilever of Figure 12-18 if the allowable shearing stress parallel to grain is 500 kPa.

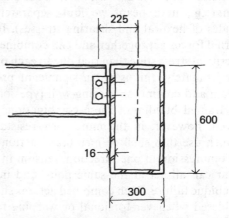

Figure 12-18. Cantilevered square section.

12-11. The steel box girder of Figure 12-19 spans 9 m between fixed supports and is loaded only by a beam reaction at midspan. The reaction is 50 kN and is eccentric by 225 mm. Determine the approximate maximum shearing stress by assuming that both torsional shear and bending shear will maximize at the supports. The bending shear force may be computed as if the beam were simply supported.

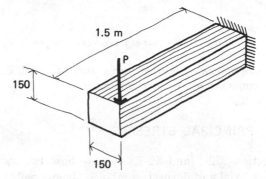

Figure 12-19. Hollow steel girder.

12-12. The built-up timber beam of Figure 12-20 cantilevers out to pick up a joist reaction from one side. Assume that the torsional stress will maximize at the glue-nailed junction of flange and stem. Determine the

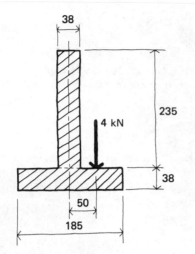

Figure 12-20. Timber T-beam cross section.

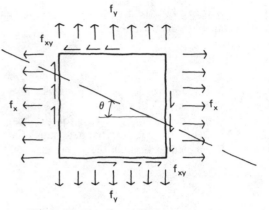

Figure 12-21. General biaxial stress state.

approximate shearing stress at that point due to combined torsion and bending.

12-4 PRINCIPAL STRESSES

In Sections 12-1 and 12-2, we saw how two normal stresses, axial and flexural, combined algebraically to act on the same fibers. Section 12-3 treated the possibility that two different kinds of tangential stress, torsional shear and shear due to bending, might act at the same point. This section will examine what happens when normal and tangential stresses get together. This, of course, would represent a more general situation than we have considered before. When a structure is loaded, all types of stresses develop in all different directions to provide the required resistance. We frequently analyze members and structures as if the various stresses occur in isolation (e.g., in a beam we look separately at the magnitudes of flexural and shearing stresses). In reality, the internal forces act together and can combine to cause a more critical stress state than that due to each one acting alone. Fortunately, this is not a significant problem in most beam and column or bearing-wall types of conventionally framed buildings. These combinations must be considered, however, in the more form-resistant structures which use thin shell or membrane action to carry loads. Compression in one direction, tension in another, and shear can all act at the same point and interact to cause a unique failure. Such combined actions should also be considered whenever torsional or warping forces are involved. The maximum stresses can easily occur on planes that do not make angles of 0 or 90° with the axis of the member.

Figure 12-21 shows a tiny element on the surface of a structural member. It is being acted upon by two normal stresses, f_x and f_y, which might have resulted

from computations involving P/A or Mc/I. There are also shearing stresses, f_{xy}, which typically could be generated from Tr/J or VQ/Ib. The sense shown is the positive one for each stress. The major question suggested before is how these stresses can combine to create a tensile stress (or a compressive one) greater than either of those now shown and which acts on some other plane at some other angle. When this happens, we need to know how great this stress is and the orientation (θ) of the plane on which it acts. Similarly, the possibility of shearing stresses greater than f_{xy} and acting on a different set of planes needs to be investigated.

As presented in Appendix G, for every state of stress such as that of Figure 12-21, there exists a maximum value of normal stress and a minimum value of normal stress. These are called *principal stresses* and act on a pair of orthogonal planes, which make angles of θ and $\theta + 90°$ with the x and y axes. The planes are called *principal planes*. (The words "maximum" and "minimum" are used algebraically in this case so that a numerically large tensile stress is greater than a small one, and a numerically small compressive stress is greater than a large compressive stress.)

In a similar fashion, the maximum shearing stresses do not necessarily act in the x and y directions. The two planes of maximum shearing stress are found to make angles of 45° with the principal planes. This set of planes is also orthogonal as required for shearing stress equilibrium. Figure 12-22 indicates some possible stress directions with the appropriate nomenclature. The maximum normal stress is called f_1 and the minimum one is f_2. The maximum shearing stress is designated f_s. Numerical values may be found in terms of the reference stresses. From the derivations in Appendix G,

$$f_{1,2} = \frac{f_x + f_y}{2} \pm \sqrt{\left(\frac{f_x - f_y}{2}\right)^2 + (f_{xy})^2} \qquad (12\text{-}4)$$

$$f_s = \sqrt{\left(\frac{f_x - f_y}{2}\right)^2 + (f_{xy})^2} \qquad (12\text{-}5)$$

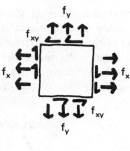

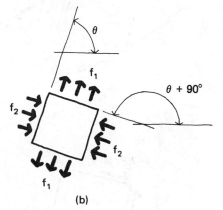

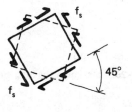

Figure 12-22. Principal stresses and maximum shearing stress: (a) reference planes; (b) principal planes; (c) maximum shearing stress planes.

The angles that the various planes make with the x and y reference axes can be obtained from

$$\tan 2\theta_{1,2} = \frac{-f_{xy}}{(f_x - f_y)/2} \qquad (12\text{-}6)$$

$$\tan 2\theta_s = \frac{(f_x - f_y)/2}{f_{xy}} \qquad (12\text{-}7)$$

These equations can help to justify some of the previous statements. The tangent function of Equations (12-6) and (12-7) is a double-valued one such that any angles called 2θ will always be 180° apart. This ensures, of course, that the angles θ will be 90° apart, thus defining orthogonal planes. Also notice for the same two equations that the terms to the right of the equal sign are

negative reciprocals of each other. This means that the angles $2\theta_{1,2}$ are 90° from the angles $2\theta_s$. Therefore, the planes defined by θ_s will be 45° away from the planes defined by $\theta_{1,2}$.

Looking at Equation (12-4), we see that the maximum and minimum stresses differ only by the sign of the second term, which is the expression for the maximum shearing stress. If we add f_1 and f_2, we get

$$f_1 + f_2 = f_x + f_y$$

which says that the sum of the principal stresses is equal to the sum of the reference stresses. This can provide a convenient check on our arithmetic when computing values of f_1 and f_2. Furthermore, if we subtract the expressions for f_1 and f_2, we find that the maximum shearing stress is equal to one-half the algebraic difference between the principal stresses. With the help of Equation (G-1b) in the Appendix, it can also be shown that the principal planes will have no shear on them. This is only common sense once we realize that any shear would have to interact with the normal stresses on those planes and cause more extreme stresses to exist elsewhere.

The following examples will illustrate the determination of principal stresses. It is important to notice how equilibrium considerations help to differentiate between the two principal planes and also to select the sense of the maximum shearing stress.

EXAMPLE 12-4

Determine the principal stresses and the maximum shearing stress for the given x and y stresses in Figure 12-23.

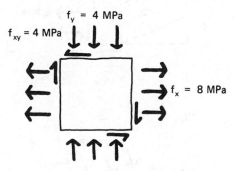

Figure 12-23. Reference stress state.

Solution: Find the maximum shearing stress first.

$$f_s = \sqrt{\left(\frac{f_x - f_y}{2}\right)^2 + (f_{xy})^2}$$

$$= \sqrt{\left(\frac{8 - (-4)}{2}\right)^2 + (4)^2}$$

$$= 7.21 \text{ MPa}$$

$$f_{1,2} = \frac{f_x + f_y}{2} \pm f_s$$

$$= \frac{8-4}{2} \pm 7.21$$

$$f_1 = 9.21 \text{ MPa}$$

$$f_2 = -5.21 \text{ MPa}$$

$$f_1 + f_2 = f_x + f_y \quad \text{check}$$

$$9.21 + (-5.21) = 8 - 4 \quad \checkmark$$

Now find the angles of the principal planes.

$$\tan 2\theta_{1,2} = \frac{-f_{xy}}{(f_x - f_y)/2}$$

$$= \frac{-4}{(8-4)/2}$$

$$= -2$$

$$2\theta_{1,2} = 116.6° \quad \text{and} \quad 296.6°$$

$$\theta_{1,2} = 58.3° \quad \text{and} \quad 148.3°$$

The principal planes are shown in Figure 12-24(b). Which stress acts on which plane can be ascertained by examining what the original stresses will cause to happen on one of the principal planes. Figure 12-24(a) shows a corner from the reference block sliced at one of the principal plane angles. By inspection (or by writing the equilibrium equations) we can determine that the plane 1–1 will need tension rather than compression to hold the corner in equilibrium. Thus, the maximum principal stress is shown on the corresponding contiguous principal plane in Figure 12-24(b).

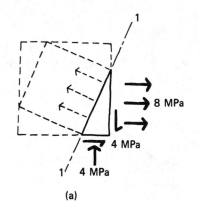

(a)

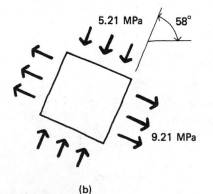

(b)

Figure 12-24. Principal planes.

The planes of maximum shearing stress will be 45° away and the correct sense is determined similarly as in Figure 12-25. The corner of the principal stress block isolated in Figure 12-25(a) will require the tangential stress to act upward and to the left for equilibrium. This same stress must act oppositely on the matching face of the maximum shear block in Figure 12-25(b).

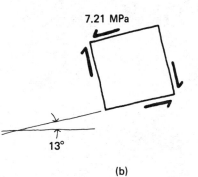

(a)

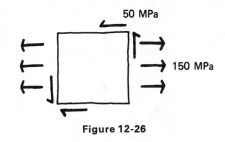

(b)

Figure 12-25. Maximum shearing stress.

EXAMPLE 12-5

Determine the principal stress and maximum shearing stress for the stress state of Figure 12-26. The f_y value is zero.

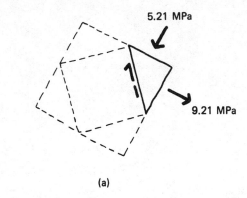

Figure 12-26

Solution:

$$f_s = \sqrt{\left(\frac{f_x - f_y}{2}\right)^2 + (f_{xy})^2}$$

$$= \sqrt{\left(\frac{150}{2}\right)^2 + (50)^2}$$

$$= 90.1 \text{ MPa}$$

$$f_{1,2} = \frac{f_x + f_y}{2} \pm f_s$$

$$= \frac{150}{2} \pm 90.1$$

$$f_1 = 165.1 \text{ MPa}$$

$$f_2 = -15.1 \text{ MPa}$$

$$f_1 + f_2 = f_x + f_y \quad \text{check}$$

$$165.1 - 15.1 = 150 + 0 \quad \checkmark$$

$$\tan 2\theta_{1,2} = \frac{-f_{xy}}{(f_x - f_y)/2}$$

$$= \frac{-(-50)}{150/2}$$

$$= \frac{2}{3}$$

$$2\theta_{1,2} = 33.7° \quad \text{and} \quad 213.7°$$

$$\theta_{1,2} = 16.9° \quad \text{and} \quad 106.9°$$

Using the technique of Example 12-4, we find the senses as shown in Figure 12-27.

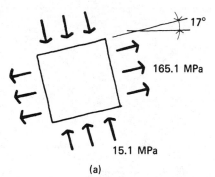

(a)

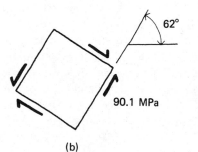

(b)

Figure 12-27. Answers for Example 12-5: (a) principal planes; (b) planes of maximum shearing stress.

EXAMPLE 12-6

Determine the principal stresses for the element of Figure 12-28, which is acted upon only by shear stresses. It was taken from the neutral axis of a beam.

Solution:

$$f_s = \sqrt{\left(\frac{f_x - f_y}{2}\right)^2 + (f_{xy})^2}$$

$$= f_{xy} = 10 \text{ MPa}$$

Figure 12-28. Pure shear.

$$f_{1,2} = \frac{f_x + f_y}{2} \pm f_s$$

$$= \pm 10$$

$$f_1 = 10 \text{ MPa}$$

$$f_2 = -10 \text{ MPa}$$

$$\tan 2\theta_{1,2} = \frac{-f_{xy}}{(f_x - f_y)/2}$$

$$= \frac{-(10)}{0}$$

$$= \infty$$

$$2\theta_{1,2} = 90° \quad \text{and} \quad 270°$$

$$\theta_{1,2} = 45° \quad \text{and} \quad 135°$$

The principal planes lie at 45° to the reference planes, as seen in Figure 12-29. The reference planes *are* the planes of maximum shear, and we can see how shear will cause diagonal normal stresses of like magnitude, as discussed in Section 6-6.

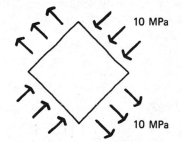

Figure 12-29. Diagonal tension and compression.

Problems

12-13. Determine the principal stresses and maximum shearing stress for the stress state in Figure 12-30.

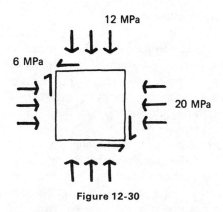

Figure 12-30

12-14. Figure 12-31 represents the tension due to bending that might occur at the bottom edge of a steel beam. Determine the principal stresses and maximum shearing stress.

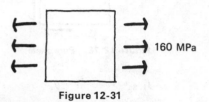

Figure 12-31

12-15. Determine the maximum shearing stress and its planes for the subsurface stress state of Figure 12-32.

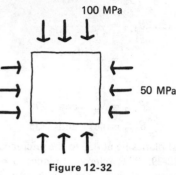

Figure 12-32

12-16. The element shown in Figure 12-33 was taken from the apex of a uniformly loaded dome. Determine the principal stresses and the maximum shearing stress.

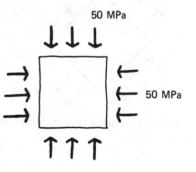

Figure 12-33. Pure compression.

12-5 THE MOHR CIRCLE

In the late nineteenth century, Otto Mohr (1835–1918), a German engineer, developed a graphical solution to determine the principal stresses. The method not only provides sufficient accuracy but is also helpful as an aid to understanding the interaction between the shearing and normal stresses.

The essence of the technique is a circle having the magnitude of the maximum shearing stress as its radius. The circle is part of a graph in which the normal stresses are measured along the abscissa, and shearing stresses are laid off as ordinates. It follows, then, that the circle

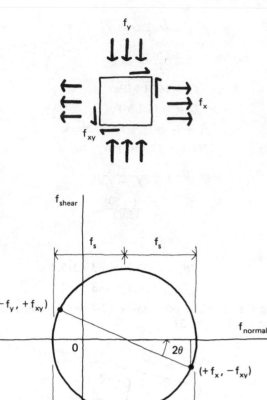

Figure 12-34. Mohr circle.

must always have its center at some point on the abscissa or normal stress axis. The reference data are plotted as in Figure 12-34. Tensile stresses plot to the right of the origin and compressive ones to the left. A special sign convention is used to graph shearing stresses on the Mohr circle. Shears that tend to rotate the element clockwise are taken as positive and those that tend to rotate the element counterclockwise are negative. In each case, a shearing stress is always associated with the normal stress on that same face. Thus, the points $(+f_x, -f_{xy})$ and $(-f_y, +f_{xy})$ are established in Figure 12-34. The two points are then connected by a straight line and its intercept with the f_{normal} axis is the center of the Mohr circle. After the circle is drawn, the principal stresses are scaled off as dimensioned in the figure. The various relationships regarding the sums and differences of the principal stresses can be seen from the graph. The triangle outlined to include the angle 2θ is the same as one used in Appendix G for the derivation of the formulas used in the preceding section. The curved arrow, showing how the diameter of the circle must be turned to get it in line with the abscissa, represents how the principal stress block should be rotated from the reference block. This will always be the case if we let f_x be the algebraically larger stress when we plot the initial two points.

EXAMPLE 12-7

Construct the Mohr circle for the data of Example 12-5.

Solution: There is no f_y stress, so we will plot the two points as $(+150, -50)$ and $(0, +50)$. The values shown in Figure 12-35 were determined by measuring from the drawing. A large scale will, of course, provide even more accuracy.

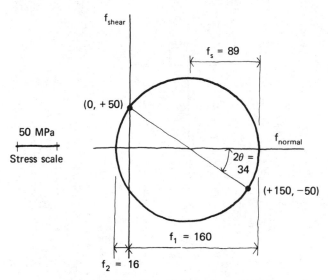

Figure 12-35. Mohr circle for Example 12-5.

Problems

12-17. Construct the Mohr circle for Example 12-6.

12-18. Construct the Mohr circle for Problem 12-14.

12-19. Use the Mohr circle to show that there is no shear on any plane for the stress state in Figure 12-33.

12-6 TORSION AND FLEXURE

Section 12-3 provides a brief look at how the torsional and bending shear stresses might act on the same plane in a beam and be directly additive. Whenever beams are loaded in both bending and torsion, it is also necessary to check for a possible interaction between that same torsional stress and the extreme fiber flexural stress. If both of these stresses are near their maximums at the same point, it is likely that a principal stress analysis will yield higher stresses of both types. This can easily happen at the fixed end of a cantilever beam, where the bending stress and torsional stress will usually maximize.

EXAMPLE 12-8

The timber signpost of Example 6-1 had a diameter of 200 mm and under load developed a torsional shearing stress on its surface of 637 kPa. If the same wind load causes a bending moment at its base of 4 kN·m, determine the principal tensile stress and the maximum shearing stress. Determine also the angles that these stresses make with the wood grain.

Solution: The extreme fiber bending stress is given by

$$f_b = \frac{Mc}{I}$$

$$I = \frac{\pi R^4}{4}$$

$$= \frac{\pi (0.100 \text{ m})^4}{4}$$

$$= 78.5(10)^{-6} \text{ m}^4$$

$$= \frac{4 \text{ kN·m}(0.100 \text{ m})}{78.5(10)^{-6} \text{ m}^4}$$

$$= 5090 \text{ kPa}$$

At the base of the signpost on the tension side, we have the x and y stresses shown in Figure 12-36. The Mohr circle technique or the following equations may be used.

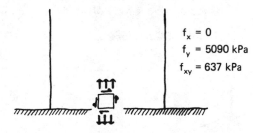

$$f_x = 0$$
$$f_y = 5090 \text{ kPa}$$
$$f_{xy} = 637 \text{ kPa}$$

Figure 12-36. Element at the base of the signpost.

$$f_s = \sqrt{\left(\frac{f_x - f_y}{2}\right)^2 + (f_{xy})^2} \qquad (12\text{-}5)$$

$$= \sqrt{\left(\frac{-5090}{2}\right)^2 + (637)^2}$$

$$= 2620 \text{ kPa}$$

$$f_1 = \frac{f_x + f_y}{2} + f_s \qquad (12\text{-}4)$$

$$= \frac{5090}{2} + 2620$$

$$= 5165 \text{ kPa}$$

The principal tensile stress is only slightly greater than the bending stress computed by Mc/I.

$$\tan 2\theta_1 = \frac{-f_{xy}}{(f_x - f_y)/2} \qquad (12\text{-}6)$$

$$= \frac{-(-637)}{(-5090)/2}$$

$$= -0.250$$

$$2\theta_1 = 166°$$

$$\theta_1 = 83°$$

Since the x direction makes an angle of 90° with the grain, the principal tension is only 7° off from the direction of the grain.

The maximum shearing stress of 2620 kPa is very high

compared to the initial f_{xy} stress of 637 kPa. However, this high stress acts on two planes that are not close to being parallel to the grain. Being 45° away from θ_1, we can determine the angles the two planes make with the x axis.

$$\theta_s = 83° - 45° \quad \text{and} \quad 83° + 45°$$
$$= 38° \quad \text{and} \quad 128°$$

As before, the x axis is at right angles to the grain so the orthogonal planes of maximum shear will make angles of 52° and 38° with the direction of the grain. Obviously, the wood is not weak in shear on these planes.

Problems

12-20. With reference to Figure 12-18, if $P = 3$ kN, determine the approximate maximum normal and shearing stresses existent anywhere in the beam.

12-21. The rectangular steel tube of Example 6-4 has an allowable shearing stress of 100 MPa. How much load P can be placed as shown in Figure 12-37 and still not exceed the allowable shearing stress at any point? Ignore the possible effects of stress concentration.

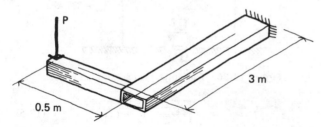

100 × 200 mm tube
Wall thickness (t) = 6 mm

Figure 12-37. Steel tube loaded in torsion and bending.

12-7 FLEXURE AND HORIZONTAL SHEAR

If the loading pattern on a beam is such that the shearing force and the moment developed are both large at the same section, it is possible for their combined action to generate large and possibly controlling stresses. Normally, the horizontal shearing stress, as computed from VQ/Ib, is not very large in the region of the extreme fibers, where bending stresses always maximize. However, certain cross sections, such as the I shape, have relatively high shearing stresses at fibers some distance from the neutral axis. As demonstrated in Section 8-5, the shearing stress will be high just inside the junction of a narrow web and a heavy flange because Q is large and b is small. These high shearing stresses can interact with the large normal stresses of flexure to cause even higher stresses. In most cases, the increase is slight, but it is good to be aware of the fact that when we design a

beam for a bending stress, as computed from Mc/I, we may not be designing for the maximum tensile and compressive stresses.

EXAMPLE 12-9

Figure 12-38 shows an I-beam built up from two 38 × 89 mm flanges and a 20-mm web piece. It spans 4.5 m on simple supports and carries two concentrated loads of 7 kN each at the third points. $I = 239(10)^6$ mm⁴.

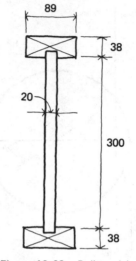

Figure 12-38. Built-up I-beam.

(a) Determine the maximum flexural stress.
(b) Determine the maximum normal stress in the web at a point just inside the flange and just outside one of the loads, as shown in Figure 12-39.

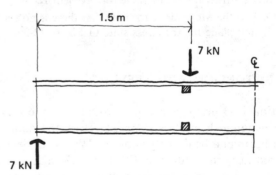

Figure 12-39. Location of points of maximum interaction between V and M.

Solution:

(a)
$$M = \frac{PL}{3}$$
$$= \frac{7 \text{ kN}(4.5 \text{ m})}{3}$$
$$= 10.5 \text{ kN·m}$$
$$f_b = \frac{Mc}{I}$$

$$= \frac{10.5 \text{ kN} \cdot \text{m}(0.188 \text{ m})}{239(10)^{-6} \text{ m}^4}$$

$$= 8260 \text{ kPa}$$

(b) First find the horizontal shearing stress at the point in question as represented by either of the small element squares in Figure 12-39.

$$f_v = \frac{VQ}{Ib}$$

$$Q = 89(38)(169)$$

$$= 572(10)^3 \text{ mm}^3$$

$$= \frac{7 \text{ kN}(572)(10)^{-6} \text{ m}^3}{239(10)^{-6} \text{ m}^4(0.020 \text{ m})}$$

$$= 838 \text{ kPa}$$

The flexural stress at that point will be less than the extreme fiber stress by the proportion

$$\frac{f_y}{f_b} = \frac{y}{c}$$

$$f_y = \frac{y}{c}f_b$$

$$= \tfrac{150}{188}(8260 \text{ kPa})$$

$$= 6590 \text{ kPa}$$

Figure 12-40 shows the stresses acting on the upper element of Figure 12-39. We can get the principal compressive stress from the formula

$$f_2 = \frac{f_x + f_y}{2} - \sqrt{\left(\frac{f_x - f_y}{2}\right)^2 + (f_{xy})^2}$$

$$= \frac{-6590}{2} - \sqrt{\left(\frac{-6590}{2}\right)^2 + (838)^2}$$

$$= -6700 \text{ kPa}$$

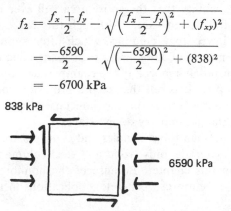

838 kPa

6590 kPa

Figure 12-40. Stresses on the *x* and *y* planes.

In this case the maximum compressive stress is that due to bending alone.

Problems

12-22. The beam in Figure 12-41 is a W410 × 46.1. It has a section modulus of $774(10)^3$ mm³ and an *I* value of $150(10)^6$ mm⁴. Its cross section has been idealized for ease of computation.

(a) Determine the maximum tensile stress due to bending alone.

(b) Determine the maximum tensile stress existent anywhere in the beam.

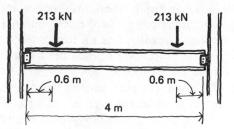

213 kN 213 kN

0.6 m 0.6 m

4 m

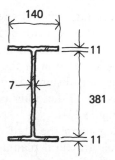

140

11

7

381

11

Figure 12-41. Steel W shape with a concentrated load.

12-23. The beam in Figure 12-42 is fabricated from two webs, each 13 mm thick, and three 38 × 89 mm pieces for each flange. It is 12 m long and must carry two concentrated loads of 20 kN each at the quarter points. Each plywood sheet is fully effective for shear, but due to cross-grain laminations, only 8 mm of its thickness can resist normal stresses. (Therefore, *I* and *Q* are reduced slightly.)

(a) Determine the maximum tensile stress due to bending.

(b) Determine the maximum tensile stress existent anywhere in the web.

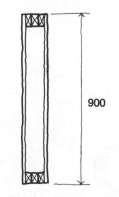

900

Figure 12-42. Plywood box beam.

13-1 COLUMNS AS BUILDING STRUCTURAL ELEMENTS

Columns are probably the most important of the various structural elements in the conventional building frame. Stacked vertically, one on top of the other, they receive live and dead loads at each floor level and must transmit these loads to the foundation system below. The spacing of columns in plan usually determines what is referred to as the *structural bay*; for example, if columns are spaced 8 m on center in one direction and 11 m in the other, the structural bay size is said to be 8 × 11 m. The size and shape of the structural bay has a great influence upon the type of framing system to be used in the floor structure.

Columns are usually designed with greater factors of safety than other structural elements, because any column failure would result in the catastrophic collapse of at least a major portion of the building frame. When a column fails, any beams or girders framing into it come down, as do all the other columns directly above, as shown in Figure 13-1.

Depending upon the skill of the designer in the initial stages of structural planning, columns can serve as valuable organizers or as ill-located hindrances to the architectural design process. Columns can be effective space dividers or modulators in large areas. Indeed, more columns than are needed structurally are sometimes used to separate one space from another functionally while preserving visual continuity.

It is most important that the designer or structural planner understand the structural behavior of columns under various kinds of loading. How long and slender can a given column be and still have a useful load capacity? When is a rectangular cross section more appropriate than a square one? How can the column work together with the horizontal spanning members that frame into it? What happens when the center of a column is removed so that services can be run vertically through it? How do the top and bottom connections affect column capacity? Can column capacity always be increased by using a stronger material? How do columns carry lateral loads? The structural planner should not only be able to answer these questions and others but should also have a real understanding of the principles that generate those answers.

Many codes include a provision for reducing the total design live load on certain structural members which have large tributary areas. This reduction (an example of which is given in Appendix O) is based on the relatively low probability that the entire area will ever be loaded to the full design value. Although this can be applicable to lower-story columns, which often support many square meters of floor area, such load reductions have been purposely ignored in the examples and problems of this chapter. It is felt that such a provision could easily lead to large errors in the nonconservative direction during the preliminary design stages.

Although the principles and concepts are the same for all materials, only wood and steel columns are analyzed in this chapter. Because of the nonhomogeneous nature of reinforced concrete, applications in this mate-

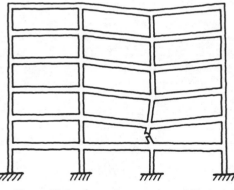

Figure 13-1. Second-story column failure.

13

Column Analysis and Design

rial require a slightly different background and approach. The behavior of such columns is discussed briefly in Chapter 17.

13-2 COLUMN FAILURE MODES

Columns are essentially compression elements and, when overloaded sufficiently, will fail by crushing or buckling or a combination of these two effects (Figure 13-2). Very short stout columns will fail by crushing, and long slender columns will fail by buckling. Actually, most columns in buildings are proportioned such that both effects would be involved.

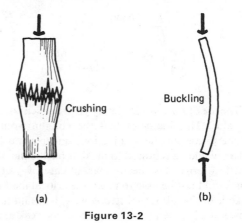

Figure 13-2

Pure crushing is a relatively easy concept to understand and a very simple design formula is available to prevent its occurrence. The designer merely provides enough cross-sectional area in the column so that the allowable bearing stress for the material is not exceeded.

$$A_r = \frac{P}{F} \tag{13-1}$$

where A_r = area required (m²)
P = total load on the column (N)
F = allowable bearing stress (Pa)

The allowable bearing stress is obtained by reducing the value of the actual crushing strength for a material by an appropriate factor of safety. (It should be noted that in the case of most steel column shapes, such crushing does not occur because a similar type of failure called *local crippling* or *buckling* occurs under a lesser load. An example of such a failure occurs when we "crush" a tin can vertically without actually crushing the material.)

13-3 THE EULER THEORY

Pure buckling or elastic buckling of long, slender columns is not so easy to understand. Here, column capacity is dependent upon the dimensions and shape of the column

and upon the stiffness of the material. Surprisingly enough, pure buckling is totally independent of the strength of the material!

The basic theory of elastic buckling was successfully formulated over 200 years ago by Leonhard Euler (1707–1783), a Swiss mathematician. Essentially, such buckling occurs because there exists more than one position of equilibrium for a long, straight compression member. The slightly deflected column shown in Figure 13-3 could carry a load and be in equilibrium just like the straight one. Conversely, this could never happen in a tension member.

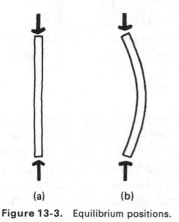

Figure 13-3. Equilibrium positions.

As you gradually increase the axial load on a long column that is initially straight, it will suddenly deflect laterally. If the load is removed, the column will return to its initial straight shape. This behavior is called *elastic buckling*. The particular value of axial load (called the critical load), which causes buckling, is given by the *Euler equation*:

$$P_{cr} = \frac{\pi^2 EI}{L^2} \tag{13-2}$$

where P_{cr} = axial load necessary to cause buckling (N)
E = modulus of elasticity of the column material (Pa)
I = moment of inertia of the column cross section (m⁴)
L = length of the column (m)

[See Appendix H for the derivation of Equation (13-2).]

Experimentally, most long columns buckle under loads that are a bit less than the value given by this equation. This is due to a number of factors, such as slight irregularities in the straightness of the member, slight eccentricity of the load, and the material being non-homogeneous.

This equation is more useful if we make a minor modification using the radius-of-gyration concept from Section 3-5,

$$r = \sqrt{\frac{I}{A}}$$

where r = radius of gyration of the column cross section (m)

A = area of the column cross section (m²)

If we solve this expression for I and substitute into Equation (13-2),

$$\left(\frac{P}{A}\right)_{cr} = \frac{\pi^2 E}{(L/r)^2} \qquad (13\text{-}3)$$

where $(P/A)_{cr}$ is the stress caused by the critical load (Pa).

The parameter L/r is called the *slenderness ratio*. The critical stress (and load) is inversely proportional to the square of this ratio.

Equations (13-2) and (13-3) are equally valid and can be used interchangeably. As stated previously, notice that neither one includes a term representing the strength of the material. Also notice that the equations give the failure loads and stresses. No factor of safety has been included.

Euler's theory assumes that the column has pinned ends that allow the column ends to rotate freely but not to translate. If the formulas are applied to columns having other end conditions, they must be adjusted by a factor to account for this change. For the following example problems of this section we shall assume pinned ends.

EXAMPLE 13-1

Determine the critical buckling stress and load for a wood column 89 × 89 mm in cross section and 3 m long. Assume that $E = 10\ 500$ MPa.

Solution: Properties of timber sections may be found in Appendix Q.

$$\left(\frac{P}{A}\right)_{cr} = \frac{\pi^2 E}{(L/r)^2}$$

$$A = 7920 \text{ mm}^2$$

$$I = 5.23(10)^6 \text{ mm}^4$$

$$r = 25.7 \text{ mm}$$

$$\frac{L}{r} = \frac{3000}{25.7} = 117$$

$$\left(\frac{P}{A}\right)_{cr} = \frac{\pi^2 (10\ 500)(10)^3 \text{ kPa}}{(117)^2}$$

$$= 7570 \text{ kPa}$$

$$P_{cr} = \left(\frac{P}{A}\right)_{cr}(A)$$

$$= (7570 \text{ kN/m}^2)(0.007\ 92 \text{ m}^2)$$

$$= 60.0 \text{ kN}$$

EXAMPLE 13-2a

Determine the critical buckling stress for a W200 × 52 steel ($F_y = 250$ MPa) column that is 9 m long.

Solution: Properties of the steel shapes used in the examples and problems of this chapter may be found in Table 2 of Appendix S. Assume E to be 200 000 MPa in all steel examples and problems.

$$\left(\frac{P}{A}\right)_{cr} = \frac{\pi^2 E}{(L/r)^2}$$

$$r_x = 89.1 \text{ mm}$$

$$r_y = 51.6 \text{ mm}$$

Compute the L/r value for each of the two axes. Substitute the larger of the two values into the Euler equation because it will yield the smaller critical stress value.

$$\frac{L}{r_x} = \frac{9000}{89.1} = 101$$

$$\frac{L}{r_y} = \frac{9000}{51.6} = 174$$

$$\left(\frac{P}{A}\right)_{cr} = \frac{\pi^2 (200)(10)^3 \text{ MPa}}{(174)^2}$$

$$= 65.2 \text{ MPa}$$

The use of L/r_x would clearly yield a much larger critical stress value. This indicates that the column would buckle about the y-axis (in the x direction) under a much smaller load than would be required to make it buckle the other way. In practical terms this means that, in case of overload, the column would not be able to reach the critical load necessary to make it buckle about its strong axis; it would have failed at a lower load value by buckling about its weak axis. Therefore, in computing critical load and stress values, always use the greater L/r value.

EXAMPLE 13-2b

Determine the critical buckling load for the column of Example 13-2a.

Solution:

$$A = 6650 \text{ mm}^2$$

$$I_y = 17.7(10)^6 \text{ mm}^4$$

$$P_{cr} = \frac{\pi^2 EI}{L^2}$$

Since L is the same for both axes, we need only I_y for use in the equation.

$$P_{cr} = \frac{\pi^2 [(200)(10)^6 \text{ kN/m}^2](17.7)(10)^{-6} \text{ m}^4}{(9 \text{ m})^2}$$

$$= 431 \text{ kN}$$

The same answer could have been obtained using the critical stress value from Example 13-2a.

$$P_{cr} = \left(\frac{P}{A}\right)_{cr}(A)$$

$$= (65\ 200 \text{ kN/m}^2)(0.006\ 65 \text{ m}^2)$$

$$= 433 \text{ kN}$$

(The discrepancy between the two answers is due to rounding error and is less than one-half of 1%.)

EXAMPLE 13-3

Determine the critical buckling load for a wood 89 × 185 mm column 4.3 m long. Assume that $E = 8000$ MPa.

Solution:

$$I_y = 10.9 \times 10^6 \text{ mm}^4$$

$$P_{cr} = \frac{\pi^2 EI}{L^2}$$

$$= \frac{\pi^2 [(8000)(10)^3 \text{ kN/m}^2](10.9)(10)^{-6} \text{ m}^4}{(4.3 \text{ m})^2}$$

$$= 46.5 \text{ kN}$$

Problems

13-1. Determine the critical buckling load for a timber column 139 × 139 mm and 5.5 m long. Assume that $E = 8000$ MPa.

13-2. Determine the critical buckling stress for a steel ($F_y = 250$ MPa) pipe column that is 5 m long. The outside diameter is 114 mm and the wall thickness is 6 mm.

13-3. Determine the critical buckling load for a single wood 38 × 89 mm stud 2.4 m long. Assume that $E = 9500$ MPa.

13-4 INFLUENCE OF DIFFERENT END CONDITIONS

How the column ends are connected to the rest of the structure has a large influence on the critical buckling load. If the column ends are restrained from rotation in some manner, the effective buckling length can be very different from the true length, as shown in Figure 13-4. True length will be called L and the effective length KL, where K is a theoretical modifier that accounts for the effect of different end conditions.

The effective length for a column with both ends fixed is just one-half that of a column with both ends pinned. The "flagpole" type of column has a K value of

2.0, which is rationalized by noting the mirror image below the fixed end needed to obtain a full buckling curve. Fortunately, this case seldom appears in building columns.

The problems presented so far have all assumed pinned ends with $K = 1.0$. Many building columns have K values that are in between the four cases shown, and judgment must be used in estimating a proper K value.

The equations presented previously should be modified to include this end condition factor.

$$P_{cr} = \frac{\pi^2 EI}{(KL)^2} \tag{13-2a}$$

$$\left(\frac{P}{A}\right)_{cr} = \frac{\pi^2 E}{(KL/r)^2} \tag{13-3a}$$

By noting that K is squared along with L, we can see the big difference these end conditions will make. For example, if we hold all other parameters constant and vary only K, then

1. A fixed-end column will support 4 times the load of one with pinned ends.
2. A pinned-end column will support 4 times the load of one with one fixed and one free end (flagpole).

Some of the examples that follow indicate fixed ends for timber columns. In actual construction detailing, this is quite difficult to achieve. However, such examples are included here to illustrate the use of the K factor.

EXAMPLE 13-4

The 139 × 139 mm timber column of Figure 13-5 is 6 m long and can be considered pinned at the lower end and effectively

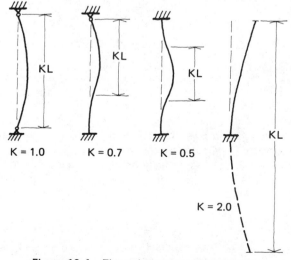

Figure 13-4. Theoretical end condition factors.

K = 1.0   K = 0.7   K = 0.5   K = 2.0

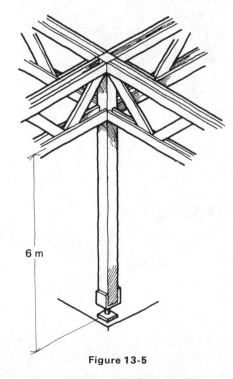

6 m

Figure 13-5

fixed by deep trusses framing into it at the top. Determine the critical buckling stress and load. Assume that $E = 11\ 000$ MPa.

Solution:

$$A = 19\ 300\ \text{mm}^2$$

$$r = 40.1\ \text{mm}$$

$$K = 0.7$$

$$\frac{KL}{r} = \frac{0.7(6000)}{40.1} = 105$$

$$\left(\frac{P}{A}\right)_{\text{cr}} = \frac{\pi^2 E}{(KL/r)^2}$$

$$= \frac{\pi^2(11\ 000)(10)^3\ \text{kPa}}{(105)^2}$$

$$= 9850\ \text{kPa}$$

$$P_{\text{cr}} = \left(\frac{P}{A}\right)_{\text{cr}}(A)$$

$$= (9850\ \text{kN/m}^2)(0.0193\ \text{m}^2)$$

$$= 190\ \text{kN}$$

EXAMPLE 13-5

A W200 × 100 section is used for the column in Figure 13-6. The bottom clip angle connection is a pin. Deep plate girders frame into the web, which serve to fix the weak axis at the top. Small bracing beams are clipped to the flanges and provide a pinned condition. Determine the critical buckling load.

Solution: From Table 2 of Appendix S,

$$r_x = 94.2\ \text{mm}$$

$$r_y = 53.9\ \text{mm}$$

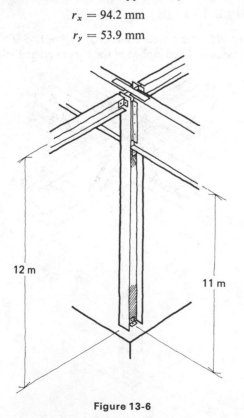

12 m

11 m

Figure 13-6

$$A = 12\ 700\ \text{mm}^2$$

$$I_x = 113(10)^6\ \text{mm}^4$$

$$I_y = 36.9(10)^6\ \text{mm}^4$$

$$L_x = 12\ \text{m}$$

$$L_y = 11\ \text{m}$$

First determine which axis is critical (i.e., which one has the greater KL/r).

$$\left(\frac{KL}{r}\right)_x = \frac{1.0(12\ 000)}{94.2} = 127$$

$$\left(\frac{KL}{r}\right)_y = \frac{0.7(11\ 000)}{53.9} = 143$$

The weak axis is critical for this column. We can now determine the critical buckling stress and multiply by the area to get the critical load. We can also find the load directly by substituting the critical axis properties into

$$P_{\text{cr}} = \frac{\pi^2 EI}{(KL)^2}$$

$$= \frac{\pi^2[200(10)^6\ \text{kN/m}^2](36.9)(10)^{-6}\ \text{m}^4}{[0.7(11\ \text{m})]^2}$$

$$= 1230\ \text{kN}$$

EXAMPLE 13-6

A steel pipe column has one end fixed and one end free. It has an outside diameter of 60.3 mm and an inside diameter of 52.5 mm. It supports an axial load of 45 kN. Determine the actual length L that this column can reach without buckling.

Solution:

$$I = \frac{\pi}{4}(R_o^4 - R_i^4)$$

$$= 0.277(10)^6\ \text{mm}^4$$

$$K = 2.0$$

$$P_{\text{cr}} = \frac{\pi^2 EI}{(KL)^2}$$

or

$$L = \frac{\sqrt{\pi^2 EI/P_{\text{cr}}}}{K}$$

$$= \frac{\sqrt{\dfrac{\pi^2[200(10)^6\ \text{kN/m}^2](0.277)(10)^{-6}\ \text{m}^4}{45\ \text{kN}}}}{2.0}$$

$$= 1.7\ \text{m}$$

EXAMPLE 13-7

A timber section 89 × 139 mm is to be used as a column 4.5 m long. The K value for the strong axis, K_x, is 1.0. At both ends, the weak axis is partially restrained, so K_y is estimated to be 0.8. Determine the critical buckling stress. Assume that $E = 8000$ MPa.

Solution:

$$r_x = 40.1\ \text{mm}$$

$$r_y = 25.7\ \text{mm}$$

Relative $\frac{1}{r}$ increased during the evolution of the classical orders.

Lower

Higher

Euler's formula, which correlates the factors principally responsible for a column's resistance to buckling, is another abstraction seemingly distant from "design," whose manipulation in fact has immediate visual consequences. The type of *end connections*—K in KL/r—and *column slenderness*—the L/r in the formula—can be seen as partial rationales underlying what seem to be merely arbitrary formal gestures or superficial modifications due only to changes in taste.

For example, a compression strut in Frei Otto's pavilion for the Museum of Modern Art garden displays a quite conscious gradation in cross section, center to ends, reflecting the fact that with pinned ends the middle of a column must resist the tendency to buckle. Alvar Aalto may have had a similar structural logic less directly in mind when he designed the columns in his 1937 Finnish Pavilion in Paris. Each has six ribs, tapering center to ends, added to a cylindrical section; yet the end connections

are certainly not pins, and the ribs may in fact add only marginally to the columns' buckling resistance. But Aalto was using our intuitive visual knowledge of behavior under load in order to involve us with the building; the ribs are a kind of plausible structural fairy tale, an invitation to empathy.

The evolution of the classical orders can be interpreted as another instance where patterns of structure coincide with patterns of visual sophistication. Despite numerous individual exceptions, the clear pattern is one of regular increase in the slenderness ratio, from the earlier Tuscan and Doric to the later Composite. To put it another way, the increase in L/r reflects both a greater technical confidence, the result of accumulated experience with columns and loads, and a greater affinity for visual lightness produced by changes in both proportion and ornamentation.

183

First determine the larger KL/r.

$$\left(\frac{KL}{r}\right)_x = \frac{1.0(4500)}{40.1} = 112$$

$$\left(\frac{KL}{r}\right)_y = \frac{0.8(4500)}{25.7} = 140$$

The weak axis is critical for this column.

$$\left(\frac{P}{A}\right)_{cr} = \frac{\pi^2 E}{(KL/r)^2}$$

$$= \frac{\pi^2(8000)(10)^3 \text{ kPa}}{(140)^2}$$

$$= 4030 \text{ kPa}$$

Problems

13-4. A steel W310 × 79 is used as a column 17 m long. Both ends are fixed. Determine the critical buckling stress and load.

13-5. An 89 × 139 mm wood post frames into stiff box beams, as shown in Figure 13-7. Its strong axis may be considered pinned at the top by a floor deck. The lower end is a simple pin for both axes. Determine the critical buckling stress and load. Assume that $E = 9000$ MPa.

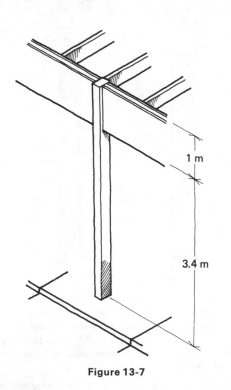

Figure 13-7

13-6. Figure 13-8 shows a 102 × 51 mm structural tube with a 6.4-mm wall thickness serving as a column 5 m long. Its upper end has pinned connections. The lower end is braced by a masonry wall so that its weak axis is fixed and the strong axis pinned. Determine the critical buckling load.

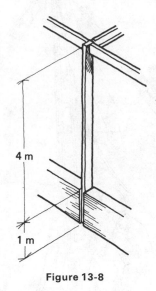

Figure 13-8

13-7. A 150-mm-diameter wood post is fixed into a large foundation pier at grade and is completely free at its upper end. How long can it be and still just support a load of 9 kN without failing? Assume that $E = 10\ 000$ MPa.

13-5 INTERMEDIATE LATERAL BRACING

We now know that if the end conditions are the same for both axes, a column will always buckle about its weak axis. A rectangular timber post will buckle in a direction parallel to its least dimension. A steel wide-flange shape will buckle in a direction parallel to its flanges. With any asymmetrical shape, we have a situation in which the full capacity of the strong axis is not normally utilized. However, there are many situations in structural frames where we can increase the capacity of such asymmetrical shapes by decreasing the effective weak-axis length. In Examples 13-5 and 13-7, this occurred to a certain degree by virtue of the different end connections. We will have a structurally more efficient column if $(KL/r)_x$ and $(KL/r)_y$ have values that are similar in magnitude. Intermediate lateral bracing members are a most effective way of doing this. Often such elements occur rather naturally for other construction reasons.

In Figure 13-9, the column is braced against weak-axis buckling by a secondary wall element. Bracing can be provided by load-carrying beams and girders as well.

It is important to realize that such members do not provide any bracing for the other axis of the column. In terms of the support provided for the column, they can be considered as two-force members (i.e., unable to resist nonaxial forces).

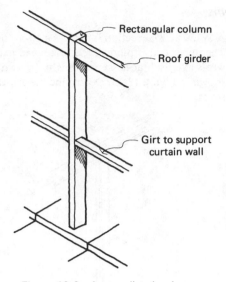

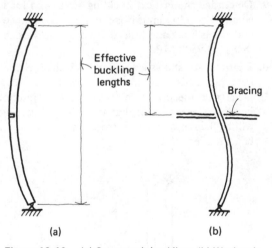

Figure 13-9. Intermediate bracing.

EXAMPLE 13-8

A wood 89 × 185 mm section is used as a column 4.3 m long. It has pinned ends and is braced against weak axis-buckling at midheight (Figure 13-10). Determine the critical buckling stress and load. Assume that $E = 8000$ MPa.

Figure 13-10. (a) Strong-axis buckling; (b) Weak-axis buckling.

Solution:

$$r_x = 53.4 \text{ mm}$$

$$r_y = 25.7 \text{ mm}$$

$$A = 16\ 500 \text{ mm}^2$$

$$\left(\frac{KL}{r}\right)_x = \frac{1.0(4300)}{53.4} = 80.5$$

$$\left(\frac{KL}{r}\right)_y = \frac{1.0(2150)}{25.7} = 83.7$$

The weak axis is critical, but not by much.

$$\left(\frac{P}{A}\right)_{cr} = \frac{\pi^2 E}{(KL/r)^2}$$

$$= \frac{\pi^2(8000)(10)^3 \text{ kPa}}{(83.7)^2} = 11\ 300 \text{ kPa}$$

$$P_{cr} = \left(\frac{P}{A}\right)_{cr}(A)$$

$$= (11\ 300 \text{ kN/m}^2)(0.0165 \text{ m}^2)$$

$$= 186 \text{ kN}$$

To see the effect of bracing the weak axis, compare the last answer with that of similar Example 13-3. With bracing, the column capacity has been increased by a factor of 4. This occurred because the effective length was cut in half.

EXAMPLE 13-9

A steel rectangular structure tube, TS 152 × 76, with a wall thickness of 12.7 mm, is used as a 6-m-long column. It has pinned ends, and its weak axis is fully braced by a masonry curtain wall, as shown in Figure 13-11. Determine the critical buckling load.

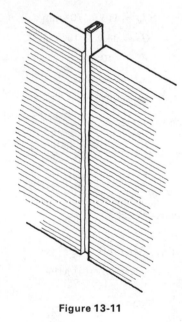

Figure 13-11

Solution: From Table 2 of Appendix S, $I_x = 10.7 \times 10^6$ mm⁴.

$$P_{cr} = \frac{\pi^2 EI}{(KL)^2}$$

$$= \frac{\pi^2[(200)(10)^6 \text{ kN/m}^2](10.7)(10)^{-6} \text{ m}^4}{[1.0(6 \text{ m})]^2}$$

$$= 587 \text{ kN}$$

EXAMPLE 13-10

A steel W250 × 73 is used as a 13.4-m-long column. It has pinned ends and its weak axis is braced at a point 7.3 m up from the lower end (see Figure 13-12). Determine the critical buckling stress and load.

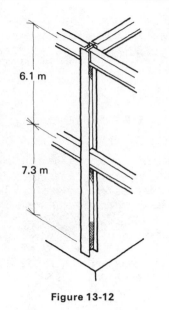

Figure 13-12

Solution:

$$I_x = 113 \times 10^6 \text{ mm}^4$$

$$I_y = 38.9 \times 10^6 \text{ mm}^4$$

$$r_x = 110 \text{ mm}$$

$$r_y = 64.5 \text{ mm}$$

$$A = 9290 \text{ mm}^2$$

First determine the larger KL/r.

$$\left(\frac{KL}{r}\right)_x = \frac{1.0(13\ 400)}{110} = 121$$

$$\left(\frac{KL}{r}\right)_y = \frac{1.0(7300)}{64.5} = 113$$

The strong axis is critical.

$$\left(\frac{P}{A}\right)_{cr} = \frac{\pi^2 E}{(KL/r)^2}$$

$$= \frac{\pi^2 (200)(10)^3 \text{ MPa}}{(121)^2}$$

$$= 135 \text{ MPa}$$

$$P_{cr} = (135 \text{ MN/m}^2)(0.009\ 29 \text{ m}^2)$$

$$= 1.25 \text{ MN}$$

or

$$P_{cr} = 1250 \text{ kN}$$

Alternatively,

$$P_{cr} = \frac{\pi^2 EI}{(KL)^2}$$

$$= \frac{\pi^2 [(200)(10)^6 \text{ kN/m}^2](113)(10)^{-6} \text{ m}^4}{[1.0(13.4 \text{ m})]^2}$$

$$= 1240 \text{ kN}$$

(The discrepancy between the two answers is due to rounding error and is less than 1 %.)

Problems

13-8. A W150 $\times$ 37.1 section is used as a 10-m-long column. The upper end is pinned, the lower end fixed, and the weak axis is braced at midheight by two angles, as shown in Figure 13-13. Determine the critical buckling stress.

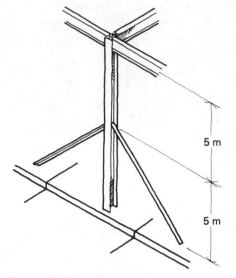

Figure 13-13. Diagonally braced column.

13-9. Determine the critical buckling stress and load for a wood 38 $\times$ 139 mm if it is 6 m long, has pinned ends, and has its weak axis braced at 1.5-m intervals. Assume that $E = 9500$ MPa.

13-10. Figure 13-14 shows a C250 $\times$ 44.8 channel used as a long pinned-end compression member of length L. Determine the optimum spacing XL of intermediate bracing elements such that the critical buckling load will be the same for both strong and weak axes. X will be a fraction of L.

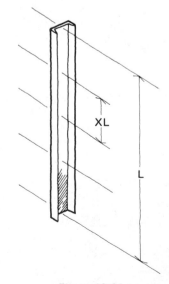

Figure 13-14

13-6 LIMITS TO THE APPLICABILITY OF THE EULER EQUATION

The plot of the Euler equation in Figure 13-15 shows that it is asymptotic to both axes. We can see that for very low values of KL/r (i.e., for short stout columns), the critical stress becomes very high. Indeed, as KL/r approaches zero, $(P/A)_{cr}$ goes to infinity. Obviously, this cannot be valid because the stresses in this region of the graph would be above the yield stress or crushing stress of the material. It is clear that the Euler equation cannot be valid if it predicts a buckling stress above the yield stress. A short column will fail by crushing under a load which is less than that predicted by the Euler equation.

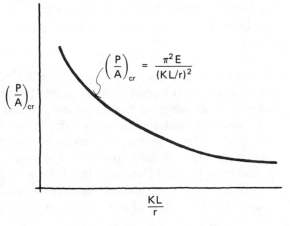

Figure 13-15. Euler equation.

The value $(P/A)_{cr}$ represents an average unit stress over the entire cross section. When a column is buckled into an arc, the stresses are not uniform over the cross section. The maximum fiber stress will be compressive, occurring on the inside of the arc. For some columns of relatively low slenderness, $(P/A)_{cr}$ may be large enough to cause a yield or crushing of these fibers. This implies that the Euler equation for elastic buckling is not completely valid except for long, thin columns. A column with a moderately (often called "intermediate") low slenderness ratio will still basically buckle rather than crush, but as this occurs some of the fibers will reach their yield stress. This type of buckling is called *inelastic buckling* and is really a combination of buckling and crushing.

In terms of developing design equations for safe loads on columns, both the timber and steel industries have come up with appropriate lower limits on KL/r. Below these values, the Euler equation cannot be used, and other methods for column design have been recommended. It is for this reason that all the previous examples and problems involved relatively long and slender columns. Methods for handling the shorter "intermediate" columns will be discussed in the following sections on timber and steel column analysis.

13-7 AXIAL LOADS ON TIMBER COLUMNS

The National Forest Products Association (NFPA) has classified timber columns into three groups based on failure mode, and we shall call these groups: short, intermediate, and long. A *short column* is one that will fail by crushing; an *intermediate column* will fail by a combination of crushing and buckling; and a *long column* will fail by Euler (or pure elastic) buckling alone. This section will examine each of the three types.

Since most timber columns are rectangular in shape, it is more convenient to work with a slenderness ratio expressed in terms of d, the cross-sectional dimension in the plane of buckling. The term L/d then is used for the slenderness ratio in timber buckling formulas as presented by the NFPA.

The changeover from a strictly crushing type of failure to one involving buckling occurs at L/d values between 5 and 12, with the higher end of the range prevailing for most species. For this reason, the NFPA has chosen an L/d value of 11 as the upper limit of slenderness ratio for which a crushing failure may be assumed. Above the limit buckling must be considered. For L/d values equal to or less than 11, the permissible stress on the cross-sectional area is taken as F_c, the allowable compressive stress parallel to grain for the species and grade of wood being used. F_c values for several species of wood are given in Appendix P.

For L/d values greater than 11 but less than a certain parameter K, the column is classified as intermediate.[1] The K value is the dividing line between intermediate and long columns and is given as

$$K = 0.671 \sqrt{\frac{E}{F_c}}$$

This value is based on the assumption that the Euler equation (after the application of an appropriate factor of safety) becomes inaccurate at slenderness ratios small enough to generate permissible stresses as high as $\frac{2}{3}F_c$. It is judged that, below this value of slenderness, enough inelastic action is taking place at failure so that the Euler equation is no longer valid.

For L/d values between 11 and K, the allowable compressive stress is given by

$$F'_c = F_c \left[1 - \frac{1}{3}\left(\frac{L/d}{K}\right)^4 \right] \qquad (13\text{-}4)$$

---

[1]This term is not to be confused with the end-conditions factor, which unfortunately has the same symbol.

where F'_c = allowable compressive stress after accounting for any buckling action

F_c = allowable stress in compression parallel to grain for the species and grade of wood being used

For L/d values greater than K, the allowable compressive stress is given by

$$F'_c = \frac{0.30E}{(L/d)^2} \qquad (13\text{-}5)$$

Equation (13-5) is actually the Euler equation with the constant π^2 incorporated into a factor to account for the reduction from critical to allowable stress and also the change from L/r to L/d as the slenderness parameter. The Euler equation can be written in terms of L/d by noting that for a solid rectangle, $r = d/\sqrt{12}$.

$$r = \sqrt{\frac{I}{A}}$$
$$= \sqrt{\frac{bd^3/12}{bd}}$$
$$= \frac{d}{\sqrt{12}}$$

We then have

$$F'_c = \frac{\pi^2 E}{[\sqrt{12}(L/d)]^2}$$

or

$$F'_c = \frac{0.824E}{(L/d)^2}$$

This critical value is then reduced by a factor of 2.74 to obtain Equation (13-5).

$$F'_c = \frac{0.824E}{2.74(L/d)^2}$$
$$= \frac{0.30E}{(L/d)^2}$$

The 2.74 reduction includes a 1.66 factor of safety and a factor that considers the statistical variation of the modulus of elasticity of visually graded lumber. For machine stress-rated and glued-laminated lumber, this value should be reduced. See the *National Design Specification* of the NFPA for further information.

A plot of the allowable stress/slenderness ratio for a typical timber column appears in Figure 13-16. The basic Euler equation is shown as a dashed line.

Several notes are in order concerning the use of Equations (13-4) and (13-5) and the dividing parameter K.

1. An L/d value greater than 50 is not permitted. This is equivalent to an L/r of 173, and it is felt that a column more slender than this is inherently unstable.

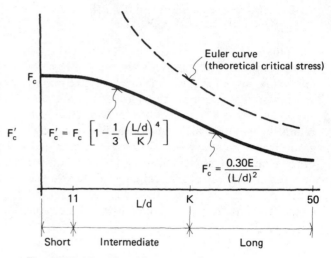

Figure 13-16. Allowable stresses for axially loaded columns.

2. The end-conditions factor is missing from the computation of the slenderness ratio, as this factor is taken as unity for most timber columns. Fixed or continuous connections are more difficult to construct in wood than in steel or concrete, and pinned conditions are normally assumed. Ignoring any probable fixity will be conservative from a design standpoint except in unusual cases such as the "flagpole," where the effective length is twice the true length.

3. The F_c value, allowable stress parallel to grain, should be modified for duration of loading and wet-use conditions as per Appendix P, but F'_c should not be modified.

4. The equations refer to solid sawn timbers, and if a member is built up by nailing several smaller pieces together, the permissible stresses should be reduced. The precise amount of reduction needed to ensure the same degree of safety present in a solid column is difficult to ascertain. It is a function of the method of joining the individual pieces, the grade of wood being used, and the column geometry. The writer feels that at least for preliminary design purposes, a reduction of 35% in F'_c is sufficient in most situations. This value will be used in the examples and problems of this text, but the reader is referred to the book *Wood Engineering*[2] for a more complete discussion.

5. Columns of circular cross section may be designed by assuming a square section of equivalent area.

6. For sections other than rectangular or circular, Equations (13-4) and (13-5) must be modified to

[2]German Gurfinkel, *Wood Engineering* (New Orleans, La.: Southern Forest Products Association, 1973), pp. 277–278.

accept the slenderness ratio as L/r. Accordingly, we get

$$F'_c = F_c\left[1 - \frac{1}{3}\left(\frac{L/r}{\sqrt{12}\,K}\right)^4\right]$$

or, if we let K, modified by the $\sqrt{12}$ factor, be called K_m, we get

$$K_m = \sqrt{12}\,(0.671)\sqrt{\frac{E}{F_c}}$$

and

$$F'_c = F_c\left[1 - \frac{1}{3}\left(\frac{L/r}{K_m}\right)^4\right] \tag{13-4a}$$

and similarly,

$$F'_c = \frac{0.30E}{(L/\sqrt{12}\,r)^2}$$

or

$$F'_c = \frac{3.60E}{(L/r)^2} \tag{13-5a}$$

7. All the timber column equations assume a full cross section of material, and this design area need not be reduced for bolt holes, etc., unless they occur within a critical part of the potential buckling length. However, the unit stress on any net section shall not exceed F_c, the allowable stress parallel to grain.

EXAMPLE 13-11

Determine the allowable stress and load for an 89 × 89 mm post of hem-fir which is 3 m long.

Solution:

$$A = 7920 \text{ mm}^2$$

$$\frac{L}{d} = \frac{3000}{89} = 33.7$$

$$K = 0.671\sqrt{\frac{E}{F_c}}$$

$$= 0.671\sqrt{\frac{10\ 300(10)^3 \text{ kPa}}{6900 \text{ kPa}}}$$

$$= 25.9$$

Since L/d is larger than K, we shall use Equation (13-5).

$$F'_c = \frac{0.30E}{(L/d)^2}$$

$$= \frac{0.30(10\ 300)(10)^3 \text{ kPa}}{(33.7)^2}$$

$$= 2720 \text{ kPa}$$

$$P = F'_c(A)$$

$$= (2720 \text{ kN/m}^2)(0.007\ 92 \text{ m}^2)$$

$$= 21.5 \text{ kN}$$

EXAMPLE 13-12

A Douglas fir section 139 × 235 mm is used as a column 9 m long. Its weak axis is braced at the third points. Determine the allowable stress and load.

Solution:

$$A = 32\ 700 \text{ mm}^2$$

First determine which axis is critical.

$$\left(\frac{L}{d}\right)_x = \frac{9000}{235} = 38.3$$

$$\left(\frac{L}{d}\right)_y = \frac{3000}{139} = 21.6$$

The strong axis controls.

$$K = 0.671\sqrt{\frac{E}{F_c}}$$

$$= 0.671\sqrt{\frac{11\ 000(10)^3 \text{ kPa}}{6900 \text{ kPa}}}$$

$$= 26.8$$

Since L/d is larger than K, Equation (13-5) will be used.

$$F'_c = \frac{0.30E}{(L/d)^2}$$

$$= \frac{0.30(11\ 000)(10)^3 \text{ kPa}}{(38.3)^2}$$

$$= 2250 \text{ kPa}$$

$$P = F'_c(A)$$

$$= (2250 \text{ kN/m}^2)(0.0327 \text{ m}^2)$$

$$= 73.6 \text{ kN}$$

EXAMPLE 13-13

An eastern spruce 89 × 139 mm section is used as a 2.5-m-long post at the end of a frame wall, as shown in Figure 13-17. Given that the narrow dimension is fully braced by the wall, determine the allowable stress and load. Assume the load to be mostly snow on the roof above.

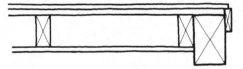

Figure 13-17. Plan of corner post.

Solution: As per Appendix P, F_c will be increased by 15% for the anticipated short duration of full load application.

$$A = 12\ 400 \text{ mm}^2$$

$$\frac{L}{d} = \frac{2500}{139} = 18.0$$

$$K = 0.671\sqrt{\frac{E}{F_c}}$$

$$= 0.671\sqrt{\frac{9600(10)^3 \text{ kPa}}{(1.15)6200 \text{ kPa}}}$$

$$= 24.6$$

In this case, L/d is less than K and the post falls into the inter-mediate category. Equation (13-4) will be used.

$$F'_c = F_c\left[1 - \frac{1}{3}\left(\frac{L/d}{K}\right)^4\right]$$

$$= 1.15(6200)\ \text{kPa}\left[1 - \frac{1}{3}\left(\frac{18.0}{24.6}\right)^4\right]$$

$$= 6450\ \text{kPa}$$

$$P = F'_c(A)$$

$$= (6450\ \text{kN/m}^2)(0.0124\ \text{m}^2)$$

$$= 80.0\ \text{kN}$$

EXAMPLE 13-14

An unbraced 4-m-long eastern hemlock post must carry a design load of 13 kN. Will an 89×89 mm section be adequate?

Solution:

$$A = 7920\ \text{mm}^2$$

$$\frac{L}{d} = \frac{4000}{89} = 44.9$$

This ratio is near the maximum L/d value permitted of 50 and is, therefore, well above the K value.

$$F'_c = \frac{0.30E}{(L/d)^2}$$

$$= \frac{0.30(8900)(10)^3\ \text{kPa}}{(44.9)^2}$$

$$= 1320\ \text{kPa}$$

$$P = F'_c(A)$$

$$= (1320\ \text{kN/m}^2)(0.007\ 92\ \text{m}^2)$$

$$= 10.5\ \text{kN}$$

The safe column capacity is less than the design load; the section is not adequate.

Perhaps an 89×139 mm section has enough area.

$$A = 12\ 400\ \text{mm}^2$$

Since the L/d remains the same, F'_c will still be 1320 kPa; and so by ratio of the cross-sectional areas, we get

$$P = \frac{12\ 400\ \text{mm}^2}{7920\ \text{mm}^2}(10.5\ \text{kN})$$

$$= 16.4\ \text{kN}$$

Therefore, the 89×139 mm post will be OK.

EXAMPLE 13-15

Determine the allowable load per linear meter (w kN/m) of a stud bearing wall 2.5 m high. The hem-fir studs are 38×89 mm in section and 400 mm on center, as shown in Figure 13-18.

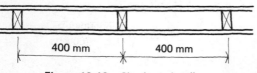

Figure 13-18.   Simple stud wall.

Solution: First determine the capacity of one stud, assuming the weak axis to be fully braced by the wallboard.

$$A = 3380\ \text{mm}^2$$

$$\frac{L}{d} = \frac{2500}{89} = 28.1$$

From Example 3-11, $K = 25.9$, so Equation (13-5) will be used.

$$F'_c = \frac{0.30E}{(L/d)^2}$$

$$= \frac{0.30(10\ 300)(10)^3\ \text{kPa}}{(28.1)^2}$$

$$= 3910\ \text{kPa}$$

$$P = F'_c(A)$$

$$= (3910\ \text{kN/m}^2)(0.003\ 38\ \text{m}^2)$$

$$= 13.2\ \text{kN}$$

The studs are placed 400 mm o.c.; therefore, the allowable load per linear meter of wall will be

$$w = \frac{1000\ \text{mm}}{400\ \text{mm}}(13.2\ \text{kN})$$

$$= 33\ \text{kN/m}$$

EXAMPLE 13-16

Determine the safe load capacity of the column section of Figure 13-19, which is constructed of Douglas fir pieces. It is 3.5 m long and has its weak axis braced at a point 2.5 m from the bottom.

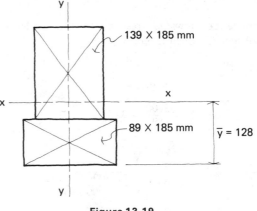

Figure 13-19

Solution: This example illustrates a situation in which an L/r expression of the slenderness ratio must be used. Also, the column is not one solid piece, os the determined stresses will be reduced by 35%, as previously indicated.

The $\bar{y}$ value is given in Figure 13-19 and using the moment of inertia values for each piece (as given in Appendix Q), we can use the parallel axis theorem to obtain I_x and I_y for the built-up section.

$$I_x = 273(10)^6\ \text{mm}^4 \qquad I_y = 88.4(10)^6\ \text{mm}^4$$

From these we get

$$r_x = 80\ \text{mm} \qquad r_y = 46\ \text{mm}$$

By virtue of the weak axis bracing,

$$\frac{L}{r_x} = \frac{3500}{80} \qquad \frac{L}{r_y} = \frac{2500}{46}$$

$$= 44 \qquad\qquad = 54$$

The weak axis is critical. Since the section is not rectangular, we shall modify the limiting value K as previously discussed, and therefore

$$K_m = (\sqrt{12})(0.671)\sqrt{\frac{E}{F_c}}$$

$$= (\sqrt{12})(0.671)\sqrt{\frac{11\ 000(10)^3\ \text{kPa}}{6900\ \text{kPa}}}$$

$$= 93$$

The column is of intermediate slenderness since 54 is less than K_m.

$$F'_c = F_c\left[1 - \frac{1}{3}\left(\frac{L/r}{K_m}\right)^4\right]$$

$$= 6900\ \text{kPa}\left[1 - \frac{1}{3}\left(\frac{54}{93}\right)^4\right]$$

$$= 6640\ \text{kPa}$$

Reducing the allowable stress because the column is a built-up one, we get

$$F'_c = 0.65(6640\ \text{kPa})$$

$$= 4320\ \text{kPa}$$

$$P = F'_c(A)$$

$$= (4320\ \text{kN/m}^2)(0.0422\ \text{m}^2)$$

$$= 182\ \text{kN}$$

Problems

13-11. A 4.3-m-long column of Douglas fir must carry a load of 62 kN. Is a 139 × 139 mm section adequate?

13-12. An eastern spruce 38 × 139 mm is used as a 3-m-long compression member. Its weak axis is braced at midlength. Determine the allowable stress and load.

13-13. Determine the allowable stress and load of the compression member in Problem 13-12 if its weak axis is braced at 1-m intervals.

13-14. Determine the allowable load on the doubled 38 × 89 mm hem-fir post in Figure 13-20. It is 2.4 m long.

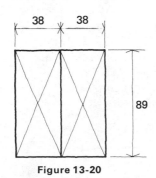

Figure 13-20

13-15. Three Douglas fir 38 × 139 mm pieces are built up, as shown in Figure 13-21. If the column is 3.7 m long, is it safe for a load of 22 kN?

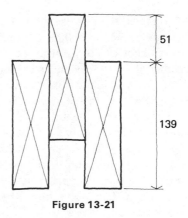

Figure 13-21

13-16. The Douglas fir stud bearing wall in Figure 13-22 is 2.4 m tall and must support a load of 15 kN per running meter. The wall is not finished by sheathing or drywall on either side, but it does have blocking at midheight. Will 38 × 89 mm studs 400 mm on center be sufficient?

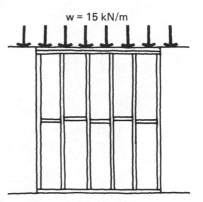

Figure 13-22. Elevation of a stud wall.

13-17. The hem-fir bearing wall of Figure 13-23 is made of 38 × 139 mm studs. How tall can the wall safely be and still support 22 kN per meter?

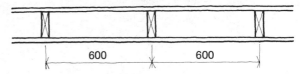

Figure 13-23. Plan of a stud wall.

13-8 AXIAL LOADS ON STEEL COLUMNS

It has been shown that the basic Euler equation for column buckling becomes invalid for low values of KL/r. This is true, of course, for steel columns as well as for timber. The American Institute of Steel Construction has made certain recommendations as to the cutoff value of KL/r, below which the Euler equation should not be used. These recommendations were based on test data collected by the Column Research Council. Many steel columns of various slenderness ratios were tested to failure to determine the lower limit of applicability of the Euler equation. That is another way of saying "at what decreasing value of KL/r does inelastic bahavior begin to take over." For KL/r values below that limit, some other procedure must be used in column analysis and design.

Based on the experimental work, it was recommended that (for steel columns) the lower limit of KL/r be the point at which the Euler equation predicted a $(P/A)_{cr}$ stress equal to one-half of the yield stress of the material. In other words, in terms of decreasing slenderness ratios, the Euler theory should not be applied when it shows an average unit stress equal to or greater than one-half of the yield stress. This will ensure that the Euler equation will only be applied to columns that are slender enough to buckle in a fully elastic manner.

The lower limit of KL/r is called C_c and is given by the following equation, which is very similar to a parameter used in timber column analysis.

$$C_c = \sqrt{\frac{\pi^2 E}{F_y/2}}$$

or

$$C_c = \sqrt{\frac{2\pi^2 E}{F_y}}$$

where F_y equals the yield stress for the column steel.

Since E is common for all structural steels, C_c will vary only with steel strength. For example, steel with an F_y of 250 MPa has a C_c value of 126 and a steel of 345 MPa has a C_c value of 107.

If the KL/r value is below C_c, an empirical equation for inelastic action, developed from the column tests, should be used. With a KL/r value above C_c, the familiar Euler equation can be used. AISC calls these equations Formula I and Formula II, respectively.

$$\frac{KL}{r} < C_c \qquad F_a = \frac{\left[1 - \frac{(KL/r)^2}{2C_c^2}\right] F_y}{\text{F.S.}} \qquad \text{AISC-I} \quad (13\text{-}6)$$

$$\frac{KL}{r} > C_c \qquad F_a = \frac{12\pi^2 E}{23(KL/r)^2} \qquad \text{AISC-II} \quad (13\text{-}7)$$

where F_a is equal to the allowable P/A stress. (There is also an AISC Formula III, which is used only for bracing or secondary members. Analysis of such members is not included in this text.)

It is easy to see that Formula II (for more slender columns) is merely the Euler equation with a factor of safety of $\frac{23}{12}$, or 1.92. The factor of safety (F.S.) in Formula I is more complicated. Rather than impose a constant factor of safety on columns that fail by inelastic buckling, it is recognized that as KL/r becomes smaller, the amount of material yielding at failure becomes greater. This implies a slower (or safer) failure such as occurs when a steel beam is failed in bending. Indeed, a very short block of steel in axial compression would fail very slowly relative to a long slender column. Therefore, a sliding factor of safety was adopted for Formula I. The F.S. value decreases as KL/r becomes less and is given by

$$\text{F.S.} = \frac{5}{3} + \frac{3(KL/r)}{8C_c} - \frac{(KL/r)^3}{8C_c^3} \qquad (13\text{-}8)$$

By substituting the appropriate limiting values of KL/r into this equation, we can see that the F.S. slides from 1.67 when $KL/r = 0$ to 1.92 when $KL/r = C_c$. A plot of Formulas I and II appears in Figure 13-24.

Just as the timber slenderness ratio was limited to a maximum of $L/d = 50$ ($L/r = 173$); steel columns having a KL/r above 200 are not permitted.

The reader should notice that, unlike Formula I, Formula II is independent of the material strength. This is consistent with previous statements about the Euler equation and the buckling strength of slender columns. It is most important to recognize that, when KL/r is greater than C_c, the capacity of a column is totally independent of the grade of steel used. It would be quite

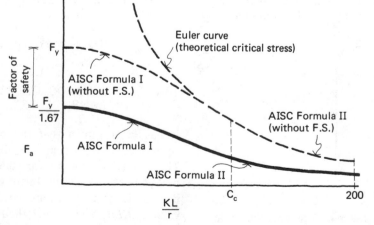

Figure 13-24. AISC column formulas.

wasteful to use high-strength steel in a long, slender column.

Before continuing with examples of the use of these formulas, a short discussion of the K factor is necessary. Through actual tests, it has been found that the theoretical K values are somewhat nonconservative for steel columns. Accordingly, the end-condition factors given in Figure 13-25 are recommended. It is easier to achieve rigid connections in steel than in wood, so the K value is not commonly dropped from the slenderness ratio. In

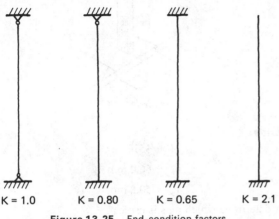

| K = 1.0 | K = 0.80 | K = 0.65 | K = 2.1 |

Figure 13-25. End-condition factors.

unbraced steel construction (that in which the lateral stability of the frame is achieved by joint continuity or moment resistance rather than a separate bracing system), K values can become quite large, owing to sidesway, and therefore very influential. Such frames must be analyzed by a technique that accounts for the relative stiffness of the connected members. The analysis of columns in such unbraced frames will not be treated here.

Unlike wood, structural steel has a constant E value (200 000 MPa). This means that, for a given steel strength, F_a is a function of KL/r alone. Tables 1 and 2 of Appendix R represent solutions of Formulas I and II for various KL/r values for two different steel strengths, $F_y = 250$ MPa and $F_y = 345$ MPa, respectively. F_a can be obtained directly from these tables, eliminating the arithmetic of the formulas. To emphasize the fact that the allowable stress does not vary with steel strength when the slenderness ratio is above C_c, F_a values are not shown above $KL/r = 126$ in the $F_y = 345$-MPa table.

Examples 13-17 and 13-18 have been solved without using Appendix R, but in Examples 13-19 through 13-22, the F_a values were taken directly from the tables.

EXAMPLE 13-17

A steel ($F_y = 250$ MPa) W310 × 97 has fixed ends and is 6 m long. Its weak axis is braced at midheight. Determine the safe load capacity for this column.

Solution:
$$A = 12\ 300\ \text{mm}^2$$
$$r_x = 134\ \text{mm}$$
$$r_y = 76.7\ \text{mm}$$

First determine the larger KL/r value.
$$\left(\frac{KL}{r}\right)_x = \frac{0.65(6000)}{134} = 29.1$$
$$\left(\frac{KL}{r}\right)_y = \frac{0.80(3000)}{76.7} = 31.3$$

The weak axis is critical, and since 31.3 is less than C_c (126), Formula I must be used. First determine the factor of safety.

$$\text{F.S.} = \frac{5}{3} + \frac{3(KL/r)}{8C_c} - \frac{(KL/r)^3}{8C_c^3}$$
$$= \frac{5}{3} + \frac{3(31.3)}{8(126)} - \frac{(31.3)^3}{8(126)^3} = 1.76$$

Then,

$$F_a = \frac{\left[1 - \frac{(KL/r)^2}{2C_c^2}\right]F_y}{\text{F.S.}}$$
$$= \frac{\left[1 - \frac{(31.3)^2}{2(126)^2}\right]250\ \text{MPa}}{1.76}$$
$$= 136\ \text{MPa}$$
$$P = F_a(A)$$
$$= (136\ \text{MN/m}^2)(0.0123\ \text{m}^2)$$
$$= 1.67\ \text{MN}$$
or
$$P = 1670\ \text{kN}$$

EXAMPLE 13-18

A nominal 150-mm-diameter standard weight pipe column of $F_y = 250$ MPa has pinned ends and is 8.5 m long. The outside diameter is 168.3 mm and the wall thickness is 7.1 mm. Will it safely support 178 kN?

Solution:
$$A = 3590\ \text{mm}^2$$
$$r = 57.1\ \text{mm}$$
$$\frac{KL}{r} = \frac{1.0(8500)}{57.1} = 149 < 200$$

Since 149 is greater than C_c (126), use Formula II.

$$F_a = \frac{12\pi^2 E}{23(KL/r)^2}$$
$$= \frac{12\pi^2[200(10)^3\ \text{MPa}]}{23(149)^2}$$
$$= 46.4\ \text{MPa}$$
$$P = F_a(A)$$
$$= (46.4\ \text{MN/m}^2)(0.003\ 59\ \text{m}^2)$$
$$= 0.167\ \text{MN}$$
or
$$P = 167\ \text{kN}$$

Since P is less than the required 178 kN, the column is not safe.

EXAMPLE 13-19

The $F_y = 250$ MPa W250 × 89 in Figure 13-26 is 6 m long and has beams framing in at the top such that the top is pinned. It must carry a load of 1250 kN. Will the lower end have to be fixed, or can it be merely a pin connection?

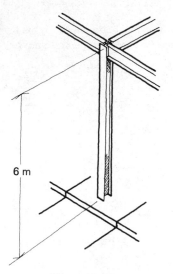

Figure 13-26

Solution:

$$r_y = 65.1 \quad \text{and} \quad A = 11\ 400\ \text{mm}^2$$

Solve for the maximum KL/r permitted by this loading. F_a must be at least equal to P/A.

$$\frac{P}{A} = \frac{1250\ \text{kN}}{0.0114\ \text{m}^2}$$

$$= 110\ 000\ \text{kPa} \quad \text{or} \quad 110\ \text{MPa}$$

From Table 1 in Appendix R, 109.6 MPa calls for a KL/r no larger than 75.

$$\frac{KL}{r} = 75$$

$$K = \frac{75r}{L}$$

$$= \frac{75(65.1)}{6000} = 0.814$$

Therefore, K can be no larger than 0.814. The lower end cannot be pinned. It must be fixed in order for this column to carry the load safely.

EXAMPLE 13-20

A steel ($F_y = 250$ MPa) 178 × 127 structural tube with a wall thickness of 6.4 mm is used as a column 5.5 m long. The ends are pinned, and the weak axis is braced 3.7 m from the lower end, as shown in Figure 13-27. Determine the safe load capacity of this column.

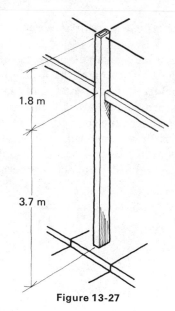

Figure 13-27

Solution:

$$A = 3570\ \text{mm}^2$$

$$r_x = 66.0\ \text{mm}$$

$$r_y = 50.8\ \text{mm}$$

First determine which axis is critical.

$$\left(\frac{KL}{r}\right)_x = \frac{1.0(5500)}{66.0} = 83.3$$

$$\left(\frac{KL}{r}\right)_y = \frac{1.0(3700)}{50.8} = 72.8$$

The strong axis is critical. From Table 1 in Appendix R,

$$F_a = 103.3\ \text{MPa}$$

$$P = F_a(A)$$

$$= 103\ 300\ \text{kN/m}^2(0.003\ 57\ \text{m})$$

$$= 369\ \text{kN}$$

EXAMPLE 13-21

An $F_y = 250$ W310 × 97 is used as a 12-m-long column supporting only a flat roof load. The ends are partially fixed and K is estimated at 0.9. If the total load of the roof is 4.0 kN/m² (including dead and live loads), how much tributary area can this column safely support? Could this area be increased if we used a steel of $F_y = 345$ MPa?

Solution:

$$r_y = 76.7\ \text{mm} \quad \text{and} \quad A = 12\ 300\ \text{mm}^2$$

$$\frac{KL}{r_y} = \frac{0.9(12\ 000)}{76.7} = 140.8$$

From Table 1 in Appendix R,

$$F_a = 51.9\ \text{MPa}$$

$$P = 51\ 900\ \text{kN/m}^2(0.0123\ \text{m}^2)$$

$$= 638\ \text{kN}$$

$$= \text{load (kN/m}^2) \times \text{area (m}^2)$$

$$638 = 4.0(A)$$
$$A = 160 \text{ m}^2$$

Therefore, example column bay dimensions could be 12.5 m square or 20 m × 8 m or 16 m × 10 m. Since the slenderness ratio is above C_c, no increase in load capacity could be achieved by using 345-MPa steel.

EXAMPLE 13-22

A 10-story office building has a bay size of 18 m by 12 m. The total load per square meter of floor or roof is 9.6 kN. An $F_y = 345$-MPa W360 × 818 was selected as the interior column for the first two stories. Will this section be adequate for a 5-m-high first story? Assume that $K = 1.0$.

Solution: First determine the total design load on an interior first floor column.

$$P = 10 \text{ stories } (18 \text{ m} \times 12 \text{ m})(9.6 \text{ kN/m}^2 \text{ per story})$$
$$= 20\ 700 \text{ kN}$$
$$r_y = 114 \text{ mm} \quad \text{and} \quad A = 105\ 000 \text{ mm}^2$$
$$\frac{KL}{r} = \frac{1.0(5000)}{114} = 43.8$$

From Table 2 in Appendix R,

$$F_a = 174.4 \text{ MPa}$$
$$P = F_a(A)$$
$$= 174\ 400 \text{ kN/m}^2(0.105 \text{ m}^2)$$
$$= 18\ 300 \text{ kN}$$
$$18\ 300 < 20\ 700$$

Therefore, the column selected is not adequate for the design loads.

Problems

13-18. Determine the permissible load on a steel ($F_y = 345$ MPa) W250 × 67 column if it is 7 m long and has pinned ends.

13-19. Determine the permissible load for the column of Problem 13-18 if its weak axis is braced at midheight.

13-20. An $F_y = 250$ MPa 230 × 30 channel is used as a column 3.6 m long. Its weak axis is fully braced and it has one pinned end and one fixed end. Determine the permissible load.

13-21. Determine the permissible load for the column of Problem 13-20 if its weak axis has no bracing.

13-22. The interior column of Figure 13-28 must support a roof load of 1.5 kN/m² snow and 2 kN/m² dead load. The bottom end is fixed and the top end pinned. Its weak axis is braced by struts at a point 2.5 m down from the top. If an $F_y = 250$ MPa W250 × 58 is used, how many square meters of roof can this column accommodate?

13-23. A 70-story building has a bay size of 13 m × 11 m. The total load per square meter of floor or roof is 7.0 kN. Will the $F_y = 250$-MPa section shown in Figure

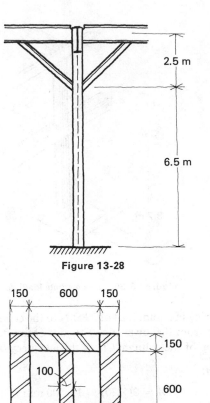

Figure 13-28

Figure 13-29.   Cross section.

13-29 be adequate for a 6-m-high interior first-story column? Assume pinned ends.

13-9   INTERMEDIATE AXIAL LOADS

Beams and girders sometimes deliver loads to columns in a manner that leaves one of the column axes unbraced. When this happens at some intermediate point in the column height, the effective buckling length of the unbraced axis can be quite difficult to determine. For preliminary design purposes, it will be sufficient (and conservative) to assume that all of the load is applied at the top of the column. This follows the recommendation of the NFPA with respect to *eccentric* intermediate loads and will not be overly conservative as long as such loads come into the column at or above midheight.

For a proper analytical determination of the true buckling length, the reader is referred to Chapter 5 of the book *Steel Structures.*[3]

EXAMPLE 13-23

The 6.7-m-long Douglas fir column of Figure 13-30 is built up from three 38 × 139 mm members. The second floor

[3]William McGuire, *Steel Structures* (Englewood Cliffs, N.J.: Prentice-Hall, Inc., 1968), pp. 574–579.

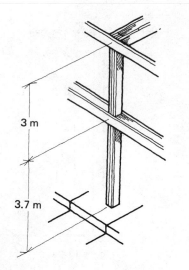

Figure 13-30. Intermediate loading.

beams bring in a total load of 8900 N to the column at a point 3.7 m up from the lower end. The roof beams deliver 5400 N to the top of the column. Check the adequacy of this design.

Solution:

$$A = 3(5280) = 15\ 800 \text{ mm}^2$$

First check the lower section, which is loaded by a total of 14.3 kN.

$$\left(\frac{L}{d}\right)_y = \frac{3700}{114} = 32.4$$

which is larger than a computed K value of 25.5; therefore

$$F'_c = \frac{0.30E}{(L/d)^2}$$

$$= \frac{0.30(12\ 400)(10)^3 \text{ kPa}}{(32.4)^2}$$

$$= 3540 \text{ kPa}$$

Reducing this because the column is built up, we get $0.65(3540) = 2300$ kPa.

$$P = F'_c(A)$$

$$= (2300 \text{ kN/m}^2)(0.0158 \text{ m}^2)$$

$$= 36.3 \text{ kN}$$

Now check the total column length assuming that the full load of 14.3 kN acts at the top. The strong axis is unbraced for its full length.

$$\left(\frac{L}{d}\right)_x = \frac{6700}{139} = 48.2$$

$$F'_c = \frac{0.30E}{(L/d)^2}$$

$$= \frac{0.30(12\ 400)(10)^3 \text{ kPa}}{(48.2)^2}$$

$$= 1600 \text{ kPa} \quad \text{which, when reduced, becomes}$$
$$0.65(1600) = 1040 \text{ kPa}$$

$$P = F'_c(A)$$

$$= (1040 \text{ kN/m}^2)(0.0158 \text{ m}^2)$$

$$= 16.4 \text{ kN}$$

Therefore, the column is adequate.

EXAMPLE 13-24

The $F_y = 345$-MPa column of Figure 13-31 is 9 m long and has its weak axis braced by floor beams at a point 4.3 m down from the top. The bottom is fixed and the top is pinned. The column directly above brings in 2200 kN, and the third floor beams deliver a total of 267 kN. The second floor spandrel beams bring in 400 kN. Is a W310 × 143 sufficient for these loads?

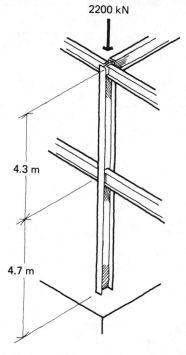

Figure 13-31

Solution:

$$A = 18\ 800 \text{ mm}^2$$

$$r_x = 138 \text{ mm}$$

$$r_y = 78.4 \text{ mm}$$

First check the weak axis under a total load of 2867 kN.

$$\left(\frac{KL}{r}\right)_y = \frac{0.80(4700)}{78.4} = 48.0$$

Using Table 2 of Appendix R,

$$F_a = 170.0 \text{ MPa}$$

$$P = F_a(A)$$

$$= (170\ 000 \text{ kN/m}^2)(0.0188 \text{ m}^2)$$

$$= 3200 \text{ kN}$$

$$3200 > 2867$$

Therefore, the weak axis is adequate. Now check the strong axis assuming that the full load of 2867 kN is applied at the top.

$$\left(\frac{KL}{r}\right)_x = \frac{0.80(9000)}{138} = 52.2$$

Using the same table,

$$F_a = 165.5 \text{ MPa}$$

$$P = F_a(A)$$

$$= (165\ 500 \text{ kN/m}^2)(0.0188 \text{ m}^2)$$

$$= 3100 \text{ kN}$$

The strong axis is also adequate.

Problems

13-24. An eastern spruce 139×139 mm must carry a roof load (mostly snow) of 13 kN and balcony load of 9 kN, as shown in Figure 13-32. Is the column section safe?

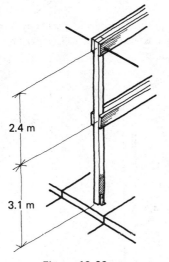

Figure 13-32

13-25. Would an 89×139 mm timber suffice as the column of Problem 13-24? Assume the section is oriented such that
(a) the 89-mm dimension is parallel to the beams.
(b) the 139-mm dimension is parallel to the beams.

13-26. Figure 13-33 shows an $F_y = 250$-MPa W310 $\times$ 179 column braced by second-floor beams that bring in 220 kN each. The load from columns and beams above is 2700 kN. If the ends are pinned, is the column section adequate?

13-10 BEAM-COLUMNS

The previous examples have been restricted to concentric loads that result in normal P/A stresses. Bending can also be a factor in column design, as flexural stresses can be generated by eccentric and/or lateral loads. The timber and steel industries have adopted procedures for handling

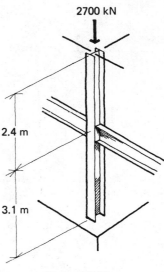

Figure 13-33

such cases, and formulas have been developed for the more frequently encountered situations. All such formulas stem from the same basic interaction concept. If both bending and axial forces act on a member, the magnitude of the axial stress present will be a certain fraction of the allowable axial stress, *and* the magnitude of the bending stress present will be a certain fraction of the allowable bending stress. The sum of these two fractions cannot exceed unity. In general terms, this can be expressed as follows:

$$\frac{f_{\text{actual axial}}}{F_{\text{allowable axial}}} + \frac{f_{\text{actual bending}}}{F_{\text{allowable bending}}} \leq 1 \qquad (13\text{-}9)$$

The right-hand side of Equation (13-9) may be modified for duration of loading and moisture conditions as appropriate.

In this text, we shall consider bending loads that act about only one cross-sectional axis. For bending about both axes, the basic formula would have a second bending term.

13-11 COMBINED LOADING ON TIMBER COLUMNS

For timber columns the National Forest Products Association has developed three sets of formulas to handle various combinations of concentric, eccentric, and lateral loads for the three different slenderness categories (Figure 13-34).

(In all the following formulas, f_{ce} is the axial stress due to the eccentric load alone, and f_c is that due to the sum of the eccentric and concentric loads.)

When L/d is 11 or less (short columns), the following formulas apply:

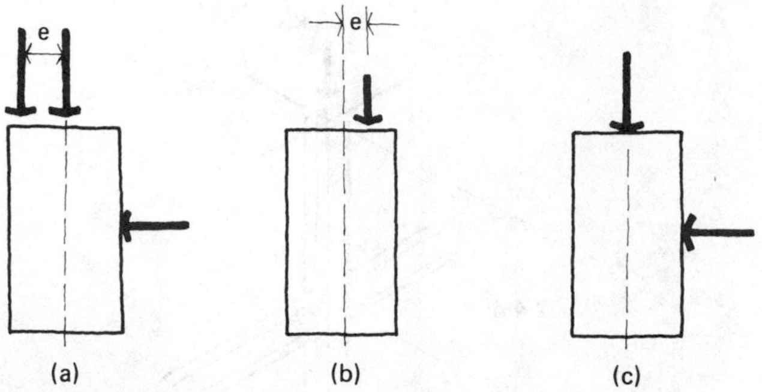

Figure 13-34. Three load combinations for Formulas (13-10), (13-11), and (13-12).

1. Combined concentric, eccentric, and lateral loads

$$\frac{f_c}{F'_c} + \frac{f_b + f_{ce}(6e/d)}{F_b} \leq 1 \qquad (13\text{-}10\text{a})$$

2. Eccentric loads alone

$$\frac{f_c}{F'_c} + \frac{f_c(6e/d)}{F_b} \leq 1 \qquad (13\text{-}10\text{b})$$

3. Concentric and lateral loads

$$\frac{f_c}{F'_c} + \frac{f_b}{F_b} \leq 1 \qquad (13\text{-}10\text{c})$$

Whe L/d is greater than 11 but less than K (intermediate columns), the following formulas apply:

1. Combined concentric, eccentric, and lateral loads

$$\frac{f_c}{F'_c} + \frac{f_b + f_{ce}(6 + 1.5J)(e/d)}{F_b - Jf_{ce}} \leq 1 \qquad (13\text{-}11\text{a})$$

2. Eccentric load alone

$$\frac{f_c}{F'_c} + \frac{f_c(6 + 1.5J)(e/d)}{F_b - Jf_c} \leq 1 \qquad (13\text{-}11\text{b})$$

3. Concentric and lateral loads

$$\frac{f_c}{F'_c} + \frac{f_b}{F_b - Jf_c} \leq 1 \qquad (13\text{-}11\text{c})$$

The new term J in Formulas (13-11) is merely a convenience parameter which represents the degree of slenderness present at that value of L/d between 11 and K.

$$J = \frac{(L/d) - 11}{K - 11}$$

where J can never take a value less than zero nor more than unity. The NFPA recommends determining the L/d, for use in obtaining J, by always taking d as the dimension in the plane of bending. (The writer likes a slightly more conservative approach and prefers to take L/d as the largest slenderness ratio present, independent of the axis of bending.)

Finally, when L/d is larger than K (long columns), the following formulas apply:

1. Combined concentric, eccentric, and lateral loads

$$\frac{f_c}{F'_c} + \frac{f_b + f_{ce}(7.5e/d)}{F_b - f_{ce}} \leq 1 \qquad (13\text{-}12\text{a})$$

2. Eccentric load alone

$$\frac{f_c}{F'_c} + \frac{f_c(7.5e/d)}{F_b - f_c} \leq 1 \qquad (13\text{-}12\text{b})$$

3. Concentric and lateral loads

$$\frac{f_c}{F'_c} + \frac{f_b}{F_b - f_c} \leq 1 \qquad (13\text{-}12\text{c})$$

These formulas are actually simplifications of more complicated theoretical ones, and the reader is referred to the *National Design Specification* of the NFPA for a complete bibliography on the subject.

EXAMPLE 13-25

Figure 13-35 shows an 89×139 mm column of northern pine, 3.7 m long, and loaded eccentrically by a beam reaction. The total load is 8 kN and is eccentric by 115 mm. Is the column adequate?

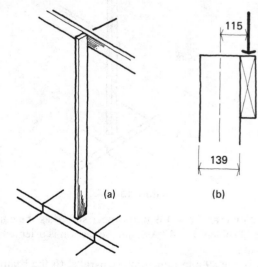

Figure 13-35. Eccentrically loaded column.

Solution: First compute the L/d to determine which formula to use.

$$\frac{L}{d} = \frac{3700}{89} = 41.6$$

$$K = 0.671\sqrt{\frac{E}{F_c}}$$

$$= 0.671\sqrt{\frac{9600(10)^3 \text{ kPa}}{6700 \text{ kPa}}}$$

$$= 25.4$$

Since L/d is larger than K, this is a long column and we shall use Formula (13-12b).

$$\frac{f_c}{F'_c} + \frac{f_c(7.5e/d)}{F_b - f_c} \leq 1$$

$A = 12\ 400\ \text{mm}^2$

$$f_c = \frac{P}{A} \qquad\qquad F_c' = \frac{0.30E}{(L/d)^2}$$

$$= \frac{8\ \text{kN}}{0.0124\ \text{m}^2} \qquad = \frac{0.30(9600)(10)^3\ \text{kPa}}{(41.6)^2}$$

$$= 645\ \text{kPa} \qquad\qquad = 1660\ \text{kPa}$$

From Appendix P, $F_b = 8300$ kPa.

$$\frac{645}{1660} + \frac{645[7.5(115)/139]}{8300 - 645} = ?$$

$$0.39 + 0.52 = 0.91$$

Since 0.91 is less than 1, the section is adequate.

EXAMPLE 13-26

The Douglas fir 89×235 mm section of Figure 13-36 is 6 m long and has its weak axis braced at midheight. The wind load is picked up by the girt and transferred to the column as a point load. If $P = 13.5$ kN and $W = 5$ kN, check the adequacy of the design.

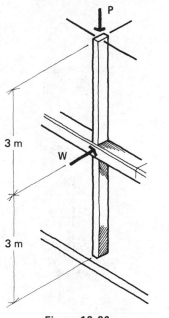

Figure 13-36

Solution: First compute the larger L/d to determine which formula to use.

$$\left(\frac{L}{d}\right)_x = \frac{6000}{235} \qquad \left(\frac{L}{d}\right)_y = \frac{3000}{89}$$

$$= 25.5 \qquad\qquad = 33.7$$

$$K = 0.671\sqrt{\frac{E}{F_c}}$$

$$= 0.671\sqrt{\frac{12\ 400(10)^3\ \text{kPa}}{8600\ \text{kPa}}}$$

$$= 25.5$$

Since 33.7 is larger than 25.5, this is a long column and Formula (13-12c) will be used.

$$\frac{f_c}{F_c'} + \frac{f_b}{F_b - f_c} \le 1$$

$A = 20\ 900\ \text{mm}^2$

$$f_o = \frac{P}{A} \qquad\qquad F_c' = \frac{0.30E}{(L/d)^2}$$

$$= \frac{13.5\ \text{kN}}{0.0209\ \text{m}^2} \qquad = \frac{0.30(12\ 400)(10)^3\ \text{kPa}}{(33.7)^2}$$

$$= 646\ \text{kPa} \qquad\qquad = 3280\ \text{kPa}$$

$$M = \frac{WL}{4}$$

$$= \frac{5\ \text{kN}(6\ \text{m})}{4}$$

$$= 7.5\ \text{kN·m}$$

$$f_b = \frac{M}{S_x} \qquad\qquad S_x = 869(10)^3\ \text{mm}^3$$

$$= \frac{7.5\ \text{kN·m}}{819(10)^{-6}\ \text{m}^3}$$

$$= 9160\ \text{kPa}$$

From Appendix P, $F_b = 10\ 300$ kPa.

$$\frac{646}{3280} + \frac{9160}{10\ 300 - 645} = ?$$

$$0.20 + 0.95 = 1.15$$

Since the right-hand side of the equation can be as large as 1.33 (because of the wind load), the column is adequate.

EXAMPLE 13-27

The southern pine column of Figure 13-37 is 139×235 mm in cross section and is subjected to a uniform wind load (acting as a negative pressure) of 3 kN/m. Additionally, the two beams together provide an axial load of 8 kN while the girder delivers 40 kN at an eccentricity of 200 mm. Exterior sheathing is assumed to provide full lateral support for the weak axis. Check the adequacy of this design.

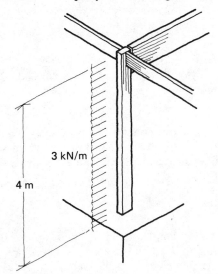

Figure 13-37. Timber column loaded by concentric, eccentric, and lateral forces.

Solution: The weak axis is fully braced so the slenderness ratio is

$$\frac{L}{d} = \frac{4000}{235} = 17.0$$

$$K = 0.671\sqrt{\frac{E}{F_c}}$$

$$= 0.671\sqrt{\frac{11\ 000(10)^3\ \text{kPa}}{6300\ \text{kPa}}}$$

$$= 28.0$$

Since L/d is less than K and more than 11, this is an intermediate column and Formula (13-11a) will be used.

$$\frac{f_c}{F'_c} + \frac{f_b + f_{ce}(6 + 1.5J)(e/d)}{F_b - Jf_{ce}} \leq 1$$

$$A = 32\ 700\ \text{mm}^2$$

$$f_c = \frac{P}{A} \qquad\qquad F'_c = F_c\left[1 - \frac{1}{3}\left(\frac{L/d}{K}\right)^4\right]$$

$$= \frac{48\ \text{kN}}{0.0327\ \text{m}^2} \qquad = 6300\ \text{kPa}\left[1 - \frac{1}{3}\left(\frac{17.0}{28.0}\right)^4\right]$$

$$= 1470\ \text{kPa} \qquad\qquad = 6010\ \text{kPa}$$

$$f_{ce} = \frac{P}{A} \qquad\qquad F_b = 9000\ \text{kPa}$$

$$= \frac{40\ \text{kN}}{0.0327\ \text{m}^2}$$

$$= 1220\ \text{kPa}$$

$$J = \frac{(L/d) - 11}{K - 11} \qquad M = \frac{wL^2}{8}$$

$$= \frac{17.0 - 11}{28.0 - 11} \qquad = \frac{(3\ \text{kN/m}^2)(4\ \text{m})^2}{8}$$

$$= 0.35 \qquad\qquad = 6\ \text{kN·m}$$

$$S_x = 1280(10)^3\ \text{mm}^3$$

$$f_b = \frac{M}{S_x}$$

$$= \frac{6\ \text{kN·m}}{1280(10)^{-6}\ \text{m}^3}$$

$$= 4700\ \text{kPa}$$

Substituting into Formula (13-11a), we get

$$\frac{1470}{6010} + \frac{4700 + 1220[6 + 1.5(0.35)](0.200/0.235)}{9000 - (0.35)1220} = ?$$

$$0.24 + 1.34 = 1.58$$

Clearly, this column is not adequate, as 1.58 exceeds the permissible 1.33 value. A 139×285 mm section has a much larger strong-axis section modulus and would probably suffice.

Problems

13-27. A 3-m-long column is built up of three hem-fir 38 mm × 89 mm pieces as shown in Figure 13-38. Is the column section adequate to carry safely a load of 6 kN at an eccentricity of 80 mm?

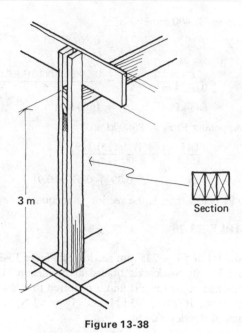

3 m   Section

Figure 13-38

13-28. An 89 × 185 mm column of southern pine is 5.5 m long and has its weak axis braced at midheight as shown in Figure 13-39. The axial load at the top is 4500 N. The eccentric load is 2000 N with an eccentricity of 140 mm. The wind load is 4000 N. Is the column safe?

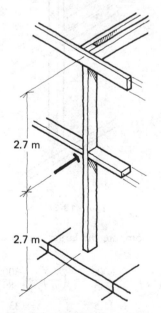

2.7 m

2.7 m

Figure 13-39. Column with concentric, eccentric, and lateral loads.

13-29. A 139 × 139 mm hem-fir post is 3 m long and must carry an axial load of 20 kN. If a uniform wind load of 3.0 kN/m acts over the length of the post, will the square section still be adequate?

13-12 COMBINED LOADING ON STEEL COLUMNS

The concepts involved in the behavior of steel columns under the combined action of axial and bending loads are very similar to those pertaining to timber columns. The basic interaction equation still holds, expressed as

$$\frac{f_a}{F_a} + \frac{f_b}{F_b} \le 1$$

where f_a = actual P/A stress

f_b = actual stress due to bending loads

F_a = allowable P/A stress consistent with the greatest KL/r

F_b = allowable bending stress, subject to all of the provisions involving compactness, unbraced length, and material strength

Because large axial loads with large slenderness ratios bring about increased lateral deflection, the bending part of the formula should be modified just as we did with wood in Section 13-11. The so-called "amplification factor" recommended by AISC to account for this increase in moment due to lateral deflection changes the formula to

$$\frac{f_a}{F_a} + \left[\frac{1}{1 - f_a/F'_e}\right]\frac{f_b}{F_b} \le 1 \qquad (13\text{-}13)$$

where $F'_e = \dfrac{12\pi^2 E}{23(KL/r)_b}$ \qquad (13-14)

in which $(KL/r)_b$ is the slenderness ratio in the plane of bending. Values of F'_e are independent of the low end cutoff provisions usually pertaining to an Euler expression. Table 3 of Appendix R gives F'_e values for various slenderness ratios.

This amplification factor can be considerably in error if the moments applied to the ends of a column (by eccentric loads or by continuity with other members) act in such a way as to stiffen the column against buckling. Therefore, a factor called C_m is introduced. The formula then becomes

$$\frac{f_a}{F_a} + \left[\frac{C_m}{1 - f_a/F'_e}\right]\frac{f_b}{F_b} \le 1.0 \qquad (13\text{-}15)$$

where C_m is defined as follows:

$$C_m = 0.6 - 0.4\frac{M_1}{M_2} \qquad (13\text{-}16)$$

in which M_1/M_2 is the ratio of the smaller end moment to the larger one. M_1/M_2 is taken as positive if the moments tend to cause reverse curvature and negative if they tend to cause single curvature. Examples are given in Figure 13-40.

This tempering factor C_m applied to the basic amplification factor should never be taken as less than

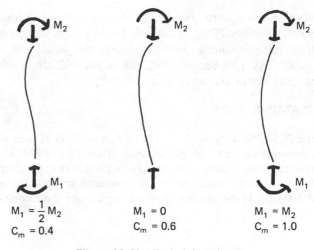

Figure 13-40. Typical C_m values.

0.4. Also, if any frame sidesway is involved, C_m should not be taken as less than 0.85, because in this case the column end points move out of alignment, causing additional moment from the axial loads. C_m becomes more complicated if the moment on the column comes from a lateral load rather than from members framing into the ends of the column. In such cases, C_m can be conservatively taken as unity.

The interaction formula, (13-15), pertains to critical buckling stresses which are assumed to occur away from the points of bracing. To guard against overstressing at one end of the column, where no buckling action is present, stresses are also limited by the following formula based on the concepts of Section 12-1.

$$\frac{f_a}{0.60F_y} + \frac{f_b}{F_b} \le 1.0 \qquad (13\text{-}17)$$

Finally, when the amount of axial load relative to the column axial capacity is low, it is recognized that no amplification factor is needed. Therefore, if $f_a/F_a < 0.15$, we can use

$$\frac{f_a}{F_a} + \frac{f_b}{F_b} = 1 \qquad (13\text{-}18)$$

instead of Formulas (13-15) and (13-17).

As with the timber interaction formulas, only one axis of bending has been considered in this presentation.

The note that follows pertains to the allowable bending stress for use in the foregoing formulas.

[The proper determination of an accurate value for the allowable bending stress F_b, for use in the interaction equations, can become unnecessarily complex. For strong-axis bending, it varies from $\frac{2}{3}F_y$ downward, depending upon compactness and lateral support. In the examples and problems of this chapter, F_b is taken as $0.60F_y$ (for strong-axis bending) so a consideration of compactness is obviated. The $0.60F_y$ value presumes a more-or-less square wide-flange section with fairly high lateral stability. This value will be too high for most deep, narrow column sections unless the weak axis is braced. As per Section 9-7, the allowable stress for bending about the weak axis is $0.75F_y$.]

EXAMPLE 13-28

The $F_y = 250$-MPa W250 × 149 of Figure 13-41 is used as a 5-m-long column with pinned ends. It must carry 1300 kN from the column directly above, plus a 270-kN reaction from the girder that frames into the column with an eccentricity of 190 mm. Is the column section adequate for these conditions?

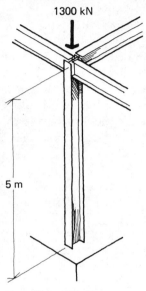

Figure 13-41

Solution:

$$A = 19\ 000\ \text{mm}^2$$
$$r_x = 117\ \text{mm}$$
$$r_y = 67.4\ \text{mm}$$

First replace the eccentric load by a concentric load and a couple. Then check to see if $f_a/F_a < 0.15$.

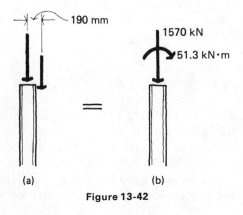

Figure 13-42

$$f_a = \frac{P}{A} = \frac{1570\ \text{kN}}{0.019\ \text{m}^2}$$
$$= 82\ 600\ \text{kPa} = 82.6\ \text{MPa}$$
$$\frac{KL}{r_y} = \frac{1.0(5000)}{67.4} = 74.3$$

From Table 1 in Appendix R,

$$F_a = 110.2\ \text{MPa}$$
$$\frac{f_a}{F_a} = \frac{82.6}{110.2} = 0.75$$
$$0.75 > 0.15$$

Check the two required interaction formulas.

$$C_m = 0.6 - 0.4\frac{M_1}{M_2}$$
$$M_1 = 0 \qquad M_2 = 51.3\ \text{kN·m}$$
$$C_m = 0.6$$
$$S_x = 1840 \times 10^3\ \text{mm}^3$$
$$f_b = \frac{M}{S} = \frac{51.3\ \text{kN·m}}{0.001\ 84\ \text{m}^3}$$
$$= 27\ 900\ \text{kPa} = 27.9\ \text{MPa}$$
$$F_b = 0.60F_y = 150\ \text{MPa}$$
$$\left(\frac{KL}{r}\right)_b = \left(\frac{KL}{r}\right)_x = \frac{1.0(5000)}{117} = 42.7$$

From Table 3 of Appendix R,

$$F'_e = 564.8\ \text{MPa}$$
$$\frac{f_a}{F_a} + \left[\frac{C_m}{1 - f_a/F'_e}\right]\frac{f_b}{F_b} = ?$$
$$0.75 + \left[\frac{0.6}{1 - 82.8/564.8}\right]\frac{27.9}{150} = ?$$
$$0.75 + 0.13 = 0.88$$
$$0.88 < 1.0 \qquad \text{OK}$$
$$\frac{f_a}{0.60F_y} + \frac{f_b}{F_b} = ?$$
$$\frac{82.8}{150} + \frac{27.9}{150} = ?$$
$$0.56 + 0.19 = 0.75$$
$$0.75 < 1.0 \qquad \text{OK}$$

The column section is safe.

EXAMPLE 13-29

A 4.2-m-long column has girders framing into it at top and bottom with moment resisting connections. It must carry an axial load of 2700 kN, including the girder and beam reactions at the top. Live-load imbalance causes a potential maximum moment at the top and bottom of 108 kN·m, as shown in the load diagram of Figure 13-43. K for the weak axis is 1.0, and K for the strong axis is estimated at 0.90. Is an $F_y = 345$-MPa W310 × 202 sufficient to carry these loads?

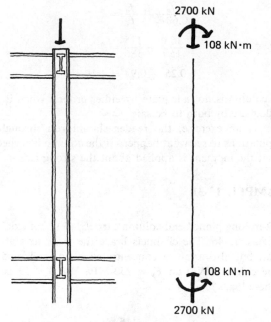

2700 kN

108 kN·m

108 kN·m

2700 kN

Figure 13-43

Solution:

$$A = 25\ 700\ \text{mm}^2$$

$$r_x = 142\ \text{mm}$$

$$r_y = 80.4\ \text{mm}$$

First check to see if $f_a/F_a < 0.15$.

$$f_a = \frac{P}{A} = \frac{2700\ \text{kN}}{0.0257\ \text{m}^2}$$

$$= 105\ 000\ \text{kPa} = 105\ \text{MPa}$$

$$\left(\frac{KL}{r}\right)_y = \frac{1.0(4200)}{80.4} = 52.3$$

From Table 2 in Appendix R,

$$F_a = 166$$

$$\frac{f_a}{F_a} = \frac{105}{166} = 0.63$$

$$0.63 > 0.15$$

Check the two required interaction formulas.

$$C_m = 0.6 - 0.4\frac{M_1}{M_2}$$

$$\frac{M_1}{M_2} = -1.0$$

$$C_m = 0.6 - 0.4(-1.0) = 1.0$$

$$S_x = 3050 \times 10^3\ \text{mm}^3$$

$$f_b = \frac{M}{S} = \frac{108\ \text{kN·m}}{0.003\ 05\ \text{m}^3}$$

$$= 35\ 400\ \text{kPa} = 35.4\ \text{MPa}$$

$$F_b = 0.60F_y = 207\ \text{MPa}$$

$$\left(\frac{KL}{r}\right)_b = \left(\frac{KL}{r}\right)_x = \frac{0.90(4200)}{142} = 26.6$$

From Table 3 of Appendix R,

$$F'_e = 1456\ \text{MPa}$$

$$\frac{f_a}{F_a} + \left[\frac{C_m}{1 - f_a/F'_e}\right]\frac{f_b}{F_b} = ?$$

$$0.63 + \left[\frac{1.0}{1 - 105/1456}\right]\frac{35.4}{207} = ?$$

$$0.63 + 0.18 = 0.81$$

$$0.81 < 1.0 \quad \text{OK}$$

$$\frac{f_a}{0.60F_y} + \frac{f_b}{F_b} = ?$$

$$\frac{105}{207} + \frac{35.4}{207} = ?$$

$$0.51 + 0.17 = 0.68$$

$$0.68 < 1.0 \quad \text{OK}$$

The column section is adequate. As an exercise, the reader may wish to check the adequacy of this same column in $F_y = 250$-MPa steel.

EXAMPLE 13-30

The $F_y = 250$-MPa W310 × 179 of Figure 13-44 is 6 m long and has pinned ends. Two beams and a girder bring in 490 kN of axial load. A column from above delivers 350 kN at an eccentricity of 460 mm. Is the column safe?

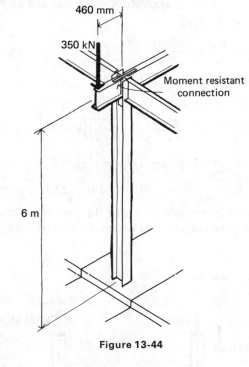

460 mm

350 kN

Moment resistant connection

6 m

Figure 13-44

Solution:

$$A = 22\ 800\ \text{mm}^2$$

$$r_y = 79.5\ \text{mm}$$

First replace the eccentric load by a concentric load and a couple. Then check to see if $f_a/F_a = < 0.15$.

$$f_a = \frac{P}{A} = \frac{840 \text{ kN}}{0.0228 \text{ m}^2}$$

$$= 36\ 900 \text{ kPa} = 36.9 \text{ MPa}$$

$$\frac{KL}{r_y} = \frac{1.0(6000)}{79.5} = 75.5$$

From Table 1 in Appendix R,

$$F_a = 109$$

$$\frac{f_a}{F_a} = \frac{36.9}{109} = 0.34$$

$$0.34 > 0.15$$

Check the two required interaction formulas.

$$C_m = 0.6 - 0.4\frac{M_1}{M_2}$$

$$M_1 = 0 \qquad M_2 = 161 \text{ kN·m}$$

$$C_m = 0.6$$

$$S_y = 918 \times 10^3 \text{ mm}^3$$

(*Note:* This is the weak-axis section modulus because the moment is acting about that axis.)

$$f_b = \frac{M}{S} = \frac{161 \text{ kN·m}}{0.000\ 918 \text{ m}^3}$$

$$= 175\ 000 \text{ kPa} = 175 \text{ MPa}$$

$$F_b = 0.75F_y \qquad \text{since this is weak-axis bending on a symmetrical shape (see Section 9-7)}$$

$$= 186 \text{ MPa}$$

$$\left(\frac{KL}{r}\right)_b = \frac{KL}{r_y} = \frac{1.0(6000)}{79.5} = 75.5$$

From Table 3 of Appendix R,

$$F'_e = 181 \text{ MPa}$$

$$\frac{f_a}{F_a} + \left[\frac{C_m}{1 - f_a/F'_e}\right]\frac{f_b}{F_b} = ?$$

$$0.34 + \left[\frac{0.6}{1 - 36.9/181}\right]\frac{175}{186} = ?$$

$$0.34 + 0.71 = 1.05$$

The column is not safe by one of the interaction formulas. For illustrative purposes, the second equation will be checked anyway.

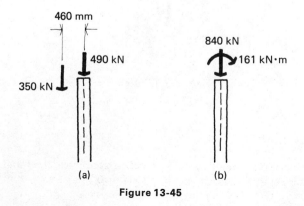

Figure 13-45

$$\frac{f_a}{0.60F_y} + \frac{f_b}{F_b} = ?$$

$$\frac{36.9}{150} + \frac{175}{186} = ?$$

$$0.25 + 0.94 = 1.19$$

This column is not adequate by either criteria when it must be adequate by both to be safe.

As an exercise, the reader should run through the computations to see what happens if the column is turned 90° so that the moment is applied about the strong axis.

EXAMPLE 13-31

A 7.2-m-long pinned end column carries 115 kN of axial load in Figure 13-46. The channels brace the weak axis at mid-height, but also apply a concentrated wind load of 50 kN to the column. Will an $F_y = 250$-MPa W200 × 59 be safe for these loads?

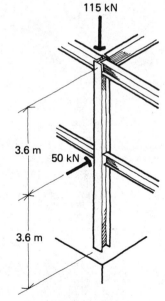

Figure 13-46

Solution:

$$A = 7550 \text{ mm}^2$$

$$r_x = 89.7 \text{ mm}$$

$$r_y = 52.0 \text{ mm}$$

First check to see if $f_a/F_a < 0.15$.

$$f_a = \frac{P}{A} = \frac{115 \text{ kN}}{0.007\ 55 \text{ m}^2}$$

$$= 15\ 200 \text{ kPa} = 15.2 \text{ MPa}$$

$$\left(\frac{KL}{r}\right)_x = \frac{1.0(7200)}{89.7} = 80.3$$

$$\left(\frac{KL}{r}\right)_y = \frac{1.0(3600)}{51.8} = 69.5$$

The strong axis is critical for axial buckling alone. From Table 1 in Appendix R,

$$F_a = 106 \text{ MPa}$$

$$\frac{f_a}{F_a} = \frac{15.2}{106} = 0.14$$

$$0.14 < 0.15$$

Therefore, check only the one interaction equation as prescribed for this case of very low axial load.

$$S_x = 582 \times 10^3 \text{ mm}^3$$

$$f_b = \frac{M}{S} = \frac{WL/4}{S}$$

$$= \frac{[50(7.2)/4] \text{ kN·m}}{0.000\ 582 \text{ m}^3}$$

$$= 155\ 000 \text{ kPa} = 155 \text{ MPa}$$

$$F_b = 0.60 F_y = 149 \text{ MPa}$$

$$\frac{f_a}{F_a} + \frac{f_b}{F_b} = ?$$

$$0.14 + \frac{155}{150} = ?$$

$$0.14 + 1.04 = 1.18$$

$$1.18 < 1.33 \quad \text{OK}$$

The column is adequate.

EXAMPLE 13-32

Figure 13-47 shows a 4-m-long column pinned at the top and fixed at the bottom. It must carry a total axial load of 1560 kN and a uniformly applied wind load of 20 kN/m. Will an $F_y = 250$ MPa W310 × 117 be adequate?

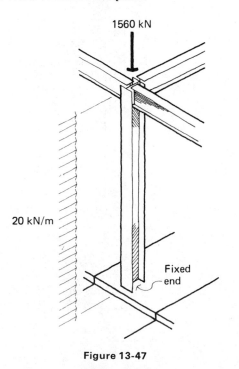

1560 kN

20 kN/m

Fixed end

Figure 13-47

Solution:

$$A = 15\ 000 \text{ mm}^2$$

$$r_x = 136 \text{ mm}$$

$$r_y = 77.4 \text{ mm}$$

First check to see if $f_a/F_a < 0.15$.

$$f_a = \frac{P}{A} = \frac{1560 \text{ kN}}{0.0150 \text{ m}^2}$$

$$= 104\ 000 \text{ kPa} = 104 \text{ MPa}$$

$$\frac{KL}{r_y} = \frac{0.80(4000)}{77.4} = 41.3$$

From Table 1 in Appendix R,

$$F_a = 132 \text{ MPa}$$

$$\frac{f_a}{F_a} = \frac{104}{132} = 0.79$$

$$0.79 > 0.15$$

Check the two required interaction formulas.

$$C_m = 1.0 \quad \text{because we have a lateral load}$$

$$S_x = 1750 \times 10^3 \text{ mm}^3$$

$$M = \frac{wL^2}{8}$$

$$f_b = \frac{M}{S} = \frac{[20(4)^2/8] \text{ kN·m}}{0.001\ 75 \text{ m}^3}$$

$$= 22\ 900 \text{ kPa} = 22.9 \text{ MPa}$$

$$F_b = 0.60 F_y = 150 \text{ MPa}$$

$$\left(\frac{KL}{r}\right)_b = \frac{KL}{r_x} = \frac{0.80(4000)}{136} = 23.6$$

From Table 3 in Appendix R,

$$F'_e = 1851 \text{ MPa}$$

$$\frac{f_a}{F_a} + \left[\frac{C_m}{1 - f_a/F'_e}\right]\frac{f_b}{F_b} = ?$$

$$0.79 + \left[\frac{1.0}{1 - 104/1851}\right]\frac{22.9}{150} = ?$$

$$0.79 + 0.16 = 0.95$$

$$0.95 < 1.33 \quad \text{OK}$$

$$\frac{f_a}{0.60 F_y} + \frac{f_b}{F_b} = ?$$

$$\frac{104}{150} + \frac{22.9}{150} = ?$$

$$0.70 + 0.15 = 0.85$$

$$0.85 < 1.33 \quad \text{OK}$$

The column is safe.

Problems

13-30. Figure 13-48 shows two beams and a girder framing into the top of an $F_y = 250$ MPa W360 × 122 column, which is 6 m long. Each beam reaction is 270 kN. The girder reaction is 900 kN with an eccentricity of 200 mm. The bottom of the column is fixed and the top is

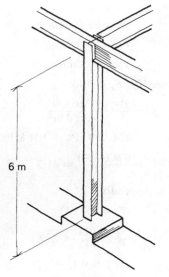

Figure 13-48

pinned and C_m may be taken as 0.4. Is the column section safe?

13-31. An $F_y = 345$-MPa W310 × 52 serves as a column in the rigid bent of Figure 13-49. It is 4 m long and fixed at the bottom. The girder loads generate the loading diagram shown. K for both axes is estimated at 0.80. Is the column section adequate?

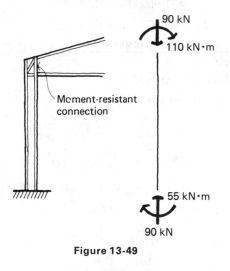

Figure 13-49

13-32. Check the adequacy of the column section in Problem 13-31 if all conditions remain the same except for the axial load, which increases to 180 kN.

13-33. An $F_y = 250$-MPa W310 × 202 is used as a pinned end column 5 m long, as shown in Figure 13-50. It must sustain a 2000-kN axial load and a wind load of $w = 20$ kN per meter applied as shown. Is the column safe?

13-34. Figure 13-51 shows an $F_y = 250$ MPa W310 × 143 column 7.3 m long with pinned ends. It must carry

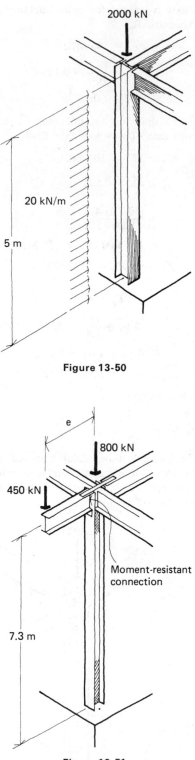

Figure 13-50

Figure 13-51

an axial load of 800 kN plus an eccentric load of 450 kN. How large can the eccentricity, e, get if the column is to remain safe?

14-1 INTRODUCTION

A truss is a lightweight frame generally used for relatively long spans in buildings and bridges. They are usually placed parallel to one another to make a one-way system for a floor or roof deck. Their lightness means they are deeper than beams would be if used on a similar span, and for this reason trusses are more frequently used in roof structures.

In the United States, trusses are almost always constructed of wood or steel, but in other countries they have also been precast in reinforced concrete. The light triangular wood truss, made of 38 × 89 mm and 38 × 139 mm pieces and placed 600 mm on centers, is used almost exclusively to make residential gable roofs in some parts of the United States. It erects rapidly and enables the floor below to be free of interior bearing partitions. Steel trusses, both flat and curved, are used to span the large majority of very long span buildings such as field houses and sports domes. In such structures, self-weight can easily become a controlling design factor, and the small span/depth ratio of a truss (with its increased building envelope) becomes a welcome trade-off to minimize this dead load.

Trusses can be fabricated in almost any shape. In technical terms, a truss is a triangulated planar framework made up of linear elements that connect at pin joints. When actually constructed, these joints are seldom truly pinned, but the initial structural analysis makes this assumption anyway. (For many trusses, the members are thin and have relatively little bending resistance, so the pinned-joint assumption causes no great error.) A few of the more commonly used truss shapes are illustrated in Figure 14-1. Some have been named for the engineer or designer who popularized that particular type.

Loaded properly, each member of a truss is (in ideal terms) a two-force member. It is either in tension or compression, and if in compression, it behaves as a slender column and must be designed with elastic buckling in mind. When trusses are used on simple spans, all the top chord members form a continuous line of compression and the entire top of the truss is subject to the lateral buckling phenomenon discussed in Section 9-2. Usually, the roof "skin" provides the required lateral bracing unless the trusses are exposed. Overhanging trusses will have compression in some bottom chord elements, and these are subject to the same buckling effects.

For the purposes of preliminary design, it is assumed that trusses are loaded by concentrated loads that act only at the joints. In actuality, most floor and roof loads are uniform, and when the deck surface is attached directly to the top chord elements, these members are subjected to the combined action of axial and bending forces. They must be finally designed using an interaction approach described in Section 13-10. The examples and problems of this chapter are concerned only with the analysis of trusses loaded through the joints, or panel points.

Almost all trusses are statically determinate with respect to the external reaction components. Depending on the manner of triangulation, trusses can also be determinate or indeterminate with respect to the internal forces in the members. Trusses with redundant members are internally statically indeterminate, and the member forces cannot be resolved using statics alone. Whether or not a truss is internally determinate can be ascertained by Equation (14-1). Trusses without enough members to make triangles using every joint will be unstable, and those with excess members are indeterminate.

$$m + 3 = 2j \qquad (14\text{-}1)$$

where m = number of members, assuming no member runs through a joint
j = number of joints

In Equation (14-1), the constant 3 represents the usual

Trusses

14

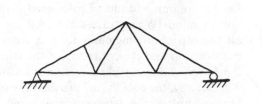

Fink

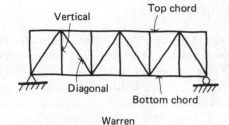

Warren

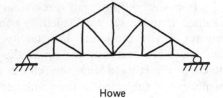

Howe

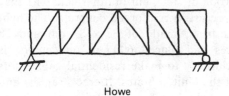

Howe

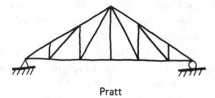

Pratt

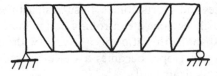

Pratt

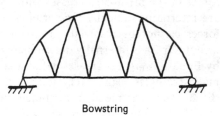

Bowstring

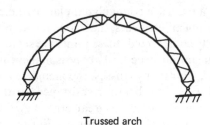

Trussed arch

Figure 14-1. Typical truss types.

three external reaction components. The concept here is that the number of unknowns equals the unknown member forces (*m*) plus the reaction components. At a planar joint, only two force equations of equilibrium, $\sum F_x = 0$ and $\sum F_y = 0$, can be written, and this means that the total number of available equations is twice the number of joints (*j*).

The trusses in Figure 14-1 are determinate, as are all of the trusses in the examples and problems. Figure 14-2 shows two indeterminate trusses. The one in Figure 14-2(b) has two diagonals, which cross without a joint. This type of truss becomes determinate if we assume that those two members are so slender and flexible as to be worthless in compression, in which case only one of them will be functional, depending upon the loading pattern. The diagonals are then called *counters*.

The geometry imposed by triangulation means that, under certain loading conditions, some of the members of a truss may have no internal force. In such

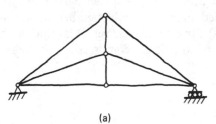

(a)

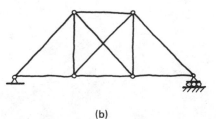

(b)

Figure 14-2. Indeterminate trusses.

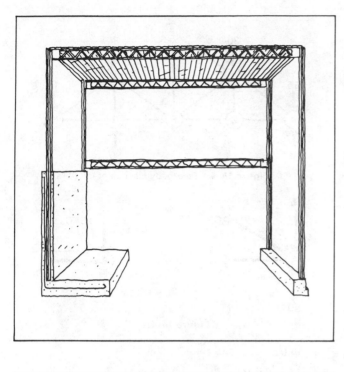

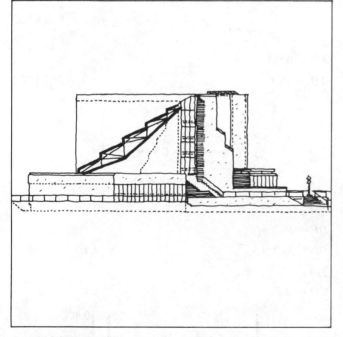

Be they straightforward or complex, trusses are relatively long-span building elements that offer considerable possibility for architectural effect along with the efficient performance of structural jobs. The variety of truss shapes, types, and adaptations is large, but even the simplest can have both visual and intellectual fascination: the attractions of a well-made puzzle, the paradox of a large strong thing made from many small weak things. Further, the usefulness of trusses in roof structures is an eternal invitation to experiments with the interacting effects of structure and light on interior space. From Charles Eames' unassumingly elegant use of stock steel bar joists in his own California house, to Frank Lloyd Wright's more spectacular (but really no more complicated) wooden trusses over the drafting room at Taliesin East, the range of expression available with simple trusses is enormous. But complexity, too, has its places and desirable effects; the technically complex trusses and the soaring space shadowed by them, in James Stirling's Cambridge History Faculty, and the decoratively complex trusses and brooding interior of Bernard Maybeck's First Church of Christ Scientist, are two diverse instances.

cases, the member acts as a bracing element and is usually needed for stability. These *zero members* could also carry force under a different loading pattern.

14-2 ANALYSIS BY JOINT EQUILIBRIUM

If we assume that all joints are pinned and loads and reactions act only at the joints, each joint becomes a small concurrent force system. It must be held in equilibrium by the known forces acting on it from the loads (including reactions) and by the unknown forces from the two-force members. Each joint can then be analyzed like the simple structures of Section 2-5. As pointed out previously, there are only two equations available for each joint, so we must move from joint to joint over the truss in such a manner as to be always working with only two unknowns. In many cases, this means starting at one of the joints at the ends of the truss and progressing toward the center.

The external reaction components should be determined before isolating the joints, and this has been done in the examples that follow. After solving for the reactions of a given truss, the reader should attempt to guess which members are in tension and compression before continuing with the solution. The answers obtained from any numerical analysis can then be rationalized with the visual analysis, and arithmetical errors can often be caught before they accumulate.

EXAMPLE 14-1

Determine the forces in each of the members of the truss in Figure 14-3.

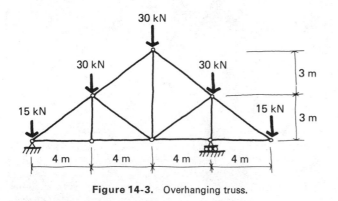

Figure 14-3. Overhanging truss.

Solution: Make a free-body diagram of each joint in turn, showing compressive arrows acting toward the joint and tensile arrows pointing away from the joint. As usual, incorrect sense assumptions will result in negative answers.

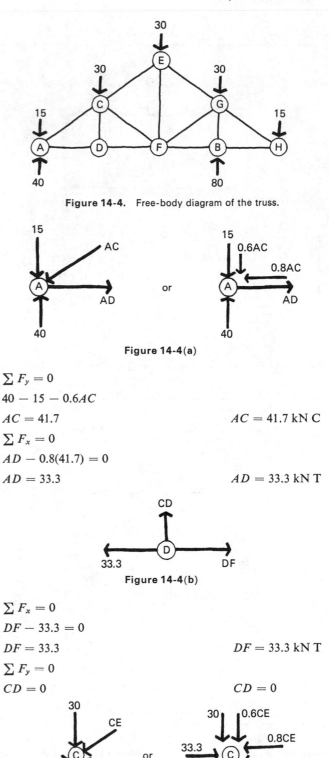

Figure 14-4. Free-body diagram of the truss.

Figure 14-4(a)

$$\sum F_y = 0$$
$$40 - 15 - 0.6AC$$
$$AC = 41.7 \qquad\qquad AC = 41.7 \text{ kN C}$$
$$\sum F_x = 0$$
$$AD - 0.8(41.7) = 0$$
$$AD = 33.3 \qquad\qquad AD = 33.3 \text{ kN T}$$

Figure 14-4(b)

$$\sum F_x = 0$$
$$DF - 33.3 = 0$$
$$DF = 33.3 \qquad\qquad DF = 33.3 \text{ kN T}$$
$$\sum F_y = 0$$
$$CD = 0 \qquad\qquad CD = 0$$

Figure 14-4(c)

$$\sum F_x = 0$$
$$33.3 - 0.8CE - 0.8CF = 0$$

$\Sigma F_y = 0$

$-30 + 25 - 0.6CE + 0.6CF = 0$

Solving simultaneously gives us

$CF = 25$ $CF = 25$ kN C

$CE = 16.7$ $CE = 16.7$ kN C

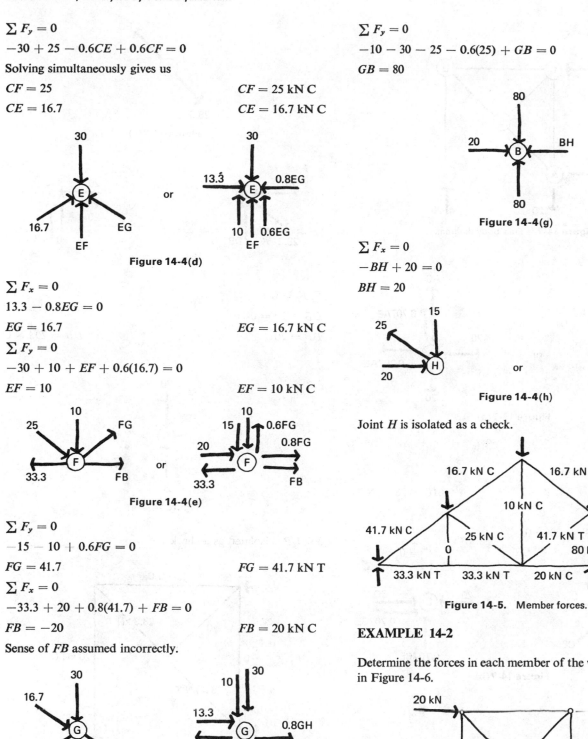

Figure 14-4(d)

$\Sigma F_x = 0$

$13.3 - 0.8EG = 0$

$EG = 16.7$ $EG = 16.7$ kN C

$\Sigma F_y = 0$

$-30 + 10 + EF + 0.6(16.7) = 0$

$EF = 10$ $EF = 10$ kN C

Figure 14-4(e)

$\Sigma F_y = 0$

$-15 - 10 + 0.6FG = 0$

$FG = 41.7$ $FG = 41.7$ kN T

$\Sigma F_x = 0$

$-33.3 + 20 + 0.8(41.7) + FB = 0$

$FB = -20$ $FB = 20$ kN C

Sense of *FB* assumed incorrectly.

Figure 14-4(f)

$\Sigma F_x = 0$

$-33.3 + 13.3 + 0.8GH = 0$

$GH = 25$ $GH = 25$ kN T

$\Sigma F_y = 0$

$-10 - 30 - 25 - 0.6(25) + GB = 0$

$GB = 80$ $GB = 80$ kN C

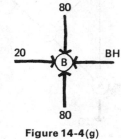

Figure 14-4(g)

$\Sigma F_x = 0$

$-BH + 20 = 0$

$BH = 20$ $BH = 20$ kN C

Figure 14-4(h)

Joint *H* is isolated as a check.

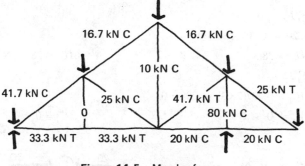

Figure 14-5. Member forces.

EXAMPLE 14-2

Determine the forces in each member of the wind bent shown in Figure 14-6.

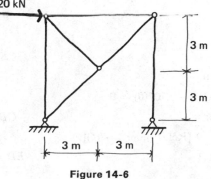

Figure 14-6

Solution:

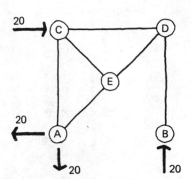

Figure 14-7. Free-body diagram.

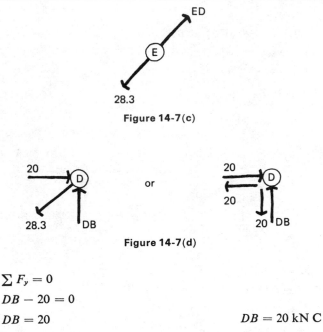

Figure 14-7(c)

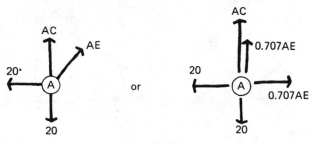

Figure 14-7(a)

$\sum F_x = 0$

$-20 + 0.707AE = 0$

$AE = 28.3$ $AE = 28.3$ kN T

$\sum F_y = 0$

$AC + 0.707(28.3) - 20 = 0$

$AC = 0$ $AC = 0$

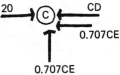

Figure 14-7(b)

$\sum F_y = 0$

$0.707CE = 0$

$CE = 0$ $CE = 0$

$\sum F_x = 0$

$+20 - CD - 0.707(0) = 0$

$CD = 20$ $CD = 20$ kN C

$\sum F_{AD} = 0$ [Ref. Figure 14-7(c)]

$ED = 28.3$ $ED = 28.3$ kN T

$\sum F_y = 0$

$DB - 20 = 0$

$DB = 20$ $DB = 20$ kN C

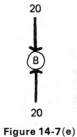

Joint *B* is isolated as a check.

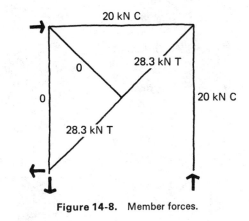

Figure 14-8. Member forces.

Problems

14-1. Determine the forces in the members of the truss in Figure 14-9.

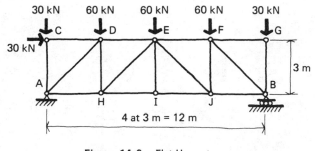

Figure 14-9. Flat Howe truss.

14-2. Determine the forces in the members of the truss in Figure 14-10.

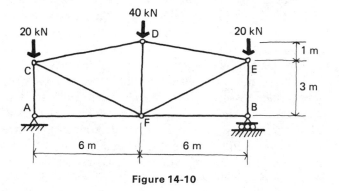

Figure 14-10

14-3. Determine the forces in the members of the truss in Figure 14-11.

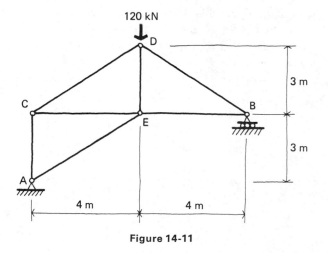

Figure 14-11

14-4. Work Problem 14-3 after adding a 20-kN load acting to the right at joint *C* in Figure 14-11.

14-5. Determine the forces in the members of the frame in Figure 14-12.

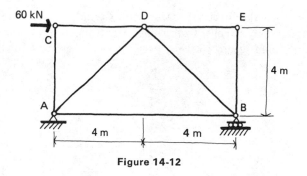

Figure 14-12

14-3 GRAPHICAL TECHNIQUES

Whenever a structure is held in static equilibrium by a number of forces, the vectors representing those forces must form a polygon that will close head to tail. This graphical statement of equilibrium is not limited by the size of the structure and is true for an entire truss as a whole free-body and for each individual joint. This makes it possible to obtain the magnitude and sense of the forces in truss members using only graphical techniques. First, a large external force polygon is drawn to a suitable force scale and then smaller polygons, one for each joint, are superimposed on the external diagram. The sides of each polygon can be scaled off for the force magnitudes, and the sense can be determined by following the arrows around the polygon to see whether a given vector points in toward a joint or out away from it. The complete diagram is called a *Maxwell diagram*, after J. Clerk Maxwell (1831–1879), a Scottish scientist.

To help with the bookkeeping, a special system of notation is sometimes used with graphical methods. In this case, as shown in Figure 14-13, a letter has been placed between every external force and a number in every internal panel space. An external force or the internal force in a member can be named by the two figures on either side of it. After the external reactions have been determined, the external force polygon is laid out, labeling each force at its head and tail by the letters

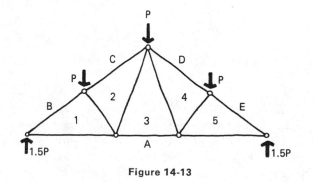

Figure 14-13

between the forces. Because the external force system is completely parallel in this case, the forces will appear as coincident vectors on the polygon (see Figure 14-14).

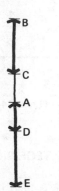

Figure 14-14. External force polygon drawn to scale.

Next, the individual joint polygons are added to the diagram to determine the member forces. (Notice that, since this truss is symmetrically configured and symmetrically loaded, only half of the members need to be diagrammed.) Just as with the algebraic method, joint polygons must be drawn in a sequence that gives us no more than two unknowns to be found by each polygon. Starting with the left-hand support joint and naming the forces by going clockwise around the joint, we have three forces: *AB*, *B*1, and 1*A*. It is important that the letters and/or numbers are taken in the same order (clockwise or counterclockwise) for each joint. The three forces in question must form a triangle, and since force *AB* is already on the diagram, the remaining lines of action must be placed as in Figure 14-14(a). They will interesect, locating the point 1.

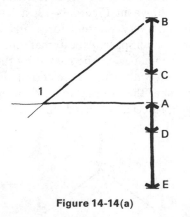

Figure 14-14(a)

The magnitudes can be scaled directly, and the sense of each force can be found by imagining an arrowhead to be located at the end of each vector [Figure 14-14(b)]. The vector *B*1 will have an arrowhead at the 1 end, clearly acting in toward the original joint. The vector 1*A* will

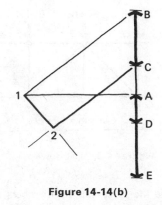

Figure 14-14(b)

have an arrow at the *A* end and will be pulling on the joint. Therefore, we conclude that *B*1 is in compression and 1*A* is in tension. It is important that arrowheads not actually be placed on the internal polygon vectors because the sense of the force in a member can only be determined with respect to one of the joints at the member's ends.

Next, move up the slope of the truss to another joint, which involves only two unknowns. Here, reading clockwise, the forces are *BC* (the known load *P*), *C*2 and 21 (both unknown), and 1*B* (just determined). Notice that for this joint the member force must be called 1*B* and not *B*1. The line of action of *C*2 is drawn through *C* and that of 21 is drawn through 1. Their intersection will establish the point 2, as shown in Figure 14-14(b), and the magnitudes of the two unknowns. The sense of each can be found in the manner previously described.

Moving down to a lower chord joint, the remaining two member forces can be resolved by establishing the point 3 in Figure 14-14(c). It is the intersection of the lines of action for 23 and 3*A*. The Maxwell diagram (for one-half the truss as required in this case) is now complete.

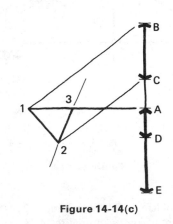

Figure 14-14(c)

As with all graphical solutions, large diagrams and drafting care will ensure reasonable accuracy. Such methods are preferred whenever a truss has a complex geometry, because odd member angles are easily accommodated.

EXAMPLE 14-3

Use the Maxwell diagram method to determine the member forces in the truss in Figure 14-15.

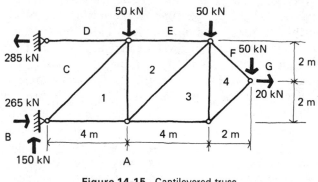

Figure 14-15. Cantilevered truss.

Solution:

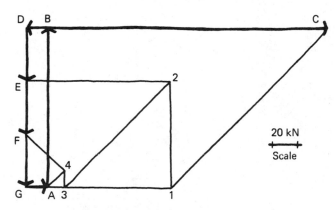

Figure 14-16. Maxwell diagram for Example 14-3.

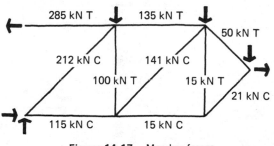

Figure 14-17. Member forces.

EXAMPLE 14-4

Use a Maxwell diagram to determine the member forces in the truss of Example 14-1.

Solution:

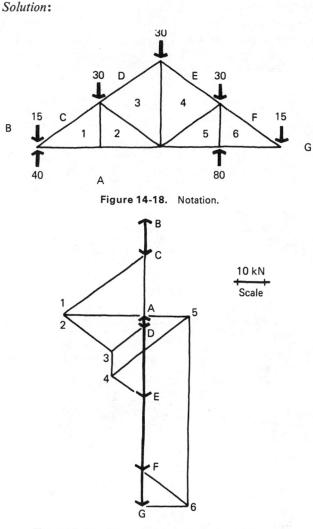

Figure 14-18. Notation.

Figure 14-19. Maxwell diagram for the truss of Example 14-1.

The answers are the same as those given in Figure 14-5, but the quantities will be slightly less precise.

Problems

14-6. Use the graphical method to find the member forces of the truss in Figure 14-9.

14-7. Determine the forces in the members of the truss in Figure 14-20.

Figure 14-20. Fan truss.

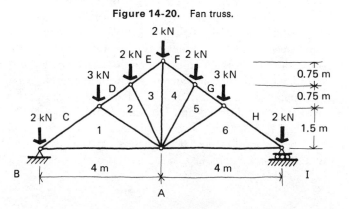

14-8. Use the graphical method to find the member forces of the truss in Figure 14-11.

14-9. Assuming the wind suction forces are normal to the roof plane, graphically determine the member forces for the truss of Figure 14-21.

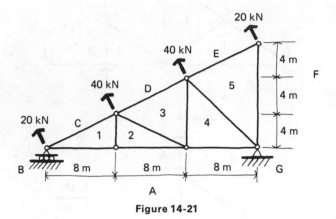

Figure 14-21

14-10. Determine the forces in the members of the arched truss of Figure 14-22.

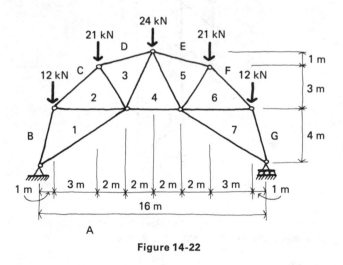

Figure 14-22

14-4 METHOD OF SECTIONS

A third approach to truss analysis, called the *method of sections*, consists of cutting sections through the truss so that a free-body diagram of a portion of the truss will involve the desired unknown member forces. In general, it is faster than either of the previous methods because it makes use of all three equations of planar static equilibrium. Both the joint equilibrium method and its graphical statement deal with concurrent forces and therefore no moment arms are available. Realizing that the entire truss is in equilibrium and that each joint is in equilibrium, it follows that larger portions of the truss will also be in equilibrium. If a truss is cut through by an imaginary cutting plane and a portion to one side of that

plane is isolated, it will be held in a state of balance by the external forces acting on the truss and the unknown forces in the cut members. Since the free-body diagram makes these internal forces external, the equations of statics can be used to find them. With three equations available, three unknown member forces can be determined with each free-body cut.

Successive cutting planes may be used to isolate increasingly larger portions of the truss, as shown in Figure 14-23. However, one of the advantages to this method is that all the member forces need not be found if we are interested only in those in one area of the truss. (Whenever a section cuts through two concurrent unknowns, as in Figure 14-23(b), this method reduces to a joint equilibrium problem. The two procedures, of course, can be used to work different parts of the same truss.)

The senses of the forces in the unknown members are assumed so that an arrow acting against the cutting plane is compressive and one pulling away from it is tensile. As usual, a negative sign in the answer will

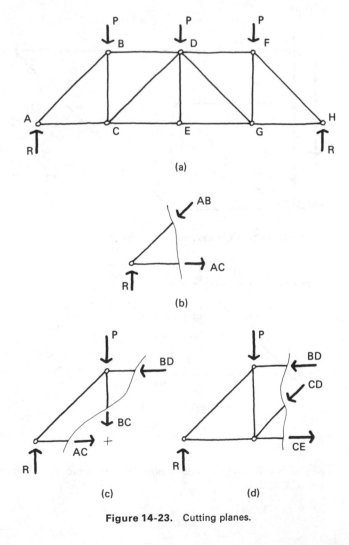

Figure 14-23. Cutting planes.

indicate an incorrect assumption. The isolated portion of the truss is treated as a rigid free body, and moment centers may be located on or off the body. The forces in cut sloping members are usually broken down into their rectangular components so that moment arms can be obtained from known dimensions. It is helpful to realize that a resultant force can be translated forward or backward along its line of action (before being replaced by its components), and this can sometimes result in convenient moment-arm distances. This translation does not in any way affect the state of equilibrium.

EXAMPLE 14-5

Determine the forces in members *CE*, *DE*, and *DF* of the truss shown in Figure 14-24.

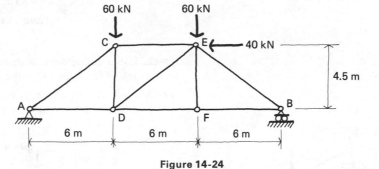

Figure 14-24

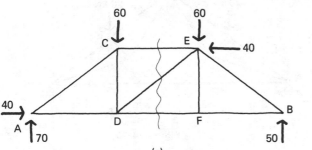

(a)

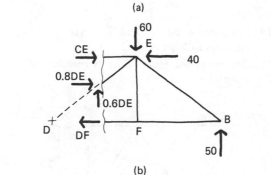

(b)

Figure 14-25. Free-body diagrams.

Solution: First find the external reactions and then cut a section through the three members.

Applying the equations of statics to the body in Figure 14-25(b), we get

$$\sum F_y = 0$$

$$-60 + 50 + 0.6DE = 0$$

$$DE = 16.7 \qquad\qquad DE = 16.7 \text{ kN C}$$

$$\sum M_E = 0$$

$$50(6) - DF(4.5) = 0$$

$$DF = 66.7 \qquad\qquad DF = 66.7 \text{ kN T}$$

$$\sum M_D = 0$$

$$-CE(4.5) - 60(6) + 40(4.5) + 50(12) = 0$$

$$CE = 93.3 \qquad\qquad CE = 93.3 \text{ kN C}$$

$$\sum F_x = 0 \qquad \text{check}$$

$$93.3 + 0.8(16.7) - 66.7 - 40 \approx 0 \quad \checkmark$$

EXAMPLE 14-6

Determine the forces in members *EG*, *FG*, and *FB* of the overhanging truss in Figure 14-26.

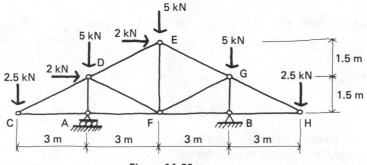

Figure 14-26

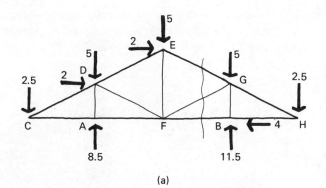

(a)

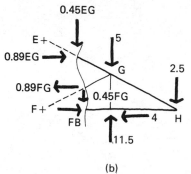

(b)

Figure 14-27. Free-body diagrams.

Solution: Using the isolated portion in Figure 14-27(b), we get

$$\sum M_G = 0$$

$$-4(1.5) - 2.5(3) + FB(1.5) = 0$$

$$FB = 9 \qquad\qquad FB = 9 \text{ kN C}$$

$$\sum M_F = 0$$

(Let the force *EG* be translated back to point *E*, where its vertical component will have no moment arm with respect to moment center *F*.)

$$-5(3) + 11.5(3) - 2.5(6) - 0.89EG(3) = 0$$

$$EG = 1.7 \qquad\qquad EG = 1.7 \text{ kN C}$$

$$\sum M_H = 0$$

(Let the force *FG* be translated forward to point *F*.)

$$5(3) - 11.5(3) + 0.45FG(6) = 0$$

$$FG = 7.2 \qquad\qquad FG = 7.2 \text{ kN T}$$

Since neither force equation was used, either will be valid for a check.

$$\sum F_x = 0 \qquad \text{check}$$

$$0.89(1.7) - 0.89(7.2) - 4 + 9 \approx 0 \quad \checkmark$$

Problems

14-11. Use the method of sections combined with joint equilibrium to determine the forces in the members of the Warren truss in Figure 14-28.

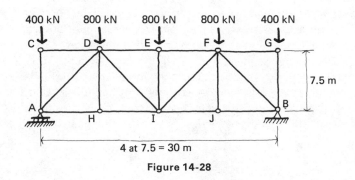

Figure 14-28

14-12. Use a cut section to determine the force in member *DE* of the truss in Figure 14-11.

14-13. Find the magnitude of the force in the tensile tie *AB* of the truss in Figure 14-29.

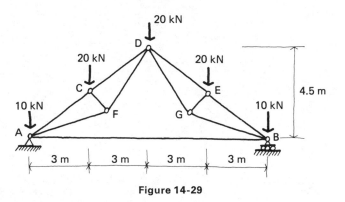

Figure 14-29

14-14. Use a cut section to find the force in member *DB* of the truss in Figure 14-12.

14-15. Determine the force in each member of the three-story wind bent of Figure 14-30.

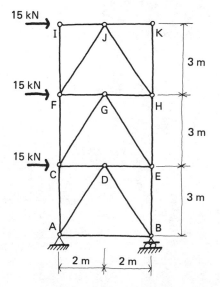

Figure 14-30. Wind bent.

14-5 PRELIMINARY DETERMINATION OF DEPTH

When used as the primary members of long-span roof structures, trusses are normally simply supported on two parallel bearing walls or *bearing lines*, composed of beams and columns. The spacing of such trusses is a function of the span and material, the load, the roof deck elements, the type of support, and, of course, the desired truss depth.

A truss, particularly a flat one with parallel top and bottom chords, behaves very much like a beam in that the top is in compression and the bottom in tension. The bending forces maximize at or near midspan, and the shear, taken by the diagonal (web) members, is critical near the end supports. The depth is usually controlled by moment, and the capacity of the resisting couple formed by the top and bottom chord (flange) elements must be at least as great as the moment caused by the external loads. For example, a vertical section cut through one of the central panels of the truss in Figure 14-28 will need a large resisting moment to maintain equilibrium. This moment can only be provided by the C and T forces shown in the free body of Figure 14-31. A simple computation shows these member forces to be 1600 kN C and 1200 kN T.

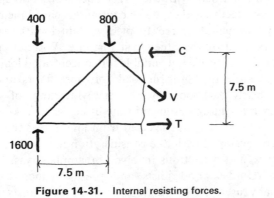

Figure 14-31. Internal resisting forces.

The top chord will usually be the critical member of the pair for two reasons: (1) it will be subject to compression buckling (at least about one axis) and (2) it may carry direct bending loads as well as an axial force from the truss action. (In spite of this, some timber trusses will have tension members that control the moment capacity. This is because of the difficulty encountered in making tensile connections when the force is applied parallel to the grain near the end of a member.) For the current example, let us assume a steel truss loaded through purlins so that the top chord elements carry only axial loads but are not braced against buckling. From Figure 14-28 we see that each top chord is 7.5 m long. If we assume pinned ends ($K = 1$ for column end fixity), how large should this top chord be? From Table 2 of

Appendix S, we can arbitrarily select a W250 × 58 with an area of 7420 mm² as a trial section. It has a least radius of gyration of 50.2 mm, which will mean a slenderness ratio of

$$\frac{KL}{r_y} = \frac{1.0(7500 \text{ mm})}{50.2 \text{ mm}}$$
$$\approx 149$$

From Table 1 of Appendix R, the allowable axial stress will be

$$F_a \approx 46 \text{ MPa}$$

The member's load capacity is then

$$P = F_a(A)$$
$$\approx 46\ 000 \text{ kPa}(0.007\ 42 \text{ m}^2)$$
$$\approx 341 \text{ kN}$$

This is way below the required value, as the C force in the top chord is 1600 kN. If this is approximately the size of member desired in the truss, clearly the trusses will have to be deeper, loaded differently, or spaced more closely together.

Moving up in size, we can try a W310 × 143. It has an area of 18 200 mm² and an r_y of 78.4 mm.

$$\frac{KL}{r_y} = \frac{1.0(7500 \text{ mm})}{78.4}$$
$$\approx 96$$

Again, from Table 1 of Appendix R, the allowable stress is

$$F_a \approx 93 \text{ MPa}$$

The load capacity is

$$P = F_a(A)$$
$$\approx 93\ 000 \text{ kPa}(0.0182 \text{ m}^2)$$
$$\approx 1750 \text{ kN}$$

This value is above the required capacity, and the member selected would even be a bit overdesigned.

This procedure can be easily reversed to provide a first approximation of a required truss depth, as illustrated by the following example.

EXAMPLE 14-7

Determine the approximate depth y needed for parallel timber roof trusses, one of which is shown in Figure 14-32. The total

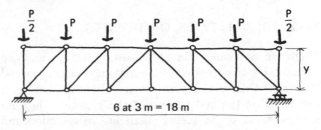

Figure 14-32. Flat Howe truss.

load is 2.5 kN/m², and the trusses are spaced 2 m on centers. It is desired that the critical top chord members be no larger in section than 89 × 185 mm. Use Douglas fir and assume no lateral support between panel points.

Solution: From the tributary area involved, each load P will be 15 kN. Taking moments about the point A in Figure 14-33,

$$\Sigma M_A = 0$$

$$-45(6) + 7.5(6) + 15(3) + C(y) = 0$$

$$C(y) = 180 \text{ kN·m}$$

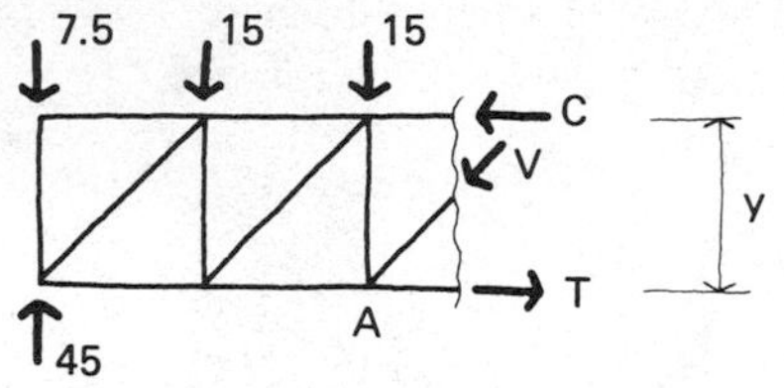

Figure 14-33. Free-body diagram.

From Appendix Q, the area of an 89 × 185 mm section is 16 500 mm², and using Equation (13-5), we can get the allowable axial stress for an unbraced length of 3 m.

$$F'_c = \frac{0.30E}{(L/d)^2} \qquad (13\text{-}5)$$

$$= \frac{0.30(12\ 400\ \text{MPa})}{(3000/89)^2}$$

$$= 3.27 \text{ MPa}$$

or

$$F'_c = 3270 \text{ kPa}$$

The member's load capacity is then

$$P = F'_c(A)$$

$$= 3270 \text{ kPa}(0.0165 \text{ m}^2)$$

$$= 54 \text{ kN}$$

Assuming the compressive force C cannot exceed this value, we can determine the needed depth

$$C(y) = 180 \text{ kN·m}$$

$$54 \text{ kN}(y) = 180 \text{ kN·m}$$

$$y = 3.33 \text{ m}$$

This means that about 3 to 3.5 m of depth is needed for these trusses or the scheme will have to be altered in some way so as to change the loading, the member size, or the bracing conditions.

14-6 SPECIAL TYPES OF TRUSSES

There are two categories of trusses which are used so frequently in construction today that they warrant special attention. One is the prefabricated light timber truss mentioned in the first section of this chapter. They are usually made up of pieces small in cross section and fastened at the joints so that all members can lie in the

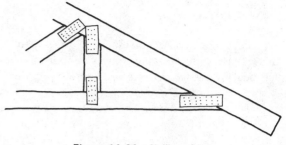

Figure 14-34. Nailing plates.

same plane. These joints are nailed together using special toothed light-gage-steel plates as seen in Figure 14-34. Whenever possible, chord members continue through joints for ease of fabrication. (The basic analysis still assumes a completely hinged joint, however.)

When fully braced by a roof plane, these trusses are very stiff and much stronger than they appear. Specifications have been set in a standard manner so that, if no special loads or unusual supports conditions are present, these trusses can be ordered almost as stock items with obvious economy.

The second type of frequently used truss is the open-web steel bar joist, often referred to simply as a bar joist. They are usually fabricated from angles and round bar stock, with the larger ones using only angles. Shop-welded together, using continuous chord members, they are manufactured to meet certain load capacities as specified by the Steel Joist Institute. Without special detailing, they are not suitable for concentrated loads but can handle the uniform loads of most floors and flat (or nearly flat) roofs over a very wide range of spans. They are seldom designed in the usual sense. Like rolled steel beams, they are selected from load tables that have been developed with due consideration for the moments, shears, and deflections involved in simple spans.

Unlike wood joists and precast concrete joists usually used on shorter spans, open web joists easily permit the through passage of wires and pipes and even small ducts. The minimum of on-site labor required for their erection means that steel joists can often provide a very economical deck system. They are particularly well suited for one-story structures with high ceilings, such as factories and gymnasiums, where fireproofing and acoustics needs are minimal.

A third type of special truss is not really a truss at all. As shown in Figure 14-35, the Vierendeel "truss" is really more like a rigid frame or a beam with large holes. The absence of triangulation and the presence of fully moment resistant joints mean that this structure is grossly misnomered when called a truss. The Vierendeel frame takes its name from its designer, Arthur Vierendeel (1852–c.1930), a Belgian engineer and builder. It is usually made of reinforced concrete, which inherently

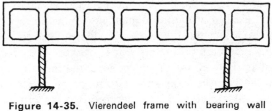

Figure 14-35. Vierendeel frame with bearing wall supports.

provides the required joint fixity but can also be fabricated from steel. It carries its load through the development of bending stresses in all or most of the segments. As the frame bends, the members assume "S" patterns for their deflected shapes because the joints apply moments to the ends of the members as they rotate.

This joint continuity makes the structure highly indeterminate.

While the Vierendeel frame is quite inefficient compared to a truss, it can be very useful in specific structural situations. The lack of diagonal members means that there are large clear openings in the frame that can be used nonstructurally. Their best application occurs when the span and loads are such that a frame equal in depth to one story height is required. If the floor plan can accommodate the web verticals, the frame will become an integrated part of the architectural section. The Vierendeel frame of Figure 14-35 is used to provide a large column-free area beneath a heavily loaded second floor.

The concepts of indeterminacy or redundancy were mentioned in Section 2-12 as part of a consideration of static equilibrium. Indeterminate beams and frames, by definition, have a larger than necessary number of support conditions or reaction components. Such structures are usually constructed with continuity or fixity at some or all of the supports and member connections. This is another way of saying that certain connections or supports are moment-resistant and not free to rotate (e.g., a fixed end).

Because these structures are redundant or "overstable," they cannot be analyzed using the concepts of static equilibrium alone, and additional information about their behavior is needed. Invariably, this includes a consideration of how such a structure or its parts deform. This was the principle behind the method of superposition of loads presented in Section 10-11 and used to solve beams with one redundant support.

A very simplistic type of indeterminate structure was analyzed in Section 4-8, the axially loaded member constructed of two materials. In this case, the analysis used the fact that the two materials must deform equally and would, therefore, develop stress in proportion to their relative stiffness (E) values.

Continuous beams and frames are approached in a similar way, in that all methods of indeterminate analysis include a consideration of the relative stiffness of each member. Since bending forces rather than axial forces are critical, relative stiffness is dependent upon I, L, and the support conditions, as well as E. In fact, the modulus of elasticity usually does not vary from member to member, so relative stiffness becomes a function of I, L, and the support conditions. A more important similarity exists, however, between the continuous beam or frame and the axially loaded composite member. The two materials in the composite member did not act independently but accepted and shared the applied load in a manner dependent upon the resistance (stiffness) of each. Likewise, the loads applied to the various members of a continuous structure are accepted and shared by those members in a manner dependent upon the relative resistance (stiffness) of each. Unlike the pinned connections of determinate structures, the continuous connections of indeterminate structures cause the members to interact with one another to share the load. In the simple column-and-beam structure of Figure 15-1(a), the beam bends independently of the columns, whereas in the frame of Figure 15-1(b), the columns also act in bending to help resist the load. Clearly, increasing the stiffness of the columns in the determinate frame would not affect the stresses or deflections of the beam, only those of the columns. Changing the stiffness of the

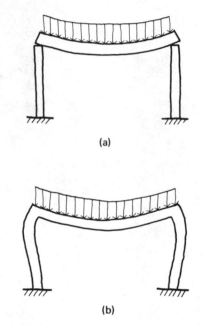

(a)

(b)

Figure 15-1. Determinate and indeterminate frames.

15 Indeterminate Beams and Frames

columns in the rigid frame, however, would definitely affect the stresses and deflections of the beam. Similarly, a change in the stiffness of the beam would affect the behavior of the columns. The major portion of this chapter involves the study of this type of interaction.

One cannot make any conclusive statements regarding the superiority or inferiority of continuous structures relative to noncontinuous structures. This is a function of the structural design objectives, types of loads present, materials and construction systems available, and other design considerations. Nevertheless, we can note the general structural advantages and disadvantages involved in the use of continuous or moment-resistant connections. There are, of course, exceptions in each case.

Advantages:

1. More even distribution of stresses, resulting in somewhat smaller members.
2. Higher overall stiffness, resulting in smaller deflections.
3. Collapse of a member usually requires failure at more than one section.
4. Designer can control moments somewhat by manipulating stiffness and end conditions.

Disadvantages:

1. Usually more difficult to analyze and construct.
2. Assumptions concerning loads and supports are more critical.
3. Shearing forces can be larger.
4. More subject to damage by foundation settlement and thermal changes.

In practical construction terms, timber structures tend to be determinate, if only because rigid joints are difficult to construct in wood. However, continuous beams spanning several supports without joints are as common in wood as they are in steel and reinforced concrete. Reinforced concrete, except that which is precast, is almost always indeterminate. The moment-resistant connection is inherent to the monolithic nature of cast-in-place reinforced concrete. Structural steel can be continuous, noncontinuous, or someplace in between. It is possible to make either bolted or welded connections that are pinned, fully moment-resistant, or possessing a specified amount of resistance. Smaller steel elements such as open-web bar joists usually have no continuity at their supports, whereas large sections for one-story long-span applications are almost always connected as rigid frames. While moment-resistant connections are common in structural steel, they are, relatively speaking, more difficult to construct than in reinforced concrete.

15-2 THEOREM OF THREE MOMENTS

A very simple analytical technique, which involves an equation called the *theorem of three moments*, can be applied to beams that have redundant support conditions. The technique can be used on a beam of only one span (indeterminate by virtue of its end conditions) but is most effectively applied to continuous members that span across several supports. In Figure 15-2(b), two spans of a uniformly loaded continuous beam have been sketched as free bodies to expose the internal moments at supports *A*, *B*, and *C*. It is seen that for each span, these support moments are redundant in terms of equilibrium. If these moments were known, each beam segment would then become determinate and the vertical support forces could be found from simple statics. The theorem of three moments can be used to determine these unknown support moments.

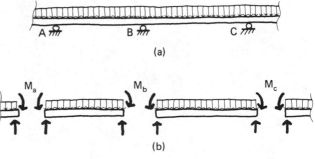

Figure 15-2. Redundant support moments.

The general theorem, as derived in Appendix I, is valid for any loading condition. As indicated in the derivation, however, a less general theorem is often used for cases involving uniform loads constant over a given span and/or concentrated loads. The theorem that results is

$$M_a \frac{L_1}{I_1} + 2M_b\left(\frac{L_1}{I_1} + \frac{L_2}{I_2}\right) + M_c\frac{L_2}{I_2}$$
$$= -\frac{w_1 L_1^3}{4I_1} - \frac{w_2 L_2^3}{4I_2} - \frac{P_1 a_1 b_1}{I_1 L_1}(L_1 + a_1)$$
$$- \frac{P_2 a_2 b_2}{I_2 L_2}(L_2 + b_2) \qquad (15\text{-}1)$$

in which M_a, M_b, and M_c are the unknown support moments and the other notation is as presented in Figure 15-3. If the beam is one of constant cross section, the theorem can be simplified by the deletion of the moment of inertia symbols, and we get Equation (15-2).

$$M_a L_1 + 2M_b(L_1 + L_2) + M_c L_2$$
$$= -\frac{w_1 L_1^3}{4} - \frac{w_2 L_2^3}{4} - \frac{P_1 a_1 b_1}{L_1}(L_1 + a_1)$$
$$- \frac{P_2 a_2 b_2}{L_2}(L_2 + b_2) \qquad (15\text{-}2)$$

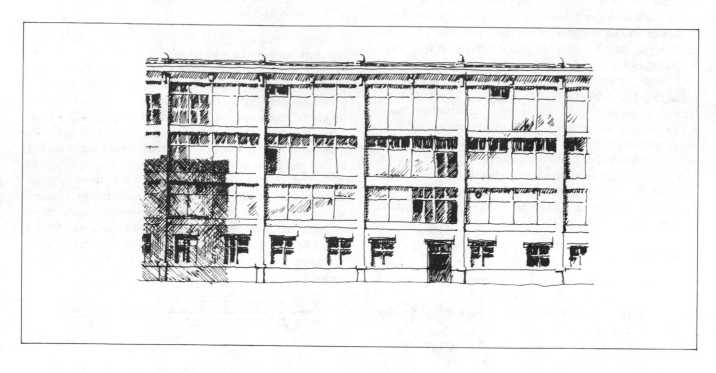

Indeterminacy is an everyday occurrence in actual building practice. Whenever beams and columns are fastened together in a continuous manner with moment-resistant connections, a statically indeterminate frame results. Such is the case with the spinning mill building in Tourcoing, France designed and constructed by François Hennibique in 1895. This building is one of the outstanding forerunners of modern reinforced concrete construction.

The roof structure of the Columbus, Indiana, Post Office by Roche and Dinkeloo is indeterminate to a lesser degree. The long beams running the length of the building are not constructed integrally with the transverse girders or piers, but they do span continuously over more than two supports. Indeterminate elements often provide visual continuity as well as structural continuity, creating a sense of unity or "wholeness."

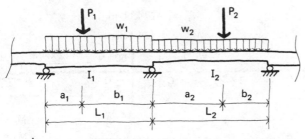

Figure 15-3. Notation for theorem of three moments.

EXAMPLE 15-1

Determine the unknown support moment at B and construct the shear and moment diagrams for the beam in Figure 15-4.

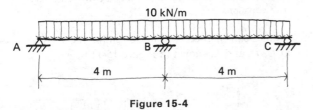

Figure 15-4

Solution: In this case, M_a and M_c are both zero and there are no concentrated loads, so the theorem of three moments reduces to

$$2M_b(L_1 + L_2) = -\frac{w_1 L_1^3}{4} - \frac{w_2 L_2^3}{4}$$

Substituting in the appropriate values, we get

$$2M_b(4 + 4) = -\frac{10(4)^3}{4} - \frac{10(4)^3}{4}$$

$$M_b = -20 \text{ kN·m}$$

Figure 15-5 shows how the beam can now be treated as two determinate spans that share a common support at B. The 20-kN·m support moment is applied to each span with a negative sense (i.e., tension in the top fiber), as indicated by the sign of M_b. Support moments should be treated as points of known moment when constructing moment diagrams.

For convenience, the reactions have been determined in parts. The row of upward-acting 20-kN forces is due to the uniform load acting alone, and the couples formed by the 5-kN forces are in response to the support moment. These component forces can be algebraically summed to get the final reaction values at each support. Notice that the center support carries more than half the total load in this case. Figure 15-6 illustrates the resulting increase in shear force present at the central support. The student should ascertain

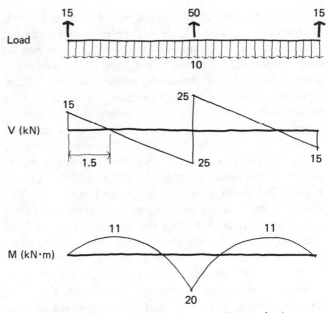

Figure 15-6. Load, shear, and moment diagrams for the beam of Example 15-1.

the full effects of continuity in this example by comparing the V and M diagrams to those that would result if this beam were constructed of two separate simple spans.

The theorem of three moments can be used to solve continuous beams of any number of spans by applying it successively to each pair of adjacent spans. Making the appropriate extensions of the notation, as illustrated in Figure 15-7, we get a set of equations equal in number to the number of unknown support moments.

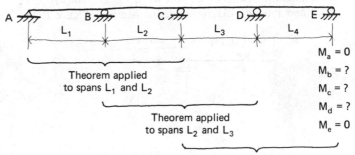

$M_a = 0$
$M_b = ?$
$M_c = ?$
$M_d = ?$
$M_e = 0$

Figure 15-7. Three unknown support moments and three equations.

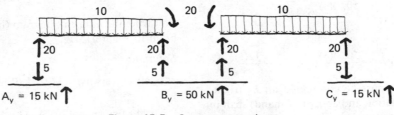

Figure 15-5. Component reactions.

The theorem can also be used for fixed-end beams of one or more spans. Here it is necessary to make use of the fact that the slope of the elastic curve is zero at such supports. This means that a fixed end can be simulated, in concept, by the central support of a set of continuous spans having mirror-image symmetry. The two-span beam of Example 15-1 has a slope of zero at support B due to such symmetry. This means that each span of the beam could be fixed at support B with no change in the elastic curve and thus no change in the shears or moments. Conversely, the fixed-end beam in Figure 15-8 could be solved using the theorem of three moments by creating an imaginary L_1 span out to the left of support B. Selecting the proper imaginary load and length for this span to achieve symmetry, the beam is then identical to the one in Example 15-1. Mathematically, the use of imaginary spans has the effect of doubling both sides of the three moments equation, and thus the lengths and loads of such spans may be taken as zero when writing the equations. Examples 15-2 and 15-3 illustrate this procedure.

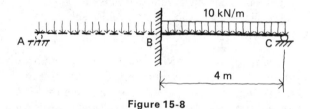

Figure 15-8

EXAMPLE 15-2

Determine the unknown support moments and construct the shear and moment diagrams for the beam of Figure 15-9.

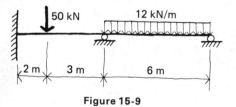

Figure 15-9

Solution: As indicated in Figure 15-10, the theorem need not be applied to spans AB and BC because for those two spans all the load terms will be zero. Writing equations for the other two pairs, we get

spans BC and CD

$$2M_c(0 + 5) + (M_d)(5) = -\frac{50(2)(3)}{5}(5 + 3)$$

spans CD and DE

$$M_c(5) + 2M_d(5 + 6) = -\frac{50(2)(3)}{5}(5 + 2) - \frac{12(6)^3}{4}$$

Notice that the span CD must be considered an L_2 (right-hand) span in the first equation and an L_1 (left-hand) span in the second equation. Solving these two simultaneously gives us

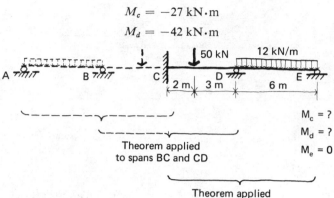

$$M_c = -27 \text{ kN·m}$$
$$M_d = -42 \text{ kN·m}$$

Figure 15-10. Two unknown support moments and two equations.

These values can then be used to determine the vertical reactions at C, D, and E, shown in Figure 15-11.

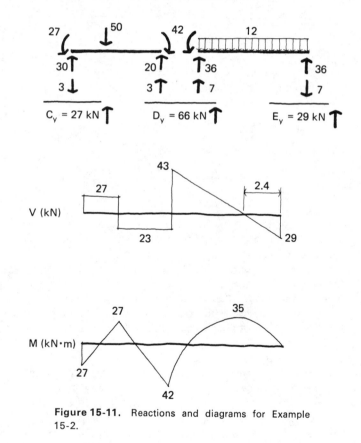

Figure 15-11. Reactions and diagrams for Example 15-2.

EXAMPLE 15-3

Construct the moment diagram (in terms of w and L) for the beam in Figure 15-12.

Solution:

(left two spans) $2M_k(0 + L) + M_q(L) = -\dfrac{wL^3}{4}$

(right two spans) $M_k(L) + 2M_q(L + 0) = -\dfrac{wL^3}{4}$

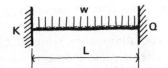

Figure 15-12.   Uniformly loaded beam with fixed ends.

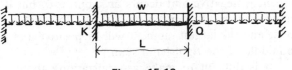

Figure 15-13

Since by symmetry, $M_k = M_q$, either equation may be used to find the value.

$$M_k = M_q = -\frac{wL^2}{12}$$

Because the end moments are equal, the vertical reactions will each be $wL/2$, which means that the shear diagram will be the same as that of a simply supported beam. The moment diagram appears in Figure 15-14, and one should notice that it is quite different from that of a simple beam. End fixity not only reduces the positive moment by a factor of three ($wL^2/8$ to $wL^2/24$) but also causes the maximum moment to be changed in location, sense, and magnitude. The absolute value of the maximum moment is, in fact, reduced by 50%.

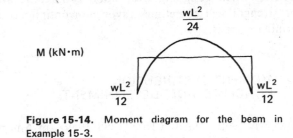

Figure 15-14.   Moment diagram for the beam in Example 15-3.

EXAMPLE 15-4

Construct the shear and moment diagrams for the beam of Figure 15-15 in which the moment of inertia of span BC is twice that of span AB.

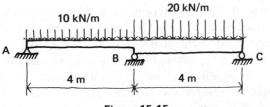

Figure 15-15

Solution: The changing beam cross section necessitates the use of Equation (15-1).

$$M_a\frac{L_1}{I_1} + 2M_b\left(\frac{L_1}{I_1} + \frac{L_2}{I_2}\right) + M_c\frac{L_2}{I_2}$$

$$= -\frac{w_1 L_1^3}{4I_1} - \frac{w_2 L_2^3}{4I_2} - \frac{P_1 a_1 b_1}{I_1 L_1}(L_1 + a_1)$$

$$- \frac{P_2 a_2 b_2}{I_2 L_2}(L_2 + b_2) \qquad (15\text{-}1)$$

Since the relative rather than actual I values influence the results, their numerical values need not be known. It is sufficient to arbitrarily let I for span AB be unity and I for span BC be twice unity.

$$2M_b\left(\frac{4}{1} + \frac{4}{2}\right) = -\frac{10(4)^3}{4(1)} - \frac{20(4)^3}{4(2)}$$

$$M_b = -27 \text{ kN·m}$$

Using the procedures of previous examples, we get the V and M diagrams of Figure 15-16.

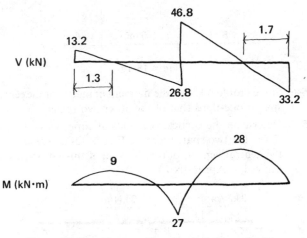

Figure 15-16.   Shear and moment diagrams for the beam of Example 15-4.

Problems

15-1. Construct the shear and moment diagrams for the beam of Example 15-4 if the moment of inertia is constant over both spans. Compare your results to those of Examples 15-1 and 15-4.

15-2. Solve Problem 10-15 using the theorem of three moments.

15-3. Construct the V and M diagrams for the beam in Figure 15-17.

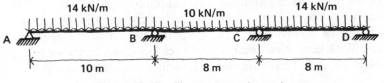

Figure 15-17.   Three-span continuous beam.

15-4. Construct the *V* and *M* diagrams for the fixed-end beam in Figure 15-18. (*Hint:* Make use of symmetry to reduce the number of equations.)

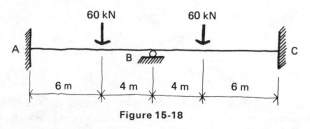

Figure 15-18

15-5. Determine the vertical reactions at supports *A*, *B*, and *C* for the beam in Figure 15-19. The moment of inertia of span *AB* is twice that of span *BC*.

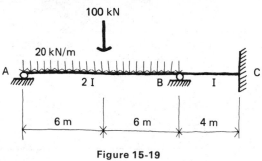

Figure 15-19

15-6. Solve Problem 15-3 if the moment of inertia of the center span is one-third that of the other two spans.

15-7. Determine the vertical reactions at supports *A*, *B*, and *C* for the two-span beam of Figure 15-20. (*Hint:* Use the general version of the theorem of three moments as derived in Appendix I.)

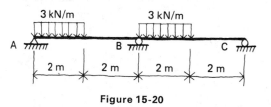

Figure 15-20

15-3 LOADING PATTERNS

Continuous and fixed-end beams, like those on simple supports, are designed for the maximum stresses and deflections. Although deflection can be important, it is less likely to be the controlling design factor because of the inherently reduced angles of slope at the supports. Continuity or fixity serves to reduce the deflections between the supports. Bending and shearing stresses, however, may be increased or decreased by this continuity, and it is sometimes necessary to study more than one loading pattern to determine which combination will generate the maximum values. With continuous beams, the critical design loading might be one of less than full

load. While the dead load is normally present on all spans, the analyst must consider the presence *and* absence of live loads. The addition or removal of a load will always change one or more moments elsewhere. As an illustration of this, look at the beam in Example 15-2. Under the given loading conditions, the maximum moment is negative and occurs at support *D*, but if we remove the 50-kN concentrated load, this value will reduce and the largest moment will be positive and near the middle of the right-hand span.

It is difficult to make generalizations about continuous beams with moments of inertia that vary from span to span, but for those of constant *I* (and *E*, of course), maximum negative moments will usually occur when adjacent spans are fully loaded. Maximum positive moments will be found when alternate spans are loaded. This is illustrated for uniform loads in Figure 15-21, where decimal coefficients of wL^2 are given for the moments in beams of three spans.

In a similar manner, it can be shown that the maximum shearing forces will generally result from loading adjacent spans. More important, these shearing forces, unlike bending moments, will generally be increased by the presence of continuity (see Example 15-1). This can be critical when designing with wood, where the low shear strength will sometimes favor noncontinuous or determinate spans.

15-4 MOMENT DISTRIBUTION CONCEPTS AND DEVELOPMENT

In the early 1930s, Hardy Cross (1885–1959), an American engineer, developed a new method called *moment distribution* for the analysis of indeterminate beams and frames. Prior to that time, obtaining the design moments for a continuous building frame was a time-consuming and complicated process, invariably involving the handling of large numbers of equations. The strength of the Hardy Cross method is that no matter how complicated or how indeterminate a frame becomes, the only mathematical skills required are those of simple arithmetic. Moment distribution is an iterative process of successive approximations and was criticized at first for not being able to provide accurate answers in a direct manner. However, it was soon realized that such accuracy is seldom if ever needed in structural engineering, and within a few years the technique had received widespread adoption.

Subsequently, the advent of large electronic computers permitted the application of matrix methods to such problems and greatly reduced the need for refined methods of hand calculation. Sophisticated programs

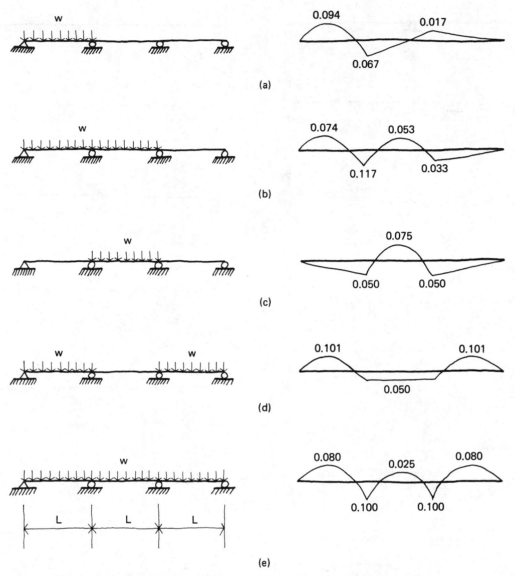

Figure 15-21. Moment coefficients for three-span continuous beams. ($M =$ coefficient $\times wL^2$).

have been developed that enable the structural designer to analyze a very complex frame in just a few seconds, and the computer has become an indispensable tool in most engineering offices.

Since most students of architecture and building construction do not have a background in matrix algebra, computer applications have not been included in this text. Emphasis has been placed instead on moment distribution because of its simplicity, and more important, because familiarity with its concepts can lead to a real understanding of the interactive nature of the members of continuous beams and frames.

While moment distribution is most advantageously used to analyze frames, the fundamental principles will be developed in this article by using continuous beams

as examples. The basic concept of moment distribution involves a study of how the different joints of a continuous structure are caused to turn or rotate under the applied loads. A joint is defined as a junction of two or more members *or* a junction of a member and a support. Members are considered to be connected to one another with full continuity such that if a joint turns through a certain angle, all members meeting there turn through that same angle.

The iterative process of distributing moments is actually a numerical procedure that includes cycles of successively "locking" and "unlocking" (preventing rotation and permitting rotation) the various joints of a structure. Figure 15-22 is a qualitative diagram of two cycles of the physical analogy of this process using a

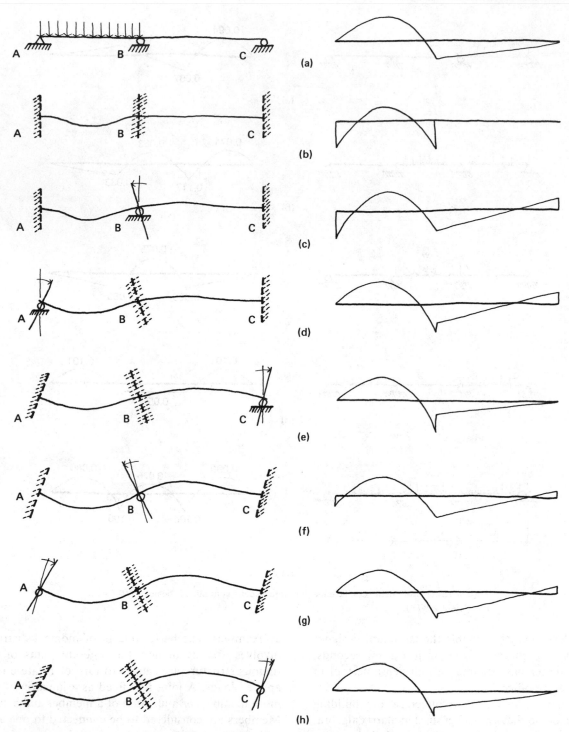

Figure 15-22. Locking and unlocking joints.

beam with three joints. The slopes and deflections have, as usual, been greatly exaggerated. Figure 15-22(a) shows the beam with its final moment diagram representing the end result of the analysis. The other sketches comprise the various steps taken in moment distribution to converge upon this result.

As seen in Figure 15-22(b), it is first assumed that

all joints are locked or fixed when the loads are applied. Moment will exist only in the loaded span. In this example, the central joint B is unlocked first, which causes the deflected shape and the moment diagram of Figure 15-22(c). The resulting rotation allows joint B to go into equilibrium or a state of balance (equal moment values just to the left and right of the joint), but also increases the moment at joint *A* and develops a new moment at joint *C*. These changes in moment at the opposite (and locked) ends of the members are called *carryover moments*. Next, joint *A* is unlocked and allowed to turn as in Figure 15-22(d). Note that the other joints remain locked, including *B* in its new position. This release at *A* does not affect span *BC* with its two locked ends, but reduces the moment at *A* to zero and causes a carryover moment at joint *B*. It is most important to notice that this carryover moment throws the joint *B* out of equilibrium (i.e., if unlocked, it would rotate some more). Finally, joint *C* is released as shown in Figure 15-22(e), and its moment goes to zero with a corresponding carryover effect at *B*. Because of the disequilibrium (lack of balance) at joint *B*, the diagram is quite different from the final one of Figure 15-22(a) and a second cycle is necessary. Joints *B*, *A*, and *C* are again unlocked and locked as seen in Figure 15-22(f), (g), and (h). This time, the effects are much smaller and joint *B* ends up only slightly out of balance. The moment diagram now approximates the final one at the top of the figure. Whether or not third and fourth cycles are necessary would depend upon the specific conditions of loads, spans, and desired accuracy level. In many cases, three balances (releases of each joint) are necessary and sufficient. The actual numerical distribution procedure is not as lengthy or drawn out as it may appear, however, because in mathematical terms, it is convenient to unlock and lock all joints simultaneously.

Before working some specific examples, we need to look further into a few definitions and procedures. It is worthwhile to note that the actual procedures of moment distribution are quite simple to perform, but the theoretical basis for those procedures is often difficult to grasp in the abstract. Thus, it is recommended that the following material be read through and then studied more thoroughly in conjunction with the example problems that follow.

The technique of moment distribution does not result in moment diagrams but instead provides the magnitude and sense of the internal moments at each joint. These joint moments are then used to obtain the shear and moment diagrams as we did with the theorem of three moments in Section 15-2. A sign convention is required which indicates how joints will rotate or (in the case of fixed joints) tend to rotate when acted upon by the joint moments. This is an arbitrary selection, and, in this text, moments that cause or tend to cause clockwise rotation of the joint are taken as positive, and moments that cause or tend to cause counterclockwise rotation are taken as negative. It is important to realize that this convention is completely independent of the usual one for bending moment, which relates moment to

curvature. The joint moment convention is a bookkeeping aid for moment distribution procedures only.

It has been mentioned that when a joint is released or balanced, a carryover moment is induced at the opposite end(s) of the member(s) coming into that joint. Figure 15-23 will be used to show that a moment induced at the locked end of a member is equal to one-half of the moment taken at the unlocked end. Since the deflection is zero at point *A*, the tangential deviation at *A* with respect

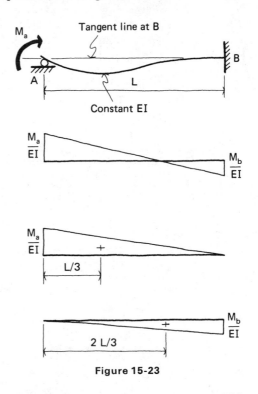

Figure 15-23

to a tangent line from *B*, $t_{a/b}$, will be zero. This means that the statical moment of the area under the M/EI curve with respect to *A* must also be zero. Using the two partial diagrams (because of their convenient centroid locations), we get

$$\frac{1}{2}\left(\frac{M_a}{EI}\right)(L)\left(\frac{L}{3}\right) - \frac{1}{2}\left(\frac{M_b}{EI}\right)(L)\left(\frac{2L}{3}\right) = 0$$

$$M_b = \tfrac{1}{2}M_a$$

Note that this coefficient, called the *carryover factor*, will always have a value of 1/2 provided that *E* and *I* are constant throughout the length of the member.

Finally, whenever a joint is released, which is being acted upon by an unbalanced moment (and is therefore not in equilibrium), it will rotate, and the members coming into it will develop moments as equilibrium is restored. The sum of these moments will equal the initial unbalanced moment and will be shared by the various members. As previously stated, the members are rigidly connected and will each turn through the same minute angle. Therefore, the amount of moment to be taken by (or distributed to) each member will be a function of the relative stiffness of each member. Stiffness, in this case, refers to the amount of resistance that a member has to the rotation of its unlocked end (i.e., for a given angle of rotation, a stiffer member will develop more moment). The stiffness of a member can be measured as the ratio of this moment to the angle. This relationship will be developed for the beam in Figure 15-24. We can solve for the angle θ_a by using the first moment-area theorem and the fact that θ_b is zero. The change in angle between points A and B is equal to θ_a, and therefore θ_a is equal to the area under the M/EI curve.

$$\theta_a = \frac{1}{2}\frac{M_a}{EI}(L) - \frac{1}{2}\frac{M_b}{EI}(L)$$

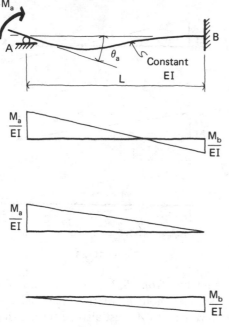

Figure 15-24

From previous work, we know that $M_b = \frac{1}{2}M_a$ and we get

$$\theta_a = \frac{1}{2}\left(\frac{M_a}{EI}\right)(L) - \frac{1}{2}\left(\frac{M_a}{2EI}\right)(L)$$

$$= \frac{M_aL}{4EI}$$

Therefore, the moment/angle ratio will be

$$\frac{M_a}{\theta_a} = \frac{4EI}{L} \qquad (15\text{-}3a)$$

This expression indicates that stiffness is a function of E, I, L and the constant 4, which is due to the fixed end condition and its carryover moment. If the members coming into a joint have the same E value and end conditions, the stiffness of the members relative to one another will be a function of I/L. Thus, whenever a joint

is unlocked and rotates to achieve equilibrium, the moment will be distributed to the members in an amount proportional to their I/L values.

In moment distribution, a distribution factor (DF) is assigned to each of the members at a joint, indicating how much of the moment is to be taken by each member. It is in reality nothing more than a decimal fraction representing how much of the total joint stiffness is contributed by that member.

Figure 15-25 shows a two-span beam in which the moment of inertia of span BC is twice that of span AB. Since only the relative stiffness is important, convenient values are often used for moments of inertia. The relative stiffness of each member is

$$\left(\frac{I}{L}\right)_{ab} = \frac{1}{4} = 0.250 \qquad \left(\frac{I}{L}\right)_{bc} = \frac{2}{5} = 0.400$$

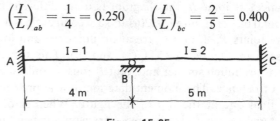

Figure 15-25

A distribution factor for each end of each member can then be found by dividing the stiffness of the member by the sum of the stiffnesses of all the members at that joint.

$$DF = \frac{I/L}{\sum (I/L)}$$

Letting the first letter of the subscript indicate the joint in question, the DF values at joint B would be

$$DF_{ba} = \frac{0.250}{0.250 + 0.400} \qquad DF_{bc} = \frac{0.400}{0.250 + 0.400}$$

$$= 0.385 \qquad\qquad = 0.615$$

The distribution factors at a given joint should always be rounded to sum to unity.

The DF value of a member at a fixed-end support, DF_{ab} or DF_{cb} for example, will be zero. Such a joint should be thought of as having two members, the member itself and the wall. Since the wall is infinitely stiff, it will take any moment applied to that joint and nothing will be distributed to the member. The opposite will be true when a pin or roller occurs at the end of a structure. Since there is only one member at such a joint, no sharing is possible, and the distribution factor for that member must be unity.

The examples that follow should serve to clarify some of the preceding material, and reference to it should be made while following the actual procedures.

Before starting a distribution, all joints are assumed to be fixed and are acted upon by moments at the ends of the loaded spans. The magnitudes of these "fixed-end moments" may be found for the more frequently encountered load situations in Appendix V. They can be determined for other loads by using the theorem of three moments.

EXAMPLE 15-5

Distribute the moments and construct the shear and moment diagrams for the continuous beam of constant *EI* shown in Figure 15-26.

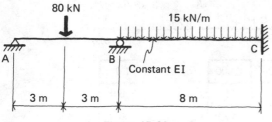

Figure 15-26

Solution: First determine the distribution factors at the three joints. Letting *I* have a value of unity, the relative stiffness of each member is

$$\left(\frac{I}{L}\right)_{ab} = \frac{1}{6} = 0.167 \qquad \left(\frac{I}{L}\right)_{bc} = \frac{1}{8} = 0.125$$

Using these to get the DF values at *B* gives us

$$\mathrm{DF}_{ba} = \frac{0.167}{0.167 + 0.125} \qquad \mathrm{DF}_{bc} = \frac{0.125}{0.167 + 0.125}$$

$$= 0.572 \qquad\qquad = 0.428$$

At supports *A* and *C*, we get

$$\mathrm{DF}_{ab} = 1.0 \quad \text{and} \quad \mathrm{DF}_{cb} = 0.0$$

The magnitudes of the fixed-end moments (FEM values) for the left and right spans can be found using cases 10 and 11, respectively, in Appendix V.

$$\mathrm{FEM}_{ab} = \mathrm{FEM}_{ba} = \frac{Pa^2b}{L^2} = \frac{80(3)^2(3)}{(6)^2} = 60 \text{ kN·m}$$

$$\mathrm{FEM}_{bc} = \mathrm{FEM}_{cb} = \frac{wL^2}{12} = \frac{15(8)^2}{12} = 80 \text{ kN·m}$$

The sign of an FEM will depend upon how it acts upon the joint, clockwise (+) and counterclockwise (−).

The completed moment distribution with three balances is shown in Figure 15-27. The student should study each balance and carryover step in some detail, paying particular attention to the signs. The special sign convention was developed so that the joints will be in equilibrium at the end of each balance. As mentioned previously, the carryover moments then act to force each joint out of equilibrium necessitating another balance. The process is continued until the desired degree of convergence is obtained. Each block is then totaled to give the final joint moments. The moment distribution sign convention is used to show how these moments act on the joints in the small free bodies at the bottom of Figure 15-27. As it must be, the resulting moment at *A* is zero.

It is important to realize that the entire moment distribution procedure is concerned with how the members act

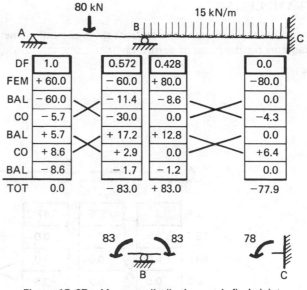

DF	1.0	0.572	0.428		0.0
FEM	+ 60.0	− 60.0	+ 80.0		−80.0
BAL	− 60.0	− 11.4	− 8.6		0.0
CO	− 5.7	− 30.0	0.0		− 4.3
BAL	+ 5.7	+ 17.2	+ 12.8		0.0
CO	+ 8.6	+ 2.9	0.0		+6.4
BAL	− 8.6	− 1.7	− 1.2		0.0
TOT	0.0	− 83.0	+ 83.0		−77.9

Figure 15-27. Moment distribution and final joint moments.

upon the joints. How those joint moments then act upon the ends of the members is shown in Figure 15-28. The moments acting on the members are used to get the component reactions so the shear and moment diagrams can be drawn. At this step, the moment distribution sign convention must be abandoned in favor of the usual one for internal bending moment. By this convention, all four of the curved arrows at joint *B* in Figure 15-28 represent a single negative (tension top fiber) value of moment occurring in the beam at joint *B*.

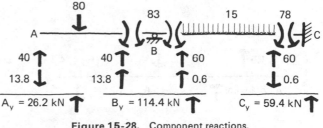

Figure 15-28. Component reactions.

The completed *V* and *M* diagrams appear in Figure 15-29.

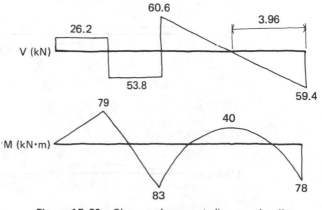

Figure 15-29. Shear and moment diagrams for the beam of Example 15-5.

EXAMPLE 15-6

Distribute the moments and construct the shear and moment
diagrams for the beam of Figure 15-30.

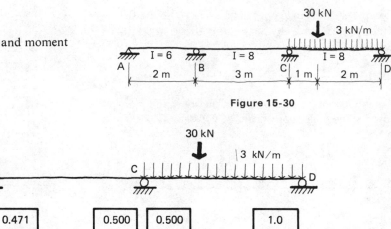

Figure 15-30

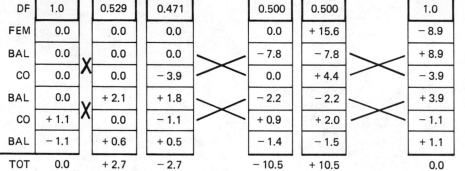

DF	1.0	0.529	0.471		0.500	0.500		1.0
FEM	0.0	0.0	0.0		0.0	+ 15.6		− 8.9
BAL	0.0	0.0	0.0		− 7.8	− 7.8		+ 8.9
CO	0.0	0.0	− 3.9		0.0	+ 4.4		− 3.9
BAL	0.0	+ 2.1	+ 1.8		− 2.2	− 2.2		+ 3.9
CO	+ 1.1	0.0	− 1.1		+ 0.9	+ 2.0		− 1.1
BAL	− 1.1	+ 0.6	+ 0.5		− 1.4	− 1.5		+ 1.1
TOT	0.0	+ 2.7	− 2.7		− 10.5	+ 10.5		0.0

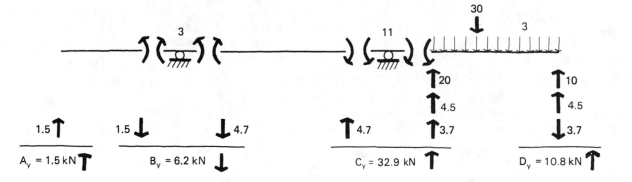

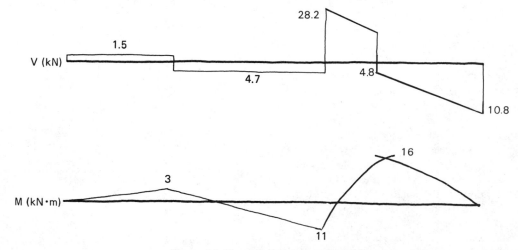

Figure 15-31. Solution to Example 15-6.

Solution: First compute the relative stiffnesses and distribution factors.

$$\left(\frac{I}{L}\right)_{ab} = \frac{6}{2} = 3.00 \qquad \left(\frac{I}{L}\right)_{bc} = \left(\frac{I}{L}\right)_{cd} = \frac{8}{3} = 2.67$$

$$DF_{ba} = \frac{3.00}{3.00 + 2.67} = 0.529$$

$$DF_{bc} = \frac{2.67}{3.00 + 2.67} = 0.471$$

$$DF_{cb} = DF_{cd} = \frac{2.67}{2.67 + 2.67} = 0.500$$

$$DF_{ab} = DF_{dc} = 1.0$$

From Appendix V, the FEM values for the loaded span are

$$FEM_{cd} = \frac{Pab^2}{L^2} + \frac{wL^2}{12}$$

$$= \frac{30(1)(2)^2}{(3)^2} + \frac{3(3)^2}{12} = 15.6 \text{ kN·m}$$

$$FEM_{dc} = \frac{Pa^2b}{L^2} + \frac{wL^2}{12}$$

$$= \frac{30(1)^2(2)}{(3)^2} + \frac{3(3)^2}{12} = 8.9 \text{ kN·m}$$

The distribution and completed diagrams are given in Figure 15-31 on page 234. Note that the moment at support *B* is positive. The student should verify that this is compatible with the beam's curvature by sketching the deflected shape.

EXAMPLE 15-7

Construct the *V* and *M* diagrams for the continuous beam in Figure 15-32.

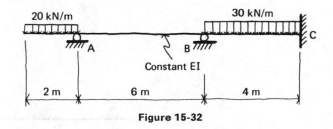

Figure 15-32

Solution: The distribution and diagrams are presented in Figure 15-33 on pages 235 and 236. Notice that the overhang is fully determinate, having shears and moments that are independent of the other two spans. It provides a fixed-end moment of 40 kN·m, but its free end prevents it from contributing any stiffness to joint *A*.

Problems

15-8. Use moment distribution to verify the results obtained in Example 15-2.

DF		1.0		0.400	0.600		0.0
FEM	−40.0	0.0		0.0	+40.0		−40.0
BAL		+40.0		−16.0	−24.0		0.0
CO		−8.0		+20.0	0.0		−12.0
BAL		+8.0		−8.0	−12.0		0.0
CO		−4.0		+4.0	0.0		−6.0
BAL		+4.0		−1.6	−2.4		0.0
TOT	−40.0	+40.0		−1.6	+1.6		−58.0

Figure 15-33. Moment distribution for Example 15-7.

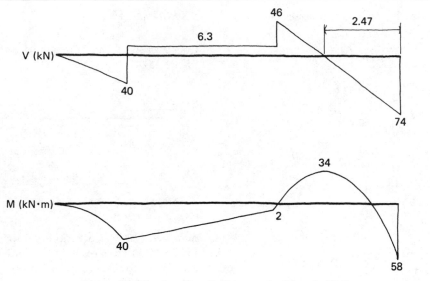

Figure 15-33. (continued) Diagrams for Example 15-7.

15-9. Construct the shear and moment diagrams for the beam in Figure 15-34.

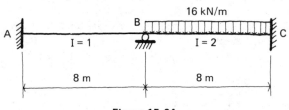

Figure 15-34

15-10. Work Problem 15-5 using moment distribution.

15-11. Construct the shear and moment diagrams for the beam in Figure 15-35.

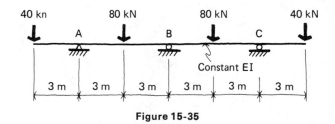

Figure 15-35

15-12. Knowing how the carryover factor was developed, determine the moment at B in Figure 15-36 by inspection and draw the moment diagram.

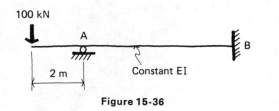

Figure 15-36

15-5 PINNED-END STIFFNESS REDUCTION

The moment distribution process can be shortened somewhat for those structures that have end spans that terminate in a pin or roller support. As illustrated in Examples 15-5 and 15-6, a distribution factor of unity at such supports is used to maintain the proper zero moment condition. This part of the distribution can be eliminated by taking into account the inherent difference in stiffness of a pinned end span as opposed to one with a fixed end. By doing this, we can leave such supports free to rotate (unlocked) from the start, thereby removing them from the balance and carryover process.

In the preceding section, it was found that the stiffness of a member with the opposite end fixed is given as

$$\frac{M_a}{\theta_a} = \frac{4EI}{L} \qquad (15\text{-}3a)$$

This will change if the member has a pin or roller end, as shown in Figure 15-37 on page 237.

Solving for θ_a using the second moment-area theorem, we get

$$\theta_a = \tan \theta_a = \frac{t_{b/a}}{L}$$

$$= \frac{[\frac{1}{2}(M_a/EI)(L)(2L/3)]}{L}$$

$$= \frac{M_a L}{3EI}$$

The stiffness will then be

$$\frac{M_a}{\theta_a} = \frac{3EI}{L} \qquad (15\text{-}3b)$$

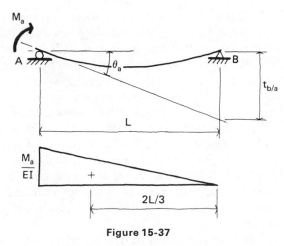

Figure 15-37

Comparing this with Equation (15-3a), we can state that the *relative* stiffness of a span that ends in a pin or roller will be $\frac{3}{4}(I/L)$.

If these supports are left unlocked for the distribution, a change must also be made in the fixed-end moment values. Previously, these end spans were assumed to have two fixed joints when the starting end moments were determined. Releasing one of the joints will permit the moment there to drop to zero. This unlocking amounts to a balance step, so one-half the moment will be carried over to the remaining fixed end. This can be verified by examining the formulas in Appendix V. Compare those cases with one end fixed and one end roller-supported to those cases with two fixed ends. The moment at the remaining fixed end is equal to the moment that was there when both ends were fixed *plus* one-half the moment that used to exist at the other end.

This shortcut or modification for spans that end in a pin or roller then consists of two parts: (1) computing the relative stiffness as $\frac{3}{4}(I/L)$, and (2) computing the fixed-end moment value at the continuous end as if the span had one end fixed and one end pinned. It is important to remember that this can only be done for spans that terminate the beam or frame with a pin or roller.

EXAMPLE 15-8

Rework the distribution part of Example 15-5 using the pinned-end modification.

Solution: The stiffness of span *AB* can be reduced while that of span *BC* remains the same.

$$\frac{3}{4}\left(\frac{I}{L}\right)_{ab} = \frac{3}{4}\left(\frac{1}{6}\right) = 0.125 \qquad \left(\frac{I}{L}\right)_{bc} = \frac{1}{8} = 0.125$$

The DF values at joint *B* will then be equal. The fixed-end moment values for span *AB* will also change. The FEM value at joint *A* will be zero while that at joint *B* can be found as case 8 of Appendix V.

$$\text{FEM}_{ba} = \frac{Pab}{2L^2}(a + L)$$

$$= \frac{80(3)(3)}{2(6)^2}(3 + 6) = 90 \text{ kN·m}$$

Comparing the distribution results in Figure 15-38 with the previous results of Figure 15-27, we see that, for this example, only two balances are now necessary to achieve the exact values. A fourth balance in the previous distribution is necessary to achieve similar results with rounding.

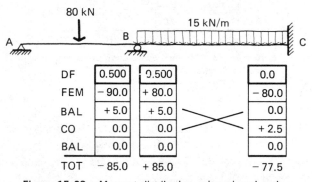

	80 kN		15 kN/m	

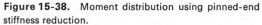

	A		B		C
DF		0.500	0.500		0.0
FEM		−90.0	+80.0		−80.0
BAL		+5.0	+5.0		0.0
CO		0.0	0.0		+2.5
BAL		0.0	0.0		0.0
TOT		−85.0	+85.0		−77.5

Figure 15-38. Moment distribution using pinned-end stiffness reduction.

EXAMPLE 15-9

Rework the distribution part of Example 15-6 using the pinned-end modification.

Solution: In this case, both end spans can make use of the shortcut, and the new stiffnesses and distribution factors will be

$$\frac{3}{4}\left(\frac{I}{L}\right)_{ab} = \frac{3}{4}\left(\frac{6}{2}\right) = 2.25 \qquad \left(\frac{I}{L}\right)_{bc} = \frac{8}{3} = 2.67$$

$$\frac{3}{4}\left(\frac{I}{L}\right)_{cd} = \frac{3}{4}\left(\frac{8}{3}\right) = 2.00$$

$$\text{DF}_{ba} = \frac{2.25}{2.25 + 2.67} = 0.457$$

$$\text{DF}_{bc} = \frac{2.67}{2.25 + 2.67} = 0.543$$

$$\text{DF}_{cb} = \frac{2.67}{2.67 + 2.00} = 0.572$$

$$\text{DF}_{cd} = \frac{2.00}{2.67 + 2.00} = 0.428$$

The modified FEM value at joint *C* can be obtained by using the "mirror images" of cases 8 and 9 in Appendix V or, more simply, from the previously computed values of Example 15-6.

$$\text{FEM}_{cd} = 15.6 + \tfrac{1}{2}(8.9)$$

$$= 20 \text{ kN·m}$$

The distribution in Figure 15-39 yields results that are essentially the same as those achieved previously using the basic method.

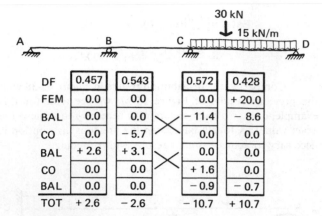

DF	0.457	0.543		0.572	0.428
FEM	0.0	0.0		0.0	+ 20.0
BAL	0.0	0.0		− 11.4	− 8.6
CO	0.0	− 5.7		0.0	0.0
BAL	+ 2.6	+ 3.1		0.0	0.0
CO	0.0	0.0		+ 1.6	0.0
BAL	0.0	0.0		− 0.9	− 0.7
TOT	+ 2.6	− 2.6		− 10.7	+ 10.7

Figure 15-39. Moment distribution using pinned-end stiffness reduction.

Problems

15-13. Verify the results of Example 15-4 by using moment distribution with pinned-end modifications.

15-14. Construct the V and M diagrams for the continuous beam of Figure 15-40.

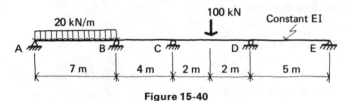

Figure 15-40

15-15. Determine the vertical reactions for the beam of constant EI in Figure 15-20.

15-16. Using the results of Example 15-3, determine the value of the moment at the wall for the beam in Figure 15-41.

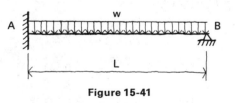

Figure 15-41

15-6 MOMENT DISTRIBUTION IN FRAMES

The best use of moment distribution is in the analysis of indeterminate frames. The principles and procedures developed for continuous beams can be applied without change, and the process is lengthened only by the size of the frame. With frames, the interaction of the members due to continuity becomes even more obvious. We shall see that moment is "drawn" to the stiffer members according to the distribution factors, and these members end up doing the most "work" to support the loads.

In this section, only frames without sidesway will be considered. Sidesway, which involves a loading pattern or configuration that causes lateral deflection of the joints and members, is discussed briefly in Section 15-10. To meet the no-sidesway condition, frames must be symmetrical and symmetrically loaded, or restrained in some manner so that the joints do not translate.

Before proceeding with the examples, it may be helpful to review Section 7-6, dealing with the shear and moment diagrams of frames. The diagrams for indeterminate frames are constructed in the same manner as those for determinate frames except that the joint moments are all known from the moment distribution procedure.

Before starting the V and M diagrams for a frame, it is helpful to make sure that the joints and members are in equilibrium by using free-body sketches. This will clarify the senses and also serve as a partial check on the distribution. It is also often helpful to sketch the probable deflected shape of the elastic curve. The senses indicated by the moment diagram must be consistent with a rational deflected shape. When sketching the deflected shape of a frame, remember that all corners remain right angles, and for frames without sidesway, corners rotate or tend to rotate but do not translate. Indicating the points of inflection on a deflected shape will also help with drawing the moment diagram.

EXAMPLE 15-10

Distribute the moments and construct the V and M diagrams for the frame in Figure 15-42.

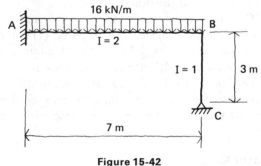

Figure 15-42

Solution: Obtain the distribution factors and fixed-end moment values.

$$\left(\frac{I}{L}\right)_{ab} = \frac{2}{7} = 0.286 \qquad \frac{3}{4}\left(\frac{I}{L}\right)_{bc} = \frac{3}{4}\left(\frac{1}{3}\right) = 0.250$$

$$\text{DF}_{ba} = \frac{0.286}{0.286 + 0.250} = 0.534$$

$$\text{DF}_{bc} = \frac{0.250}{0.286 + 0.250} = 0.466$$

$$\text{DF}_{ab} = 0.0$$

$$\text{FEM}_{ab} = \text{FEM}_{ba} = \frac{wL^2}{12} = \frac{16(7)^2}{12} = 65.3 \text{ kN·m}$$

The distribution and V and M diagrams are given in Figure 15-43. Reactions are presented in the free-body sketches as internal shears, to avoid confusion at the corners. The reader should take care to note all signs and senses and their consistency with the diagrams. Note particularly that the moments must be equal at a two-member corner.

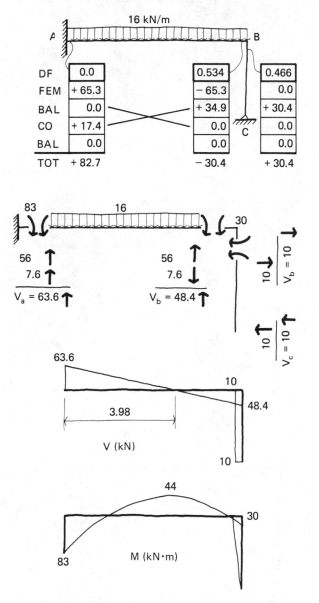

Figure 15-43. Moment distribution and V and M diagrams.

For frames, it is often easier to plot moment diagrams on the convex or tension side of the curvature, as discussed in Section 7-7. This diagram and the deflected shape of the frame appear in Figure 15-44.

EXAMPLE 15-11

Construct the shear and tension side moment diagram for the point-loaded frame in Figure 15-45.

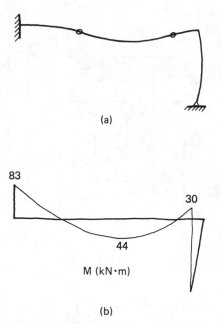

Figure 15-44. Deflected shape and tension side moment diagram for the frame of Example 15-10.

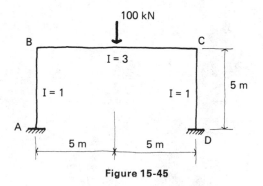

Figure 15-45

Solution: The distribution and diagrams appear in Figure 15-46. Notice that the procedures could have been shortened somewhat by taking advantage of symmetry. Also notice that the final distribution moments at the column bases are approximately one-half the moments at the column tops. This relationship will be exact if the final carryover step is performed and will hold for any unloaded span with a fixed end. The lower distribution blocks could have been deleted and one-half the final moment carried over, as illustrated in the free-body sketches.

The stiffer members of a frame as determined by I, L, and the end conditions will take more moment in the distribution process. If we change the stiffness of one of the members of a frame, we can change the entire moment diagram. Moment will be "drawn" away from the flexible members to the stiffer ones. It is possible to reduce peak moments in continuous structures by *reducing* the stiffness of the affected members. Stiffnesses can be changed by reducing or tapering the section, using pins or partially resistant connections and by changing the span.

The student should experiment with the simple frame of Example 15-11 to see the effects on the moment diagram

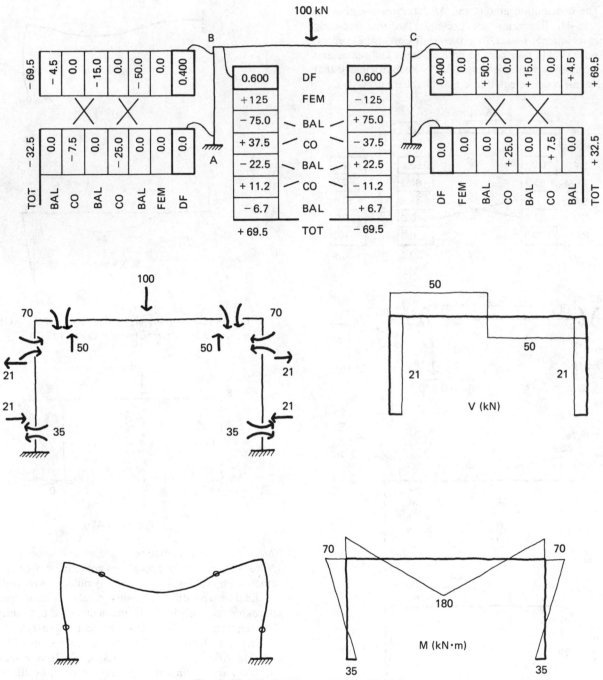

Figure 15-46. Solution to Example 15-11.

of changing the relative beam and column stiffnesses. For example, check to see if increasing the cross section of the columns will effectively reduce the large moment at midspan.

EXAMPLE 15-12

Construct the moment diagram for the frame in Figure 15-47.

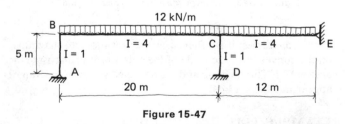

Figure 15-47

Solution: The distribution and diagrams are given in Figure 15-48. The distribution factors at joint C each represent the ratio of the stiffness of the member in question to the sum of all three stiffnesses. Each balance is then distributed to all three members. Partial shear diagrams are included to locate the points of maximum positive moment.

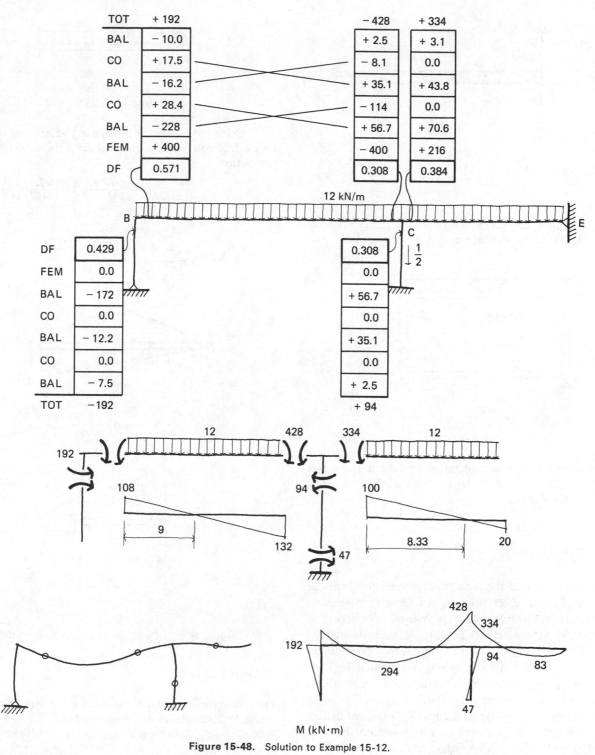

Figure 15-48. Solution to Example 15-12.

Problems

15-17. Rework Example 15-10 if the moments of inertia of the beam and column are made equal in value.

15-18. Distribute the moments and construct the moment diagram for the frame in Figure 15-49.

15-19. Construct the moment diagram for the frame in Figure 15-50. Assume *EI* as constant for all members.

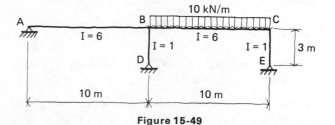

Figure 15-49

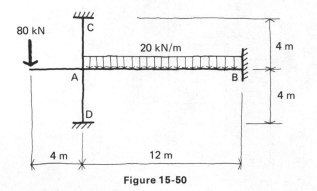

Figure 15-50

15-20. Determine the magnitude of moment that exists in side AD of the continuous box in Figure 15-51.

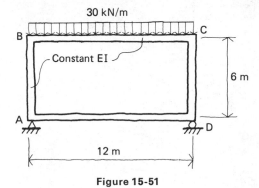

Figure 15-51

15-21. Construct the moment diagram for the continuous box in Figure 15-51 if the bottom side AD is also loaded by 30 kN/m.

15-7 DEFLECTION

Elastic deflections of the members between the joints or supports of continuous beams and frames can be computed using the conventional techniques developed in Chapter 10. As mentioned previously, such deflections are usually smaller than in comparable determinate structures, by virtue of the restraint provided by continuity. However, the lateral deflections of frames subject to sidesway can be considerable, often becoming major design factors in high-rise buildings. This type of deflection is related to joint translation and will not be considered here. Such deflections could, however, be determined by the same methods.

EXAMPLE 15-13

Determine the midspan deflection of the beam in Figure 15-52 in terms of w, L, and EI.

Solution: Use a conjugate beam with component M/EI loading.

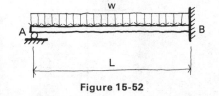

Figure 15-52

Using the free body in Figure 15-53(b), we can solve for the midspan moment that will equal the deflection in the real beam.

$$M_m = \frac{wL^3}{48EI}\left(\frac{L}{2}\right) + \frac{wL^3}{64EI}\left(\frac{L}{6}\right) - \frac{wL^3}{24EI}\left(\frac{3L}{16}\right)$$

$$= \frac{wL^4}{192EI}$$

$$\Delta_m = \frac{wL^4}{192EI}$$

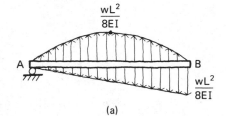

(a)

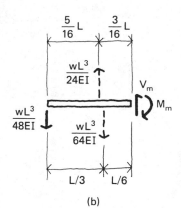

(b)

Figure 15-53. Conjugate beam with M/EI loading.

EXAMPLE 15-14

Determine the deflection of the beam at the load point for the frame in Example 15-11. Assume that I for the beam is $300(10)^6$ mm⁴, I for each column is $100(10)^6$ mm⁴, and $E = 200$ GPa.

Solution: Use moment-area techniques to find the rotation of one of the upper joints and establish a tangential deviation for the elastic curve at the load point.

Referring to Figure 15-54(a), the deflection at M is

$$\Delta_m = \nabla_m + t_{m/c}$$

which assumes that the tangential deviation will fall below the tangent line. Using the component moment diagrams in Figure 15-54(b) and the first moment-area theorem, we can find θ_c.

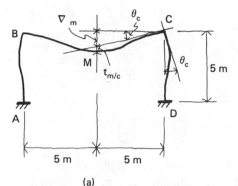

(a)

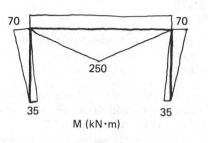

M (kN·m)

(b)

Figure 15-54

$$\theta_c = \frac{1}{2}\left(\frac{70}{EI}\right)(5) - \frac{1}{2}\left(\frac{35}{EI}\right)(5)$$

$$= \frac{87.5}{EI} \text{ kN·m}^2$$

Letting the moment of inertia of the beam be represented as $3I$ (where I is the column moment of inertia), we can find ∇_m and $t_{m/c}$.

$$\nabla_m = \theta_c(5)$$

$$= \frac{87.5}{EI}(5)$$

$$= \frac{437.5}{EI} \text{ kN·m}^3$$

From the second moment-area theorem and recognizing that areas of positive curvature will cause upward deviations and areas of negative curvature will cause downward deviations,

$$t_{m/c} = \frac{1}{2}\left(\frac{250}{3EI}\right)(5)\left(\frac{5}{3}\right) - \frac{70}{3EI}(5)\left(\frac{5}{2}\right) = \frac{55.5}{EI} \text{ kN·m}^3 \text{ up}$$

Therefore, the $t_{m/c}$ is actually subtractive from ∇_m and not additive as assumed in Figure 15-54(a).

$$\Delta_m = \frac{437.5}{EI} - \frac{55.5}{EI}$$

$$= \frac{382}{EI} \text{ kN·m}^3$$

$$= \frac{382 \text{ kN·m}^3}{[200(10)^6 \text{ kN/m}^2][100(10)^{-6} \text{ m}^4]}$$

$$= 0.019 \text{ m}$$

$$= 19 \text{ mm}$$

Problems

15-22. Use moment-area or conjugate beam techniques to show that the midspan deflection of a uniformly loaded fixed-end beam is $wL^4/384EI$.

15-23. Compute the deflection (as a function of EI) at the free end of the beam of Example 15-7.

15-24. Determine the deflection at midspan of the beam BC in the frame of Example 15-12. Assume that I for the beam is $400(10)^6$ mm^4, I for each column is $100(10)^6$ mm^4, and E equals 200 GPa.

15-8 SUPPORT SETTLEMENT

In Section 15-1, it was mentioned that structures with continuity are more subject to damage by foundation settlement. That this is the case is easily seen in Figure 15-55. The determinate spans in Figure 15-55(a) are able to accommodate the slight change in support heights with virtually no additional stresses, while the continuous spans in Figure 15-55(b) assume S-shaped curvatures and develop moment accordingly. Depending on the severity of the settlement, the loading conditions, and the stiffness of the members, these moments can precipi-

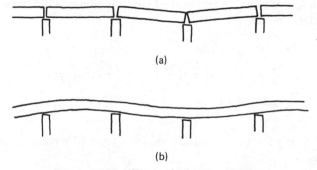

(a)

(b)

Figure 15-55. Effects of support settlement.

tate a structural failure. Reinforced concrete structures present a particular concern because of the placement of reinforcing bars to receive the tensile stresses of bending. Under normal loading conditions, the support moments will be negative and the steel placed near the top of the cross section. If settlement occurs, it is possible that this moment could change in sign, placing the unreinforced bottom fibers in tension. This is one of the reasons why most structural concrete codes require some reinforcing at these points.

Independent of the superstructure material, foundations are always designed to avoid or minimize differential settlements, because such changes invariably act to increase the moment at one or more critical sections. These increases can be analyzed using moment distribution if the settlements can be predicted or assumed. If the joints at the two end supports of a span are assumed to be locked and one support is displaced an amount Δ with respect to the other, the joints will develop equal fixed-end moments. For the displacement shown in Figure 15-56, the FEM values will be positive by our moment distribution convention as the member attempts

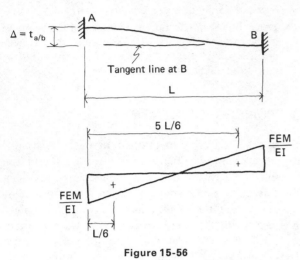

Figure 15-56

to turn each of the joints in a clockwise manner. The relationship between the displacement and the moment developed can be established using the second moment-area theorem.

$$\Delta = t_{a/b}$$
$$= \frac{1}{2}\left(\frac{FEM}{EI}\right)\left(\frac{L}{2}\right)\left(\frac{5L}{6}\right) - \frac{1}{2}\left(\frac{FEM}{EI}\right)\left(\frac{L}{2}\right)\left(\frac{L}{6}\right)$$
$$= \frac{FEM(L)^2}{6EI}$$

Solving for the magnitude of the fixed-end moment, we get

$$FEM = \frac{6EI\Delta}{L^2} \qquad (15\text{-}4a)$$

A similar relationship can be found for a pinned-end span with its lesser stiffness. Referring to Figure 15-57, we get

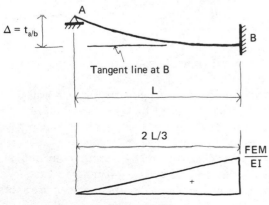

Figure 15-57

$$\Delta = t_{a/b}$$
$$= \frac{1}{2}\left(\frac{FEM}{EI}\right)(L)\left(\frac{2L}{3}\right)$$
$$= \frac{FEM(L)^2}{3EI}$$

or

$$FEM = \frac{3EI\Delta}{L^2} \qquad (15\text{-}4b)$$

Once the fixed-end moment values have been determined, the moments can be distributed to determine the final moments due to the settlement.

EXAMPLE 15-15

Determine the moments that result in the beam of Figure 15-26 if support B undergoes a settlement of 30 mm. Let E equal 20 GPa and I equal $3000(10)^6$ mm⁴.

Solution: First determine the moment diagram due to settlement alone, and then add these moments to the ones previously obtained and given in Figure 15-29.

Figure 15-58(a) shows the settlement at support B with the joint locked to get the fixed-end moments. The different end conditions will result in different FEM values.

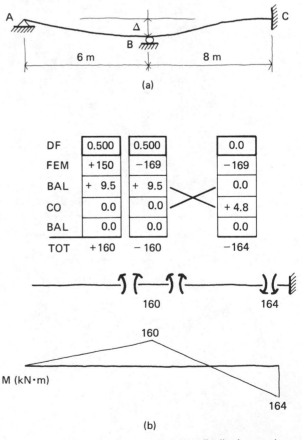

(a)

DF	0.500	0.500		0.0
FEM	+150	−169		−169
BAL	+ 9.5	+ 9.5		0.0
CO	0.0	0.0		+ 4.8
BAL	0.0	0.0		0.0
TOT	+160	− 160		−164

(b)

Figure 15-58. Settlement moment distribution and diagram.

$$\text{FEM}_{ba} = \frac{3EI\Delta}{L^2}$$

$$= \frac{3[20(10)^6 \text{ kN/m}^2][3000(10)^{-6} \text{ m}^4]0.030 \text{ m}}{(6 \text{ m})^2}$$

$$= 150 \text{ kN·m}$$

$$\text{FEM}_{bc} = \text{FEM}_{cb} = \frac{6EI\Delta}{L^2}$$

$$= \text{FEM}_{cb} = \frac{6[20(10)^6 \text{ kN/m}^2][3000(10)^{-6} \text{ m}^4]0.030 \text{ m}}{(8 \text{ m})^2}$$

$$= \text{FEM}_{cb} = 169 \text{ kN·m}$$

The distribution and final moments due to settlement are shown in Figure 15-58(b). The distribution factors were obtained using the pinned-end modification.

The final V and M diagrams due to the load and the settlement acting together are shown in Figure 15-59, and it is easy to see that a settlement of this magnitude can have serious consequences.

EXAMPLE 15-16

Construct the final moment diagram for the frame of Example 15-12 if the left-hand column settles an amount equal to 30 mm. Assume that I for the beam is $400(10)^6$ mm⁴, I for each column is $100(10)^6$ mm⁴, and E equals 200 GPa.

Solution: The fixed-end moments that result in the beam due to a displacement of 30 mm with the joints locked are obtained as

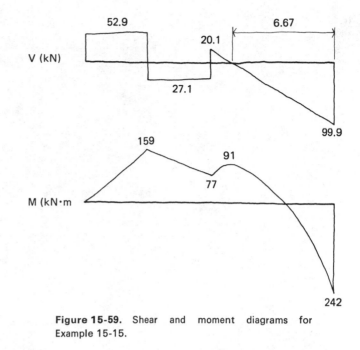

Figure 15-59. Shear and moment diagrams for Example 15-15.

$$\text{FEM}_{bc} = \text{FEM}_{cb} = \frac{6EI\Delta}{L^2}$$

$$= \frac{6[200(10)^6 \text{ kN/m}^2][400(10)^{-6} \text{ m}^4]0.030 \text{ m}}{(20 \text{ m})^2}$$

$$= 36 \text{ kN·m}$$

The distribution and moment diagram for the effects of settlement alone are given in Figure 15-60 on pages 245 and 246.

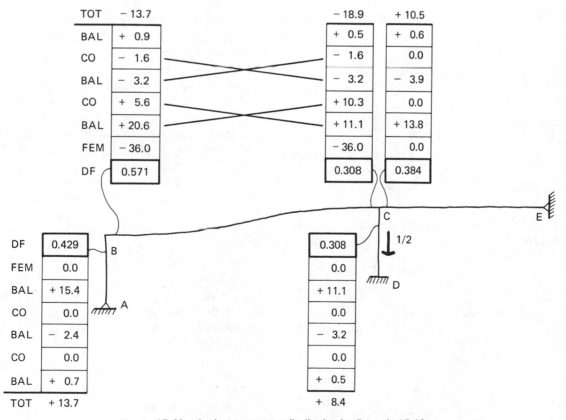

Figure 15-60. Settlement moment distribution for Example 15-16.

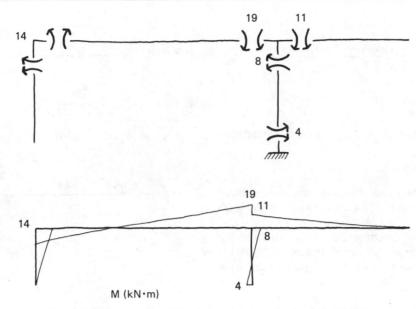

Figure 15-60. (continued) Settlement moments for Example 15-16.

These moments can be added to those previously obtained due to the loads, which will result in the final diagram in Figure 15-61.

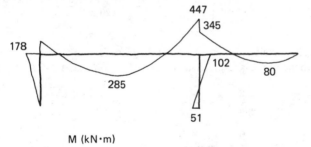

M (kN·m)

Figure 15-61. Solution to Example 15-16.

Problems

15-25. Construct the final moment diagram for the continuous beam of Example 15-6 if the support at *C* settles downward a distance of 20 mm. Assume that *E* equals 10 000 MPa and *I* equals 50(10)⁶ mm⁴.

15-26. Rework Example 15-16 if the right-hand column is displaced instead of the left-hand one.

15-27. Construct the moment diagram due to the lateral load in Figure 15-62 if it displaces the column tops by

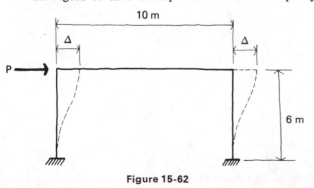

Figure 15-62

10 mm. Let *EI* be constant for the entire frame at 40 000 kN·m².

15-28. Using the results of Problem 15-27, determine the magnitude of the load *P* necessary to establish horizontal equilibrium of the entire frame in Figure 15-62.

15-9 ESTIMATING FRAME MOMENTS

After some practice with moment distribution and moment diagrams, it becomes possible to make reasonably accurate "guesses" as to the magnitudes and senses of the moment ordinates. This is especially true of simple frames of one or two bays carrying uniform loads. The deflected shape of such a frame is relatively easy to visualize, and, using the principles of joint equilibrium and the relationship between moment and curvature, a *qualitative* moment diagram can be sketched. This type of moment diagram represents approximate magnitudes graphically and has no numbers. In terms of investigating the structural implications of alternative design configurations, such sketches can be most valuable. Knowing where the moments are high and low and how a frame is bending provides a much quicker insight into how the structure is "working" than any moment distribution or other numerical procedure.

Figure 15-63 shows three simple frames with their deflected shapes and qualitative tension-side moment diagrams. The dimensions are relative but no moments of inertia have been provided. In general, one can assume that beams and girders have larger cross sections than do columns. The reader should study these frames and attempt to rationalize the diagrams. Particular attention should be paid to the way in which the moment ordinates act to maintain rotational equilibrium at the joints. The

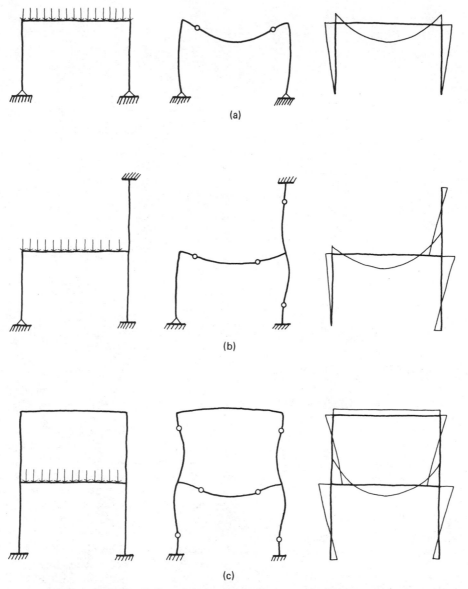

Figure 15-63. Deflected shapes and qualitative moment diagrams.

diagrams also attempt to reflect the relative stiffness (resistance to rotation) of the joints. For example, the right end of the beam in Figure 15-63(b) is connected to a much stiffer joint than is the left end. The right end approximates a fixed end, while the left end acts much more like a pin connection and the moment diagram reflects this difference in the magnitudes of the end moments. Similarly, compare the moment diagrams for the beams of Figure 15-63(a) and (c). The ends of the beam in the one-story frame have less resistance to rotation than those in the two-story frame, where two columns are present at each joint. This means that the one-story roof beam will deflect more and have a large positive moment at midspan, unlike the two-story floor beam, which has less deflection and larger negative end moments.

It can be seen that uniformly loaded beams having continuity with columns and other beams of similar loads and spans will generally have moment diagrams bounded by the extremes given in Figure 15-64. End moments can be estimated as fractions of wL^2, depending upon the stiffness of the end connections compared to these three cases. This information, coupled with the fact that equilibrium of the joints must always be maintained, enables us to make educated guesses about the magnitudes of these moment ordinates. Positive moments can then be approximated using component diagrams.

After studying the examples that follow, the student can practice by estimating the moments for the frames of the examples and problems of Section 15-6 for which the answers are given. The author has found that after some practice many students, particularly those with a good grasp of the concepts of moment distribution, can usually estimate the larger moment values within 15

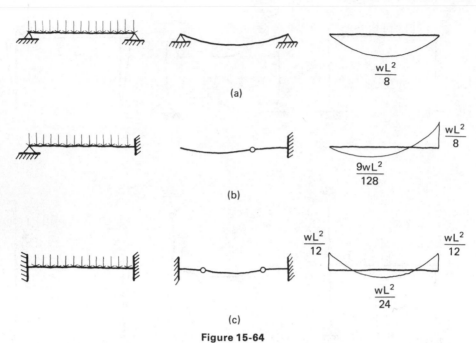

Figure 15-64

or 20%. Smaller moments are much more difficult to assess, but then, of course, these are seldom critical to the design.

In making estimates, it can help to keep the following points in mind:

1. Beams are longer than columns but usually have I values several times as large.
2. Start by ascertaining which way the joints will rotate or tend to rotate under the loads.
3. Joint equilibrium must be maintained.
4. Spans of dissimilar length and/or uneven loads will often cause end moments larger than those due to full fixity.
5. The principle of superposition applies, and loads can be treated one at a time.
6. Moments in overhangs are always determinate.

EXAMPLE 15-17

Estimate the moments for the two frames in Figure 15-65 and sketch the approximate moment diagrams.

Solution: First draw the deflected shapes and the qualitative moment diagrams. Note that in each case, the load will rotate joint A clockwise and joint B counterclockwise. The joints of the one-story frame will rotate more than those of the two-story frame because of the difference in restraint provided by the columns (see Figure 15-66).

Now compare the end joints of the two beams with respect to fixity, recognizing that the negative moment in each beam would be $wL^2/12$ if fully fixed and would approach zero if the connection acted like a pin. Obviously, the ends of the beam are less "fixed" in the one-story frame than in the two-story frame. While the end moments in both cases will be less than $wL^2/12$, they are clearly not equal. In this case, accurate estimates would be about $wL^2/30$ and $wL^2/20$,

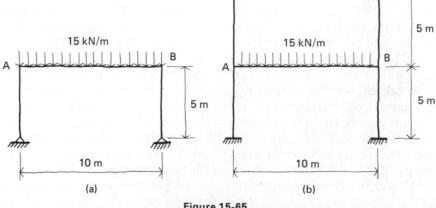

Figure 15-65

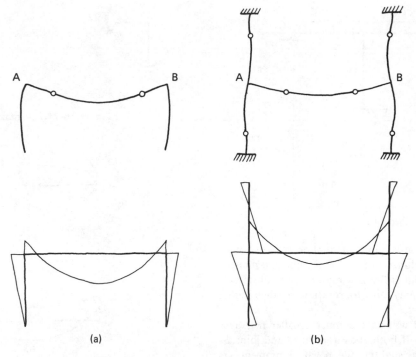

Figure 15-66. Deflected shapes and qualitative moment diagrams.

respectively. For the loads given, the equivalent numerical values are 50 kN·m and 75 kN·m.

Joint equilibrium at *A* for each frame is established in Figure 15-67. Since the upper and lower columns of the two-story frame are of equal stiffness, they will act equally to oppose the beam moment.

The positive moment values can be found by algebraically adding the simple beam moments to those created by the end fixity. The column end moments for the two-story frame are found using the carryover factor. Final diagrams are given in Figure 15-68, where the values have been rounded to whole numbers. In reality, rounding the values even further, say to the nearest 10 kN·m in this case, would better reflect the accuracy of such estimations.

EXAMPLE 15-18

Construct an estimated moment diagram for the frame in Figure 15-69.

Solution: Sketch the deflected shape noting the difference in stiffness between joints *A* and *B*. Joint *B* will probably rotate counterclockwise a small amount, removing most of the positive curvature (and moment) from span *BC*. The

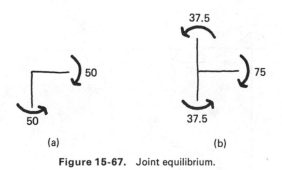

Figure 15-67. Joint equilibrium.

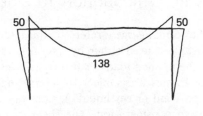

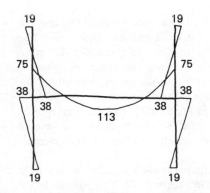

Figure 15-68. Estimated moment values for Example 15-17.

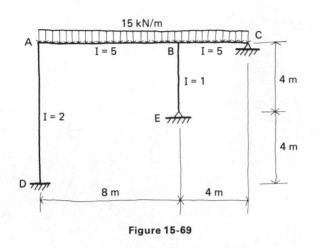

Figure 15-69

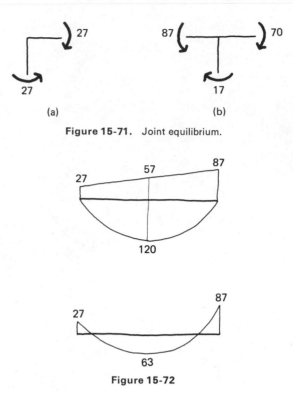

Figure 15-71. Joint equilibrium.

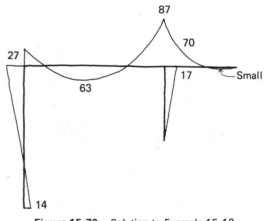

Figure 15-72

two beams will have negative moments that are almost equal at joint B because the column with its low I value and pinned end adds little to the joint stiffness. Columns without lateral load develop moment only due to rotation of their ends caused by other members.

Clearly, beam AB will have a much smaller negative moment at A than at B. If both ends were fixed and joint B rotated counterclockwise slightly, the negative moment at B would decrease from $wL^2/12$ to about $wL^2/13$ or $wL^2/14$. But the end at A is not fixed. Considering the other extreme, if A acted like a pin, the negative moment at B would be $wL^2/8$ or slightly less, say, $wL^2/9$. This indicates the moment at B will be someplace between $wL^2/9$ and $wL^2/14$, say $wL^2/11$, or about $87\ kN \cdot m$. Since the long column at A provides the only restraint to this end of the beam, the moment should be small, say $wL^2/35$, or about $27\ kN \cdot m$.

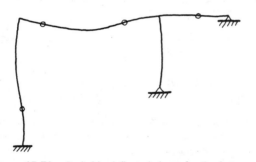

Figure 15-70. Probable deflected shape for the frame of Example 15-18.

The span BC is like a beam with one fixed end and one pinned end except that the fixed end has been rotated to create even more negative moment in this short stiff span. This is consistent with our previous reasoning regarding the inability of the column at B to take much moment, so the beam moments would have to be of similar magnitude. Joint moment values are given in Figure 15-71 to force joint equilibrium. The distribution of the 87-kN·m moment at joint B is made so it corresponds roughly to the different member stiffnesses.

The midspan moment in span AB is easily obtained from the component diagrams in Figure 15-72. This will not be the maximum positive moment because of the lack of symmetry,

but will be reasonably close. The positive moment in span BC will be very small.

The final results appear in Figure 15-73 and the values are reasonably correct when compared to those achieved by moment distribution.

Figure 15-73. Solution to Example 15-18.

15-10 INTRODUCTION TO SIDESWAY

The term *sidesway* refers to the lateral displacement of a frame caused either by lateral loads or by asymmetry in the applied loads or frame stiffness. Since most building frames are subject to lateral loading of some type (e.g., wind or earthquake), sidesway can be a significant design consideration. The shears, moments, and deflections must be absorbed by sidesway of the frame itself or a secondary bracing system. Approximate techniques for determining sidesway forces are presented in Chapter 16, and these are more than sufficient for the purposes of most preliminary designs.

If necessary, a more accurate analysis can be made using the concepts developed in Section 15-8 on support settlement. Using a one-story frame as an example, the frame is first analyzed for gravity loads as if some unknown horizontal restraining force was acting to prevent sidesway. From equilibrium of the column moments and shears, the magnitude and sense of this imaginary restraining force can be determined. Next, it is assumed that the frame carries no load but that the upper joints are displaced laterally, causing arbitrary but relative moments in the columns. After these moments are distributed, the resulting column moments can again be used to determine the force that caused the displacement. The final moments are achieved by adding the moments from the gravity loads alone (sidesway prevented) to a certain fraction of the sidesway moments. This fraction is the ratio of the restraining force to the displacing force.

These procedures become more complicated with frames of several stories and are considerably beyond the scope of this text. The interested reader is urged to pursue the subject by consulting one of the many texts devoted to the analysis of indeterminate structures.

16-1 INTRODUCTION

There are two major sources of lateral loads on buildings: wind and earthquake. The intensity and frequency of these loads in various regions of the United States are depicted in the maps of Appendix N. It can be seen that many areas have either high winds or significant earthquake activity or both. Building codes generally do not require that a structure be designed to resist a simultaneous occurrence of critical wind and earthquake forces. Such a combination is highly improbable. By the same token, local codes frequently specify design loads that are above those recommended by "model" codes for wind and occasionally for earthquakes. Maps such as those in Appendix N are only best estimates and precedence is given to the applicable local or municipal code.

While these two phenomena are very different in their nature, development, behavior, and effects on structures, they do have two factors in common. First, they are both lateral forces that must be resisted in some manner by the building structure, either through the development of additional stresses in the gravity load-carrying elements, or by a separate lateral bracing system, or both. Second, the magnitudes of the forces involved generally increase with building height (i.e., wind and earthquake forces play a greater role in the design of tall buildings than in low buildings).

Lateral loads have several effects on a building frame. They usually increase certain axial forces, shears, and bending moments and decrease others. Of these various effects, increase in bending moment is the least tolerable. The design of moment-resisting frames above four or five stories in height can easily be governed by the lateral loads, even though appropriate increases in allowable stresses or decreases in load factors are included. Lateral loads also cause deflection or "drift," which can become important in terms of damage to partitions and building services by racking. Additionally, in tall buildings, continuous sway under high wind load could reach the level where the accompanying acceleration is perceptible and therefore physically uncomfortable.

In designing for lateral load, Figure 16-1 shows qualitatively the influence of height on the weight (and cost) of building structure. Depending on the particular structural systems and techniques selected for resisting the effects of gravity and lateral loads, and the magnitude of those loads, the premium for increased height can be significant.

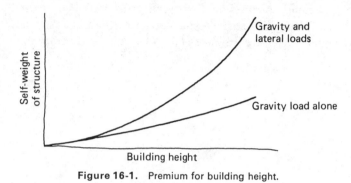

Figure 16-1. Premium for building height.

16-2 WIND LOADS AND DISTRIBUTION

As expected, wind pressures vary with wind velocity, although not in a proportional manner. Equation (16-1) expresses this relationship as measured from wind tunnel tests. The constant, 0.000 047, accounts for the change in units. The wind pressure q is usually modified by factors to account for the effect of gusting and building shape.

$$q = 0.000\ 047V^2 \qquad (16\text{-}1)$$

where q = wind pressure on a surface normal to the wind (kN/m²)
V = wind velocity (km/hr)

16

Consideration of Lateral Loads

As determined empirically, wind velocities vary with the height above grade and the surface roughness. In general, the wind speed and the corresponding pressure will increase with height up to a point referred to as the *gradient height*, h_g. The gradient height is the altitude at which the wind velocity is no longer affected by the surface features of the ground. This gradient altitude will be much higher over an urban area with many closely spaced tall buildings, than it will be over a flat open terrain without obstructions. Gradient heights have been estimated to be approximately 500 m above major cities, 400 m over suburban areas and 300 m over open terrain. It may be assumed that at these altitudes the wind velocities will be equal.

For each situation, the wind velocities below the gradient height will vary exponentially with the degree of surface roughness. This relationship is given by Equation (16-2) and is shown graphically in Figure 16-2(a)

$$V_1 = V_g \left(\frac{h_1}{h_g}\right)^\alpha \qquad (16\text{-}2)$$

where V_1 = velocity at height h_1

V_g = velocity at height h_g, the gradient height

and α is a factor which accounts for surface roughness. Typical values for α are $\frac{1}{3}$ for urban areas, $\frac{1}{5}$ for suburban areas, and $\frac{1}{7}$ for open terrain.

The wind velocity map in Appendix N provides design wind speeds over flat open terrain at an altitude of approximately 10 m. Equation (16-2) can be used to establish the velocity at the gradient height of 300 m for open terrain using an α value of $\frac{1}{7}$. From this the velocities for other altitudes and other roughness conditions can be obtained. For example, if the design wind value for a given region is 130 km/hr as measured 10 m above a flat plane, then Equation (16-2) tells us that the wind velocity at the gradient height is 210 km/hr. This means that the wind speed is about 210 km/hr at 300 m

above flat terrain, 400 m above a suburban area, and 500 m above a large city. Using the same equation with different α values and gradient heights, we can generate the values shown in Table 16-1. These velocities can be translated into pressures using Equation (16-1) and modified, as previously mentioned, for the effects of gusting and building shape. Since curved pressure distributions are awkward to work with, the design pressures are often presented as step-functions, such as the one shown in Figure 16-2(b).

TABLE 16-1 *Wind Velocities for a Design Wind of 130 km/hr*

	Wind velocity (km/hr)		
Height (m)	*Open terrain*	*Suburban*	*Urban*
10	130	100	60
30	150	125	80
90	175	155	120
300	210	200	175
400	210	210	195
500	210	210	210

Once the pressures that act on the side of a building are known, the uniform loads are converted to a series of concentrated loads to act on the building frame. This is done by using the tributary area of the exterior wall so the magnitude of each load is usually a direct function of the column spacing.

Wind creates pressures or suctions on building surfaces, depending upon the angles of incidence between the wind direction and the surfaces. In general, pressures are created on windward surfaces that have an included angle of more than about 30° between the wind direction and the surface plane. Suctions are generated on all parallel and leeward surfaces. Such suction forces can be considerable and become critical with respect to the

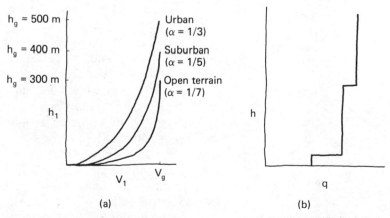

Figure 16-2. Actual wind velocity curves versus a typical code-specified pressure distribution.

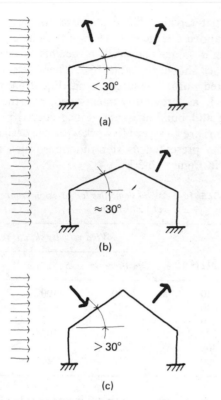

Figure 16-3. Wind effects on gable angles.

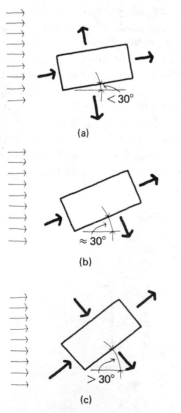

Figure 16-4. Wind effects on plan orientation.

fastening of the skin or cladding to the building frame. Lightweight residential and commercial siding or curtain-wall components are often pulled off at building corners by the powerful "eddy" forces there. Tornados and hurricanes can lift entire roofs from small buildings by airfoil action unless proper anchorage is provided.

16-3 EARTHQUAKES

It is now generally accepted that earthquakes are caused by movements of the large plates that make up the upper mantle or crust of the earth. As one plate moves with respect to another, fault systems are developed along their common edges and these constitute the location of the more severe earthquakes. The crust of the earth, like most materials, is somewhat elastic, and as this gradual plate motion takes place, elastic strains build up along the faulted areas. When the inevitable slippage takes place, this stored energy is suddenly released, resulting in an earthquake. The phenomenon can be conceptualized as the same kind of action that takes place when you bend a plastic ruler back with your forefinger. Eventually, the end of the ruler slips out from under your finger and energy is released through vibration.

The frequency and magnitude of earthquakes is directly related to plate activity. Currently, the two most active areas are along the boundaries of the Pacific plate (one large sea-floor plate) and at the junction of the African plate and the Eurasian plate. Thus, we have many quakes along the western borders of the Americas, the eastern edges of Asia, and in the eastern Mediterranean countries. Seismic activity is by no means limited to these locations, however, and some of the biggest earthquakes have occurred elsewhere. The zone map in Appendix N provides a measure of previous activity for various regions of the United States, and it is easily seen that earthquakes are not restricted to the West Coast states.

Actually, most quakes do very little damage. Thousands occur annually but are so small as to be hardly noticed. The amount of energy released from a particular earthquake and its consequent damage potential are functions of the depth of the focus (place of rupture), the local soil conditions, and the type and size of the fault system. In some cases, earthquakes of only moderate intensity, in terms of energy release, can be just as destructive as larger ones.

Earthquake intensity can be measured by two different scales. One is the *Richter scale* (after Charles Richter, an American seismologist), which provides a relative measure of the total energy release by using seismograph readings. The Richter magnitude of an earthquake is defined as the logarithm of the amplitude of the largest shock wave measured at a normalized distance from the epicenter. The logarithmic effect and the fact that total energy release is not proportional to amplitude combines to give us the end result that each whole number on the Richter scale represents an approximate 30-fold increase in energy output. Thus, a Richter reading of 8 means an energy release about 30 times greater than a Richter 7 and about 900 times greater than a Richter 6. This extreme degree of nonlinearity must be kept in mind; there would be little difference between a 5.5 and a 5.6 quake, but an 8.6 would be much more destructive than an 8.5.

The other scale is called the *Modified Mercalli* or *MM scale* and is named for Giuseppe Mercalli (1850–1914), an Italian scientist. It was modified by others in 1931. It is based on observations made by trained observers in the area of ground motion and has 12 levels of intensity, designated by Roman numerals. The full scale of effects can be found in any book devoted to earthquakes or seismic design, and only a few representative notations are given here. For example, an MM IV would be designated if minor tremors can be felt by most people, windows rattle, and wooden walls and frames creak; MM VII would indicate that people become frightened, pictures fall, furniture shifts, and cracks develop in some masonry walls; and an MM X would mean general panic, cracks open in the ground, and many buildings collapse.

The largest shock amplitudes generally occur soon after the start of the quake motion, which may have a duration of several seconds to somewhat less than a minute. However, many earthquakes are accompanied by significant "aftershocks" occurring from several hours to several days after the main shock. These "secondary" adjustments in the earth's crust can disrupt rescue and salvage operations and cause further damage to already weakened structures.

With respect to buildings, earthquakes can precipitate four kinds of damaging effects:

1. The actual displacement that occurs along the fault line.
2. Ground shaking or vibration.
3. Ground failure, such as landslides and liquefaction.
4. Tsunamis, or large sea waves.

Of these effects, the damage is usually greatest from numbers 2 and 3. Ground slippage along fault planes can be very dramatic but seldom affects a large number of structures. Tsunamis can be very destructive in low-lying coastal areas and can be generated by earthquakes far away. However, in many cases, warning and evacuation are possible, minimizing the loss of life.

Ground shaking, on the other hand, can be widespread and very destructive, depending upon its magnitude and duration. Without special considerations, most materials cannot withstand many cycles of loading at high stress levels, and structural design efforts have typically been directed at controlling these stresses.

Ground failure is also recognized as a major cause of earthquake damage. Liquefaction, or the saturation of granular bearing soils, can be particularly destructive. It is caused by vibration that results in a "suspension" of granular or sandy soils, making them behave much like quicksand.

16-4 EARTHQUAKE LOADS AND DISTRIBUTION

Currently, there is considerable research activity in the field of aseismic or earthquake resistant design. Studies involve site selection, soil properties, structural behavior, building configuration, and policy implementation. Therefore, any design approach or method is subject to considerable change in the near future. The most frequently used approach to the quantification of earthquake design loads was developed by the Structural Engineers Association of California (SEAOC) in the late 1950s and has been revised about every three years since then. Most model codes have adopted the revisions as they appear, and it is likely that such updating will continue as we learn more from the many research efforts in progress.

Buildings respond differently to ground motion, depending upon many factors. One of the most important of these involves the natural frequency of the building, which, in turn, is a function of many parameters, including building height, plan dimensions, and frame stiffness. This natural or first harmonic frequency, the distribution of mass, and the damping characteristics of the construction system will all influence the various modes of vibration that the building will develop in response to an earthquake. The ground acceleration results from vibration, so it is cyclic, reversing direction in fractions of a second (Figure 16-5). Unlike wind loads, the forces acting on the various parts of a building are inertial and are directly related to the mass and acceleration of that part.

The first step in quantifying these forces is to establish a value for the design shear force at grade: How much force does the ground mass suddenly apply to the base of the structure? This can be approximated for design purposes by the formula

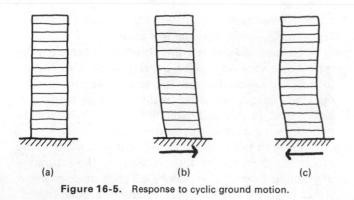

Figure 16-5. Response to cyclic ground motion.

$$V = ZIKCSW \qquad (16\text{-}3)$$

where V = base shear force (N)

Z = coefficient based upon seismic zone map

I = occupancy importance factor

K = coefficient representing seismic resistance of building structural system

C = coefficient based upon predicted natural period of building

S = coefficient based upon site and structure resonance

W = total dead weight of the building (including mechanical equipment) (N)

As indicated in this formula, the design shear force will be a certain fraction of the total dead weight, as determined by the five coefficients. The seismic zone for any place in the United States may be obtained from Appendix N, and Z is then evaluated from Table 16-2. The factors I and K can be read from Tables 16-3 and 16-4, respectively.

TABLE 16-2 *Seismic Zone Coefficient*

Z	*Earthquake zone*
0	0
0.1875	1
0.375	2
0.75	3
1.00	4

TABLE 16-3 *Occupancy Importance Factors*

I	*Type of occupancy*
1.5	Essential facilities, such as hospitals, police and fire stations, and municipal disaster stations
1.25	Places of public assembly for more than 300 persons
1.0	All others

TABLE 16-4 *Structural System Factors*

K	*Lateral load system*
1.33	Separate bracing system to take all lateral loads; shear wall systems
0.80	Combination shear wall, shear truss (or other lateral bracing system) and moment resisting frame; shear system designed to resist 100% of forces and frame designed to resist 25% of forces
0.67	Ductile moment resisting frame designed to take 100% of lateral forces
1.00	Other building systems
2.50	Elevated tanks
2.00	Nonbuilding structures

The coefficient C can be obtained as

$$C = \frac{1}{15\sqrt{T}} \qquad (16\text{-}4)$$

where T equals predicted natural period of vibration of the building (s). C is never taken as greater than 0.12.

The value of T can be approximated by Equation (16-5a) or (16-5b) whichever is applicable, but is not to be taken as less than 0.3 s in any event. For most buildings,

$$T = \frac{0.09h}{\sqrt{D}} \qquad (16\text{-}5a)$$

where h = building height (m)

D = plan dimension of building at grade in a direction parallel to the lateral forces (m)

For buildings with a 100% ductile moment resisting frame ($K = 0.67$), T is better approximated by

$T = 0.10$ times the number of stories above grade

$$(16\text{-}5b)$$

The coefficient S for building and site interaction can be computed by Equation (16-6a) or (16-6b), depending upon the ratio of the building period to the characteristic site period, T_s. However, S is never to be taken as less than 1.0. The value of T_s can be established by a geotechnical analysis of the site and is limited to the range 0.5 to 2.5 s. When

$$\frac{T}{T_s} \le 1.0, \quad S = 1.0 + \frac{T}{T_s} - 0.5\left(\frac{T}{T_s}\right)^2 \qquad (16\text{-}6a)$$

When

$$\frac{T}{T_s} > 1.0, \quad S = 1.2 + 0.6\frac{T}{T_s} - 0.3\left(\frac{T}{T_s}\right)^2 \qquad (16\text{-}6b)$$

In the absence of a proper determination of the value of T_s, S is to be taken as 1.5.

The following example will illustrate the determination of the base shear for a typical rectangular building block. The ground acceleration has been assumed parallel to the building's long dimension, as this is usually the critical direction.

EXAMPLE 16-1

Determine the base shear force V for the 14-story commercial building in Figure 16-6. It is located in San Francisco and the characteristic site frequency, T_s, has been determined as 2.0 s. It has a separate core system to carry the full lateral load and a moment resisting frame designed for 25% of these loads. A typical floor (and the roof) has a dead load value of 6 kN/m², which includes an allowance for all structural members. The seventh floor has some heavy mechanical equipment, so the average dead load for that floor is 9 kN/m².

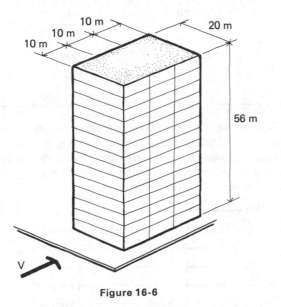

Figure 16-6

Solution: First compute the total dead weight above grade. Assume the first floor to be at grade and therefore not included. Twelve floors and one roof gives us a dead weight of

$$13 \times 20\text{ m} \times 30\text{ m} \times 6\text{ kN/m}^2 = 46\ 800\text{ kN}$$

The mechanical floor weighs

$$1 \times 20\text{ m} \times 30\text{ m} \times 9\text{ kN/m}^2 = \underline{5\ 400\text{ kN}}$$
$$\text{Total } W = \overline{52\ 200\text{ kN}}$$

From the map in Appendix N, San Francisco is located in Zone 4, so the value of Z is 1.0. From Table 16-3, a commerical building does not qualify for an increased occupancy importance factor, so $I = 1$. From Table 16-4 and the building description, $K = 0.80$.

The fundamental period, using Equation (16-5a), is

$$T = \frac{0.09h}{\sqrt{D}}$$
$$= \frac{0.09(56)}{\sqrt{30}}$$
$$= 0.92\text{ s } (>0.3,\text{ OK})$$

Using Equation (16-4), we find

$$C = \frac{1}{15\sqrt{T}}$$
$$= \frac{1}{15\sqrt{0.92}}$$
$$= 0.0695\ (<0.12,\text{ OK})$$

If $T_s = 2.0$ s, then

$$\frac{T}{T_s} = \frac{0.92}{2.0} = 0.46$$

which is less than unity, so we use Equation (16-6a) to establish the coefficient S.

$$S = 1.0 + \frac{T}{T_s} - 0.5\left(\frac{T}{T_s}\right)^2$$
$$= 1.0 + 0.46 - 0.5(0.46)^2$$
$$= 1.35$$

We can now find V using Equation (16-3).

$$V = ZIKCSW$$
$$= 1.0(1.0)(0.80)(0.0695)(1.35)(52\ 200\text{ kN})$$
$$= 3920\text{ kN}$$

Problems

16-1. Determine the base shear force for the Boston city police station, shown schematically in Figure 16-7. The building is square in plan 25 m × 25 m at the ground level and 40 m × 40 m at the fifth floor and roof levels. It has a fully moment resistant frame. The total dead load of each deck is 7 kN/m² except for the roof, which is 4 kN/m². No data are available regarding the natural period of the site.

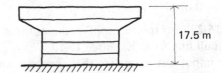

Figure 16-7. Section through a square building.

16-2. Solve Problem 16-1 if the building is located in Washington, D.C., and uses only shear walls to resist the lateral loads.

16-3. Compute the value of V for the shorter plan dimension of the building of Example 16-1.

16-4. Determine V for the Chicago hospital shown schematically in Figure 16-8. The building is a square pyra-

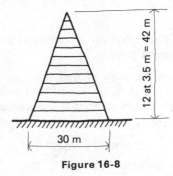

Figure 16-8

mid and ultilizes a fully moment resistant frame. Each floor has a dead load of 4 kN/m² except for the sixth floor, which has some heavy equipment, making its total value 8 kN/m². The characteristic site period has been found to be 1.0 s.

After the base shear has been computed, it is distributed as inertia forces which act at each floor level, and these constitute the lateral design loads for the building frame. In distributing these forces, both the height and weight of the different floors need to be considered, and Equation (16-7) has been developed for this purpose. Each level takes a certain fraction of V determined by its height and weight. The equation includes a term F_t, which is a portion of V to be applied to the top of the structure in addition to the force normally distributed to that level. This extra force is included to account for the "whiplash" effect at the top of tall structures and may be found from Equation (16-8). The value of F_t is not to exceed $0.25V$, and it may be taken as zero when T is 0.7 s or less.

$$F_x = \frac{(V - F_t)w_x h_x}{\sum\limits_{i=1}^{n} w_i h_i} \qquad (16\text{-}7)$$

where F_x = lateral force at level x, to be distributed horizontally according to the weight distribution at that level (N)

w_x = dead weight of building attributed to level x (N)

h_x = height of level x (m)

$F_t = 0.07TV$

Example 16-2 illustrates the application of these formulas using the building from Example 16-1.

It is important to realize that the brief analysis of earthquake forces presented in this section is but an introduction to the subject. In the interest of simplicity, the writer has deliberately ignored some important topics, such as frequency-response spectra, dynamic modal analysis, and the analysis of forces on parts of structures. The quantitative analysis provided here is intended only as part of an overview of earthquake forces and the factors that influence their magnitudes.

EXAMPLE 16-2

Determine the forces that act at each level for the 14-story building of Example 16-1.

Solution: From the work of that example, $V = 3920$ kN and $T = 0.92$ s. Equation (16-8) will then give us the additional force that must be applied at the roof level.

$$F_t = 0.07 \ TV \qquad (16\text{-}8)$$
$$= 0.07(0.92)(3920 \text{ kN})$$
$$= 252 \text{ kN } (<0.25 \text{ V, OK})$$

The remainder of the base shear, $V - F_t$, or 3668 kN, is distributed to all levels, including the roof. Table 16-5 pro-

TABLE 16-5   *Data for Equation (16-7)*

Floor level, x	w_x	h_x	$w_x h_x$	F_x (kN)
2	3600	4	14 400	34
3	3600	8	28 800	68
4	3600	12	43 200	102
5	3600	16	57 600	136
6	3600	20	72 000	170
7	5400	24	129 600	306
8	3600	28	100 800	238
9	3600	32	115 200	272
10	3600	36	129 600	306
11	3600	40	144 000	340
12	3600	44	158 400	373
13	3600	48	172 800	407
14	3600	52	187 200	441
R	3600	56	201 600	475

$$\sum_{i=1}^{n} (w_x h_x) = 1 \ 555 \ 200$$

vides a convenient way of keeping the data for use in Equation (16-7). The final design forces are shown in Figure 16-9. Notice the influence of the extra mass located at the seventh-floor level. Also notice how the inclusion of F_t significantly amplifies the roof-level design load.

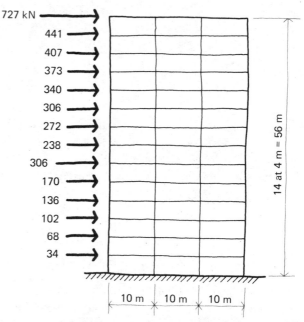

727 kN
441
407
373
340
306
272
238
306
170
136
102
68
34

14 at 4 m = 56 m

10 m   10 m   10 m

Figure 16-9.   Earthquake design loads.

Problems

16-5. Determine the distribution of lateral forces for the building of Problem 16-1.

16-6. Recompute the roof level force in Example 16-2 if the mechanical equipment is placed on the roof instead of the seventh floor.

16-7. Determine the distribution of lateral forces for the pyramidal building of Problem 16-4.

16-5 EARTHQUAKE DESIGN PRINCIPLES

The major goal of aseismic design is energy absorption. The building should be able to withstand the accelerations due to the predicted ground motion without structural failures and without nonstructural failures that might endanger the occupants. It is well known that, during the period of actual ground shaking, the stresses and deformations that occur are many times those that would be caused by the calculated design loads of the previous section. It is also known that buildings designed for those design loads generally behave in a satisfactory manner (at least structurally) in an earthquake. This is true essentially for two reasons. First, there is considerable damping action and energy absorption from the nonstructural building systems. Second, properly designed structures have continuity and ductility, so that strain levels well beyond the elastic range can take place repeatedly without material failure.

Overall building configuration can also play a large role in a structure's ability to withstand earthquake loads. Simple symmetrical volumes perform much better than schemes with many reentrant corners and odd plan shapes. Figure 16-10 illustrates how stresses become amplified at the junctions of different building masses. Asymmetrical placement of shear walls or lateral bracing systems can cause large torsional forces and deforma-

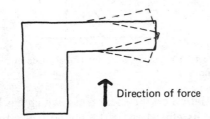

Figure 16-10. Irregular shapes cause stress concentrations at junctions.

tions, as shown in Figure 16-11. Overhangs, setbacks, cantilevers, and parapets should be avoided, as they represent changes in rigidity from one part of a building to the next and prevent a uniformity of energy absorption. Similarly, it must be recognized that certain rigid nonstructural elements, such as masonry interior or exterior walls, can act to stiffen the structural frames at their locations and draw forces to parts of a frame not designed for those loads. For example, this can easily happen to the structural members adjacent to a stiff vertical circulation core.

Foundations also need special design consideration. If practical, the elements should be tied together to pre-

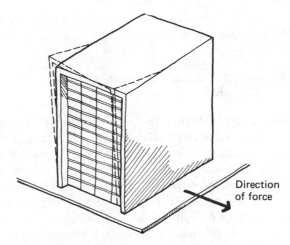

Figure 16-11. Deformation of a building with three rigid walls and one "open" wall.

vent differential movement. Extra connections are also needed between the superstructure and the foundation.

Proper design calls for careful detailing to ensure continuity in all structural connections; heavy members merely clipped together invite disaster. It is also important to pay special attention to all fastenings in the nonstructural systems. This is an area of design that has been underemphasized, and some of the most significant hazards to life safety have occurred when curtain walls, partitions, and ceiling systems were shaken loose from the structure. In such cases, the frame performs adequately because of its special design, but no special attention was given to the other systems.

Ceiling and partition systems must be designed to accommodate the motion of the building structure. Clearances must be detailed between infill partitions, glazing, ceiling panels, and the structure to avoid damage by wracking. Extra anchors and attachments are needed for exterior veneers and panels, and panel joints must allow for abnormal movement. Special hangers are needed for ceiling systems, pipes, ducts, and lighting fixtures. Emergency power and lighting systems must remain functional. Elevators must continue to operate.

The requirement for a ductile structural system does not necessarily imply one of great flexibility and large deformations. It is obvious that excessive deformation can result in significant detailing problems for the nonstructural systems. Tall buildings with moment-resisting frames often require a separate lateral bracing system merely to control drift or sway.

It is important to understand that building safety in an earthquake means much more than just structural safety. Perhaps the greatest need is not for more accurate analytical procedures but for closer attention to details and better construction supervision and inspection. Studies have shown that buildings constructed according to stringent code provisions and with great care fare much better than those that have been hastily erected with many "shortcuts."

16-6 LATERAL LOAD BRACING SYSTEMS

As illustrated in Figure 16-1, the amount of structure needed to resist wind or earthquake loads increases with height. A considerable premium is paid to build a tall building that will not sway excessively. However, the desirability of an urban location and the high cost of land means that such projects remain economically sound from an overall standpoint. Therefore, architects and engineers continue to search for efficient means of providing lateral load resistance.

The simplest means of countering lateral forces is through moment-resisting connections of beams and girders to columns. This provides for so-called rigid frame or portal action but has severe height limitations, because the moments, and therefore the lateral deflections, can become very large. The first tall buildings had little difficulty with this because the interior and exterior walls were generally very heavy and gave considerable stiffness to the frame. By today's standards, the frames themselves were also often overdesigned. With the advent of lightweight partitions and curtain walls and the development of better analytical techniques, the inclusion of a separate bracing system became necessary for tall buildings.

There are essentially two actions that take place in a moment-resisting frame subjected to lateral load. They are shown in Figure 16-12 and consist of shear wracking and cantilever bending. Shear wracking causes moments in the girders and columns, and the cantilever action results in additional column axial loads and deformations.

The most obvious means of stiffening a frame is by placing rigid shear walls at selected locations to maintain the rectangular shape of each story. In reinforced concrete construction, these walls are usually cast in place

monolithically with the girders and columns, and in steel buildings the wall is actually a shear truss. Such trusses can have full diagonals or K braces, which allow greater flexibility in the placement of openings in the wall. Naturally, the size of openings in a shear wall or truss is limited because it reduces the effectiveness of the system. In concrete, these walls are often made part of a vertical circulation core, where the stairwells must be walled in for fire protection anyway. When a shear truss is used in a steel building, the girder-to-column framing can be done with simple clip angles, avoiding the use of expensive moment-resistant connections. In both steel and concrete, the lateral bracing system can be reduced in size as it goes up the building and the cumulative loads become smaller. Figure 16-13 shows a typical K-braced shear truss in a steel building. Such trusses can have many different configurations and combinations of diagonals.

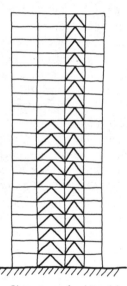

Figure 16-13. Shear truss for lateral loads in a steel building.

A variation on the shear truss, which has been used to improve its efficiency, is the belted truss. In this system, as shown in Figure 16-14(a), deep horizontal trusses connect the vertical shear truss to the exterior columns at one or more locations over the building height. As lateral sway is induced, the exterior columns act to restrain the belt trusses, which, in turn, cause changes in curvature and reduced bending loads in the shear truss. Figure 16-14(c) provides a comparison between bending in the core trusses with and without the belt trusses.

In an effort to free the interior of high-rise office and apartment buildings to permit more flexibility in space planning, designers have found ways to keep the lateral bracing system within the exterior walls. One such technique creates a framed tube by using closely spaced exterior columns. The spandrel beams then become very short and stiff, as shown in Figure 16-15.

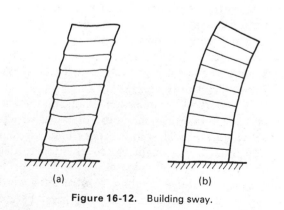

(a)   (b)

Figure 16-12. Building sway.

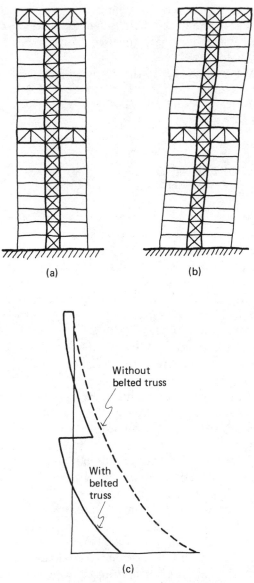

(a)   (b)

(c)

Figure 16-14. Belted truss system.

Without belted truss

With belted truss

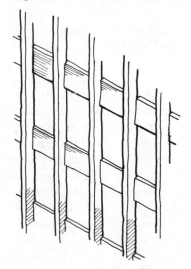

Figure 16-15. Framed tube exterior wall.

Using moment-resisting connections at every column and spandrel intersection (as in a Vierendeel frame) means that the moments due to lateral loads are distributed over many intersections. Such a system behaves like a shear wall with many small openings. In fact, it can be argued that this kind of wall is conceptually a bearing wall rather than a framed wall because the columns cannot behave independently of one another. A heavy vertical load on one column will be partly transferred to the adjacent columns by shear via the spandrel beams.

The framed tube exterior wall is often combined with a core, which carries only gravity loads, creating a tube within a tube system. The distance between the two tubes is left column-free by using long-span floor trusses or girders.

One of the limitations of the framed tube system involves a phenomenon called *shear lag*, which results in an uneven distribution of column loads. The tube acts like a cantilevered box beam when subjected to lateral loads (i.e., the two walls that are parallel to the wind act as webs and the windward and leeward walls serve as flanges). Following conventional beam theory, the columns in the webs should show a linear variation in axial load, while the columns in the flanges should be uniformly stressed. This condition is represented by the dashed line in Figure 16-16. The walls, however, are not homogeneous and isotropic as assumed for beam theory; they are perforated by many small openings. Consequently, the bending strains are not linear, because

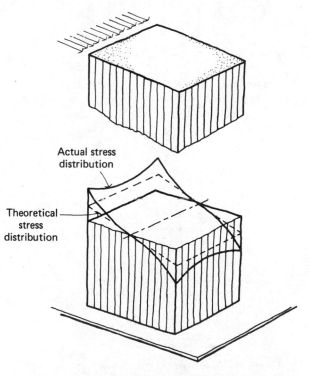

Actual stress distribution

Theoretical stress distribution

Figure 16-16. Effects of shear lag in framed tube.

wracking occurs as the columns and spandrels bend, preventing proper shear transfer. This results in the corner columns having to do more than their share of the work, as shown by the solid-line stress distribution in Figure 16-16.

To overcome the shear lag problem, which becomes severe in very tall structures, two approaches have been taken. One is to use interior stiffening frames parallel to the outside walls. Such frames serve as additional webs in the box-beam analogy, creating several smaller peak values in the distribution of column loads. The system has been called the "bundled tube concept," because the structural partitions divide the building plan into a series of adjacent tubes. This has the advantage of providing convenient modules for building setback as the building increases in height (see Figure 16-17).

The other means of overcoming shear lag is through the use of diagonals in the outside walls of the framed tube. The walls then become huge trusses, as illustrated

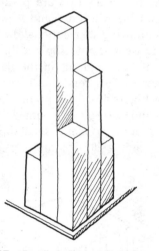

Figure 16-17. Bundled tube configuration as used in the Sears Tower in Chicago.

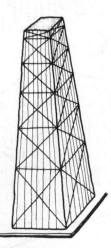

Figure 16-18. Trussed walls as used in the John Hancock Building in Chicago.

in Figure 16-18, and wracking (and the consequent shear lag) is minimized. The system becomes even more efficient if the diagonals are used to carry part of the gravity load as well.

Many of the recent developments in tall building structures, including the belted truss, bundled tube, and exterior trussing concepts, have been pioneered by Fazlur Khan, an American engineer.

16-7 PORTAL METHOD FOR APPROXIMATE ANALYSIS

A proper analysis of the effects of lateral loads in a rigid or moment resisting frame requires the use of an indeterminate procedure and, in the case of larger structures, the use of a computer. However, it is possible to make an approximate analysis using either of two very simple techniques. One is called the *portal method* and is generally favored for structures up to about 25 stories; the other, called the *cantilever method*, is considered better for very tall structures. Reasonable accuracy can be achieved by either method for straightforward, repetitive frames.

The principal assumption made by either procedure is that under lateral loads a point of inflection will develop at the midlength of every beam and column. This will be more or less true depending upon the uniformity of member stiffness over the building frame. With an assumed hinge in every member, a highly indeterminate frame becomes determinate.

The portal method makes assumptions regarding the distribution of the lateral forces into column shears, and the cantilever method requires assumptions about the distribution of the column axial loads. The two methods are very similar, both in concept and use, and only the portal method will be looked at in more detail.

The hinge assumption dictates a zero moment condition at the midheight of every column. This means that partial free-body diagrams sketched for each story level as in Figure 16-19(c) will show *no unknown moments*. In the portal method, it is assumed that the column shears, which act to maintain equilibrium at each level, are developed in each column in direct proportion to its tributary floor area. Thus, in the case of equal bay sizes, interior columns will take twice as much shear force as exterior columns. This is rationalized somewhat by relative column size and stiffness, but more so by the fact that interior columns function as part of *two* portals. Notice from Figure 16-19(c) that the shear forces in the second story columns must sum to the value F_r, whereas those in the first story will sum to the value $F_2 + F_r$. As expected, lateral loads generate large forces and

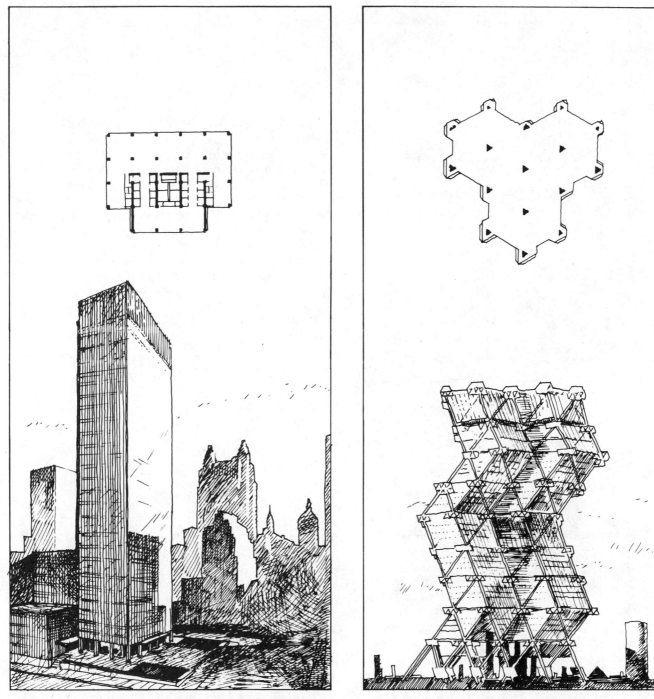

It is clear that the choice of a lateral bracing system for a tall building almost inevitably has visual consequences. It may even be decided that the bracing system will become the most prominent feature of the building's architectural character. This is the case in, for example, SOM's Chicago Hancock Tower of Figure 16-18 and Louis Kahn's project for the Philadelphia Municipal Building. Kahn's design was for an eccentrically irregular vertical space truss (that is, a truss whose pattern of triangulation is three-dimensional), one which would have

revealed to its viewers the fact that tall buildings must deal with lateral forces, not just accumulated weight acting straight down. Mies van der Rohe's and Philip Johnson's Seagram Building chooses, for equally good reasons, to do exactly the opposite. It is as reticent as possible about the presence of its elevator-core/shear wall lateral bracing. Shown in most photographs as a prismatic slab, Seagram is actually T-shaped in plan, with the blank side walls of the T working as shear-wall extensions of the core, acting to brace the "slab's" weaker axis.

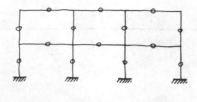

(a)

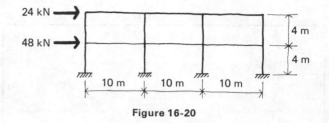

Figure 16-20

Solution: Isolate the roof and second floor levels as free bodies. Since, in this case, the tributary floor area of an interior column is twice that of an exterior one, the column shears will develop as per the proportional relationship 1 : 2 : 2 : 1. This results in the forces shown in Figure 16-21(a). (Notice that for each story the sum of the column shears must equal the sum of the lateral loads above that level.) From these values the compressive axial forces in the six girders may be found by cutting a free-body section at the midspan inflection point of each girder. In each case an axial force will develop to create horizontal equilibrium with the external lateral load and the column shears. For the roof girders, left to right,

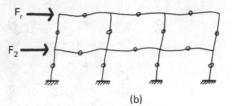

(b)

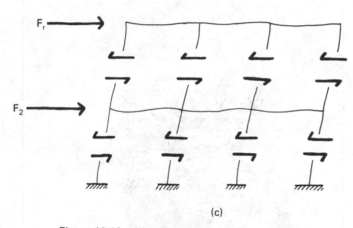

(c)

Figure 16-19. Hinge assumptions for approximate analysis.

moments in the lower stories of buildings and are less critical at the upper levels. The following examples provide applications of the portal method. In the first example, the axial forces and shears, as well as the moments, are found for each member. However, it is usually the moments that are critical, and the large values in the examples and problems will serve to explain why separate lateral bracing is usually necessary.

EXAMPLE 16-3

The frame shown in Figure 16-20 is one of many placed 12 m on center. Therefore, based on the tributary area in elevation, a 1-kN/m² wind load will result in the two concentrated loads given. Determine the approximate axial forces, shears, and moments in this frame due to the lateral load.

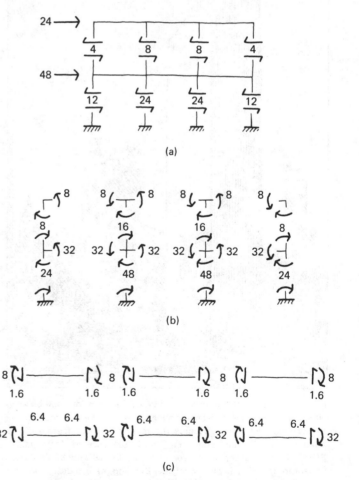

Figure 16-21. Portal analysis free-body diagrams: (a) column shears (kN); (b) joint moments (kN · m); (c) girder moments (kN · m) and shears (kN).

these values will be 20, 12, and 4 kN, and for the floor girder we get 40, 24, and 8 kN.

Using the same column shears and making a free body of each joint, we can get all the joint moments, as shown in Figure 16-21(b). In each case, the moment at the top or bottom of a column will be the shear force times half the column height. The girder moments are found by using joint equilibrium and the fact that, because of the midspan location of the point of inflection, the moments at the two ends of any member must be equal.

When the girder moments are then applied to the ends of the girders, the girder shear forces needed for rotational equilibrium can be determined, as shown in Figure 16-21(c). Finally, these girder shears, if applied to the joints, will result in axial forces in the columns. In this case, owing to the equal bay sizes, the interior columns will develop no axial forces due to the wind load. The leeward columns will go into compression and the windward columns into tension, in this case 1.6 kN for the second story and 8.0 kN for the first story. The final forces and moments are given in Figure 16-22.

EXAMPLE 16-4

Use the portal method to find the lateral load moments in the asymmetrical frame of Figure 16-23.

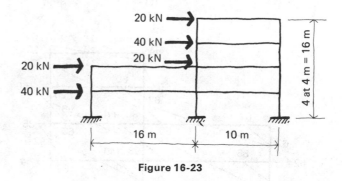

Figure 16-23

Solution: The column shear forces are distributed as shown in Figure 16-24(a). For the lower two stories, the tributary areas of the columns have the ratio 8 : 13 : 5 based on the column spacing, so the forces shown are in that ratio (rounded to the nearest kN). The resulting joint moments and the moment diagram are shown in Figure 16-24(b) and (c), respectively, which appears on page 266.

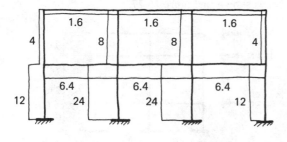

(a)

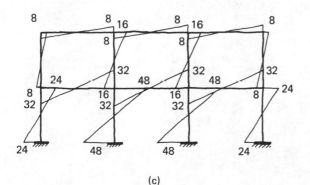

(b)

(c)

Figure 16-22. Results of Example 16-3: (a) axial forces (kN); (b) shear forces (kN); (c) bending moments (kN · m).

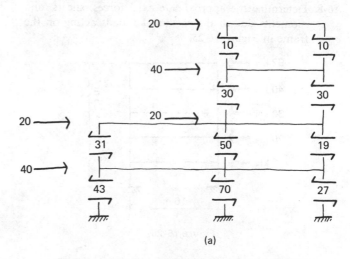

(a)

Figure 16-24. Moments by portal analysis: (a) Column shears (kN).

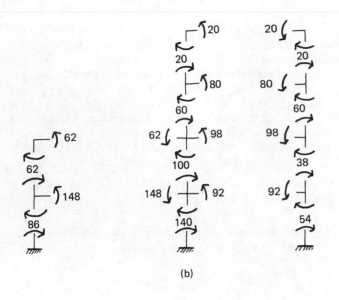

(b)

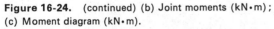

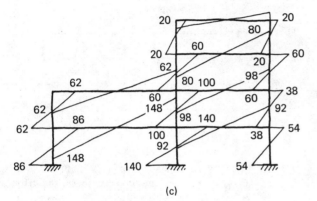

(c)

Figure 16-24. (continued) (b) Joint moments (kN·m);
(c) Moment diagram (kN·m).

Problems

16-8. Determine the approximate axial forces, shears, and moments due to the earthquake loads acting on the frame in Figure 16-25.

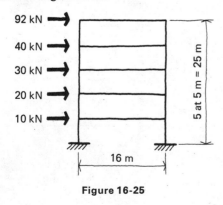

Figure 16-25

16-9. In Example 16-1, it was stated that the 14-story building of Figure 16-6 had a moment-resisting frame capable of taking 25% of the earthquake loads. Assuming that the loads give in Figure 16-9 will be shared by two parallel frames, determine the moments in the second-story girders due to 25% of the lateral load.

16-10. Use the portal method to construct a tension side moment diagram for the building frame in Figure 16-26. Assume that the frame is typical of many spaced 8 m on center.

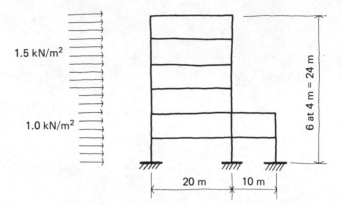

Figure 16-26. Wind pressures on a six-story building.

16-11. Determine the approximate frame moments due to the loads shown in Figure 16-27.

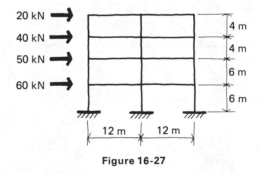

Figure 16-27

17-1 INTRODUCTION TO REINFORCED CONCRETE

The structural behavior of a composite material, such as reinforced concrete, is quite different from that of homogeneous materials. Much of conventional theory developed for the analysis of stresses and deflections is predicated upon an assumption as to the uniformity of properties throughout a given structure or element. When two dissimilar materials, such as steel and concrete, are used together, the conventional means of analysis cannot be directly applied. As explained in Section 4-8, when two different materials are subjected to the same strain, they will develop different stresses, depending upon their E values. This means that in a beam, for example, even though both materials might be located the same distance from the neutral axis and therefore have the same strain, they would not develop the same stresses. This is discussed briefly in Section 9-14, which deals with beams of two materials.

The situation is further complicated by the nature of concrete itself. First, concrete is very weak in tension and cracks under very low loads. When this occurs, the tensile forces must be carried entirely by the reinforcing bars. Second, as shown in Figure 4-8, concrete in compression does not have a linear relationship between stress and strain. While its stress–strain curve is approximately linear for low loads, gradual but significant yielding takes place after the stresses reach about one-half their ultimate value. For many years, "working stress" or "service load" design techniques were applied to reinforced concrete and the allowable stresses were restricted to values below this level so that the concrete could be considered approximately elastic. The more rational "strength design" approach accurately considers the inelastic nature of concrete.

The ultimate crushing strength of structural concrete is measured by standard test cylinders and will vary with age and the length of curing time as well as the mix proportions and quality of ingredients. Since the strength gain is exponential and very little takes place after the first 4 weeks, a cylinder test at 28 days has been adopted as standard by the American Society for Testing and Materials (ASTM), the Portland Cement Association (PCA), and the American Concrete Institute (ACI). This 28-day crushing strength is designated as f'_c and is used as a reference value to express the tensile strength, shearing strength, and even the modulus of elasticity of the concrete. The f'_c value for structural concrete of normal density (about 2300 kg/m³) varies in practice from about 15 MPa to about 35 MPa, but higher strengths are often used in prestressed concrete and in columns. Depending upon how the values are measured, the tensile strength will range from 0.4 to 0.8 times $\sqrt{f'_c}$ and the shearing strength from 0.2 to 0.4 times $\sqrt{f'_c}$. The modulus of elasticity is a function of both density and strength and for stone concrete is given approximately by $E = 4730 \sqrt{f'_c}$. In these empirical assessments all values are expressed in MPa and it is understood that such units are not affected by the radical sign.

Reinforcing bars come in sizes ranging from 100 mm² to 2500 mm² in cross-sectional area, as given in Appendix T. The two largest bar sizes are usually used only in columns. Two different grades of yield strength are used for "re-bars" in building structures, 300 and 400 MPa, with the latter value most prevalent by far.

Besides individual bars, prewelded mats of heavy wire mesh are sometimes used for the reinforcing in large surfaces such as flat slabs. This type of reinforcing is called *welded wire fabric.*

Reinforcing steel must be detailed according to the applicable code provisions so that

1. Adequate space exists in between and around the bars to permit the proper placement of fresh concrete. (The usually results in clear spaces of 25 to 40 mm between bars.)

Reinforced Concrete and Prestressed Concrete Concepts

17

2. Adequate concrete cover for the steel is provided to prevent damage by fire or corrosion. (This often means a clear distance between the inside of the formwork and the main steel of about 50 mm for columns and beams and about 20 mm for slabs.)
3. Adequate bond is developed between the steel and the concrete to permit the necessary transfer of forces. (This can restrict the distribution and size of bars in a given area and require that certain bars be made longer to gain adequate anchorage.)

The American Concrete Institute publishes the booklet *Building Code Requirements for Reinforced Concrete*, which is referred to as the "ACI Code." This document serves as a guide for the structural analysis and design of all types of concrete structures and is referenced by most model and local building codes. Its purpose is to specify standard procedures and practices to be followed to produce structures that are both safe and economical. It is recommended that this booklet and its companion, the *Commentary on Building Code Requirements for Reinforced Concrete*, be purchased by the serious designer of concrete structures. In addition, the Concrete Reinforcing Steel Institute (CRSI) and the ACI both publish worthwhile design aids, which can serve to reduce the number of required computations in common situations.

17.2 LOAD FACTORS

As mentioned in Section 4-10, the concept of strength design or ultimate strength design is not based upon an allowable stress level. Instead, the service loads are multiplied by various load factors to convert them to ultimate or failure loads, and the structure or element is then designed to fail under these loads. The load factors constitute a factor of safety against the effects of overload and the simplifying assumptions usually made in structural design.

The ACI Code recommends the use of different factors for various kinds of loads, and some of these are presented in Table 17-1. The letter U represents the required ultimate strength while D, L, W, and E represent the actual effects of dead, live, wind, and earthquake loads, respectively. The differences in load factors are generally intended to reflect the accuracy with which such loads can be predicted. In all cases, the most stringent or "worst case" is to be used except that the effects of wind and earthquake need not be combined. Notice that for lateral loads two possibilities are included to reflect the presence *or* the absence of full live load. Also, notice that the required strength is reduced by about 25% in such cases to reflect the increased ability

of materials to withstand loads applied for brief time periods.

TABLE 17-1 *American Concrete Institute Load Factors*

Gravity loads	$U = 1.4D + 1.7L$
Lateral loads	$U = 0.75(1.4D + 1.7L + 1.7W)$
(Earthquake forces may be considered by substituting $1.1E$ for W.)	$U = 0.9D + 1.3W$

In addition to the load factors, the ACI Code further increases the margin of safety by specifying the use of "capacity reduction factors" to account for the fact that the actual strength of a member might not be as great as its theoretical capacity. These are called ϕ *factors* and, as seen in Table 17-2, they generally reflect the relative importance of a member to the overall structural integrity of the building and the nature of possible failures. As explained in Section 13-1, a column failure does more damage to a building than do most beam failures, and in succeeding sections it will be shown that bending failures in reinforced concrete are more ductile (and therefore slower) than failures in shear or compression. The ϕ factors are also intended to provide for slight variations in the quality of materials and workmanship which could accumulate in a detrimental manner.

TABLE 17-2 *American Concrete Institute ϕ Factors*

Structural behavior	ϕ Factor
Bending	0.90
Shear	0.85
Axial compression	
With lateral ties	0.70
With spiral ties	0.75

Since the ϕ factor is used to reduce the theoretical ultimate capacity of a member and the load factors increase the actual loads present, the effective factor of safety can be determined by dividing the load factor by the ϕ factor.

17-3 ULTIMATE MOMENT CAPACITY

Use of the strength design method for flexural analysis requires that we be able to estimate accurately the ultimate bending moment capacity of a given section. In this text, we shall restrict our consideration to rectangular sections utilizing tensile reinforcement only. For the analysis of other cross sections, such as T-beams, and beams with compression reinforcement, the reader should consult one of the many texts on reinforced concrete. In such cases, the procedures involve a few additional terms but are based on the concepts developed in this article.

In all situations involving flexure, the externally applied forces that cause bending are resisted by an internal couple. In a reinforced concrete beam, this couple is provided by the steel reinforcing bars acting in tension and the concrete acting in compression. Since concrete is quite weak in tension, it is assumed that cracks are present in the tensile areas of the cross section and the tensile force is carried completely by the steel. In regions of high moment, it is assumed (slightly conservatively) that such cracks extend from the extreme fibers up to, or down to, the neutral axis. Figure 17-1 shows these cracks in a beam with end fixity. Assuming the maintenance of a proper bond between the concrete and steel, these cracks are closely spaced and almost invisible under service loads.

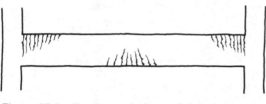

Figure 17-1. Tensile cracks in a reinforced concrete beam.

As the loads increase, causing increased bending strain, these cracks widen and propagate further, and when the ultimate capacity is reached, failure can occur in one of two ways: the concrete will crush in compression or the steel will yield in tension. If the amount of reinforcing is relatively small, guaranteeing a high stress level, the steel will yield before the concrete crushes. On the other hand, if a large amount of steel is present, the steel stress will be low and failure will occur by concrete crushing. As seen in Figure 4-9, mild steel is a very ductile material capable of developing large strains after the yield point. Elongations as long as 25% ($\epsilon = 0.25$) are sustained before actual rupture takes place. Concrete, however, is much less ductile and crushes rather abruptly at low strain levels. Stress–strain curves in compression for several different concrete strengths are shown in Figure 17-2, and it is commonly assumed that crushing takes place at a strain level of about 3% ($\epsilon = 0.003$).

Clearly, if the steel yields before the concrete crushes, large bending strains will take place, cracks will open widely, and the consequent large deflections will provide a warning of the impending collapse. Given an overload situation, such a failure is far preferable to one precipitated by concrete crushing, and for this reason the ACI Code limits the amount of tensile reinforcement

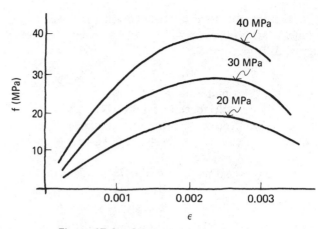

Figure 17-2. Concrete stress–strain curves.

in all beams. This important Code provision is discussed in the following article and investigated more thoroughly in Appendix J.

Once we are assured that the amount of tensile reinforcing present in any given section is small enough so that failure is forced to occur by tension, we can easily develop an expression for the ultimate moment capacity. Figure 17-3 illustrates the stress state within

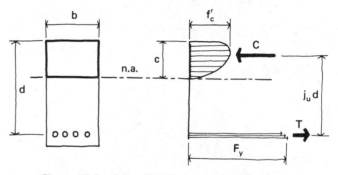

Figure 17-3. Stress distribution under ultimate moment conditions.

the beam at failure. The steel stress upon reaching yield is assumed to remain constant (a conservative assumption that ignores the strain-hardening characteristics of mild steel), while the strain in both materials continues, causing increased deflection. Collapse will finally take place when the concrete stress distribution looks approximately like that of a stress–strain curve and crushing at the extreme fiber results. The two forces C and T must at all times be equal (to ensure static equilibrium in the horizontal direction) and are assumed to be constant once the steel yields. During the interval between failure (steel first reaches yield) and final collapse, the resisting couple will increase slightly, owing to an increase in the moment arm. This moment arm, denoted as $j_u d$, must increase slightly for the compressive force C to remain constant. As the concrete stresses increase toward f'_c, the neutral axis moves so as to reduce the compressive area, thereby enabling the force to remain constant. The moment at failure, including the capacity reduction factor, ϕ, is given as

$$M_u = \phi T j_u d \qquad (17\text{-}1)$$

where M_u = ultimate moment (N·m)
  T = tensile force at failure (N)
  d = effective depth, the distance from the extreme compressive fiber to the centroid of the steel (m)
  j_u = a decimal fraction of d which depends upon the material strengths and the amount of reinforcing

In Equation (17-1), T is used instead of the compressive force C because it is easy to evaluate as the product of the steel area and the yield strength, and therefore

$$M_u = \phi A_s F_y j_u d$$

where A_s = area of tensile reinforcement (m²)
  F_y = yield strength of the steel (Pa)

Furthermore, it is often convenient to express the steel area as a fraction of the effective beam area, excluding the protective concrete cover. This unitless value is called ρ, the *steel ratio*, and is defined as

$$\rho = \frac{A_s}{bd} \qquad (17\text{-}2)$$

where b is the beam width (m). Letting $A_s = \rho bd$ and substituting, we get

$$M_u = \phi \rho F_y bd^2 j_u \qquad (17\text{-}3)$$

Equation (17-3) constitutes an easy-to-use expression for the ultimate moment capacity of a given section. Only the value j_u needs to be determined.

As derived in Appendix J,

$$j_u = 1 - 0.59\rho\frac{F_y}{f'_c} \qquad (17\text{-}4)$$

and is a decimal fraction that measures the size of the moment arm between C and T. Values of j_u for $F_y = 400$-MPa steel and several concrete strengths are presented in tabular form in Appendix U.

EXAMPLE 17-1

Compute the ultimate moment capacities for the beam sections in Figure 17-4. Assume that $F_y = 400$ MPa and $f'_c = 25$ MPa.

Solution: In each case, obtain the values of ρ and j_u for use in Equation (17-3). The indicated steel areas may be found from Appendix U. For the first beam section [Figure 17-4(a)], we have

$$\rho = \frac{A_s}{bd}$$

$$= \frac{4(300 \text{ mm}^2)}{(300 \text{ mm})(500 \text{ mm})}$$

$$= 0.008$$

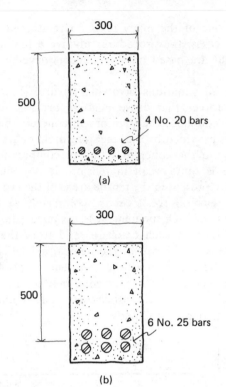

Figure 17-4. Reinforced concrete beam sections.

$$j_u = 1 - 0.59\rho\frac{F_y}{f'_c}$$

$$= 1 - 0.59(0.008)\frac{400 \text{ MPa}}{25 \text{ MPa}}$$

$$= 0.924$$

Taking $\phi = 0.90$ from Table 16-2, we get the ultimate moment as

$$M_u = \phi \rho F_y bd^2 j_u$$

$$= 0.90(0.008)(400\ 000 \text{ kPa})(0.300 \text{ m})(0.500 \text{ m})^2 0.924$$

$$= 200 \text{ kN·m}$$

The same procedures may be followed for the second beam section [Figure 17-4(b)].

$$\rho = \frac{A_s}{bd}$$

$$= \frac{6(500 \text{ mm}^2)}{(300 \text{ mm})(500 \text{ mm})}$$

$$= 0.020$$

$$j_u = 1 - 0.59\rho\frac{F_y}{f'_c}$$

$$= 1 - 0.59(0.020)\frac{400 \text{ MPa}}{25 \text{ MPa}}$$

$$= 0.811$$

$$M_u = \phi \rho F_y bd^2 j_u$$

$$= 0.90(0.020)(400\ 000 \text{ kPa})(0.300 \text{ m})(0.500 \text{ m})^2 0.811$$

$$= 438 \text{ kN·m}$$

The reader should verify that in each case the value of j_u could have been obtained directly from Appendix U.

EXAMPLE 17-2

If the beam section in Figure 17-4(a) is used on a 7-m simple span, determine the ultimate uniform load w_u in kN/m.

Solution: The maximum moment occurs at midspan and has a value of $wL^2/8$. From the work of Example 17-1, the ultimate moment is 200 kN·m.

$$w_u = \frac{8M_u}{L^2}$$

$$= \frac{8(200 \text{ kN} \cdot \text{m})}{(7 \text{ m})^2}$$

$$= 32.7 \text{ kN/m}$$

EXAMPLE 17-3

The ends of the beam in Figure 17-5 may be taken as fixed. The live load is 14 kN/m and the dead load is 10 kN/m. Ascertain that the ultimate moment capacity of the section shown will accommodate these loads and the weight of the beam itself.

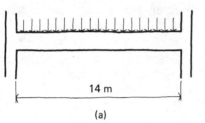

14 m

(a)

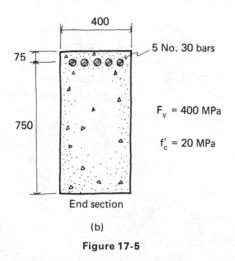

400

75

5 No. 30 bars

750

F_y = 400 MPa

f'_c = 20 MPa

End section

(b)

Figure 17-5

Solution: It is common practice to take the density of reinforced concrete as 2400 kg/m³, which includes a small allowance for the mass of the steel. The mass of the section per running meter is then

$$(0.400 \text{ m})(0.825 \text{ m})(2400 \text{ kg/m}^3) = 792 \text{ kg/m}$$

Converting this to weight, we get

$$w = (792 \text{ kg/m})(9.8 \text{ N/kg})$$

$$= 7760 \text{ N/m}$$

$$= 7.76 \text{ kN/m}$$

This should be added to the dead load before the load factors are applied. From Table 17-1,

$$w_u = 1.4(D) + 1.7(L)$$

$$= 1.4(10 + 7.76) + 1.7(14)$$

$$= 48.7 \text{ kN/m}$$

From case 11 of Appendix V, the maximum moment is $wL^2/12$ and occurs at either end of the beam.

$$M_u = \frac{w_u L^2}{12}$$

$$= \frac{48.7(14)^2}{12}$$

$$= 795 \text{ kN} \cdot \text{m required}$$

To accommodate the given loads safely, the section must provide at least this much capacity.

$$\rho = \frac{A_s}{bd}$$

$$= \frac{5(700)}{400(750)}$$

$$= 0.0117$$

Using Appendix U and interpolating, we get $j_u = 0.862$ and the ultimate capacity is

$$M_u = \phi \rho F_y b d^2 j_u$$

$$= 0.90(0.0117)(400\ 000 \text{ kPa})(0.400 \text{ m})(0.750 \text{ m})^2 0.862$$

$$= 817 \text{ kN} \cdot \text{m} \quad \text{provided}$$

Since this is greater than the moment required, the section will be adequate.

Problems

17-1. Determine the ultimate moment capacity of the beam section in Figure 17-5(b) if the concrete used has an f'_c of 30 MPa.

17-2. The section shown in Figure 17-4(b) is used to span between simple supports and must carry an ultimate load (including the effect of its own weight) of $w_u = 30$ kN/m. How far apart can the supports be placed? Assume moment controls.

17-3. The simple beam in Figure 17-6 is used to span 9 m and supports two concentrated loads at the third points. Each load has a service value of 90 kN, made up of

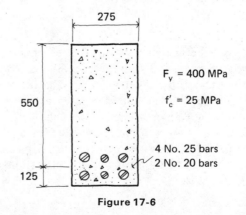

275

550

F_y = 400 MPa

f'_c = 25 MPa

125

4 No. 25 bars
2 No. 20 bars

Figure 17-6

one-half dead load and one-half live load. Is the section adequate to carry these loads and itself?

17-4. Figure 17-7 shows a partial section of a floor deck that must support a service live load of 3 kN/m² and a service dead load of 1 kN/m² (not including the weight of the construction itself). The reinforced concrete slabs span 4 m from beam to beam and the beams in turn span 10 m to girders. An indeterminate analysis indicates that the critical beam moment occurs where the beam joins the girder and is approximately $wL^2/11$. If $F_y = 400$ MPa and $f'_c = 25$ MPa, is the beam adequately reinforced?

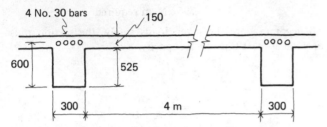

Figure 17-7.   Floor construction (end section).

17-5. Using the data of Problem 17-4, determine the maximum safe distance that the beams could cantilever beyond the supporting girder. Assume moment controls.

17-4 AMOUNT OF REINFORCEMENT

As mentioned in the previous section, it is important to limit the amount of tensile reinforcement in a beam so that if failure ever does occur, it will result from a yielding of the steel rather than a crushing of the concrete. A small percentage of reinforcing means that steel yield will occur before the concrete crushes, whereas a large percentage will result in concrete crushing prior to steel yield. Obviously, there is some specific amount of reinforcement that results in the simultaneous failure of both materials. This is referred to as a *balanced failure* and occurs when the amount of tensile steel is equal to ρ_b, the balanced steel ratio. As derived in Appendix J, by using equilibrium considerations and the compatibility of strains,

$$\rho_b = \frac{0.003}{0.003 + F_y/E_s} \frac{\beta_1 0.85 f'_c}{F_y} \qquad (17\text{-}5)$$

where β_1 is a factor that accounts for the skewed shape of the concrete stress distribution at failure. As determined empirically, β_1 has a value of 0.85 for concrete strengths up to 30 MPa but decreases at the rate of 0.008 for each MPa increase in strength above that level. The ACI Code specifies a minimum value for β_1 of 0.65. Since the modulus of elasticity of the steel E_s is constant at 200 GPa, ρ_b is easily evaluated as a function of the material strengths.

Presumably any beam with a steel ratio smaller than ρ_b will fail in a slow ductile manner if subjected to the ultimate load. Such beams are said to be *underreinforced*, while those having steel ratios greater than ρ_b are called *overreinforced*. Overreinforced beams fail abruptly without excessive deflection and are not permitted by the ACI Code. Moreover, because of the inherent variability in material properties, the Code stipulates that the steel percentage not approach ρ_b but instead be held to 75% of that value. Accordingly, the maximum value of steel percentage permitted for beams with tensile reinforcement only[1] is

$$\rho_{\max} = 0.75\rho_b \qquad (17\text{-}6)$$

Values of $\rho_{\max}$ for 20, 25, 30, and 35 MPa concrete used with $F_y = 400$ MPa steel are given in Appendix U, and these values have not been exceeded in the examples and problems of Section 17-3.

The Code also provides a similar restriction on the minimum amount of reinforcement to be used in a beam. This is done to ensure that the ultimate moment of any reinforced section will be at least as great as that of the corresponding unreinforced section, computed by using regular flexure theory and the tensile strength of plain concrete. For a steel strength of 400 MPa, $\rho_{\min}$ is about 0.0034.

17-5 DESIGN FOR FLEXURE

The size of reinforced concrete beams and girders is usually governed by moment rather than by shear or deflection. Once the maximum design moment is known, the section is proportioned so that it will have enough depth, width, and reinforcing steel to accommodate this moment.

For ease of construction, the width of a beam framing into a column is often made equal to the column dimension. This, of course, assumes that the required column section is known or can be estimated. Deep, narrow beams are seldom used because the reinforcing steel then has to be stacked in many rows, making concrete placement difficult. Thus, lateral stability is seldom a problem with reinforced concrete as beam widths are generally in the neighborhood of 1/4 to 1/2 of the depth.

The smallest overall cross section is achieved by using the maximum permitted amount of steel (i.e., $\rho_{\max}$). However, this does not necessarily result in design economy because of the higher cost of steel compared to concrete and because of the increased shear and deflection

---

[1] Although such cases will not be treated here, the reader should rationalize why it might be permissible to increase the percentage of tensile reinforcement if compressive reinforcement is also provided.

problems of smaller members. For preliminary sizing purposes, some designers recommend setting ρ somewhat less than ρ_{max}, say, $\rho = \frac{2}{3}\rho_{max}$, which is the same as $\frac{1}{2}\rho_b$. This procedure provides an advantage during the final design calculations in that a beam's depth can be reduced slightly (or its capacity increased) if needed merely by increasing the steel ratio.

Reinforced concrete beams are usually continuous, having negative moments at the supports and positive moments in the central portion of each span. Tensile steel is placed near the top or bottom of the section as required by these moments. Once the overall dimensions have been determined by the largest moment (of either sense), smaller amounts of steel are used at other sections to carry the smaller moments. In actual construction practice, most beams have some steel that runs the full length of the beam, top and bottom. To guard against moment reversals and shifts in peak moments due to unexpected loading patterns, the Code requires a certain fraction of the positive moment steel to run the full beam length and some negative steel to be continued into the zones of positive moment. Longitudinal steel also acts as supports for the shear stirrups.

For design purposes, it is convenient to lump all of the materials parameters in Equation (17-3) into one value. Letting this value be called K_u, the width and depth needed for a given moment then becomes

$$bd^2 = \frac{M_u}{K_u} \qquad (17\text{-}7)$$

where $K_u = \phi\rho F_y j_u$. Values of K_u in units of MPa are tabulated in Appendix U for a range of steel percentages. Once a percentage is selected, the required size of cross section is readily found by using that table and Equation (17-7).

It is important to remember to include an allowance for member self-weight in the dead load before computing the design moment. In doing this and in finding the dead load of floor slabs, etc., it may be helpful to work with the weight of a cubic meter of material rather than with its mass. Accordingly, the dead load or weight density of reinforced concrete is 2400 kg/m³ × 0.0098 kN/kg, or about 23.5 kN/m³.

EXAMPLE 17-4

A reinforced concrete beam is used on an 8-m simple span. It must support a concentrated dead load at midspan of 100 kN and a uniform load of 12 kN/m, half of which is dead and half of which is live. (Assume, for this example, that an allowance for the beam self-weight has been included in the uniform dead load.) Determine the required overall depth h if $b = 350$ mm, $F_y = 400$ MPa, $f'_c = 20$ MPa, and $\rho = \frac{2}{3}\rho_{max}$.

Solution: First determine the required effective depth d. The ultimate loads will be as follows:

$$P_u = 1.4P = 1.4(100)$$
$$= 140 \text{ kN}$$
$$w_u = 1.4w_D + 1.7w_L$$
$$= 1.4(6) + 1.7(6)$$
$$= 18.6 \text{ kN/m}$$

The maximum moment occurs at midspan and is given by

$$M_u = \frac{P_u L}{4} + \frac{w_u L^2}{8}$$
$$= \frac{140(8)}{4} + \frac{18.6(8)^2}{8}$$
$$= 429 \text{ kN·m required}$$

From Appendix U, ρ_{max} for the given materials is 0.0163, and two-thirds of that value is 0.0109. From the same table, $K_u = 3.42$ MPa.

$$bd^2 = \frac{M_u}{K_u}$$
$$= \frac{429 \text{ kN·m}}{3420 \text{ kN/m}^2}$$
$$= 0.125 \text{ m}^3$$

If $b = 350$ mm, then

$$d^2 = \frac{0.125 \text{ m}^3}{0.350 \text{ m}}$$
$$d = 0.598 \text{ m}$$
$$= 600 \text{ mm}$$

The value is rounded to the nearest 5 mm to be consistent with the probable precision of field construction techniques. The required area of steel is computed from

$$A_s = \rho bd$$
$$= 0.0109(350)(600)$$
$$= 2290 \text{ mm}^2$$

Two No. 25 and two No. 30 bars will provide 2400 mm², more than sufficient steel, and will not be too crowded in a single row. A minimum of 50 mm clear distance between these bars and the edge of the beam is required to allow space for the shear stirrups and provide adequate coverage. The diameter of a No. 30 bar is 30 mm, so the minimum distance from the centroid of the steel to the concrete surface is 15 plus 50, or 65 mm. A sketch of the cross section showing an overall depth h of 665 mm is given in Figure 17-8.

EXAMPLE 17-5

Using the same materials, determine the minimum required effective depth d for the beam in Example 17-4. Assume that the width must remain at 350 mm.

Solution: Let $\rho = \rho_{max}$ and, extrapolating from Appendix U, $K_u = 4.74$ MPa.

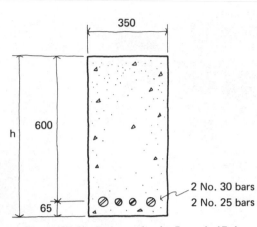

Figure 17-8. Beam section for Example 17-4.

$$bd^2 = \frac{M_u}{K_u}$$

$$= \frac{429 \text{ kN·m}}{4740 \text{ kN/m}^2}$$

If $b = 0.350$ m, then

$$d = 0.509 \text{ m}$$
$$= 510 \text{ mm}$$

The overall depth h will be larger than d, of course, and when using the maximum steel ratio, this difference can be considerable, as more than one row of bars is usually required. An even smaller depth is obtainable by increasing the width and the concrete strength while maintaining a high steel percentage. Such a cross section would be structurally inefficient and more costly.

EXAMPLE 17-6

A continuous beam spanning 9 m between columns must support a plank-with-topping floor deck, as shown in Figure 17-9. The prestressed planks span to similar beams spaced 11 m on centers and carry a live load of 4 kN/m² and a miscellaneous dead load of 0.5 kN/m². The floor construction itself weighs 3.5 kN/m². The critical moment occurs where the beam meets a column and is estimated at $wL^2/10$. If $F_y = 400$ MPa, $f'_c = 30$ MPa, and $\rho = \frac{2}{3}\rho_{max}$, determine the effective depth d.

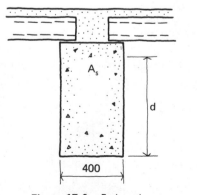

Figure 17-9. End section.

First compute the uniform service live and dead loads from an 11-m tributary strip.

$$w_L = 11(4) = 44 \text{ kN/m}$$
$$w_D = 11(0.5 + 3.5) = 44 \text{ kN/m}$$

The beam size should be estimated in order to include an allowance for the beam self-weight. Reinforced concrete beams usually have span/depth ratios between 10 and 20, and since the tributary area is large in this case, let the depth be assumed at one-tenth the span, or 0.9 m. The cross-sectional area is then 0.4 times 0.9, or 0.36 m², and the weight of the beam per unit length is

$$w_{s.w.} = 0.36 \text{ m}^2(23.5 \text{ kN/m}^3) = 8.5 \text{ kN/m}$$

The ultimate uniform load is

$$w_u = 1.4(44 + 8.5) + 1.7(44)$$
$$= 148 \text{ kN/m}$$

and the ultimate moment is

$$M_u = \frac{w_u L^2}{10}$$
$$= \frac{148(9)^2}{10}$$
$$= 1200 \text{ kN·m required}$$

Using Appendix U, $\frac{2}{3}\rho_{max}$ is 0.0162 and therefore $K_u = 5.08$ MPa.

$$bd^2 = \frac{M_u}{K_u}$$
$$= \frac{1200 \text{ kN·m}}{5080 \text{ kN/m}^2}$$

Since $b = 0.400$ m,

$$d = 0.768 \text{ m}$$
$$= 770 \text{ mm}$$

Considering the requirements for concrete cover, the estimate of the beam depth was sufficiently accurate to avoid any recomputation.

EXAMPLE 17-7

If the effective depth d of the beam in Example 17-6 is limited to 660 mm, determine the required steel ratio and select suitable reinforcing bars.

Solution: With this value of d, the overall depth will be about 750 mm. Although it probably will not change the moment by much, the reduced self-weight is

$$w_{s.w.} = 0.400 \text{ m}(0.750 \text{ m})(23.5 \text{ kN/m}^3) = 7 \text{ kN/m}$$

and the revised load is

$$w_u = 1.4(44 + 7) + 1.7(44)$$
$$= 146 \text{ kN/m}$$

Proportioning our previous moment, we get

$$M_u = \frac{146}{148}(1200) = 1180 \text{ kN·m required}$$

The required value of ρ can be found from Appendix U if we know K_u, which we do because

$$K_u = \frac{M_u}{bd^2}$$

$$= \frac{1180 \text{ kN} \cdot \text{m}}{(0.400 \text{ m})(0.660 \text{ m})^2}$$

$$= 6770 \text{ kPa}$$

$$= 6.77 \text{ MPa}$$

The needed steel ratio is very close to ρ_{max} at about 0.023.

$$A_s = \rho bd$$

$$= 0.023(400)(660)$$

$$= 6070 \text{ mm}^2$$

This can be provided by five No. 35 bars and four No. 20 bars, as shown in Figure 17-10. Because two layers of steel are needed to maintain the proper clearance between the bars, the overall depth will be about 750 mm, as predicted.

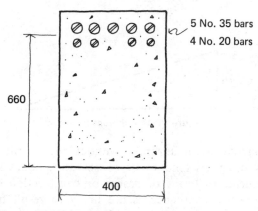

Figure 17-10. Reinforcing steel pattern for the beam in Example 17-7.

Problems

17-6. A reinforced concrete beam section must resist an ultimate moment of 500 kN·m, which includes the effects of beam weight. If $F_y = 400$ MPa, $f'_c = 25$ MPa, and $\rho = \frac{2}{3}\rho_{max}$, determine the required effective depth for
(a) $b = 250$ mm
(b) $b = 300$ mm
(c) $b = 350$ mm

17-7. The beam in the rigid frame of Figure 17-11 supports a service dead load of 20 kN/m (not including self-

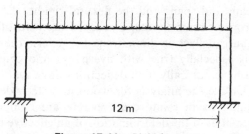

Figure 17-11. Rigid frame.

weight) and a service live load of 16 kN/m. An indeterminate analysis shows that the negative end moments provided by the columns are valued at $wL^2/20$ each. Find the midspan positive moment and determine the required effective depth. Assume that $b = 400$ mm, $F_y = 400$ MPa, $f'_c = 30$ MPa, and let $\rho = \rho_{max}$.

17-8. The two cantilever beams in Figure 17-12 must support a live load of 5 kN/m² over the balcony surface plus the concrete slab and the brick wall. Determine the effective depth, d, of the beams if $F_y = 400$ MPa, $f'_c = 25$ MPa, and $\rho = \frac{2}{3}\rho_{max}$. (The approximate density of masonry may be found in Appendix K.)

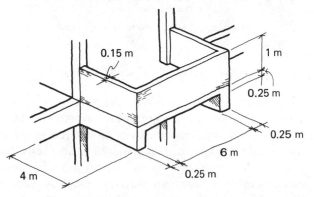

Figure 17-12. Balcony with masonry wall.

17-9. The girder in Figure 17-13 must carry several beam reactions plus its own self-weight. Let $F_y = 400$ MPa, $f'_c = 25$ MPa, and $b = d/2$. The ultimate load R_u is 112 kN.
(a) Determine the required effective depth for the maximum moment using $\rho = 0.018$.
(b) Using the dimensions found in part (a), determine the required steel ratio at another critical moment location.

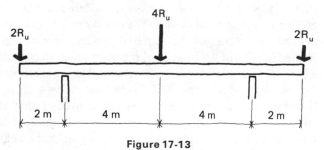

Figure 17-13

17-10. The reinforced concrete floor deck in Figure 17-14 has a 120-mm-thick one-way slab that spans 3 m from beam to beam. The floor carries a live load of 3 kN/m² and a miscellaneous dead load of 0.7 kN/m². Assume that $F_y = 400$ MPa, $f'_c = 30$ MPa, and let $\rho = 0.020$. Estimate beam weights as necessary.
(a) Determine the effective depth of typical beam AB by estimating the negative end moments as $M_A = wL^2/9$ and $M_B = wL^2/24$.
(b) Determine the effective depth of girder CD. Assume that the columns provide fixed ends for the beam.

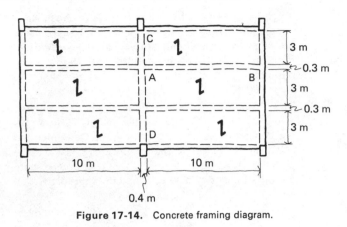

Figure 17-14. Concrete framing diagram.

17-6 INTRODUCTION TO BEAM SHEAR

As mentioned in Section 6-6, shearing forces develop diagonal tensile and compressive stresses in beams. Because of the inherent weakness of concrete in tension, special reinforcing is usually required to help resist these stresses. Rectangular "hoops" called *stirrups*, usually made from No. 10 bars, are placed vertically, as shown in Figure 17-15. Stirrups are spaced near to one another or far apart, depending upon the amount of shear force present at that section and the strength of the concrete. Stirrups are also used to resist the shearing stresses due to the presence of torsion, such as exists in spandrel and other beams loaded from one side only.

Figure 17-15 shows one-half of a uniformly loaded beam and its shear diagram. As expected, the spacing between stirrups increases as the shear forces diminish. Since shear seldom governs the size of a concrete beam, stirrup placement is not usually considered a part of preliminary structural design. The equations and analysis needed to determine the required spacing will not be treated here, and the interested reader is urged to consult a text on reinforced concrete structures. There are numerous requirements in the ACI Code concerning stirrups, the most important of which is the provision that if stirrups are needed, the maximum spacing permitted is one-half of the effective depth. This assumes that cracks caused by diagonal tension will form on angles of about 45° and thus a maximum spacing of $d/2$ ensures that any given crack must cross at least one stirrup. In a manner similar to the analysis for shear in timber beams, it is also recognized that such cracks are resisted by localized vertical compressive stresses that exist near the supports. The Code does not permit the absence of stirrups in such areas but stipulates that the spacing need not be controlled by these points of peak shear. Instead, the required spacing is relaxed to that needed for the shear force at a section d distance from the support.

Finally, it is important to realize that shear failures

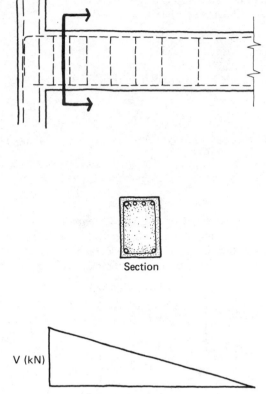

Figure 17-15. Stirrups for shear.

in concrete occur abruptly, without any warning, and many designers tend to be conservative about stirrup placement. In terms of design or construction errors, more severe consequences are likely to result from a missing stirrup than from a missing flexural rebar.

17-7 INTRODUCTION TO BEAM DEFLECTION

The continuity of the monolithic construction generally used with cast-in-place concrete makes deflection a less critical design parameter for this material than for wood or steel. The usually negative end moments reduce the midspan deflection, and for many beams a deflection computation is unnecessary. However, in designing for moment, relatively small cross sections are possible with the use of strength design methods and high steel ratios. As with any material, beam deflection is a function of the loads and spans and the flexural rigidity *EI*. Under the proper circumstances, a reduced moment of inertia can cause deflection limitations to govern the design. This is especially true with overhangs and cantilevers, which have naturally high deflections anyway.

Unlike the analysis for wood and steel, deflection computations in reinforced concrete are hampered by uncertainties in the determination of an effective moment of inertia. Under normal service loads, tensile cracks exist due to bending and shear, and the length and frequency of these cracks depends upon the magnitude and placement of the loads. Thus, the moment of inertia available to control deflection varies over the length of the beam and is a function of the loading history. While approximate methods have been developed for computing effective moments of inertia, the procedures are somewhat complicated and beyond the limited scope of this chapter. Briefly, the amount of cross section that can contribute to the moment of inertia is a function of the size of the actual moment relative to the smaller moment required to crack the section. If the "cracking moment" is large and the actual moment small, the effective I will be large. The resistance of a section to cracking can be increased by increasing the overall dimensions and/or by specifying stronger concrete. The placement of steel in the compressive area of the section will also enable the beam to take more load before developing flexural cracks.

This latter procedure is also helpful in combatting the effects of creep, which occurs in concrete in the presence of sustained compressive stress. Depending on the magnitude of such stresses, the long-term deflection due to creep can actually be twice that of the initial elastic deformation. When a large portion of the design load will be applied over long time periods, as is the case with high dead loads or the live loads in storage areas, compression steel can be used to reduce the concrete stress and the effects of creep. As indicated previously, compression steel is also sometimes used to increase bending capacity. It is worthwhile to note that whenever reinforcing carries compressive forces, the shear stirrups serve the added and necessary function of providing lateral support for the long slender bars. Without this containment, the bars would easily buckle outward in spite of the concrete cover.

17-8 CONSIDERATIONS IN COLUMN DESIGN

Most columns in reinforced concrete are loaded in both compression and bending. Because of the continuity of the beam-to-column connections, moment is usually applied to a column at each floor level (see Figure 7-51). Even in symmetrical situations (e.g., where beams of equal span frame into the opposite sides of a column), the potential difference in live loads on the two spans will require an analysis for moment. Even where computations and details provide that all the load be concentric, the ACI Code specifies a decrease in axial capacity to guard against the effects of imperfect materials and/or improper positioning of members and reinforcing.

Columns placed in a rectangular grid are designed

for primary bending about one or two axes, depending upon loading and framing patterns. The concept is similar to the one developed for combined stresses in Section 12-2 in that different amounts of resistance may be required of the column section for the two axes. Rectangular cross sections and different reinforcing patterns can be used to provide the proper response to these moments.

There are two basic kinds of reinforced concrete columns: those with lateral ties and those with spiral ties. Figure 17-16 provides an example of each. Laterally tied columns are usually square or rectangular, and those with spiral ties are usually circular, but exceptions are found in each case. The purpose of either type of tie is to prevent the buckling of the longitudinal bars in compression, as the concrete cover required for moisture and fire protection is too thin to provide the necessary restraint. The spacing and configuration of the lateral

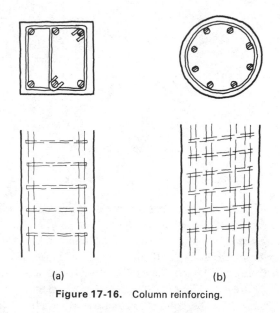

(a)   (b)

Figure 17-16. Column reinforcing.

ties or the pitch of the spiral is carefully controlled by the Code as a function of the number and size of the longitudinal bars. Columns with lateral ties are easier to construct and are usually less expensive than those with spirals. However, the continuous spiral tie imparts a certain ductility to a column under overload conditions. At failure, a spirally tied column will continue to deflect (shorten) while maintaining a high load capacity, whereas a laterally tied column will fail without exhibiting this "yielding" characteristic. In certain cases, the advantages provided by this type of ductile failure will outweigh the extra expense.

The different behavior of the two column types is recognized by the Code by providing different ϕ factors (see Section 17-2) and by specifying different amounts of reduction for possible accidental eccentricities. The eccentricity reduction factors to be used for the design of "axially loaded" columns are, respectively, 0.80 for laterally tied columns and 0.85 for spirally tied columns.

For either type of column, the Code also spells out minimum and maximum steel percentages and makes numerous provisions regarding the detailing of reinforcing patterns and connections. A full consideration of these requirements is more properly included in a text dealing exclusively with reinforced concrete, where a chapter or more could be devoted to column design. Only the fundamental concepts are included here, and a proper quantitative analysis with examples has been deliberately avoided.

The behavior of a reinforced concrete column is a function of the relative amounts of bending moment and axial load. (Eccentric loads can always be converted to an axial load and a moment.) Figure 17-17 shows a

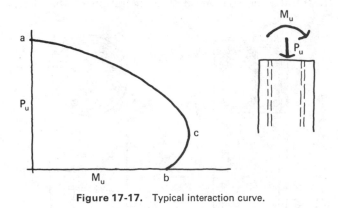

Figure 17-17. Typical interaction curve.

plot of axial load versus moment for a column with bending about one axis. Such a diagram is called a *column interaction curve* and portrays the influence of moment upon axial capacity, and vice versa. The point labeled *a* on the ordinate represents the strength of the column under pure axial load and the point labeled *b* on the abscissa is the bending capacity of the section under pure moment. For an ideal homogeneous and isotropic material, with equal resistance to the effects of tensile and compressive stress, the curve would assume a straight line between *a* and *b*. For reinforced concrete, hardly such a material, the diagram is curved. Since by Code provision bending failures are forced to occur by yield of the tensile steel, the largest moment capacity for a given section will exist under the action of some axial load. An axial load places all the concrete (and reinforcing bars) in compression and effectively increases the amount of tension that can be sustained in bending. In effect, the existing compressive stress in the tensile steel must be brought to zero ("using up" some of the bending load) before these bars can go into tension due to the balance of the moment. In this case, point *c* represents the maximum moment capacity of the section.

(The compressive stress may be thought of as a kind of "prestress" and, in fact, the fundamental idea of prestressed concrete, presented in the next section, has the same basis.) The shape of these interaction curves is a function of the amount of reinforcing and its location, strength of the materials, and shape of the cross section. In general, moment will reduce the capacity of a column to withstand axial loads. Under overload, the column will fail by concrete crushing and compressive steel yield due to the additive effects of axial and bending forces. However, when the moment is relatively large (high eccentricity), a small amount of axial load is actually desirable.

To make column design less tedious, certain design aids have been developed by the American Concrete Institute and others. These usually consist of a series of curves, such as the one in Figure 17-17, in either graphical or tabular form. Using these aids, it is relatively easy to select a column of the appropriate dimensions and steel percentage once the ultimate axial load and moment are known.

The theoretical capacity of a short column under axial load is easy to compute because the stress is uniform and both materials will be taken to their maximum possible values.

$$P_u = 0.85f'_c A_c + F_y A_s \qquad (17\text{-}8)$$

where P_u = ultimate axial load (N)
A_c = area of the concrete (m²)
A_s = area of the steel (m²)

In this equation, the concrete strength is usually reduced by a factor of 0.85, as it is here. This is because tests have shown that the strength of concrete under slowly applied loads (as in a column) is less than that of a cylinder test, where the load is relatively rapidly applied.

It is important to realize that Equation (17-8) cannot be used for design purposes, even for axial loads, unless the P_u value is further reduced by the previously mentioned eccentricity factor and the appropriate ϕ factor. Most concrete columns are subjected to applied moments of considerable magnitude at both top and bottom by virtue of their continuity with beams and girders. Interactive concepts will then control the design rather than axial capacity. It is also important to realize that the equation totally ignores column slenderness, a factor that can have a large influence on the ultimate axial load, bending moment included or not.

As with steel columns, the effect of end rigidity will influence the ultimate buckling load of a slender concrete column. As pointed out in Section 13-8 pertaining to steel columns, the end-conditions factor K can become quite large if a column is in a frame subjected to sidesway. Most steel structures have a separate bracing system to prevent sidesway due to lateral loads and asymmetrical loading. Concrete frames, on the other hand, especially those in low- and medium-rise buildings, frequently use the continuity of the beam-to-column connections to resist such forces. As shown in Figure 17-18, the column ends will move out of vertical alignment and the ends will rotate due to sidesway. The effective K value can then be considerably greater than unity and is dependent upon the relative stiffnesses of the column and the flexural members. If the frame is braced, however, K is unity or even less.

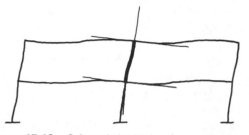

Figure 17-18. Column behavior in a frame with side-sway.

For this reason, the Code specifies different design procedures, sometimes quite involved, to evaluate the effects of slenderness in braced and unbraced frames. The end result is to magnify the maximum column moment from the framing members by a factor that accounts for the severity of the slenderness and the direction of the moments. The column section is then designed in the usual manner for the axial load and the magnified moment.

It is also recognized that many concrete columns are stocky enough so that the slenderness effects can be ignored altogether and the time-consuming analysis avoided. In a braced frame, for example, it has been found that slenderness effects will not be critical for a column with an unbraced length not greater than about seven times its least dimension. Depending upon the end moments and stiffnesses, this value can rise to about 15 or even higher. It is quite logical to assume that columns in unbraced frames cannot be as slender as those in braced frames.

17-9 INTRODUCTION TO PRESTRESSING

The fundamental principle behind prestressing is presented in Section 12-1, which deals with combined axial and bending stresses. The stresses due to bending are added algebraically to the axial stresses, and the member is designed for the maximum tensile and compressive stresses that result. If the axial stress is compressive, as in Figure 12-1, the extreme fiber stress in compression will be increased and the extreme fiber stress in tension will be reduced. One can readily see the beneficial effects of placing a concrete beam in compression before applying any bending loads. The net effect will be a reduction in the tensile stresses that cause concrete to crack.

Prestressing may be defined as the purposeful introduction of stresses into a member so that undesirable stresses that result from the applied loads may be reduced.

While the idea of prestressing concrete was explored much earlier, the most significant developments took place in Europe in the 1930s and were often pioneered by Eugene Freysinnet (1879–1962), a French engineer.

Prestressed concrete is usually more expensive than regular reinforced concrete but it has a number of distinct advantages. It can span further with less depth. Tension cracks can be reduced or eliminated. Beam deflection can be reduced or eliminated. The smaller cross sections also mean less structural dead weight, always a concern with concrete structures.

The higher cost is due, in part, to the fact that higher-strength materials are required to obtain the benefits of prestressing. The prestress force is usually imparted to the concrete by embedded steel strands which are stretched elastically by hydraulic jacks. When the jacking force is removed, the steel strand attempts to return to its original length but is prevented from doing so by the concrete, which goes into compression. Ordinary steel cannot be used for prestressing, for the simple reason that it will not strain very much before yielding. If a reinforcing bar with a yield strength of 400 MPa is stretched so that it has a tensile stress of 200 MPa, its strain level will be about 0.0010. This is about equal to the strain that would result in the concrete due to shrinkage and creep. In other words, in time, the concrete would shorten about as much as we had stretched the steel, and there would be no prestress left. If, however, high-strength cable steel is used, with a yield value of 1000 MPa or greater, and it is stressed to 500 MPa, there will still be plenty of prestress left after the concrete shortens. The high prestress forces needed to make the steel effective also result in the need for higher-strength concrete, and f'_c values of 40 and 50 MPa are not uncommon. Depending upon the application, the higher cost of these materials can be more than offset by the advantages of prestressing.

There are essentially two kinds of prestressing used with concrete: pretensioning and posttensioning. The prefix relates to the time at which the steel is stretched (i.e., before or after the concrete is placed). In *pretensioning*, the technique usually used with precast beams, many steel strands about 10 mm in diameter are stretched between two rigid steel abutments on a prestressing bed. The most commonly used strand is composed of seven wires, six of which spiral around a center one.

The distance between the abutments.may be 100 m or more in length as several members placed end to end can be made at one time with this technique. A schematic diagram of this arrangement is shown in Figure 17-19. After the strands are all stretched to the desired tension and held by the abutments, the concrete is placed in the

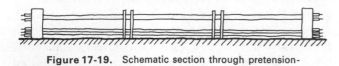

Figure 17-19. Schematic section through pretensioning bed.

steel forms and cured to the minimum strength necessary to accept the prestress force. The strands are then cut between each of the members and the prestress force is imparted to the concrete by bond. The members are removed from the forms for further curing, enabling the forms to be reused immediately. Pretensioning has the high level of quality control normally associated with factory production environments.

Posttensioning can be used with cast-in-place concrete and is done by placing the concrete around one or more tendons that have been positioned in the form. These tendons, often about 50 mm in diameter, are normally draped as shown in Figure 17-20 and are coated

Figure 17-20. Posttensioning tendons.

or sheathed with some plastic material to prevent bonding with the concrete. Alternatively, they are placed in conduits or passageways left in the concrete. After the concrete has been cured to the desired strength level, the tendons are stretched and fixed to anchorage plates at their ends. The prestress force is imparted to the concrete via these end anchorages. The lack of bond between the tendons and the concrete means that tensioning can occur in stages if required by the design. (It is sometimes desirable to introduce further prestress force after some of the dead loads have been applied to the beam.)

Whether pretensioned or posttensioned, all prestressed members have other reinforcing as well, sometimes for flexure and usually for shear. Pretensioned members must be reinforced for handling and posttensioned members for the high localized anchorage stresses.

Because posttensioning is done on site, it is generally used with regular monolithic concrete construction. After construction is complete, it is usually not possible to tell whether a beam is posttensioned or not except perhaps by its high span/depth ratio. The nature of the

building is still characteristically concrete and usually has the continuity achievable with this material. Precast and pretensioned construction, on the other hand, assumes a different nature. The architecture that results is often one which reflects the fact that the building is made from prefabricated pieces or parts. In this respect, the design vocabulary is similar to that of wood and steel and less like concrete in the usual sense. The real structural design issues are often associated with how the pieces join rather than how they affect one another in terms of moments and deflections. These are general observations, of course, and are subject to exception. For instance, posttensioning techniques are sometimes used to "fasten" precast segments of buildings together at the site, and a different kind of continuity results.

The location of the prestressing steel is very important in both pretensioning and posttensioning. With a concentric prestress force, the distribution of the axial stresses is uniform over the cross section, as in Figure 12-1. This means that the compressive stress will always be increased by the same amount that the tensile stress is reduced. A large prestress force in combination with bending stresses could result in an overstress of the concrete in compression. This can be avoided by moving the prestress force away from the centroid toward the tension side of the beam. It is then called an *eccentric prestress force*, and its effects are shown in Figure 17-21.

An eccentric force can be treated as having two components, an axial force and a couple. By changing the eccentricity e, it is possible to manipulate the prestress distribution. A prestress force placed below the centroid will result in a slight upward camber in the beam (depending upon the magnitude of the self-weight), and it is usually considered desirable to induce a little tension in what will become the extreme compressive fiber.

In the dual signs of the following equation, the top sign refers to the top fiber stress and the bottom sign to the bottom fiber stress. As in Figure 17-21, it has been assumed that the gravity loads will result in positive moment.

$$f_p = -\frac{P}{A} \pm \frac{Pec}{I} \qquad (17\text{-}9)$$

where $f_p =$ top and bottom stresses due to prestress (Pa). Equation (17-9) is based on those of Section 12-2. As usual, the positive sign denotes tension and the negative sign, compression.

The addition of the regular bending stresses f_b from the live and dead loads is shown in Figure 17-22. Once again, by proper location of the prestress force, the final stresses can be manipulated. It is even possible to have a section completely in compression under all the

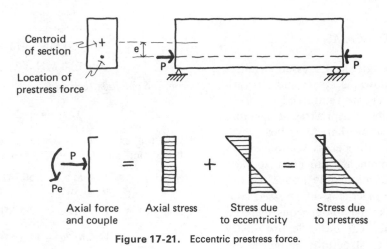

Centroid
of section

Location of
prestress force

Axial force   Axial stress   Stress due   Stress due
and couple   to eccentricity   to prestress

Figure 17-21. Eccentric prestress force.

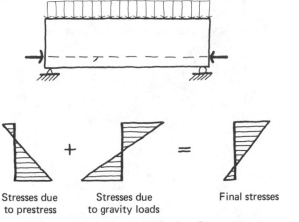

Stresses due   Stresses due   Final stresses
to prestress   to gravity loads

Figure 17-22. Prestresses plus bending stresses.

loads. Since $f_b = Mc/I$, the final stresses are obtained as follows:

$$f = -\frac{P}{A} \pm \frac{Pec}{I} \pm \frac{Mc}{I} \qquad (17\text{-}10)$$

where f represents the final top and bottom stresses (Pa).

Obviously, it would seem ideal to be able to vary the location of the prestress force over the length of the beam in response to a changing gravity load moment. This is relatively easy to do with the draped tendons used in posttensioning, and continuous beams are often prestressed using continuous tendons such as that of Figure 17-23. Even the necessarily straight tendons used in pretensioning are often placed in a triangular pattern in elevation so that the maximum eccentricity occurs at the point of greatest moment.

Figure 17-23. Varying tendon eccentricity (shown greatly exaggerated).

Prestressed concrete is used for floor slabs as well as beams. Many flat plate systems are constructed with posttensioning tendons running in both directions. They are spaced over the entire floor and are often continuous from one side of the building to the other, moving up and down within the slab as required by the moments. For buildings having a relatively constant structural bay size with no unusual loads or conditions, the use of precast pretensioned planks can often result in considerable savings. Under light floor or roof loads, a highly prestressed plank system can span up to about 12 m.

Most manufacturers of pretensioned concrete have standard planks and other sections, such as the typical ones shown in Figure 17-24. In many cases, they can be selected directly from load tables provided by the manufacturer. Because of the cost of transportation, such precast sections are usually more popular for building sites that are not great distances from the precasting plant.

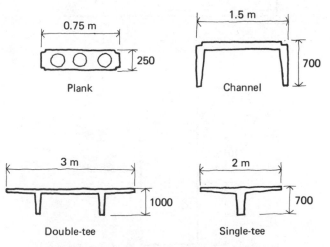

0.75 m   1.5 m
         250   700
Plank   Channel

3 m   2 m
          1000   700
Double-tee   Single-tee

Figure 17-24. Typical standard precast sections with representative dimensions.

17-10 BASIC ANALYSIS OF PRESTRESSED BEAMS

The complete analysis and design of prestressed members calls for the use of both allowable stress and strength design procedures. Unlike regular reinforced concrete, the cracks on the tension side of a prestressed member are infrequent, if not absent altogether. Most beams will have compression over the entire cross section except at locations of maximum moment, and even at these points tensile stresses will develop only under the full service load. In the absence of cracks, prestressed concrete behaves much more like a homogeneous material than like reinforced concrete. The basic flexure theory has more validity, and many structural designers use allowable or working stress techniques to proportion members and strength methods as a final check on their capacities. In the brief introduction provided in this section and the one that follows, we shall use only working stress methods and check only a few stresses. A thorough analysis of prestressed concrete behavior is well beyond the intent of this text and can be found in numerous books that are devoted entirely to the subject.

EXAMPLE 17-8

The prestressed beam in Figure 17-25 has two tendons for a total area of 2500 mm². The stress in the tendons is 600 MPa. Assuming that the uniform load shown includes the beam self-weight, find the top and bottom fiber stresses at midspan.

Solution: First find the stresses due to the prestress force alone.

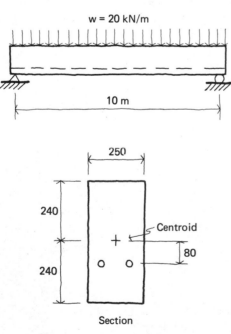

Figure 17-25. Prestressed beam.

$$P = F_s A_s$$
$$= 600 \text{ MN/m}^2(0.0025 \text{ m}^2)$$
$$= 1.50 \text{ MN}$$

From the previous section,

$$f_p = -\frac{P}{A} \pm \frac{Pec}{I} \tag{17-9}$$

Using the entire cross section, we can find that $A = 120\,000 \text{ mm}^2$ and $I = 2300(10)^6 \text{ mm}^4$.

$$f_p = -\frac{1.50 \text{ MN}}{0.120 \text{ m}^2} \pm \frac{1.50 \text{ MN}(0.080 \text{ m})(0.240 \text{ m})}{0.002\,30 \text{ m}^4}$$

$$f_p \atop \text{top} = -12.5 \text{ MPa} + 12.5 \text{ MPa} = 0$$

$$f_p \atop \text{bottom} = -12.5 \text{ MPa} - 12.5 \text{ MPa} = -25 \text{ MPa}$$

These prestresses are shown in Figure 17-26(a) and are constant over the full length of the beam.

The midspan bending stresses are given by

$$f_b = \pm \frac{Mc}{I}$$

$$M = \frac{wL^2}{8}$$

$$= \frac{20 \text{ kN/m}(10 \text{ m})^2}{8}$$

$$= 250 \text{ kN} \cdot \text{m}$$

$$= \mp \frac{0.250 \text{ MN} \cdot \text{m}(0.240 \text{ m})}{0.002\,30 \text{ m}^4}$$

$$f_b \atop \text{top} = -26 \text{ MPa}$$

$$f_b \atop \text{bottom} = +26 \text{ MPa}$$

These stresses are shown in Figure 17-26(b), and the combined stress distribution appears in Figure 17-26(c).

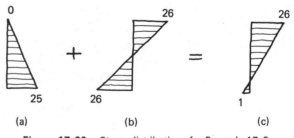

(a)   (b)   (c)

Figure 17-26. Stress distributions for Example 17-8.

Problems

17-11. The pretensioned beam in Figure 17-27 has a group of six deflected tendons. The load w is 16 kN/m, which includes the beam self-weight. Let the prestress force be 700 kN and determine the midspan extreme fiber stresses.

17-12. The T-beam of Figure 17-28 has a prestress force of 6 MN. The maximum allowable tensile stress in the concrete used is 2 MPa at the time of tensioning. If

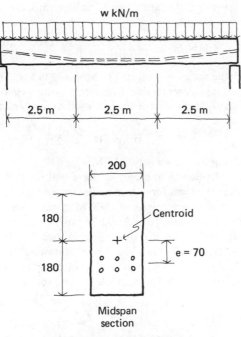

Figure 17-27. Prestressed beam.

the only load on the beam is its own self-weight, compute the maximum permissible tendon eccentricity at midspan.

17-13. The T-beam of Figure 17-28 has a prestress force of 8 MN with a midspan eccentricity of 200 mm. How much load w kN/m, including the self-weight, can be placed on this beam if the concrete stresses at the time of loading are limited to 20 MPa in compression and 4 MPa in tension? Assume that the midspan section controls.

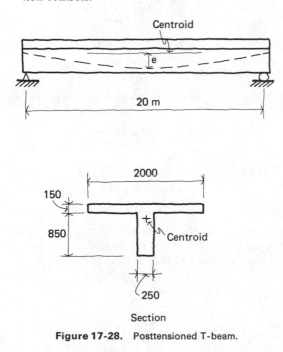

Figure 17-28. Posttensioned T-beam.

17-11 INITIAL AND FINAL STRESSES

The basis for any type of working stress or service load design is that the allowable stresses for the material(s) never be exceeded, that is, that the factor of safety inherent in these stresses must not be reduced under the most severe of anticipated loading conditions. It is important to recognize that with prestressed concrete there are at least two stages that may be critical. The first occurs when the prestress is initially applied to the concrete. With pretensioning, this is referred to as the time of transfer; with posttensioning, it happens when the tendons are "jacked." Usually at this time, the concrete is not fully cured and may be quite weak. The economics of construction do not permit the lapse of several weeks before stressing the concrete. With eccentrically located tendons, tension will usually exist on the far edge of member and compression on the edge nearest the tendons. At this stage, the self-weight of the member is usually the only load that is acting to reduce these stresses, so this condition could become critical. It must also be remembered that the prestress values usually vary over the length of beam as do the self-weight stresses.

The second and more obvious stage occurs when the beam is finally loaded with the full service load. Now the concrete has presumably reached its full (28-day) strength. The load acts in opposition to the prestress, and what was the tensile fiber before goes into compression, and vice versa. These final stresses must not exceed the allowable values.

The American Concrete Institute has provided two sets of allowable stresses for use with prestressed members, one for the initial application of the prestressing force and a second for the final loading stage. These are summarized in Table 17-3. The quantity f'_{ci} refers to the cylinder strength of the concrete at the time of prestress.

TABLE 17-3 *ACI Allowable Stresses for Prestressed Concrete*

Stage	*Allowable stresses (MPa)*	
	Tension	*Compression*
Initial (at prestress)	$+0.25\sqrt{f'_{ci}}$	$-0.60f'_{ci}$
Final (at service load)	$+0.50\sqrt{f'_c}$	$-0.45f'_c$

This analysis at more than one stage of loading is further complicated by the fact that the prestress force is not constant. It drops considerably between the initial and final stages, the difference being called the *prestress loss.* The amount of this loss depends upon many factors, including shrinkage, creep, elastic shortening, and friction, and is generally about 15 or 20%. It is clear that different values of the force must be used for the different stress checks. The initial prestress force is usually denoted as P_i and the final force as P when using Equations (17-9) and (17-10).

The Code recommends allowable steel stresses that are quite high, 70 or 80% of the ultimate stress, for two reasons. First, the steel stress will always drop from its initial value, and second, the stress is known with much more than the usual order of construction accuracy. For one thing, it is very easy to measure the steel elongation during the jacking operation and use the modulus of elasticity to get the stress.

EXAMPLE 17-9

The beam section in Figure 17-29 is pretensioned with straight strands, stressed to their maximum allowable value of 1000 MPa. The span is 7 m. Use the allowable stresses in Table 17-3.

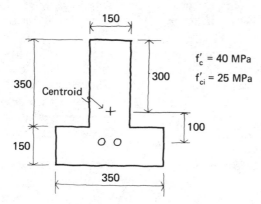

Figure 17-29. Inverted T-beam.

(a) Determine the maximum permitted area of prestressing steel.
(b) If the prestress losses are 20%, find the maximum uniform load that can safely be applied to this beam.

Solution: The area of the cross section is 105 000 mm² and the moment of inertia is 2270(10)⁶ mm⁴. The eccentricity of the steel is 100 mm.

(a) The amount of steel will be controlled by the initial allowable stresses at a section near the end of the beam where the prestress is not tempered by the self-weight. It could be controlled by either the tensile stress or the compressive stress. The extreme fiber stresses at the time of prestress are measured by

$$f_p = -\frac{P_i}{A} \pm \frac{P_i e c}{I} \qquad (17\text{-}9)$$

From Table 17-3, the allowable tensile stress is $0.25\sqrt{f'_{ci}}$; the allowable compressive stress is $0.60 f'_{ci}$. In this case, the needed values are, respectively, 1.25 MPa and 15 MPa. If the tensile stress at the top governs, then by

substituting the appropriate values into the equation above, we get

$$+1.25 \text{ MN/m}^2 = -\frac{P_i}{0.105 \text{ m}^2} + \frac{P_i(0.100 \text{ m})(0.300 \text{ m})}{2270(10)^{-6} \text{ m}^4}$$

Solving for P_i gives us 0.338 MN or 338 kN. The initial allowable compressive stress (note the negative sign) at the bottom fiber is limited by the same equation:

$$-15 \text{ MN/m}^2 = -\frac{P_i}{0.105 \text{ m}^2} - \frac{P_i(0.100 \text{ m})(0.200 \text{ m})}{2270(10)^{-6} \text{ m}^{-4}}$$

Solving for P_i, we get 0.818 MN or 818 kN.

Evidently, the tensile stress will control, and the initial prestress force can be no larger than 0.338 MN. If the steel is stressed to 1000 MPa (as given), its area can be no larger than 0.000 338 m², or 338 mm².

(b) After losses, the prestressing force becomes 0.80 times 338 kN, or 270 kN. The Code allowable stresses are $0.50\sqrt{f'_c}$ in tension and $0.45 f'_c$ in compression, or, in this case, 3.16 MPa and 18 MPa, respectively.

$$f = -\frac{P}{A} \pm \frac{P e c}{I} \mp \frac{M c}{I} \qquad (17\text{-}10)$$

We can use Equation (17-10) to determine the largest permissible gravity load moment. If the bottom fiber tension controls, then

$$3.16 \text{ MN/m}^2 = -\frac{0.270 \text{ MN}}{0.105 \text{ m}^2}$$
$$-\frac{0.270 \text{ MN}(0.100 \text{ m})(0.200 \text{ m})}{2270(10)^{-6} \text{ m}^4}$$
$$+\frac{M(0.200 \text{ m})}{2270(10)^{-6} \text{ m}^4}$$

Solving for M, we find

$$M = 0.092 \text{ MN·m}$$
$$= 92 \text{ kN·m}$$

If the top fiber compressive stresses control, then

$$-18 \text{ MN/m}^2 = -\frac{0.270 \text{ MN}}{0.105 \text{ m}^2}$$
$$+\frac{0.270 \text{ MN}(0.100 \text{ m})(0.300 \text{ m})}{2270(10)^{-6} \text{ m}^4}$$
$$-\frac{M(0.300 \text{ m})}{2270(10)^{-6} \text{ m}^4}$$

Solving for M gives us

$$M = 0.144 \text{ MN·m}$$
$$= 144 \text{ kN·m}$$

Again, the tensile stress will control. The maximum moment is 92 kN·m and the maximum permissible load is readily computed for the simple beam as

$$w = \frac{8M}{L^2}$$
$$= \frac{8(92 \text{ kN·m})}{(7 \text{ m})^2}$$
$$= 15 \text{ kN/m}$$

The self-weight of the beam is 0.105 m² × 23.5 kN/m³, or 2.5 kN/m. Therefore, the net load that can be carried by the beam is 15 less 2.5, or 12.5 kN/m.

Problems

17-14. The roof plank in Figure 17-30 must carry a load of $w = 4$ kN/m, which includes its own self-weight. Its design is based on the ACI allowable stresses.

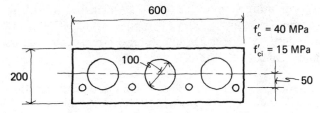

Figure 17-30. Precast plank cross section.

(a) Determine the maximum permitted prestress force.

(b) If the prestress loss is 18%, how far can the plank safely span under the given load?

17-15. The cross section in Figure 3-38 is inverted and used for a simply supported girder spanning 20 m. In addition to its own weight, it must carry an applied live load of 5 kN/m and an applied dead load of 10 kN/m. Assume that the design is governed by the ACI allowable stresses and that the concrete has its full strength of 50 MPa at the time of jacking (i.e., $f'_{ci} = f'_c = 50$ MPa). Assume that the stresses at midspan will control.

(a) If P_i is 3 MN, determine the maximum permissible eccentricity if the load on the member is its own weight plus the dead load of 10 kN/m.

(b) If the prestress loss is 20%, are the stresses within the allowables under the full load?

What Is SI Metric?

SI metric is the name given to the new measurement system which is being adopted on a worldwide basis. It differs somewhat from the long-standing European metric system. SI stands for Le Système International d'Unités, a name generated by the 36 nations meeting at the 11th General Conference on Weights and Measures (CGPM) in 1960.

SI is a coherent means of measurement based on the meter–kilogram–second–ampere system of fundamental units. Conversions within the system (e.g., ounces to pounds and inches to feet, as we do in the customary system) are never necessary.

How New Is the Metric System to the United States?

In 1866, Congress made the metric system a legal system of units for U.S. use. In 1875 the United States and 16 other nations formed the General Conference on Weights and Measures (CGPM). The United States has been active in the periodic meetings of this group.

In 1893, an Executive Order made the meter and the kilogram fundamental standards from which the pound and the yard would henceforth be derived.

In 1960 the CGPM established the SI system and has subsequently modified it in several meetings.

Who Is in Charge of Metric Conversion in the U.S. Construction Industry?

The American National Standards Institute (ANSI) is directly responsible to the U.S. Congress for metric conversion in general. ANSI established the American National Metrication Council (ANMC), which in turn set up five national committees, one of which is for the construction industry. This is the Construction Industries Coordinating Committee (CICC), which has seven subcommittees now at work: Designers (A/E), Codes and Standards, Product Manufacturers, Users, Contractors, Labor, and Real Estate.

What Are the Principal Units Used in Structures Which Will Be of Concern to the Architect?

Name	Symbol	Use
Meter	m	Site plan dimensions, building plans
Millimeter	mm	Building plans and details
Square millimeters	mm^2	Small areas
Square meters	m^2	Large areas
Hectare	ha	Very large areas (1 hectare equals 10^4 m^2)
Cubic millimeters	mm^3	Small volumes
Cubic meters	m^3	Large volumes
Section modulus	mm^3	Property of cross section
Moment of inertia	mm^4	Property of cross section
Kilogram	kg	Mass of all building materials
Newton	N	Force (all structural computations)
Pascal	Pa	Stress or pressure (all structural computations; one pascal equals one newton per square meter)
Mass density	kg/m^3	Density of materials
Degree Celsius	°C	Temperature measurement

Appendices

What Are the Common Prefixes?

Multiplication factors	Prefix	Symbol
10^{12}	tera	T
10^9	giga (jĭga)	G
10^6	mega	M
10^3	kilo	k
10^2	hecto	h
10^1	deka	da
10^{-1}	deci	d
10^{-2}	centi	c
10^{-3}	milli	m
10^{-6}	micro	m
10^{-9}	nano (năno)	n
10^{-12}	pico (pēco)	p
10^{-15}	femto	f
10^{-18}	atto	a

frequently used by architects

*To be consistant and avoid confusion, prefixes should change in steps of 10^3; therefore, these four should be avoided if at all possible.

What Are Some Rules of "Grammar"?

Double prefixes should never be used; e.g., use Gm (gigameter), not Mkm (megakilometer).

Base units are not capitalized unless you are writing a *symbol* that is derived from a proper name; e.g., 12 meters or 12 m, 60 newtons or 60 N.

Plurals are accomplished normally except for quantities less than 1. In such cases the "s" is deleted; e.g., 2.6 meters and 0.6 meter.

Prefix symbols are not capitalized except for M (mega), G (giga), and T (tera). This avoids confusion with m (meter), g (gram), and t (metric ton). One metric ton (t) is equal to one megagram (Mg).

Periods are not used after symbols except at the end of a sentence. Commas should not be used to clarify groups of digits; instead, use spaced groups of three on each side of the decimal point.

832 604.789 06   not   832,604.78906

20 800   not   20,800

Exception: The space is optional in groups of four digits; e.g.,

1486   or   1 486

0.3248   or   0.324 8

Division is indicated by a slash; e.g., a certain steel beam has a mass of 100 kg/m.

Multiplication is indicated by a dot placed at mid-height of the letters; e.g., a certain moment or torque might be given as 100 kN·m.

Decimals (not dual units) should be used; e.g., for the length of one side of a building lot, state 118.6 m rather than 118 m, 600 mm.

All dimensions on a given drawing should have the same units.

In Terms of Concepts Used in Structures, What Is the Major Change from the Customary System to SI?

In the SI metric system of units, there is a clear distinction made between mass and force. The customary system treated mass and force as if they both had force units; i.e., we said that a beam weighed 100 *lb* per foot and that the force in a truss member was 1800 *lb*. It was correct to use pounds for force but not for weight (mass). In the European metric system, we said that the beam weighed 149 *kg* per meter and that the force in a truss member was 818 *kg of force* (kgf). It was correct to use kilograms for weight (mass) but not for force.

F is equal to *MA*   *F* is not equal to *M*

SI units do not confuse the two terms. We can "weigh" items such as cubic meters of concrete by establishing their mass in kilograms, but force is expressed in newtons and pressure (stress) is in newtons per square meter (pascals).

A commonly used illustration to explain the difference between force and mass is to look at what happens in different fields of gravity. Assume that you are holding a 1-kg mass in the palm of your hand. On earth, the kg would exert a force of 9.8 N downward on your hand. (This would vary slightly, depending upon whether you were located at sea level or on top of Mt. Everest.) At Tranquility Base on our moon it would push with a force of 1.6 N, and on the surface of Jupiter you would feel a force of 24.1 N!

For structural engineering purposes on earth, we can multiply our loads (if given in kg) by 9.8 to get the number of newtons of force which we must design for.

How Will the New Units Modify Design Drawings?

Conceptually, the square meter is the new unit of plan area replacing the square foot. Length measurements may be in meters or millimeters, except that it is desirable to express all the measurements on a single drawing in the same units. (Among other advantages, this obviates the need for placing m or mm as a suffix to each dimension.) The millimeter is preferred for all detail, section, and plan drawings up through the scale of 1:200. On plans, this results in small numbers for wall thicknesses and large numbers for room dimensions, but eliminates the need for fractions. Even on details, the millimeter is small enough so that, with few exceptions, fractions can be avoided.

(In this text, beam spans and column heights are given in meters for computational ease. The fact that stress is expressed in terms of newtons per square meter means that most dimensions should be converted to meters for use in formulas and equations.)

The basic building modules recommended are 100 mm and 300 mm. The 300-mm dimension is very close to 12 inches and will be an easy concept to adopt. At the same time, it is much more flexible than the foot, in that it is *evenly* divisible by 2, 3, 4, 5, 6, 10, 15, 20, 25, 30, 50, 60, 100, and 150.

Commonly Used Scales

Customary	Nearest convenient ratio	Metric equivalent
$\frac{1}{16}'' = 1' - 0''$	1 : 200	5 mm = 1 m
$\frac{1}{8}'' = 1' - 0''$	1 : 100	10 mm = 1 m
$\frac{1}{4}'' = 1' - 0''$	1 : 50	20 mm = 1 m
$\frac{1}{2}'' = 1' - 0''$	1 : 20	50 mm = 1 m
$\frac{3}{4}'' = 1' - 0''$	1 : 10	100 mm = 1 m
$1\frac{1}{2}'' = 1' - 0''$	1 : 10	100 mm = 1 m
$3'' = 1' - 0''$	1 : 5	200 mm = 1 m
$1'' = 20'$	1 : 200	5 mm = 1 m
$1'' = 50'$	1 : 500	2 mm = 1 m

How Is Conversion to SI Being Made in the Building Materials Industry?

There are two ways to convert. *Soft* conversion means only paper dimensions and properties change; *hard* conversion means the physical piece changes dimensions. Because of its size and diversity, the construction industry will probably lag behind others in making the changeover. A lot of coordination between the various technical committees must take place before jumping ahead; e.g., suppose the concrete block industry decides to hard-convert, this will mean that window-frame producers are not free to soft-convert.

Initially, it appears as though most structural materials manufacturers are soft-converting, and this text has been written with that in mind. Framing lumber cross sections have been soft-converted to the nearest millimeter. Sheet materials may actually hard-convert. The same is true at this writing for the masonry industries and concrete-reinforcing-bar producers. The steel industry is initially soft-converting but will probably undertake a hard conversion at a later date, reducing the number of sections available. The steel cross-sectional dimensions and properties used in this text have been obtained by converting the customary values.

Are There Some Conversion Factors That We Can Use While Becoming Familiar with the New Units?

There are endless tables of conversion factors available. However, the more we use conversion factors, the longer it will be before we are able to "think" in metric. In any event, one must keep the desired level of accuracy in mind when making conversions. For example, suppose that you are working with a reinforced concrete beam 12×20 inches in cross section. You wish to convert its area in square inches to millimeters squared. (The dimensions imply an accuracy of plus or minus 1 square inch, or about 0.4%.) Following the table below, you could convert to metric by multiplying 240 by 6.451 600 E+02 to get an area of 154 838 mm². To use this quantity would be deceiving in terms of accuracy because it is subject to the same $\pm 0.4\%$ tolerance level, or in this case about 600 mm². In other words, the area could range from approximately 154 200 to about 155 400. Expressing the converted area as simply 155 000 mm² would be much more consistent.

A few conversion factors that may prove useful in structural analysis are presented below.

To convert from	to	Multiply by
inches	mm	2.540 000 E+01
feet	m	3.048 000 E−01
in.²	mm²	6.451 600 E+02
ft²	m²	9.290 304 E−02
in.³	mm³	1.638 706 E+04
ft³	m³	2.831 685 E−02
in.⁴	mm⁴	4.162 314 E+05
°F	°C	$t°C = (t°F - 32)/1.8$
lb (mass) per foot	kg/m	1.488 163 E+00
lb (force) per foot	N/m	1.459 390 E+01
strain/°F (thermal expansion)	strain/°C	1.800 000 E+00
lb (force)	N	4.448 222 E+00
kip (force)	kN	4.448 222 E+00
lb-ft (moment)	N·m	1.355 818 E+00
kip-ft (moment)	kN·m	1.355 818 E+00
psi (stress)	kPa	6.894 757 E+00
ksi (stress)	MPa	6.894 757 E+00
psf (uniform load)	kN/m²	4.788 026 E−02

References

Metric Practice Guide, Bulletin E 380–76, American Society for Testing and Materials, 19 Race Street, Philadelphia, Pa. 19103.

Recommended Practice for the Use of Metric (SI) Units in Building Design and Construction, NBS Technical Note 938, U.S. Government Printing Office, Washington, D.C. 20402 (SD Cat. No. C13.46: 938).

APPENDIX B
SELECTED BIBLIOGRAPHY

List 1 Qualitative

AIA RESEARCH CORPORATION. *Earthquakes and Architects.* Washington, D.C.: AIA Research Corporation, 1975.

AMBROSE, JAMES E. *Building Structures Primer.* New York: Wiley, 1963.

BILL, MAX, ED. *Robert Maillart.* Zurich: d'Architecture (Artemis), 1949.

CASSIE, W. FISHER, AND NAPPER, J. H. *Structure in Building.* London: Architectural Press, 1952.

COLLINS, PETER. *Concrete—The Vision of a New Architecture.* New York: Horizon Press, 1959.

CORKILL, PHILIP A., PUDERBAUGH, HOMER L., AND SAWYERS, H. KEITH. *Structure and Architectural Design.* Iowa City, Ia.: Bawden Brothers, 1974.

ENGEL, HEINRICH. *Structure Systems.* New York: Praeger, 1968.

FABER, COLIN. *Candela: The Shell Builder.* New York: Reinhold, 1963.

GAKKAI, NIHON. *Design Essentials in Earthquake Resistant Buildings.* New York: Elsevier, 1970.

HERTEL, HEINRICH. *Structure, Form and Movement.* New York: Reinhold, 1966.

HOWARD, H. SEYMOUR, JR. *Structures: An Architect's Approach.* New York: McGraw-Hill, 1966.

JOEDICKE, JURGEN. *Shell Architecture.* New York: Reinhold, 1963.

KEPES, GYORGY, ED. *Structure in Art and in Science.* New York: Braziller, 1965.

MAINSTONE, ROWLAND. *Developments in Structural Form.* Cambridge, Mass.: MIT Press, 1975.

NERVI, PIER LUIGI. *Buildings, Projects, Structures, 1953–1963.* New York: Praeger, 1963.

NERVI, PIER LUIGI. *Structures.* New York: McGraw-Hill, 1956.

RANDALL, FRANK A., and PANANESE, WILLIAM C. *Concrete Masonry Handbook.* Skokie, Ill.: Portland Cement Association, 1976.

ROSENTHAL, H. WERNER. *Structural Decisions.* London: Chapman & Hall, 1962.

SALVADORI, MARIO G., AND HELLER, ROBERT. *Structure in Architecture.* Englewood Cliffs, N.J.: Prentice-Hall, 1963.

SIEGEL, CURT. *Structure and Form in Modern Architecture.* New York: Reinhold, 1962.

THOMPSON, D'ARCY WENTWORTH. *On Growth and Form.* Abridged edition by John Tyler Bonner. Cambridge: Cambridge University Press, 1961.

TIMOSHENKO, STEPHEN P. *History of Strength of Materials.* New York: McGraw-Hill, 1953.

TORROJA, EDUARDO. *Philosophy of Structures.* Berkeley, Calif.: University of California Press, 1958.

TORROJA, EDUARDO. *The Structures of Eduardo Torroja.* New York: McGraw-Hill, 1958.

WACHSMANN, KONRAD. *The Turning Point of Building: Structure and Design.* New York: Reinhold, 1961.

ZUK, WILLIAM. *Concepts of Structures.* New York: Reinhold, 1963.

ZUK, WILLIAM, AND CLARK, ROGER H. *Kinetic Architecture.* New York: Van Nostrand–Reinhold, 1970.

List 2 Quantitative

AMERICAN CONCRETE INSTITUTE. *Building Code Requirements for Reinforced Concrete* (ACI 318–77). Detroit, Mich.: American Concrete Institute, 1977.

AMERICAN CONCRETE INSTITUTE. *Commentary on Building Code Requirements for Reinforced Concrete* (ACI 318–77). Detroit, Mich.: American Concrete Institute, 1977.

AMERICAN CONCRETE INSTITUTE. *Design Handbook* (SP-17). Detroit, Mich.: American Concrete Institute, 1973.

AMERICAN INSTITUTE OF STEEL CONSTRUCTION. *Manual of Steel Construction.* New York: American Institute of Steel Construction, 1970.

AMERICAN INSTITUTE OF TIMBER CONSTRUCTION. *Manual of Timber Construction.* Englewood, Colo.: American Institute of Timber Construction, 1974.

AMRHEIN, JAMES E. *Reinforced Masonry Engineering Handbook.* Los Angeles: Masonry Institute of America, 1973.

APPLIED TECHNOLOGY COUNCIL. *Tentative Provisions for the Development of Seismic Regulations for Buildings.* Washington, D.C.: U.S. Government Printing Office, 1978.

BAKOS, JACK D., JR. *Structural Analysis for Engineering Technology.* Columbus, Ohio: Merrill, 1973.

BASSIN, MILTON G., AND BRODSKY, STANLEY M. *Statics and Strength of Materials.* New York: McGraw-Hill, 1969.

BEER, FERDINAND P., AND JOHNSTON, RUSSELL E., JR. *Mechanics for Engineers, Statics and Dynamics.* New York: McGraw-Hill, 1962.

BENJAMIN, BEZALEEL S. *Structural Design with Plastics.* New York: Van Nostrand–Reinhold, 1969.

BENJAMIN, BEZALEEL S. *Structures for Architects.* Lawrence, Kans.: Ashnorjen Bezaleel Publishing Co., 1974.

BRICK INSTITUTE OF AMERICA. *Recommended Practice for Engineered Brick Masonry.* McLean, Va.: Brick Institute of America, 1975.

CONCRETE REINFORCING STEEL INSTITUTE. *CRSI Handbook.* Chicago: Concrete Reinforcing Steel Institute, 1975.

COWAN, HENRY J. *Architectural Structures, An Introduction to Structural Mechanics.* New York: American Elsevier, 1976.

CRAWLEY, STANLEY M., AND DILLON, ROBERT M. *Steel Buildings: Analysis and Design*. New York: Wiley, 1970.

FERGUSON, PHIL M. *Reinforced Concrete Fundamentals*. New York: Wiley, 1965.

FINTEL, MARK, ED. *Handbook of Concrete Engineering*. New York: Van Nostrand–Reinhold, 1974.

FITZGERALD, ROBERT W. *Strength of Materials*. Reading, Mass.: Addison-Wesley, 1967.

GURFINKEL, GERMAN. *Wood Engineering*. New Orleans, La.: Southern Forest Products Association, 1973.

HIGDON, ARCHIE, OHLSEN, EDWARD H., AND STILES, WILLIAM B. *Mechanics of Materials*. New York: Wiley, 1976.

HILL, LOUIS A., JR. *Fundamentals of Structural Design: Steel, Concrete, and Timber*. Scranton, Pa.: Intext Educational, 1975.

JENSEN, ALFRED, AND CHENOWETH, HARRY H. *Statics and Strength of Materials*. New York: McGraw-Hill, 1967.

LEVINSON, IRVING J. *Mechanics of Materials*. Englewood Cliffs, N.J.: Prentice-Hall, 1963.

LIBBY, JAMES R. *Modern Prestressed Concrete*. New York: Van Nostrand–Reinhold, 1977.

MARCUS, SAMUEL H. *Basics of Structural Steel Design*. Reston, Va.: Reston Publishing Co., 1977.

McCORMAC, JACK C. *Structural Analysis*. Scranton, Pa.: Intext Educational, 1975.

McCORMAC, JACK C. *Structural Steel Design*. Scranton, Pa.: Intext Educational, 1971.

MERRITT, FREDERICK S., ED. *Building Construction Handbook*. New York: McGraw-Hill, 1975.

MILLER, F. E., AND DOERINGSFELD, H. A. *Mechanics of Materials*. Scranton, Pa.: International Textbook, 1962.

MOTT, ROBERT L. *Applied Strength of Materials*. Englewood Cliffs, N.J.: Prentice-Hall, 1978.

NATIONAL CONCRETE MASONRY ASSOCIATION. *Specification for the Design and Construction of Load-Bearing Concrete Masonry*. McLean, Va.: National Concrete Masonry Association, 1975.

NATIONAL FOREST PRODUCTS ASSOCIATION. *National Design Specification for Stress-Grade Lumber and Its Fastenings*. Washington, D.C.: National Forest Products Association, 1977.

NATIONAL FOREST PRODUCTS ASSOCIATION. *Wood Structural Design Data*. Washington, D.C.: National Forest Products Association, 1970.

NORRIS, CHARLES H., WILBUR, JOHN B., AND UTKU, SENOL. *Elementary Structural Analysis*. New York: McGraw-Hill, 1976.

PETERSON, ALDOR C. *Applied Mechanics: Strength of Materials*. Boston: Allyn and Bacon, 1969.

PRESTRESSED CONCRETE INSTITUTE. *Fundamentals of Prestressed Concrete Design*. Chicago: Prestressed Concrete Institute, 1964.

SALVADORI, MARIO G., AND LEVY, MATTHYS. *Structural Design in Architecture*. Englewood Cliffs, N.J.: Prentice-Hall, 1967.

SIMIU, EMIL, AND SCANLON, ROBERT H. *Wind Effects on Structures*. New York: Wiley, 1978.

SCHUELLER, WOLFGANG. *High-Rise Building Structures*. New York: Wiley, 1977.

STEEL JOIST INSTITUTE. *Standard Specifications and Load Tables*. Arlington, Va.: Steel Joist Institute, 1977.

TIMOSHENKO, STEPHEN P., AND YOUNG, D. H. *Elements of Strength of Materials*. New York: Van Nostrand, 1968.

TRATHEN, ROLAND H. *Statics and Strength of Materials*. New York: Wiley, 1954.

WINTER, GEORGE, AND NILSON, ARTHUR. *Design of Reinforced Concrete Structures*. New York: McGraw-Hill, 1975.

APPENDIX C
DERIVATION OF BASIC TORSIONAL STRESS EXPRESSIONS

Polar Moment of Inertia

The general expression for polar moment of inertia is

$$J = \int_0^A r^2 \, dA$$

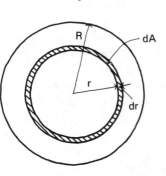

Figure C-1. Differential ring.

where r is the distance from the axis of rotation to the element dA. For the solid circle in Figure C-1, $dA = 2\pi r \, dr$, so that

$$J = \int_0^R r^2 \, 2\pi r \, dr$$

or

$$J = 2\pi \int_0^R r^3 \, dr$$

$$= 2\pi \left[\frac{r^4}{4} \right]_0^R$$

$$= \frac{\pi R^4}{2}$$

Torsional Stress

The differential torque produced on the ring element dA by the stress f_v will be

$$dT = rf_v\, 2\pi r\, dr$$

or

$$dT = 2\pi r^2 f_v\, dr$$

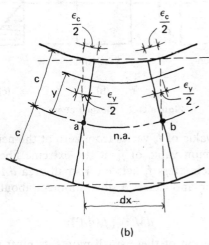

Figure C-2. Torsional stresses on a circular cross section.

If the stress distribution is linear, as shown in Figure C-2, then by similar triangles,

$$\frac{f_v}{r} = \frac{f_{v_{max}}}{R}$$

then

$$f_v = \frac{rf_{v_{max}}}{R}$$

where f_v varies but $f_{v_{max}}$ is constant for a given torque and cross section. Substituting into the expression for dT, we get

$$dT = \frac{2\pi r^3 f_{v_{max}}}{R}\, dr$$

The summation of dT will give us

$$T = \frac{2\pi f_{v_{max}}}{R} \int_0^R r^3\, dr$$

Performing the integration yields

$$T = \frac{2\pi f_{v_{max}}}{R}\left[\frac{r^4}{4}\right]_0^R$$

but

$$2\pi\left[\frac{r^4}{4}\right]_0^R = J$$

so

$$T = \frac{f_{v_{max}} J}{R}$$

Solving for f_v, we get

$$f_{v_{max}} = \frac{TR}{J} \qquad (6\text{-}1)$$

The foregoing derivation assumes that

1. Plane transverse sections remain plane after the torque forces have been applied.
2. The value of $f_{v_{max}}$ does not exceed the proportional limit of the material.

APPENDIX D
DERIVATION OF BASIC FLEXURAL STRESS EQUATION

The beam in Figure D-1 has a rectangular cross section, which has been specified here for the sake of convenience and clarity. The beam cross section can be any shape and the following derivation will still be valid. It is necessary, however, to make a number of other assumptions concerning the material and the geometry, and these will be listed at the end of this appendix. The most important of these is that "planes before bending remain plane after bending," which is stated graphically in Figure D-1(b).

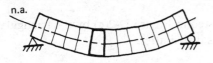

(a)

(b)

Figure D-1. Flexural strain.

To understand this, visualize a straight unloaded beam and make a series of imaginary slices through it quite close together. The planes made by the imaginary slicer should be parallel to each other and normal to the beam axis. When the beam is bent under load, as in Figure D-1(a), the planes will not warp or twist out of shape but will merely tilt toward one another. They will remain flat, getting closer together where the fibers are in compression and farther apart where tension occurs. This assumption is quite valid and can be proven visually using a material of low stiffness.

There will be a horizontal plane, designated ab in Figure D-1(b) and called the neutral axis, which will neither lengthen nor shorten. The fact that "planes remain plane" ensures that the unit strain, ϵ, will be proportional to its distance from the neutral axis. The fiber located y distance above the n.a. in Figure D-1(b) has an original unit length of dx and has a total strain of ϵ_y. Likewise, the top fiber of the beam, c distance from the n.a., has the same original unit length and a total strain of ϵ_c. By similar triangles

$$\frac{\epsilon_y}{\epsilon_c} = \frac{y}{c} \tag{D-1}$$

Since stress is proportional to strain by Hooke's law (if we keep the stresses in the elastic region for the material), then

$$\frac{f_y}{f_c} = \frac{y}{c} \tag{D-2}$$

as illustrated in Figure D-2(c) by the triangular, straight-line stress distribution.

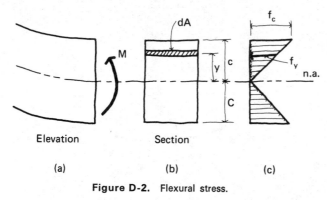

Elevation   Section

(a)   (b)   (c)

Figure D-2. Flexural stress.

The value of f_y varies from zero at the neutral axis to a maximum value of f_c at the extreme fibers of the section. Each stress f_y acts on a small area dA of beam cross section and causes a small moment about the neutral axis.

$$dM = [f_y(dA)]y$$

The summation of these small moments must equal the couple M, which is caused by the external loads. (The value of M, of course, varies along the length of a beam as represented by a moment diagram.)

$$M = \int_0^A f_y y \, dA$$

The variable f_y can be eliminated by using Equation D-2,

$$f_y = f_c\left(\frac{y}{c}\right)$$

giving us

$$M = \int_0^A \frac{f_c}{c} y^2 \, dA$$

Removing the constants, we get

$$M = \frac{f_c}{c} \int_0^A y^2 \, dA$$

in which the quantity $\int_0^A y^2 \, dA$ is the moment of inertia of the cross section taken with respect to the neutral axis. Making the change, we get

$$M = \frac{f_c}{c} I_{n.a.}$$

Solving for bending stress, we get

$$f_c = \frac{Mc}{I_{n.a.}} \tag{D-3}$$

where f_c is the extreme fiber bending stress. (*Note:* f_c is often written as f_b with b understood to mean "extreme fiber bending.")

It will be proven that the neutral axis is coincident with the centroidal axis, as implied by the dimensions labeled c in Figure D-1(b). Therefore, $I_{n.a.} = I_{c.g.}$ and the subscripts are usually deleted,

$$f = \frac{Mc}{I} \tag{8-1a}$$

The stress at some fiber other than the top or bottom locations is found as

$$f_y = \frac{My}{I} \tag{8-1}$$

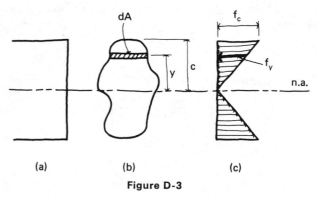

(a)   (b)   (c)

Figure D-3

To show that the neutral axis is a centroidal one, examine Figure D-3. The forces, $f_y \, dA$, must algebraically add to zero to ensure horizontal equilibrium ($\sum F_x = 0$) for the beam section on which they act.

$$\int_0^A f_y \, dA = 0$$

However, $f_y = f_c(y/c)$ as before, so

$$\frac{f_c}{c} \int_0^A y \, dA = 0$$

The quantity f_c/c is clearly not equal to zero; therefore,

$$\int_0^A y\, dA = 0$$

From Chapter 3 the reader should recall that this integral is the expression for the statical moment of the area in Figure D-3(b), using the neutral axis as the reference axis. The only way the statical moment of an area can be zero is if the reference axis is a centroidal axis.

The general formula for flexural stress developed here is subject to the following idealistic restrictions:

1. Transverse sections remain plane.
2. The beam is straight, of constant cross section, and does not twist under load.
3. The material is homogeneous and isotropic in the direction of stress.
4. The proportional limit is not exceeded.
5. The deformations are small.

APPENDIX E
DERIVATION OF BASIC HORIZONTAL SHEARING STRESS EQUATION

As with the derivation of the flexural stress formula, a rectangular cross section will be used here. This is done only for simplicity and the formula so developed is not restricted as to cross-sectional shape.

The beam shown with its moment diagram in Figure E-1(a) is typical in that its moment varies from one transverse section to another, e.g., from section 1 to section 2. In this case, M_2 is slightly greater than M_1, by the amount dM.

Figure E-2 shows this difference in moment between sections 1 and 2 by showing the normal stresses that act on those sections. There is an increase in these stresses acting on the transverse sections containing the element dA as we move from plane 1 to plane 2. This change in stress will result in an unbalanced force on the block

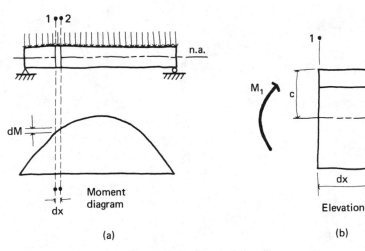

(a)   (b)

Figure E-1. Change in bending moment.

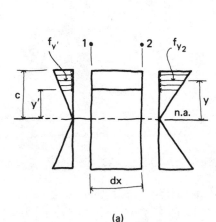

(a)   (b)

Figure E-2. Change in bending stress.

that has dimensions b, $c - y'$, and dx. Therefore, a stress f_v is developed to put this block back in equilibrium. The magnitude of this horizontal shearing stress at level y can be determined from the basic equilibrium equation,

$$\sum F_x = 0$$
$$f_v b\, dx = C_2 - C_1 \qquad \text{(E-1)}$$

where C_2 and C_1 of Figure E-3 are resultants or summations of the normal stresses, shown in Figure E-2(b) acting on the elemental areas dA.

$$C_2 = \int_{y'}^{c} f_{y_2}\, dA$$

$$C_1 = \int_{y'}^{c} f_{y_1}\, dA$$

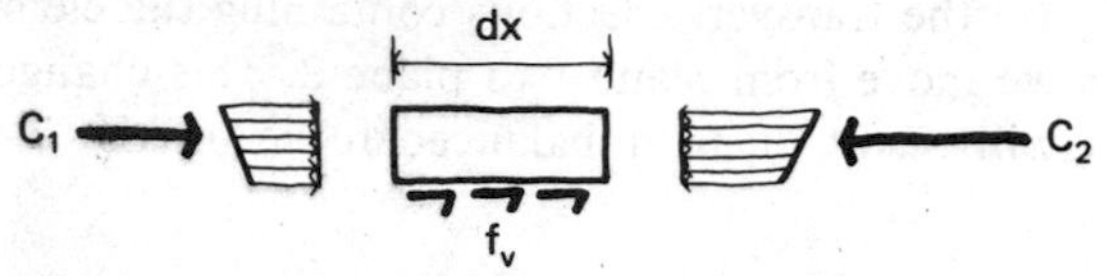

Figure E-3. Development of horizontal shearing stress.

In these equalities, f_y can be replaced by the appropriate values of My/I, where M is a constant for a given section and I is presumed constant for the entire beam.

$$C_2 = \frac{M_2}{I} \int_{y'}^{c} y\, dA$$

$$C_1 = \frac{M_1}{I} \int_{y'}^{c} y\, dA$$

Substituting into Equation (E-1), we get

$$f_v b\, dx = \frac{M_2 - M_1}{I} \int_{y'}^{c} y\, dA$$

where $M_2 - M_1 = dM$, as previously indicated. Solving for the shearing stress at level y yields

$$f_v = \frac{dM}{dx\, Ib} \int_{y'}^{c} y\, dA$$

where $dM/dx = V$, the vertical shearing force:

$$f_v = \frac{V}{Ib} \int_{y'}^{c} y\, dA$$

The expression $\int_{y'}^{c} y\, dA$ has been given the symbol Q. It is the statical moment of that portion of the cross section which lies between level y' (where we are finding the stress) and level c (the edge of the section), taken with respect to the neutral axis. Using the symbol Q for this statical moment, the complete formula is

$$f_v = \frac{VQ}{Ib} \qquad \text{(8-4)}$$

Because the flexure formula, $f_y = My/I$, was used in this derivation, the shearing stress formula is subject to the same assumptions or restrictions listed in Appendix D.

APPENDIX F
PROOF OF MOMENT-AREA THEOREMS

First Moment-Area Theorem

The basic equation developed in Section 10-4 can be written as

$$\frac{d(dy/dx)}{dx} = \frac{M}{EI}$$

For the small slopes of elastic curves assumed previously, $dy/dx = \tan \theta = \theta$. Then

$$\frac{d^2y}{dx^2} = \frac{d\theta}{dx}$$

Also,

$$\frac{d\theta}{dx} = \frac{M}{EI}$$

which can be written as

$$d\theta = \frac{M}{EI}\, dx$$

which is valid for a small length of beam dx. It states that a small change in angle is equal to a small area. Integrating both sides of the equation with finite limits determined by the portion of the beam shown in Figure F-1, we get that the change in angle θ from point A to point B is equal to the shaded area under the M/EI curve.

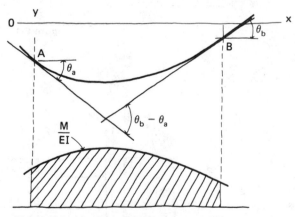

Figure F-1. Portion of elastic curve and M/EI diagram.

Second Moment-Area Theorem

Two tangent lines to the elastic curve at infinitesimally close points c and d will subtend a distance dt on the vertical line through B, as shown in Figure F-2.

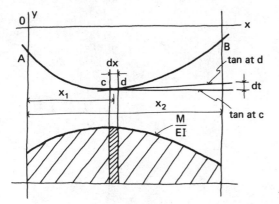

Figure F-2. Portion of elastic curve and *M/EI* diagram.

$$\tan d\theta = \frac{dt}{x_2 - x_1}$$

Since for small values of θ, the tangent function equals the angle itself, we can say that

$$d\theta = \frac{dt}{x_2 - x_1}$$

Previously, $d\theta$ was declared equal to $(M/EI)\,dx$; therefore,

$$dt = (x_2 - x_1)\frac{M}{EI}dx$$

This states that a small vertical distance on a line through B is equal to a small area, $(M/EI)\,dx$, times the distance from the line to the centroid of the area, $x_2 - x_1$. Integrating both sides of the equation with finite limits determined by the portion of the beam shown in Figure F-2, we get that the distance $t_{b/a}$ along a vertical line through B is equal to the shaded area times the distance from the vertical line to the centroid of the shaded area (see Figure F-3).

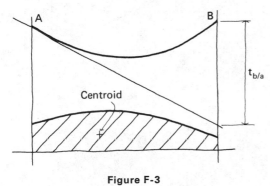

Figure F-3

APPENDIX G
DERIVATION OF PRINCIPAL STRESS EQUATIONS

Figure G-1 shows a small element of dimensions $(dx)(dy)(dz)$ being acted upon by normal stresses and shearing stresses. The senses shown are taken as positive.

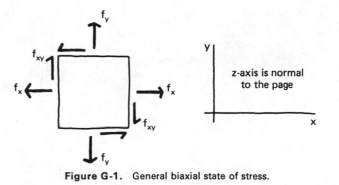

Figure G-1.   General biaxial state of stress.

First, let us obtain expressions for the stresses on any plane through the block (e.g., the plane that makes the angle θ with the vertical plane). In general, such a plane will be acted upon by a normal stress and a shearing stress as shown in Figure G-2. We can find f_n and f_{nv} by writing equilibrium equations in the n and v directions. Using the FBD of Figure G-3 and multiplying stress times area

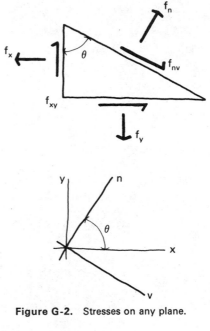

Figure G-2.   Stresses on any plane.

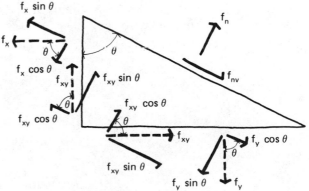

Figure G-3.   Free-body diagram.

to get the force in each case, we get

$$\sum F_n = 0$$

$$f_n \, dv \, dz + f_{xy} \sin \theta \, dy \, dz + f_{xy} \cos \theta \, dx \, dz$$
$$- f_y \sin \theta \, dx \, dz - f_x \cos \theta \, dy \, dz = 0$$

Dividing through by dz and dv,

$$f_n + f_{xy} \sin \theta \frac{dy}{dv} + f_{xy} \cos \theta \frac{dx}{dv} - f_y \sin \theta \frac{dx}{dv}$$
$$- f_x \cos \theta \frac{dy}{dv} = 0$$

But $dy/dv = \cos \theta$ and $dx/dv = \sin \theta$; therefore,

$$f_n + f_{xy} \sin \theta \cos \theta + f_{xy} \cos \theta \sin \theta - f_y \sin^2 \theta$$
$$- f_x \cos^2 \theta = 0$$

or

$$f_n = f_x \cos^2 \theta + f_y \sin^2 \theta - 2f_{xy} \sin \theta \cos \theta$$

If we write $\sum F_v = 0$ and simplify in the same manner, we get

$$f_{nv} = (f_x - f_y) \sin \theta \cos \theta + f_{xy}(\cos^2 \theta - \sin^2 \theta)$$

Using the following three trigonometric identities, we can further simplify these equations.

$$\cos^2 \theta = \frac{1}{2}(1 + \cos 2\theta)$$

$$\sin^2 \theta = \frac{1}{2}(1 - \cos 2\theta)$$

$$\sin \theta \cos \theta = \frac{1}{2} \sin 2\theta$$

The stresses on any plane making the angle θ with the plane acted upon by f_x will then be

$$f_n = \frac{f_x + f_y}{2} + \frac{f_x - f_y}{2} \cos 2\theta - f_{xy} \sin 2\theta \quad \text{(G-1a)}$$

$$f_{nv} = \frac{f_x - f_y}{2} \sin 2\theta + f_{xy} \cos 2\theta \quad \text{(G-1b)}$$

In order to obtain the principal stresses and the maximum shearing stress, we need to determine the particular values of θ that will cause Equation (G-1) to maximize. To do this, we can take the first derivative of each and set it equal to zero. For Equation (G-1a), we get

$$\frac{df_n}{d} = -\frac{f_x - f_y}{2} \sin 2\theta - f_{xy} \cos 2\theta = 0$$

Dividing through by $\cos 2\theta$,

$$\frac{\sin 2\theta}{\cos 2\theta} = \frac{-f_{xy}}{(f_x - f_y)/2}$$

or

$$\tan 2\theta_{1,2} = \frac{-2f_{xy}}{f_x - f_y} \quad \text{(12-6)}$$

where the subscripts 1 and 2 denote the principal planes. Since the tangent function is double valued, $2\theta_{1,2}$ defines

angles 180° apart, which means that $\theta_{1,2}$ represents two angles 90° apart. The principal planes then must be mutually perpendicular. The smaller angle of $\theta_{1,2}$ is the angle one of the principal planes makes with the vertical and is also the angle made by the other principal plane with the horizontal. These planes could also be defined as in Figure G-4. The normal stresses acting on

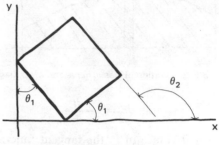

Figure G-4. Principal planes.

these planes are the algebraic maximum and minimum values for the general biaxial state of stress. To find the magnitudes of these principal stresses, we need to substitute the values of $\theta_{1,2}$ into Equation (G-1a). First, we can break $\tan 2\theta_{1,2}$ into its sine and cosine values. If we let

$$\tan 2\theta_{1,2} = \frac{-f_{xy}}{(f_x - f_y)/2}$$

and the triangle of Figure G-5 be used to define $2\theta_{1,2}$ graphically, then the Pythagorean theorem will give us

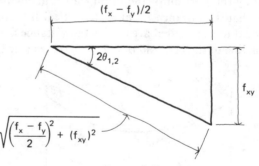

Figure G-5

$$\sin 2\theta_{1,2} = \pm \frac{f_{xy}}{\sqrt{\left(\dfrac{f_x - f_y}{2}\right)^2 + (f_{xy})^2}}$$

and

$$\cos 2\theta_{1,2} = \pm \frac{f_x - f_y}{2\sqrt{\left(\dfrac{f_x - f_y}{2}\right)^2 + (f_{xy})^2}}$$

Substituting these quantities into Equation (G-1a) at the appropriate places will give us

$$f_{1,2} = \frac{f_x + f_y}{2} \pm \sqrt{\left(\frac{f_x - f_y}{2}\right)^2 + (f_{xy})^2} \quad \text{(12-4)}$$

in which $f_{1,2}$ are the principal values of f_n.

Following the same procedure with Equation (G-1b) and setting the first derivative equal to zero will give us

$$\tan 2\theta_s = \frac{f_x - f_y}{2f_{xy}} \qquad (12\text{-}7)$$

This quantity is the negative reciprocal of Equation (12-6) [in other words, $2\theta_s$ is always 90° from $2\theta_{1,2}$], which means that the planes acted upon by the maximum shearing stresses make angles of 45° with the principal planes. Using the Pythagorean theorem as we did before to eliminate the tangent function gives us

$$\sin 2\theta_s = \pm \frac{f_x - f_y}{2\sqrt{\left(\dfrac{f_x - f_y}{2}\right)^2 + (f_{xy})^2}}$$

and

$$\cos 2\theta_s = \pm \frac{f_{xy}}{\sqrt{\left(\dfrac{f_x - f_y}{2}\right)^2 + (f_{xy})^2}}$$

If we substitute these values into Equation (G-1b), we get

$$f_s = \pm \sqrt{\left(\frac{f_x - f_y}{2}\right)^2 + (f_{xy})^2} \qquad (12\text{-}5)$$

in which f_s is the maximum value of f_{nv}. Note that this is the second term of the principal stress equation.

This derivation and the examples of Chapter 12 do not address stresses on planes that are not perpendicular to the xy plane. It should be noted that in certain cases where the normal stresses are of like sign but not equal in magnitude, it will be possible for the maximum shearing stress to occur on a plane that is perpendicular to the xz or yz planes. Such cases and the more general triaxial stress state have been deliberately ignored in this beginning text.

APPENDIX H
DERIVATION OF EULER COLUMN BUCKLING EQUATION

Under the application of a certain critical load, a column can be in equilibrium in the curved (buckled) position. In this buckled position, an increase in P will cause an increase in the lateral deflection (leading to failure), and a decrease in P will cause the column to return to its initially straight position. It is this critical value of P that is quantified by the Euler equation.

Just as in a beam, the rate of change of slope of the column is directly proportional to the bending moment and inversely proportional to the stiffness. With respect to the free-body diagram in Figure H-1(b), this relationship is given by

$$-\frac{d^2 y}{dx^2} = \frac{Py}{EI}$$

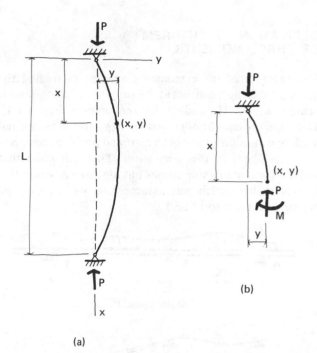

Figure H-1. Forces involved in column buckling.

(The negative sign is present because of the selection of the origin for the coordinate axes.) As x increases, the slope decreases; thus, the rate of change of slope is negative. The equation can be rewritten as

$$\frac{d^2 y}{dx^2} + \frac{P}{EI} y = 0 \qquad (\text{H-1})$$

If we let $m = \sqrt{P/EI}$ such that

$$\frac{d^2 y}{dx^2} + m^2 y = 0 \qquad (\text{H-2})$$

the solution of the differential equation is of the form

$$y = A \cos mx + B \sin mx \qquad (\text{H-3})$$

which involves two arbitrary constants, A and B. That this is a valid solution for y may be verified by taking the second derivative of Equation (H-3) and substituting it into Equation (H-2).

To evaluate the constants A and B, we can use the boundary condition of $y = 0$ when $x = 0$, from which we get $A = 0$, and therefore $y = B \sin mx$. Likewise, $y = 0$ when $x = L$ or $B \sin mL = 0$. If B is to have a value, then $\sin mL$ must be zero. This is only true if $mL = 0, \pi, 2\pi, 3\pi$, etc. The coefficient of π represents the buckling mode. For the single wave mode of our column, $mL = \pi$. Replacing m by $\sqrt{P/EI}$ and solving for P, we get

$$P = \frac{\pi^2 EI}{L^2} \qquad (13\text{-}2)$$

where P is the critical buckling load.

APPENDIX I
DERIVATION OF THEOREM
OF THREE MOMENTS

The theorem of three moments enables us to find the internal bending moments at the supports of a continuous beam (i.e., M_a, M_b, and M_c for the beam in Figure I-1). These quantities, although usually negative under normal loading conditions, have been assumed positive (compression top fiber) in this derivation. This will mean that when a computed value comes out algebraically negative (opposite that which was assumed), it will actually *be* negative (tension top fiber).

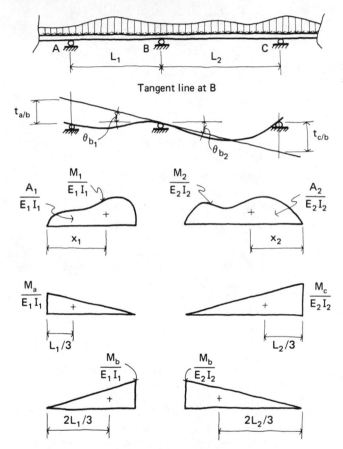

Figure I-1. Continuous beam with a general load and assumed M/EI diagram (in parts).

Figure I-1 shows a continuous beam under a general load. The elastic curve shows an arbitrary slope, θ_b, at the central support, and the continuity present ensures that the slopes of the two spans are equal at this point. Using this equality and moment-area theory, we can derive an equation involving the three unknown support moments.

The moment diagram for each span has been drawn in parts to separate the moment due to the simple beam loads from that due to continuity at the supports. Since for small angles, an angle is equal to its own tangent and

$$\theta_{b_1} = \theta_{b_2}$$

then

$$\tan \theta_{b_1} = \tan \theta_{b_2}$$

Assuming the two tangential deviations to be of opposite sign,

$$\frac{t_{a/b}}{L_1} = -\frac{t_{c/b}}{L_2}$$

Using the second moment-area theorem and letting the areas under the simple beam M/EI curves be given by A_1/E_1I_1 and A_2/E_2I_2, respectively, we get

$$\frac{\dfrac{A_1}{E_1I_1}(x_1) + \dfrac{1}{2}\left(\dfrac{M_a}{E_1I_1}\right)(L_1)\left(\dfrac{L_1}{3}\right) + \dfrac{1}{2}\left(\dfrac{M_b}{E_1I_1}\right)(L_1)\left(\dfrac{2L_1}{3}\right)}{L_1}$$

$$= \frac{-\dfrac{A_2}{E_2I_2}(x_2) - \dfrac{1}{2}\left(\dfrac{M_c}{E_2I_2}\right)(L_2)\left(\dfrac{L_2}{3}\right) - \dfrac{1}{2}\left(\dfrac{M_b}{E_2I_2}\right)(L_2)\left(\dfrac{2L_2}{3}\right)}{L_2}$$

Simplifying and assuming that E is constant for both spans gives us the general theorem of three moments.

$$M_a\frac{L_1}{I_1} + 2M_b\left(\frac{L_1}{I_1} + \frac{L_2}{I_2}\right) + M_c\frac{L_2}{I_2} = -\frac{6A_1x_1}{I_1L_1} - \frac{6A_2x_2}{I_2L_2}$$

For the frequently occurring uniform and concentrated loads, Figure I-2 shows how the general load terms on

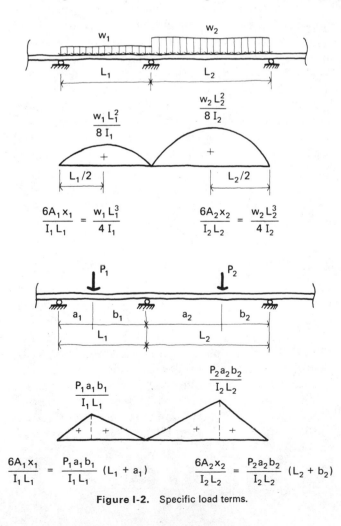

Figure I-2. Specific load terms.

the right-hand side of the equation can be replaced by ones more suitable for direct substitution. This gives us

$$M_a\frac{L_1}{I_1} + 2M_b\left(\frac{L_1}{I_1} + \frac{L_2}{I_2}\right) + M_c\frac{L_2}{I_2}$$

$$= -\frac{w_1 L_1^3}{4I_1} - \frac{w_2 L_2^3}{4I_2} - \frac{P_1 a_1 b_1}{I_1 L_1}(L_1 + a_1)$$

$$- \frac{P_2 a_2 b_2}{I_2 L_2}(L_2 + b_2) \quad (15\text{-}1)$$

APPENDIX J
DERIVATION OF ULTIMATE MOMENT CAPACITY TERMS

In Section 17-3, the ultimate moment capacity for beams that fail by tensile yield is developed as

$$M_u = \phi\rho F_y bd^2 j_u \quad (17\text{-}3)$$

The unknown fraction j_u can most easily be ascertained by using the concept of the equivalent rectangular stress block shown in Figure J-1(c). It must be emphasized that the actual stress distribution at failure approximates the parabolic curve shown in Figure J-1(b) and that the rectangular distribution is a conceptual tool only. It is used because its geometrical properties are easier to deal with than those of a curved distribution. In order to have the same volume as the real stress block, one side of the rectangle represents an "average" of the peak stresses and takes a value of $0.85f'_c$. Similarly, the depth of the rectangle does not extend all the way to the neutral axis, in order to reflect the skewed shape of the real distribution. Because the degree of "skewness" varies with concrete strength (as shown in the stress–strain curves of Figure 17-2), the dimension, a, is expressed as $a = \beta_1 c$, in which β_1 depends upon f'_c. Experimentally, β_1 has a value of 0.85 for concrete strengths up to 30 MPa but

decreases at the rate of 0.008 for each MPa increase in strength above that level. The ACI Code specifies a minimum value for β_1 of 0.65.

Since the compressive force resultant C acts through the centroid of the stress block, it will be located at a distance of $a/2$ from the extreme compressive fiber. If the moment arms in Figures J-1(b) and (c) are to be equal, we get

$$j_u d = d - \frac{a}{2}$$

or

$$j_u = 1 - \frac{a}{2d}$$

By virtue of horizontal equilibrium, the compressive force resultant must equal the tensile force resultant, and this equality can be used to evaluate the distance, a. Assuming that the stress distribution acts on a beam of width b, we get

$$C = T$$

$$0.85f'_c ab = A_s F_y$$

$$a = \frac{A_s F_y}{0.85f'_c b}$$

Letting $A_s = \rho bd$, then

$$a = \frac{\rho F_y d}{0.85f'_c}$$

Substituting this into the expression for j_u, we get

$$j_u = 1 - 0.59\rho\frac{F_y}{f'_c} \quad (17\text{-}4)$$

The equivalent rectangular stress block was first proposed by Charles S. Whitney (1892–1959), an American engineer and pioneer in the development of ultimate strength theory.

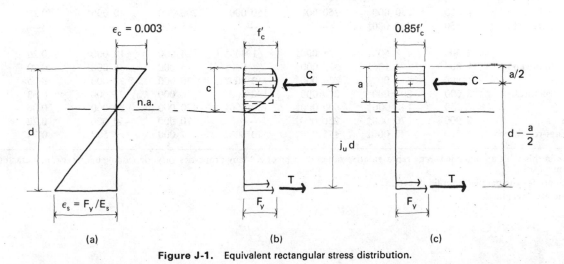

Figure J-1. Equivalent rectangular stress distribution.

In Section 17-4, ρ_b is defined as the particular value of ρ that will result in a simultaneous failure of the steel in tension and the concrete in compression. The equilibrium considerations used in evaluating j_u can be used to derive an expression for ρ_b. Letting ρ take the value of ρ_b, we get

$$a = \frac{\rho_b F_y d}{0.85 f'_c}$$

Since $a = \beta_1 c$, we can solve for ρ_b and get

$$\rho_b = \frac{c \beta_1 f'_c}{F_y d}$$

Since it is assumed that concrete crushes at a strain of 0.003 and that the flexural strain distribution is linear at failure, Figure J-1(a) can be used to evaluate the distance c. From similar triangles,

$$c = \frac{0.003d}{0.003 + F_y/E_s}$$

Substituting this into the previous equation gives us

$$\rho_b = \frac{0.003}{0.003 + F_y/E_s} \frac{\beta_1 0.85 f'_c}{F_y} \qquad (17\text{-}5)$$

APPENDIX K
MASS DENSITIES OF SELECTED BUILDING MATERIALS*†

Aluminum	2600
Brick masonry construction	1900
Cement plaster	1900
Concrete masonry construction, hollow blocks	1300
Concrete, stone, reinforced	2400
Concrete, structural lightweight, reinforced	1800
Earth, sand, loose	1600
Earth, topsoil, packed	1500
Glass	2900
Gypsum board	800
Insulation, rigid	300
Plywood	600
Steel	7850
Stone	2600
Wood, Douglas fir	500
Wood, oak	700
Wood, redwood	400
Water, fresh	1000

*Values in this table are intended to be representative rather than precise. Most material densities vary considerably, depending upon type and/or ambient conditions.

†Values given are in kg/m³.

APPENDIX L
PROPERTIES OF MATERIALS*

Material	Density (kg/m³)	Strength (kPa) (yield values except where noted)			Modulus of elasticity (E) (MPa)	Modulus of rigidity (G) (MPa)	Poisson's ratio (v) (stress ‖ to grain)	Coefficient of thermal expan. (°C⁻¹)(10⁻⁶)
		Tension	Compression	Shear				
Wood (dry)†								
Douglas fir	500	40 000	25 000	3 500	12 000	700	0.4	4
Redwood	400	45 000	30 000	3 000	9 000	500	0.4	4
Southern pine	350	60 000	35 000	4 000	12 000	700	0.4	4
Steel								
Mild, low-carbon	7 850	250 000	250 000	150 000	200 000	80 000	0.28	11.7
Cable, high-strength	7 850	1 800 000‡	—	—	165 000	—	—	11.7
Concrete								
Stone	2 300	1 500‡	25 000‡	1 400‡	24 000	10 000	0.20	10
Structural, lightweight	1 800	1 100‡	25 000‡	900‡	15 000	6 000	0.20	10
Brick masonry	1 900	2 000‡	30 000‡	2 000‡	30 000	12 000	0.25	6
Aluminum, structural	2 600	200 000	200 000	140 000	70 000	26 000	0.33	22
Iron, cast	7 250	140 000‡	600 000‡	180 000‡	170 000	80 000	0.06	11
Glass, plate	2 900	70 000‡	250 000‡	—	70 000	30 000	0.22	8
Polyester, glass-reinforced	1 700	70 000‡	175 000‡	70 000‡	7 000	3 500	0.24	60

*Values given in this table are intended to be representative rather than precise. Many properties vary, depending upon type, manufacturing process, and conditions of use.

†Values given are for the parallel-to-grain direction.

‡Denotes ultimate strength.

APPENDIX M
PROPERTIES OF AREAS

TABLE M-1 *Areas and Centroids*

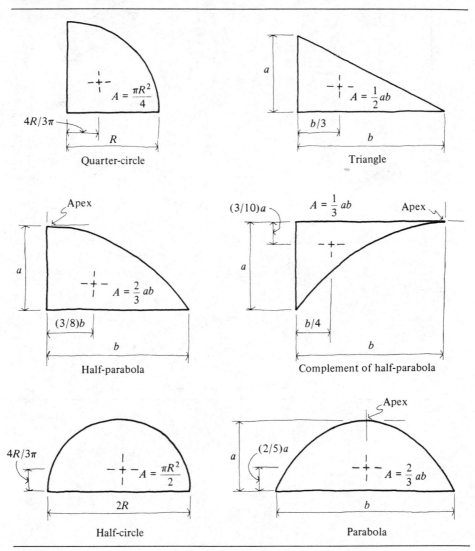

Quarter-circle

Triangle

Half-parabola

Complement of half-parabola

Half-circle

Parabola

TABLE M-2   *Moments of Inertia*

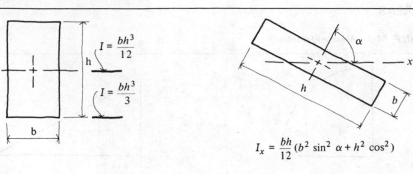

$$I_x = \frac{bh}{12}(b^2 \sin^2 \alpha + h^2 \cos^2)$$

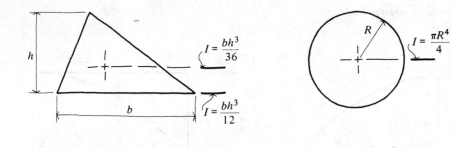

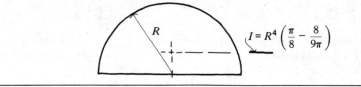

Map N-1. Snow. Snow load in kilonewtons per square meter on the ground, 50-year recurrence level. Note that roof live-load design values less than 1 kN/m² are not permitted by most codes. (This material is adapted with permission from American National Standard A58.1 copyright 1972 by ANSI, copies of which may be purchased from the American National Standards Institute, 1430 Broadway, New York, New York 10018.)

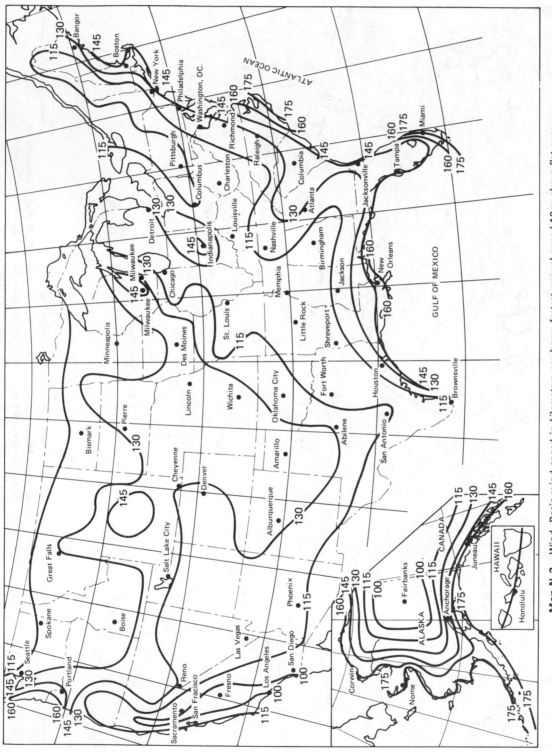

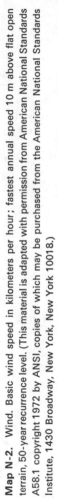

Map N-2. Wind. Basic wind speed in kilometers per hour; fastest annual speed 10 m above flat open terrain, 50-year recurrence level. (This material is adapted with permission from American National Standards A58.1 copyright 1972 by ANSI, copies of which may be purchased from the American National Standards Institute, 1430 Broadway, New York, New York 10018.)

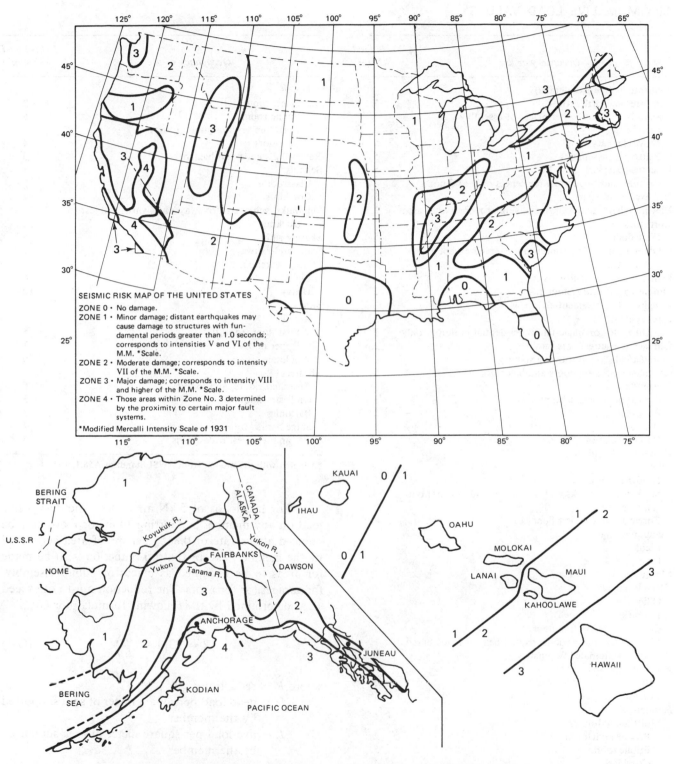

SEISMIC RISK MAP OF THE UNITED STATES

ZONE 0 · No damage.
ZONE 1 · Minor damage; distant earthquakes may
cause damage to structures with fundamental periods greater than 1.0 seconds;
corresponds to intensities V and VI of the
M.M. *Scale.
ZONE 2 · Moderate damage; corresponds to intensity
VII of the M.M. *Scale.
ZONE 3 · Major damage; corresponds to intensity VIII
and higher of the M.M. *Scale.
ZONE 4 · Those areas within Zone No. 3 determined
by the proximity to certain major fault
systems.

*Modified Mercalli Intensity Scale of 1931

Map N-3. Earthquake. (Adapted from the 1976 edition of the Uniform Building
Code, copyright 1976, with permission of the publisher, The International Conference
of Building Officials.)

APPENDIX O
MINIMUM LIVE LOAD VALUES*

Occupancy or use	Live load (kN/m²)
Apartments (*see* Residential)	
Armories and drill rooms	7
Assembly halls and other places of assembly	
Fixed seats	3
Movable seats	5
Platforms (assembly)	5
Balcony (exterior)	5
On one- and two-family residences only and not exceeding 10 m²	3
Bowling alleys, poolrooms, and similar recreational areas	3.5
Corridors	
First floor	5
Other floors, same as occupancy served except as indicated	
Dance halls and ballrooms	5
Dining rooms and restaurants	5
Dwellings (*see* Residential)	
Fire escapes	5
On multi- or single-family residential buildings only	2
Garages (passenger cars only)	2.5
Grandstands (*see* Reviewing stands)	
Gymnasiums, main floors and balconies	5
Hospitals	
Operating rooms, laboratories	3
Private rooms	2
Wards	2
Corridors, above first floor	4
Hotels (*see* Residential)	
Libraries	
Reading rooms	3
Stack rooms (books and shelving at 1000 kg/m³) but not less than	7
Corridors, above first floor	4
Manufacturing	
Light	6
Heavy	12
Marquees	3.5
Office buildings	
Offices	2.5
Lobbies	5
Corridors, above first floor	4
File and computer rooms require heavier loads based upon anticipated occupancy	
Penal institutions	
Cell blocks	2
Corridors	5
Residential	
Multifamily houses	
Private apartments	2
Public rooms	5
Corridors	4
Dwellings	
First floor	2
Second floor and habitable attics	1.5
Uninhabitable attics	1

Occupancy or use	Live load (kN/m²)
Hotels	
Guest rooms	2
Public rooms	5
Corridors serving public rooms	5
Corridors	4
Reviewing stands and bleachers	5
Schools	
Classrooms	2
Corridors	4
Sidewalks, vehicular driveways, and yards, subject to trucking	12
Skating rinks	5
Stairs and exitways	5
Storage warehouse	
Light	6
Heavy	12
Stores	
Retail	
First floor, rooms	5
Upper floors	3.5
Wholesale	6
Theaters	
Aisles, corridors, and lobbies	5
Orchestra floors	3
Balconies	3
Stage floors	7
Yards and terraces, pedestrians	5

*Adapted with permission from ANSI Standard A58.1, 1972.

For live loads of 5 kN/m² or less, the design live load on any member supporting 14 m² or more may be reduced at the rate of 0.86% per m² of area supported by the member, except that no reduction is to be made for areas to be occupied as places of public assembly, for garages, or for roofs. The reduction must not exceed R, as determined by the following formula, nor 60%.

$$R = 23\left(1 + \frac{D}{L}\right) \tag{O-1}$$

where R = reduction (%)
  D = dead load per square meter of area supported by the member
  L = live load per square meter of area supported by the member

When live loads exceed 5 kN/m², no reduction may be made, except that the live loads on columns may be reduced 20%.

APPENDIX P
ALLOWABLE STRESS VALUES
FOR SELECTED WOODS*

Species and size	F_b (kPa)	F_b (kPa) (repetitive)†	F_v (kPa)	F_c (kPa)	E (MPa)
Douglas fir No. 1					
thickness ≤ 89 mm	10 300	12 000	650	8 600	12 400
> 89 mm	8 900	—	600	6 900	11 000
Eastern spruce No. 1					
thickness ≤ 89 mm	7 500	8 600	450	6 200	9 600
> 89 mm	6 500	—	400	5 000	8 300
Hem-fir No. 1					
thickness ≤ 89 mm	8 300	9 600	500	6 900	10 300
> 89 mm	6 900	—	500	5 800	9 600
Northern pine No. 1					
thickness ≤ 89 mm	8 300	9 600	500	6 700	9 600
> 89 mm	7 200	—	450	5 500	8 900
Southern pine No. 1					
thickness ≤ 89 mm	10 300	12 000	600	8 600	12 400
> 89 mm	9 000	—	750	6 300	11 000
Eastern hemlock No. 1					
thickness ≤ 89 mm	8 900	10 300	600	8 900	8 900
> 89 mm	8 300	—	600	6 000	8 900

*For each species the values given assume a No. 1 grade designation.
†Repetitive members in bending are ones that are closely enough spaced or tied sufficiently to avoid independent action, e.g., residential floor joists with bridging and subfloor.

When the duration of loading is known, the allowables may be modified by the following factors:

Two months (snow)	1.15
Seven days	1.25
Wind or earthquake	1.33
Impact	2.00

If the *full* load is to be applied, continuously or cumulatively, for more than 10 years, the allowable stresses should be multiplied by 0.90. The modulus of elasticity values are not subject to such modifications.

When lumber is to be used where it will be continuously or intermittently wet, the values in the table should be decreased as follows:

Thickness (mm)	Decrease factor			
	F_b	F_v	F_c	E
≤89	0.86	0.97	0.70	0.97
>89	1.00	1.00	0.91	1.00

When lumber 139 mm and wider is used in bending about the *minor* axis, the allowable bending stress may be increased as follows:

Thickness (mm)	Increase factor
38	1.22
89	1.11
>89	1.00

APPENDIX Q
WOOD SECTION PROPERTIES (*continued on page 308*)

Size (mm)	Area (mm²)	$S_x(10^3\ mm^3)$	$S_y(10^3\ mm^3)$	$I_x(10^6\ mm^4)$	$I_y(10^6\ mm^4)$
38 × 89	3 380	50.1	21.4	2.23	0.407
38 × 139	5 280	122	33.5	8.51	0.636
38 × 185	7 030	217	44.5	20.1	0.846
38 × 235	8 930	350	56.6	41.1	1.07
38 × 285	10 800	514	68.6	73.3	1.30
89 × 89	7 920	118	118	5.23	5.23
89 × 139	12 400	287	184	19.9	8.17
89 × 185	16 500	508	244	47.0	10.9
89 × 235	20 900	819	310	96.3	13.8
89 × 285	25 400	1 210	376	172	16.7
89 × 335	29 800	1 660	442	279	19.7
89 × 385	34 300	2 200	508	423	22.6

(*Tabled values continued on page 308.*)

APPENDIX Q   (continued)

Size (mm)	Area (mm²)	S_x(10³ mm³)	S_y(10³ mm³)	I_x(10⁶ mm⁴)	I_y(10⁶ mm⁴)
139 × 139	19 300	448	448	31.1	31.1
139 × 185	25 700	793	596	73.3	41.4
139 × 235	32 700	1 280	757	150	52.6
139 × 285	39 600	1 880	918	268	63.8
139 × 335	46 600	2 600	1 080	435	75.0
139 × 385	53 500	3 430	1 240	661	86.2
139 × 495	68 800	5 680	1 590	1 400	111
139 × 595	82 700	8 200	1 920	2 440	133
185 × 185	34 200	1 060	1 060	97.6	97.6
185 × 235	43 500	1 700	1 340	200	124
185 × 285	52 700	2 500	1 630	357	150
185 × 335	62 000	3 460	1 910	580	177
185 × 385	71 200	4 570	2 200	880	203
185 × 495	91 600	7 550	2 820	1 870	261
185 × 595	110 000	10 900	3 390	3 250	314

APPENDIX R
VALUES FOR STEEL COLUMN ANALYSIS

TABLE R-1 F_a Values for F_y = 250 MPa

Main and secondary members: $\frac{KL}{r}$ not over 120						Main members: $\frac{KL}{r}$ 121 to 200			
$\frac{KL}{r}$	F_a (MPa)	$\frac{KL}{r}$	F_a (MPa)	$\frac{KL}{r}$	F_a (MPa)	$\frac{KL}{r}$	F_a (MPa)	$\frac{KL}{r}$	F_a (MPa)
1	148.6	41	131.8	81	105.1	121	69.9	161	39.7
2	148.4	42	131.2	82	104.3	122	68.9	162	39.2
3	148.1	43	130.7	83	103.6	123	67.9	163	38.8
4	147.8	44	130.0	84	102.7	124	66.9	164	38.3
5	147.5	45	129.5	85	102.0	125	65.8	165	37.9
6	147.2	46	128.9	86	101.2	126	64.9	166	37.4
7	146.9	47	128.3	87	100.4	127	63.9	167	36.9
8	146.5	48	127.8	88	99.6	128	62.8	168	36.5
9	146.2	49	127.1	89	98.7	129	61.9	169	36.1
10	145.9	50	126.5	90	97.9	130	61.0	170	35.7
11	145.5	51	125.9	91	97.2	131	60.0	171	35.2
12	145.1	52	125.3	92	96.3	132	59.1	172	34.8
13	144.8	53	124.7	93	95.4	133	58.2	173	34.4
14	144.5	54	124.0	94	94.6	134	57.4	174	34.0
15	144.0	55	123.4	95	93.8	135	56.5	175	33.7
16	143.6	56	122.8	96	92.9	136	55.6	176	33.2
17	143.3	57	122.1	97	92.1	137	54.9	177	32.9
18	142.9	58	121.5	98	91.2	138	54.1	178	32.5
19	142.5	59	120.9	99	90.3	139	53.3	179	32.1
20	142.0	60	120.2	100	89.5	140	52.5	180	31.8
21	141.6	61	119.5	101	88.6	141	51.8	181	31.4
22	141.2	62	118.9	102	87.7	142	51.1	182	31.1
23	140.7	63	118.2	103	86.8	143	50.3	183	30.8
24	140.3	64	117.5	104	86.0	144	49.6	184	30.4
25	139.8	65	116.8	105	85.0	145	49.0	185	30.1
26	139.4	66	116.1	106	84.1	146	48.3	186	29.8
27	138.9	67	115.4	107	83.2	147	47.6	187	29.5
28	138.5	68	114.7	108	82.3	148	47.0	188	29.2
29	138.0	69	114.0	109	81.4	149	46.4	189	28.8
30	137.5	70	113.3	110	80.5	150	45.8	190	28.5
31	137.0	71	112.6	111	79.6	151	45.2	191	28.2

(*Tabled values continue on page 309.*)

TABLE R-1 (continued)

$\frac{KL}{r}$	F_a (MPa)	$\frac{KL}{r}$	F_a (MPa)	$\frac{KL}{r}$	F_a (MPa)	$\frac{KL}{r}$	F_a (MPa)	$\frac{KL}{r}$	F_a (MPa)
32	136.5	72	111.8	112	78.6	152	44.5	192	27.9
33	136.0	73	111.1	113	77.6	153	44.0	193	27.7
34	135.5	74	110.4	114	76.7	154	43.4	194	27.4
35	135.0	75	109.6	115	75.8	155	42.9	195	27.1
36	134.5	76	108.9	116	74.8	156	42.3	196	26.8
37	133.9	77	108.2	117	73.8	157	41.8	197	26.5
38	133.4	78	107.4	118	72.9	158	41.2	198	26.3
39	132.9	79	106.7	119	71.9	159	40.8	199	26.0
40	132.3	80	105.9	120	70.9	160	40.2	200	25.7

TABLE R-2 F_a Values for $F_y = 345$ MPa

Main and secondary members: $\frac{KL}{r}$ not over 120						Main members: $\frac{KL}{r}$ 121 to 126	
$\frac{KL}{r}$	F_a (MPa)	$\frac{KL}{r}$	F_a (MPa)	$\frac{KL}{r}$	F_a (MPa)	$\frac{KL}{r}$	F_a (MPa)
1	206.4	41	177.1	81	129.7	121	70.3
2	206.0	42	176.2	82	128.3	122	69.2
3	205.5	43	175.1	83	126.9	123	68.1
4	205.0	44	174.2	84	125.5	124	67.0
5	204.5	45	173.1	85	124.0	125	65.9
6	204.0	46	172.1	86	122.7	126	64.9
7	203.4	47	171.1	87	121.2		
8	202.8	48	170.0	88	119.8		
9	202.3	49	169.0	89	118.3		
10	201.7	50	167.9	90	116.8		
11	201.1	51	166.8	91	115.3		
12	200.5	52	165.8	92	113.8		
13	199.9	53	164.7	93	112.3		
14	199.3	54	163.5	94	110.7		
15	198.6	55	162.4	95	109.2		
16	197.9	56	161.3	96	107.7		
17	197.2	57	160.1	97	106.1		
18	196.6	58	159.0	98	104.6		
19	195.8	59	157.8	99	103.0		
20	195.1	60	156.7	100	101.4		
21	194.4	61	155.5	101	99.8		
22	193.6	62	154.2	102	98.2		
23	192.9	63	153.1	103	96.5		
24	192.1	64	151.8	104	94.9		
25	191.3	65	150.7	105	93.3		
26	190.5	66	149.4	106	91.6		
27	189.7	67	148.2	107	89.9		
28	188.9	68	146.9	108	88.3		
29	188.1	69	145.6	109	86.7		
30	187.2	70	144.4	110	85.1		
31	186.4	71	143.1	111	83.6		
32	185.5	72	141.8	112	82.1		
33	184.6	73	140.5	113	80.6		
34	183.7	74	139.2	114	79.2		
35	182.8	75	137.8	115	77.8		
36	181.9	76	136.5	116	76.5		
37	181.0	77	135.2	117	75.2		
38	180.0	78	133.8	118	73.9		
39	179.1	79	132.5	119	72.7		
40	178.1	80	131.1	120	71.5		

TABLE R-3 *F'_e Values for All Grades of Steel*

$\frac{KL_b}{r_b}$	F'_e (MPa)	$\frac{KL_b}{r_b}$	F'_e (MPa)	$\frac{KL_b}{r_b}$	F'_e (MPa)	$\frac{KL_b}{r_b}$	F'_e (MPa)	$\frac{KL_b}{r_b}$	F'_e (MPa)	$\frac{KL_b}{r_b}$	F'_e (MPa)
21	2334.7	51	395.8	81	156.9	111	83.6	141	51.8	171	35.2
22	2127.3	52	380.8	82	153.1	112	82.1	142	51.1	172	34.8
23	1946.3	53	366.5	83	149.5	113	80.6	143	50.3	173	34.4
24	1787.5	54	353.1	84	145.9	114	79.2	144	49.6	174	34.0
25	1647.4	55	340.4	85	142.5	115	77.8	145	49.0	175	33.6
26	1523.1	56	328.3	86	139.2	116	76.5	146	48.3	176	33.2
27	1412.3	57	316.9	87	136.0	117	75.2	147	47.6	177	32.9
28	1313.2	58	306.1	88	132.9	118	73.9	148	47.0	178	32.5
29	1224.2	59	295.8	89	130.0	119	72.7	149	46.4	179	32.1
30	1144.0	60	286.0	90	127.1	120	71.5	150	45.8	180	31.8
31	1071.4	61	277.7	91	124.3	121	70.3	151	45.2	181	31.4
32	1005.5	62	267.9	92	121.6	122	69.2	152	44.5	182	31.1
33	945.5	63	259.4	93	119.1	123	68.1	153	44.0	183	30.8
34	890.7	64	251.4	94	116.5	124	67.0	154	43.4	184	30.4
35	840.5	65	243.7	95	114.1	125	65.9	155	42.9	185	30.1
36	794.4	66	236.4	96	111.7	126	64.9	156	42.3	186	29.8
37	752.1	67	229.4	97	109.4	127	63.9	157	41.8	187	29.4
38	713.1	68	222.6	98	107.2	128	62.8	158	41.2	188	29.1
39	676.9	69	216.3	99	105.1	129	61.9	159	40.8	189	28.8
40	643.5	70	210.2	100	102.9	130	61.0	160	40.2	190	28.5
41	612.5	71	204.2	101	100.9	131	60.0	161	39.7	191	28.2
42	583.6	72	198.6	102	98.9	132	59.1	162	39.2	192	27.9
43	556.8	73	193.2	103	97.1	133	58.2	163	38.8	193	27.7
44	531.8	74	188.0	104	95.2	134	57.4	164	38.3	194	27.4
45	508.4	75	183.1	105	93.4	135	56.5	165	37.9	195	27.1
46	486.6	76	178.2	106	91.6	136	55.6	166	37.4	196	26.8
47	466.1	77	173.7	107	89.9	137	54.9	167	36.9	197	26.5
48	446.9	78	169.2	108	88.3	138	54.1	168	36.5	198	26.3
49	428.9	79	165.0	109	86.7	139	53.3	169	36.1	199	26.0
50	411.8	80	160.9	110	85.1	140	52.5	170	35.7	200	25.7

APPENDIX S
STEEL SECTION PROPERTIES

Table S-1 is arranged in order of decreasing strong-axis section modulus values. In each group the bold faced section is the lightest. Sections marked with an asterisk (*) are noncompact in $F_y = 345$ MPa steel. The section marked with a double asterisk (**) is noncompact in $F_y = 250$ MPa steel. A noncompact section will have a reduction in allowable bending stress of up to 10%. Shapes are designated by nominal depth and mass per meter.

TABLE S-1 *Beam Selection*

S_x (10^3 mm³)	Designation	I_x (10^6 mm⁴)	S_y (10^3 mm³)	I_y (10^6 mm⁴)	A (mm²)	d (mm)
18 200	**W920 × 446**	8450	2560	541	57 000	933
16 900	**W920 × 417**	7870	2360	499	53 200	928
15 600	**W920 × 387**	7200	2160	454	49 400	921
14 700	**W920 × 365**	6700	2020	420	46 500	916
13 700	**W920 × 342**	6240	1870	391	43 600	912
13 600	W840 × 359	5910	1930	388	45 700	868
12 400	**W840 × 329**	5330	1740	350	41 900	862
11 800	**W920 × 313**	5490	1110	171	39 900	932
11 600	W360 × 634	2750	4640	982	80 600	474

TABLE S-1 (continued)

S_x (10³ mm³)	Designation	I_x (10⁶ mm⁴)	S_y (10³ mm³)	I_y (10⁶ mm⁴)	A (mm²)	d (mm)
11 200	**W840 × 299**	4790	1560	312	38 100	855
10 900	**W920 × 289**	5040	1010	156	36 900	927
10 900	W760 × 314	4290	1640	315	40 000	786
10 700	W360 × 592	2500	4290	903	75 500	465
10 200	**W920 × 271**	4700	944	144	34 600	923
9 950	W360 × 551	2260	3950	828	70 300	455
9 800	W760 × 284	3820	1570	280	36 200	779
9 500	**W920 × 253**	4370	872	133	32 300	919
9 160	W360 × 509	2040	3620	753	65 200	446
8 880	**W920 × 238**	4060	805	123	30 300	915
8 830	W760 × 257	3410	1310	249	32 800	773
8 290	W360 × 463	1800	3260	670	59 000	435
8 260	**W920 × 223**	3760	739	112	28 500	911
8 230	W690 × 265	2910	1290	231	33 700	706
7 980	W840 × 226	3400	773	114	28 800	851
7 520	W360 × 421	1600	2930	599	53 700	425
7 460	W690 × 240	2610	1160	207	30 600	701
7 340	**W840 × 210**	3100	700	102	26 800	846
7 190	**W920 × 201**	3250	618	93.7	25 600	903
6 800	W360 × 382	1420	2640	537	48 800	416
6 780	W610 × 241	2150	1120	184	30 800	635
6 740	W690 × 217	2340	1040	184	27 700	695
6 650	**W840 × 193**	2790	621	90.7	24 700	840
6 230	W760 × 196	2400	610	81.6	25 100	770
6 150	W360 × 347	1250	2380	479	44 200	407
6 080	W610 × 217	1910	991	163	27 700	628
5 880	**W840 × 176**	2460	534	77.8	22 400	835
5 820	W760 × 185	2230	564	75.3	23 500	766
5 540	W360 × 314	1110	2130	429	40 000	399
5 390	**W760 × 173**	2050	513	68.3	22 100	762
5 390	W610 × 195	1670	869	142	24 800	622
5 390	W530 × 219	1520	985	156	27 900	560
5 080	W360 × 287	1000	1950	388	36 600	393
4 900	**W760 × 161**	1860	457	60.8	20 500	758
4 900	W690 × 170	1700	516	66.1	21 600	693
4 830	W530 × 196	1340	877	139	25 000	554
4 770	W610 × 174	1470	762	124	22 200	616
4 600	W360 × 262	891	1750	345	33 400	387
4 470	W530 × 182	1230	806	127	23 200	551
4 410	**W760 × 147**	1660	401	53.3	18 800	753
4 380	W690 × 152	1510	456	57.9	19 400	688
4 310	W310 × 283	787	1520	245	36 000	365
4 230	W610 × 155	1290	667	108	19 700	611
4 160	W360 × 237	791	1580	311	30 100	380
4 130	S610 × 179	1260	342	35.0	22 800	610
4 080	W530 × 165	1110	729	114	21 100	546
3 980	**W690 × 140**	1360	406	51.6	17 900	684
3 870	S610 × 158	1180	324	32.5	20 100	610
3 850	W310 × 253	687	1350	215	32 300	356
3 800	W360 × 216	712	1430	282	27 500	375
3 790	W460 × 177	912	736	105	22 600	482
3 720	W530 × 150	1010	660	103	19 200	543
3 640	**W610 × 140**	1120	393	45.4	17 900	617

TABLE S-1 (continued)

S_x $(10^3 mm^3)$	Designation	I_x $(10^6 mm^4)$	S_y $(10^3 mm^3)$	I_y $(10^6 mm^4)$	A (mm^2)	d (mm)
3 490	**W690 × 125**	1190	347	44.1	16 000	678
3 420	W360 × 196	637	1220	228	25 000	372
3 420	W310 × 226	595	1190	189	28 800	348
3 340	W460 × 158	795	646	91.6	20 100	476
3 260	S610 × 149	995	216	19.9	19 000	610
3 210	**W610 × 125**	986	342	39.3	15 900	612
3 150	W530 × 138	862	362	38.7	17 600	549
3 110	W360 × 179	574	1110	206	22 800	368
3 080	W460 × 144	728	592	83.7	18 400	472
3 060	S610 × 134	937	206	18.7	17 100	610
3 050	W310 × 202	516	1050	166	25 700	341
2 880	**W610 × 113**	874	302	34.3	14 500	608
2 870	S610 × 119	878	198	17.6	15 200	610
2 870	W410 × 149	620	585	77.4	19 000	431
2 830	W360 × 162	516	1000	186	20 600	364
2 800	W530 × 123	762	320	33.9	15 700	544
2 720	W460 × 128	637	518	72.8	16 300	467
2 670	W310 × 179	445	918	144	22 800	333
2 640	S510 × 141	670	226	20.7	18 000	508
2 570	W360 × 147*	462	905	167	18 800	360
2 540	W410 × 132	541	515	67.8	16 900	425
2 520	**W610 × 101**	762	257	29.3	13 000	603
2 490	S510 × 127	633	215	19.2	16 100	508
2 470	W530 × 109	666	279	29.4	13 900	539
2 390	W460 × 113	554	452	63.3	14 400	463
2 380	W310 × 158	388	808	125	20 100	327
2 340	W360 × 134*	416	818	151	17 100	356
2 290	**W530 × 101**	616	257	26.9	12 900	537
2 200	W410 × 114	462	441	57.4	14 600	420
2 150	**W610 × 92**	645	161	14.4	11 700	603
2 150	W310 × 143	347	728	112	18 200	323
2 100	S510 × 112	533	152	12.3	14 300	508
2 080	**W530 × 92**	554	228	23.9	11 800	533
2 080	W460 × 106	487	259	25.1	13 400	469
2 060	W250 × 167	298	742	98.2	21 200	289
2 020	W360 × 122	367	480	61.6	15 500	363
1 930	S510 × 97.3	491	144	11.4	12 400	508
1 930	W310 × 129	308	651	100	16 500	318
1 920	W460 × 97	445	236	22.8	12 300	466
1 920	W410 × 100	397	380	49.5	12 700	415
1 870	**W610 × 82**	562	136	12.1	10 500	599
1 840	W360 × 110	331	436	55.8	14 100	360
1 840	W250 × 149	259	655	86.2	19 000	282
1 820	W530 × 85	487	153	12.7	10 800	535
1 770	W460 × 89	410	218	20.9	11 400	463
1 750	W310 × 117	276	587	89.9	15 000	314
1 690	W360 × 101	301	397	50.4	12 900	357
1 690	S460 × 104	385	127	10.0	13 300	457
1 610	W250 × 131	222	570	74.5	16 700	275
1 610	**W460 × 82**	370	195	18.7	10 500	460
1 600	W310 × 107	248	531	81.2	13 600	311
1 550	**W530 × 74**	410	125	10.4	9 480	529
1 510	W410 × 85	316	198	17.9	10 800	417
1 510	W360 × 91	266	352	44.5	11 500	353

TABLE S-1 (continued)

S_x (10^3 mm^3)	Designation	I_x (10^6 mm^4)	S_y (10^3 mm^3)	I_y (10^6 mm^4)	A (mm^2)	d (mm)
1 460	**W460 × 74**	333	175	16.7	9 480	457
1 460	S460 × 81.4	335	114	8.66	10 400	457
1 440	W310 × 97*	222	477	72.4	12 300	308
1 410	W250 × 115	189	493	64.1	14 600	269
1 340	**W530 × 66**	351	104	8.62	8 390	525
1 330	W410 × 75	274	172	15.5	9 480	413
1 290	W460 × 68	296	122	9.37	8 710	459
1 280	W310 × 86	198	351	44.5	11 000	310
1 270	W360 × 79	225	234	24.0	10 100	354
1 240	W250 × 101	164	433	55.8	12 900	264
1 230	MC460 × 86	281	87.2	7.41	11 000	457
1 190	W410 × 67	244	153	13.7	8 580	410
1 160	W310 × 79	177	315	39.9	10 100	306
1 150	W360 × 72	202	210	21.4	9 100	350
1 140	MC460 × 77.2	261	83.1	6.83	9 870	457
1 120	**W460 × 60**	255	104	7.95	7 610	455
1 090	W250 × 89	142	377	48.3	11 400	260
1 060	**W410 × 60**	216	135	12.0	7 610	407
1 060	S380 × 74	202	91.3	6.53	9 480	381
1 060	W310 × 74	164	228	23.4	9 480	310
1 050	MC460 × 68.2	241	79.0	6.29	8 710	457
1 030	W360 × 64	178	185	18.8	8 130	347
1 010	MC460 × 63.5	231	76.9	5.99	8 130	457
990	W200 × 100	113	351	36.9	12 700	229
983	W250 × 80	126	338	42.9	10 200	256
977	S380 × 64	186	85.7	5.99	8 130	381
952	W310 × 67	146	203	20.8	8 520	306
944	**W460 × 52**	212	83.9	6.37	6 650	450
926	W410 × 53	186	115	10.2	6 840	403
895	W360 × 57	160	129	11.1	7 230	358
895	W250 × 73	113	306	38.9	9 290	253
882	C380 × 74	168	61.9	4.58	9 480	381
852	W200 × 86	94.9	300	31.3	11 000	222
850	W310 × 60	129	180	18.4	7 610	303
833	S310 × 74	127	94.1	6.53	9 480	305
805	W250 × 67	103	218	22.2	8 580	257
796	**W360 × 51**	142	113	9.70	6 450	355
773	**W410 × 46.1**	156	73.6	5.16	5 880	403
762	C380 × 60	145	55.1	3.84	7 610	381
747	W310 × 52	119	122	10.2	6 650	317
744	S310 × 60.7	113	84.6	5.66	7 740	305
710	W200 × 71	76.6	246	25.3	9 100	216
690	W250 × 58	87.0	185	18.7	7 420	252
688	**W360 × 44.8**	121	95.4	8.16	5 710	352
688	C380 × 50.4	132	51.0	3.38	6 430	381
633	**W310 × 44.5**	99.1	102	8.45	5 670	313
629	**W410 × 38.8**	125	57.2	3.99	4 950	399
626	S310 × 52	95.3	63.7	4.11	6 640	305
597	S310 × 47.3	90.7	61.3	3.90	6 030	305
582	W200 × 59	60.8	200	20.4	7 550	210
578	**W360 × 39.0**	102	58.0	3.71	4 960	353
574	W250 × 49.1	70.8	151	15.2	6 260	247
547	**W310 × 38.7**	84.9	87.5	7.2	4 940	310
531	W250 × 44.8	70.8	94.2	6.95	5 700	266
511	W200 × 52	52.9	174	17.7	6 650	206
482	S250 × 52	61.2	55.4	3.48	6 640	254

TABLE S-1 (continued)

S_x (10^3 mm^3)	Designation	I_x (10^6 mm^4)	S_y (10^3 mm^3)	I_y (10^6 mm^4)	A (mm^2)	d (mm)
475	**W360 × 32.9**	82.8	45.9	2.92	4 190	349
457	W250 × 38.5	59.9	80.1	5.87	4 910	262
450	W200 × 46.1	45.8	152	15.4	5 890	203
443	C310 × 45	67.4	33.8	2.14	5 690	305
436	M250 × 43.3	54.5	61.6	4.66	5 520	251
416	**W310 × 32.7**	64.9	37.9	1.94	4 180	313
405	S250 × 37.8	51.6	47.7	2.83	4 810	254
398	W200 × 41.7	40.8	109	9.03	5 320	205
395	C310 × 37	59.9	30.8	1.86	4 740	305
387	M250 × 34.1	48.7	57.0	4.16	4 340	251
380	**W250 × 32.7**	49.1	65.0	4.75	4 190	258
353	**C310 × 30.8**	53.7	28.3	1.61	3 930	305
349	**W310 × 28.3**	54.1	30.8	1.57	3 590	309
346	**M360 × 25.6**	61.2	21.8	1.10	3 260	356
342	W200 × 35.9	34.5	92.3	7.62	4 570	201
339	C250 × 45	42.9	27.0	1.64	5 690	254
308	**W250 × 28.4**	40.1	35.1	1.79	3 630	260
298	W200 × 31.3	31.3	60.8	4.07	3 970	210
298	C250 × 37	38.0	24.3	1.40	4 740	254
280	**W310 × 23.8**	42.9	23.1	1.17	3 040	305
274	W150 × 37.1	22.2	91.9	7.12	4 740	162
266	S200 × 34	27.0	33.9	1.79	4 370	203
265	W250 × 25.3	34.1	29.2	1.48	3 220	257
259	C250 × 30	32.8	21.6	1.17	3 790	254
249	W200 × 26.6	25.8	49.8	3.32	3 390	207
244	**W310 × 21.0**	36.9	19.5	0.982	2 680	303
236	S200 × 27.4	24.0	30.5	1.55	3 480	203
226	W250 × 22.3	28.7	23.8	1.20	2 850	254
221	C250 × 22.8	28.1	19.0	0.949	2 900	254
221	C230 × 30	25.3	19.2	1.01	3 800	229
220	W150 × 29.8	17.2	72.3	5.54	3 790	157
198	S180 × 30	17.6	26.9	1.32	3 790	178
197	**M310 × 17.6**	29.9	10.5	0.408	2 240	305
193	W200 × 22.5	20.0	27.9	1.42	2 860	206
185	C230 × 22	21.2	16.6	0.803	2 850	229
180	C200 × 27.9	18.3	16.6	0.824	3 560	203
179	W250 × 17.9*	22.4	18.0	0.907	2 280	251
174	C230 × 19.9	19.9	15.8	0.733	2 540	229
172	S180 × 22.8	15.3	23.6	1.10	2 890	178
167	W150 × 24.0	13.4	51.0	1.84	3 060	160
167	W130 × 28.1	10.9	59.5	3.80	3 590	131
162	W200 × 19.3	16.5	22.5	1.14	2 480	203
159	W150 × 22.5**	12.1	36.1	3.88	2 860	152
158	M130 × 28.1	10.0	51.4	3.27	3 580	127
151	**MC310 × 15.8**	23.1	5.08	0.159	2 000	305
149	C200 × 20.5	15.0	14.0	0.637	2 610	203
144	S150 × 25.7	10.9	21.3	0.961	3 270	152
140	W130 × 23.8	8.91	49.2	3.13	3 040	127
133	C200 × 17.1	13.6	12.8	0.549	2 180	203
128	**W200 × 15.0***	12.8	17.4	0.870	1 910	200
128	C180 × 22.0	11.3	12.8	0.574	2 790	178
127	**M250 × 13.4**	16.1	7.42	0.253	1 710	254
121	S150 × 18.6	9.20	17.9	0.758	2 360	152
120	W150 × 18.0	9.20	24.6	1.24	2 290	153
114	C180 × 18.2	10.1	11.5	0.487	2 320	178

TABLE S-1 (*continued*)

S_x (10^3 mm^3)	Designation	I_x (10^6 mm^4)	S_y (10^3 mm^3)	I_y (10^6 mm^4)	A (mm^2)	d (mm)
105	**MC250 $\times$ 12.5**	13.3	4.42	0.137	1 590	254
99.8	S130 $\times$ 22.0	6.33	16.6	0.695	2 800	127
99.7	C180 $\times$ 14.6	8.87	10.2	0.403	1 850	178
95.1	C150 $\times$ 19.3	7.24	10.5	0.437	2 470	152
91.1	W150 $\times$ 13.5	6.83	18.2	0.916	1 730	150
89.5	W100 $\times$ 19.3	4.70	31.1	1.61	2 470	106
82.9	C150 $\times$ 15.6	6.33	9.24	0.360	1 990	152
80.6	S130 $\times$ 15	5.12	13.3	0.508	1 880	127
75.7	**M200 $\times$ 9.7**	7.70	5.62	0.143	1 240	203
72.4	MC250 $\times$ 9.7	9.20	1.93	0.047	1 240	254
71.8	C150 $\times$ 12.2	5.45	8.06	0.288	1 550	152
58.3	C130 $\times$ 13.4	3.70	7.36	0.263	1 700	127
56.4	**M180 $\times$ 8.2**	4.99	4.08	0.104	1 050	178
55.6	S100 $\times$ 14.1	2.83	10.6	0.376	1 800	102
49.8	S100 $\times$ 11.5	2.53	9.41	0.318	1 450	102
49.2	C130 $\times$ 10.0	3.12	6.19	0.199	1 270	127
39.3	**M150 $\times$ 6.5**	3.00	2.93	0.069	832	152
37.5	C100 $\times$ 10.8	1.91	5.62	0.180	1 370	102
32.0	S75 $\times$ 11.2	1.22	7.67	0.244	1 430	76
31.6	C100 $\times$ 8.0	1.60	4.64	0.133	1 030	102
27.5	S75 $\times$ 8.5	1.05	6.39	0.189	1 080	76
22.6	C75 $\times$ 8.9	0.862	4.39	0.127	1 140	76
18.4	C75 $\times$ 7.4	0.770	3.82	0.103	948	76
19.2	C75 $\times$ 6.1	0.691	3.31	0.082	781	76

Structural tubes are designated by overall dimensions and wall thickness; channels and W shapes by nominal depth and mass per meter. Table S-2 includes only a few of the many available column sections and is intended only for use with the examples and problems of Chapter 13.

TABLE S-2 *Selected Column Sections*

Designation	Area (mm^2)	I_x (10^6 mm^4)	S_x (10^3 mm^3)	r_x (mm)	I_y (10^6 mm^4)	S_y (10^3 mm^3)	r_y (mm)
TS 102 $\times$ 51 $\times$ 6.4	1 670	1.95	38.5	34.3	0.64	25.2	19.6
TS 152 $\times$ 76 $\times$ 12.7	4 610	10.7	141	48.3	3.51	92.3	27.7
TS 178 $\times$ 127 $\times$ 6.4	3 570	15.6	175	66	9.28	146	50.8
C230 $\times$ 30	3 800	25.3	221	81.8	1.01	19.2	16.3
C250 $\times$ 44.6	5 690	42.9	339	86.9	1.64	27.0	17.0
W150 $\times$ 37.1	4 740	22.2	274	68.3	7.12	91.9	38.9
W200 $\times$ 52	6 650	52.9	511	89.2	17.7	174	51.6
W200 $\times$ 59	7 550	60.8	582	89.7	20.4	200	52.0
W200 $\times$ 100	12 700	113	990	94.2	36.9	351	53.9
W250 $\times$ 58	7 420	87	690	108	18.7	185	50.2
W250 $\times$ 67	8 580	103	805	110	22.2	218	50.9
W250 $\times$ 73	9 290	113	895	110	38.9	306	64.2
W250 $\times$ 89	11 400	142	1 090	112	48.3	377	65.1
W250 $\times$ 149	19 000	259	1 840	117	86.2	655	67.4
W310 $\times$ 52	6 650	119	747	134	10.2	122	39.2
W310 $\times$ 79	10 100	177	1 160	132	39.9	315	62.9
W310 $\times$ 97	12 300	222	1 440	134	72.4	477	76.7
W310 $\times$ 117	15 000	276	1 750	136	89.9	587	77.4
W310 $\times$ 143	18 200	347	2 150	138	112	728	78.4
W310 $\times$ 179	22 800	445	2 670	140	144	918	79.5
W310 $\times$ 202	25 700	516	3 050	142	166	1050	80.4
W360 $\times$ 122	15 500	367	2 020	154	61.6	480	63.0
W360 $\times$ 134	17 100	416	2 340	156	151	818	94.2
W360 $\times$ 818	105 000	3930	15 300	193	1360	6190	114

APPENDIX T
REINFORCING BAR SIZES

Designation	Area (mm^2)	Diameter (mm)
10	100	11.3
15	200	16.0
20	300	19.5
25	500	25.2
30	700	29.9
35	1000	35.7
45	1500	43.7
55	2500	56.4

APPENDIX U
VALUES FOR STRENGTH DESIGN
OF REINFORCED CONCRETE BEAMS*

	$F_y = 400\ MPa$							
	$f'_c = 20\ MPa$ $\rho_{max} = 0.0163$		$f'_c = 25\ MPa$ $\rho_{max} = 0.0203$		$f'_c = 30\ MPa$ $\rho_{max} = 0.0244$		$f'_c = 35\ MPa$ $\rho_{max} = 0.0270$	
$\rho = \dfrac{A_s}{bd}$	j_u	$K_u\ (MPa)$	j_u	$K_u\ (MPa)$	j_u	$K_u\ (MPa)$	j_u	$K_u\ (MPa)$
0.004	0.953	1.37	0.962	1.39	0.969	1.40	0.973	1.40
0.005	0.941	1.69	0.953	1.72	0.961	1.73	0.966	1.74
0.006	0.929	2.01	0.943	2.04	0.953	2.06	0.960	2.07
0.007	0.917	2.31	0.934	2.35	0.945	2.38	0.953	2.40
0.008	0.906	2.61	0.924	2.66	0.937	2.70	0.946	2.72
0.009	0.894	2.90	0.915	2.96	0.929	3.01	0.939	3.04
0.010	0.882	3.18	0.906	3.26	0.921	3.32	0.933	3.36
0.011	0.870	3.45	0.896	3.55	0.913	3.62	0.926	3.67
0.012	0.858	3.71	0.887	3.83	0.906	3.91	0.919	3.97
0.013	0.847	3.96	0.877	4.10	0.898	4.20	0.912	4.27
0.014	0.835	4.21	0.868	4.37	0.890	4.49	0.906	4.57
0.015	0.823	4.44	0.858	4.63	0.882	4.76	0.899	4.85
0.016	0.811	4.67	0.849	4.89	0.874	5.03	0.892	5.14
0.017			0.840	5.14	0.866	5.30	0.885	5.42
0.018			0.830	5.38	0.858	5.56	0.879	5.70
0.019			0.821	5.62	0.851	5.82	0.872	5.96
0.020			0.811	5.84	0.843	6.07	0.865	6.23
0.021					0.835	6.31	0.858	6.49
0.022					0.827	6.55	0.852	6.75
0.023					0.819	6.78	0.845	7.00
0.024					0.811	7.01	0.838	7.24
0.025							0.831	7.48
0.026							0.825	7.72
0.027							0.818	7.95

$$M_u = K_u bd^2 \qquad K_u = \phi \rho F_y j_u \qquad j_u = 1 - 0.59\rho \frac{F_y}{f'_c}$$
$$\phi = 0.90$$

*Values of j and K_u for steel percentages above ρ_{max} or below ρ_{min} are not shown.

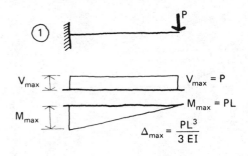

① $V_{max} = P$

$M_{max} = PL$

$\Delta_{max} = \dfrac{PL^3}{3\,EI}$

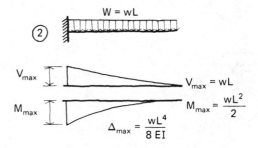

② $W = wL$

$V_{max} = wL$

$M_{max} = \dfrac{wL^2}{2}$

$\Delta_{max} = \dfrac{wL^4}{8\,EI}$

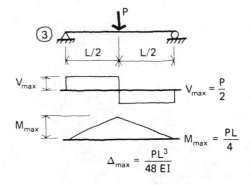

③ $\dfrac{L}{2} \quad \dfrac{L}{2}$

$V_{max} = \dfrac{P}{2}$

$M_{max} = \dfrac{PL}{4}$

$\Delta_{max} = \dfrac{PL^3}{48\,EI}$

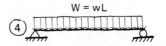

④ $W = wL$

$V_{max} = \dfrac{wL}{2}$

$M_{max} = \dfrac{wL^2}{8}$

$\Delta_{max} = \dfrac{5\,wL^4}{384\,EI}$

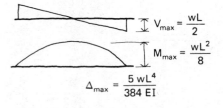

⑤ $(a < b)$

$V_{max} = \dfrac{Pb}{L}$

$M_{max} = \dfrac{Pab}{L}$

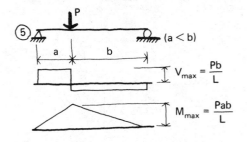

⑥ $W = \dfrac{1}{2} wL$

$V_{max} = \dfrac{wL}{3}$

$M_{max} = \dfrac{wL^2}{9\sqrt{3}}$

$\Delta_{max} = \dfrac{0.0652\,wL^4}{EI}$

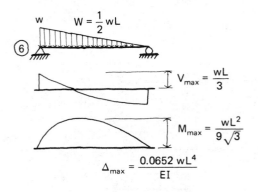

⑦ $W = wa \quad (a < b)$

$V_{max} = \dfrac{wa}{2L}(2L - a)$

$M_{max} = \left[\dfrac{wa}{2L}(2L - a)\right]^2 \Big/ 2a$

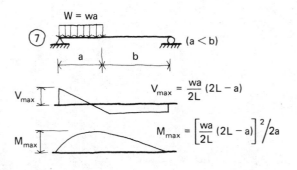

⑧

$V_l = \dfrac{Pb^2}{2L^3}(a + 2L)$

$V_r = \dfrac{Pa}{2L^3}(3L^2 - a^2)$

$M_p = \dfrac{Pab^2}{2L^3}(a + 2L)$

$M_r = \dfrac{Pab}{2L^2}(a + L)$

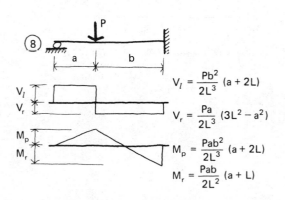

317

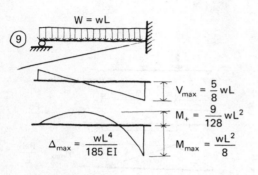

⑨

$$V_{max} = \frac{5}{8} wL$$

$$M_+ = \frac{9}{128} wL^2$$

$$\Delta_{max} = \frac{wL^4}{185\, EI}$$

$$M_{max} = \frac{wL^2}{8}$$

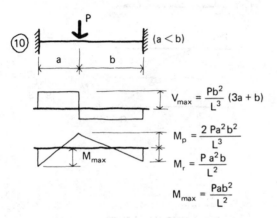

⑩ (a < b)

$$V_{max} = \frac{Pb^2}{L^3} (3a + b)$$

$$M_p = \frac{2\, Pa^2 b^2}{L^3}$$

$$M_r = \frac{P\, a^2 b}{L^2}$$

$$M_{max} = \frac{Pab^2}{L^2}$$

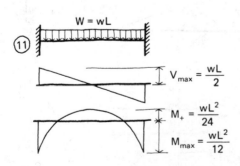

⑪

$$V_{max} = \frac{wL}{2}$$

$$M_+ = \frac{wL^2}{24}$$

$$M_{max} = \frac{wL^2}{12}$$

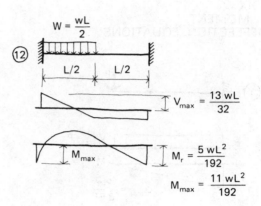

⑫

$$V_{max} = \frac{13\, wL}{32}$$

$$M_r = \frac{5\, wL^2}{192}$$

$$M_{max} = \frac{11\, wL^2}{192}$$

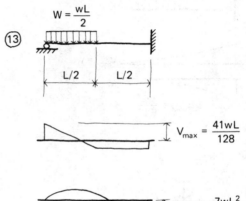

⑬

$$V_{max} = \frac{41 wL}{128}$$

$$M_{max} = \frac{7 wL^2}{128}$$

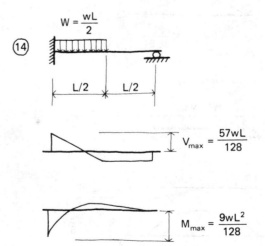

⑭

$$V_{max} = \frac{57 wL}{128}$$

$$M_{max} = \frac{9 wL^2}{128}$$

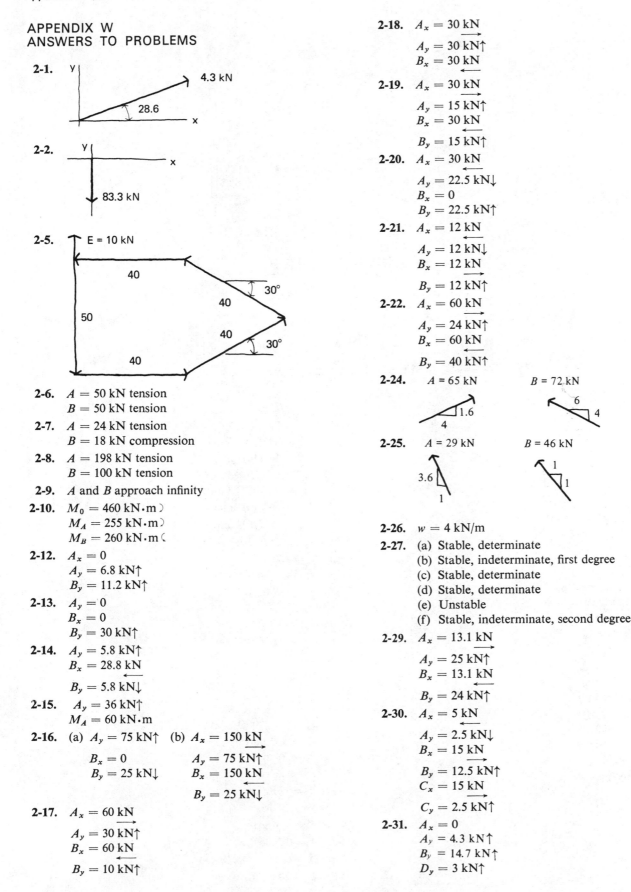

APPENDIX W
ANSWERS TO PROBLEMS

2-1.

y, 4.3 kN, 28.6, x

2-2.

y, x, 83.3 kN

2-5. E = 10 kN

40, 50, 40, 40, 40, 30°, 30°

2-6. $A = 50$ kN tension
$B = 50$ kN tension

2-7. $A = 24$ kN tension
$B = 18$ kN compression

2-8. $A = 198$ kN tension
$B = 100$ kN tension

2-9. A and B approach infinity

2-10. $M_0 = 460$ kN·m ⟩
$M_A = 255$ kN·m ⟩
$M_B = 260$ kN·m ⟨

2-12. $A_x = 0$
$A_y = 6.8$ kN↑
$B_y = 11.2$ kN↑

2-13. $A_y = 0$
$B_x = 0$
$B_y = 30$ kN↑

2-14. $A_y = 5.8$ kN↑
$B_x = 28.8$ kN←
$B_y = 5.8$ kN↓

2-15. $A_y = 36$ kN↑
$M_A = 60$ kN·m

2-16. (a) $A_y = 75$ kN↑   (b) $A_x = 150$ kN→
$B_x = 0$ $A_y = 75$ kN↑
$B_y = 25$ kN↓ $B_x = 150$ kN←
                $B_y = 25$ kN↓

2-17. $A_x = 60$ kN→
$A_y = 30$ kN↑
$B_x = 60$ kN←
$B_y = 10$ kN↑

2-18. $A_x = 30$ kN→
$A_y = 30$ kN↑
$B_x = 30$ kN←

2-19. $A_x = 30$ kN→
$A_y = 15$ kN↑
$B_x = 30$ kN←
$B_y = 15$ kN↑

2-20. $A_x = 30$ kN←
$A_y = 22.5$ kN↓
$B_x = 0$
$B_y = 22.5$ kN↑

2-21. $A_x = 12$ kN←
$A_y = 12$ kN↓
$B_x = 12$ kN→
$B_y = 12$ kN↑

2-22. $A_x = 60$ kN→
$A_y = 24$ kN↑
$B_x = 60$ kN←
$B_y = 40$ kN↑

2-24. $A = 65$ kN $B = 72$ kN
1.6, 4, 6, 4

2-25. $A = 29$ kN $B = 46$ kN
3.6, 1, 1, 1

2-26. $w = 4$ kN/m

2-27. (a) Stable, determinate
(b) Stable, indeterminate, first degree
(c) Stable, determinate
(d) Stable, determinate
(e) Unstable
(f) Stable, indeterminate, second degree

2-29. $A_x = 13.1$ kN→
$A_y = 25$ kN↑
$B_x = 13.1$ kN←
$B_y = 24$ kN↑

2-30. $A_x = 5$ kN←
$A_y = 2.5$ kN↓
$B_x = 15$ kN→
$B_y = 12.5$ kN↑
$C_x = 15$ kN→
$C_y = 2.5$ kN↑

2-31. $A_x = 0$
$A_y = 4.3$ kN↑
$B_y = 14.7$ kN↑
$D_y = 3$ kN↑

2-32.

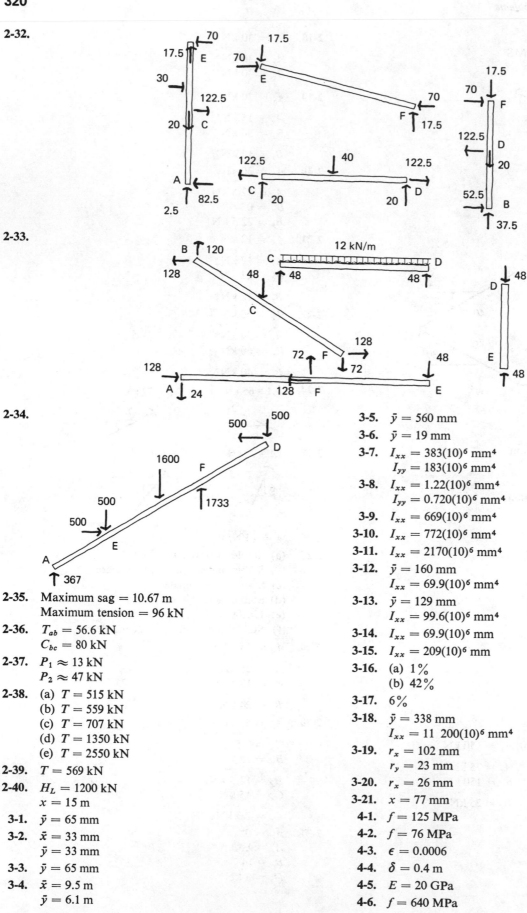

2-33.

2-34.

2-35. Maximum sag = 10.67 m
Maximum tension = 96 kN

2-36. $T_{ab} = 56.6$ kN
$C_{bc} = 80$ kN

2-37. $P_1 \approx 13$ kN
$P_2 \approx 47$ kN

2-38. (a) $T = 515$ kN
(b) $T = 559$ kN
(c) $T = 707$ kN
(d) $T = 1350$ kN
(e) $T = 2550$ kN

2-39. $T = 569$ kN

2-40. $H_L = 1200$ kN
$x = 15$ m

3-1. $\bar{y} = 65$ mm

3-2. $\bar{x} = 33$ mm
$\bar{y} = 33$ mm

3-3. $\bar{y} = 65$ mm

3-4. $\bar{x} = 9.5$ m
$\bar{y} = 6.1$ m

3-5. $\bar{y} = 560$ mm

3-6. $\bar{y} = 19$ mm

3-7. $I_{xx} = 383(10)^6$ mm⁴
$I_{yy} = 183(10)^6$ mm⁴

3-8. $I_{xx} = 1.22(10)^6$ mm⁴
$I_{yy} = 0.720(10)^6$ mm⁴

3-9. $I_{xx} = 669(10)^6$ mm⁴

3-10. $I_{xx} = 772(10)^6$ mm⁴

3-11. $I_{xx} = 2170(10)^6$ mm⁴

3-12. $\bar{y} = 160$ mm
$I_{xx} = 69.9(10)^6$ mm⁴

3-13. $\bar{y} = 129$ mm
$I_{xx} = 99.6(10)^6$ mm⁴

3-14. $I_{xx} = 69.9(10)^6$ mm

3-15. $I_{xx} = 209(10)^6$ mm

3-16. (a) 1%
(b) 42%

3-17. 6%

3-18. $\bar{y} = 338$ mm
$I_{xx} = 11\ 200(10)^6$ mm⁴

3-19. $r_x = 102$ mm
$r_y = 23$ mm

3-20. $r_x = 26$ mm

3-21. $x = 77$ mm

4-1. $f = 125$ MPa

4-2. $f = 76$ MPa

4-3. $\epsilon = 0.0006$

4-4. $\delta = 0.4$ m

4-5. $E = 20$ GPa

4-6. $f = 640$ MPa

4-7. $D = 111$ mm

4-8. $\delta = 4$ mm

4-9. $f_c = 8.96$ MPa
$f_s = 89.6$ MPa

4-10. Cable A, $P = 720$ kN
Cable B, $P = 80$ kN

4-11. Cable A, $P = 779$ kN
Cable B, $P = 701$ kN

4-12. At $-10°C$, $L = 124.95$ m
At $70°C$, $L = 125.06$ m

4-13. Width $= 10$ mm

4-14. $f = 234$ MPa

4-15. 1.90 m

4-16. $f = 46.5$ MPa

4-17. $A = 67\ 500$ mm²

4-18. $A = 1.18$ m²

4-19. $D = 28$ mm

4-20. $D = 370$ mm

6-1. $f_v = 67.0$ MPa

6-2. $R = 147$ mm

6-3. $T_{hole} = \frac{15}{16}T_{solid}$

6-4. $\theta = 4$ degrees

6-5. $T = 65$ N·m

6-6. $f_v \approx 772$ kPa

6-7. $T_{ultimate} \approx 24$ kN·m

6-8. $f_v = 98.7$ MPa

6-9. $T_{hollow} \approx 5T_{solid}$

6-10. $T \approx 516$ N·m

6-11. 97% reduction

6-12. $T_{\substack{welded \\ channels}} \approx 32T_{wide\ flange} \approx 48T_{\substack{channels \\ not\ welded}}$

7-1.

7-2.

7-3.

7-4. V (kN)

7-5.

7-6.

7-7. $M_{max} = 39$ kN·m

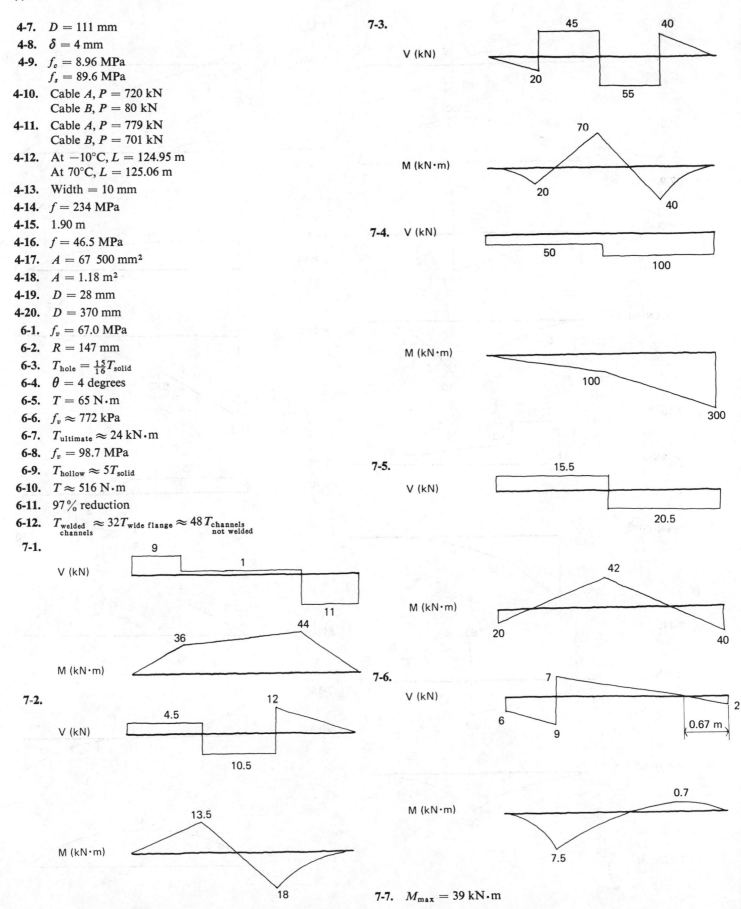

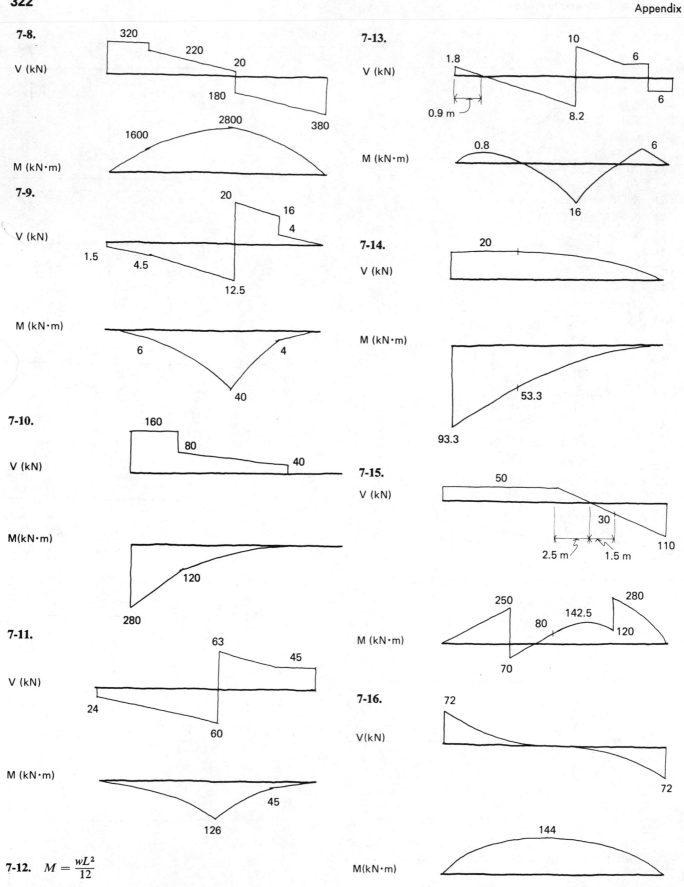

7-8.

V (kN) 320 220 20 180 380

M (kN·m) 1600 2800

7-9.

V (kN) 20 16 4 1.5 4.5 12.5

M (kN·m) 6 4 40

7-10.

V (kN) 160 80 40

M(kN·m) 120 280

7-11.

V (kN) 63 45 24 60

M (kN·m) 45 126

7-12. $M = \dfrac{wL^2}{12}$

7-13.

V (kN) 10 1.8 6 0.9 m 8.2 6

M (kN·m) 0.8 6 16

7-14.

V (kN) 20

M (kN·m) 53.3 93.3

7-15.

V (kN) 50 30 110 2.5 m 1.5 m

M (kN·m) 250 80 142.5 280 70 120

7-16.

V(kN) 72 72

M(kN·m) 144

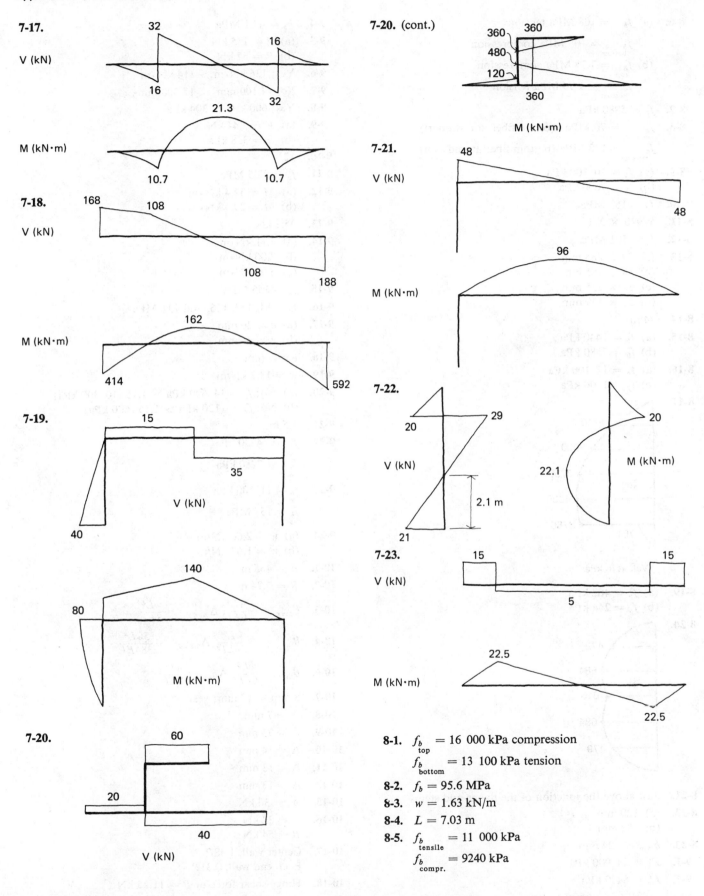

7-17.

V (kN)

32
16
16
32

M (kN·m)

21.3
10.7   10.7

7-18.

V (kN)

168
108
108
188

M (kN·m)

162
414   592

7-19.

15
35
V (kN)
40

140
80
M (kN·m)

7-20.

60
20
40
V (kN)

7-20. (cont.)

360   360
480
120
360
M (kN·m)

7-21.

V (kN)

48
48

96
M (kN·m)

7-22.

20   29
V (kN)
2.1 m
21

20
22.1   M (kN·m)

7-23.

15   15
V (kN)
5

22.5
M (kN·m)
22.5

8-1. $f_{b_{top}}$ = 16 000 kPa compression

$f_{b_{bottom}}$ = 13 100 kPa tension

8-2. f_b = 95.6 MPa

8-3. w = 1.63 kN/m

8-4. L = 7.03 m

8-5. $f_{b_{tensile}}$ = 11 000 kPa

$f_{b_{compr.}}$ = 9240 kPa

8-6. (a) $f_{b_{top}}$ = 108 MPa tension

$f_{b_{bottom}}$ = 108 MPa compression

(b) $f_{b_{top}}$ = 7.74 MPa compression

$f_{b_{bottom}}$ = 7.74 MPa tension

8-7. f_b = 5980 kPa

8-8. $f_{b_{compr.}}$ = 70 MPa (bottom fiber at a support)

$f_{b_{tension}}$ = 143 MPa (bottom fiber at midspan)

8-9. (a) f_b = 10 100 kPa

(b) f_b = 7600 kPa

8-10. f_b = 152 MPa

8-11. W920 × 271

8-12. f_b = 101 MPa

8-13. (a) 38 × 285 mm

(b) 38 × 185 mm

(c) 38 × 235 mm

(d) 38 × 139 mm

8-14. 74 m

8-15. (a) f_b = 1440 kPa

(b) f_b = 7580 kPa

8-16. (a) f_b = 12 100 kPa

(b) f_y = 1600 kPa

8-17.

1750
3000
3750
4000
3750
751

Values in kPa

8-19. (a) f_v = 462 kPa

(b) f_v = 244 kPa

8-20.

479
684
616
684
479

8-21. Just above the junction of the flange and stems

8-22. (a) 120 mm

(b) 52 mm

8-23. b_{min} = 124 mm

9-1. F'_b = 14 900 kPa

9-2. F'_b = 8470 kPa

9-4. F_b = 43.1 MPa

9-5. (a) P = 155 kN

(b) P = 52 kN

9-6. Yes; 136 kN·m > 114 kN·m

9-7. No; 14 100 mm² < 17 300 mm²

9-8. Yes; 600 kPa > 304 kPa

9-9. (a) V = 2.44 kN

(b) f_v = 338 kPa

9-10. 12%

9-11. f_v = 93.5 MPa

9-12. (a) M = 32.4 kN·m

(b) M = 29.5 kN·m

9-13. 35.2 kN

9-14. (a) 7.11 kN·m

(b) 2.00 kN·m

(c) 8.00 kN·m

9-15. f_b = 155 MPa

9-16. f_b = 81, 113, 126, and 131 MPa

9-17. (a) $e \approx$ 20 mm

(b) $e \approx$ 46 mm

9-18. $e \approx$ 7 mm

9-19. w = 13.2 kN/m

9-20. (a) No; f_b = 14 600 kPa > 1.15 (10 300 kPa)

(b) No; f_v = 1120 kPa > 1.15 (600 kPa)

9-21. 3.5 m

9-22. $f_{b_{E.S.}}$ = 4730 kPa

$f_{b_{S.P.}}$ = 7280 kPa

9-23. f_{b_w} = 11 100 kPa

f_{b_s} = 157 MPa

9-24. (a) w = 2.66 kN/m

(b) w = 1.67 kN/m

10-1. R = 465 m

10-2. R = 7.74 m

10-3. $\theta_{max} = -\dfrac{wL^3}{6EI}$, $\Delta_{max} = -\dfrac{wL^4}{8EI}$

10-4. $\theta_{max} = \mp\dfrac{wL^3}{24EI}$, $\Delta_{max} = -\dfrac{5wL^4}{384EI}$

10-6. $\theta_{max} = \dfrac{wL^3}{6EI}$, $\Delta_{max} = \dfrac{wL^4}{8EI}$

10-7. 8 mm < 17 mm; yes

10-8. Δ = 7 mm

10-9. Δ = 73 mm

10-10. Δ = 14 mm

10-11. Δ = 13 mm

10-12. Δ = 13 mm

10-15. A_y = 30 kN

10-16. A = 32 kN

B = 54 kN

10-17. Center wall, 1.38P

Each end wall, 0.31P

10-18. Hinge shear force at B = 11.25 kN

11-1. Joist, 38 × 139 mm
Header, two 38 × 235 mm
Lintel, two 38 × 235 mm

11-2. Joist, 38 × 235 mm
Beam, 38 × 285 mm

11-3. Beam, 89 × 285 mm
Girder, 139 × 235 mm

11-5. *AB*, W610 × 113
AC, W460 × 60

11-6. *AB*, W530 × 196

11-7. *AB*, W760 × 147
CD, W920 × 446

12-1. $f_{top} = 9130$ kPa
$f_{bottom} = 9630$ kPa

12-2. $f_{max \atop tensile} = 145$ MPa
$f_{max \atop compr.} = 192$ MPa

12-3. $f_{max \atop tensile} = 7090$ kPa
$f_{max \atop compr.} = 7450$ kPa

12-4. $f_{max \atop tensile} = 13\ 200$ kPa
$f_{max \atop compr.} = 15\ 300$ kPa

12-5. $f_a = 11\ 200$ kPa compression
$f_b = 1600$ kPa compression
$f_c = 8020$ kPa tension
$f_d = 1600$ kPa compression

12-6. $e_y = 230$ mm

12-7. Yes; 267 kPa > 200 kPa

12-8. $e = \dfrac{R}{4}$

12-9. $f_{max \atop compr.} = 5760$ kPa

12-10. $P = 3$ kN

12-11. $f_{v \atop max} \approx 2660$ kPa

12-12. $f_v \approx 1400$ kPa

12-13.

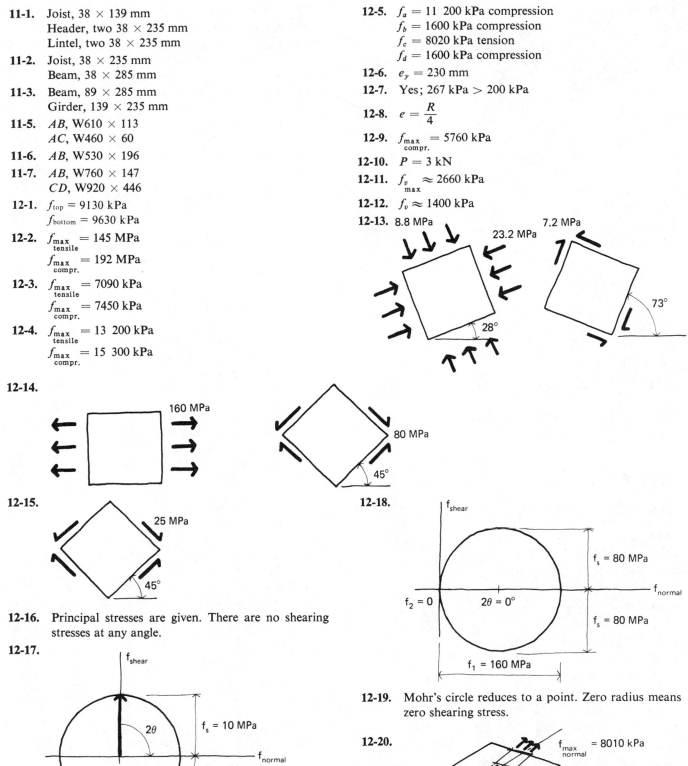

12-14.

12-15.

12-16. Principal stresses are given. There are no shearing stresses at any angle.

12-17.

12-18.

12-19. Mohr's circle reduces to a point. Zero radius means zero shearing stress.

12-20.

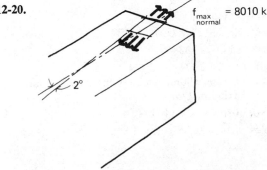

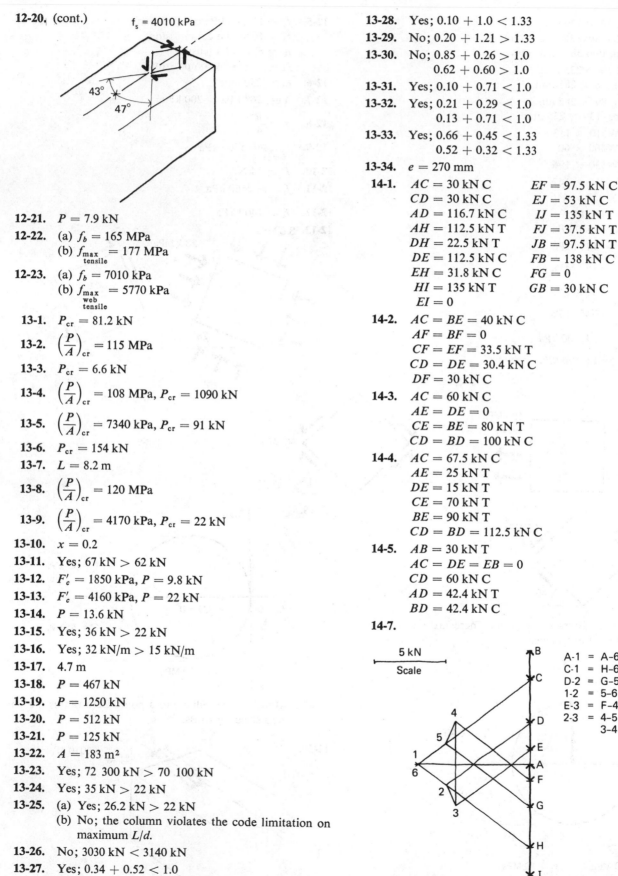

12-20. (cont.)

$f_s = 4010$ kPa

43°

47°

12-21. $P = 7.9$ kN

12-22. (a) $f_b = 165$ MPa
(b) $f_{\max \atop \text{tensile}} = 177$ MPa

12-23. (a) $f_b = 7010$ kPa
(b) $f_{\max \atop \substack{\text{web} \\ \text{tensile}}} = 5770$ kPa

13-1. $P_{cr} = 81.2$ kN

13-2. $\left(\dfrac{P}{A}\right)_{cr} = 115$ MPa

13-3. $P_{cr} = 6.6$ kN

13-4. $\left(\dfrac{P}{A}\right)_{cr} = 108$ MPa, $P_{cr} = 1090$ kN

13-5. $\left(\dfrac{P}{A}\right)_{cr} = 7340$ kPa, $P_{cr} = 91$ kN

13-6. $P_{cr} = 154$ kN

13-7. $L = 8.2$ m

13-8. $\left(\dfrac{P}{A}\right)_{cr} = 120$ MPa

13-9. $\left(\dfrac{P}{A}\right)_{cr} = 4170$ kPa, $P_{cr} = 22$ kN

13-10. $x = 0.2$

13-11. Yes; 67 kN > 62 kN

13-12. $F'_c = 1850$ kPa, $P = 9.8$ kN

13-13. $F'_c = 4160$ kPa, $P = 22$ kN

13-14. $P = 13.6$ kN

13-15. Yes; 36 kN > 22 kN

13-16. Yes; 32 kN/m > 15 kN/m

13-17. 4.7 m

13-18. $P = 467$ kN

13-19. $P = 1250$ kN

13-20. $P = 512$ kN

13-21. $P = 125$ kN

13-22. $A = 183$ m²

13-23. Yes; 72 300 kN > 70 100 kN

13-24. Yes; 35 kN > 22 kN

13-25. (a) Yes; 26.2 kN > 22 kN
(b) No; the column violates the code limitation on maximum L/d.

13-26. No; 3030 kN < 3140 kN

13-27. Yes; 0.34 + 0.52 < 1.0

13-28. Yes; 0.10 + 1.0 < 1.33

13-29. No; 0.20 + 1.21 > 1.33

13-30. No; 0.85 + 0.26 > 1.0
0.62 + 0.60 > 1.0

13-31. Yes; 0.10 + 0.71 < 1.0

13-32. Yes; 0.21 + 0.29 < 1.0
0.13 + 0.71 < 1.0

13-33. Yes; 0.66 + 0.45 < 1.33
0.52 + 0.32 < 1.33

13-34. $e = 270$ mm

14-1. $AC = 30$ kN C $\quad$ $EF = 97.5$ kN C
$CD = 30$ kN C $\quad$ $EJ = 53$ kN C
$AD = 116.7$ kN C $\quad$ $IJ = 135$ kN T
$AH = 112.5$ kN T $\quad$ $FJ = 37.5$ kN T
$DH = 22.5$ kN T $\quad$ $JB = 97.5$ kN T
$DE = 112.5$ kN C $\quad$ $FB = 138$ kN C
$EH = 31.8$ kN C $\quad$ $FG = 0$
$HI = 135$ kN T $\quad$ $GB = 30$ kN C
$EI = 0$

14-2. $AC = BE = 40$ kN C
$AF = BF = 0$
$CF = EF = 33.5$ kN T
$CD = DE = 30.4$ kN C
$DF = 30$ kN C

14-3. $AC = 60$ kN C
$AE = DE = 0$
$CE = BE = 80$ kN T
$CD = BD = 100$ kN C

14-4. $AC = 67.5$ kN C
$AE = 25$ kN T
$DE = 15$ kN T
$CE = 70$ kN T
$BE = 90$ kN T
$CD = BD = 112.5$ kN C

14-5. $AB = 30$ kN T
$AC = DE = EB = 0$
$CD = 60$ kN C
$AD = 42.4$ kN T
$BD = 42.4$ kN C

14-7.

5 kN

Scale

A-1 = A-6 = 8 kN T
C-1 = H-6 = 10 kN C
D-2 = G-5 = 7.5 kN C
1-2 = 5-6 = 2.5 kN C
E-3 = F-4 = 6.7 kN C
2-3 = 4-5 = 1.6 kN C
3-4 = 6 kN T

14-9.

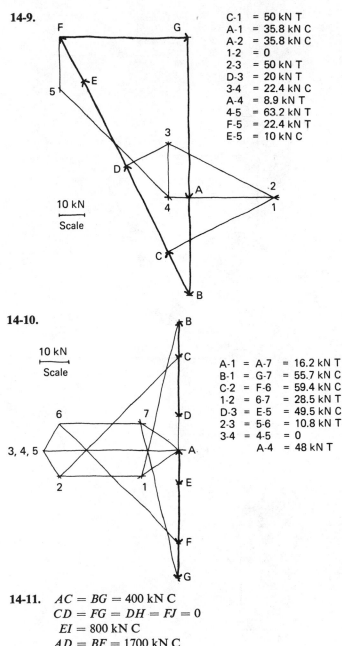

C-1	=	50 kN T
A-1	=	35.8 kN C
A-2	=	35.8 kN C
1-2	=	0
2-3	=	50 kN T
D-3	=	20 kN T
3-4	=	22.4 kN C
A-4	=	8.9 kN T
4-5	=	63.2 kN T
F-5	=	22.4 kN T
E-5	=	10 kN C

14-10.

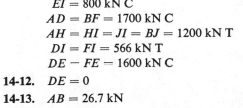

A-1 = A-7	=	16.2 kN T
B-1 = G-7	=	55.7 kN C
C-2 = F-6	=	59.4 kN C
1-2 = 6-7	=	28.5 kN T
D-3 = E-5	=	49.5 kN C
2-3 = 5-6	=	10.8 kN T
3-4 = 4-5	=	0
A-4	=	48 kN T

14-11. $AC = BG = 400$ kN C
$CD = FG = DH = FJ = 0$
$EI = 800$ kN C
$AD = BF = 1700$ kN C
$AH = HI = JI = BJ = 1200$ kN T
$DI = FI = 566$ kN T
$DE - FE = 1600$ kN C

14-12. $DE = 0$

14-13. $AB = 26.7$ kN

14-14. $DB = 42.4$ kN C

14-15.
$IJ = 15$ kN C	$GE = 27.04$ kN C
$IF = KJ = KH = 0$	$GC = 27.04$ kN T
$JH = 13.5$ kN C	$CD = 30$ kN C
$JF = 13.5$ kN T	$CA = 33.75$ kN T
$FG = 22.5$ kN C	$DE = 15$ kN T
$FC = 11.25$ kN T	$EB = 33.75$ kN C
$GH = 7.5$ kN T	$DB = 40.6$ kN C
$HE = 11.25$ kN C	$DA = 40.6$ kN T
	$AB = 22.5$ kN T

15-1.

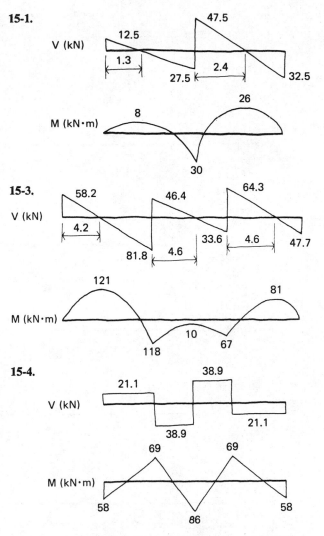

15-3.

15-4.

15-5. $R_A = 137$ kN↑; $R_B = 349$ kN↑; $R_C = 146$ kN↑

15-6.

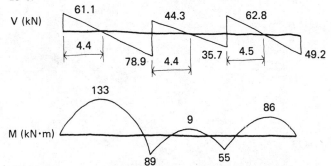

15-7. $R_A = 3.75$ kN↑; $R_B = 7.5$ kN↑; $R_C = 0.75$ kN↑

15-9.

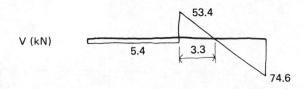

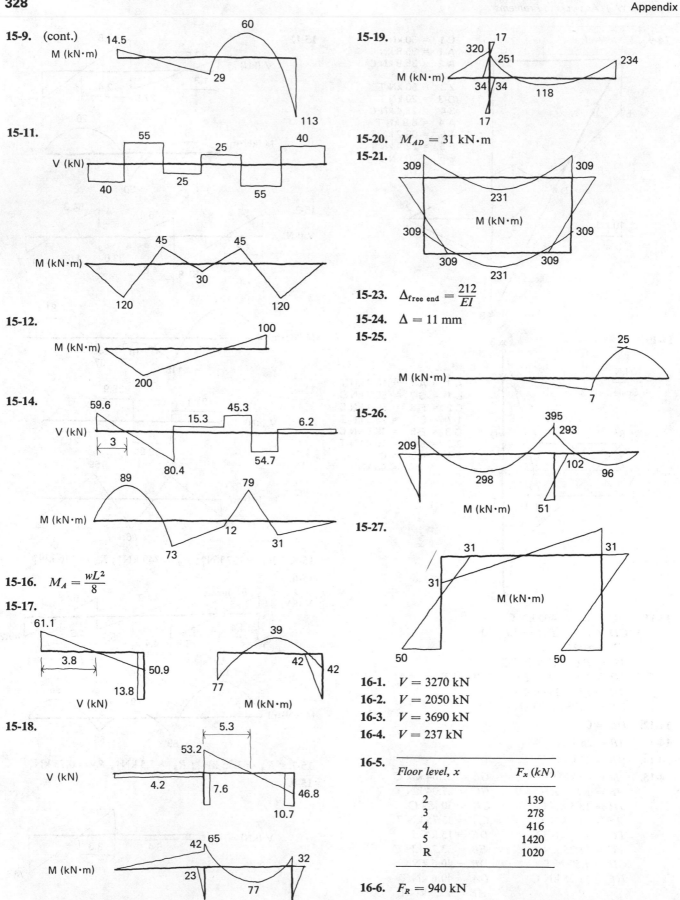

15-9. (cont.)   M (kN·m)

15-11.   V (kN)

M (kN·m)

15-12.   M (kN·m)

15-14.   V (kN)

M (kN·m)

15-16. $M_A = \dfrac{wL^2}{8}$

15-17.   V (kN)   M (kN·m)

15-18.   V (kN)

M (kN·m)

15-19.   M (kN·m)

15-20. $M_{AD} = 31$ kN·m

15-21.   M (kN·m)

15-23. $\Delta_{\text{free end}} = \dfrac{212}{EI}$

15-24. $\Delta = 11$ mm

15-25.   M (kN·m)

15-26.   M (kN·m)

15-27.   M (kN·m)

16-1. $V = 3270$ kN
16-2. $V = 2050$ kN
16-3. $V = 3690$ kN
16-4. $V = 237$ kN

16-5.

Floor level, x	F_x (kN)
2	139
3	278
4	416
5	1420
R	1020

16-6. $F_R = 940$ kN

16-7.

Floor level, x	F_x (kN)
2	13
3	22
4	27
5	28
6	54
7	24
8	19
9	14
10	9
11	4
12	1
R	20

16-8.

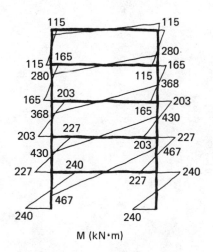

Axials (kN)

V (kN)

M (kN·m)

16-9. $M = 325$ kN·m

16-10.

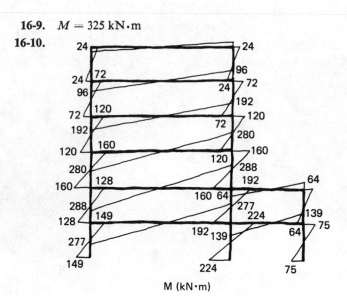

M (kN·m)

16-11.

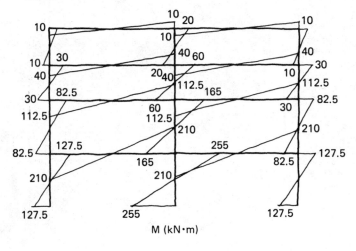

M (kN·m)

17-1. $M_u = 860$ kN·m

17-2. $L = 10.8$ m

17-3. No; 432 kN·m < 480 kN·m

17-4. Yes; 514 kN·m > 452 kN·m

17-5. $L_{max} = 4.5$ m

17-6. (a) $d = 690$ mm
  (b) $d = 630$ mm
  (c) $d = 580$ mm

17-7. $d \approx 490$ mm

17-8. $d \approx 715$ mm

17-9. (a) $d \approx 565$ mm
  (b) $\rho = 0.0168$

17-10. (a) $d = 575$ mm
  (b) $d = 610$ mm

17-11. $f_b \atop \text{top} = 24.4$ MPa compression

$f_b \atop \text{bottom} = 4.9$ MPa tension

17-12. $e_{max} = 460$ mm

17-13. $w = 45.8$ kN/m

17-14. (a) $P_{max} = 370$ kN, tension controls
  (b) $L_{max} = 8.9$ m

17-15. (a) $e_{max} = 305$ mm
  (b) Yes; 21.6 MPa compression < 22.5 MPa compression; 6.9 MPa compression < 3.5 MPa tension

A

Aalto, Alvar, 183
Accuracy of computations, 11
Aftershock, 255
Allowable stress, 62
   steel, 114
   wood, duration of loading, 307
   wood (table) 307
American Concrete Institute, 62, 267, 283
American Institute of Steel Construction, 67, 114, 191
American Institute of Timber Construction, 65, 111, 113
American National Metrication Council, 286
American National Standards Institute, 286, 303, 304
Angle of twist, 74
Answers to problems, 319
Area:
   first moment of, 42
   properties of, 301
   second moment of, 46
   statical moment of, 46
Average unit strain, 54
Axial stress (*see* Stress)

B

Bartning, Otto, 69
Beam-column, 197
Beams:
   deflection of, 133
     equations for, 317
   efficiency of, 150
   flitch plate, 129
   "ideal," 150
   lateral bracing, 111
   lateral buckling, 110

Beams *(cont.)*:
   lateral stability, 110, 114
   local buckling, steel, 114
   minor axis bending, 117, 307
   selection of, 155
   self-weight, 101, 104
   size effect, wood, 113
     factors (table), 113
   slenderness factor, wood, 111
   on a slope, 120
   of two materials, 129
   variable moment of inertia, 123
Bearing lines, 219
Bending, structural inefficiency of, 99
Building Code Requirements for Reinforced Concrete, 268
Building codes, 10
Built-up column, load reduction for, 188
Bundled tube, 81, 262

C

Cable, 37
Carryover factor, 231
Carryover moments, 231
Center of gravity, 42
Centroid, 42
Centroid location (table), 301
Columbus, Indiana, Post Office, 224
Columns:
   bracing of, 184
   combined loading, 197, 201
   effective length, 181
   elastic buckling, 179
   end conditions, 181
   failure modes, 179
   inelastic buckling, 187
   radius of gyration, 179

Index

Columns *(cont.)*:
  slenderness ratio, 180
    steel, maximum, 192
    wood, maximum, 188
  steel, 191, 201
    table of values, 308
  wood, 187, 197
Combined stresses:
  axial and flexural, 164
  flexure and horizontal shear, 176
  torsion and horizontal shear, 168
  torsion and flexure, 175
Compact section, 113, 310
Component (*see* Force)
Concrete:
  characteristics of, 65
  curing of, 66
  reinforced (*see* Reinforced concrete)
Concrete Reinforcing Steel Institute, 268
Conjugate beam method, 141
Connections:
  moment resistant, 94
  symbols for, 23
Construction Industries Coordinating Committee, 286
Continuity, 222, 225, 228, 238
Continuous beam, 223
Crawley, S. W., 128
Creep, definition of, 68
Cross, Hardy, 228
Cross section, 42
Cross-shears, 75
Crown Hall, 111
Counters, 208
Couples, 20
Cuvier, Georges, 7

D

Deflection:
  approximate determination, 145
  equations, 145, 317
  limitations (table), 133
  maximum, 144
Density (*see* Mass density)
Determinacy, 31
Diagonal buckling, 76
Diagonal tension, 76
Dillon, R. M., 128
Dinkeloo, John, 224
Double integration, 135
Drift, 252

E

Eames, Charles, 209
Earthquake:
  building natural frequency, 255
  design principles, 259
  loads, 254
  map, 305
  occupancy importance factors (table), 256
  seismic zone coefficients (table), 256
  structural system factors (table), 256
Eccentric loading, 166, 168, 197, 201
Economy of structure, 3
Effective length (*see* Columns)
Efficiency, structural, 62
Elastic buckling (*see* Columns)
Elastic curve, 134, 238
End conditions (*see* Columns)
Equilibrium:
  concurrent forces, 16
  graphical statement, 18
  simple cables, 37
  single members, 24
  two-force members, 27
Euler equation, 179
  AISC Formula II, 192
  derivation of, 297
  limits of applicability, 187
Euler, Leonhard, 135, 179

F

Factor of safety:
  definition of, 62
  reasons for, 63
  steel columns, 192
  wood columns, 188
Finnish Pavilion, 183
Fire resistance, 3
First moment (*see* Area)
Flexural stress (*see* Stress)
Flexure formula, 100
  derivation of, 297
Flitch plate, 129
Force:
  components, 13
  definition of, 12
  direction of, 12
  equilibrant, 15
  graphical polygon, 14, 30
  moment of, 19
  reactions, 24
  redundant, 146, 222

Force *(cont.):*
  resultant, 13
  sense of, 12
Frames:
  deflected shapes, 256
  deflection of, 242
  determinate, 93
  estimating moments in, 246
  sidesway, 238, 250
Framing, 149
Free-body diagram, 24

G

Gradient height, 253
Gurfinkel, German, 188

H

Hancock Building (Chicago), 81, 262
Hennibique, Francois, 224
Hooke, Robert, 55
Horizontal shear *(see* Stress)

I

Indeterminate structures *(see* Structures)
Inelastic buckling *(see* Columns)
International Conference of Building Officials, 305

J

Johnson, Philip, 263
Joint equilibrium (trusses), 230

K

Kahn, Louis, 263
Kern, 167
Khan, Fazlur, 262

L

Lateral bracing, 111, 184
Lateral buckling, 110
Lateral loads *(see* Loads)
Lateral stability, 110, 114
Laugier, Abbe, 2
Le Corbusier, 2, 154
Line of action, 12
Liquefaction, 255

Loads:
  lateral:
    bracing for, 184 , 260
    earthquake, 252, 254
    portal method for, 262
    wind, 4, 252
      intensity map, 304
      velocity (table), 253
  live:
    reduction for, 178
    table of, 306
    patterns of, 228
    snow intensity map, 303
    tributary areas, 151
    types of, 4
Local buckling, steel, 114

M

McGuire, William, 195
Maisons Dom-ino, 2
Manual of Steel Construction, 114, 120, 159, 163
Manual of Timber Construction, 112
Mass densities (table), 300
Masonry:
  characteristics of, 67
  reinforced, 67
Materials:
  characteristics of, 65, 150
  properties (table), 300
Maxwell, J. Clerk, 213
Maxwell diagram, 213
Maybeck, Bernard, 209
Mercalli, Giuseppe, 255
Middle-third rule, 167
Mies van der Rohe, 111, 263
Minor axis bending, 117, 307
Modified Mercalli Scale, 255
Modular ratio, 129
Modulus of elasticity, 56
Modulus of rigidity, 74
Mohr, Otto, 174
Mohr circle, 174
Moment, definition of, 19
Moment-area method, 137
Moment-area theorems, proof of, 294
Moment arm, 19
Moment diagrams:
  cable analogy, 97
  component form, 140
  for indeterminate frames, 238
  maximum value, 92

Moment diagrams *(cont.)*:
   moment and shear relationships, 88
   sign convention, 82
   tension side, 96, 239
Moment distribution:
   beams, 233
   concepts, 228
   frames, 238
   pinned-end stiffness reduction, 236
   sign convention, 233
Moment of inertia:
   defined, 45
   formulas (table), 301
   parallel axis theorem, 49
   polar, 73
Munday, Richard, 69
Museum of Modern Art, 183

N

National Design Specification (timber), 188, 198
National Forest Products Association, 65, 187, 197
Navier, Claude L. M. H., 56, 100
Neutral axis, 99
Notre-Dame du Raincy Church, 69

O

Otto, Frei, 183

P

Parallel axis theorem, 49
Parent, Antoine, 100
Pascal, Blaise, 53
Perret, Auguste, 69
Philadelphia Municipal Building, 263
Pin joint, 35
Plastic hinge, 113
Plastics, structural, 67
Point of concurrency, 30
Point of inflection, 83
Poisson, S. D., 55
Polar moment of inertia, 73
Ponding, 133
Portal method, 262
Portland cement, 66
Portland Cement Association, 66, 267
Prestressed concrete:
   allowable stresses (table), 283
   initial and final stresses, 283
   posttensioned, 279
   prestress loss, 284
   pretensioned, 279

Principal axes, 46, 126, 164
Principal planes, 170
Principal stresses:
   defined, 170
   derivation of equations, 295
Problem answers, 319
Properties of areas, 301
Properties of materials (table), 300
Properties of sections:
   steel (table), 310
   wood (table), 307

R

Radius of gyration, 53, 179
Redundant forces, 146, 222
Reinforced concrete:
   beams:
      balanced failure, 272
      deflection, 276
      effective depth, 270
      maximum steel ratio, 272
      overreinforced, 272
      shear stirrups, 76, 273, 276
      steel ratio, 270
      ultimate moment capacity, 268
        derivation of equation, 299
      underreinforced, 272
      values for strength design (table), 316
   capacity reduction factors (table), 268
   characteristics, 66
   columns, 277
   load factors (table), 268
   reinforcing bars, 267
      sizes (table), 316
Relative stiffness, 232, 237, 279
Resultant *(see* Force)
Richter, Charles, 254
Richter Scale, 254
Rigid body, 24
Roche, Kevin, 224

S

Ste. Chapelle Church, 69
Saint-Venant, Barre de, 137
Seagram Building, 263
Sears Tower, 81, 262
Second moment *(see* Area)
Section modulus, 104
Self-weight, 101, 104
Settlement, 243
Shear and moment diagrams:
   equations for, 81
   relationships, 88
   sign convention, 82

Shear center, 124
Shear flow, 81
Shearing stress (*see* Stress)
Shear lag, 261
Shear stirrups, 76, 273, 276
Shear truss, 260
Sidesway, 193, 238, 250, 279
SI metric system:
    conversion factors (table), 288
    introduction, 286
    prefixes (table), 287
    scales (table), 288
    units (table), 286
Slenderness factor (*see* Beams)
Slenderness ratio (*see* Columns)
Snow load (*see* Loads)
Span/depth ratio, 207
    table, 8
Span range (table), 8
Stability, 1, 31
Statical moment (*see* Area)
Static equilibrium (*see* Equilibrium)
Statics, definition of, 12
Steel:
    characteristics of, 66
    section properties (table), 310
    yield strength, 67
Steel Church, 69
Steel Joist Institute, 220
Steel ratio (*see* Reinforced concrete)
Stiffness, 3, 56 (*see also* Relative stiffness)
Stirling, James, 209
Strain:
    average unit, 54
    flexural, 99
    lateral, 55
    shearing, 54
    thermal, 60
    total, 54
Strength design:
    definition, 62
    in reinforced concrete, 267
        values for (table), 316
Strength of structure, 3
Stress:
    axial, 53
        in bending members, 164
        in columns, 179, 278
        in prestressing, 279
    concentration, 68
    critical buckling, 180
    flexural, 82, 99
        derivation of formula, 297
    horizontal shearing, 106
        derivation of formula, 293

Stress *(cont.):*
    horizontal shearing *(cont.):*
        steel, 119
        wood, 117
    normal, 53
    shearing, 53, 82
    stress-strain curve, 55
    tangential, 53
    thermal, 60
    torsional, 72
        derivation of equations, 290
    yield point, 55
    (*see also* Combined stresses)
Strong axis, 180
Structural analysis, definition of, 62
Structural bay, 178
Structural design, definition of, 62
Structural Engineers Association of California, 255
Structural systems:
    compatibility, 10
    characteristics (table), 8
Structure:
    cost of, 10
    economy of, 3
    efficiency of, 62, 99
    fire resistance of, 3
    forms in nature, 5
    indeterminate:
        advantages and disadvantages, 223
        defined, 32
        method of superposition, 146
        moment distribution, 228
        theorem of three moments, 223
    integrity of, 1
    planning of, 3, 149, 151
    psychological safety of, 3
Superposition:
    and indeterminate structures, 146
    principle of, 140
Support:
    fixed end, 24
    ideal, 22
    pin, 23
    roller, 23
    settlement, 243

                    T

Taliesin East, 209
Tangential deviation, 137
Temperature:
    effects of, 60
    (*see also* Stress)
Theorem of three moments, 223
    derivation of, 298

Three-hinged arch, 33
Timber:
 allowable stresses (table), 307
 characteristics of, 65
 section properties (table), 307
Torque force, 74
Torsion, effective shapes for, 81
Torsional stress (*see* Stress)
Transformed section, 129
Tributary area, 151
Tributary strip, 151
Trinity Church, 69
Truss:
 defined, 207
 graphical solution, 213
 joint equilibrium, 210
 method of sections, 216
Tsunami, 255
Two-force member, 27, 184, 207

U

Ultimate moment capacity (*see* Reinforced concrete)
Ultimate strength design (*see* Strength design)
Unit strain, 54

V

Varignon, Pierre, 20
Varignon's theorem, 20
Vierendeel, Arthur, 220
Vierendeel "truss," 220
Villa Savoye, 154

W

Weak axis, 180, 184
Welded wire fabric, 267
Wind load (*see* Loads)
Wood (*see* Timber)
Wood Structural Design Data, 163
World Trade Center, 81
Wright, Frank Lloyd, 209

Y

Yield point, 55
Young, Thomas, 56
Young's modulus, 56